International Financial Management

Eighth Edition

The McGraw-Hill/Irwin Series in Finance, Insurance, and Real Estate

Stephen A. Ross
Franco Modigliani Professor of Finance and Economics
Sloan School of Management
Massachusetts Institute of Technology
Consulting Editor

FINANCIAL MANAGEMENT

Block, Hirt, and Danielsen
Foundations of Financial Management
Sixteenth Edition

Brealey, Myers, and Allen
Principles of Corporate Finance
Twelfth Edition

Brealey, Myers, and Allen
Principles of Corporate Finance, Concise
Second Edition

Brealey, Myers, and Marcus
Fundamentals of Corporate Finance
Eighth Edition

Brooks
FinGame Online 5.0

Bruner
Case Studies in Finance: Managing for Corporate Value Creation
Eighth Edition

Cornett, Adair, and Nofsinger
Finance: Applications and Theory
Fourth Edition

Cornett, Adair, and Nofsinger
Finance: M Book
Third Edition

DeMello
Cases in Finance
Third Edition

Grinblatt (editor)
Stephen A. Ross, Mentor: Influence through Generations

Grinblatt and Titman
Financial Markets and Corporate Strategy
Second Edition

Higgins
Analysis for Financial Management
Eleventh Edition

Ross, Westerfield, Jaffe, and Jordan
Corporate Finance
Eleventh Edition

Ross, Westerfield, Jaffe, and Jordan
Corporate Finance: Core Principles and Applications
Fifth Edition

Ross, Westerfield, and Jordan
Essentials of Corporate Finance
Ninth Edition

Ross, Westerfield, and Jordan
Fundamentals of Corporate Finance
Eleventh Edition

Shefrin
Behavioral Corporate Finance: Decisions that Create Value
Second Edition

INVESTMENTS

Bodie, Kane, and Marcus
Essentials of Investments
Tenth Edition

Bodie, Kane, and Marcus
Investments
Tenth Edition

Hirt and Block
Fundamentals of Investment Management
Tenth Edition

Jordan, Miller, and Dolvin
Fundamentals of Investments: Valuation and Management
Eighth Edition

Stewart, Piros, and Heisler
Running Money: Professional Portfolio Management
First Edition

Sundaram and Das
Derivatives: Principles and Practice
Second Edition

FINANCIAL INSTITUTIONS AND MARKETS

Rose and Hudgins
Bank Management and Financial Services
Ninth Edition

Rose and Marquis
Financial Institutions and Markets
Eleventh Edition

Saunders and Cornett
Financial Institutions Management: A Risk Management Approach
Ninth Edition

Saunders and Cornett
Financial Markets and Institutions
Sixth Edition

INTERNATIONAL FINANCE

Eun and Resnick
International Financial Management
Eighth Edition

REAL ESTATE

Brueggeman and Fisher
Real Estate Finance and Investments
Fifteenth Edition

Ling and Archer
Real Estate Principles: A Value Approach
Fifth Edition

FINANCIAL PLANNING AND INSURANCE

Allen, Melone, Rosenbloom, and Mahoney
Retirement Plans: 401(k) s, IRAs, and Other Deferred Compensation Approaches
Eleventh Edition

Altfest
Personal Financial Planning
Second Edition

Harrington and Niehaus
Risk Management and Insurance
Second Edition

Kapoor, Dlabay, Hughes and Hart
Focus on Personal Finance: An Active Approach to Help You Develop Successful Financial Skills
Fifth Edition

Kapoor, Dlabay, Hughes, and Hart
Personal Finance
Eleventh Edition

Walker and Walker
Personal Finance: Building Your Future
Second Edition

International Financial Management

Eighth Edition

Cheol S. Eun
Georgia Institute of Technology

Bruce G. Resnick
Wake Forest University

McGraw Hill Education

INTERNATIONAL FINANCIAL MANAGEMENT

Published by McGraw-Hill Education, 2 Penn Plaza, New York, NY 10121. Copyright
© 2018 by McGraw-Hill Education. All rights reserved. Printed in the United States
of America. No part of this publication may be reproduced or distributed in any form
or by any means, or stored in a database or retrieval system, without the prior written
consent of McGraw-Hill Education, including, but not limited to, in any network or other
electronic storage or transmission, or broadcast for distance learning.

Some ancillaries, including electronic and print components, may not be available to
customers outside the United States.

This book is printed on acid-free paper.

4 5 6 7 8 9 LWI 21 20 19 18

ISBN 978-1-259-92219-0
MHID 1-259-92219-7

The Internet addresses listed in the text were accurate at the time of publication. The
inclusion of a website does not indicate an endorsement by the authors or McGraw-
Hill Education, and McGraw-Hill Education does not guarantee the accuracy of the
information presented at these sites.

mheducation.com/highered

About the Authors

Cheol S. Eun,
Georgia Institute of Technology

Cheol S. Eun (Ph.D., NYU) is the Thomas R. Williams Chair and Professor of Finance at the Scheller College of Business, Georgia Institute of Technology. Before joining Georgia Tech, he taught at the University of Minnesota and the University of Maryland. He also taught at the Wharton School of the University of Pennsylvania, Korea Advanced Institute of Science and Technology (KAIST), Singapore Management University, and the Esslingen University of Technology (Germany) as a visiting professor. He has published extensively on international finance issues in such major journals as the *Journal of Finance, Journal of Financial Economics, JFQA, Journal of Banking and Finance, Journal of International Money and Finance, Management Science,* and *Oxford Economic Papers.* Also, he has served on the editorial boards of the *Journal of Banking and Finance, Journal of Financial Research, Journal of International Business Studies,* and *European Financial Management.* His research is widely quoted and referenced in various scholarly articles and textbooks in the United States as well as abroad.

Dr. Eun is the founding chair of the *Fortis/Georgia Tech Conference on International Finance.* The key objectives of the conference are to promote research on international finance and provide a forum for interactions among academics, practitioners, and regulators who are interested in vital current issues of international finance.

Dr. Eun has taught a variety of courses at the undergraduate, graduate, and executive levels, and was the winner of the Krowe Teaching Excellence Award at the University of Maryland. He also has served as a consultant to many national and international organizations, including the World Bank, Apex Capital, and the Korean Development Institute, advising on issues relating to capital market liberalization, global capital raising, international investment, and exchange risk management. In addition, he has been a frequent speaker at academic and professional meetings held throughout the world.

Bruce G. Resnick,
Wake Forest University

Bruce G. Resnick is the Joseph M. Bryan Jr. Professor of Banking and Finance at the Wake Forest University School of Business in Winston-Salem, North Carolina. He has a D.B.A. (1979) in finance from Indiana University. Additionally, he has an M.B.A. from the University of Colorado and a B.B.A. from the University of Wisconsin at Oshkosh. Prior to coming to Wake Forest, he taught at Indiana University for ten years, the University of Minnesota for five years, and California State University for two years. He has also taught as a visiting professor at Bond University, Gold Coast, Queensland, Australia, and at the Helsinki School of Economics and Business Administration in Finland. Additionally, he served as the Indiana University resident director at the Center for European Studies at Maastricht University, the Netherlands. He also served as an external examiner to the Business Administration Department of Singapore Polytechnic and as the faculty advisor on Wake Forest University study trips to Japan, China, and Hong Kong.

Dr. Resnick teaches M.B.A. courses at Wake Forest University. He specializes in the areas of investments, portfolio management, and international financial management. Dr. Resnick's research interests include market efficiency studies of options and financial futures markets and empirical tests of asset pricing models. A major interest has been the optimal design of internationally diversified portfolios constructed to control for parameter uncertainty and exchange rate risk. In recent years, he has focused on information transmission in the world money markets and yield spread comparisons of domestic and international bonds. His research articles have been published in most of the major academic journals in finance. His research is widely referenced by other researchers and textbook authors. He is an associate editor for the *Emerging Markets Review, Journal of Economics and Business,* and the *Journal of Multinational Financial Management.*

Preface

Our Reason for Writing this Textbook

Both of us have been teaching international financial management to undergraduates and M.B.A. students at Georgia Institute of Technology, Wake Forest University, and at other universities we have visited for three decades. During this time period, we conducted many research studies, published in major finance and statistics journals, concerning the operation of international financial markets. As one might imagine, in doing this we put together an extensive set of teaching materials that we used successfully in the classroom. As the years went by, we individually relied more on our own teaching materials and notes and less on any one of the major existing textbooks in international finance (most of which we tried at some point).

As you may be aware, the scope and content of international finance have been fast evolving due to deregulation of financial markets, product innovations, and technological advancements. As capital markets of the world are becoming more integrated, a solid understanding of international finance has become essential for astute corporate decision making. Reflecting the growing importance of international finance as a discipline, we have seen a sharp increase in the demand for experts in the area in both the corporate and academic worlds.

In writing *International Financial Management,* Eighth Edition, our goal was to provide well-organized, comprehensive, and up-to-date coverage of the topics that take advantage of our many years of teaching and research in this area. We hope the text is challenging to students. This does not mean that it lacks readability. The text discussion is written so that a self-contained treatment of each subject is presented in a *user-friendly* fashion. The text is intended for use at both the advanced undergraduate and M.B.A. levels.

The Underlying Philosophy

International Financial Management, Eighth Edition, like the first seven editions, is written based on two tenets: emphasis on the basics and emphasis on a managerial perspective.

Emphasis on the Basics

We believe that any subject is better learned if one first is well grounded in the basics. Consequently, we initially devote several chapters to the fundamental concepts of international finance. After these are learned, the remaining material flows easily from them. We always bring the reader back, as the more advanced topics are developed, to their relationship to the fundamentals. By doing this, we believe students will be left with a framework for analysis that will serve them well when they need to apply this material in their careers in the years ahead.

We believe this approach has produced a successful textbook: *International Financial Management* is used in many of the best business schools in the world. Various editions of the text have been translated into Spanish and two dialects of Chinese. There is a global edition. In addition, local co-authors have assisted in preparing a Canadian, Malaysian, Indonesian, and Indian adaptations.

Eighth Edition Organization

International Financial Management, Eighth Edition, has been completely updated. All data tables and statistics are the most current available when the text went to press. Additionally, the chapters incorporate several new International Finance in Practice boxes that contain real-world illustrations of chapter topics and concepts. In the margins below, we highlight specific changes in the Eighth Edition.

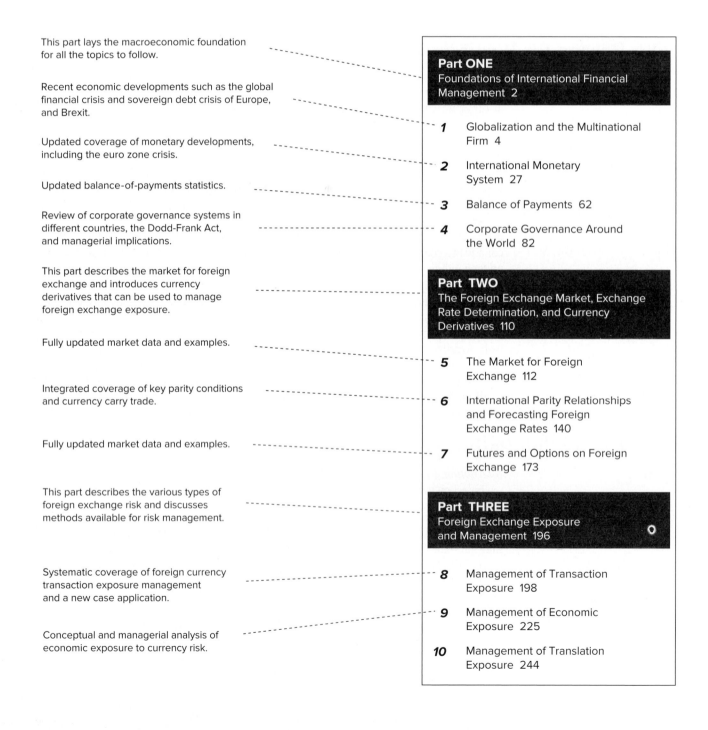

This part lays the macroeconomic foundation for all the topics to follow.

Recent economic developments such as the global financial crisis and sovereign debt crisis of Europe, and Brexit.

Updated coverage of monetary developments, including the euro zone crisis.

Updated balance-of-payments statistics.

Review of corporate governance systems in different countries, the Dodd-Frank Act, and managerial implications.

This part describes the market for foreign exchange and introduces currency derivatives that can be used to manage foreign exchange exposure.

Fully updated market data and examples.

Integrated coverage of key parity conditions and currency carry trade.

Fully updated market data and examples.

This part describes the various types of foreign exchange risk and discusses methods available for risk management.

Systematic coverage of foreign currency transaction exposure management and a new case application.

Conceptual and managerial analysis of economic exposure to currency risk.

Part ONE
Foundations of International Financial Management 2

1   Globalization and the Multinational Firm 4

2   International Monetary System 27

3   Balance of Payments 62

4   Corporate Governance Around the World 82

Part TWO
The Foreign Exchange Market, Exchange Rate Determination, and Currency Derivatives 110

5   The Market for Foreign Exchange 112

6   International Parity Relationships and Forecasting Foreign Exchange Rates 140

7   Futures and Options on Foreign Exchange 173

Part THREE
Foreign Exchange Exposure and Management 196

8   Management of Transaction Exposure 198

9   Management of Economic Exposure 225

10 Management of Translation Exposure 244

A Managerial Perspective

The text presentation never loses sight of the fact that it is teaching students how to make managerial decisions. *International Financial Management,* Eighth Edition, is founded in the belief that the fundamental job of the financial manager is to maximize shareholder wealth. This belief permeates the decision-making process we present from cover to cover. To reinforce the managerial perspective, we provide numerous "real-world" stories whenever appropriate.

This part provides a thorough discussion of international financial institutions, assets, and marketplaces.

Fully updated market data and statistics. Updated discussion on Basel III capital adequacy standards. Updated discussion on the causes and consequences of the global financial crisis. New section on ICE Libor.

Fully updated market data and examples.

New statistical presentation of market capitalizations and liquidity measurement in developed and developing countries. Updated discussion of market consolidations and mergers.

Fully updated market data and statistics. New discussion on swap trading practices under new financial regulation. New International Finance in Practice box on trading swaps via a clearing-house.

Updated statistical analysis of international markets and diversification with small-cap stocks.

This part covers topics on financial management practices for the multinational firm.

Updated trends in cross-border investment and M&A deals. Updated political risk scores for countries.

New analysis of home bias and the cost of capital around the world. Also, comparison of capital structure across countries.

Fully updated comparative national income tax rate table with updated examples. New section on tax inversion maneuvers.

Key Features

EXAMPLE | 11.1: Rollover Pricing of a Eurocredit

Teltrex International can borrow $3,000,000 at LIBOR plus a lending margin of 0.75 percent per annum on a three-month rollover basis from Barclays in London. Suppose that three-month LIBOR is currently 5.53 percent. Further suppose that over the second three-month interval LIBOR falls to 5.12 percent. How much will Teltrex pay in interest to Barclays over the six-month period for the Eurodollar loan?

Solution: $3,000,000 × (.0553 + .0075)/4 + $3,000,000 × (.0512 + .0075)/4 = $47,100 + $44,025 = $91,125

INTERNATIONAL FINANCE IN PRACTICE

FX Market Volumes Surge

The FX market is growing at record levels, according to figures released by the CME Group, the largest regulated foreign exchange market in the world.

Last month the CME Group reported average daily notional volume at a record level of $121 billion, up 82 percent compared to a year earlier.

With a number of indicators at play, like the news of Greece's credit concerns and the continued appetite for high-yielding currencies like the Australian dollar and the Canadian dollar, the CME saw record volumes and notional values in the euro and Australian and Canadian dollars. Euro FX futures and options saw total average daily volume of 362,000 contracts with total notional ADV of slightly over $62 billion.

Australian dollar futures and options climbed to nearly 119,000 contracts in average daily volume with almost $11 billion in total notional ADV, and Canadian dollar futures

and options surpassed 88,000 contracts in ADV and $8 billion in total notional ADV.

With foreign currency futures going from strength to strength, the CME Group recently published a white paper outlining the benefits of FX futures.

"These contracts provide an ideal tool to manage currency or FX risks in an uncertain world," it said. "Product innovation, liquidity, and financial surety are the three pillars upon which the CME Group has built its world-class derivatives market. The CME Group provides products based on a wide range of frequently transacted currencies, liquidity offered on the state-of-the-art CME Globex electronic trading platform, and financial sureties afforded by its centralized clearing system."

Source: Global Investor, March 2010. All rights reserved. Used with permission.

In More Depth

European Option-Pricing Formula

In the last section, we examined a simple one-step version of binomial option-pricing model. Instead, we could have assumed the stock price followed a multiplicative binomial process by subdividing the option period into many subperiods. In this case, S_T and C_T could be many different values. When the number of subperiods into which the option period is subdivided goes to infinity, the European call and put pricing formulas presented in this section are obtained. Exact European call and put pricing formulas are:[5]

$$C_e = S_t e^{-r_f T} N(d_1) - E e^{-r_\$ T} N(d_2) \qquad (7.12)$$

and

$$P_e = E e^{-r_\$ T} N(-d_2) - S_t e^{-r_f T} N(-d_1) \qquad (7.13)$$

The interest rates $r_\$$ and r_f are assumed to be annualized and constant over the term-to-maturity T of the option contract, which is expressed as a fraction of a year.

Invoking IRP, where with continuous compounding $F_T = S_t e^{(r_\$ - r_f)T}$, C_e and P_e in Equations 7.12 and 7.13 can be, respectively, restated as:

$$C_e = [F_T N(d_1) - E N(d_2)] e^{-r_\$ T} \qquad (7.14)$$

and

$$P_e = [E N(-d_2) - F_T N(-d_1)] e^{-r_\$ T} \qquad (7.15)$$

where

$$d_1 = \frac{\ln(F_T/E) + .5\sigma^2 T}{\sigma \sqrt{T}}$$

and

$$d_2 = d_1 - \sigma \sqrt{T}$$

$N(d)$ denotes the cumulative area under the standard normal density function from $-\infty$ to d_1 (or d_2). The variable σ is the annualized volatility of the change in exchange rate $\ln(S_{t+1}/S_t)$. Equations 7.14 and 7.15 indicate that C_e and P_e are functions of only five variables: F_T, E, $r_\$$, T, and σ. It can be shown that both C_e and P_e increase when σ becomes larger.

QUESTIONS	1. How would you define *transaction exposure*? How is it different from economic exposure?
	2. Discuss and compare hedging transaction exposure using the forward contract versus money market instruments. When do alternative hedging approaches produce the same result?
	3. Discuss and compare the costs of hedging by forward contracts and options contracts.
PROBLEMS	The spreadsheet TRNSEXP.xls may be used in solving parts of problems 2, 3, 4, and 6.
	1. Cray Research sold a supercomputer to the Max Planck Institute in Germany on credit and invoiced €10 million payable in six months. Currently, the six-month forward exchange rate is $1.10/€ and the foreign exchange adviser for Cray Research predicts that the spot rate is likely to be $1.05/€ in six months.
	a. What is the expected gain/loss from a forward hedge?
	b. If you were the financial manager of Cray Research, would you recommend hedging this euro receivable? Why or why not?

Questions and Problems—Each chapter contains a set of Questions and Problems. This material can be used by students on their own to test their understanding of the material, or as homework exercises assigned by the instructor. Questions and Problems relating to the In More Depth sections of the text are indicated by *blue type*.

Questions with Excel Software—An icon in the margin indicates that the end-of-chapter question is linked to an Excel program created by the authors. See the Ancillary Materials section for more information on the software.

CFA Questions—Many chapters include problems from CFA Program Curriculum study materials. These CFA problems, indicated with the CFA logo, show students the relevancy of what is expected of certified professional analysts.

Case Applications—Case Applications are incorporated within selected chapters throughout the text in order to enhance specific topics and help students apply theories and concepts to "real-world" situations.

CASE APPLICATION	**Richard May's Options**
	It is Tuesday afternoon, February 14, 2012. Richard May, Assistant Treasurer at American Digital Graphics (ADG), sits in his office on the thirty-fourth floor of the building that dominates Rockefeller Plaza's west perimeter. It's Valentine's Day, and Richard and his wife have dinner reservations with another couple at Balthazar at 7:30. I must get this hedging memo done, thinks May, and get out of here. Foreign exchange options? I had better get the story straight before someone in the Finance Committee starts asking questions. Let's see, there are two ways in which I can envision us using options now. One is to hedge a dividend due on September 15th from ADG Germany. The other is to hedge our upcoming payment to Matsumerda for their spring RAM chip statement. With the yen at 78 and increasing I'm glad we haven't covered the payment so far, but now I'm getting nervous and I would like to protect my posterior. An option to buy yen on June 10 might be just the thing.

MINI CASE	**Airbus' Dollar Exposure**
	Airbus sold an A400 aircraft to Delta Airlines, a U.S. company, and billed $30 million payable in six months. Airbus is concerned about the euro proceeds from international sales and would like to control exchange risk. The current spot exchange rate is $1.05/€ and the six-month forward exchange rate is $1.10/€. Airbus can buy a six-month put option on U.S. dollars with a strike price of €0.95/$ for a premium of €0.02 per U.S. dollar. Currently, six-month interest rate is 2.5 percent in the euro zone and 3.0 percent in the United States.
	1. Compute the guaranteed euro proceeds from the American sale if Airbus decides to hedge using a forward contract.
	2. If Airbus decides to hedge using money market instruments, what action does Airbus need to take? What would be the guaranteed euro proceeds from the American sale in this case?
	3. If Airbus decides to hedge using put options on U.S. dollars, what would be the "expected" euro proceeds from the American sale? Assume that Airbus regards the current forward exchange rate as an unbiased predictor of the future spot exchange rate.
	4. At what future spot exchange do you think Airbus will be indifferent between the option and money market hedge?

Mini Cases—Almost every chapter includes a mini case for student analysis of multiple concepts covered throughout the chapter. These Mini Case problems are "real-world" in nature to show students how the theory and concepts in the textbook relate to the everyday world.

McGraw-Hill Connect®
Learn Without Limits

Connect is a teaching and learning platform that is proven to deliver better results for students and instructors.

Connect empowers students by continually adapting to deliver precisely what they need, when they need it, and how they need it, so your class time is more engaging and effective.

73% of instructors who use **Connect** require it; instructor satisfaction **increases** by 28% when **Connect** is required.

Connect's Impact on Retention Rates, Pass Rates, and Average Exam Scores

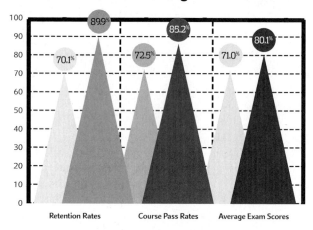

Using **Connect** improves retention rates by **19.8%**, passing rates by **12.7%**, and exam scores by **9.1%**.

Analytics

Connect Insight®

Connect Insight is Connect's new one-of-a-kind visual analytics dashboard—now available for both instructors and students—that provides at-a-glance information regarding student performance, which is immediately actionable. By presenting assignment, assessment, and topical performance results together with a time metric that is easily visible for aggregate or individual results, Connect Insight gives the user the ability to take a just-in-time approach to teaching and learning, which was never before available. Connect Insight presents data that empowers students and helps instructors improve class performance in a way that is efficient and effective.

Impact on Final Course Grade Distribution

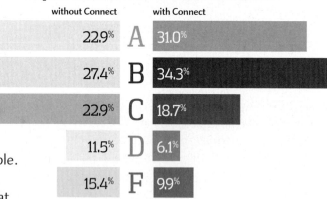

without Connect		with Connect
22.9%	A	31.0%
27.4%	B	34.3%
22.9%	C	18.7%
11.5%	D	6.1%
15.4%	F	9.9%

Students can view their results for any **Connect** course.

Mobile

Connect's new, intuitive mobile interface gives students and instructors flexible and convenient, anytime–anywhere access to all components of the Connect platform.

Adaptive

THE **ADAPTIVE** **READING EXPERIENCE**
DESIGNED TO TRANSFORM THE WAY STUDENTS READ

More students earn **A's** and **B's** when they use McGraw-Hill Education **Adaptive** products.

SmartBook®

Proven to help students improve grades and study more efficiently, SmartBook contains the same content within the print book, but actively tailors that content to the needs of the individual. SmartBook's adaptive technology provides precise, personalized instruction on what the student should do next, guiding the student to master and remember key concepts, targeting gaps in knowledge and offering customized feedback, and driving the student toward comprehension and retention of the subject matter. Available on tablets, SmartBook puts learning at the student's fingertips—anywhere, anytime.

Over **8 billion questions** have been answered, making McGraw-Hill Education products more intelligent, reliable, and precise.

www.mheducation.com

Ancillary Materials

To assist in course preparation, the following instructor ancillaries are within the Instructor Library in Connect:

- **Solutions Manual**—Includes detailed suggested answers and solutions to the end-of-chapter questions and problems, written by the authors.
- **Lecture Outlines**—Chapter outlines, learning objectives, and teaching notes for each chapter.
- **Test Bank**—True/false and multiple-choice test questions for each chapter prepared by Courtney Baggett, Butler University. Available as Word documents and assignable within Connect.
- **PowerPoint Presentations**—PowerPoint slides for each chapter to use in classroom lecture settings, created by John Stansfield, University of Missouri.

The resources also include the International Finance Software that can be used with this book. This Excel software has four main programs:

- A currency options pricing program allows students to price put and call options on foreign exchange.
- A hedging program allows the student to compare forward, money market instruments, futures, and options for hedging exchange risk.
- A currency swap program allows students to calculate the cash flows and notional values associated with swapping fixed-rate debt from one currency into another.
- A portfolio optimization program based on the Markowitz model allows for examining the benefits of international portfolio diversification.

The four programs can be used to solve certain end-of-chapter problems (marked with an Excel icon) or assignments the instructor devises. A User's Manual and sample projects are included in the Instructor Resources.

Acknowledgments

We are indebted to the many colleagues who provided insight and guidance throughout the development process. Their careful work enabled us to create a text that is current, accurate, and modern in its approach. Among all who helped in this endeavor for the Eighth Edition:

Richard Ajayi
University of Central Florida

Lawrence A. Beer
Arizona State University

Nishant Dass
Georgia Institute of Technology

John Hund
Rice University

Irina Khindanova
University of Denver

Gew-rae Kim
University of Bridgeport

Jaemin Kim
San Diego State University

Yong-Cheol Kim
University of Wisconsin, Milwaukee

Yen-Sheng Lee
Bellevue University

Charmen Loh
Rider University

Atsuyuki Naka
University of New Orleans

Richard L. Patterson
Indiana University, Bloomington

Adrian Shopp
Metropolitan State University of Denver

H. Douglas Witte
Missouri State University

John Wald
University of Texas at San Antonio

Many people assisted in the production of this textbook. At the risk of overlooking some individuals, we would like to acknowledge Brian Conzachi for the outstanding job he did proofreading the entire manuscript. Additionally, we thank Yusri Zaro for his hard work checking the accuracy of the solutions manual. Rohan-Rao Ganduri, Kristen Seaver, Milind Shrikhande, Jin-Gil Jeong, Sanjiv Sabherwal, Sandy Lai, Jinsoo Lee, Hyung Suk Choi, Teng Zhang, Minho Wang, and Victor Huang provided useful inputs into the text. Professor Martin Glaum of the Giessen University (Germany) also provided valuable comments.

We also wish to thank the many professionals at McGraw-Hill Education for their time and patience with us. Charles Synovec, executive brand manager; Noelle Bathurst, senior product developer; and Tara Slagle and Debra Boxill, content project managers have done a marvelous job guiding us through this edition, as has Melissa Leick, as content project manager.

Last, but not least, we would like to thank our families, Christine, James, and Elizabeth Eun and Donna Resnick, for their tireless love and support, without which this book would not have become a reality. Special thanks go to Christine Eun who came up with an excellent design for the book cover.

We hope that you enjoy using *International Financial Management,* Eighth Edition. In addition, we welcome your comments for improvement. Please let us know either through McGraw-Hill Education, c/o Editorial, or at our e-mail addresses provided below.

Cheol S. Eun
cheol.eun@scheller.gatech.edu

Bruce G. Resnick
resnickbg@wfu.edu

Contents
in Brief

Contents

PART FOUR   World Financial Markets and Institutions

International Financial Management

Eighth Edition

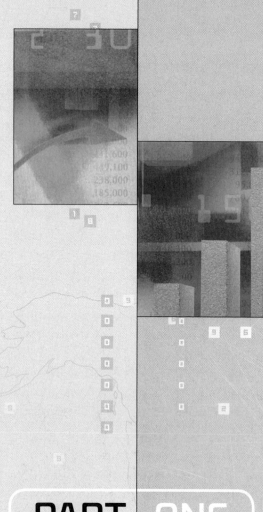

PART ONE

Foundations of International Financial Management

PART ONE lays the macroeconomic and institutional foundation for all the topics to follow. A thorough understanding of this material is essential for understanding the advanced topics covered in the remaining sections.

CHAPTER 1 provides an introduction to *International Financial Management*. The chapter discusses why it is important to study international finance and distinguishes international finance from domestic finance.

CHAPTER 2 introduces the various types of international monetary systems under which the world economy can function and has functioned at various times. The chapter traces the historical development of the world's international monetary systems from the early 1800s to the present. Additionally, a detailed discussion of the European Monetary Union is presented.

CHAPTER 3 presents balance-of-payment concepts and accounting. The chapter shows that even a country must keep its "economic house in order" or else it will experience current account deficits that will undermine the value of its currency.

CHAPTER 4 provides an overview of corporate governance around the world. Corporate governance structure varies greatly across countries, reflecting diverse cultural, economic, political, and legal environments.

Globalization and the Multinational Firm

AS THE TITLE *International Financial Management* indicates, in this book we are concerned with financial management in an international setting. Financial management is mainly concerned with how to *optimally* make various corporate financial decisions, such as those pertaining to investment, financing, dividend policy, and working capital management, with a view to achieving a set of given corporate objectives. In Anglo-American countries as well as in many advanced countries with well-developed capital markets, maximizing shareholder wealth is generally considered the most important corporate objective.

Why do we need to study "international" financial management? The answer to this question is straightforward: We are now living in a highly **globalized and integrated world economy**. American consumers, for example, routinely purchase oil imported from Saudi Arabia and Nigeria, TV sets from Korea, automobiles from Germany and Japan, garments from China, shoes from Indonesia, handbags from Italy, and wine from France. Foreigners, in turn, purchase American-made aircraft, software, movies, jeans, smartphones, and other products. Continued liberalization of international trade is certain to further internationalize consumption patterns around the world.

Like consumption, production of goods and services has become highly globalized. To a large extent, this has happened as a result of multinational corporations' (MNCs) relentless efforts to source inputs and locate production anywhere in the world where costs are lower and profits are higher. For example, personal computers sold in the world market might have been assembled in Malaysia with Taiwanese-made monitors, Korean-made keyboards, U.S.-made chips, and preinstalled software packages that were jointly developed by U.S. and Indian engineers. It has often become difficult to clearly associate a product with a single country of origin.

Recently, financial markets have also become highly integrated. This development allows investors to diversify their investment portfolios internationally. In 2016, for instance, U.S. investors collectively invested $154 billion in foreign securities, such as stocks and bonds, whereas foreigners invested $276 billion in U.S. securities.[1] In particular, Asian and Middle Eastern investors are investing heavily in U.S. and other foreign financial markets in efforts to recycle their large trade surpluses. In addition, many major corporations of the world, such as IBM, Toyota, and British Petroleum, have their shares cross-listed on foreign stock exchanges, thereby rendering their shares internationally tradable and gaining access to foreign capital as well. Consequently, Toyota's venture, say, in China can be financed partly by American investors who purchase Toyota shares traded on the New York Stock Exchange.

---

[1]This information is from *International Financial Statistics*, 2016.

Undoubtedly, we are now living in a world where all the major economic functions—consumption, production, and investment—are highly globalized. It is thus essential for financial managers to fully understand vital international dimensions of financial management. This *global shift* is in marked contrast to a few decades ago, when the authors of this book were learning finance. At that time, most professors customarily (and safely, to some extent) ignored international aspects of finance. This parochial attitude has become untenable since then.

What's Special about International Finance?

Although we may be convinced of the importance of studying international finance, we still have to ask ourselves, what's special about international finance? Put another way, how is international finance different from purely domestic finance (if such a thing exists)? Three major dimensions set international finance apart from domestic finance. They are:

1. Foreign exchange and political risks.
2. Market imperfections.
3. Expanded opportunity set.

As we will see, these major dimensions of international finance largely stem from the fact that sovereign nations have the right and power to issue currencies, formulate their own economic policies, impose taxes, and regulate movements of people, goods, and capital across their borders. Before we move on, let us briefly describe each of the key dimensions of international financial management.

Foreign Exchange and Political Risks

Suppose Mexico is a major export market for your company and the Mexican peso depreciates drastically against the U.S. dollar, as it did in December 1994. This means that your company's products can be priced out of the Mexican market, as the peso price of American imports will rise following the peso's fall. If such countries as Indonesia, Thailand, and Korea are major export markets, your company would have faced the same difficult situation in the wake of the Asian currency crisis of 1997. In integrated financial markets, individuals or households may also be seriously exposed to uncertain exchange rates. For example, since the EU accession, many Hungarians have borrowed in terms of the euro or Swiss franc to purchase houses. They were initially attracted by the easy availability and low interest rates for foreign currency mortgage loans. However, as the Hungarian currency, forint, was falling against the euro and Swiss franc during the recent global financial crisis, the burden of mortgage payments in terms of forint has increased sharply, forcing many borrowers to default. The preceding examples suggest that when firms and individuals are engaged in cross-border transactions, they are potentially exposed to **foreign exchange risk** that they would not normally encounter in purely domestic transactions.

Currently, the exchange rates among such major currencies as the U.S. dollar, Japanese yen, British pound, and euro fluctuate continuously in an unpredictable manner. This has been the case since the early 1970s, when fixed exchange rates were abandoned. As can be seen from Exhibit 1.1, exchange rate volatility has exploded since 1973. Exchange rate uncertainty will have a pervasive influence on all the major economic functions, including consumption, production, and investment.

Another risk that firms and individuals may encounter in an international setting is political risk. **Political risk** ranges from unexpected changes in tax rules to outright expropriation of assets held by foreigners. Political risk arises from the fact that a sovereign country can change the "rules of the game" and the affected parties may not have effective recourse. In 1992, for example, the Enron Development Corporation, a subsidiary of a Houston-based energy company, signed a contract to build India's largest power plant. After Enron had spent nearly $300 million, the project

https:// www.cia.gov/library /publications/the-world-factbook

Website of *The World Factbook* published by the CIA provides background information, such as geography, government, and economy, of countries around the world.

5

EXHIBIT 1.1

Monthly Percentage Change in Japanese Yen-U.S. Dollar Exchange Rate

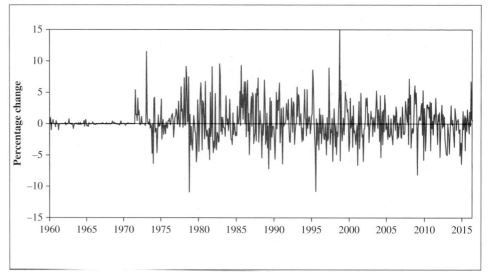

Source: International Monetary Fund, *International Financial Statistics,* various issues.

was canceled in 1995 by nationalist politicians in the Maharashtra state who argued India didn't need the power plant. For another example, in April 2012 the Argentine goverment nationalized a majority stake in YPF, the country's largest oil company, worth approximately $10 billion, held by the Spanish parent company, Repsol, accusing the latter for underproducing oil in Argentina. Broadly, the seizure of YPF is a part of the campaign to bring strategic industries under government control. Both the Enron and Repsol episodes illustrate the difficulty of enforcing contracts in foreign countries.[2]

Multinational firms and investors should be particularly aware of political risk when they invest in those countries without a tradition of the rule of law. The meltdown of Yukos, the largest Russian oil company, provides a compelling example. Following the arrest of Mikhail Khodorkovsky, the majority owner and a critic of the government, on fraud and tax evasion charges, the Russian authorities forced Yukos into bankruptcy. The authorities sued the company for more than $20 billion in back taxes and auctioned off its assets to cover the alleged tax arrears. This government action against Yukos, widely viewed as politically motivated, inflicted serious damage on international shareholders of Yukos, whose investment values were wiped out. It is important to understand that the property rights of shareholders and investors are not universally respected.

Market Imperfections

Although the world economy is much more integrated today than was the case 10 or 20 years ago, a variety of barriers still hamper free movements of people, goods, services, and capital across national boundaries. These barriers include legal restrictions, excessive transaction and transportation costs, information asymmetry, and discriminatory taxation. The world markets are thus highly imperfect. As we will discuss later in this book, **market imperfections**, which represent various frictions and impediments preventing markets from functioning perfectly, play an important role in motivating MNCs to locate production overseas. Honda, a Japanese automobile company, for instance, decided to establish production facilities in Ohio, mainly to circumvent trade barriers. One might even say that MNCs are a gift of market imperfections.

Imperfections in the world financial markets tend to restrict the extent to which investors can diversify their portfolios. An interesting example is provided by the Nestlé Corporation, a well-known Swiss MNC. Nestlé used to issue two different classes of common stock, bearer shares and registered shares, and foreigners were allowed to hold

---

[2]Since then, Enron has renegotiated the deal with the Maharashtra state while the Spanish government retaliated by restricting imports from Argentina.

EXHIBIT 1.2

Daily Prices of Nestlé's Bearer and Registered Shares

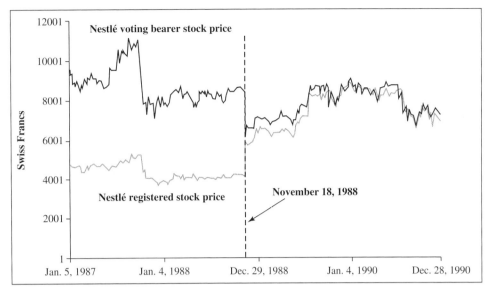

Source: Reprinted from *Journal of Financial Economics,* Volume 37, Issue 3, Claudio Loderer and Andreas Jacobs, "The Nestlé Crash," pp. 315–39, 1995, with kind permission from Elsevier Science S.A., P.O. Box 564, 1001 Lausanne, Switzerland.

only bearer shares. As Exhibit 1.2 shows, bearer shares used to trade for about twice the price of registered shares, which were exclusively reserved for Swiss residents.[3] This kind of price disparity is a uniquely international phenomenon that is attributable to market imperfections.

On November 18, 1988, however, Nestlé lifted restrictions imposed on foreigners, allowing them to hold registered as well as bearer shares. After this announcement, the price spread between the two types of Nestlé shares narrowed drastically. As Exhibit 1.2 shows, the price of bearer shares declined sharply, whereas that of registered shares rose sharply. This implies that there was a major transfer of wealth from foreign shareholders to domestic shareholders. Foreigners holding Nestlé bearer shares were exposed to political risk in a country that is widely viewed as a haven from such risk. The Nestlé episode illustrates both the importance of considering market imperfections in international finance and the peril of political risk.

Expanded Opportunity Set

When firms venture into the arena of global markets, they can benefit from an **expanded opportunity set**. As previously mentioned, firms can locate production in any country or region of the world to maximize their performance and raise funds in any capital market where the cost of capital is the lowest. In addition, firms can gain from greater economies of scale when their tangible and intangible assets are deployed on a global basis. A real-world example showing the gains from a global approach to financial management is provided by the following excerpt from *The Wall Street Journal* (April 9, 1996):

> Another factor binding bond markets ever closer is large companies' flexibility to issue bonds around the world at will, thanks to the global swap market. At the vanguard are companies such as General Electric of the U.S. Mark VanderGriend, who runs the financing desk at Banque Paribas, says it took "about 15 minutes" to put together a four billion franc ($791.6 million) deal for GE. By raising the money in francs and swapping into dollars instantly, GE will save five hundredths of a percentage point—or about $400,000 annually on the nine-year deal. "They have such a huge requirement for capital that they are constantly looking for arbitrages," adds Mr. VanderGriend. "And they don't care much how they get there."

---

[3]It is noted that bearer and registered shares of Nestlé had the same claims on dividends but differential voting rights. Chapter 17 provides a detailed discussion of the Nestlé case.

Individual investors can also benefit greatly if they invest internationally rather than domestically. Suppose you have a given amount of money to invest in stocks. You may invest the entire amount in U.S. (domestic) stocks. Alternatively, you may allocate the funds across domestic and foreign stocks. If you diversify internationally, the resulting international portfolio may have a lower risk or a higher return (or both) than a purely domestic portfolio. This can happen mainly because stock returns tend to covary less across countries than within a given country. Once you are aware of overseas investment opportunities and are willing to diversify internationally, you face a much expanded opportunity set and you can benefit from it. It just doesn't make sense to play in only one corner of the sandbox. Thus, an important "normative" theme we will study throughout this book is: how to maximize the benefits from the global opportunity set, while judiciously controlling currency and political risks and managing various market imperfections.

Goals for International Financial Management

The foregoing discussion implies that understanding and managing foreign exchange and political risks and coping with market imperfections have become important parts of the financial manager's job. *International Financial Management* is designed to provide today's financial managers with an understanding of the fundamental concepts and the tools necessary to be effective global managers. Throughout, the text emphasizes how to deal with exchange risk and market imperfections, using the various instruments and tools that are available, while at the same time maximizing the benefits from an expanded global opportunity set.

Effective financial management, however, is more than the application of the newest business techniques or operating more efficiently. There must be an underlying goal. *International Financial Management* is written from the perspective that the fundamental goal of sound financial management is shareholder wealth maximization. **Shareholder wealth maximization** means that the firm makes all business decisions and investments with an eye toward making the owners of the firm—the shareholders—better off financially, or more wealthy, than they were before.

Whereas shareholder wealth maximization is generally accepted as the ultimate goal of financial management in "Anglo-Saxon" countries, such as Australia, Canada, the United Kingdom, and especially the United States, it is not as widely embraced a goal in other parts of the world. In countries like France and Germany, for example, shareholders are generally viewed as one of the "stakeholders" of the firm, others being employees, customers, suppliers, banks, and so forth. European managers tend to consider the promotion of the firm's stakeholders' overall welfare as the most important corporate goal. In Japan, on the other hand, many companies form a small number of interlocking business groups called *keiretsu*, such as Mitsubishi, Mitsui, and Sumitomo, which arose from consolidation of family-owned business empires. Although *keiretsu* have weakened in recent years, Japanese managers still tend to regard the prosperity and growth of their *keiretsu* as the critical goal; for instance, they tend to strive to maximize market share, rather than shareholder wealth.

It is pointed out, however, that as capital markets are becoming more liberalized and internationally integrated in recent decades, even managers in France, Germany, Japan, and other non-Anglo-Saxon countries are beginning to pay serious attention to shareholder wealth maximization. In Germany, for example, companies are now allowed to repurchase stocks, if necessary, for the benefit of shareholders. In accepting an unprecedented $203 billion takeover offer by Vodafone AirTouch, a leading British wireless phone company, Klaus Esser, CEO of Mannesmann of Germany, cited shareholder interests: "The shareholders clearly think that this company, Mannesmann, a great company, would be better together with Vodafone AirTouch. . . . The final decision belongs to shareholders."[4]

---

[4]The source for this information is *The New York Times*, February 4, 2000, p. C9.

Obviously, the firm could pursue other goals. This does not mean, however, that the goal of shareholder wealth maximization is merely an alternative, or that the firm should enter into a debate as to its appropriate fundamental goal. Quite the contrary. If the firm seeks to maximize shareholder wealth, it will most likely simultaneously be accomplishing other legitimate goals that are perceived as worthwhile. Shareholder wealth maximization is a long-run goal. A firm cannot stay in business to maximize shareholder wealth if it treats employees poorly, produces shoddy merchandise, wastes raw materials and natural resources, operates inefficiently, or fails to satisfy customers. Only a well-managed business firm that profitably produces what is demanded in an efficient manner can expect to stay in business in the long run and thereby provide employment opportunities.

While managers are hired to run the company for the interests of shareholders, there is no guarantee that they will actually do so. As shown by a series of corporate scandals at companies like Enron, WorldCom, and Global Crossing, managers may pursue their own private interests at the expense of shareholders when they are not closely monitored. This so-called agency problem is a major weakness of the public corporation. Extensive corporate malfeasance and accounting manipulations at these companies eventually drove them into financial distress and bankruptcy, devastating shareholders and employees alike. Lamentably, some senior managers and corporate insiders enriched themselves enormously in the process. Clearly, the boards of directors, the ultimate guardians of the interests of shareholders, failed to perform their duties at these companies. In the wake of these corporate calamities that have undermined the credibility of the free market system, the society has painfully learned the importance of **corporate governance**, that is, the financial and legal framework for regulating the relationship between a company's management and its shareholders. Needless to say, the corporate governance problem is not confined to the United States. In fact, it can be a much more serious problem in many other parts of the world, especially emerging and transition economies, such as Indonesia, Korea, China, Italy, and Russia, where legal protection of shareholders is weak or virtually nonexistent.

As we will discuss in Chapter 4 in detail, corporate governance structure varies greatly across countries, reflecting different cultural, legal, economic, and political environments in different countries. In many countries where shareholders do not have strong legal rights, corporate ownership tends to be concentrated. The concentrated ownership of the firm, in turn, may give rise to the conflicts of interest between dominant shareholders (often the founding family) and small outside shareholders. The collapse of Parmalat, a family-controlled Italian company, after decades of accounting frauds, provides an example of corporate governance risk. The company allegedly hid debts, "invented" assets, and diverted funds to bail out failing ventures of the family members. Because only the Tanzi (founding) family and close associates knew how the company was run, it was possible to hide the questionable practices for decades. Outside shareholders who collectively control a 49 percent stake did not know how Parmalat was operating. Franco Ferrarotti, professor of sociology at the University of Rome, was quoted as saying, "The government is weak, there is no sense of state, public services are bad and social services are weak. The family is so strong because it is the only institution that doesn't let you down."[5]

Shareholders are the owners of the business; it is their capital that is at risk. It is only equitable that they receive a fair return on their investment. Private capital may not have been forthcoming for the business firm if it had intended to accomplish any other objective. As we will discuss shortly, the massive privatization that has been taking place in developing and formerly socialist countries, which will eventually enhance the standard of living of these countries' citizens, depends on private investment. It is thus vitally important to strengthen corporate governance so that shareholders receive fair returns on their investments. In what follows, we are going to discuss in detail: (i) the globalization of the world economy, and (ii) the growing role of MNCs in the world economy.

---

[5]*USA Today*, February 4, 2004, p. 2B.

Globalization of the World Economy: Major Trends and Developments

The term "globalization" became a popular buzzword for describing business practices in the last few decades, and it appears as if it will continue to be a key word for describing business management throughout the current century. In this section, we review several key trends and developments of the world economy: (i) the emergence of globalized financial markets, (ii) the emergence of the euro as a global currency, (iii) Europe's sovereign debt crisis of 2010, (iv) continued trade liberalization and economic integration, (v) large-scale privatization of state-owned enterprises, and (vi) the global financial crisis of 2008–2009.

Emergence of Globalized Financial Markets

The 1980s and 90s saw a rapid integration of international capital and financial markets. The impetus for globalized financial markets initially came from the governments of major countries that had begun to deregulate their foreign exchange and capital markets. For example, in 1980 Japan deregulated its foreign exchange market, and in 1985 the Tokyo Stock Exchange admitted as members a limited number of foreign brokerage firms. Additionally, the London Stock Exchange (LSE) began admitting foreign firms as full members in February 1986.

Perhaps the most celebrated deregulation, however, occurred in London on October 27, 1986, and is known as the "Big Bang." On that date, as on "May Day" in 1975 in the United States, the London Stock Exchange eliminated fixed brokerage commissions. Additionally, the regulation separating the order-taking function from the market-making function was eliminated. In Europe, financial institutions are allowed to perform both investment-banking and commercial-banking functions. Hence, the London affiliates of foreign commercial banks were eligible for membership on the LSE. These changes were designed to give London the most open and competitive capital markets in the world. It has worked, and today the competition in London is especially fierce among the world's major financial centers. The United States repealed the Glass-Steagall Act, which restricted commercial banks from investment banking activities (such as underwriting corporate securities), further promoting competition among financial institutions. Even developing countries such as Chile, Mexico, and Korea began to liberalize by allowing foreigners to directly invest in their financial markets.

www.imf.org

Offers an overview of globalization and financial development.

Deregulated financial markets and heightened competition in financial services provided a natural environment for financial innovations that resulted in the introduction of various instruments. Examples of these innovative instruments include currency futures and options, multicurrency bonds, international mutual funds, country funds, exchange-traded funds (ETFs), and foreign stock index futures and options. Corporations also played an active role in integrating the world financial markets by listing their shares across borders. Such well-known non-U.S. companies as BHP Billiton, Petrobras, China Mobile, Novartis, Wipro, Honda Motor, Telmex, ING, BP, Korea Telecom, and UBS are directly listed and traded on the New York Stock Exchange. At the same time, U.S. firms such as IBM and GE are listed on the Frankfurt, London, and Paris stock exchanges. Such cross-border listings of stocks allow investors to buy and sell foreign shares as if they were domestic shares, facilitating international investments.[6]

Last but not least, advances in computer and telecommunications technology contributed in no small measure to the emergence of global financial markets. These technological advancements, especially Internet-based information technologies, gave investors around the world immediate access to the most recent news and information

---

[6]Various studies indicate that the liberalization of capital markets tends to lower the cost of capital. See, for example, Peter Henry, "Stock Market Liberalization, Economic Reform, and Emerging Market Equity Prices," *Journal of Finance* (2000), pp. 529–64.

affecting their investments, sharply reducing information costs. Also, computerized order-processing and settlement procedures have reduced the costs of international transactions. Based on the U.S. Department of Commerce computer price deflator, the relative cost index of computing power declined from a level of 100 in 1960 to 15.6 in 1970, 2.9 in 1980, and only 0.5 by 1999. As a result of these technological developments and the liberalization of financial markets, cross-border financial transactions have exploded in recent years.

Emergence of the Euro as a Global Currency

The advent of the euro at the start of 1999 represents a momentous event in the history of the world financial system that has profound ramifications for the world economy. Currently, more than 300 million Europeans in 19 countries (Austria, Belgium, Cyprus, Estonia, Finland, France, Germany, Greece, Ireland, Italy, Latvia, Lithuania, Luxembourg, Malta, the Netherlands, Portugal, Slovakia, Slovenia, and Spain) are using the common currency on a daily basis. No single currency has circulated so widely in Europe since the days of the Roman Empire. Considering that many new members of the EU, including the Czech Republic, Hungary, and Poland, may adopt the euro eventually, the **transactions domain** of the euro may become larger than that of the U.S. dollar in the future.

Once a country adopts the common currency, it obviously cannot have its own monetary policy. The common monetary policy for the euro zone is now formulated by the **European Central Bank** (ECB) that is located in Frankfurt and closely modeled after the Bundesbank, the German central bank. ECB is legally mandated to achieve price stability for the euro zone. Considering the sheer size of the euro zone in terms of population, economic output, and world trade share, the euro has a potential for becoming another global currency rivaling the U.S. dollar for dominance in international trade and finance. Reflecting the significance of the euro's introduction, Professor Robert Mundell, who is often referred to as the intellectual father of the euro, stated: "The creation of the euro area will eventually, but inevitably, lead to competition with the dollar area, both from the standpoint of excellence in monetary policy, and in the enlistment of other currencies."[7] If the euro maintains its credibility, the world faces the prospect of a bipolar international monetary system.

Since its inception in 1999, the euro has already brought about revolutionary changes in European finance. For instance, by redenominating corporate and government bonds and stocks from many different currencies into the common currency, the euro has precipitated the emergence of continentwide capital markets in Europe that are comparable to U.S. markets in depth and liquidity. Companies all over the world can benefit from this development as they can raise capital more easily on favorable terms in Europe. In addition, the recent surge in European M&A activities, cross-border alliances among financial exchanges, and lessening dependence on the banking sectors for capital raising are all manifestations of the profound effects of the euro.

Since the end of World War I, the U.S. dollar has played the role of the dominant global currency, displacing the British pound. As a result, foreign exchange rates of currencies are often quoted against the dollar, and the lion's share of currency trading involves the dollar on either the buy or sell side. Similarly, international trade in primary commodities, such as petroleum, coffee, wheat, and gold, is conducted using the U.S. dollar as the invoice currency. Reflecting the dominant position of the dollar in the world economy, central banks of the world hold a major portion of their external reserves in dollars. The ascendance of the dollar reflects several key factors such as the dominant size of the U.S. economy, mature and open capital markets, price stability, and the political and military power of the United States. It is noted that the dominant global currency status of the dollar confers upon the United States

---

[7]Source: Robert Mundell, 2000, "Currency Area, Volatility and Intervention," *Journal of Policy Modeling 22* (3), 281–99.

many special privileges, such as the ability to run trade deficits without having to hold much in foreign exchange reserves, that is, "deficits without tears," and to conduct a large portion of international transactions in dollars, without bearing exchange risks. However, once economic agents start to use the euro in earnest as an invoice and reserve currency, the dollar may have to share the aforementioned privileges with the euro.

Europe's Sovereign Debt Crisis of 2010

The euro's emergence as a global currency, however, was dealt a serious setback in the midst of Europe's sovereign debt crisis. The crisis started in December 2009 when the new Greek government revealed that its budget deficit for the year would be 12.7 percent of GDP, not the 3.7 percent previously forecast. The previous government had falsified the national account data. Unbeknownst to the outside world, Greece was in a serious violation of Europe's stability pact, which limits the annual budget deficit of a euro-zone country to a maximum of 3 percent of GDP. This news surprised financial markets and prompted investors, who became worried about sovereign default, to sell off Greek government bonds. The Greek predicament is attributable to excessive borrowing and spending, with wages and prices rising faster than productivity. With the adoption of the euro, Greece no longer can use the traditional means of restoring competitiveness, i.e., depreciation of the national currency.

The panic spread to other weak European economies, especially Ireland, Portugal, and Spain. In the spring of 2010, both Standard & Poor's and Moody's, credit rating agencies, downgraded the government bonds of the affected countries, making borrowing and refinancing more costly. In particular, the Greek government bond was downgraded to "junk," ineligible for institutional investment. The unfolding "Greek drama" is illustrated in Exhibit 1.3, which plots the two-year government bond yields for Greece and Germany, as well as the dollar-euro exchange rate. As can be seen from the exhibit, Greece paid a minimal or practically nonexistent premium above the German interest rate until December 2009. This was possible owing to Greece's membership in the euro club. However, the Greek interest rate began to rise sharply thereafter, reaching 18.3 percent on May 7, 2010, before it fell following the announcement of the bailout package on May 9. Also, the specter of chaotic sovereign defaults led to a sharp fall of the euro's exchange value in currency markets.

EXHIBIT 1.3

The Greek Drama

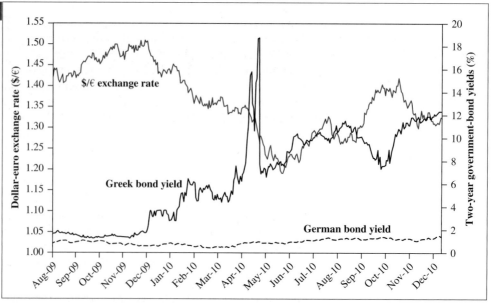

Source: Bloomberg.

The sovereign debt crisis in Greece, which accounts for only about 2.5 percent of euro-zone GDP, quickly escalated to a Europe-wide debt crisis, threatening the nascent recovery of the world economy from the severe global financial crisis of 2008–2009. Facing the spreading crisis, the European Union (EU) countries, led by France and Germany, jointly with the International Monetary Fund (IMF), put together a massive €750 billion package to bail out Greece and other weak economies. It is noted that Europe's lack of political union and fragmented decision-making structure made it slow and contentious for EU countries to reach agreement on the bailout plan, making the rescue more expensive than it may otherwise have been.

Europe's sovereign-debt crisis of 2010 revealed a profound weakness of the euro as the common currency: Euro-zone countries have achieved monetary integration by adopting the euro, but without fiscal integration. While euro-zone countries share the common monetary policy, fiscal policies governing taxation, spending, and borrowing firmly remain under the control of national governments. Hence, a lack of fiscal discipline in a euro-zone country can always become a Europe-wide crisis, threatening the value and credibility of the common currency. The long-term viability of the euro and its potential as a global currency thus critically depend on how this disparity between monetary and fiscal integration will be addressed. Regarding this challenge, Jean-Claude Trichet, former president of the European Central Bank (ECB), recently called for making a "quantum leap" in the euro zone's economic governance and urged Europe to form a "fiscal confederation." It remains to be seen whether Europe will be able to meet these challenges.

Trade Liberalization and Economic Integration

International trade, which has been the traditional link between national economies, has continued to expand. As Exhibit 1.4 shows, the ratio of merchandise exports to GDP for the world has increased from 7.0 percent in 1950 to 26.2 percent in 2014. This implies that, over the same time period, international trade increased nearly three times as fast as world GDP. For some countries, international trade grew much faster; for Germany, the ratio rose from 6.2 percent to 51.1 percent, while for Korea it grew from 1.0 percent to 50.1 percent over the same time period. Latin American countries such as Argentina, Brazil, and Mexico used to have relatively low export-to-GDP ratios. In 1973, for example, the export-to-GDP ratio was 2.1 percent for Argentina, 2.6 percent for Brazil, and 2.2 percent for Mexico. This reflects the inward-looking, protectionist economic policies these countries pursued in the past. Even these once-protectionist countries are now increasingly pursuing free-market and open-economy

EXHIBIT 1.4

Long-Term Openness in Perspective (merchandise exports/GDP at 1990 prices, in percent)

Country	1870	1913	1929	1950	1973	2014
United States	2.5	3.7	3.6	3.0	5.0	13.8
Canada	12.0	12.2	15.8	13.0	19.9	32.1
Australia	7.4	12.8	11.2	9.1	11.2	21.0
United Kingdom	12.0	17.7	13.3	11.4	14.0	28.6
Germany	9.5	15.6	12.8	6.2	23.8	51.1
France	4.9	8.2	8.6	7.7	15.4	27.9
Spain	3.8	8.1	5.0	1.6	5.0	32.1
Japan	0.2	2.4	3.5	2.3	7.9	17.6
Korea	0.0	1.0	4.5	1.0	8.2	50.1
Thailand	2.1	6.7	6.6	7.0	4.5	62.3
Argentina	9.4	6.8	6.1	2.4	2.1	11.0
Brazil	11.8	9.5	7.1	4.0	2.6	10.8
Mexico	3.7	10.8	14.8	3.5	2.2	32.0
World	5.0	8.7	9.0	7.0	11.2	26.2

Source: Various issues of *World Financial Markets*, JP Morgan, *World Development Indicators*, *International Trade Statistics*, and *International Financial Statistics*, IMF.

policies because of the gains from international trade. In 2014, the export-to-GDP ratio was 11.0 percent for Argentina, 10.8 percent for Brazil, and 32.0 percent for Mexico.

The principal argument for international trade is based on the **theory of comparative advantage**, which was advanced by David Ricardo in his seminal book, *Principles of Political Economy* (1817). According to Ricardo, it is mutually beneficial for countries if they specialize in the production of those goods they can produce most efficiently and trade those goods among them. Suppose England produces textiles most efficiently, whereas France produces wine most efficiently. It then makes sense if England specializes in the production of textiles and France in the production of wine, and the two countries then trade their products. By doing so, the two countries can increase their combined production of textiles and wine, which, in turn, allows both countries to consume more of both goods. This argument remains valid even if one country can produce both goods more efficiently than the other country.[8] Ricardo's theory has a clear policy implication: *Liberalization of international trade will enhance the welfare of the world's citizens.* In other words, international trade is not a "zero-sum" game in which one country benefits at the expense of another country—the view held by the "mercantilists." Rather, international trade could be an "increasing-sum" game at which all players become winners.

Although the theory of comparative advantage is not completely immune to valid criticism, it nevertheless provides a powerful intellectual rationale for promoting free trade among nations. Currently, international trade is becoming further liberalized at both the global and regional levels. At the global level, the **General Agreement on Tariffs and Trade (GATT)**, which is a multilateral agreement among member countries, has played a key role in dismantling barriers to international trade. Since it was founded in 1947, GATT has been successful in gradually eliminating and reducing tariffs, subsidies, quotas, and other barriers to trade. Under the auspices of GATT, the Uruguay Round launched in 1986 aims to (i) reduce import tariffs worldwide by an average of 38 percent, (ii) increase the proportion of duty-free products from 20 percent to 44 percent for industrialized countries, and (iii) extend the rules of world trade to cover agriculture, services such as banking and insurance, and intellectual property rights. It also created a permanent **World Trade Organization (WTO)** to replace GATT. The WTO has more power to enforce the rules of international trade. China joined the WTO in 2001. China's WTO membership will further legitimize the idea of free trade. The latest round of talks, the Doha Round commenced at Doha, Qatar, in 2001, is still continuing. Its objective is to lower trade barriers around the world, promoting free trade between developed and developing countries. However, negotiations have stalled over a divide between the developed countries led by the United States, European Union, and Japan and the developing countries led by Brazil, China, and India. The main disagreements are over opening up agricultural and industrial markets of various countries and how to reduce rich countries' agricultural subsidies.

Inspired by Deng Xiaoping's pragmatic policies, that is, "to get rich is glorious," China began to implement market-oriented economic reforms in the late 1970s. Since then, the Chinese economy has grown rapidly, often at an astounding rate of 10 percent per annum, and in the process has lifted tens of millions of local citizens from poverty. China's impressive economic growth has been driven by burgeoning international trade and foreign direct investment. China's demand for natural resources, capital goods, and technologies, in turn, has boosted exports to China from the rest of the world. India has also joined China in recent years in opening its economy and attracting foreign investment. India has implemented its own market-oriented reforms since the early 1990s, gradually dismantling the "license-raj" or quota system in all economic spheres and encouraging private entrepreneurship. As is well known, India has emerged as the most important center for outsourcing

www.wto.org

The World Trade Organization website covers news and data about international trade development.

---

[8]Readers are referred to Appendix 1A for a detailed discussion of the theory of comparative advantage.

information technology (IT) services, back-office support, and R&D functions. The huge supplies of labor, highly skilled and disciplined, in China and India are bound to alter the structure of the world economy in a major way. China already is the second largest economy in the world, second only to the United States. India, on the other hand, is the third largest economy ahead of Japan in terms of purchasing power. The importance of China and India is likely to grow further, profoundly altering the pattern of international production, trade, and investment.

On the regional level, formal arrangements among countries have been instituted to promote economic integration. The **European Union (EU)** is a prime example. The European Union is the direct descendent of the European Community (formerly the European Economic Community), which was established to foster economic integration among the countries of Western Europe. Today the EU includes 28 member states that have eliminated barriers to the free flow of goods, capital, and people. The member states of the EU hope this move will strengthen its economic position relative to the United States, China, and Japan. In January 1999, 11 member countries of the EU successfully adopted a single common currency, the euro, which may potentially rival the U.S. dollar as a dominant currency for international trade and investment. Greece joined the euro club in January 2001. Subsequently, five more EU member countries—Cyprus, Estonia, Malta, Slovenia, and Slovakia—adopted the euro. The launch of the euro has spurred a rush by European companies into seeking pan-European and global alliances. Merger and acquisition (M&A) deals in Europe have become comparable to the figure for U.S. deals in recent years.

Whereas the economic and monetary union planned by the EU is one of the most advanced forms of economic integration, a free trade area is the most basic. In 1994, Canada, the United States, and Mexico entered into the **North American Free Trade Agreement (NAFTA)**. Canada is the United States' largest trading partner and Mexico is the third largest. In a free trade area, most impediments to trade, such as tariffs and import quotas, are eliminated among members. The terms of NAFTA call for phasing out tariffs over a 15-year period. Many observers believe that NAFTA will foster increased trade among its members, resulting in an increase in the number of jobs and the standard of living in all member countries. It is interesting to note from Exhibit 1.4 that for Mexico, the ratio of export to GDP has increased dramatically from 2.2 percent in 1973 to 32.0 percent in 2014. This dramatic increase in Mexico's propensity to trade should be attributed to NAFTA.

Recently, the process of global and regional economic integration was dealt a major setback when the majority of Britons voted to leave the EU, an event known as "Brexit." The unexpected outcome of the British referendum, held on June 23, 2016, concerning the EU membership can mark the inflection point of the globalization process that has taken place for the last 60 years or so. Brexit is likely to weaken both the United Kingdom and the European Union, economically and politically. Also, London's position as the dominant center of European finance may deteriorate if the UK loses unrestricted access to Europe's single market. In fact, one cannot completely discount the possibility that Brexit may trigger slow disintegration of the EU under the worst-case scenario.

It is ironic that Britain, the country that championed free trade and liberal capitalism, became the first country to voluntarily leave the EU, the most ambitious globalization project. How did it happen? The answer for the question also seems a bit ironic: Brexit happened, to a certain extent, because globalization succeeded. As European integration deepened, London emerged as the capital of European finance, benefiting London tremendously. But the rest of England did not share the fruits of this success. It is highly instructive that although 60 percent of Londoners voted for remaining in the EU, only 45 percent of voters throughout the rest of England voted the same way. Basically, the majority of voters outside of London felt alienated from the globalized economy and were concerned about competition for jobs from the immigrants.

www.lib.berkeley.edu/doemoff/govinfo/intl/gov_eu.html

The University of California at Berkeley library provides a web guide to resources related to the European Union.

Brexit also revealed some of the difficulties associated with free trade and global economic integration that espouse free movements of goods, capital, and people. Although international trade contributes a great deal to economic growth, lifting tens of millions of people from poverty around the world, it also produces clear winners and losers. As a result, unless losers are compensated by transfer payment and retraining, free trade is likely to encounter political opposition. It is thus important for countries to pay attention to "shared growth" to continue to benefit from free trade and economic integration and fend off protectionism. If protectionism wins over free trade, as happened in the 1930s, everybody may end up becoming losers.

Privatization

The economic integration and globalization that began in the 1980s picked up speed in the 1990s via privatization. Through **privatization**, a country divests itself of the ownership and operation of a business venture by turning it over to the free market system. Privatization did not begin with the fall of the Berlin Wall; nevertheless, its pace has quickly accelerated since the collapse of communism in the Eastern Bloc countries. It is ironic that the very political and economic system that only a short while ago extolled the virtues of state ownership should so dramatically be shifting toward capitalism by shedding state-operated businesses. President Calvin Coolidge once said that the business of America is business. One might now say that business is the business of the world.

Privatization can be viewed in many ways. In one sense it is a denationalization process. When a national government divests itself of a state-run business, it gives up part of its national identity. Moreover, if the new owners are foreign, the country may simultaneously be importing a cultural influence that did not previously exist. Privatization is frequently viewed as a means to an end. One benefit of privatization for many less-developed countries is that the sale of state-owned businesses brings to the national treasury hard-currency foreign reserves. The sale proceeds are often used to pay down sovereign debt that has weighed heavily on the economy. Additionally, privatization is often seen as a cure for bureaucratic inefficiency and waste; some economists estimate that privatization improves efficiency and reduces operating costs by as much as 20 percent.

There is no one single way to privatize state-owned operations. The objectives of the country seem to be the prevailing guide. For the Czech Republic, speed was the overriding factor. To accomplish privatization en masse, the Czech government essentially gave away its businesses to the Czech people. For a nominal fee, vouchers were sold that allowed Czech citizens to bid on businesses as they went on the auction block. From 1991 to 1995, more than 1,700 companies were turned over to private hands. Moreover, three-quarters of the Czech citizens became stockholders in these newly privatized firms.

In Russia, there has been an "irreversible" shift to private ownership, according to the World Bank. More than 80 percent of the country's nonfarm workers are now employed in the private sector. Eleven million apartment units have been privatized, as have half of the country's 240,000 other business firms. Additionally, via a Czech-style voucher system, 40 million Russians now own stock in more than 15,000 medium- to large-size corporations that became privatized through mass auctions of state-owned enterprises.

In China, privatization has proceeded by way of listing state-owned enterprises (SOEs) on the organized exchanges, thereby making SOEs eligible for private ownership. In the early 1980s, China launched two stock exchanges—the Shanghai Stock Exchange and the Shenzhen Stock Exchange—as a part of concerted efforts toward market-oriented reform. Since their inception, the Chinese stock markets have grown at a phenomenal pace, becoming some of the largest stock markets in Asia in terms of capitalization. Currently, more than 2,000 companies are listed on China's stock exchanges. China's stock markets now play a vital role in privatization of SOEs, raising new capital for business investments and ventures, and propagating corporate ownership among citizens. Foreigners may also participate in the ownership of Chinese firms mainly by investing in the so-called B-shares listed on the Shanghai or Shenzen stock exchanges or in those shares that are directly listed on the Hong Kong Stock Exchange (H-shares), New York Stock Exchange, or other international exchanges. It is noted that A-shares of Chinese firms are mostly reserved for domestic investors. While individual and institutional investors are now actively investing in Chinese shares, the Chinese government still retains the majority stakes in most public firms.

For some countries, privatization has meant globalization. For example, to achieve fiscal stability, New Zealand had to open its once-socialist economy to foreign capital. Australian investors now control its commercial banks, and U.S. firms purchased the national telephone company and timber operations. While workers' rights have changed under foreign ownership and a capitalist economy, New Zealand now ranks high among the most competitive market environments. Fiscal stability has also been realized. In 1994, New Zealand's economy grew at a rate of 6 percent and inflation was under control. As can be seen from the experiences of New Zealand, privatization has spurred a tremendous increase in cross-border investment.

Global Financial Crisis of 2008–2009

The subprime mortgage crisis in the United States that began in the summer of 2007 led to a severe credit crunch, making borrowing and refinancing difficult for households, firms, and banks. The credit crunch, in turn, escalated to a full-blown global financial crisis in 2008–2009. The defining moment of the crisis came on September 14, 2008, when Lehman Brothers, a major U.S. investment bank with a global presence, went bankrupt. The abrupt failure of an iconic U.S. bank touched off a major crisis of confidence in financial markets and institutions around the world. Stock prices fell precipitously. Output fell and unemployment rose sharply. As shown in Exhibit 1.5, the Dow Jones Industrial Average (DJIA), a popular U.S. stock market index, fell rapidly from a peak of 14,164 reached on October 9, 2007, to a trough of 7,062 on February 27, 2009, a 50 percent decline, while the U.S. unemployment rate began to rise from 4.4 percent in May 2007 to reach 10.1 percent in October 2009. At the same time, international trade has been shrinking rapidly. The crisis engulfed not only the advanced economies, such as the United States, Japan, and the European Union, but also many emerging

EXHIBIT 1.5

U.S. Unemployment Rate and Dow Jones Industrial Average (DJIA)

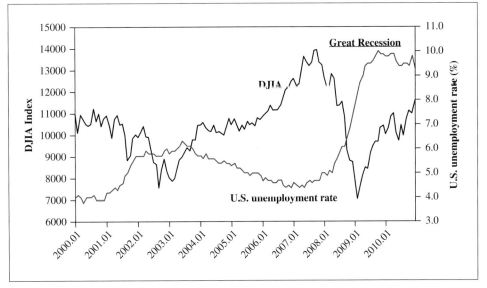

Source: Bloomberg.

economies, including Brazil, China, and Russia, albeit less severely. The world was sliding into the "Great Recession," the most serious, synchronized economic downturn since the Great Depression.

Subprime mortgages are a financial instrument designed to facilitate home ownership for low and modest income households. Most subprime mortgages are adjustable-rate mortgages and are refinanced relatively frequently. Mortgage banks raise funds for making subprime loans mainly by securitization. Once subprime mortgage loans are originated, they are pooled and packaged into a variety of mortgage-backed securities and sold to various institutional investors in the United States and abroad. Subprime mortgages worked as designed while house prices were rising during 1996–2005. But as U.S. interest rates began to rise in early 2004 due to the tightening monetary policy of the Federal Reserve, house prices stopped rising and began to decline in 2006. Subsequently, subprime borrowers started to default, spreading risk among investors and eroding the bank capital base in the United States and abroad.

What caused the global financial crisis? While it may be early to provide a definitive answer for this important question, it is possible to identify several factors that are likely to have contributed to the crisis. First, households and financial institutions borrowed too much and took too much risk. This excessive borrowing and risk taking is, in turn, attributable to the ample supply of liquidity and credit that is due to (i) the "easy money" policy of the Federal Reserve Bank, a legacy of its former chairman, Allan Greenspan, and also (ii) the massive inflow of foreign money associated with the recycling of trade surpluses of Asian countries, including China, Japan, and Korea, and the oil-exporting countries in the Middle East. Second, the crisis was amplified manyfold and transmitted globally by securitization. Securitization allows loan originators to avoid bearing the default risk, which leads to a compromised lending standard and increased moral hazard. Also, financial engineers designed opaque and complex mortgage-based securities that could be used for excessive risk-taking. These securities were traded infrequently and were often difficult to value. Third, the "invisible hands" of free markets apparently failed to self-regulate its excesses, contributing to the banking crisis. At the same time, "light touch" regulations by government agencies, such as the Securities and Exchange Commission (SEC) and the Federal Reserve, led to a failure to detect the rising risk in the financial system and to take regulatory actions in a timely fashion to prevent the crisis. This laissez-faire regulatory stance reflects the broad deregulation of the U.S. economy that has taken place since the 1980s. The repeal of the Glass-Steagall Act in 1999 is the *prima facie* example of the deregulatory trend in the United States. The Act, which was adopted in the wake of the Great Depression, built a firewall between commercial and investment banking activities. Its repeal may have encouraged banks to take risks excessively. Fourth, international financial markets are highly interconnected and integrated nowadays. Defaults of subprime mortgages in the United States came to threaten the solvency of the teachers' retirement program in Norway as the latter invested in U.S. mortgage-backed securities. The U.S. government was compelled to rescue AIG, a U.S. insurance company, with a $180 billion package, the most costly bailout of a single firm in history, as it feared that if AIG were allowed to fail, it might start a chain reaction of bankruptcies of AIG's international counterparties that included Goldman Sachs, Deutsche Bank, Barclays, Union Bank of Switzerland (UBS), Société Générale, and Merrill Lynch. So AIG was found to be not only too big, but also too interconnected to fail. In the contemporary world economy, a local financial shock originating in a market can quickly be transmitted to other markets through contagion and other channels. No market or institution is an island in an integrated world.

Facing the severe credit crunch and economic downturn, the U.S. government took forceful actions to save the banking system and stimulate the economy. As a matter of fact, the government acted as the lender of last resort as well as the spender of last resort to keep the economy floating. Specifically, the Bush administration-implemented Troubled Asset Relief Program (TARP), which was enacted in October 2008. Seven hundred billion dollars of the TARP fund were injected into the financial system to buy nonperforming assets and mortgage-related securities from banks and also to directly strengthen banks' capital reserves. The Obama administration, in turn, implemented an $850 billion economic stimulus program to boost economic activities and create jobs. Many governments around the world, notably the U.K., France, Germany, China, and Korea, implemented similar stimulating measures. In addition, to prevent future financial crises and costly bailouts, the U.S. government adopted much tighter rules of finance in July 2010. Among other things, the new rules prohibit banks from making risky investments with their own money, which may endanger the core capital of banks. In addition, a new independent Consumer Financial Protection Bureau was set up to protect consumers from predatory lending. Also, a new Financial Stability Oversight Council of regulators chaired by the Treasury secretary would be responsible for carefully monitoring the **systemic risk** affecting the entire financial market.

Lastly, it is noteworthy that during the course of the global financial crisis of 2008–2009, the G-20, composed of both leading developed countries, such as Germany, Japan, and the United States, and major developing countries, such as Brazil, China, India, Korea, and South Africa, has emerged as the premier forum for discussing international economic issues and coordinating financial regulations and macroeconomic policies. We will revisit and discuss these and other related issues in greater detail in Chapter 11.

Multinational Corporations

In addition to international trade, foreign direct investment by MNCs is a major force driving globalization of the world economy. According to a UN report, there are about 60,000 MNCs in the world with over 500,000 foreign affiliates.[9] Since the 1990s, foreign direct investment by MNCs grew at the annual rate of about 10 percent. In comparison, international trade grew at the rate of 3.5 percent during the same period.

A **multinational corporation (MNC)** is a business firm incorporated in one country that has production and sales operations in many other countries. The term suggests a firm obtaining raw materials from one national market and financial capital from another, producing goods with labor and capital equipment in a third country, and selling the finished product in yet other national markets. Indeed, some MNCs have operations in dozens of different countries. MNCs obtain financing from major money centers around the world in many different currencies to finance their operations. Global operations force the treasurer's office to establish international banking relationships, place short-term funds in several currency denominations, and effectively manage foreign exchange risk.

Exhibit 1.6 lists the top 40 of the largest 100 MNCs ranked by the size of foreign assets. The list was compiled by the United Nations Conference on Trade and Development (UNCTAD). Many of the firms on the list are well-known MNCs with household names because of their presence in consumer product markets. For example, General Electric (GE), General Motors, British Petroleum (BP), Toyota, BMW, Apple, Walmart, Procter & Gamble, Nestlé, Pfizer, and Siemens are names recognized by most people. By country of origin, U.S. MNCs, with 17 out of the total of 100, constitute the largest group. The U.K. has 16 MNCs and France 11 in the

www.unctad.org/wir

This UNCTAD website provides a broad coverage of cross-border investment activities by multinational corporations.

---

[9]The source for this information is the United Nations' *World Investment Report*, various issues.

EXHIBIT 1.6   **The World's Top 40 Nonfinancial MNCs, Ranked by Foreign Assets, 2013**

Ranking by Foreign Assets	Corporation	Country	Industry	Assets (in $ Billions)		Sales (in $ Billions)		Employment (in Thousands)	
				Foreign	Total	Foreign	Total	Foreign	Total
1	General Electric Co	United States	Electrical and electronic equipment	331.16	656.56	74.38	142.94	135.00	307.00
2	Royal Dutch Shell Plc	United Kingdom	Petroleum expl./ref./distr.	301.90	357.51	275.65	451.24	67.00	92.00
3	Toyota Motor Corp	Japan	Motor vehicles	274.38	403.09	171.23	256.38	137.00	333.50
4	Exxon Mobil Corp	United States	Petroleum expl./ref./distr.	231.03	346.81	237.44	390.25	45.22	75.00
5	Total SA	France	Petroleum expl./ref./distr.	226.72	238.87	175.70	227.90	65.60	98.80
6	BP Plc	United Kingdom	Petroleum expl./ref./distr.	202.90	305.69	250.37	379.14	64.30	83.90
7	Vodafone Group Plc	United Kingdom	Telecommunications	182.84	202.76	59.06	69.28	83.42	91.27
8	Volkswagen Group	Germany	Motor vehicles	176.66	446.56	211.49	261.56	317.80	572.80
9	Chevron Corp	United States	Petroleum expl./ref./distr.	175.74	253.75	122.98	211.66	32.60	64.60
10	Eni SpA	Italy	Petroleum expl./ref./distr.	141.02	190.13	109.89	152.31	56.51	83.89
11	Enel SpA	Italy	Electricity, gas and water	140.40	226.01	61.87	106.92	37.13	71.39
12	Glencore Xstrata Plc	Switzerland	Mining and quarrying	135.08	154.93	153.91	232.69	180.53	190.00
13	Anheuser-Busch InBev NV	Belgium	Food, beverages and tobacco	134.55	141.67	39.41	43.20	144.89	154.59
14	EDF SA	France	Utilities (electricity, gas and water)	130.16	353.57	46.98	100.36	28.98	158.47
15	Nestlé SA	Switzerland	Food, beverages and tobacco	124.73	129.97	98.03	99.67	323.00	333.00
16	E.ON AG	Germany	Utilities (electricity, gas and water)	124.43	179.99	115.07	162.57	49.81	62.24
17	GDF Suez	France	Utilities (electricity, gas and water)	121.40	219.76	72.13	118.56	73.00	147.20
18	Deutsche Telekom AG	Germany	Telecommunications	120.35	162.67	50.05	79.84	111.95	228.60
19	Apple Computer Inc	United States	Electrical and electronic equipment	119.92	207.00	104.71	170.91	50.32	84.40
20	Honda Motor Co Ltd	Japan	Motor vehicles	118.48	151.97	96.06	118.18	120.99	190.34
21	Mitsubishi Corp	Japan	Wholesale trade	112.76	148.75	17.64	75.73	19.79	65.98
22	Siemens AG	Germany	Electrical and electronic equipment	110.46	137.86	85.44	99.54	244.00	362.00
23	ArcelorMittal	Luxembourg	Metal and metal products	109.60	112.31	74.37	79.44	175.56	232.00
24	Iberdrola SA	Spain	Utilities (electricity, gas and water)	108.68	127.24	23.53	44.11	18.70	30.68
25	Johnson & Johnson	United States	Pharmaceuticals	96.80	132.68	39.40	71.31	75.22	128.10
26	Nissan Motor Co Ltd	Japan	Motor vehicles	95.23	143.03	81.17	104.61	93.24	160.53
27	Hutchison Whampoa Ltd	Hong Kong, China	Diversified	91.44	105.17	26.13	33.04	215.27	260.00
28	Fiat S.p.A.	Italy	Motor vehicles	90.98	119.47	106.05	115.26	163.08	225.59
29	Pfizer Inc	United States	Pharmaceuticals	90.40	172.10	31.31	51.58	48.27	77.70
30	BMW AG	Germany	Motor vehicles	88.37	190.51	85.32	100.98	80.67	110.35
31	Wal-Mart Stores Inc	United States	Retail and trade	88.21	204.75	137.61	476.29	800.00	2200.00
32	Daimler AG	Germany	Motor vehicles	87.26	232.02	116.53	156.64	107.10	274.62
33	Telefonica SA	Spain	Telecommunications	87.16	163.65	58.24	75.76	76.97	126.73
34	Mitsui & Co Ltd	Japan	Wholesale trade	86.02	107.02	22.21	57.29	36.29	45.15
35	Ford Motor Co	United States	Motor vehicles	79.09	203.75	61.46	146.92	97.00	181.00
36	CITIC Group	China	Diversified	78.60	565.88	9.56	55.49	25.29	125.22
37	Statoil ASA	Norway	Petroleum expl./ref./distr.	78.18	144.74	23.95	105.45	3.08	23.41
38	Airbus Group NV	France	Aircraft	77.61	128.47	72.53	78.67	89.55	144.06
39	Novartis AG	Switzerland	Pharmaceuticals	71.94	126.25	57.19	57.92	73.08	135.70
40	Procter & Gamble Co	United States	Diversified	70.98	139.26	51.34	84.17	88.75	121.00

Source: *World Investment Report 2014*, UNCTAD.

top 100, followed by Germany and Japan with 10 each, and Switzerland with 5. It is interesting to note that some Swiss firms are extremely multinational. Nestlé, for instance, derives about 98 percent of its sales from overseas markets, and employs about 322,996 workers, 97 percent of its total employment, outside Switzerland. Obviously, MNCs make a significant contribution to the creation of job opportunities around the world.

MNCs may gain from their global presence in a variety of ways. First of all, MNCs can benefit from the economy of scale by (i) spreading R&D expenditures and advertising costs over their global sales, (ii) pooling global purchasing power over suppliers, (iii) utilizing their technological and managerial know-how globally with minimum additional costs, and so forth. Furthermore, MNCs can use their global presence to take advantage of underpriced labor services available in certain developing countries, and gain access to special R&D capabilities residing in advanced foreign countries. MNCs can indeed leverage their global presence to boost their profit margins and create shareholder value.

In recent years, companies are increasingly using offshore outsourcing as a way of saving costs and boosting productivity. For example, when Microsoft entered the video game market, it decided to **outsource** production of the Xbox gaming console to Flextronics, a Singapore-based contract manufacturer. Flextronics, in turn, decided to manufacture all Xbox consoles in China. This outsourcing decision allows Microsoft, a company mainly known for its strength in software, to benefit from the manufacturing and logistics capabilities of Flextronics and low labor costs in China. Like Microsoft, many companies around the world are using outsourcing to enhance their competitive positions in the marketplace.

SUMMARY

This chapter provided an introduction to *International Financial Management.*

1. It is essential to study "international" financial management because we are now living in a highly globalized and integrated world economy. Owing to the (a) continuous liberalization of international trade and investment, and (b) rapid advances in telecommunications and transportation technologies, the world economy will become even more integrated.

2. Three major dimensions distinguish international finance from domestic finance. They are (a) foreign exchange and political risks, (b) market imperfections, and (c) an expanded opportunity set.

3. Financial managers of MNCs should learn how to manage foreign exchange and political risks using proper tools and instruments, deal with (and take advantage of) market imperfections, and benefit from the expanded investment and financing opportunities. By doing so, financial managers can contribute to shareholder wealth maximization, which is the ultimate goal of international financial management.

4. The theory of comparative advantage states that economic well-being is enhanced if countries produce those goods for which they have comparative advantages and then trade those goods. The theory of comparative advantage provides a powerful rationale for free trade. Currently, international trade is becoming liberalized at both the global and the regional levels. At the global level, WTO plays a key role in promoting free trade. At the regional level, the European Union and NAFTA play a vital role in dismantling trade barriers within regions.

www.mhhe.com/er8e

5. The subprime mortgage crisis in the United States that began in the summer of 2007 led to a severe credit crunch. The credit crunch, in turn, escalated to a major global financial crisis in 2008–2009. The global financial crisis may be attributable to several factors, including (i) excessive borrowing and risk taking by both households and banks, (ii) failure of government regulators to detect the rising risk in the financial system and take timely preventive actions, and (iii) the interconnected and integrated nature of financial markets. In addition, the world economy was buffeted by Europe's sovereign-debt crisis. The crisis started in Greece in December 2009 when it was disclosed that the country's budget deficit would be far worse than previously forecasted. The panic spread among weak European economies. The interest rates in these countries rose sharply and, at the same time, the euro depreciated sharply in currency markets, hurting its credibility as a major global currency.

6. A major economic trend of the recent decades is the rapid pace with which former state-owned businesses are being privatized. With the fall of communism, many Eastern Bloc countries began stripping themselves of inefficient business operations formerly run by the state. Privatization has placed a new demand on international capital markets to finance the purchase of the former state enterprises, and it has also brought about a demand for new managers with international business skills.

7. In modern times, it is not a country per se but rather a controller of capital and know-how that gives the country in which it is domiciled a comparative advantage over another country. These controllers of capital and technology are multinational corporations (MNCs). Today, it is not uncommon for an MNC to produce merchandise in one country, on capital equipment financed by funds raised in a number of different currencies, through issuing securities to investors in many countries and then selling the finished product to customers all over the world.

KEY WORDS

corporate governance, 9
European Central Bank, 11
European Union (EU), 15
expanded opportunity set, 7
foreign exchange risk, 5
General Agreement on Tariffs and Trade (GATT), 14

globalized and integrated world economy, 4
market imperfections, 6
multinational corporation (MNC), 19
North American Free Trade Agreement (NAFTA), 15
outsource, 21
political risk, 5

privatization, 16
shareholder wealth maximization, 8
systemic risk, 19
theory of comparative advantage, 14
transactions domain, 11
World Trade Organization (WTO), 14

QUESTIONS

1. Why is it important to study international financial management?
2. How is international financial management different from domestic financial management?
3. Discuss the major trends that have prevailed in international business during the last two decades.
4. How is a country's economic well-being enhanced through free international trade in goods and services?
5. What considerations might limit the extent to which the theory of comparative advantage is realistic?

6. What are multinational corporations (MNCs) and what economic roles do they play?

7. Ross Perot, a former presidential candidate of the Reform Party, which was a third political party in the United States, had strongly objected to the creation of the North American Free Trade Agreement (NAFTA), which nonetheless was inaugurated in 1994. Perot feared the loss of American jobs to Mexico, where it is much cheaper to hire workers. What are the merits and demerits of Perot's position on NAFTA? Considering the recent economic developments in North America, how would you assess Perot's position on NAFTA?

8. In 1995, a working group of French chief executive officers was set up by the Confederation of French Industry (CNPF) and the French Association of Private Companies (AFEP) to study the French corporate governance structure. The group reported the following, among other things: "The board of directors should not simply aim at maximizing share values as in the U.K. and the U.S. Rather, its goal should be to serve the company, whose interests should be clearly distinguished from those of its shareholders, employees, creditors, suppliers, and clients but still equated with their general common interest, which is to safeguard the prosperity and continuity of the company." Evaluate the above recommendation of the working group.[10]

9. Emphasizing the importance of voluntary compliance, as opposed to enforcement, in the aftermath of such corporate scandals as those involving Enron and WorldCom, U.S. President George W. Bush stated that while tougher laws might help, "ultimately, the ethics of American business depends on the conscience of America's business leaders." Describe your view on this statement.

10. Suppose you are interested in investing in shares of Samsung Electronics of Korea, which is a world leader in mobile phones, TVs, and home appliances. But before you make an investment decision, you would like to learn about the company. Visit the website of Yahoo (finance.yahoo.com) and collect information about Samsung Electronics, including the recent stock price history and analysts' views of the company. Discuss what you learn about the company. Also discuss how the instantaneous access to information via Internet would affect the nature and workings of financial markets.

INTERNET EXERCISES

WWW

1. Visit the corporate websites of Nestlé, one of the most multinational companies in the world, and study the scope of geographical diversification of its sales and revenues. Also, gather and evaluate the company's financial information from the related websites. You may use such Internet search engines as Google and Yahoo.

MINI CASE

Nike and Sweatshop Labor

Nike, a company headquartered in Beaverton, Oregon, is a major force in the sports footwear and fashion industry, with annual sales exceeding $30 billion, more than half of which now come from outside the United States. The company was co-founded in 1964 by Phil Knight, a CPA at Price Waterhouse, and Bill Bowerman, college track coach, each investing $500 to start. The company, initially called Blue Ribbon Sports, changed its name to

[10]This question draws on the article by François Degeorge, "French Boardrooms Wake Up Slowly to the Need for Reform," in the Complete MBA Companion in Global Business, *Financial Times*, 1999, pp. 156–60.

Nike in 1971 and adopted the "Swoosh" logo—recognizable around the world—originally designed by a college student for $35. Nike became highly successful in designing and marketing mass-appealing products such as the Air Jordan, the best-selling athletic shoe of all time.

Nike has no production facilities in the United States. Rather, the company manufactures athletic shoes and garments in such Asian countries as China, Indonesia, and Vietnam using subcontractors, and sells the products in the U.S. and international markets. In each of those Asian countries where Nike has production facilities, the rates of unemployment and under-employment are relatively high. The wage rate is very low in those countries by U.S. standards—the hourly wage rate in the manufacturing sector is less than $2 in those countries, compared with about $35 in the United States. In addition, workers in those countries often operate in poor and unhealthy environments and their rights are not particularly well protected. Understandably, host countries are eager to attract foreign investments like Nike's to develop their economies and raise the living standards of their citizens. Recently, however, Nike came under worldwide criticism for its practice of hiring workers for such a low rate of pay—"next to nothing" in the words of critics—and overlooking poor working conditions in host countries.

Initially, Nike denied the sweatshop charges and lashed out at critics. But later, the company began monitoring the labor practices at its overseas factories and grading the factories in order to improve labor standards. Nike also agreed to random factory inspections by disinterested parties.

Discussion Points

1. Do you think the criticism of Nike is fair, considering that the host countries are in dire needs of creating jobs?

2. What do you think Nike's executives might have done differently to prevent the sensitive charges of sweatshop labor in overseas factories?

3. Do firms need to consider the so-called corporate social responsibilities in making investment decisions?

REFERENCES & SUGGESTED READINGS

Basic Finance References

Bodie, Zvi, Alex Kane, and Alan J. Marcus. *Investments*, 9th ed. New York: Irwin/McGraw-Hill, 2010.

Ross, Stephen A., Randolph W. Westerfield, and Jeffrey F. Jaffee. *Corporate Finance*, 9th ed. New York: Irwin/McGraw-Hill, 2011.

International Accounting References

Choi, Frederick D.S. *International Accounting*, 5th ed. Pearson Education, 2007.

Meuller, Gerhard G., Helen Gernon, and Gary Meek. *Accounting: An International Perspective*, 5th ed. Burr Ridge, Ill.: Richard D. Irwin, 2000.

International Economics References

Baker, Stephen A. *An Introduction to International Economics*. San Diego: Harcourt Brace Jovanovich, 1990.

Husted, Steven, and Michael Melvin. *International Economics,* 9th ed. Pearson, 2012.

Krugman, Paul R., and Maurice Obstfeld. *International Economics: Theory and Policy*, 8th ed. Reading, Mass.: Addison-Wesley, 2008.

Rivera-Batiz, Francisco L., and Luis Rivera-Batiz. *International Finance and Open Economy Macroeconomics*, 2nd ed. Upper Saddle River, N.J.: Prentice Hall, 1994.

1A Gain from Trade: The Theory of Comparative Advantage

The theory of comparative advantage was originally advanced by the 19th-century economist David Ricardo as an explanation for why nations trade with one another. The theory claims that economic well-being is enhanced if each country's citizens produce that which they have a comparative advantage in producing relative to the citizens of other countries, and then trade products. Underlying the theory are the assumptions of free trade between nations and that the factors of production (land, labor, technology, and capital) are relatively immobile. Consider the example described in Exhibit A.1 as a vehicle for explaining the theory.

Exhibit A.1 assumes two countries, A and B, which each produce only food and textiles, but they do not trade with one another. Country A and B each have 60,000,000 units of input. Each country presently allocates 40,000,000 units to the production of food and 20,000,000 units to the production of textiles. Examination of the exhibit shows that Country A can produce five pounds of food with one unit of production or three yards of textiles. Country B has an absolute advantage over Country A in the production of both food and textiles. Country B can produce 15 pounds of food or four yards of textiles with one unit of production. When all units of production are employed, Country A can produce 200,000,000 pounds of food and 60,000,000 yards of textiles. Country B can produce 600,000,000 pounds of food and 80,000,000 yards of textiles. Total output is 800,000,000 pounds of food and 140,000,000 yards of textiles. Without trade, each nation's citizens can consume only what they produce.

While it is clear from the examination of Exhibit A.1 that Country B has an absolute advantage in the production of food and textiles, it is not so clear that Country A (B) has a relative advantage over Country B (A) in producing textiles (food). Note that in using units of production, Country A can "trade off" one unit of production needed to produce five pounds of food for three yards of textiles. Thus, a yard of textiles has an *opportunity cost* of $5/3 = 1.67$ pounds of food, or a pound of food has an opportunity cost of $3/5 = .60$ yards of textiles. Analogously, Country B has an opportunity cost of $15/4 = 3.75$ pounds of food per yard of textiles, or $4/15 = .27$ yards of textiles per pound of food. When viewed in terms of opportunity costs it is clear that Country A

| | | Country | | |
		A	B	Total
I.	Units of input (000,000)			
	Food	40	40	
	Textiles	20	20	
II.	Output per unit of input (lbs. or yards)			
	Food	5	15	
	Textiles	3	4	
III.	Total output (lbs. or yards) (000,000)			
	Food	200	600	800
	Textiles	60	80	140
IV.	Consumption (lbs. or yards) (000,000)			
	Food	200	600	800
	Textiles	60	80	140

		Country A	Country B	Total
I.	Units of input (000,000)			
	Food	20	50	
	Textiles	40	10	
II.	Output per unit of input (lbs. or yards)			
	Food	5	15	
	Textiles	3	4	
III.	Total output (lbs. or yards) (000,000)			
	Food	100	750	850
	Textiles	120	40	160
IV.	Consumption (lbs. or yards) (000,000)			
	Food	225	625	850
	Textiles	70	90	160

is relatively more efficient in producing textiles and Country B is relatively more efficient in producing food. That is, Country A's (B's) opportunity cost for producing textiles (food) is less than Country B's (A's). A *relative efficiency* that shows up via a lower opportunity cost is referred to as a comparative advantage.

Exhibit A.2 shows that when there are no restrictions or impediments to free trade, such as import quotas, import tariffs, or costly transportation, the economic well-being of the citizens of both countries is enhanced through trade. Exhibit A.2 shows that Country A has shifted 20,000,000 units from the production of food to the production of textiles where it has a comparative advantage and that Country B has shifted 10,000,000 units from the production of textiles to the production of food where it has a comparative advantage. Total output is now 850,000,000 pounds of food and 160,000,000 yards of textiles. Suppose that Country A and Country B agree on a price of 2.50 pounds of food for one yard of textiles, and that Country A sells Country B 50,000,000 yards of textiles for 125,000,000 pounds of food. With free trade, Exhibit A.2 makes it clear that the citizens of each country have increased their consumption of food by 25,000,000 pounds and textiles by 10,000,000 yards.

PROBLEMS

1. Country C can produce seven pounds of food or four yards of textiles per unit of input. Compute the opportunity cost of producing food instead of textiles. Similarly, compute the opportunity cost of producing textiles instead of food.

2. Consider the no-trade input/output situation presented in the following table for countries X and Y. Assuming that free trade is allowed, develop a scenario that will benefit the citizens of both countries.

		Country X	Country Y	Total
I.	Units of input (000,000)			
	Food	70	60	
	Textiles	40	30	
II.	Output per unit of input (lbs. or yards)			
	Food	17	5	
	Textiles	5	2	
III.	Total output (lbs. or yards) (000,000)			
	Food	1,190	300	1,490
	Textiles	200	60	260
IV.	Consumption (lbs. or yards) (000,000)			
	Food	1,190	300	1,490
	Textiles	200	60	260

2 International Monetary System

THIS CHAPTER EXAMINES the **international monetary system**, which defines the overall financial environment in which multinational corporations and international investors operate. As mentioned in Chapter 1, the exchange rates among major currencies, such as the U.S. dollar, British pound, Swiss franc, and Japanese yen, have been fluctuating since the fixed exchange rate regime was abandoned in 1973. Consequently, corporations nowadays are operating in an environment in which exchange rate changes may adversely affect their competitive positions in the marketplace. This situation, in turn, makes it necessary for many firms to carefully measure and manage their exchange risk exposure. Similarly, international investors face the problem of fluctuating exchange rates affecting their portfolio returns. As we will discuss shortly, however, many European countries have adopted a common currency called the **euro**, rendering intra-European trade and investment much less susceptible to exchange risk. The complex international monetary arrangements imply that for adroit financial decision making, it is essential for managers to understand, in detail, the arrangements and workings of the international monetary system.

The international monetary system can be defined as the *institutional framework within which international payments are made, movements of capital are accommodated*, and *exchange rates among currencies are determined*. It is a complex whole of agreements, rules, institutions, mechanisms, and policies regarding exchange rates, international payments, and the flow of capital. The international monetary system has evolved over time and will continue to do so in the future as the fundamental business and political conditions underlying the world economy continue to shift. In this chapter, we will review the history of the international monetary system and contemplate its future prospects. In addition, we will compare and contrast the alternative exchange rate systems, that is, fixed versus flexible exchange rates. For astute financial management, it is important to understand the dynamic nature of international monetary environments.

Evolution of the International Monetary System

The international monetary system went through several distinct stages of evolution. These stages are summarized as follows:

1. Bimetallism: Before 1875.
2. Classical gold standard: 1875–1914.

3. Interwar period: 1915–1944.

4. Bretton Woods system: 1945–1972.

5. Flexible exchange rate regime: Since 1973.

We now examine each of the five stages in some detail.

Bimetallism: Before 1875

Prior to the 1870s, many countries had **bimetallism**, that is, a double standard in that free coinage was maintained for both gold and silver. In Great Britain, for example, bimetallism was maintained until 1816 (after the conclusion of the Napoleonic Wars) when Parliament passed a law maintaining free coinage of gold only, abolishing the free coinage of silver. In the United States, bimetallism was adopted by the Coinage Act of 1792 and remained a legal standard until 1873, when Congress dropped the silver dollar from the list of coins to be minted. France, on the other hand, introduced and maintained its bimetallism from the French Revolution to 1878. Some other countries such as China, India, Germany, and Holland were on the silver standard.

The international monetary system before the 1870s can be characterized as "bimetallism" in the sense that both gold and silver were used as international means of payment and that the exchange rates among currencies were determined by either their gold or silver contents.[1] Around 1870, for example, the exchange rate between the British pound, which was fully on a gold standard, and the French franc, which was officially on a bimetallic standard, was determined by the gold content of the two currencies. On the other hand, the exchange rate between the franc and the German mark, which was on a silver standard, was determined by the silver content of the currencies. The exchange rate between the pound and the mark was determined by their exchange rates against the franc. It is also worth noting that, due to various wars and political upheavals, some major countries such as the United States, Russia, and Austria-Hungary had irredeemable currencies at one time or another during the period 1848–1879. One might say that the international monetary system was less than fully *systematic* up until the 1870s.

Countries that were on the bimetallic standard often experienced the well-known phenomenon referred to as **Gresham's law**. Since the exchange ratio between the two metals was fixed officially, only the abundant metal was used as money, driving more scarce metal out of circulation. This is Gresham's law, according to which "bad" (abundant) money drives out "good" (scarce) money. For example, when gold from newly discovered mines in California and Australia poured into the market in the 1850s, the value of gold became depressed, causing overvaluation of gold under the French official ratio, which equated a gold franc to a silver franc 15½ times as heavy. As a result, the franc effectively became a gold currency.

Classical Gold Standard: 1875–1914

Mankind's fondness for gold as a storage of wealth and means of exchange dates back to antiquity and was shared widely by diverse civilizations. Christopher Columbus once said, "Gold constitutes treasure, and he who possesses it has all he needs in this world." The first full-fledged **gold standard**, however, was not established until 1821 in Great Britain, when notes from the Bank of England were made fully redeemable for gold. As previously mentioned, France was effectively on the gold standard beginning in the 1850s and formally adopted the standard in 1878. The newly emergent German empire, which was to receive a sizable war indemnity from France, converted

---

[1]This does not imply that each individual country was on a bimetallic standard. In fact, many countries were on either a gold standard or a silver standard until the 1870s.

to the gold standard in 1875, discontinuing free coinage of silver. The United States adopted the gold standard in 1879, Russia and Japan in 1897.

One can say roughly that the *international* gold standard existed as a historical reality during the period 1875–1914. The majority of countries got off gold in 1914 when World War I broke out. The classical gold standard as an international monetary system thus lasted for about 40 years. During this period, London became the center of the international financial system, reflecting Britain's advanced economy and its preeminent position in international trade.

An *international* gold standard can be said to exist when, in most major countries, (i) gold alone is assured of unrestricted coinage, (ii) there is two-way convertibility between gold and national currencies at a stable ratio, and (iii) gold may be freely exported or imported. In order to support unrestricted convertibility into gold, banknotes need to be backed by a gold reserve of a minimum stated ratio. In addition, the domestic money stock should rise and fall as gold flows in and out of the country. The above conditions were roughly met between 1875 and 1914.

Under the gold standard, the exchange rate between any two currencies will be determined by their gold content. For example, suppose that the pound is pegged to gold at six pounds per ounce, whereas one ounce of gold is worth 12 francs. The exchange rate between the pound and the franc should then be two francs per pound. To the extent that the pound and the franc remain pegged to gold at given prices, the exchange rate between the two currencies will remain stable. There were indeed no significant changes in exchange rates among the currencies of such major countries as Great Britain, France, Germany, and the United States during the entire period. For example, the dollar–sterling exchange rate remained within a narrow range of $4.84 and $4.90 per pound. Highly stable exchange rates under the classical gold standard provided an environment that was conducive to international trade and investment.

Under the gold standard, misalignment of the exchange rate will be automatically corrected by cross-border flows of gold. In the above example, suppose that one pound is trading for 1.80 francs at the moment. Because the pound is undervalued in the exchange market, people will buy pounds with francs, but not francs with pounds. For people who need francs, it would be cheaper first to buy gold from the Bank of England and ship it to France and sell it for francs. For example, suppose that you need to buy 1,000 francs using pounds. If you buy 1,000 francs in the exchange market, it will cost you £555.56 at the exchange rate of Fr1.80/£. Alternatively, you can buy 83.33 = 1,000/12 ounces of gold from the Bank of England for £500:

$$£500 = (1,000/12) \times 6$$

Then you could ship it to France and sell it to the Bank of France for 1,000 francs. This way, you can save about £55.56.[2] Since people only want to buy, not sell, pounds at the exchange rate of Fr1.80/£, the pound will eventually appreciate to its fair value, namely, Fr2.0/£.

Under the gold standard, international imbalances of payment will also be corrected automatically. Consider a situation where Great Britain exported more to France than the former imported from the latter. This kind of trade imbalance will not persist under the gold standard. Net export from Great Britain to France will be accompanied by a net flow of gold in the opposite direction. This international flow of gold from France to Great Britain will lead to a lower price level in France and, at the same time, a higher price level in Great Britain. (Recall that under the gold standard, the domestic money stock is supposed to rise or fall as the country experiences an inflow or outflow of gold.) The resultant change in the relative price level, in turn, will slow exports from Great Britain and encourage exports from France. As a result, the initial net

---

[2]In this example, we ignored shipping costs. But as long as the shipping costs do not exceed £55.56, it is still advantageous to buy francs via "gold export" than via the foreign exchange market.

export from Great Britain will eventually disappear. This adjustment mechanism is referred to as the **price-specie-flow mechanism**, which is attributed to David Hume, a Scottish philosopher.[3]

Despite its demise a long time ago, the gold standard still has ardent supporters in academic, business, and political circles, which view it as an ultimate hedge against price inflation. Gold has a natural scarcity and no one can increase its quantity at will. Therefore, if gold serves as the sole base for domestic money creation, the money supply cannot get out of control and cause inflation. In addition, if gold is used as the sole international means of payment, then countries' balance of payments will be regulated automatically via the movements of gold.[4] As a result, no country may have a persistent trade deficit or surplus.

The gold standard, however, has a few key shortcomings. First of all, the supply of newly minted gold is so restricted that the growth of world trade and investment can be seriously hampered for the lack of sufficient monetary reserves. The world economy can face deflationary pressures. Second, whenever the government finds it politically necessary to pursue national objectives that are inconsistent with maintaining the gold standard, it can abandon the gold standard. In other words, the international gold standard per se has no mechanism to compel each major country to abide by the rules of the game.[5] For such reasons, it is not very likely that the classical gold standard will be restored in the foreseeable future.

Interwar Period: 1915–1944

World War I ended the classical gold standard in August 1914, as major countries such as Great Britain, France, Germany, and Russia suspended redemption of banknotes in gold and imposed embargoes on gold exports. After the war, many countries, especially Germany, Austria, Hungary, Poland, and Russia, suffered hyperinflation. The German experience provides a classic example of hyperinflation: By the end of 1923, the wholesale price index in Germany was more than 1 trillion (!) times as high as the prewar level. Freed from wartime pegging, exchange rates among currencies were fluctuating in the early 1920s. During this period, countries widely used "predatory" depreciations of their currencies as a means of gaining advantages in the world export market.

As major countries began to recover from the war and stabilize their economies, they attempted to restore the gold standard. The United States, which replaced Great Britain as the dominant financial power, spearheaded efforts to restore the gold standard. With only mild inflation, the United States was able to lift restrictions on gold exports and return to a gold standard in 1919. In Great Britain, Winston Churchill, the chancellor of the Exchequer, played a key role in restoring the gold standard in 1925. Besides Great Britain, such countries as Switzerland, France, and the Scandinavian countries restored the gold standard by 1928.

The international gold standard of the late 1920s, however, was not much more than a facade. Most major countries gave priority to the stabilization of domestic economies and systematically followed a policy of **sterilization of gold** by matching inflows and outflows of gold respectively with reductions and increases in domestic money and credit. The Federal Reserve of the United States, for example, kept some

---

[3]The price-specie-flow mechanism will work only if governments are willing to abide by the rules of the game by letting the money stock rise and fall as gold flows in and out. Once the government demonetizes (neutralizes) gold, the mechanism will break down. In addition, the effectiveness of the mechanism depends on the price elasticity of the demand for imports.

[4]The balance of payments will be discussed in detail in Chapter 3.

[5]This point need not be viewed as a weakness of the gold standard per se, but it casts doubt on the long-term feasibility of the gold standard.

gold outside the credit base by circulating it as gold certificates. The Bank of England also followed the policy of keeping the amount of available domestic credit stable by neutralizing the effects of gold flows. In a word, countries lacked the political will to abide by the "rules of the game," and so the automatic adjustment mechanism of the gold standard was unable to work.

Even the facade of the restored gold standard crumbled down in the wake of the Great Depression and the accompanying financial crises. Following the stock market crash and the onset of the Great Depression in 1929, many banks, especially in Austria, Germany, and the United States, suffered sharp declines in their portfolio values, touching off runs on the banks. Against this backdrop, Britain experienced a massive outflow of gold, which resulted from chronic balance-of-payment deficits and lack of confidence in the pound sterling. Despite coordinated international efforts to rescue the pound, British gold reserves continued to fall to the point where it was impossible to maintain the gold standard. In September 1931, the British government suspended gold payments and let the pound float. As Great Britain got off gold, countries such as Canada, Sweden, Austria, and Japan followed suit by the end of 1931. The United States got off gold in April 1933 after experiencing a spate of bank failures and outflows of gold. Lastly, France abandoned the gold standard in 1936 because of the flight from the franc, which, in turn, reflected the economic and political instability following the inception of the socialist Popular Front government led by Leon Blum. Paper standards came into being when the gold standard was abandoned.

In sum, the interwar period was characterized by economic nationalism, halfhearted attempts and failure to restore the gold standard, economic and political instabilities, bank failures, and panicky flights of capital across borders. No coherent international monetary system prevailed during this period, with profoundly detrimental effects on international trade and investment. It is during this period that the U.S. dollar emerged as the dominant world currency, gradually replacing the British pound for the role.

Bretton Woods System: 1945–1972

In July 1944, representatives of 44 nations gathered at Bretton Woods, New Hampshire, to discuss and design the postwar international monetary system. After lengthy discussions and bargains, representatives succeeded in drafting and signing the Articles of Agreement of the International Monetary Fund (IMF), which constitutes the core of the **Bretton Woods system**. The agreement was subsequently ratified by the majority of countries to launch the IMF in 1945. The IMF embodied an explicit set of rules about the conduct of international monetary policies and was responsible for enforcing these rules. Delegates also created a sister institution, the International Bank for Reconstruction and Development (IBRD), better known as the World Bank, that was chiefly responsible for financing individual development projects.

In designing the Bretton Woods system, representatives were concerned with how to prevent the recurrence of economic nationalism with destructive "beggar-thy-neighbor" policies and how to address the lack of clear rules of the game plaguing the interwar years. The British delegates led by John Maynard Keynes proposed an international clearing union that would create an international reserve asset called "bancor." Countries would accept payments in bancor to settle international transactions, without limit. They would also be allowed to acquire bancor by using overdraft facilities with the clearing union. On the other hand, the American delegates, headed by Harry Dexter White, proposed a currency pool to which member countries would make contributions and from which they might borrow to tide themselves over during short-term balance-of-payments deficits. Both delegates desired exchange rate stability without restoring an international gold standard. The American proposal was largely incorporated into the Articles of Agreement of the IMF.

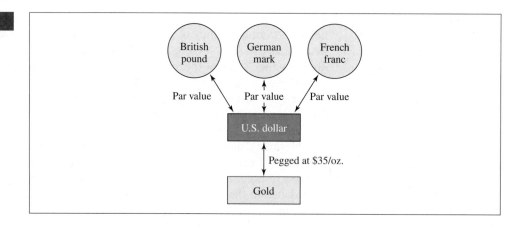

Under the Bretton Woods system, each country established a **par value** in relation to the U.S. dollar, which was pegged to gold at $35 per ounce. This point is illustrated in Exhibit 2.1. Each country was responsible for maintaining its exchange rate within ±1 percent of the adopted par value by buying or selling foreign exchanges as necessary. However, a member country with a "fundamental disequilibrium" may be allowed to make a change in the par value of its currency. Under the Bretton Woods system, the U.S. dollar was the only currency that was fully convertible to gold; other currencies were not directly convertible to gold. Countries held U.S. dollars, as well as gold, for use as an international means of payment. Because of these arrangements, the Bretton Woods system can be described as a dollar-based **gold-exchange standard**. A country on the gold-exchange standard holds most of its reserves in the form of currency of a country that is *really* on the gold standard.

Advocates of the gold-exchange system argue that the system economizes on gold because countries can use not only gold but also foreign exchanges as an international means of payment. Foreign exchange reserves offset the deflationary effects of limited addition to the world's monetary gold stock. Another advantage of the gold-exchange system is that individual countries can earn interest on their foreign exchange holdings, whereas gold holdings yield no returns. In addition, countries can save transaction costs associated with transporting gold across countries under the gold-exchange system. An ample supply of international monetary reserves coupled with stable exchange rates provided an environment highly conducive to the growth of international trade and investment throughout the 1950s and 1960s.

Professor Robert Triffin warned, however, that the gold-exchange system was programmed to collapse in the long run. To satisfy the growing need for reserves, the United States had to run balance-of-payments deficits continuously, thereby supplying the dollar to the rest of the world. Yet if the United States ran perennial balance-of-payments deficits, it would eventually impair the public confidence in the dollar, triggering a run on the dollar. Under the gold-exchange system, the reserve-currency country should run balance-of-payments deficits to supply reserves, but if such deficits are large and persistent, they can lead to a crisis of confidence in the reserve currency itself, causing the downfall of the system. This dilemma, known as the **Triffin paradox**, was indeed responsible for the eventual collapse of the dollar-based gold-exchange system in the early 1970s.

The United States began to experience trade deficits with the rest of the world in the late 1950s, and the problem persisted into the 1960s. By the early 1960s the total value of the U.S. gold stock, when valued at $35 per ounce, fell short of foreign dollar holdings. This naturally created concern about the viability of the dollar-based system. Against this backdrop, President Charles de Gaulle prodded the Bank of France to buy gold from the U.S. Treasury, unloading its dollar holdings. Efforts to remedy the problem centered on (i) a series of dollar defense measures taken by the U.S. government and (ii) the creation of a new reserve asset, **special drawing rights (SDRs)**, by the IMF.

In 1963, President John Kennedy imposed the Interest Equalization Tax (IET) on U.S. purchases of foreign securities in order to stem the outflow of dollars. The IET was designed to increase the cost of foreign borrowing in the U.S. bond market. In 1965, the Federal Reserve introduced the U.S. voluntary Foreign Credit Restraint Program (FCRP), which regulated the amount of dollars U.S. banks could lend to U.S. multinational companies engaged in foreign direct investments. In 1968, these regulations became legally binding. Such measures as IET and FCRP lent a strong impetus to the rapid growth of the Eurodollar market, which is a transnational, unregulated fund market.

www.imf.org/external/fin.htm

Provides detailed information about the SDR, such as SDR exchange rates, interests, allocations, etc.

To partially alleviate the pressure on the dollar as the central reserve currency, the IMF created an artificial international reserve called the SDR in 1970. The SDR, which is a basket currency comprising major individual currencies, was allotted to the members of the IMF, who could then use it for transactions among themselves or with the IMF. In addition to gold and foreign exchanges, countries could use the SDR to make international payments.

Initially, the SDR was designed to be the weighted average of 16 currencies of those countries whose shares in world exports were more than 1 percent. The percentage share of each currency in the SDR was about the same as the country's share in world exports. In 1981, however, the SDR was greatly simplified to comprise only five major currencies: U.S. dollar, German mark, Japanese yen, British pound, and French franc. As Exhibit 2.2 shows, the weight for each currency is updated periodically, reflecting the relative importance of each country in the world trade of goods and services and the amount of the currencies held as reserves by the members of the IMF. With the advent of the euro in 1999, the SDR became composed of just four major currencies: the U.S. dollar, the euro, the British pound, and the Japanese yen. In 2016, the Chinese yuan was added to the SDR basket. As a result, the SDR is currently composed of the U.S. dollar (41.73 percent weight), euro (30.93 percent), Chinese yuan (10.92 percent), Japanese yen (8.33 percent), and British pound (8.00 percent).

The SDR is used not only as a reserve asset but also as a denomination currency for international transactions. Because the SDR is a "portfolio" of currencies, its value tends to be more stable than the value of any individual currency included in the SDR. The portfolio nature of the SDR makes it an attractive denomination currency for international commercial and financial contracts under exchange rate uncertainty.

The efforts to support the dollar-based gold-exchange standard, however, turned out to be ineffective in the face of expansionary monetary policy and rising inflation in the United States, which were related to the financing of the Vietnam War and the Great Society program. In the early 1970s, it became clear that the dollar was over-valued, especially relative to the mark and the yen. As a result, the German and Japanese central banks had to make massive interventions in the foreign exchange market to maintain their par values. Given the unwillingness of the United States to control its monetary expansion, the repeated central bank interventions could not solve

EXHIBIT 2.2	The Composition of the Special Drawing Right (SDR)[a]						
Currencies	1986–1990	1991–1995	1996–2000	2001–2005	2006–2010	2011–2015	2016–2020
U.S. dollar	42%	40%	39%	45%	44%	41.9%	41.73%
Euro	—	—	—	29	34	37.4	30.93
German mark	19	21	21	—	—	—	—
Japanese yen	15	17	18	15	11	9.4	8.33
British pound	12	11	11	11	11	11.3	8.09
French franc	12	11	11	—	—	—	—
Chinese renminbi	—	—	—	—	—	—	10.92

[a]The composition of the SDR changes every 5 years.
Source: International Monetary Fund.

the underlying disparities. In August 1971, President Richard Nixon suspended the convertibility of the dollar into gold and imposed a 10 percent import surcharge. The foundation of the Bretton Woods system began to crack under the strain.

In an attempt to save the Bretton Woods system, 10 major countries, known as the Group of Ten, met at the Smithsonian Institution in Washington, D.C., in December 1971. They reached the **Smithsonian Agreement**, according to which (i) the price of gold was raised to $38 per ounce, (ii) each of the other countries revalued its currency against the U.S. dollar by up to 10 percent, and (iii) the band within which the exchange rates were allowed to move was expanded from 1 percent to 2.25 percent in either direction.

The Smithsonian Agreement lasted for little more than a year before it came under attack again. Clearly, the devaluation of the dollar was not sufficient to stabilize the situation. In February 1973, the dollar came under heavy selling pressure, again prompting central banks around the world to buy dollars. The price of gold was further raised from $38 to $42 per ounce. By March 1973, European and Japanese currencies were allowed to float, completing the decline and fall of the Bretton Woods system. Since then, the exchange rates among such major currencies as the dollar, the mark (later succeeded by the euro), the pound, and the yen have been fluctuating against each other.

The Flexible Exchange Rate Regime: 1973–Present

The flexible exchange rate regime that followed the demise of the Bretton Woods system was ratified after the fact in January 1976 when the IMF members met in Jamaica and agreed to a new set of rules for the international monetary system. The key elements of the **Jamaica Agreement** include

1. Flexible exchange rates were declared acceptable to the IMF members, and central banks were allowed to intervene in the exchange markets to iron out unwarranted volatilities.

2. Gold was officially abandoned (i.e., demonetized) as an international reserve asset. Half of the IMF's gold holdings were returned to the members and the other half were sold, with the proceeds to be used to help poor nations.

3. Non-oil-exporting countries and less-developed countries were given greater access to IMF funds.

The IMF continued to provide assistance to countries facing balance-of-payments and exchange rate difficulties. The IMF, however, extended assistance and loans to the member countries on the condition that those countries follow the IMF's macroeconomic policy prescriptions. This "conditionality," which often involves deflationary macroeconomic policies and elimination of various subsidy programs, provoked resentment among the people of developing countries receiving the IMF's balance-of-payments loans.

As can be expected, exchange rates have become substantially more volatile since March 1973 than they were under the Bretton Woods system. Exhibit 2.3 summarizes the behavior of the dollar exchange rate since 1960. The exhibit shows the exchange rate between the U.S. dollar and a weighted basket of 21 other major currencies. The decline of the dollar between 1970 and 1973 represents the transition from the Bretton Woods to the flexible exchange rate system. The most conspicuous phenomena shown in Exhibit 2.3 are the dollar's spectacular rise between 1980 and 1984 and its equally spectacular decline between 1985 and 1988. These unusual episodes merit some discussion.

Following the U.S. presidential election of 1980, the Reagan administration ushered in a period of growing U.S. budget deficits and balance-of-payments deficits. The U.S. dollar, however, experienced a major appreciation throughout the first half of the 1980s

www.federalreserve.gov
/releases/h10/hist

Provides historical exchange rates.

EXHIBIT 2.3 **The Trade-Weighted Value of the U.S. Dollar since 1964[a]**

[a]The value of the U.S. dollar represents the nominal exchange rate index (2010 = 100) with weights derived from trade among 27 industrialized countries.

Source: Bank for International Settlements.

because of the large-scale inflows of foreign capital caused by unusually high real interest rates available in the United States. To attract foreign investment to help finance the budget deficit, the United States had to offer high real interest rates. The heavy demand for dollars by foreign investors pushed up the value of the dollar in the exchange market.

The value of the dollar reached its peak in February 1985 and then began a persistent downward drift until it stabilized in 1988. The reversal in the exchange rate trend partially reflected the effect of the record-high U.S. trade deficit, about $160 billion in 1985, brought about by the soaring dollar. The downward trend was also reinforced by concerted government interventions. In September 1985, the so-called G-5 countries (France, Japan, Germany, the U.K., and the United States) met at the Plaza Hotel in New York and reached what became known as the **Plaza Accord**. They agreed that it would be desirable for the dollar to depreciate against most major currencies to solve the U.S. trade deficit problem and expressed their willingness to intervene in the exchange market to realize this objective. The slide of the dollar that had begun in February was further precipitated by the Plaza Accord.

As the dollar continued its decline, the governments of the major industrial countries began to worry that the dollar may fall too far. To address the problem of exchange rate volatility and other related issues, the G-7 economic summit meeting was convened in Paris in 1987.[6] The meeting produced the **Louvre Accord**, according to which:

1. The G-7 countries would cooperate to achieve greater exchange rate stability.
2. The G-7 countries agreed to more closely consult and coordinate their macroeconomic policies.

The Louvre Accord marked the inception of the **managed-float system** under which the G-7 countries would jointly intervene in the exchange market to correct over- or undervaluation of currencies. Following the Louvre Accord, exchange rates became relatively more stable for a while. During the period 1996–2001, however, the U.S. dollar generally appreciated, reflecting a robust performance of the U.S. economy fueled by the technology boom. During this period, foreigners invested heavily in the

---

[6]The G-7 is composed of Canada, France, Japan, Germany, Italy, the U.K., and the United States.

United States to participate in the booming U.S. economy and stock markets. This helped the dollar to appreciate. In 2001, however, the U.S. dollar began to depreciate due to a sharp stock market correction, the ballooning trade deficits, and the increased political uncertainty following the September 11 incident.

The Current Exchange Rate Arrangements

Although the most actively traded currencies of the world, such as the dollar, the yen, the pound, and the euro, may be fluctuating against each other, a significant number of the world's currencies are pegged to single currencies, particularly the U.S. dollar and the euro, or baskets of currencies such as the SDR. The current exchange rate arrangements as classified by the IMF are provided in Exhibit 2.4. The classification system used in Exhibit 2.4 is based on IMF member countries' actual, *de facto* arrangements, as identified by IMF staff, which can be different from the officially announced, *de jure* arrangements. The system classifies exchange rate arrangements primarily based on the degree to which the exchange rate is determined by the market rather than by official government action, with market-determined rates generally being more flexible.

As can be seen from the exhibit, the IMF currently classifies exchange rate arrangements into 10 separate regimes:[7]

No separate legal tender: The currency of another country circulates as the sole legal tender. Adopting such an arrangement implies complete surrender of the monetary authorities' control over the domestic monetary policy. Examples include Ecuador, El Salvador, and Panama.

Currency board: A **currency board** arrangement is a monetary arrangement based on an explicit legislative commitment to exchange domestic currency for a specified foreign currency at a fixed exchange rate, combined with restrictions on the issuing authority to ensure the fulfillment of its legal obligation. This implies that domestic currency is usually fully backed by foreign assets, eliminating traditional central bank functions such as monetary control and lender of last resort, and leaving little room for discretionary monetary policy. Examples include Hong Kong, Bulgaria, and Brunei.

Conventional peg: For this category the country formally (de jure) pegs its currency at a fixed rate to another currency or a basket of currencies, where the basket is formed, for example, from the currencies of major trading or financial partners and weights reflect the geographic distribution of trade, services, or capital flows. The anchor currency or basket weights are public or notified to the IMF. The country authorities stand ready to maintain the fixed parity through direct intervention (i.e., via sale or purchase of foreign exchange in the market) or indirect intervention (e.g., via exchange-rate-related use of interest rate policy, imposition of foreign exchange regulations, exercise of moral suasion that constrains foreign exchange activity, or intervention by other public institutions). There is no commitment to irrevocably keep the parity, but the formal arrangement must be confirmed empirically: the exchange rate may fluctuate within narrow margins of less than ±1 percent around a central rate—or the maximum and minimum value of the spot market exchange rate must remain within a narrow margin of 2 percent for at least six months. Examples include Jordan, Saudi Arabia, and Morocco.

Stabilized arrangement: Classification as a *stabilized arrangement* entails a spot market exchange rate that remains within a margin of 2 percent for 6 months or more (with the exception of a specified number of outliers or step adjustments)

---

[7]We draw on IMF classifications provided in *Annual Report on Exchange Arrangements and Exchange Restrictions 2015.*

EXHIBIT 2.4 De Facto Classification of Exchange Rate Arrangements and Monetary Policy Frameworks (as of April 30, 2015)

Exchange rate arrangement (number of countries)	Monetary Policy Framework						
	Exchange rate anchor				Monetary aggregate target	Inflation-targeting framework	Other[1]
	U.S. dollar (42)	Euro (25)	Composite (12)	Other (8)	(25)	(36)	(43)
No separate legal tender (13)	Ecuador El Salvador Marshall Islands Micronesia	Kosovo Montenegro		Kiribati Tuvalu			
		San Marino					
Currency board (11)	Djibouti Hong Kong SAR ECCU Antigua and Barbuda Dominica Grenada St. Kitts and Nevis St. Lucia St. Vincent and the Grenadines	Bosnia and Herzegovina Bulgaria		Brunei Darussalam			
Conventional peg (44)	Aruba The Bahamas Bahrain Barbados Belize Curaçao and Sint Maarten Eritrea Iraq (01/12) Jordan Oman Qatar Saudi Arabia South Sudan Turkmenistan United Arab Emirates Venezuela	Cabo Verde Comoros Denmark[2] Sao Tome and Príncipe WAEMU Benin BurkinaFaso Cote d'Ivoire Guinea Bissau Mali Niger Senegal Togo CEMAC Cameroon Central African Rep. Chad. Rep. of Congo Equatorial Guinea Gabon	Fiji Kuwait Morocco[3] Samoa	Bhutan Lesotho Namibia Nepal Swaziland			Solomon Islands[4]
Stabilized arrangement (22)	Cambocia (01/14) Guyana Lebanon Maldives Suriname Trinidad and Tobago	FYR Macedonia	Singapore Vietnam[5]		Bangladesh[5] Bolivia[5] Burundi[5] Democratic Rep. of the Congo[5] Guinea[5] Sri Lanka[5] Yemen[5]	Czech Rep.[6] (11/13)	Costa Rica (04/14) Azerbaijan[5] Egypt[5] Kazakhstan[8] (02/14) Mauritania[6] (11/13)

(Continued)

EXHIBIT 2.4 De Facto Classification of Exchange Rate Arrangements and Monetary Policy Frameworks (as of April 30, 2015) (continued)

Exchange rate arrangement (number of countries)	Monetary Policy Framework						
	Exchange rate anchor				Monetary aggregate target (25)	Inflation-targeting framework (36)	Other[1] (43)
	U.S. dollar (42)	Euro (25)	Composite (12)	Other (8)			
Crawling peg (3)	Honduras[6] (07/11) Nicaragua		Botswana				
Crawl-like arrangement (20)	Jamaica[8]	Croatia	Iran[5,6,9] (03/14) Libya (03/14)		Belarus[5] China[5] Ethiopia[5] Uzbekistan[5] Rwanda[6] (09/13) Tajikistan[5] (05/14)	Armenia[5] Dominican Republic[5] Guatemala[5]	Angola[5] (09/14) Argentina[5] Haiti[5] Lao P.D.R.[5] Papua New Guinea (04/14) Switzerland[7] Tunisia[4,8]
Pegged exchange rate whithin horizontal bands (1)			Tonga				
Other managed arrangement (10)	Liberia		Algeria Syria		Myanmar Nigeria		Kyrgyz Rep. Malaysia Pakistan Sudan Vanuatu
Floating (37)					Afghanistan The Gambia (01/14) Madagascar Malawi Mozambique Seychelles (03/14) Sierra Leone Tanzania Ukraine (02/14) Uruguay	Albania Brazil Colombia Georgia Ghana Hungary Iceland India Indonesia Israel Korea Moldova New Zealand Paraguay Peru Philippines	Kenya[8] Mauritius Mongolia Zambia

Free floating (30)		
Romania	Australia	Somalia
Russia (11/14)	Canada	United States
Serbia	Chile	**EMU**
South Africa	Japan	Austria
Thailand	Mexico	Belgium
Turkey	Norway	Cyprus
Uganda	Poland	Estonia
	Sweden	Finland
	United Kingdom	France
		Germany
		Greece
		Ireland
		Italy
		Latvia (01/14)
		Lithuania (01/15)
		Luxembourg
		Malta
		Netherlands
		Portugal
		Slovak Rep.
		Slovenia
		Spain

Source: IMF staff.

Note: If the member country's de facto exchange rate arrangement has been reclassified during the reporting period, the date of change is indicated in parentheses.

CEMAC = Central African Economic and Monetary Community; ECCU = Eastern Caribbean Currency Union; EMU = European Economic and Monetary Union; WAEMU = West African Economic and Monetary Union.

[1]Includes countries that have not explicitly stated nominal anchor, but rather monitor various indicators in conducting monetary policy.

[2]The member participates in the European Exchange Rate Mechanism (ERM II).

[3]Within the framework of an exchange rate fixed to a currency composite, the Bank Al-Maghrib adopted a monetary policy framework in 2006 based on various inflation indicators with the overnight interest rate as its operational target to pursue its main objective of price stability.

[4]The country maintains a de facto exchange rate anchor to a composite.

[5]The country maintains a de facto exchange rate anchor to the U.S. dollar.

[6]The exchange rate arrangement or monetary policy framework was reclassified retroactively, overriding a previously published classification.

[7]The country maintains a de facto exchange rate anchor to the euro.

[8]The central bank has taken preliminary steps toward inflation targeting.

[9]The exchange rate arrangement was reclassified twice during this reporting period, reverting to the classification in the previous year's report.

and is not floating. The required margin of stability can be met either with respect to a single currency or a basket of currencies, where the anchor currency or the basket is ascertained or confirmed using statistical techniques. Examples are Cambodia, Singapore, and Lebanon.

Crawling peg: Classification as a *crawling peg* involves the confirmation of the country authorities' de jure exchange rate arrangement. The currency is adjusted in small amounts at a fixed rate or in response to changes in selected quantitative indicators, such as past inflation differentials vis-à-vis major trading partners or differentials between the inflation target and expected inflation in major trading partners. Examples are Honduras and Nicaragua.

Crawl-like arrangement: The exchange rate must remain within a narrow margin of 2 percent relative to a statistically identified trend for six months or more (with the exception of a specified number of outliers), and the exchange rate arrangement cannot be considered as floating. Usually, a minimum rate of change greater than allowed under a stabilized (peg-like) arrangement is required. Ethiopia, China, and Croatia are examples.

Pegged exchange rate within horizontal bands: The value of the currency is maintained within certain margins of fluctuation of at least ±1 percent around a fixed central rate, or the margin between the maximum and minimum value of the exchange rate exceeds 2 percent. Tonga is the only example.

Other managed arrangement: This category is a residual, and is used when the exchange rate arrangement does not meet the criteria for any of the other categories. Arrangements characterized by frequent shifts in policies may fall into this category. Examples are Algeria, Nigeria, and Malaysia.

Floating: A floating exchange rate is largely market determined, without an ascertainable or predictable path for the rate. In particular, an exchange rate that satisfies the statistical criteria for a stabilized or a crawl-like arrangement will be classified as such unless it is clear that the stability of the exchange rate is not the result of official actions. Foreign exchange market intervention may be either direct or indirect, and serves to moderate the rate of change and prevent undue fluctuations in the exchange rate, but policies targeting a specific level of the exchange rate are incompatible with floating. Examples include Brazil, Korea, Turkey, and India.

Free floating: A floating exchange rate can be classified as *free floating* if intervention occurs only exceptionally and aims to address disorderly market conditions and if the authorities have provided information or data confirming that intervention has been limited to at most three instances in the previous six months, each lasting no more than three business days. Examples are Canada, Mexico, Japan, the U.K., United States, and euro zone.

As of April 2015, a large number of countries (30), including Australia, Canada, Japan, the United Kingdom, euro area, and the United States, allow their currencies to float freely against other currencies; the exchange rates of these countries are essentially determined by market forces. Thirty-seven countries, including India, Brazil, and Korea, adopt floating exchange rates that are largely market determined. In contrast, 13 countries do not have their own national currencies. For example, Panama and Ecuador are using the U.S. dollar. Eleven countries, including Bulgaria, Hong Kong SAR, and Dominica, on the other hand, maintain national currencies, but they are permanently fixed to such hard currencies as the U.S. dollar or euro. The remaining countries adopt a mixture of fixed and floating exchange rate regimes. As is well known, the European Union has pursued Europe-wide monetary integration by first establishing the European Monetary System and then the European Monetary Union. These topics deserve a detailed discussion.

European Monetary System

According to the Smithsonian Agreement, which was signed in December 1971, the band of exchange rate movements was expanded from the original plus or minus 1 percent to plus or minus 2.25 percent. Members of the European Economic Community (EEC), however, decided on a narrower band of ±1.125 percent for their currencies. This scaled-down, European version of the (quasi-) fixed exchange rate system that arose concurrently with the decline of the Bretton Woods system was called the **snake**. The name "snake" was derived from the way the EEC currencies moved closely together within the wider band allowed for other currencies like the dollar.

The EEC countries adopted the snake because they felt that stable exchange rates among the EEC countries were essential for promoting intra-EEC trade and deepening economic integration. The snake arrangement was replaced by the **European Monetary System (EMS)** in 1979. The EMS, which was originally proposed by German Chancellor Helmut Schmidt, was formally launched in March 1979. Among its chief objectives are

1. To establish a "zone of monetary stability" in Europe.
2. To coordinate exchange rate policies vis-à-vis the non-EMS currencies.
3. To pave the way for the eventual European monetary union.

At the political level, the EMS represented a Franco-German initiative to speed up the movement toward European economic and political unification. All EEC member countries, except the United Kingdom and Greece, joined the EMS. The two main instruments of the EMS are the European Currency Unit and the Exchange Rate Mechanism.

The **European Currency Unit (ECU)** is a "basket" currency constructed as a weighted average of the currencies of member countries of the European Union (EU). The weights are based on each currency's relative GNP and share in intra-EU trade. The ECU serves as the accounting unit of the EMS and plays an important role in the workings of the exchange rate mechanism.

The **Exchange Rate Mechanism (ERM)** refers to the procedure by which EMS member countries collectively manage their exchange rates. The ERM is based on a "parity grid" system, which is a system of par values among ERM currencies. The par values in the parity grid are computed by first defining the par values of EMS currencies in terms of the ECU.

When the EMS was launched in 1979, a currency was allowed to deviate from the parities with other currencies by a maximum of plus or minus 2.25 percent, with the exception of the Italian lira, for which a maximum deviation of plus or minus 6 percent was allowed. In September 1993, however, the band was widened to a maximum of plus or minus 15 percent. When a currency is at the lower or upper bound, the central banks of both countries are required to intervene in the foreign exchange markets to keep the market exchange rate within the band. To intervene in the exchange markets, the central banks can borrow from a credit fund to which member countries contribute gold and foreign reserves.

Since the EMS members were less than fully committed to coordinating their economic policies, the EMS went through a series of realignments. The Italian lira, for instance, was devalued by 6 percent in July 1985 and again by 3.7 percent in January 1990. In September 1992, Italy and the U.K. pulled out of the ERM as high German interest rates were inducing massive capital flows into Germany. Following German reunification in October 1990, the German government experienced substantial budget deficits, which were not accommodated by the monetary policy. Germany would not lower its interest rates for fear of inflation, and the U.K. and Italy were not willing to raise their interest rates (which was necessary to maintain their exchange rates) for fear of higher unemployment. Italy, however, rejoined the ERM in December 1996 in an effort to participate in the European monetary union. However, the U.K. still remains outside the European monetary union.

Despite the recurrent turbulence in the EMS, European Union members met at Maastricht (Netherlands) in December 1991 and signed the **Maastricht Treaty**. According to the treaty, the EMS would irrevocably fix exchange rates among the member currencies by January 1, 1999, and subsequently introduce a common European currency, replacing individual national currencies. The European Central Bank, to be located in Frankfurt, Germany, would be solely responsible for the issuance of common currency and conducting monetary policy in the euro zone. National central banks of individual countries then would function pretty much like regional member banks of the U.S. Federal Reserve System. Exhibit 2.5 provides a chronology of the European Union.

To pave the way for the European Monetary Union (EMU), the member countries of the European Monetary System agreed to closely coordinate their fiscal, monetary, and exchange rate policies and achieve a *convergence* of their economies. Specifically, each member country shall strive to: (i) keep the ratio of government budget deficits

---

EXHIBIT 2.5

Chronology of the European Union

1951	The treaty establishing the European Coal and Steel Community (ECSC), which was inspired by French Foreign Minister Robert Schuman, was signed in Paris by six countries: France, Germany, Italy, Netherlands, Belgium, and Luxembourg.
1957	The treaty establishing the European Economic Community (EEC) was signed in Rome.
1968	The Custom Union became fully operational; trade restrictions among the EEC member countries were abolished and a common external tariff system was established.
1973	The U.K., Ireland, and Denmark became EEC members.
1978	The EEC became the European Community (EC).
1979	The European Monetary System (EMS) was established for the purpose of promoting exchange rate stability among the EC member countries.
1980	Greece became an EC member.
1986	Portugal and Spain became EC members.
1987	The Single European Act was adopted to provide a framework within which the common internal market could be achieved by the end of 1992.
1991	The Maastricht Treaty was signed and subsequently ratified by 12 member states. The treaty establishes a timetable for fulfilling the European Monetary Union (EMU). The treaty also commits the EC to political union.
1994	The European Community was renamed the European Union (EU).
1995	Austria, Finland, and Sweden became EU members.
1999	A common European currency, the euro, was adopted by 11 EU member countries.
2001	Greece adopted the euro on January 1.
2002	Euro notes and coins were introduced; national currencies were withdrawn from circulation.
2004	EU expanded by admitting 10 new member countries: Cyprus, Czech Republic, Estonia, Hungary, Latvia, Lithuania, Malta, Poland, Slovak Republic, and Slovenia.
2007	Bulgaria and Romania were admitted to the EU. Slovenia adopted the euro.
2008	Cyprus and Malta adopted the euro.
2009	Slovakia adopted the euro.
2010	Europe's sovereign debt crisis.
2011	Estonia adopted the euro.
2013	Croatia joined the EU.
2014	Latvia adopted the euro.
2015	Lithuania adopted the euro.
2016	The United Kingdom decided to leave the EU, following the referendum on Brexit.

to gross domestic product (GDP) below 3 percent, (ii) keep gross public debts below 60 percent of GDP, (iii) achieve a high degree of price stability, and (iv) maintain its currency within the prescribed exchange rate ranges of the ERM. Currently, "convergence" is the buzz word in such countries as the Czech Republic, Hungary, and Poland that may join the EMU in the future.

The Euro and the European Monetary Union

On January 1, 1999, an epochal event took place in the arena of international finance: Eleven of 15 EU countries adopted a common currency called the euro, voluntarily giving up their monetary sovereignty. The original euro-11 includes Austria, Belgium, Finland, France, Germany, Ireland, Italy, Luxembourg, the Netherlands, Portugal, and Spain. Four member countries of the European Union—Denmark, Greece, Sweden, and the United Kingdom—did not join the first wave. Greece, however, joined the euro club in 2001 when it could satisfy the convergence criteria. Subsequently, Slovenia adopted the euro in 2007, and Cyprus and Malta did so in 2008. Slovakia adopted the euro in 2009 and Estonia did the same in 2011. Lastly, Latvia adopted the euro in 2014 and Lithuania did the same in 2015. Currently, the euro zone comprises 19 countries.

The advent of a European single currency, which may potentially rival the U.S. dollar as a global currency, has profound implications for various aspects of international finance. In this section, we are going to (i) describe briefly the historical background for the euro and its implementation process, (ii) discuss the potential benefits and costs of the euro from the perspective of the member countries, and (iii) investigate the broad impacts of the euro on international finance in general.

A Brief History of the Euro

Considering that no European currency has been in circulation since the fall of the Roman Empire, the advent of the euro in January 1999 indeed qualifies as an epochal event. The Roman emperor Gaius Diocletianus, A.D. 286–301, reformed the coinage and established a single currency throughout the realm. The advent of the euro also marks the first time that sovereign countries voluntarily have given up their monetary independence to foster economic integration. The euro thus represents a historically unprecedented experiment, the outcome of which will have far-reaching implications. If the experiment succeeds, for example, both the euro and the dollar will dominate the world of international finance. In addition, a successful euro may give a powerful impetus to the political unionization of Europe.

The euro should be viewed as a product of historical evolution toward an ever deepening integration of Europe, which began in earnest with the formation of the European Economic Community in 1958. As discussed previously, the European Monetary System (EMS) was created in 1979 to establish a European zone of monetary stability; members were required to restrict fluctuations of their currency exchange rates. In 1991, the Maastricht European Council reached agreement on a draft Treaty on the European Union, which called for the introduction of a single European currency by 1999. With the launching of the euro on January 1, 1999, the **European Monetary Union (EMU)** was created. The EMU is a logical extension of the EMS, and the European Currency Unit (ECU) was the precursor of the euro. Indeed, ECU contracts were required by EU law to be converted to euro contracts on a one-to-one basis.

As the euro was introduced, each national currency of the euro-11 countries was *irrevocably* fixed to the euro at a conversion rate as of January 1, 1999. The conversion rates are provided in Exhibit 2.6. On January 1, 2002, euro notes and coins were introduced to circulation while national bills and coins were being gradually withdrawn. Once the changeover was completed by July 1, 2002, the legal-tender status of national currencies was canceled, leaving the euro as the sole legal tender in the euro-zone countries.

EXHIBIT 2.6

Euro Conversion Rates

1 Euro Is Equal to	
Austrian schilling	13.7603
Belgian franc	40.3399
Dutch guilder	2.20371
Finnish markka	5.94573
French franc	6.55957
German mark	1.95583
Irish punt	0.78756
Italian lira	1936.27
Luxembourg franc	40.3399
Portuguese escudo	200.482
Spanish peseta	166.386

Source: *The Wall Street Journal.*

www.ecb.int

Website of the European Central Bank offers a comprehensive coverage of the euro and links to EU central banks.

Monetary policy for the euro zone countries is now conducted by the **European Central Bank (ECB)** headquartered in Frankfurt, Germany, whose primary objective is to maintain price stability. The independence of the ECB is legally guaranteed so that in conducting its monetary policy, it will not be unduly subjected to political pressure from any member countries or institutions. By and large, the ECB is modeled after the German Bundesbank, which was highly successful in achieving price stability in Germany. Willem (Wim) Duisenberg, the first president of the ECB, who previously served as the president of the Dutch National Bank, defined "price stability" as an annual inflation rate of "less than but close to 2 percent."

The national central banks of the euro zone countries will not disappear. Together with the European Central Bank, they form the **Eurosystem**, which is in a way similar to the Federal Reserve System of the United States. The tasks of the Eurosystem are threefold: (i) to define and implement the common monetary policy of the Union; (ii) to conduct foreign exchange operations; and (iii) to hold and manage the official foreign reserves of the euro member states. In addition, governors of national central banks will sit on the Governing Council of the ECB. Although national central banks will have to follow the policies of the ECB, they will continue to perform important functions in their jurisdiction such as distributing credit, collecting resources, and managing payment systems.

Before we proceed, let us briefly examine the behavior of exchange rate between the dollar and euro. Panel A of Exhibit 2.7 plots the daily dollar–euro exchange rate since the inception of the euro, whereas Panel B plots the rate of change of the exchange rate. As can be seen from Panel A, since its introduction at $1.18 per euro in January 1999, the euro was steadily depreciating against the dollar, reaching a low point of $0.83 per euro in October 2000. The depreciation of the euro during this period reflects the robust performance of the U.S. economy and massive European investments in the United States. From the start of 2002, however, the euro began to appreciate against the dollar, reaching a rough parity by July 2002. This, in turn, reflects a slowdown of the U.S. economy and lessening European investments in the United States. The euro continued to strengthen against the dollar, reaching $1.60 per euro in July 2008 before it started to fall as the global financial crisis spread. During a crisis period, the dollar tends to become stronger, reflecting investors' preference for the dollar as a safe haven. Although the euro began to rebound in early 2009, it started to fall again against the dollar as Europe's sovereign debt crisis hurt the euro's credibility. Panel B confirms that the dollar–euro exchange rate is highly volatile.

What Are the Benefits of Monetary Union?

The euro zone countries obviously decided to form a monetary union with a common currency because they believed the benefits from such a union would outweigh the associated costs—in contrast to those eligible countries that chose not to adopt the

EXHIBIT 2.7	The Daily Dollar–Euro Exchange Rate since the euro's Inception

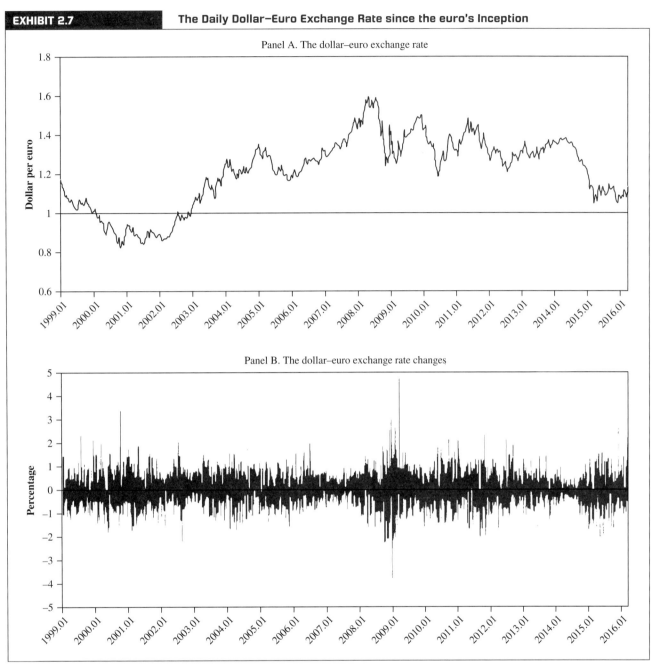

Source: Datastream.

single currency. It is thus important to understand the potential benefits and costs of monetary union.

What are the main benefits from adopting a common currency? The most direct and immediate benefits are reduced transaction costs and the elimination of exchange rate uncertainty. There was a popular saying in Europe that if one travels through all EU countries, changing money in each country but not actually spending it, one returns home with only half the original amount. Once countries use the same currency, transactions costs will be reduced substantially. These savings will accrue to practically all economic agents, benefiting individuals, companies, and governments. Although it is difficult to estimate accurately the magnitude of foreign exchange transaction costs, a consensus estimation was around 0.4 percent of Europe's GDP.

Economic agents should also benefit from the elimination of exchange rate uncertainty. Companies will not suffer currency loss anymore from intra–euro zone transactions. Companies that used to hedge exchange risk will save hedging costs. As price comparison becomes easier because of the common currency, consumers can benefit from comparison shopping. Increased price transparency will promote Europe-wide competition, exerting a downward pressure on prices. Reduced transaction costs and the elimination of currency risk together will have the net effect of promoting cross-border investment and trade within the euro zone. By furthering the economic integration of Europe, the single currency will promote corporate restructuring via mergers and acquisitions, encourage optimal business location decisions, and ultimately strengthen the international competitive position of European companies. Thus, the enhanced efficiency and competitiveness of the European economy can be regarded as the third major benefit of the monetary union.

The advent of the common European currency also helps create conditions conducive to the development of continental capital markets with depth and liquidity comparable to those of the United States. In the past, national currencies and a localized legal/regulatory framework resulted in largely illiquid, fragmented capital markets in Europe, which prevented European companies from raising capital on competitive terms. The common currency and the integration of European financial markets pave the way for a European capital market in which both European and non-European companies can raise money at favorable rates. A study by Bris, Koskinen, and Nilsson (2004) indeed documents that the adoption of the euro as the common European currency has lowered firms' cost of capital in the euro zone and enhanced the firm value by about 17 percent on average. The increases in firm valuation are larger for firms that were exposed to intra-European currency risks, that is, those firms that were expected to benefit more from the common currency.

Last but not least, sharing a common currency should promote political cooperation and peace in Europe. The founding fathers of the European Union, including Jean Monnet, Paul-Henri Spaak, Robert Schuman, and their successors, took a series of economic measures designed to link European countries together. They envisioned a new Europe in which economic interdependence and cooperation among regions and countries would replace nationalistic rivalries, which so often led to calamitous wars in the past. In this context Helmut Kohl, a former German chancellor, said that the European Monetary Union was a "matter of war and peace." If the euro proves to be successful in the long run, it will advance the political integration of Europe in a major way, even making a "United States of Europe" eventually feasible.

Costs of Monetary Union

The main cost of monetary union is the loss of national monetary and exchange rate policy independence. Suppose Finland, a country heavily dependent on the paper and pulp industries, faces a sudden drop in world paper and pulp prices. This price drop could severely hurt the Finnish economy, causing unemployment and income decline while scarcely affecting other euro-zone countries. Finland thus faces an "asymmetric shock." Generally speaking, a country is more prone to asymmetric shocks the less diversified and more trade-dependent its economy is.

If Finland maintained monetary independence, the country could consider lowering domestic interest rates to stimulate the weak economy as well as letting its currency depreciate to boost foreigners' demand for Finnish products. But because Finland has joined the EMU, the country no longer has these policy options at its disposal. Further, with the rest of the euro zone unaffected by Finland's particular problem, the ECB is not likely to tune its monetary policy to address a local Finnish shock. In other words, a common monetary policy dictated in Frankfurt cannot address asymmetric economic shocks that affect only a particular country or subregion; it can only effectively deal with euro zone–wide shocks.

If, however, wage and price levels in Finland are flexible, then the country may still be able to deal with an asymmetric shock; lower wage and price levels in Finland would have economic effects similar to those of a depreciation of the Finnish currency. Furthermore, if capital flows freely across the euro zone and workers are willing to relocate to where jobs are, then again much of the asymmetric shock can be absorbed without monetary adjustments. If these conditions are not met, however, the asymmetric shock can cause a severe and prolonged economic dislocation in the affected country. In this case, monetary union will become a costly venture. According to the theory of **optimum currency areas**, originally conceived by Professor Robert Mundell of Columbia University, the relevant criterion for identifying and designing a common currency zone is the degree of factor (i.e., capital and labor) mobility within the zone; a high degree of factor mobility would provide an adjustment mechanism, providing an alternative to country-specific monetary/currency adjustments.

Considering the high degree of capital and labor mobility in the United States, one might argue that the United States approximates an optimum currency area; it would be suboptimal for each of the 50 states to issue its own currency. In contrast, unemployed workers in Helsinki, for example, are not very likely to move to Amsterdam or Stuttgart for job opportunities because of cultural, religious, linguistic, and other barriers. The stability pact of EMU, designed to discourage irresponsible fiscal behavior in the post-EMU era, also constrains the Finnish government to restrict its budget deficit to 3 percent of GDP at most. At the same time, Finland cannot expect to receive a major transfer payment from Brussels, because of a rather low degree of fiscal integration among EU countries. These considerations taken together suggest that the European Monetary Union will involve significant economic costs. Due to the sluggish economic conditions, France and Germany often let the budget deficit exceed the 3 percent limit. This violation of the stability pact compromises the fiscal discipline necessary for supporting the euro.

An empirical study by von Hagen and Neumann (1994) identified Austria, Belgium, France, Luxembourg, the Netherlands, and Germany as nations that satisfy the conditions for an optimum currency area. However, Denmark, Italy, and the United Kingdom do not. It is noted that Denmark and the United Kingdom actually chose to stay out of the EMU. Von Hagen and Neumann's study suggests that Italy joined the EMU prematurely. It is interesting to note that some politicians in Italy blame the country's economic woes on the adoption of the euro and argue for the restoration of Italian lira. The International Finance in Practice box, "Mundell Wins Nobel Prize in Economics," explains Professor Mundell's view on the monetary union.

Prospects of the Euro: Some Critical Questions

Will the euro survive and succeed in the long run? The first real test of the euro will come when the euro zone experiences major asymmetric shocks. A successful response to these shocks will require wage, price, and fiscal flexibility. A cautionary note is in order: Asymmetric shocks can occur even within a country. In the United States, for example, when oil prices jumped in the 1970s, oil-consuming regions such as New England suffered a severe recession, whereas Texas, a major oil-producing state, experienced a major boom. Likewise, in Italy, the highly industrialized Genoa–Milan region and the southern Mezzogiorno, an underdeveloped region, can be in very different phases of the business cycle. But these countries have managed their economies with a common national monetary policy. Although asymmetric shocks are no doubt more serious internationally, one should be careful not to exaggerate their significance as an impediment to monetary union. In addition, since the advent of the EMS in 1979, the EMU member countries have restricted their monetary policies in order to maintain exchange rate stability in Europe. Considering that intra-euro zone trade accounts for about 60 percent of foreign trade of the euro-zone countries, benefits from the EMU may exceed the associated costs. Furthermore, leaders in political and business circles in Europe have invested substantial political capital in the success of the euro. So long

Mundell Wins Nobel Prize in Economics

Robert A. Mundell, one of the intellectual fathers of both the new European common currency and Reagan-era supply-side economics, won the Nobel Memorial Prize in Economic Science.

Mr. Mundell conducted innovative research into common currencies when the idea of the euro, Europe's new currency, was still a fantasy. The 66-year-old Columbia University professor, a native of Canada, also examined the implications of cross-border capital flows and flexible foreign-exchange rates when capital flows were still restricted and currencies still fixed to each other.

"Mundell chose his problems with uncommon—almost prophetic—accuracy in terms of predicting the future development of international monetary arrangements and capital markets," the selection committee said in announcing the prize.

An eccentric, white-haired figure who once bought an abandoned Italian castle as a hedge against inflation, Mr. Mundell later became a hero of the economic Right with his dogged defense of the gold standard and early advocacy of the controversial tax-cutting, supply-side economics that became the hallmark of the Reagan administration.

While the Nobel committee sidestepped his political impact in awarding Mr. Mundell the $975,000 prize for his work in the 1960s, his conservative fans celebrated the award as an endorsement of supply-side thinking.

"I know it will take a little longer, but history eventually will note that it was Mundell who made it possible for Ronald Reagan to be elected president," by providing the intellectual backing for the Reagan tax cuts, wrote conservative economist Jude Wanniski on his website.

Mr. Mundell's advocacy of supply-side economics sprang from his work in the 1960s examining what fiscal and monetary

Mundell's View

Great currencies and great powers according to Robert Mundell:

Country	Period
Greece	7th–3rd C. B.C.
Persia	6th–4th C. B.C.
Macedonia	4th–2nd C. B.C.
Rome	2nd C. B.C.–4th C.
Byzantium	5th–13th C.
Franks	8th–11th C.
Italian city states	13th–16th C.
France	13th–18th C.
Holland	17th–18th C.
Germany (thaler)	14th–19th C.
France (franc)	1803–1870
Britain (pound)	1820–1914
U.S. (dollar)	1915–present
E.U. (euro)	1999

Source: The Euro and the Stability of the International Monetary System, Robert Mundell, Columbia University.

policies are appropriate if exchange rates are either fixed—as they were prior to the collapse of the gold-based Bretton Woods system in the early 1970s—or floating, as they are in the U.S. and many other countries today.

One major finding has since become conventional wisdom: When money can move freely across borders, policy makers

as Europe can resolve internal frictions and imbalances as revealed in the Greek debt crisis, the euro can survive. Despite the bailout funds and austerity programs, however, if southern European countries, that is, Greece, Portugal, and Spain, fail to reduce debts and restart economic growth in the near future, they may reach the tipping point where people can no longer sustain job loss and other economic pains and demand the exit from euro zone. Thus, the future of the euro as the common currency critically depends on whether or not these countries can find a way of growing their economies while retaining the euro. At the moment, the jury is still out on this question.

Will the euro become a global currency rivaling the U.S. dollar? The U.S. dollar has been the dominant global currency since the end of the First World War, replacing the British pound as the currency of choice in international commercial and financial transactions. Even after the dollar got off the gold anchor in 1971, it retained its dominant position in the world economy. This dominance was possible because the dollar was backed by the sheer size of the U.S. economy and the relatively sound monetary policy of the Federal Reserve. Now, as can be seen from Exhibit 2.8, the euro zone is comparable to the United States in terms of population size, GDP, and international trade share. Exhibit 2.8 also shows that the euro is as important a denomination currency as the dollar in international bond markets. In contrast, the Japanese yen plays an insignificant role in international bond markets. As previously discussed, there is

must choose between exchange-rate stability and an independent monetary policy. They can't have both.

Mr. Mundell's work has long had an impact on policy makers. In 1962, he wrote a paper addressing the Kennedy administration's predicament of how to spur the economy while facing a balance-of-payments deficit. "The only correct way to do it was to have a tax cut and then protect the balance of payments by tight money," he recalled in a 1996 interview. The Kennedy administration eventually came around to the same way of thinking.

Mr. Mundell traces the supply-side movement to a 1971 meeting of distinguished economists, including Paul Volcker and Paul Samuelson, at the Treasury Department. At the time, most economists were stumped by the onset of stagflation—a combination of inflationary pressures, a troubled dollar, a worsening balance of payments and persistent unemployment. They thought any tightening of monetary or fiscal policy would bolster the dollar and improve the balance of payments, but worsen unemployment. An easing of monetary or fiscal policy might generate jobs, but weaken the dollar, lift prices and expand the balance-of-payments deficit.

Mr. Mundell suggested a heretical solution: Raise interest rates to protect the dollar, but cut taxes to spur the economy. Most others in the room were aghast at the idea, fearing tax cuts would lead to a swelling budget deficit—something many nonsupply-siders believe was exactly what happened during the Reagan years.

"I knew I was in the minority," he said in an 1988 interview. "But I thought my vote should count much more than the others because I understood the subject."

At the University of Chicago early in his career, Mr. Mundell befriended a student named Arthur Laffer, and together they were at the core of the supply-side movement. Even today, Mr. Mundell predicts similar policies will be necessary to keep the U.S. economic expansion going. "Monetary policy isn't going to be enough to stay up there and avoid a recession," he said in an interview yesterday. "We'll have to have tax reduction, too."

While in Chicago, he found himself constantly at odds with Milton Friedman, who advocated monetary rules and floating exchange rates. Mr. Mundell joined Columbia in 1974, two years before Mr. Friedman won the economics Nobel.

Ever the maverick, Mr. Mundell remains a fan of the gold standard and fixed exchange rates at a time when they're out of favor with most other economists. "You have fixed rates between New York and California, and it works perfectly," he said.

The Nobel committee also praised Mr. Mundell's research into common currency zones, which laid the intellectual foundation for the 11-country euro. In 1961, when European countries still clung to their national currencies, he described the circumstances in which nations could share a common currency.

"At the time, it just seemed like such a wacko thing to work on, and that's why it's so visionary," said Kenneth Rogoff, a Harvard economist.

In particular, Mr. Mundell argued that in any successful currency zone, workers must be able to move freely from areas that are slowing to areas that are booming. Some critics suggest the euro nations don't fit his description.

But Mr. Mundell believes the new currency will eventually challenge the dollar for global dominance. "The benefits will derive from transparency of pricing, stability of expectations and lower transactions costs, as well as a common monetary policy run by the best minds that Europe can muster," Mr. Mundell wrote last year. He began working on the euro project as a consultant to European monetary authorities in 1969.

Outside academia, Mr. Mundell has led a colorful life. Worried about the onset of inflation in the late 1960s, he bought and renovated a 16th century Italian castle originally built for Pandolfo Petrucci, the "Strong Man of Siena." Mr. Mundell has four children, who range in age from one to 40.

EXHIBIT 2.8

Macroeconomic Data for Major Economies[a]

Economy	Population (Million)	GDP ($ Trillion)	Annual Inflation	World Trade Share	International Bonds Outstanding ($ Billion)
United States	318	17.4	2.2%	10.6%	8,816
Euro zone	339	12.5	1.8%	14.8%	8,092
China	1,355	11.0	2.2%	11.3%	n.a.
Japan	127	4.1	0.1%	3.9%	402
United Kingdom	64	2.7	2.1%	3.1%	1,988

[a]The inflation rate is the average from 1999 to 2015. The international bonds outstanding refer to international bonds and notes outstanding as of June 2015. The world trade share is based on data in 2014. The remaining data are 2015 figures.

Source: Adapted from IMF, World Trade Organization, Bank for International Settlements, and European Commission: Economic and Financial Affairs.

little doubt that the ECB will pursue a sound monetary policy. Reflecting both the size of the euro-zone economy and the mandate of the ECB, the euro is emerging as the second global currency, challenging the dollar's sole dominance. Given its relatively small transactions domain and limited international usage, the Japanese yen is likely to be a junior partner in the dollar–euro condominium. The Chinese yuan, on the other hand, has a large transactions domain in terms of population and GDP and thus can become a major global currency. At the moment, however, the currency is in the early stage of internationalization.

The Mexican Peso Crisis

On December 20, 1994, the Mexican government under new president Ernesto Zedillo announced its decision to devalue the peso against the dollar by 14 percent. This decision, however, touched off a stampede to sell pesos as well as Mexican stocks and bonds. As Exhibit 2.9 shows, by early January 1995 the peso had fallen against the U.S. dollar by as much as 40 percent, forcing the Mexican government to float the peso. As concerned international investors reduced their holdings of emerging market securities, the peso crisis rapidly spilled over to other Latin American and Asian financial markets.

Faced with an impending default by the Mexican government and the possibility of a global financial meltdown, the Clinton administration, together with the International Monetary Fund (IMF) and the Bank for International Settlement (BIS), put together a $53 billion package to bail out Mexico.[8] As the bailout plan was put together and announced on January 31, the world's, as well as Mexico's, financial markets began to stabilize.

The Mexican peso crisis is significant in that it is perhaps the first serious international financial crisis touched off by cross-border flight of portfolio capital. International mutual funds are known to have invested more than $45 billion in Mexican securities during a three-year period prior to the peso crisis. As the peso fell, fund managers quickly liquidated their holdings of Mexican securities as well as other emerging market securities. This had a highly destabilizing, contagious effect on the world financial system.

As the world's financial markets are becoming more integrated, this type of contagious financial crisis is likely to occur more often. Two lessons emerge from the peso

EXHIBIT 2.9

U.S. Dollar versus Mexican Peso Exchange Rate (November 1, 1994– January 31, 1995)

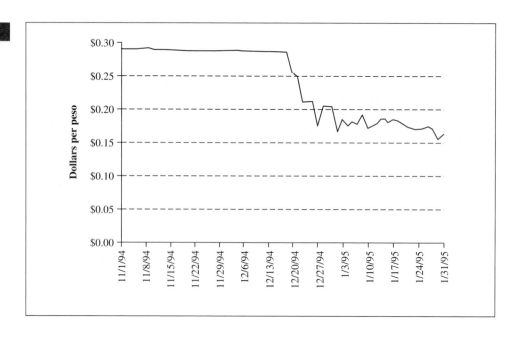

[8]The United States contributed $20 billion out of its Exchange Stabilization Fund, whereas IMF and BIS contributed, respectively, $17.8 billion and $10 billion. Canada, Latin American countries, and commercial banks collectively contributed $5 billion.

crisis. First, it is essential to have a multinational safety net in place to safeguard the world financial system from the peso-type crisis. No single country or institution can handle a potentially global crisis alone. In addition, the usually slow and parochial political processes cannot cope with rapidly changing market conditions. In fact, the Clinton administration faced stiff opposition in Congress and from foreign allies when it was working out a bailout package for Mexico. As a result, early containment of the crisis was not possible. Fortunately, the G-7 countries endorsed a $50 billion bailout fund for countries in financial distress, which would be administered by the IMF, and a series of increased disclosure requirements to be followed by all countries. The reluctance of the outgoing Salinas administration to disclose the true state of the Mexican economy, that is, the rapid depletion of foreign exchange reserves and serious trade deficits, contributed to the sudden collapse of the peso. Transparency always helps prevent financial crises.

Second, Mexico excessively depended on foreign portfolio capital to finance its economic development. In hindsight, the country should have saved more domestically and depended more on long-term rather than short-term foreign capital investments. As Professor Robert MacKinnon of Stanford University pointed out, a flood of foreign money had two undesirable effects. It led to an easy credit policy on domestic borrowings, which caused Mexicans to consume more and save less.[9] Foreign capital influx also caused a higher domestic inflation and an overvalued peso, which hurt Mexico's trade balances.

The Asian Currency Crisis

On July 2, 1997, the Thai baht, which had been largely fixed to the U.S. dollar, was suddenly devalued. What at first appeared to be a local financial crisis in Thailand quickly escalated into a global financial crisis, first spreading to other Asian countries—Indonesia, Korea, Malaysia, and the Philippines—then far afield to Russia and Latin America, especially Brazil. As can be seen from Exhibit 2.10, at the height

EXHIBIT 2.10

Asian Currency Crisis

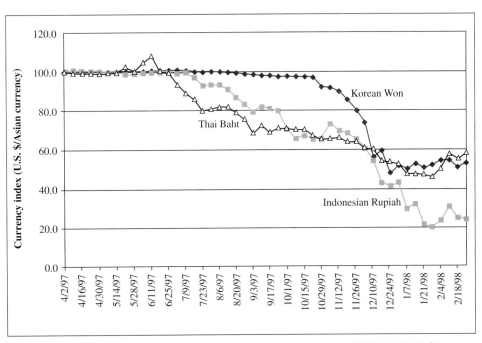

Exchange rates are indexed (U.S. $/Asian currency on 4/2/97 100). Exchange rates on 4/2/97: 0.00112 U.S. $/Korean won, 0.03856 U.S. $/Thai baht, and 0.00041 U.S. $/Indonesian rupiah.

---

[9]See "Flood of Dollars, Sunken Pesos," *New York Times*, January 20, 1995, p. A2g.

of the crisis the Korean won fell by about 50 percent in its dollar value from its precrisis level, whereas the Indonesian rupiah fell an incredible 80 percent.

The 1997 Asian crisis was the third major currency crisis of the 1990s, preceded by the crises of the European Monetary System (EMS) of 1992 and the Mexican peso in 1994–95. The Asian crisis, however, turned out to be far more serious than its two predecessors in terms of the extent of contagion and the severity of resultant economic and social costs. Following the massive depreciations of local currencies, financial institutions and corporations with foreign-currency debts in the afflicted countries were driven to extreme financial distress and many were forced to default. What's worse, the currency crisis led to an unprecedentedly deep, widespread, and long-lasting recession in East Asia, a region that, for the last few decades, has enjoyed the most rapidly growing economy in the world. At the same time, many lenders and investors from the developed countries also suffered large capital losses from their investments in emerging-market securities. For example, Long Term Capital Management (LTCM), one of the largest and, until then, profitable hedge funds, experienced a near bankruptcy due to its exposure to Russian bonds. In mid-August 1998, the Russian ruble fell sharply from 6.3 rubles per dollar to about 20 rubles per dollar. The prices of Russian stocks and bonds also fell sharply. The Federal Reserve System, which feared a domino-like systemic financial failure in the United States, orchestrated a $3.5 billion bailout of LTCM in September 1998.

Given the global effects of the Asian currency crisis and the challenges it poses for the world financial system, it would be useful to understand its origins and causes and discuss how similar crises might be prevented in the future.

Origins of the Asian Currency Crisis

Several factors are responsible for the onset of the Asian currency crisis: a weak domestic financial system, free international capital flows, the contagion effects of changing market sentiment, and inconsistent economic policies. In recent decades, both developing and developed countries were encouraged to liberalize their financial markets and allow free flows of capital across countries. As capital markets were liberalized, both firms and financial institutions in the Asian developing countries eagerly borrowed foreign currencies from U.S., Japanese, and European investors, who were attracted to these fast-growing emerging markets for extra returns for their portfolios. In 1996 alone, for example, five Asian countries—Indonesia, Korea, Malaysia, the Philippines, and Thailand—experienced an inflow of private capital worth $93 billion. In contrast, there was a net outflow of $12 billion from the five countries in 1997.

Large inflows of private capital resulted in a credit boom in the Asian countries in the early and mid-1990s. The credit boom was often directed to speculations in real estate and stock markets as well as to investments in marginal industrial projects. Fixed or stable exchange rates also encouraged unhedged financial transactions and excessive risk-taking by both lenders and borrowers, who were not much concerned with exchange risk. As asset prices declined (as happened in Thailand prior to the currency crisis) in part due to the government's effort to control the overheated economy, the quality of banks' loan portfolios also declined as the same assets were held as collateral for the loans. Clearly, banks and other financial institutions in the afflicted countries practiced poor risk management and were poorly supervised. In addition, their lending decisions were often influenced by political considerations, likely leading to suboptimal allocation of resources. However, the so-called crony capitalism was not a new condition, and the East Asian economies achieved an economic miracle under the same system.

Meanwhile, the booming economy with a fixed or stable nominal exchange rate inevitably brought about an appreciation of the real exchange rate. This, in turn, resulted in a marked slowdown in export growth in such Asian countries as Thailand and Korea. In addition, a long-lasting recession in Japan and the yen's depreciation against the dollar hurt Japan's neighbors, further worsening the trade balances of the Asian developing countries. If the Asian currencies had been allowed to depreciate in real terms, which

EXHIBIT 2.11

Financial Vulnerability Indicators

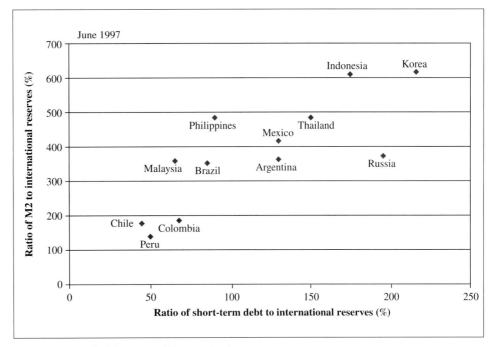

June 1997

Source: The World Bank, International Monetary Fund.

was not possible because of the fixed nominal exchange rates, such catastrophic, sudden changes of the exchange rates as observed in 1997 might have been avoided.

In Thailand, as the run on the baht started, the Thai central bank initially injected liquidity to the domestic financial system and tried to defend the exchange rate by drawing on its foreign exchange reserves. With its foreign reserves declining rapidly, the central bank eventually decided to devalue the baht. The sudden collapse of the baht touched off a panicky flight of capital from other Asian countries with a high degree of financial vulnerability. It is interesting to note from Exhibit 2.11 that the three Asian countries hardest hit by the crisis are among the most financially vulnerable as measured by (i) the ratio of short-term foreign debts to international reserve and (ii) the ratio of broad money, M2 (which represents the banking sector's liabilities) to international reserve. Contagion of the currency crisis was caused at least in part by the panicky, indiscriminate flight of capital from the Asian countries for fear of a spreading crisis. Fear thus became self-fulfilling. As lenders withdrew their capital and refused to renew short-term loans, the former credit boom turned into a credit crunch, hurting creditworthy as well as marginal borrowers.

As the crisis unfolded, the International Monetary Fund (IMF) came to rescue the three hardest-hit Asian countries—Indonesia, Korea, and Thailand—with bailout plans. As a condition for the bailing out, however, the IMF imposed a set of austerity measures, such as raising domestic interest rates and curtailing government expenditures, that were designed to support the exchange rate. Because these austerity measures, contractionary in nature, were implemented when the economies had already been contracting because of a severe credit crunch, the Asian economies consequently suffered a deep, long-lasting recession. According to a World Bank report (1999), one-year declines in industrial production of 20 percent or more in Thailand and Indonesia are comparable to those in the United States and Germany during the Great Depression. One can thus argue that the IMF initially prescribed the wrong medicine for the afflicted Asian economies. The IMF bailout plans were also criticized on another ground: moral hazard. IMF bailouts may breed dependency in developing countries and encourage risk-taking on the part of international lenders. There is a sentiment that taxpayers' money should not be used to bail out "fat-cat" investors. Former U.S. senator Lauch Faircloth was quoted as saying: "Through the IMF we have privatized profits and socialized losses." No bailout, however, can be compared with the proposal to get rid of the only fire department in town so that people will be more careful about fire.

Lessons from the Asian Currency Crisis

www.adb.org

Provides a broad coverage of Asian financial developments.

Generally speaking, liberalization of financial markets when combined with a weak, underdeveloped domestic financial system tends to create an environment susceptible to currency and financial crises. Interestingly, both Mexico and Korea experienced a major currency crisis within a few years after joining the OECD, which required a significant liberalization of financial markets. It seems safe to recommend that countries first strengthen their domestic financial system and then liberalize their financial markets.

A number of measures can and should be undertaken to strengthen a nation's domestic financial system. Among other things, the government should strengthen its system of financial-sector regulation and supervision. One way of doing so is to sign on to the "Core Principle of Effective Banking Supervision" drafted by the Basle Committee on Banking Supervision and to monitor its compliance with the principle. In addition, banks should be encouraged to base their lending decisions solely on economic merits rather than political considerations. Furthermore, firms, financial institutions, and the government should be required to provide the public with reliable financial data in a timely fashion. A higher level of disclosure of financial information and the resultant transparency about the state of the economy will make it easier for all the concerned parties to monitor the situation better and mitigate the destabilizing cycles of investor euphoria and panic accentuated by the lack of reliable information.

Even if a country decides to liberalize its financial markets by allowing cross-border capital flows, it should encourage foreign direct investments and equity and long-term bond investments; it should not encourage short-term investments that can be reversed overnight, causing financial turmoil. As Chile has successfully implemented, some form of **"Tobin tax"** on the international flow of hot money can be useful. Throwing some sand in the wheels of international finance can have a stabilizing effect on the world's financial markets.

A fixed but adjustable exchange rate is problematic in the face of integrated international financial markets. Such a rate arrangement often invites speculative attack at the time of financial vulnerability. Countries should not try to restore the same fixed exchange rate system unless they are willing to impose capital controls. According to the so-called "trilemma" that economists are fond of talking about, a country can attain only two of the following three conditions: (i) a fixed exchange rate, (ii) free international flows of capital, and (iii) an independent monetary policy. It is very difficult, if not impossible, to have all three conditions. This difficulty is also known as the **incompatible trinity**. If a country would like to maintain monetary policy independence to pursue its own domestic economic goals and still would like to keep a fixed exchange rate between its currency and other currencies, then the country should restrict free flows of capital. China and India were not noticeably affected by the Asian currency crisis because both countries maintain capital controls, segmenting their capital markets from the rest of the world. Hong Kong was less affected by the crisis for a different reason. Hong Kong has firmly fixed its exchange rate to the U.S. dollar via a currency board and allowed free flows of capital; in consequence, Hong Kong gave up its monetary independence. A currency board is an extreme form of the fixed exchange rate regime under which local currency is "fully" backed by the dollar (or another chosen standard currency). Hong Kong has essentially dollarized its economy.

As previously mentioned, China maintained a fixed exchange rate between its currency, renminbi (RMB), otherwise known as the yuan, and the U.S. dollar at 8.27 RMB per dollar for a long while. As can be seen from Exhibit 2.12, however, the RMB was allowed to appreciate from mid-July 2005 for about three years before it reverted back to a (quasi-) fixed rate at around 6.82RMB per dollar in mid-July 2008. This reversion is attributable to the heightened economic uncertainty associated with the global financial crisis. But from

EXHIBIT 2.12

Renminbi (RMB) versus U.S. Dollar Exchange Rate

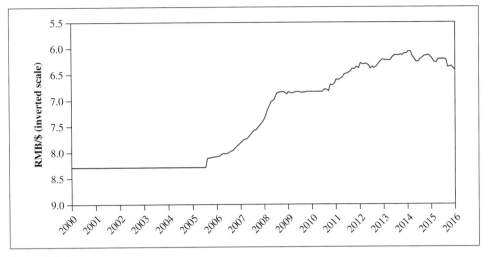

Source: Datastream.

late June 2010, RMB began to float again. The latest floating decision is related to the mounting pressure from China's trading partners for a stronger RMB as a way of reducing their trade deficits vis-à-vis China. But it is also related to China's own broad move toward liberalized capital markets. In recent years, China has been gradually lowering barriers to international capital flows. At the same time, China has been promoting a greater usage of the RMB in international transactions, with the long-term goal of establishing the RMB as a major global currency like the U.S. dollar. As previously mentioned, considering the large transactions domain of the RMB, measured in terms of population, GDP, or international trade share, China's currency has the potential to become a global currency. However, for the RMB to become a full-fledged global currency, China will need to meet a few critical, related conditions, such as (i) full convertibility of its currency, (ii) open capital markets with depth and liquidity, and (iii) the rule of law and protection of property rights. Note that the United States and euro zone satisfy these conditions.

The Argentine Peso Crisis

The 2002 crisis of the Argentine peso, however, shows that even a currency board arrangement cannot be completely safe from a possible collapse. Exhibit 2.13 shows how the peso–dollar exchange rate, fixed at parity throughout much of the 1990s,

EXHIBIT 2.13

Collapse of the Currency Board Arrangement in Argentina

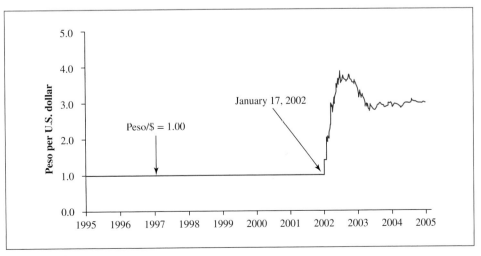

Source: Bloomberg.

collapsed in January 2002. Short of a complete dollarization (as is the case with Panama, for example), a currency board arrangement can collapse unless the arrangement is backed by the political will and economic discipline to defend it.

When the peso was first linked to the U.S. dollar at parity in February 1991 under the Convertibility Law, initial economic effects were quite positive: Argentina's chronic inflation was curtailed dramatically and foreign investment began to pour in, leading to an economic boom. Over time, however, the peso appreciated against the majority of currencies as the U.S. dollar became increasingly stronger in the second half of the 1990s. A strong peso hurt exports from Argentina and caused a protracted economic downturn that eventually led to the abandonment of the peso–dollar parity in January 2002. This change, in turn, caused severe economic and political distress in the country. The unemployment rate rose above 20 percent and inflation reached a monthly rate of about 20 percent in April 2002. In contrast, Hong Kong was able to successfully defend its currency board arrangement during the Asian financial crisis, a major stress test for the arrangement.

Although there is no clear consensus on the causes of the Argentine crisis, there are at least three factors that are related to the collapse of the currency board system and ensuing economic crisis: (i) the lack of fiscal discipline, (ii) labor market inflexibility, and (iii) contagion from the financial crises in Russia and Brazil. Reflecting the traditional sociopolitical divisions in the Argentine society, competing claims on economic resources by different groups were accommodated by increasing public sector indebtedness. Argentina is said to have a "European-style welfare system in a Third World economy." The federal government of Argentina borrowed heavily in dollars throughout the 1990s. As the economy entered a recession in the late 1990s, the government encountered increasing difficulty with rising debts, eventually defaulting on its internal and external debts. The hard fixed exchange rate that Argentina adopted under the currency board system made it impossible to restore competitiveness by a traditional currency depreciation. Further, a powerful labor union also made it difficult to lower wages and thus cut production costs that could have effectively achieved the same real currency depreciation with the fixed nominal exchange rate. The situation was exacerbated by a slowdown of international capital inflows following the financial crises in Russia and Brazil. Also, a sharp depreciation of the Brazil real in 1999 hampered exports from Argentina.

While the currency crisis is over, the debt problem has not been completely resolved. The government of Argentina ceased all debt payments in December 2001 in the wake of persistent recession and rising social and political unrest. It represents the largest sovereign default in history. Argentina faces a complex task of restructuring over $100 billion borrowed in seven different currencies and governed by the laws of eight legal jurisdictions. In June 2004, the Argentine government made a "final" offer amounting to a 75 percent reduction in the net present value of the debt. Foreign bondholders rejected this offer and asked for an improved offer. In early 2005, bondholders finally agreed to the restructuring, under which they took a cut of about 70 percent on the value of their bond holdings.

Fixed versus Flexible Exchange Rate Regimes

Since some countries, including the United States, the United Kingdom, and possibly Japan, prefer flexible exchange rates, while others, notably the members of the EMU and many developing countries, would like to maintain fixed exchange rates, it is worthwhile to examine some of the arguments advanced in favor of fixed versus flexible exchange rates.

The key arguments for flexible exchange rates rest on (i) easier external adjustments and (ii) national policy autonomy. Suppose a country is experiencing a balance-of-payments deficit at the moment. This means that there is an excess supply of the country's currency at the prevailing exchange rate in the foreign exchange market. Under a flexible exchange rate regime, the external value of the country's currency will simply

EXHIBIT 2.14

External Adjustment
Mechanism: Fixed versus
Flexible Exchange Rates

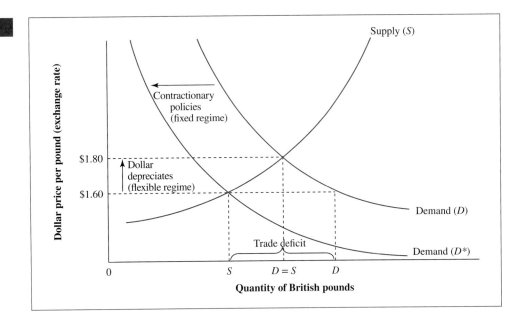

depreciate to the level at which there is no excess supply of the country's currency. At the new exchange rate level, the balance-of-payments disequilibrium will disappear.

As long as the exchange rate is allowed to be determined according to market forces, external balance will be achieved automatically. Consequently, the government does not have to take policy actions to correct the balance-of-payments disequilibrium. With flexible exchange rates, therefore, the government can use its monetary and fiscal policies to pursue whatever economic goals it chooses. Under a fixed rate regime, however, the government may have to take contractionary (expansionary) monetary and fiscal policies to correct the balance-of-payments deficit (surplus) at the existing exchange rate. Since policy tools need to be committed to maintaining the exchange rate, the government cannot use the same policy tools to pursue other economic objectives. As a result, the government loses its policy autonomy under a fixed exchange rate regime.

Using the British pound as the representative foreign exchange, Exhibit 2.14 illustrates the preceding discussion on how the balance-of-payment disequilibrium is corrected under alternative exchange rate regimes. Note that in Exhibit 2.14, the dollar price of the British pound, which is the exchange rate, is measured vertically, whereas the quantity of British pounds demanded or supplied at different exchange rates is measured horizontally. As is the case with most other commodities, the demand for British pounds would be downward sloping, whereas the supply of British pounds would be upward sloping. Suppose that the exchange rate is $1.60/£ at the moment. As can be seen from the exhibit, the demand for British pounds far exceeds the supply (i.e., the supply of U.S. dollars far exceeds the demand) at this exchange rate. The United States experiences trade (or balance of payment) deficits. Under the flexible exchange rate regime, the dollar will simply depreciate to a new level of exchange rate, $1.80/£, at which the excess demand for British pounds (and thus the trade deficit) will disappear. Now, suppose that the exchange rate is "fixed" at $1.60/£, and thus the excess demand for British pounds cannot be eliminated by the exchange rate adjustment. Facing this situation, the U.S. Federal Reserve Bank may initially draw on its foreign exchange reserve holdings to satisfy the excess demand for British pounds. If the excess demand persists, however, the U.S. government may have to resort to contractionary monetary and fiscal policies so that the demand curve can shift to the left (from D to D* in the exhibit) until the excess demand for British pounds can be eliminated at the fixed exchange rate, $1.60/£. In other words, it is necessary for the government to take policy actions to maintain the fixed exchange rate.

A possible drawback of the flexible exchange rate regime is that exchange rate uncertainty may hamper international trade and investment. Proponents of the fixed exchange rate regime argue that when future exchange rates are uncertain, businesses tend to shun foreign trade. Since countries cannot fully benefit from international trade under exchange rate uncertainty, resources will be allocated suboptimally on a global basis. Proponents of the fixed exchange rate regime argue that fixed exchange rates eliminate such uncertainty and thus promote international trade. However, to the extent that firms can hedge exchange risk by means of currency forward or options contracts, uncertain exchange rates do not necessarily hamper international trade.

As the preceding discussion suggests, the choice between the alternative exchange rate regimes is likely to involve a trade-off between national policy independence and international economic integration. If countries would like to pursue their respective domestic economic goals, they are likely to pursue divergent macroeconomic policies, rendering fixed exchange rates infeasible. On the other hand, if countries are committed to promoting international economic integration (as is the case with the core members of the European Union like France and Germany), the benefits of fixed exchange rates are likely to outweigh the associated costs.

A "good" (or ideal) international monetary system should provide (i) liquidity, (ii) adjustment, and (iii) confidence. In other words, a good IMS should be able to provide the world economy with sufficient monetary reserves to support the growth of international trade and investment. It should also provide an effective mechanism that restores the balance-of-payments equilibrium whenever it is disturbed. Lastly, it should offer a safeguard to prevent crises of confidence in the system that result in panicked flights from one reserve asset to another. Politicians and economists should keep these three criteria in mind when they design and evaluate the international monetary system.

SUMMARY

This chapter provides an overview of the international monetary system, which defines an environment in which multinational corporations and international investors operate.

1. The international monetary system can be defined as the institutional framework within which international payments are made, the movements of capital are accommodated, and exchange rates among currencies are determined.

2. The international monetary system went through five stages of evolution: (a) bimetallism, (b) classical gold standard, (c) interwar period, (d) Bretton Woods system, and (e) flexible exchange rate regime.

3. The classical gold standard spanned 1875 to 1914. Under the gold standard, the exchange rate between two currencies is determined by the gold contents of the currencies. Balance-of-payments disequilibrium is automatically corrected through the price-specie-flow mechanism. The gold standard still has ardent supporters who believe that it provides an effective hedge against price inflation. Under the gold standard, however, the world economy can be subject to deflationary pressure due to the limited supply of monetary gold.

4. To prevent the recurrence of economic nationalism with no clear "rules of the game" witnessed during the interwar period, representatives of 44 nations met at Bretton Woods, New Hampshire, in 1944 and adopted a new international monetary system. Under the Bretton Woods system, each country established a par value in relation to the U.S. dollar, which was fully convertible to gold. Countries used foreign exchanges, especially the U.S. dollar, as well as gold as international means of payments. The Bretton Woods system was designed to maintain stable exchange rates and economize on gold. The Bretton Woods system eventually collapsed in 1973 mainly because of U.S. domestic inflation and the persistent balance-of-payments deficits.

5. The flexible exchange rate regime that replaced the Bretton Woods system was ratified by the Jamaica Agreement. Following a spectacular rise and fall of the U.S. dollar in the 1980s, major industrial countries agreed to cooperate to achieve greater exchange rate stability. The Louvre Accord of 1987 marked the inception of the managed-float system under which the G-7 countries would jointly intervene in the foreign exchange market to correct over- or undervaluation of currencies.

6. In 1979, the EEC countries launched the European Monetary System (EMS) to establish a "zone of monetary stability" in Europe. The two main instruments of the EMS are the European Currency Unit (ECU) and the Exchange Rate Mechanism (ERM). The ECU is a basket currency comprising the currencies of the EMS members and serves as the accounting unit of the EMS. The ERM refers to the procedure by which EMS members collectively manage their exchange rates. The ERM is based on a parity grid that the member countries are required to maintain.

7. On January 1, 1999, 11 European countries, including France and Germany, adopted a common currency called the euro. Greece adopted the euro in 2001. Subsequently, five other countries—Cyprus, Malta, Slovakia, Slovenia, and Estonia—adopted the euro. The advent of a single European currency, which may eventually rival the U.S. dollar as a global vehicle currency, will have major implications for the European as well as world economy. Euro-zone countries will benefit from reduced transaction costs and the elimination of exchange rate uncertainty. The advent of the euro will also help develop continentwide capital markets where companies can raise capital at favorable rates.

8. Under the European Monetary Union (EMU), the common monetary policy for the euro-zone countries is formulated by the European Central Bank (ECB) located in Frankfurt. The ECB is legally mandated to maintain price stability in Europe. Together with the ECB, the national central banks of the euro-zone countries form the Eurosystem, which is responsible for defining and implementing the common monetary policy for the EMU.

9. While the core EMU members, including France and Germany, apparently prefer the fixed exchange rate regime, other major countries such as the United States and Japan are willing to live with flexible exchange rates. Under the flexible exchange rate regime, governments can retain policy independence because the external balance will be achieved by the exchange rate adjustments rather than by policy intervention. Exchange rate uncertainty, however, can potentially hamper international trade and investment. The choice between the alternative exchange rate regimes is likely to involve a trade-off between national policy autonomy and international economic integration.

KEY WORDS

bimetallism, *28*
Bretton Woods system, *31*
currency board, *36*
euro, *27*
European Central Bank (ECB), *44*
European Currency Unit (ECU), *41*
European Monetary System (EMS), *41*
European Monetary Union (EMU), *43*
Exchange Rate Mechanism (ERM), *41*

Eurosystem, *44*
gold-exchange standard, *32*
gold standard, *28*
Gresham's law, *28*
incompatible trinity, *54*
international monetary system, *27*
Jamaica Agreement, *34*
Louvre Accord, *35*
Maastricht Treaty, *42*
managed-float system, *35*
optimum currency areas, *47*

par value, *32*
Plaza Accord, *35*
price-specie-flow mechanism, *30*
Smithsonian Agreement, *34*
snake, *41*
special drawing rights (SDRs), *33*
sterilization of gold, *30*
"Tobin tax," *54*
Triffin paradox, *32*

www.mhhe.com/er8e

QUESTIONS

1. Explain Gresham's law.

2. Explain the mechanism that restores the balance-of-payments equilibrium when it is disturbed under the gold standard.

3. Suppose that the pound is pegged to gold at 6 pounds per ounce, whereas the franc is pegged to gold at 12 francs per ounce. This, of course, implies that the equilibrium exchange rate should be two francs per pound. If the current market exchange rate is 2.2 francs per pound, how would you take advantage of this situation? What would be the effect of shipping costs?

4. Discuss the advantages and disadvantages of the gold standard.

5. What were the main objectives of the Bretton Woods system?

6. Comment on the proposition that the Bretton Woods system was programmed to an eventual demise.

7. Explain how special drawing rights (SDRs) are constructed. Also, discuss the circumstances under which the SDRs were created.

8. Explain the arrangements and workings of the European Monetary System (EMS).

9. There are arguments for and against the alternative exchange rate regimes.

   a. List the advantages of the flexible exchange rate regime.

   b. Criticize the flexible exchange rate regime from the viewpoint of the proponents of the fixed exchange rate regime.

   c. Rebut the above criticism from the viewpoint of the proponents of the flexible exchange rate regime.

10. In an integrated world financial market, a financial crisis in a country can be quickly transmitted to other countries, causing a global crisis. What kind of measures would you propose to prevent the recurrence of an Asia-type crisis?

11. Discuss the criteria for a "good" international monetary system.

12. Once capital markets are integrated, it is difficult for a country to maintain a fixed exchange rate. Explain why this may be so.

13. Assess the possibility for the euro to become another global currency rivaling the U.S. If the euro really becomes a global currency, what impact will it have on the U.S. dollar and the world economy?

INTERNET EXERCISES

1. Using the data from federalreserve.gov/releases/h10/hist, first plot the monthly exchange rate between the euro and the U.S. dollar since January 2000, and try to explain why the exchange rate behaved the way it did.

MINI CASE

Grexit or Not?

When the euro was introduced in 1999, Greece was conspicuously absent from the list of the EU member countries adopting the common currency. The country was not ready. In a few short years, however, European leaders, probably motivated by their political agenda, allowed Greece to join the euro club in 2001 although it was not entirely clear if the country satisfied the entry conditions. In any case, joining the euro club allowed the Greek government, households, and firms to gain easy access to plentiful funds at historically low interest rates, ushering in a period of robust credit growth. For a while, Greeks enjoyed what seemed to be the fruits of becoming a full-fledged member of

Europe. In December 2009, however, the new Greek government revealed that the government budget deficit would be 12.7 percent for 2009, not 3.7 percent as previously announced by the outgoing government, far exceeding the EU's convergence guideline of keeping the budget deficit below 3.0 percent of the GDP. As the true picture of the government finance became known, the prices of Greek government bonds began to fall sharply, prompting panic selling among international investors, threatening the sovereign defaults.

Several years into the crisis, the Greek government debt stands at around 180 percent of GDP and the jobless rate among youth is above 50 percent. The country's GDP declined by about 25 percent. Severe austerity measures, such as sharply raised taxes and much reduced pension benefits, were imposed on Greece as conditions for the bailouts arranged by the EU, IMF, and the European Central Bank. In addition, people were allowed to have only restricted access to their bank deposits, to prevent bank runs. Opinion polls indicate that the majority of people in Germany, the main creditor nation for Greece, prefer the Greek exit from the euro zone, popularly called Grexit, while some people in Greece are demanding Grexit themselves and restoration of the national currency, the drachma.

Discussion points: (i) the root causes of the Greek predicaments, (ii) the costs and benefits of staying in the euro zone for Greece, (iii) the measures that need to be taken to keep Greece in the euro zone in the long run if that is desirable, (iv) If you were a disinterested outside advisor for the Greek government, would you advise Grexit or not? Why or why not?

REFERENCES & SUGGESTED READINGS

Bris, Arturo, Yrjö Koskinen, and Mattias Nilsson. The Euro and Corporate Valuation. Working Paper (2004).

Chinn, Menzie, and Jeffrey Frankel. "Why the Euro Will Rival the Dollar," *International Finance* 11 (2008), pp. 49–73.

Cooper, Richard N. *The International Monetary System: Essays in World Economics.* Cambridge, Mass.: MIT Press, 1987.

Eichengreen, Barry. *The Gold Standard in Theory and History.* Methuen: London, 1985, pp. 39–48.

Eichengreen, Barry. *Exorbitant Privilege: The Rise and Fall of the Dollar and the Future of the International Monetary System.* Oxford University Press, 2011.

Friedman, Milton. *Essays in Positive Economics.* Chicago: University of Chicago Press, 1953.

Jorion, Philippe. "Properties of the ECU as a Currency Basket." *Journal of Multinational Financial Management* 1 (1991), pp. 1–24.

Machlup, Fritz. *Remaking the International Monetary System: The Rio Agreement and Beyond.* Baltimore: Johns Hopkins Press, 1968.

Mundell, Robert. "A Theory of Optimum Currency Areas." *American Economic Review* 51 (1961), pp. 657–65.

———. "Currency Areas, Volatility and Intervention," *Journal of Policy Modeling* 22 (2000), pp. 281–99.

Nurkse, Ragnar. *International Currency Experience: Lessons of the Interwar Period.* Geneva: League of Nations, 1944.

Obstfeld, Maurice, Jay Shambaugh, and Alan Taylor. "The Trilemma in History: Tradeoffs among Exchange Rates, Monetary Policies, and Capital Mobility." *Review of Economics and Statistics.* 87 (2005), pp. 423–38.

Solomon, Robert. *The International Monetary System, 1945–1981.* New York: Harper & Row, 1982.

Stiglitz, Joseph. "Reforming the Global Economic Architecture: Lessons from Recent Crisis." *Journal of Finance* 54 (1999), pp. 1508–21.

Tobin, James. "Financial Globalization," Unpublished manuscript presented at American Philosophical Society, 1998.

Triffin, Robert. *Gold and the Dollar Crisis.* New Haven, Conn.: Yale University Press, 1960.

3 Balance of Payments

THE TERM balance of payments is often mentioned in the news media and continues to be a popular subject of economic and political discourse around the world. It is not always clear, however, exactly what is meant by the term when it is mentioned in various contexts. This ambiguity is often attributable to misunderstanding and misuse of the term. The balance of payments, which is a statistical record of a country's transactions with the rest of the world, is worth studying for a few reasons.

First, the balance of payments provides detailed information concerning the demand and supply of a country's currency. For example, if the United States imports more than it exports, then this means that the supply of dollars is likely to exceed the demand in the foreign exchange market, *ceteris paribus*. One can thus infer that the U.S. dollar would be under pressure to depreciate against other currencies. On the other hand, if the United States exports more than it imports, then the dollar would be more likely to appreciate.

Second, a country's balance-of-payment data may signal its potential as a business partner for the rest of the world. If a country is grappling with a major balance-of-payment difficulty, it may not be able to expand imports from the outside world. Instead, the country may be tempted to impose measures to restrict imports and discourage capital outflows in order to improve the balance-of-payment situation. On the other hand, a country experiencing a significant balance-of-payment surplus would be more likely to expand imports, offering marketing opportunities for foreign enterprises, and less likely to impose foreign exchange restrictions.

Third, balance-of-payments data can be used to evaluate the performance of the country in international economic competition. Suppose a country is experiencing trade deficits year after year. This trade data may then signal that the country's domestic industries lack international competitiveness. To interpret balance-of-payments data properly, it is necessary to understand how the balance-of-payments account is constructed.

Balance-of-Payments Accounting

The balance of payments can be formally defined as *the statistical record of a country's international transactions over a certain period of time presented in the form of double-entry bookkeeping.* Examples of international transactions include import and export of goods and services and cross-border investments in businesses, bank accounts, bonds, stocks, and real estate. Since the balance of payments is recorded over a certain period of time (i.e., a quarter or a year), it has the same time dimension as national income accounting.[1]

---

[1]In fact, the current account balance, which is the difference between a country's exports and imports, is a component of the country's GNP. Other components of GNP include consumption and investment and government expenditure.

Generally speaking, any transaction that results in a receipt from foreigners will be recorded as a credit, with a positive sign, in the U.S. balance of payments, whereas any transaction that gives rise to a payment to foreigners will be recorded as a debit, with a negative sign. Credit entries in the U.S. balance of payments result from foreign sales of U.S. goods and services, goodwill, financial claims, and real assets. Debit entries, on the other hand, arise from U.S. purchases of foreign goods and services, goodwill, financial claims, and real assets. Further, credit entries give rise to the demand for dollars, whereas debit entries give rise to the supply of dollars. Note that the demand (supply) for dollars is associated with the supply (demand) of foreign exchange.

Since the balance of payments is presented as a system of double-entry bookkeeping, every credit in the account is balanced by a matching debit and vice versa.

EXAMPLE | 3.1

For example, suppose that Boeing Corporation exported a Boeing 747 aircraft to Japan Airlines for $50 million, and that Japan Airlines pays from its dollar bank account kept with Chase Manhattan Bank in New York City. Then, the receipt of $50 million by Boeing will be recorded as a credit (+), which will be matched by a debit (−) of the same amount representing a reduction of the U.S. bank's liabilities.

EXAMPLE | 3.2

Suppose, for another example, that Boeing imports jet engines produced by Rolls-Royce for $30 million, and that Boeing makes payment by transferring the funds to a New York bank account kept by Rolls-Royce. In this case, payment by Boeing will be recorded as a debit (−), whereas the deposit of the funds by Rolls-Royce will be recorded as a credit (+).

As shown by the preceding examples, every credit in the balance of payments is matched by a debit somewhere to conform to the principle of double-entry bookkeeping.

Not only international trade, that is, exports and imports, but also cross-border investments are recorded in the balance of payments.

EXAMPLE | 3.3

Suppose that Thomson Corporation, a U.S. information services company, acquires Reuters, a British news agency, for $750 million, and that Reuters deposits the money in Barclays Bank in London, which, in turn, uses the sum to purchase U.S. treasury notes. In this case, the payment of $750 million by Thomson will be recorded as a debit (−), whereas Barclays' purchase of the U.S. Treasury notes will be recorded as a credit (+).

The above examples can be summarized as follows:

Transactions	Credit	Debit
Boeing's export	+$50 million	
Withdrawal from U.S. bank		−$50 million
Boeing's import		−$30 million
Deposit at U.S. bank	+$30 million	
Thomson's acquisition of Reuters		−$750 million
Barclays' purchase of U.S. securities	+$750 million	

Balance-of-Payments Accounts

Since the balance of payments records all types of international transactions a country consummates over a certain period of time, it contains a wide variety of accounts. However, a country's international transactions can be grouped into the following three main types:

1. The current account.
2. The capital account.
3. The official reserve account.

The **current account** includes the export and import of goods and services, whereas the **capital account** includes all purchases and sales of assets such as stocks, bonds, bank accounts, real estate, and businesses. The **official reserve account**, on the other hand, covers all purchases and sales of international reserve assets such as dollars, foreign exchanges, gold, and special drawing rights (SDRs).

Let us now examine a detailed description of the balance-of-payments accounts. Exhibit 3.1 summarizes the U.S. balance-of-payments accounts for the year 2015 that we are going to use as an example.

The Current Account   Exhibit 3.1 shows that U.S. exports were $3,044.1 billion in 2015, while U.S. imports were $3,362.1 billion. The current account balance, which is defined as exports minus imports plus unilateral transfers, that is, (1) + (2) + (3) in Exhibit 3.1, was negative, −$463.0 billion. The United States thus had a balance-of-payments deficit on the current account in 2015. The current account deficit implies that the United States used

EXHIBIT 3.1

A Summary of the U.S. Balance of Payments for 2015 (in $ billion)

			Credits	Debits
Current Account				
[1]	Exports		3,044.1	
	[1.1]	Merchandise	1,510.3	
	[1.2]	Services	750.9	
	[1.3]	Factor income	782.9	
[2]	Imports			−3,362.1
	[2.1]	Merchandise		−2,272.9
	[2.2]	Services		−488.7
	[2.3]	Factor income		−600.5
[3]	Unilateral transfer		128.6	−273.6
	Balance on current account			−463.0
	[[1] + [2] + [3]]			
Capital Account				
[4]	Direct investment		379.4	−348.6
[5]	Portfolio investment		276.3	−154.0
	[5.1]	Equity securities	−178.3	−202.6
	[5.2]	Debt securities	429.2	48.6
	[5.3]	Derivatives, net	25.4	
[6]	Other investment		270.9	−235.1
	Balance on capital account		188.9	
	[[4] + [5] + [6]]			
[7]	Statistical discrepancies		267.8	
	Overall balance			−6.3
Official Reserve Account			6.3	

Source: IMF, *International Financial Statistics Yearbook, 2016.*

www.bea.gov

Website of the Bureau of
Economic Analysis, U.S.
Department of Commerce,
provides data related to the
U.S. balance of payments.

up more output than it produced.[2] Since a country must finance its current account deficit either by borrowing from foreigners or by drawing down on its previously accumulated foreign wealth, a current account deficit represents a reduction in the country's net foreign wealth. On the other hand, a country with a current account surplus acquires IOUs from foreigners, thereby increasing its net foreign wealth.

The current account is divided into four finer categories: merchandise trade, services, factor income, and unilateral transfers. **Merchandise trade** represents exports and imports of tangible goods, such as oil, wheat, clothes, automobiles, computers, and so on. As Exhibit 3.1 shows, U.S. merchandise exports were $1,510.3 billion in 2015 while imports were $2,272.9 billion. The United States thus had a deficit on the **trade balance** or a trade deficit. The trade balance represents the net merchandise export. As is well known, the United States has experienced persistent trade deficits since the early 1980s, whereas such key trading partners as China, Japan, and Germany have generally realized trade surpluses. This persistent trade imbalance between the United States and her key trading partners has been a source of international contention.

Services, the second category of the current account, include payments and receipts for legal, consulting, and engineering services, royalties for patents and intellectual properties, insurance premiums, shipping fees, and tourist expenditures. These trades in services are sometimes called **invisible trade**. In 2015, U.S. service exports were $750.9 billion and imports were $488.7 billion, realizing a surplus of $262.2 billion. Clearly, the United States performed better in services than in merchandise trade. It is noted that thanks to the rapid advancement of information technology (IT), many services that were previously nontradable are becoming tradable. For example, X-ray pictures taken at a local hospital in the United States may be transmitted overnight via the Internet to an IT outsourcing center in India. Then, doctors there would examine the digital images and data and e-mail their diagnosis back to the U.S. hospital for a fee. In this case, the United States effectively imported medical service from India.

Factor income, the third category of the current account, consists largely of payments and receipts of interest, dividends, and other income on foreign investments that were previously made. If U.S. investors receive interest on their holdings of foreign bonds, for instance, it will be recorded as a credit in the balance of payments. On the other hand, interest payments by U.S. borrowers to foreign creditors will be recorded as debits. In 2015, U.S. residents paid out $600.5 billion to foreigners as factor income and received $782.9 billion, realizing a $182.4 billion surplus. Considering, however, that the United States has heavily borrowed from foreigners in recent years, U.S. payments of interest and dividends to foreigners are likely to rise significantly. This can increase the U.S. current account deficit in the future, *ceteris paribus*.

Unilateral transfers, the fourth category of the current account, involve "unrequited" payments. Examples include foreign aid, reparations, official and private grants, and gifts. Unlike other accounts in the balance of payments, unilateral transfers have only one-directional flows, without offsetting flows. In the case of merchandise trade, for example, goods flow in one direction and payments flow in the opposite direction. For the purpose of preserving the double-entry bookkeeping rule, unilateral transfers are regarded as an act of buying *goodwill* from the recipients. So a country that gives foreign aid to another country can be viewed as importing goodwill from the latter. As can be expected, the United States made a net unilateral transfer of $145.0 billion, which is the receipt of transfer payments ($128.6 billion) minus transfer payments to foreign entities ($273.6 billion).

---

[2]The current account balance (BCA) can be written as the difference between national output (Y) and domestic absorption, which comprises consumption (C), investment (I), and government expenditures (G):

$$BCA = Y - (C + I + G)$$

If a country's domestic absorption falls short of its national output, the country's current account must be in surplus, for more detailed discussion, refer to Appendix 3A.

EXHIBIT 3.2

A Currency Depreciation and the Time-Path of the Trade Balance: The J-Curve Effect

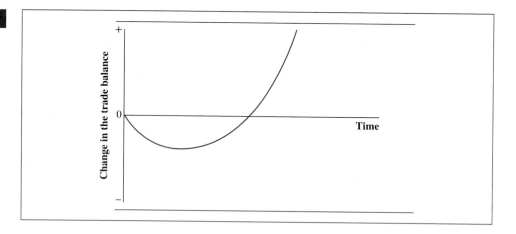

The current account balance, especially the trade balance, tends to be sensitive to exchange rate changes. When a country's currency depreciates against the currencies of major trading partners, the country's exports tend to rise and imports fall, improving the trade balance. For example, Mexico experienced continuous deficits in its trade balance of about $4.5 billion per quarter throughout 1994. Following the depreciation of the peso in December 1994, however, Mexico's trade balance began to improve immediately, realizing a surplus of about $7 billion for the year 1995.

The effect of currency depreciation on a country's trade balance can be more complicated than the case described above. Indeed, following a depreciation, the trade balance may at first deteriorate for a while. Eventually, however, the trade balance will tend to improve over time. This particular reaction pattern of the trade balance to a depreciation is referred to as the **J-curve effect**, which is illustrated in Exhibit 3.2. The curve shows the initial deterioration and the eventual improvement of the trade balance following a depreciation. The J-curve effect received wide attention when the British trade balance worsened after a devaluation of the pound in 1967. Sebastian Edwards (1989) examined various cases of devaluations carried out by developing countries from the 1960s through the 1980s, and confirmed the existence of the J-curve effect in about 40 percent of the cases.

A depreciation will begin to improve the trade balance immediately if imports and exports are *responsive* to the exchange rate changes. On the other hand, if imports and exports are inelastic, the trade balance will worsen following a depreciation. Following a depreciation of the domestic currency and the resultant rise in import prices, domestic residents may still continue to purchase imports because it is difficult to change their consumption habits in a short period of time. With higher import prices, the domestic country comes to spend more on imports. Even if domestic residents are willing to switch to less expensive domestic substitutes for foreign imports, it may take time for domestic producers to supply import substitutes. Likewise, foreigners' demand for domestic products, which become less expensive with a depreciation of the domestic currency, can be inelastic essentially for the same reasons. In the long run, however, both imports and exports tend to be responsive to exchange rate changes, exerting positive influences on the trade balance.

The Capital Account

The capital account balance measures the difference between U.S. sales of assets to foreigners and U.S. purchases of foreign assets. U.S. sales (or exports) of assets are recorded as credits, as they result in *capital inflow*. On the other hand, U.S. purchases (imports) of foreign assets are recorded as debits, as they lead to *capital outflow*. Unlike trades in goods and services, trades in financial assets affect future payments and receipts of factor income.

Exhibit 3.1 shows that the United States had a capital account surplus of $188.9 billion in 2015, implying that capital inflow to the United States far exceeded capital outflow. Clearly, the current account deficit was substantially offset by the capital account surplus.

As previously mentioned, a country's current account deficit must be paid for either by borrowing from foreigners or by selling off past foreign investments. In the absence of the government's reserve transactions, the current account balance must be equal to the capital account balance but with the opposite sign. When nothing is excluded, a country's balance of payments must necessarily balance. In 2015, however, the capital account surplus ($188.9 billion) falls much short of the current account deficit ($463.0 billion) in magnitude. But at the same time, the statistical discrepancies ($267.8 billion), including errors and omissions that tend to occur mostly in the capital account transactions, are unusually large. It is noted that the sum of the capital account surplus and the statistical discrepancies, $456.7 billion (= $188.9 billion + $267.8 billion), is very close to the current account deficit, $463.0 billion.

The capital account can be divided into three categories: direct investment, portfolio investment, and other investment. Direct investment occurs when the investor acquires a measure of control of the foreign business. In the U.S. balance of payments, acquisition of 10 percent or more of the voting shares of a business is considered giving a measure of control to the investor.

When Honda, a Japanese automobile manufacturer, built an assembly factory in Ohio, it was engaged in **foreign direct investment (FDI)**. Another example of direct investment was provided by Nestlé Corporation, a Swiss multinational firm, when it *acquired* Carnation, a U.S. firm. Of course, U.S. firms also are engaged in direct investments in foreign countries. For instance, Coca-Cola built bottling facilities all over the world. In recent years, many U.S. corporations moved their production facilities to Mexico and China, in part, to take advantage of lower costs of production. Generally speaking, foreign direct investments take place as firms attempt to take advantage of various market imperfections, such as underpriced labor services and protected markets. In 2015, U.S. direct investment overseas was $348.6 billion, whereas foreign direct investment in the United States was $379.4 billion.

Firms undertake foreign direct investments when the expected returns from foreign investments exceed the cost of capital, allowing for foreign exchange and political risks. The expected returns from foreign projects can be higher than those from domestic projects because of lower wage rates and material costs, subsidized financing, preferential tax treatment, exclusive access to local markets, and the like. The volume and direction of FDI can also be sensitive to exchange rate changes. For instance, Japanese FDI in the United States soared in the latter half of the 1980s, partly because of the sharp appreciation of the yen against the dollar. With a stronger yen, Japanese firms could better afford to acquire U.S. assets that became less expensive in terms of the yen. The same exchange rate movement discouraged U.S. firms from making FDI in Japan because Japanese assets became more expensive in terms of the dollar.

Portfolio investment, the second category of the capital account, mostly represents sales and purchases of foreign financial assets such as stocks and bonds that do not involve a transfer of control. International portfolio investments have boomed in recent years, partly due to the general relaxation of capital controls and regulations in many countries, and partly due to investors' desire to diversify risk globally. Portfolio investment comprises equity, debt, and derivative securities. Exhibit 3.1 shows that in 2015, foreigners invested $276.3 billion in U.S. financial securities, whereas Americans invested $154.0 billion in foreign securities, realizing a surplus, $122.3 billion, for the United States. Much of the surplus represents foreigners' investment in U.S. debt securities and U.S. liquidation and repatriation of foreign debt securities. Exhibit 3.1 shows that foreigners invested $429.2 billion in U.S. debt securities in 2015, whereas U.S. investors divested $48.6 billion in foreign debt securities. It is also noted that foreigners divested $178.3 billion in U.S. equities.

Investors typically diversify their investment portfolios to reduce risk. Since security returns tend to have relatively low correlations among countries, investors can reduce risk more effectively if they diversify their portfolio holdings internationally rather than purely domestically. In addition, investors may be able to benefit from higher expected returns from some foreign markets.[3]

In recent years, government-controlled investment funds, known as *sovereign wealth funds* (SWFs), are playing an increasingly visible role in international investments. SWFs are mostly domiciled in Asian and Middle Eastern countries and usually are responsible for recycling foreign exchange reserves of these countries swelled by trade surpluses and oil revenues. It is noted that SWFs invested large sums of money in many western banks that were severely affected by subprime mortgage-related losses (i.e., housing loans made to borrowers with marginal creditworthiness). For example, Abu Dhabi Investment Authority invested $7.5 billion in Citigroup, which needed to replenish its capital base in the wake of subprime losses, whereas Temasek Holdings, Singapore's state-owned investment company, injected $5.0 billion into Merrill Lynch, one of the largest investment banks in the United States. Although SWFs play a positive role in stabilizing the global banking system and help the balance-of-payment situations of the host countries, they are increasingly under close scrutiny due to their sheer size and the lack of transparency about the way these funds are operating.

The third category of the capital account is **other investment**, which includes transactions in currency, bank deposits, trade credits, and so forth. These investments are quite sensitive to both changes in relative interest rates between countries and the anticipated change in the exchange rate. If the interest rate rises in the United States while other variables remain constant, the United States will experience capital inflows, as investors would like to deposit or invest in the United States to take advantage of the higher interest rate. On the other hand, if a higher U.S. interest rate is more or less offset by an expected depreciation of the U.S. dollar, capital inflows to the United States will not materialize.[4] Since both interest rates and exchange rate expectations are volatile, these capital flows are highly reversible. In 2015, the United States experienced a major inflow of $270.9 billion in this category, while U.S. investors invested $235.1 billion in their holdings of foreign assets in this category.

Statistical Discrepancy

Exhibit 3.1 shows that there was a statistical discrepancy of $267.8 billion in 2015, representing omitted and misrecorded transactions. Recordings of payments and receipts arising from international transactions are done at different times and places, possibly using different methods. As a result, these recordings, upon which the balance-of-payments statistics are constructed, are bound to be imperfect. While merchandise trade can be recorded with a certain degree of accuracy at the customs houses, provisions of invisible services like consulting can escape detection. Cross-border financial transactions, a bulk of which might have been conducted electronically, are far more difficult to keep track of. For this reason, the balance of payments always presents a "balancing" debit or credit as a statistical discrepancy.[5] As was previously mentioned, the sum of the balance on capital account and the statistical discrepancy largely offset the balance of current account in magnitude, −$463.0 billion. This suggests that financial transactions may be mainly responsible for the discrepancy.

When we compute the *cumulative* balance of payments including the current account, capital account, and the statistical discrepancies, we obtain the so-called **overall balance** or **official settlement balance**. All the transactions comprising the

---

[3]Refer to Chapter 15 for a detailed discussion of international portfolio investment.

[4]We will discuss the relationship between the relative interest rates and the expected exchange rate change in Chapter 6.

[5]Readers might wonder how to compute the statistical discrepancies in the balance of payments. Statistical discrepancies, which represent errors and omissions, by definition, cannot be known. Since, however, the balance of payments must balance to zero when every item is included, one can determine the statistical discrepancies in the "residual" manner.

overall balance take place *autonomously* for their own sake.[6] The overall balance is significant because it indicates a country's international payment gap that must be *accommodated* with the government's official reserve transactions.

It is also indicative of the pressure that a country's currency faces for depreciation or appreciation. If, for example, a country continuously realizes deficits on the overall balance, the country will eventually run out of reserve holdings and its currency may have to depreciate against foreign currencies. In 2015, the United States had a $6.3 billion deficit on the overall balance. This means that the United States made a net payment equal to that amount to the rest of the world. If the United States had realized a surplus on the overall balance, the United States would have received a net payment from the rest of the world.

Official Reserve Account

When a country must make a net payment to foreigners because of a balance-of-payments deficit, the central bank of the country (the Federal Reserve System in the United States) should either run down its **official reserve assets**, such as gold, foreign exchanges, and SDRs, or borrow anew from foreign central banks. On the other hand, if a country has a balance-of-payments surplus, its central bank will either retire some of its foreign debts or acquire additional reserve assets from foreigners. Exhibit 3.1 shows that to deal with a $6.3 billion balance-of-payment deficit, the United States decreased its external reserve holdings by the same amount by, for example, liquidating foreign exchange reserves.

The official reserve account includes transactions undertaken by the authorities to finance the overall balance and intervene in foreign exchange markets. When the United States and foreign governments wish to support the value of the dollar in the foreign exchange markets, they sell foreign exchanges, SDRs, or gold to "buy" dollars. These transactions, which give rise to the demand for dollars, will be recorded as a positive entry under official reserves. On the other hand, if governments would like to see a weaker dollar, they "sell" dollars and buy gold, foreign exchanges, and so forth. These transactions, which give rise to the supply of dollars, will be recorded as a negative entry under official reserves. The more actively governments intervene in the foreign exchange markets, the greater the official reserve changes.

On September 6, 2011, the Swiss National Bank (SNB), the central bank of Switzerland, surprised financial markets by announcing that it will intervene in currency markets "without limit" in order to keep the Swiss franc from appreciating beyond SFr1.20/€, which is equivalent to about €0.833/SFr. The central bank announced that "with immediate effect, the bank will no longer tolerate an exchange rate in the euro against the Swiss franc below the minimum rate of SFr1.20. The SNB will enforce this minimum rate with the utmost determination and is prepared to buy foreign currency in unlimited quantities." As Switzerland was receiving safe-haven investment flows from the euro zone uncertainties, the Swiss franc has been steadily appreciating from €0.61 per Swiss franc in early 2008 to a near-parity with the euro in August 2011, hurting the export-driven economy of Switzerland. To prevent the appreciation of the Swiss franc, the SNB has been buying up euros by printing and selling francs. The intervention was focused on the euro because the euro zone is by far the largest export market for the Swiss products. As can be seen in Exhibit 3.3, the official reserve assets of Switzerland were essentially constant in 2008, implying non-intervention, but began to rise fast since 2009, reflecting the SNB intervention. Despite the intervention, the Swiss franc continued to appreciate against the euro, pushing the Swiss economy toward recession. Against this backdrop, the SNB announced the drastic measure to intervene in currency markets without limit in order to keep the minimum exchange rate of SFr1.20 against the euro. Exhibit 3.3 shows that the Swiss franc fell sharply upon the announcement and the SNB was successful in keeping the Swiss franc at the minimum rate. As a result of the central bank interventions over the years, the official reserve assets of Switzerland have increased from under $50 billion in 2008 to nearly $500 billion in 2013. The "minimum rate" policy of SNB

---

[6]Autonomous transactions refer to those transactions that occur without regard to the goal of achieving the balance-of-payments equilibrium.

EXHIBIT 3.3

Swiss Intervention in
Foreign Exchange Markets

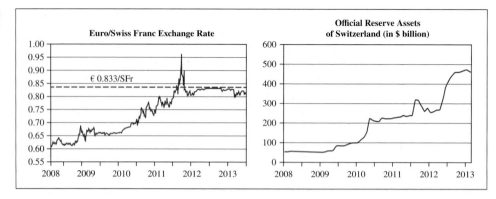

Source: Datastream and International Financial Statistics.

continued until January 2015. The Swiss episode shows that the negative effect of the so-called "market-determined exchange rate" on the real economy can force the government to tie up the "invisible hands" of the market.

Until the advent of the Bretton Woods System in 1945, gold was the predominant international reserve asset. After 1945, however, international reserve assets comprise

1. Gold.
2. Foreign exchanges.
3. Special drawing rights (SDRs).
4. Reserve positions in the International Monetary Fund (IMF).

As can be seen from Exhibit 3.4, the relative importance of gold as an international means of payment has steadily declined, whereas the importance of foreign exchanges has grown substantially. As of 2015, foreign exchanges account for about 95 percent of the total reserve assets held by IMF member countries, with gold accounting for less than 1 percent of the total reserves. Similar to gold, the relative importance of SDRs and reserve positions in the IMF have steadily declined. However, due to the IMF's issuance of $250 billion in new SDRs, SDRs' share in global reserves rose to about 4 percent in 2009. The new issuance of SDRs was based on the recommendation of the G-20 summit meeting held in London in April 2009. The objective of the new issuance was to boost global liquidity.

As can be seen from Exhibit 3.5, the U.S. dollar's share in the world's foreign exchange reserves was 56.2 percent in 1993, followed by the German mark (14.1 percent), ECU (8.3 percent), Japanese yen (8.0 percent), British pound (3.1 percent), French franc (2.2 percent), Swiss franc (1.2 percent), and Dutch guilder (0.6 percent). The "predecessor" currencies of the euro, including the German mark, French franc, Dutch guilder, and ECU, collectively received a substantial weight, about 25 percent, in the world's foreign exchange reserves. For comparison, in 1997, the world's reserves comprised the U.S. dollar (65.1 percent), German mark (14.5 percent), Japanese yen (5.8 percent), British pound (2.6 percent), French franc (1.4 percent), ECU (6.1 percent), Swiss franc (0.3 percent), Dutch guilder (0.5 percent), and miscellaneous currencies (3.9 percent). In other words, the U.S. dollar's share increased substantially throughout the 1990s at the expense of other currencies. This change could be attributed to a strong performance of the dollar in the 1990s and the uncertainty associated with the introduction of the new currency, that is, the euro. In 2015, the world reserves comprised the U.S. dollar (64.1 percent), euro (19.9 percent), Japanese yen (4.1 percent), British pound (4.9 percent), Swiss franc (0.3 percent), and miscellaneous currencies (6.8 percent). The dollar's dominant position in the world's reserve holdings may decline to a certain extent as the euro becomes a more stable and better "known quantity" and central banks wish to diversify their reserve holdings. In fact, the euro's share has increased from 17.9 percent in 1999 to 27.7 percent in 2009. By 2015, however, it declined significantly to 19.9 percent due to the euro-zone debt crisis.

EXHIBIT 3.4

Composition of Total Official Reserves (in percent)

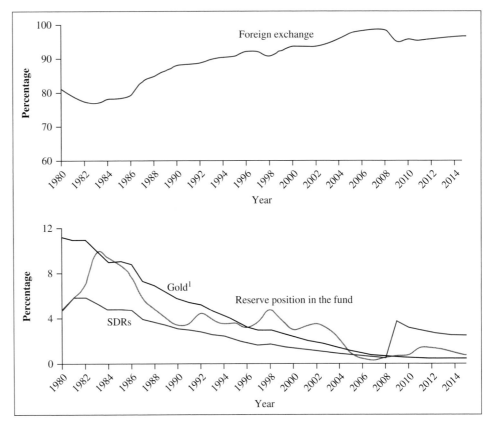

¹Values at SDR 35 per ounce. USD values are obtained by applying the USD/SDR exchange rate at the end of the period.
Source: IMF, *International Financial Statistics.*

EXHIBIT 3.5

Currency Composition of the World's Foreign Exchange Reserves (percent of total)

Currency	1993	1995	1997	1999	2001	2003	2005	2007	2009	2011	2013	2015
U.S. dollar	56.2	59.0	65.1	71.0	71.5	65.4	66.5	63.9	62.1	62.6	61.2	64.1
Japanese yen	8.0	6.8	5.8	6.4	5.0	4.4	4.0	3.2	2.9	3.6	3.8	4.1
Pound sterling	3.1	2.1	2.6	2.9	2.7	2.9	3.7	4.8	4.2	3.8	4.0	4.9
Swiss franc	1.2	0.3	0.3	0.2	0.2	0.2	0.1	0.2	0.1	0.1	0.3	0.3
Euro	—	—	—	17.9	19.2	25.0	23.9	26.1	27.7	24.4	24.2	19.9
Deutsche mark	14.1	15.8	14.5	—	—	—	—	—	—	—	—	—
French franc	2.2	2.4	1.4	—	—	—	—	—	—	—	—	—
Dutch guilder	0.6	0.3	0.4	—	—	—	—	—	—	—	—	—
ECU	8.3	8.5	6.1	—	—	—	—	—	—	—	—	—
Other currencies	6.2	4.9	3.9	1.6	1.3	2.0	1.7	1.8	3.0	5.5	6.5	6.8

Source: IMF eLibrary

In addition to the emergence of the euro as a credible reserve currency, continued U.S. trade deficits and foreigners' desire to diversify their currency holdings away from U.S. dollars could further diminish the position of the U.S. dollar as the dominant reserve currency. Particularly, the value of the U.S. dollar would also be very much affected by the currency diversification decisions of Asian central banks. These banks collectively hold an enormous amount of foreign currency reserves, mostly in dollars, arising from trade surpluses. Asian central banks also purchase U.S. dollars in foreign exchange markets in order to limit appreciation of their local currencies against the dollar.

The Balance-of-Payments Identity

When the balance-of-payments accounts are recorded correctly, the combined balance of the current account, the capital account, and the reserves account must be zero, that is,

$$BCA + BKA + BRA = 0 \tag{3.1}$$

where

BCA = balance on the current account
BKA = balance on the capital account
BRA = balance on the reserve account

The balance on the reserves account, BRA, represents the change in the official reserves.

Equation 3.1 is the **balance-of-payments identity (BOPI)** that must necessarily hold. The BOPI equation indicates that a country can run a balance-of-payments surplus or deficit by increasing or decreasing its official reserves. Under the fixed exchange rate regime, countries maintain official reserves that allow them to have balance-of-payments disequilibrium, that is, BCA + BKA is nonzero, without adjusting the exchange rate. Under the fixed exchange rate regime, the combined balance on the current and capital accounts will be equal in size, but opposite in sign, to the change in the official reserves:

$$BCA + BKA = -BRA \tag{3.2}$$

For example, if a country runs a deficit on the overall balance, that is, BCA + BKA is negative, the central bank of the country can supply foreign exchanges out of its reserve holdings. But if the deficit persists, the central bank will eventually run out of its reserves, and the country may be forced to devalue its currency. This is roughly what happened to the Mexican peso in December 1994.

Under the *pure* flexible exchange rate regime, central banks will not intervene in the foreign exchange markets. In fact, central banks do not need to maintain official reserves. Under this regime, the overall balance thus must necessarily balance, that is,

$$BCA = -BKA \tag{3.3}$$

In other words, a current account surplus or deficit must be matched by a capital account deficit or surplus, and vice versa. In a *dirty* floating exchange rate system under which the central banks discreetly buy and sell foreign exchanges, Equation 3.3 will not hold tightly.

Being an identity, Equation 3.3 does not imply a causality by itself. A current account deficit (surplus) may cause a capital account surplus (deficit), or the opposite may hold. It has often been suggested that the persistent U.S. current account deficits made it necessary for the United States to run matching capital account surpluses, implying that the former *causes* the latter. One can argue, with equal justification, that the persistent U.S. capital account surpluses, which may have been caused by high U.S. interest rates, have caused the persistent current account deficits by strengthening the value of the dollar. The issue can be settled only by careful empirical studies.

Balance-of-Payments Trends in Major Countries

Considering the significant attention that balance-of-payments data receive in the news media, it is useful to closely examine balance-of-payments trends in some of the major countries. Exhibit 3.6 provides the balance on the current account (BCA) as well as the balance on the capital account (BKA) for each of the five key countries, China, Japan, Germany, the United Kingdom, and the United States, during the period 1982–2015.

Exhibit 3.6 shows first that the United States has experienced continuous deficits on the current account since 1982 and continuous surpluses on the capital account. Clearly, the magnitude of U.S. current account deficits is far greater than any that other countries

EXHIBIT 3.6	Balances on the Current (BCA) and Capital (BKA) Accounts of Five Major Countries: 1982–2015 ($ billion)[a]									
	China		Japan		Germany		United Kingdom		United States	
Year	BCA	BKA	BCA	BKA	BCA	BKA	BCA	BKA	BCA	BKA
1982	5.7	0.6	6.9	−11.6	4.9	−2.0	8.0	−10.6	−11.6	16.6
1983	4.2	−0.1	20.8	−19.3	4.6	−6.6	5.3	−7.1	−44.2	45.4
1984	2.0	−1.9	35.0	−32.9	9.6	−9.9	1.8	−2.8	−99.0	102.1
1985	−11.4	9.0	51.1	−51.6	17.6	−15.4	3.3	−0.7	−124.5	128.3
1986	−7.0	5.0	85.9	−70.7	40.9	−35.5	−1.3	5.0	−150.5	150.2
1987	0.3	4.5	84.4	−46.3	46.4	−24.9	−8.1	28.2	−166.5	157.3
1988	−3.8	6.2	79.2	−61.7	50.4	−66.0	−29.3	33.9	−127.7	131.6
1989	−4.3	3.8	63.2	−76.3	57.0	−54.1	−36.7	28.6	−104.3	129.5
1990	12.0	0.1	44.1	−53.2	48.3	−41.1	−32.5	32.5	−94.3	96.5
1991	13.3	1.3	68.2	−76.6	−17.7	11.5	−14.3	19.0	−9.3	3.5
1992	6.4	−8.5	112.6	−112.0	−19.1	56.3	−18.4	11.7	−61.4	57.4
1993	−11.6	13.4	131.6	−104.2	−13.9	−0.3	−15.5	21.0	−90.6	91.9
1994	6.9	23.5	130.3	−105.0	−20.9	18.9	−2.3	3.8	−132.9	127.6
1995	1.6	20.9	111.0	−52.4	−22.6	29.8	−5.9	5.0	−129.2	138.9
1996	7.2	24.5	65.9	−30.7	−13.8	12.6	−3.7	3.2	−148.7	142.1
1997	29.7	6.1	94.4	−87.8	−1.2	2.6	6.8	−11.0	−166.8	167.8
1998	31.5	−6.3	120.7	−116.8	−6.4	17.6	−8.0	0.2	−217.4	151.6
1999	21.1	5.2	106.9	−31.1	−18.0	−40.5	−31.9	31.0	−324.4	367.9
2000	20.5	2.0	116.9	−75.5	−18.7	13.2	−28.8	26.2	−444.7	443.6
2001	17.4	34.8	87.8	−51.0	1.7	−24.1	−32.1	31.5	−385.7	419.9
2002	35.4	32.3	112.4	−66.7	43.4	−70.4	−26.2	17.3	−473.9	572.7
2003	45.9	52.7	136.2	67.9	54.9	−79.3	−30.5	24.8	−530.7	541.2
2004	68.7	110.7	172.1	22.5	120.3	−146.9	−35.2	10.4	−640.2	553.9
2005	160.8	58.9	165.8	−122.7	131.8	−151.2	−55.0	73.8	−754.9	763.3
2006	249.9	6.0	170.5	−102.3	150.8	−179.8	−77.6	49.0	−811.5	830.8
2007	371.8	70.4	210.5	−187.2	263.1	−325.3	−74.7	66.2	−726.6	663.7
2008	426.1	18.9	156.6	−172.6	243.9	−300.8	−39.9	21.5	−706.1	509.9
2009	297.1	144.8	142.2	−130.2	168.0	−185.9	−28.7	38.1	−419.8	474.9
2010	237.8	229.2	203.9	−155.1	200.7	−194.8	−75.2	79.5	−470.9	472.5
2011	201.7	180.6	119.1	57.1	204.3	−201.2	−46.0	51.2	−473.4	489.5
2012	215.4	−36.0	60.1	−91.3	248.9	−184.1	−97.1	95.5	−446.5	444.9
2013	148.2	343.0	46.4	43.0	253.5	−290.2	−119.9	130.8	−366.4	387.9
2014	277.4	−51.4	36.0	−49.9	281.3	−327.2	−139.7	139.9	−392.1	283.8
2015	330.6	−485.6	135.6	−170.0	285.1	−252.4	−153.1	183.4	−463.0	456.7

[a]The balance on the capital account (BKA) in this table includes statistical discrepancies. Most discrepancies occur in the capital account.

Source: IMF, *International Financial Statistics Yearbook*, various issues.

ever experienced during the 34-year sample period. In 2006, the U.S. current account deficit reached $812 billion before it started to decline due to the recession. The U.S. balance-of-payments trend is illustrated in Exhibit 3.7. The exhibit shows that the U.S. current account deficit has increased sharply since 1997. This situation has led some politicians and commentators to lament that Americans are living far beyond their means. As a matter of fact, the net international investment position of the United States turned negative in 1987 for the first time in decades and continued to deteriorate. The overseas debt burden of the United States—the difference between the value of foreign-owned assets in the United States and the value of U.S.-owned assets abroad—reached about $2,540 billion at the end of 2006, when valued by the replacement cost of the investments made abroad and at home. As recently as 1986, the United States was considered a net creditor nation, with about $35 billion more in assets overseas than foreigners owned in the United States. The International Finance in Practice box "The Dollar and the Deficit" addresses the issues associated with the U.S. trade deficit. Since 2006, however, the current account deficit has declined for the United States, reflecting the effect of the "Great Recession."

The Dollar and the Deficit

The dollar is looking vulnerable. It is propped up not by the strength of America's exports, but by vast imports of capital. America, a country already rich in capital, has to borrow from abroad almost $2 billion net every working day to cover a current-account deficit forecast to reach almost $500 billion this year.

To most economists, this deficit represents an unsustainable drain on world savings. If the capital inflows were to dry up, some reckon that the dollar could lose a quarter of its value. Only Paul O'Neill, America's treasury secretary, appears unruffled. The current-account deficit, he declares, is a "meaningless concept," which he talks about only because others insist on doing so.

The dollar is not just a matter for America, because the dollar is not just America's currency. Over half of all dollar bills in circulation are held outside American's borders, and almost half of America's Treasury bonds are held as reserves by foreign central banks. The euro cannot yet rival this global reach. International financiers borrow and lend in dollars, and international traders use dollars, even if Americans are at neither end of the deal. No asset since gold has enjoyed such widespread acceptance as a medium of exchange and store of value. In fact, some economists, such as Paul Davidson of the University of Tennessee and Ronald McKinnon of Stanford University, take the argument a step further (see references at end). They argue that the world is on a de facto dollar standard, akin to the 19th-century gold standard.

For roughly a century up to 1914, the world's main currencies were pegged to gold. You could buy an ounce for about four pounds or twenty dollars. The contemporary "dollar standard" is a looser affair. In principle, the world's currencies float in value against each other, but in reality few float freely. Countries fear losing competitiveness on world markets if their currency rises too much against the greenback; they fear inflation if it falls too far. As long as American prices remain stable, the dollar therefore provides an anchor for world currencies and prices, ensuring that they do not become completely unmoored.

In the days of the gold standard, the volume of money and credit in circulation was tied to the amount of gold in a country's vaults. Economies laboured under the "tyranny" of the gold regime, booming when gold was abundant, deflating when it was scarce. The dollar standard is a more liberal system. Central banks retain the right to expand the volume of domestic credit to keep pace with the growth of the home economy.

Eventually, however, growth in the world's economies translates into a growing demand for dollar assets. The more money central banks print, the more dollars they like to hold in reserve to underpin their currency. The more business is done across borders, the more dollars traders need to cover their transactions. If the greenback is the new gold, Alan Greenspan, the Federal Reserve chairman, is the world's alchemist, responsible for concocting enough liquidity to keep world trade bubbling along nicely.

But America can play this role only if it is happy to allow foreigners to build up a huge mass of claims on its assets—and if foreigners are happy to go along. Some economists watch with consternation as the rest of the world's claims on America outstrip America's claims on the rest of the world. As they point out, even a dollar bill is an American liability, a promise of ultimate payment by the US Treasury. Can America keep making these promises to foreigners, without eventually emptying them of value?

According to Mr. Davidson, the world cannot risk America stopping. America's external deficit means an extra $500 billion is going into circulation in the world economy each year. If America reined in its current account, international commerce would suffer a liquidity crunch, as it did periodically under the gold standard. Hence America's deficit is neither a "meaningless concept" nor a lamentable drain on world savings. It is an indispensable fount of liquidity for world trade.

Spigot by Nature

But is the deficit sustainable? Many of America's creditors, Mr. McKinnon argues, have a stake in preserving the dollar standard, whatever the euro's potential charms. In particular, a large share of America's more liquid assets are held by foreign central banks, particularly in Asia, which dare not offload them for fear of undermining the competitiveness of their own currencies. "Willy nilly," Mr. McKinnon says, "foreign governments cannot avoid being important creditors of the United States." China, for one, added $60 billion to its reserves in the year to June by ploughing most of its trade surplus with America back into American assets.

This is not the first time America's external deficits have raised alarm. In 1966, as America's post-war trade surpluses began to dwindle, *The Economist* ran an article entitled "The dollar and world liquidity: a minority view." According to this view, the build-up of dollar claims by foreigners was not a "deficit" in need of "correction." Rather, the American capital market was acting like a global financial intermediary, providing essential liquidity to foreign governments and enterprises. In their own ways, Mr. Davidson and Mr. McKinnon echo this minority view today. A "correction" of America's current deficit, they say, would create more problems than it would solve. Whether the world's holders of dollars will always agree remains to be seen.

"Financial Markets, Money and the Real World" by Paul Davidson. Edward Elgar 2002.

"The International Dollar Standard and Sustainability of the U.S. Current Account Deficit" by Ronald McKinnon 2001.

Source: © The Economist Newspaper Limited, London, September 14, 2002.

EXHIBIT 3.7    Balance-of-Payments Trends: 1982–2015

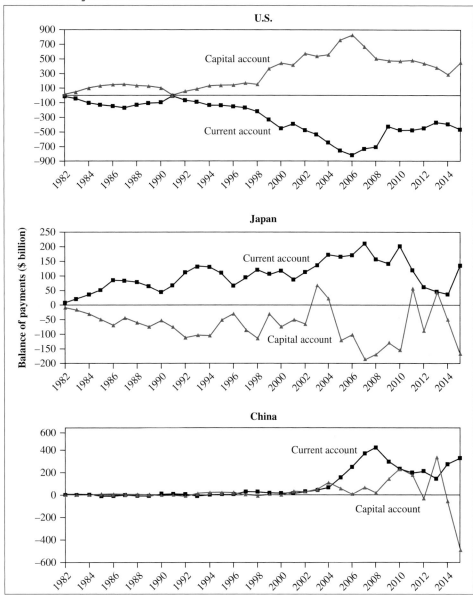

Source: IMF, *International Financial Statistics.*

Second, Exhibit 3.6 reveals that Japan has had an unbroken string of current account surpluses since 1982 despite the fact that the value of the yen rose steadily until the mid-1990s. The same point can be seen clearly from Exhibit 3.7. As can be expected, during this period Japan realized capital account deficits in most years; Japan invested heavily in foreign stocks and bonds, businesses, real estates, art objects, and the like to recycle its huge, persistent current account surpluses. Consequently, Japan emerged as the world's largest creditor nation, whereas the United States became the largest debtor nation. Japan had a capital account surplus in 2003, 2004, 2011 and 2013, reflecting increased foreign investments in Japanese securities and businesses. The persistent current account disequilibrium was a major source of friction between Japan and its key trading partners, especially the United States. In fact, Japan has often been criticized for pursuing **mercantilism** to ensure continuous trade surpluses.[7] In more recent years, however, China replaced Japan as the trading partner, realizing the largest trade surplus with the United States. As a result, China has been under pressure to let its currency appreciate against the dollar.

Third, like the United States, the United Kingdom recently experienced continuous current account deficits, coupled with capital account surpluses. The magnitude, however, is far less than that of the United States. Germany, on the other hand, traditionally had current account surpluses. Since 1991, however, Germany has been experiencing current account deficits. This is largely due to German reunification and the resultant need to absorb more output domestically to rebuild the East German region. This has left less output available for exports. Since 2001, however, Germany began to realize current account surpluses and capital account deficits, returning to the earlier pattern.

Fourth, like Japan, China tends to have a balance-of-payment surplus on the current account. Unlike Japan, however, China tends to realize a surplus on the capital account as well until recently. In 2011, for instance, China had a $201.7 billion surplus on the current account and, at the same time, a $180.6 billion surplus on the capital account. This implies that China's official reserve holdings must have gone up for the year. In fact, China's official reserves have increased sharply, reaching $3.30 trillion as of the end of 2012. In more recent years, however, China's capital account balance turned negative. In 2015, for example, the capital account balance was −$485.6 billion, reflecting China's rapidly rising foreign investments.

It is clear from Exhibit 3.6 that the United States and United Kingdom tend to realize current account deficits, whereas China, Japan, and Germany tend to realize current account surpluses. This "global imbalance" implies that the United States and United Kingdom generally use up more outputs than they produce, whereas the opposite holds for China, Japan, and Germany. Thus, if the global imbalance is to be reduced, it would be desirable for deficit countries to consume less and save more and for surplus countries to consume more and save less.[8]

While perennial balance-of-payments deficits or surpluses can be a problem, each country need not achieve balance-of-payments equilibrium every year. Suppose a country is currently experiencing a trade deficit because of the import demand for capital goods that are necessary for economic development projects. In this case, the trade deficit can be self-correcting in the long run because once the projects are completed, the country may be able to export more or import less by substituting domestic products for foreign imports. In contrast, if the trade deficit is the result of importing consumption goods, the situation may not correct itself. Thus, what matters is the nature and causes of the disequilibrium.

Lastly, let us briefly examine which countries the United States trades with most actively. Exhibit 3.8 provides the list of top 15 trading partners of the United States in terms of merchandise imports and exports. As shown in the exhibit, the United States trades most actively with China, the second largest economy in the world, importing $481.9 billion and exporting $116.2 billion in 2015. Obviously, there is a large trade imbalance between the two countries. Canada and Mexico, both of which are neighboring countries and also members of the North American Free Trade Agreements (NAFTA), are the next most important trading partners for the United States. The trade volume between the United States and each of the two neighboring countries exceeded $500 billion in 2015. These statistics imply that the trading volumes between

www.ecb.int/stats

This website provides balance-of-payment data on the euro-zone countries.

---

[7]Mercantilism, which originated in Europe during the period of absolute monarchies, holds that precious metals like gold and silver are the key components of national wealth, and that a continuing trade surplus should be a major policy goal as it ensures a continuing inflow of precious metals and thus continuous increases in national wealth. Mercantilists, therefore, abhor trade deficits and argue for imposing various restrictions on imports. Mercantilist ideas were criticized by such British thinkers as David Hume and Adam Smith. Both argued that the main source of wealth of a country is its productive capacity, not precious metals.

[8]The current account balance (BCA) is equal to national output (Y) minus domestic absorption (which comprises consumption, investment, and government expenditure), i.e., $BCA = Y - (C + I + G)$.

EXHIBIT 3.8

Top U.S. Trading Partners, 2015 (in billions of dollars)

Rank	Country	Imports	Exports	Trade Balance	Total Trade
1	China	481.9	116.2	−365.7	598.1
2	Canada	295.2	280.3	−14.9	575.5
3	Mexico	294.7	236.4	−58.4	531.1
4	Japan	131.1	62.5	−68.6	193.6
5	Germany	124.1	49.9	−74.2	174.1
6	Korea, Republic	71.8	43.5	−28.3	115.3
7	United Kingdom	57.8	56.4	−1.5	114.2
8	France	47.6	30.1	−17.6	77.7
9	Taiwan	40.7	25.9	−14.8	66.6
10	India	44.7	21.5	−23.2	66.3
11	Italy	44.0	16.2	−27.8	60.3
12	Brazil	27.4	31.7	4.3	59.1
13	Netherlands	16.8	40.7	24.0	57.5
14	Belgium	19.5	34.1	14.6	53.6
15	Switzerland	31.2	22.3	−8.9	53.5

Source: Census Bureau.

countries may largely depend on the size of the economies and the geographical distances between them, consistent with the gravity model of trade.[9] After the top three countries mentioned above come Japan, Germany, Korea, and the United Kingdom as the next major trading partners for the United States. Each of these four countries had two-way trading volume with the United States exceeding $100 billion in 2015. The exhibit also shows that the United States had sizable trade deficits with each of the top trading partners in 2015.

SUMMARY

1. The balance of payments can be defined as the statistical record of a country's international transactions over a certain period of time presented in the form of double-entry bookkeeping.

2. In the balance of payments, any transaction resulting in a receipt from foreigners is recorded as a credit, with a positive sign, whereas any transaction resulting in a payment to foreigners is recorded as a debit, with a minus sign.

3. A country's international transactions can be grouped into three main categories: the current account, the capital account, and the official reserve account. The current account includes exports and imports of goods and services, whereas the capital account includes all purchases and sales of assets such as stocks, bonds, bank accounts, real estate, and businesses. The official reserve account covers all purchases and sales of international reserve assets, such as dollars, foreign exchanges, gold, and SDRs.

4. The current account is divided into four subcategories: merchandise trade, services, factor income, and unilateral transfers. Merchandise trade represents exports and imports of tangible goods, whereas trade in services includes payments and receipts for legal, engineering, consulting, and other performed services and tourist expenditures. Factor income consists of payments and receipts of interest, dividends, and other income on previously made foreign investments. Lastly, unilateral transfer involves unrequited payments such as gifts, foreign aid, and reparations.

[9]The gravity model of international trade holds that trade flows depend on the economic sizes (masses) and distance between countries.

www.mhhe.com/er8e

5. The capital account is divided into three subcategories: direct investment, portfolio investment, and other investment. Direct investment involves acquisitions of controlling interests in foreign businesses. Portfolio investment represents investments in foreign stocks and bonds that do not involve acquisitions of control. Other investment includes bank deposits, currency investment, trade credit, and the like.

6. When we compute the cumulative balance of payments including the current account, capital account, and the statistical discrepancies, we obtain the overall balance or official settlement balance. The overall balance is indicative of a country's balance-of-payments gap that must be accommodated by official reserve transactions. If a country must make a net payment to foreigners because of a balance-of-payments deficit, the country should either run down its official reserve assets, such as gold, foreign exchanges, and SDRs, or borrow anew from foreigners.

7. A country can run a balance-of-payments surplus or deficit by increasing or decreasing its official reserves. Under the fixed exchange rate regime, the combined balance on the current and capital accounts will be equal in size, but opposite in sign, to the change in the official reserves. Under the pure flexible exchange rate regime where the central bank does not maintain any official reserves, a current account surplus or deficit must be matched by a capital account deficit or surplus.

KEY WORDS

balance of payments, 62	invisible trade, 65	official settlement
balance-of-payments	J-curve effect, 66	balance, 68
identity (BOPI), 72	mercantilism, 75	other investment, 68
capital account, 64	merchandise trade, 65	overall balance, 68
current account, 64	official reserve	portfolio investment, 67
factor income, 65	account, 64	services, 65
foreign direct investment	official reserve	trade balance, 65
(FDI), 67	assets, 69	unilateral transfers, 65

QUESTIONS

1. Define *balance of payments*.

2. Why would it be useful to examine a country's balance-of-payments data?

3. The United States has experienced continuous current account deficits since the early 1980s. What do you think are the main causes for the deficits? What would be the consequences of continuous U.S. current account deficits?

4. In contrast to the United States, Japan has realized continuous current account surpluses. What could be the main causes for these surpluses? Is it desirable to have continuous current account surpluses?

5. Comment on the following statement: "Since the United States imports more than it exports, it is necessary for the United States to import capital from foreign countries to finance its current account deficits."

6. Explain how a country can run an overall balance-of-payments deficit or surplus.

7. Explain *official reserve assets* and its major components.

8. Explain how to compute the overall balance and discuss its significance.

9. Since the early 1980s, foreign portfolio investors have purchased a significant portion of U.S. Treasury bond issues. Discuss the short-term and long-term effects of foreigners' portfolio investment on the U.S. balance of payments.

10. Describe the *balance-of-payments identity* and discuss its implications under the fixed and flexible exchange rate regimes.

11. Exhibit 3.6 indicates that in 1999, Germany had a current account deficit and at the same time a capital account deficit. Explain how this can happen.

12. Explain how each of the following transactions will be classified and recorded in the debit and credit of the U.S. balance of payments:

   a. A Japanese insurance company purchases U.S. Treasury bonds and pays out of its bank account kept in New York City.

   b. A U.S. citizen consumes a meal at a restaurant in Paris and pays with her American Express card.

   c. An Indian immigrant living in Los Angeles sends a check drawn on his LA bank account as a gift to his parents living in Mumbai.

   d. A U.S. computer programmer is hired by a British company for consulting and gets paid from the U.S. bank account maintained by the British company.

13. Construct a balance-of-payments table for Germany for the year 2010 which is comparable in format to Exhibit 3.1, and interpret the numerical data. You may consult *International Financial Statistics* published by IMF or search for useful websites for the data yourself.

14. Discuss the possible strengths and weaknesses of SDRs versus the dollar as the main reserve currency. Do you think the SDR should or could replace the U.S. dollar as the main global reserve currency?

PROBLEMS

1. Examine the following summary of the U.S. balance of payments for 2000 (in $ billion) and fill in the blank entries.

	Credits	Debits
Current Account		
(1) Exports	1,418.64	
(1.1) Merchandise	774.86	
(1.2) Services	290.88	
(1.3) Factor income	352.90	
(2) Imports		−1,809.18
(2.1) Merchandise		☐
(2.2) Services		−217.07
(2.3) Factor income		−367.68
(3) Unilateral transfer	10.24	−64.39
Balance on current account		☐
Capital Account		
(4) Direct investment	287.68	−152.44
(5) Portfolio investment	474.59	−124.94
(5.1) Equity securities	193.85	−99.74
(5.2) Debt securities	280.74	−25.20
(6) Other investment	262.64	−303.27
Balance on capital account	☐	
(7) Statistical discrepancies	☐	
Overall balance	0.30	
Official Reserve Account		−0.30

Source: IMF, *International Financial Statistics Yearbook, 2001.*

1. Study the website of the International Monetary Fund (IMF), www.imf.org, and discuss the role of the IMF in dealing with balance-of-payment and currency crises.

www.mhhe.com/er8e

MINI CASE

Mexico's Balance-of-Payments Problem

Mexico experienced large-scale trade deficits, depletion of foreign reserve holdings, and a major currency devaluation in December 1994, followed by the decision to freely float the peso. These events also brought about a severe recession and higher unemployment in Mexico. Since the devaluation, however, the trade balance has improved.

Investigate the Mexican experiences in detail and write a report on the subject. In the report, you may:

1. Document the trend in Mexico's key economic indicators, such as the balance of payments, the exchange rate, and foreign reserve holdings, during the period 1994.1 through 1995.12.

2. Investigate the causes of Mexico's balance-of-payments difficulties prior to the peso devaluation.

3. Discuss what policy actions might have prevented or mitigated the balance-of-payments problem and the subsequent collapse of the peso.

4. Derive lessons from the Mexican experience that may be useful for other developing countries.

In your report, you may identify and address any other relevant issues concerning Mexico's balance-of-payments problem. *International Financial Statistics* published by the IMF provides basic macroeconomic data on Mexico.

REFERENCES & SUGGESTED READINGS

Edwards, Sebastian. *Real Exchange Rates, Devaluation and Adjustment: Exchange Rate Policy in Developing Countries.* Cambridge, Mass.: MIT Press, 1989.

Grabbe, Orlin. *International Financial Markets.* New York: Elsevier, 1991.

Kemp, Donald. "Balance of Payments Concepts—What Do They Really Mean?" *Federal Reserve Bank of St. Louis Review,* July 1975, pp. 14–23.

Ohmae, Kenichi. "Lies, Damned Lies and Statistics: Why the Trade Deficit Doesn't Matter in a Borderless World." *Journal of Applied Corporate World,* Winter 1991, pp. 98–106.

Salop, Joan, and Erich Spitaller. "Why Does the Current Account Matter?" International Monetary Fund, *Staff Papers,* March 1980, pp. 101–34.

U.S. Department of Commerce. "Report of the Advisory Committee on the Presentation of the Balance of Payments Statistics." *Survey of Current Business,* June 1991, pp. 18–25.

Yeager, Leland. *International Monetary Relations.* New York: Harper & Row, 1965.

3A The Relationship Between Balance of Payments and National Income Accounting

This section is designed to explore the mathematical relationship between balance-of-payments accounting and national income accounting and to discuss the implications of this relationship. National income (Y), or gross domestic product (GDP), is identically equal to the sum of nominal consumption (C) of goods and services, private investment expenditures (I), government expenditures (G), and the difference between exports (X) and imports (M) of goods and services:

$$GDP \equiv Y \equiv C + I + G + X - M. \tag{3A.1}$$

Private savings (S) is defined as the amount left from national income after consumption and taxes (T) are paid:

$$S \equiv Y - C - T, \text{ or} \tag{3A.2}$$

$$S \equiv C + I + G + X - M - C - T. \tag{3A.3}$$

Noting that the BCA $\equiv$ X $-$ M, equation (3A.3) can be rearranged as

$$(S - I) + (T - G) \equiv X - M \equiv BCA. \tag{3A.4}$$

Equation (3A.4) shows that there is an intimate relationship between a country's BCA and how the country finances its domestic investment and pays for government expenditures. In equation (3A.4), (S − I) is the difference between a country's savings and investment. If (S − I) is negative, it implies that a country's domestic savings is insufficient to finance domestic investment. Similarly, (T − G) is the difference between tax revenue and government expenditures. If (T − G) is negative, it implies that tax revenue is insufficient to cover government spending and a government budget deficit exists. This deficit must be financed by the government issuing debt securities.

Equation (3A.4) also shows that when a country imports more than it exports, its BCA will be negative because through trade foreigners obtain a larger claim to domestic assets than the claim the country's citizens obtain to foreign assets. Consequently, when BCA is negative, it implies that government budget deficits and/or part of domestic investment are being financed with foreign-controlled capital. In order for a country to reduce a BCA deficit, one of the following must occur:

1. For a given level of S and I, the government budget deficit (T − G) must be reduced.
2. For a given level of I and (T − G), S must be increased.
3. For a given level S and (T − G), I must fall.

Corporate Governance Around the World

IN CHAPTER 1, we argue that the key goal of financial management should be shareholder wealth maximization. In reality, however, there is no guarantee that managers would run the company to maximize the welfare of shareholders. In fact, the recent spate of corporate scandals and failures, including Enron, WorldCom, and Global Crossing in the United States, Daewoo Group (a major *chaebol*) in Korea, Parmalat in Italy, and HIH (a major insurance group) in Australia, has raised serious questions about the way public corporations are governed around the world. When "self-interested" managers take control of the company, they sometimes engage in actions that are profoundly detrimental to the interests of shareholders and other stakeholders. For example, such managers may give themselves excessive salaries and indulgent perquisites, squander resources for corporate empire building, divert the company's cash and assets for private benefits, engage in cronyism, and steal business opportunities from the company. An article in the *Harvard Business Review* (January 2003) describes how American executives "treat their companies like ATMs, awarding themselves millions of dollars in corporate perks." In many less developed and transitional countries, corporate governance mechanisms are either very weak or virtually nonexistent. In Russia, for example, a weak corporate governance system allows managers to divert assets from newly privatized companies on a large scale.

When managerial self-dealings are excessive and left unchecked, they can have serious negative effects on corporate values and the proper functions of capital markets. In fact, there is a growing consensus around the world that it is vitally important to strengthen **corporate governance** to protect **shareholder rights**, curb managerial excesses, and restore confidence in capital markets. *Corporate governance* can be defined as *the economic, legal, and institutional framework in which corporate control and cash flow rights are distributed among shareholders, managers, and other stakeholders of the company.* Other stakeholders may include workers, creditors, banks, customers, and even the government. As we will see later, corporate governance structure varies a great deal across countries, reflecting divergent cultural, economic, political, and legal environments. It is thus essential for international investors and multinational corporations to have a solid understanding of the corporate governance environments around the world. An example of governance risk is provided by Citigroup's dealings with Parmalat. According to BBC News (March 18, 2005), William Mills of Citigroup said, "Citigroup is a victim of Parmalat's fraud and lost more than 500 million euros as a result…. If Citigroup had known the truth, it would not have done business with Parmalat."

Governance of the Public Corporation: Key Issues

The **public corporation**, which is jointly owned by a multitude of shareholders protected by limited liability, is a major organizational innovation with powerful economic consequences. The majority of global corporations that drive economic growth and innovations worldwide, such as Apple, Google, General Electric (GE), IBM, Toyota, Samsung Electronics, British Petroleum (BP), and BMW, are chartered as public corporations rather than as private companies. The first public company was organized in 1602 when the Dutch East India Company was chartered with monopoly power over Dutch spice trade in South Asia. The company issued shares for the first time in history to finance expensive and highly risky ventures that involved trading with remote, unknown foreign regions while competing with powerful rivals like England, France, Portugal, and China in Asia. The genius of public corporations stems from their capacity to allow efficient sharing or spreading of risk among many investors, who can buy and sell their ownership shares on liquid stock exchanges and let professional managers run the company on behalf of shareholders. This efficient risk-sharing mechanism enables public corporations to raise large amounts of capital at relatively low costs and undertake many investment projects that individual entrepreneurs or private investors might eschew because of the costs and/or risks. Public corporations have played a pivotal role in spreading economic growth and capitalism worldwide for the last few centuries.[1]

However, the public corporation has a key weakness—namely, the conflicts of interest between managers and shareholders. The separation of the company's ownership and control, which is especially prevalent in such countries as the United States and the United Kingdom, where corporate ownership is highly diffused, gives rise to possible conflicts between shareholders and managers. In principle, shareholders elect the board of directors of the company, which in turn hires managers to run the company for the interests of shareholders. In the United States, managers are legally bound by the "duty of loyalty" to shareholders. Managers are thus supposed to be agents working for their principals, that is, shareholders, who are the real owners of the company. In a public company with diffused ownership, the board of directors is entrusted with the vital tasks of monitoring the management and safeguarding the interests of shareholders.

In reality, however, management-friendly insiders often dominate the board of directors, with relatively few outside directors who can independently monitor the management. In the case of Enron and similarly dysfunctional companies, the boards of directors grossly failed to safeguard shareholder interests. Furthermore, with diffused ownership, few shareholders have strong enough incentive to incur the costs of monitoring management themselves when the benefits from such monitoring accrue to all shareholders alike. The benefits are shared, but not the costs. When company ownership is highly diffused, this "free-rider" problem discourages shareholder activism. As a result, the interests of managers and shareholders are often allowed to diverge. With an ineffective and unmotivated board of directors, shareholders are basically left without effective recourse to control managerial self-dealings. Recognition of this key weakness of the public corporation can be traced at least as far back as Adam Smith's *Wealth of Nations* (1776), which stated:

> The directors of such joint-stocks companies, however, being the managers rather of other people's money than of their own, it cannot well be expected that they should watch over it with the same anxious vigilance with which the partners of a private copartnery frequently watch over their own. . . . Negligence and profusion, therefore, must always prevail, more or less, in the management of the affairs of such a company.

---

[1]The Dutch East India Company is often regarded as the first multinational company (MNC) in the modern sense of the word. The company established a thriving Asian headquarters in Batavia, which is today's Jakarta, and built a trading empire stretching from South Africa to Japan. Within a century since its founding, the company became the wealthiest company in the world, employing about 50,000 employees worldwide, and had more than 150 merchant ships at its disposal.

Two hundred years later, Jensen and Meckling (1976) provided a formal analysis of the "agency problem" of the public corporation in their celebrated paper "Theory of the Firm: Managerial Behavior, Agency Costs, and Ownership Structure." The Jensen-Meckling agency theory drew attention to this vitally important corporate finance problem.

It is suggested, however, that outside the United States and the United Kingdom, diffused ownership of the company is more the exception than the rule. In Italy, for instance, the three largest shareholders control, on average, about 60 percent of the shares of a public company. The average comparable ownership by the three largest shareholders is 54 percent in Hong Kong, 64 percent in Mexico, 48 percent in Germany, 40 percent in India, and 51 percent in Israel.[2] These large shareholders (often including founding families of the company) effectively control managers and may run the company for their own interests, expropriating outside shareholders in one way or another. In many countries with concentrated corporate ownership, conflicts of interest are greater between large controlling shareholders and small outside shareholders than between managers and shareholders.

In a series of influential studies, La Porta, Lopez-de-Silanes, Shleifer, and Vishny (LLSV, hereafter) document sharp differences among countries with regard to (i) corporate ownership structure, (ii) depth and breadth of capital markets, (iii) access of firms to external financing, and (iv) dividend policies. LLSV argue that these differences among countries can be explained largely by how well investors are protected by law from expropriation by the managers and controlling shareholders of firms. LLSV also argue that the degree of legal protection of investors significantly depends on the "legal origin" of countries. Specifically, English common law countries, such as Canada, the United States, and the United Kingdom, provide the strongest protection for investors, whereas French civil law countries, such as Belgium, Italy, and Mexico, provide the weakest. We will revisit the issue of law and corporate governance later in the chapter.

Shareholders in different countries may indeed face divergent corporate governance systems. However, the central problem in corporate governance remains the same everywhere: *how to best protect outside investors from expropriation by the controlling insiders so that the investors can receive fair returns on their investments.* How to deal with this problem has enormous practical implications for shareholder welfare, corporate allocation of resources, corporate financing and valuation, development of capital markets, and economic growth. In the rest of this chapter, we will discuss the following issues in detail:[3]

- Agency problem
- Remedies for the agency problem
- Law and corporate governance
- Consequences of law
- Corporate governance reform

The Agency Problem

Suppose that the manager (or entrepreneur) and the investors sign a contract that specifies how the manager will use the funds and also how the investment returns will be divided between the manager and the investors. If the two sides can write a **complete contract** that specifies exactly what the manager will do under each of all possible

www.ecgi.org

This site provides an overview of corporate governance in European countries.

---

[2]Source: R. La Porta, F. Lopez-de-Silanes, A. Shleifer, and R. Vishny, "Law and Finance," *Journal of Political Economy* 106 (1998), pp. 1113–55.

[3]Our discussion here draws on the contributions of Jensen and Meckling (1976), Jensen (1989), La Porta, Lopez-de-Silanes, Shleifer, and Vishny (1997–2002), and Denis and McConnell (2002).

future contingencies, there will be no room for any conflicts of interest or managerial discretion. Thus, under a complete contract, there will be no **agency problem**. However, it is practically impossible to foresee all future contingencies and write a complete contract. This means that the manager and the investors will have to allocate the rights (control) to make decisions under those contingencies that are not specifically covered by the contract. Because the outside investors may be neither qualified nor interested in making business decisions, the manager often ends up acquiring most of this **residual control right**. The investors supply funds to the company but are not involved in the company's daily decision making. As a result, many public companies come to have "strong managers and weak shareholders." The agency problem refers to the possible conflicts of interest between self-interested managers as agents and shareholders of the firm who are the principals.

Having captured residual control rights, the manager can exercise substantial discretion over the disposition and allocation of investors' capital. Under this situation, the investors are no longer assured of receiving fair returns on their funds. In the contractual view of the firm described above, the agency problem arises from the difficulty that outside investors face in assuring that they actually receive fair returns on their capital.[4]

With the control rights, the manager may allow himself or herself to consume exorbitant perquisites. For example, Steve Jobs, the former CEO of Apple Inc., reportedly had a $90 million company jet at his disposal.[5] Sometimes, the manager simply steals investors' funds. Alternatively, the manager may use a more sophisticated scheme, setting up an independent company that he owns and diverting to it the main company's cash and assets through *transfer pricing*. For example, the manager can sell the main company's output to the company he owns at below market prices, or buy the output of the company he owns at above market prices. Some Russian oil companies are known to sell oil to manager-owned trading companies at below market prices and not always bother to collect the bills.[6]

Self-interested managers may also waste funds by undertaking unprofitable projects that benefit themselves but not investors. For example, managers may misallocate funds to take over other companies and overpay for the targets if it serves their private interests. Needless to say, this type of investment will destroy shareholder value. What is more, the same managers may adopt antitakeover measures for their own company in order to ensure their personal job security and perpetuate private benefits. In the same vein, managers may resist any attempts to be replaced even if shareholders' interests will be better served by their dismissal. These **managerial entrenchment** efforts are clear signs of the agency problem.

As pointed out by Jensen (1989), the agency problem tends to be more serious in companies with "free cash flows." **Free cash flows** represent a firm's internally generated funds in excess of the amount needed to undertake all profitable investment projects, that is, those with positive net present values (NPVs). Free cash flows tend to be high in mature industries with low future growth prospects, such as the steel, chemical, tobacco, paper, and textile industries. It is the *fiduciary duty* of managers to return free cash flows to shareholders as dividends. However, managers in these cash-rich and mature industries will be most tempted to waste cash flows to undertake unprofitable projects, destroying shareholders' wealth but possibly benefiting themselves.

There are a few important incentives for managers to retain cash flows. First, cash reserves provide corporate managers with a measure of independence from the capital markets, insulating them from external scrutiny and discipline. This will make life easier for managers. Second, growing the size of the company via retention of cash tends to have the effect of raising managerial compensation. As is well known, executive

---

[4]The contractual view of the firm was developed by Coase (1937) and Jensen and Meckling (1976).
[5]Source: *Financial Times*, November 27, 2002, p. 15.
[6]Source: A. Shleifer and R. Vishny, "A Survey of Corporate Governance," *Journal of Finance* (1997).

compensation depends as much on the size of the company as on its profitability, if not more. Third, senior executives can boost their social and political power and prestige by increasing the size of their company. Executives presiding over large companies are likely to enjoy greater social prominence and visibility than those running small companies. Also, the company's size itself can be a way of satisfying the executive ego.

In the face of strong managerial incentives for retaining cash, few effective mechanisms exist that can compel the managers to disgorge cash flows to shareholders. Jensen cites a revealing example of this widespread problem (1989, p. 66):

> A vivid example is the senior management of Ford Motor Company, which sits on nearly $15 billion in cash and marketable securities in an industry with excess capacity. Ford's management has been deliberating about acquiring financial service companies, aerospace companies, or making some other multibillion-dollar diversification move—rather than deliberating about effectively distributing Ford's excess cash to its owners so they can decide how to reinvest it.

He also points out that in the 1980s, many Japanese public companies retained enormous amounts of free cash flow, far exceeding what they needed to finance profitable internal projects. For example, Toyota Motor Company, with a cash hoard of more than $10 billion, was known as the "Toyota Bank." Lacking effective internal control and external monitoring mechanisms, these companies went on an overinvestment binge in the 1980s, engaging in unprofitable acquisitions and diversification moves. This wasteful corporate spending is, at least in part, responsible for the economic slump that Japan has experienced since the early 1990s.

The preceding examples show that the heart of the agency problem is the conflicts of interest between managers and the outside investors over the disposition of free cash flows. However, in high-growth industries, such as biotechnology, financial services, and pharmaceuticals, where companies' internally generated funds fall short of profitable investment opportunities, managers are less likely to waste funds in unprofitable projects. After all, managers in these industries need to have a "good reputation," as they must repeatedly come back to capital markets for funding. Once the managers of a company are known for wasting funds for private benefits, external funding for the company may dry up quickly. The managers in these industries thus have an incentive to serve the interests of outside investors and build a reputation so that they can raise the funds needed for undertaking their "good" investment projects.

Remedies for the Agency Problem

Obviously, it is a matter of vital importance for shareholders to control the agency problem; otherwise, they may not be able to get their money back. It is also important for society as a whole to solve the agency problem, since the agency problem leads to waste of scarce resources, hampers capital market functions, and retards economic growth. Several governance mechanisms exist to alleviate or remedy the agency problem:

1. Independent board of directors
2. Incentive contracts
3. Concentrated ownership
4. Accounting transparency
5. Debt
6. Overseas stock listings
7. Market for corporate control

In the following sections, we discuss the corporate governance role of each of these mechanisms.

Board of Directors

In the United States, shareholders have the right to elect the board of directors, which is legally charged with representing the interests of shareholders. If the board of directors remains independent of management, it can serve as an effective mechanism for curbing the agency problem. For example, studies show that the appointment of outside directors is associated with a higher turnover rate of CEOs following poor firm performances, thus curbing managerial entrenchment. In the same vein, in a study of corporate governance in the United Kingdom, Dahya, McConnell, and Travlos (2002) report that the board of directors is more likely to appoint an outside CEO after an increase in outsiders' representation on the board. But due to the diffused ownership structure of the public company, management often gets to choose board members who are likely to be friendly to management. As can be seen from the International Finance in Practice box "When Boards Are All in the Family," the insider-dominated board becomes a poor governance mechanism.

The structure and legal charge of corporate boards vary greatly across countries. In Germany, for instance, the corporate board is not legally charged with representing the interests of shareholders. Rather, it is charged with looking after the interests of stakeholders (e.g., workers, creditors) in general, not just shareholders. In Germany, there are two-tier boards consisting of supervisory and management boards. Based on the German *codetermination* system, the law requires that workers be represented on the supervisory board. Likewise, some U.S. companies have labor union representatives on their boards, although it is not legally mandated. In the United Kingdom, the majority of public companies voluntarily abide by the *Code of Best Practice* on corporate governance recommended by the *Cadbury Committee*. The code recommends that there should be at least three outside directors and that the board chairman and the CEO should be different individuals. Apart from outside directors, separation of the chairman and CEO positions can further enhance the independence of the board of directors. In Japan, most corporate boards are insider-dominated and are primarily concerned with the welfare of the *keiretsu* to which the company belongs.

Incentive Contracts

As previously discussed, managers capture residual control rights and thus have enormous discretion over how to run the company. But they own relatively little of the equity of the company they manage. To the extent that managers do not own equity shares, they do not have cash flow rights. Although managers run the company at their own discretion, they may not significantly benefit from the profit generated from their efforts and expertise. Jensen and Murphy (1990) show that the pay of American executives changes only by about $3 per every $1,000 change of shareholder wealth; executive pay is nearly insensitive to changes in shareholder wealth. This situation implies that managers may not be very interested in the maximization of shareholder wealth. This "wedge" between managerial control rights and cash flow rights may exacerbate the agency problem. *When professional managers have small equity positions of their own in a company with diffused ownership, they have both power and a motive to engage in self-dealings.*

Aware of this situation, many companies provide managers with **incentive contracts**, such as stocks and stock options, in order to reduce this wedge and better align the interests of managers with those of investors. With the grant of stocks or stock options, managers can be given an incentive to run the company in such a way that enhances shareholder wealth as well as their own. Against this backdrop, incentive contracts for senior executives have become common among public companies in the United States. As we have seen lately, however, senior executives can abuse incentive contracts by artificially manipulating accounting numbers, sometimes with the connivance of auditors (e.g., Arthur Andersen's involvements with the Enron debacle), or by altering investment policies so that they can reap enormous personal benefits. It is thus important for the board of directors to set up an independent compensation committee that can carefully design incentive contracts for executives and diligently monitor their actions.

When Boards Are All in the Family

There is much talk these days about the need to increase the independence of directors on company boards. That has been obvious for a long time. Indeed, it is fairly easy to spot those boards for which chief executives have handpicked friends or business associates who are not truly independent.

This characteristic is a reliable indicator of whether a chief executive acts as a baronial owner of the company, or as one chosen by—and responsible to—the stakeholders. In fact, one can argue that making boards more independent is the single most important thing we can do in the current reform climate to restore public confidence.

By now it is well documented that boards dominated by their chief executives are prone to trouble. W.R. Grace is a good example. Peter Grace, the company's chief executive, was too powerful. He controlled his board as if the enterprise were his personal fief.

Even though the business was foundering in the late 1990s, the board allowed Mr. Grace to negotiate a retirement package that included generous perks—including use of a corporate jet and a company-owned apartment. The directors also sold a subsidiary to Mr. Grace's son and bestowed other benefits that they neglected to disclose to shareholders. This non-disclosure was against the law and resulted in an SEC-type enforcement action.

Another example is Apple, whose board I was once asked, briefly, to consider joining. Apart from Steve Jobs, the CEO, the board currently has only four members while Mr. Jobs searches for a replacement for his friend Larry Ellison of Oracle, who resigned from Apple's board in September.

That is all to the good, as Mr. Ellison attended fewer than half of Apple's board meetings anyway. Bill Campbell, another director, is nominally independent but may not be truly so. Mr. Campbell, who chairs the company's audit committee, qualifies as an independent director, because he is not currently connected with Apple. But he formerly worked at Apple and sold his software company, Claris, to Apple.

Another member of Apple's audit committee, Jerome York, is the chief executive of MicroWarehouse, whose Mac Warehouse catalogue was responsible for nearly $150m of Apple's $5.4bn sales in 2001. As a former chief financial officer for International Business Machines and Chrysler Mr. York is well qualified but his presence on the all-important audit committee had to be treated as an exceptional circumstance by the NASDAQ market.

Such choices, to my mind, can yield bad judgment. In January 2000, for example, Apple's board awarded Mr. Jobs 20m shares, worth $550m if the share price increased 5 percent over 10 years. They also authorised the company to buy a $90m Gulfstream jet for him. The share price sank, putting Mr. Jobs's options under water. So the board granted him 7.5m more shares. At the time of the grant, Apple shares were underperforming other stocks in their industry sub-class by 28 percent.

There is plenty of evidence that public scrutiny and a spotlight can help improve corporate governance. The California Public Employees' Retirement System began pressing underperforming companies to change the composition of their boards in 1993. Calpers drew up a list of corporate governance standards: make independent directors a majority on boards; let these directors meet the chief executive separately three times a year; make boards perform an annual assessment of their own performance, and so on.

A study by Wilshire Associates looked at the performance of 62 companies named by Calpers as poor performers. These companies' stocks underperformed the Standard & Poor's 500 index by an average of 89 percent in the five years before they were singled out. After the spotlight was shone on them, they outperformed the index by an average of 23 percent over five years.

This does not, of course, mean all companies will fail without a model board of directors. At Warren Buffett's Berkshire Hathaway, the seven directors include Mr. Buffet's wife, his son, his business partner Charlie Munger, a partner at his company's law firm and a co-investor with Berkshire Hathaway in other companies.

Mr. Buffett makes a persuasive argument that the best directors may well be those who have the greatest personal economic stake in the company. But the correlation of seduced boards with underperforming or ethically flawed enterprises suggests that independent overseers are much less likely to give in to temptation or corruption.

Concentrated Ownership

An effective way to alleviate the agency problem is to concentrate shareholdings. If one or a few large investors own significant portions of the company, they will have a strong incentive to monitor management. For example, if an investor owns 51 percent of the company, he or she can definitely control the management (he can easily hire or fire managers) and will make sure that shareholders' rights are respected in the conduct of the company's affairs. With **concentrated ownership** and high stakes, the free-rider problem afflicting small, atomistic shareholders dissipates.

In the United States and the United Kingdom, concentrated ownership of a public company is relatively rare. Elsewhere in the world, however, concentrated ownership is the norm. In Germany, for example, commercial banks, insurance companies, other companies, and families often own significant blocks of company stock. Similarly, extensive cross-holdings of equities among *keiretsu* member companies and main banks are commonplace in Japan. Also in France, cross-holdings and "core" investors are common. In Asia and Latin America, many companies are controlled by founders or their family members. In China, the government is often the controlling shareholder for public companies. Previous studies indicate that concentrated ownership has a positive effect on a company's performance and value. For example, Kang and Shivdasani (1995) report such positive effects for Japan, and Gorton and Schmid (2000) for Germany. This suggests that large shareholders indeed play a significant governance role.

Of particular interest here is the effect of managerial equity holdings. Previous studies suggest that there can be a nonlinear relationship between managerial ownership share and firm value and performance. Specifically, as the managerial ownership share increases, firm value may initially increase, since the interests of managers and outside investors become better aligned (thus reducing agency costs). But if the managerial ownership share exceeds a certain point, firm value may actually start to decline as managers become more entrenched. With larger shareholdings, for example, managers may be able to more effectively resist takeover bids and extract larger private benefits at the expense of outside investors. If the managerial ownership share continues to rise, however, the alignment effect may become dominant again. When managers are large shareholders, they do not want to rob themselves. To summarize, there can be an "interim range" of managerial ownership share over which the entrenchment effect is dominant.

This situation is illustrated in Exhibit 4.1, depicting a possible relationship between managerial ownership share and firm value. According to Morck, Shleifer, and Vishny (1988), who studied the relationship for *Fortune* 500 U.S. companies, the first turning point (*x*) is reached at about 5 percent and the second (*y*) at about 25 percent. This means that the "entrenchment effect" is roughly dominant over the range of managerial ownership between 5 percent and 25 percent, whereas the "alignment effect" is dominant for

EXHIBIT 4.1

The Alignment versus Entrenchment Effects of Managerial Ownership

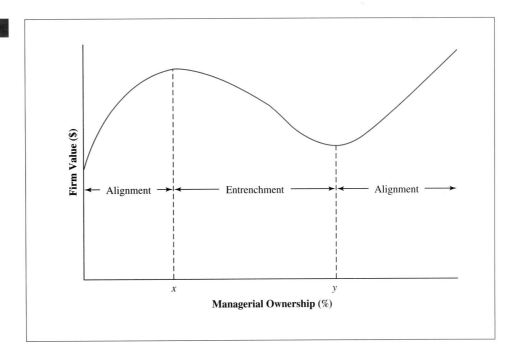

the ownership shares less than 5 percent and exceeding 25 percent.[7] The relationship between managerial ownership and firm value is likely to vary across countries. For instance, Short and Keasey (1999) indicate that the inflection point (x) is reached at 12 percent in the United Kingdom, a much higher level of managerial ownership than in the United States. They attribute this difference to more effective monitoring by U.K. institutional investors and the lesser ability of U.K. managers to resist takeover.

Accounting Transparency

Considering that major corporate scandals, such as Enron and Parmalat, are associated with massive accounting frauds, strengthening accounting standards can be an effective way of alleviating the agency problem. Self-interested managers or corporate insiders can have an incentive to "cook the books" (e.g., inflating earnings and hiding debts) to extract private benefits from the company. The managers need a veil of opaque accounting numbers to pursue their own interests at the expense of shareholders. Therefore, if companies are required to release more accurate accounting information in a timely fashion, managers may be less tempted to take actions that are detrimental to the interests of shareholders. Basically, a greater accounting transparency will reduce the information asymmetry between corporate insiders and the public and discourage managerial self-dealings.

To achieve a greater transparency, however, it is important for (i) countries to reform the accounting rules and (ii) companies to have an active and qualified audit committee. As we will discuss later in this chapter, the Sarbanes-Oxley Act of 2002 aims, among other things, to promote a greater accounting transparency in the United States.

Debt

Although managers have discretion over how much of a dividend to pay to shareholders, debt does not allow such managerial discretion. If managers fail to pay interest and principal to creditors, the company can be forced into bankruptcy and its managers may lose their jobs. Borrowing and the subsequent obligation to make interest payments on time can have a major disciplinary effect on managers, motivating them to curb private perks and wasteful investments and trim bloated organizations. In fact, debt can serve as a substitute for dividends by forcing managers to disgorge free cash flow to outside investors rather than wasting it. For firms with free cash flows, debt can be a stronger mechanism than stocks for credibly bonding managers to release cash flows to investors.[8]

Excessive debt, however, can create its own problem. In turbulent economic conditions, equities can buffer the company against adversity. Managers can pare down or skip dividend payments until the situation improves. With debt, however, managers do not have such flexibility and the company's survival can be threatened. Excessive debt may also induce the risk-averse managers to forgo profitable but risky investment projects, causing an underinvestment problem. For this reason, debt may not be such a desirable governance mechanism for young companies with few cash reserves or tangible assets. In addition, companies can misuse debt to finance corporate empire building. Daewoo, a Korean *chaebol*, borrowed excessively to finance global expansion until it went into bankruptcy; its debt-to-equity ratio reached 600 percent before bankruptcy.

Overseas Stock Listings

Companies domiciled in countries with weak investor protection, such as Italy, Korea, and Russia, can bond themselves credibly to better investor protection by listing their stocks in countries with strong investor protection, such as the United States and the

---

[7]It is noted that the authors actually used "Tobin's q" to measure firm value. Tobin's q is the ratio of the market value of company assets to the replacement costs of the assets.

[8]Leveraged buyouts (LBOs) can also be viewed as a remedy for the agency problem. LBOs involve managers or buyout partners acquiring controlling interests in public companies, usually financed by heavy borrowing. Concentrated ownership and high level of debt associated with LBOs can be effective in solving the agency problem.

United Kingdom. In other words, foreign firms with weak governance mechanisms can opt to outsource a superior corporate governance regime available in the United States via cross-listings. Suppose that Fiat, an Italian automobile company, announces its decision to list its stock on the New York Stock Exchange (NYSE).[9] Because the level of shareholder protection afforded by the U.S. Securities and Exchange Commission (SEC) and the NYSE is much higher than that provided in Italy, the action will be interpreted as signaling the company's commitment to shareholder rights. Then, investors both in Italy and abroad will be more willing to provide capital to the company and value the company shares more. Generally speaking, the beneficial effects from U.S. listings will be greater for firms from countries with weaker governance mechanisms.

Studies confirm the effects of cross-border listings. Specifically, Doidge, Karolyi, and Stulz (2002) report that foreign firms listed in the United States are valued more than those from the same countries that are not listed in the United States. They argue that firms listed in the United States can take better advantage of growth opportunities and that controlling shareholders cannot extract as many private benefits. It is pointed out, however, that foreign firms in mature industries with limited growth opportunities are not very likely to seek U.S. listings, even though these firms face more serious agency problems than firms with growth opportunities that are more likely to seek U.S. listings. In other words, firms with more serious problems are less likely to seek the remedies.

Emerging stock markets, such as China, India, Russia, and Vietnam, are highly imperfect, reflecting inadequate disclosure and regulation, opaque legal and governance framework, and ownership restrictions. In the case of China, for example, stock markets are dominated by a multitude of small individual investors who are neither well informed nor protected. So far, institutional investors, such as mutual funds, pension funds, and insurance companies, who can produce high-quality information about listed companies and effectively protect shareholders' rights, play a relatively minor role in China. However, public Chinese companies can offer the so-called "B-shares" to foreign investors that are listed on domestic stock exchanges alongside A-shares for local investors, or directly list their shares on the Hong Kong Stock Exchange as "H-shares" or on other foreign stock exchanges, including the New York Stock Exchange. Eun and Huang (2007) found that domestic Chinese investors pay higher prices for local A-shares of those Chinese companies that offer B- or H-shares to international investors. This is in recognition of the facts that (i) the issuance of international shares, that is, B-shares and H-shares, is subject to much more stringent disclosure and listing standards, making more information available to shareholders; and (ii) that foreign shareholders, especially institutional investors, may provide more rigorous monitoring of the management, thereby benefiting Chinese local shareholders as well. The Eun and Huang study also found that *ceteris paribus*, Chinese investors pay a premium for dividend-paying stocks as dividends convincingly signal the management's willingness to return cash flows to outside shareholders, rather than expropriating them.

Market for Corporate Control

Suppose a company continually performs poorly and all of its internal governance mechanisms fail to correct the problem. This situation may prompt an outsider (another company or investor) to mount a takeover bid. In a hostile takeover attempt, the bidder typically makes a tender offer to the target shareholders at a price substantially exceeding the prevailing share price. The target shareholders thus have an opportunity to sell their shares at a substantial premium. If the bid is successful, the bidder will acquire the control rights of the target and restructure the company. Following a successful takeover, the bidder often replaces the management team, divests some assets or divisions, and trims employment in an effort to enhance efficiency. If these efforts are successful, the combined market value of the acquirer and target companies will become higher than the sum of stand-alone values of the two companies, reflecting the

---

[9]Fiat is actually listed on the New York Stock Exchange.

synergies created. The market for corporate control, if it exists, can have a disciplinary effect on managers and enhance company efficiency.

In the United States and the United Kingdom, hostile takeovers can serve as a drastic governance mechanism of the last resort. Under the potential threat of take-over, managers cannot take their control of the company for granted. In many other countries, however, hostile takeovers are relatively rare. This is so partly because of concentrated ownership in these countries and partly because of cultural values and political environments disapproving hostile corporate takeovers. But even in these countries, the incidence of corporate takeovers has been gradually increasing. This can be due, in part, to the spreading of equity culture and the opening and deregulation of capital markets. In Germany, for instance, takeovers are carried out through trans-fer of block holdings. In Japan, as in Germany, interfirm cross-holdings of equities are loosening, creating capital market conditions that are more conducive to takeover activities. To the extent, however, that companies with poor investment opportunities and excess cash initiate takeovers, it may be a symptom, rather than a cure, of the agency problem.

Law and Corporate Governance

When outside investors entrust funds to the company, they receive certain rights that are legally protected. Among these are the rights to elect the board of directors, receive dividends on a pro-rata basis, participate in shareholders' meetings, and sue the company for expropriation. These rights empower investors to extract from man-agement fair returns on their funds. However, the content of law protecting investors' rights and the quality of law enforcement vary a great deal across countries. Accord-ing to the studies of La Porta, Lopez-de-Silanes, Shleifer, and Vishny (LLSV), many of the observed differences in international corporate governance systems arise from the differences in how well outside investors are protected by law from expropriation by managers and other corporate insiders. LLSV argue that the legal protection of investor rights systematically varies, depending on the historical origins of national legal systems.

Legal scholars show that the commercial legal systems (e.g., company, security, bankruptcy, and contract laws) of most countries derive from relatively few **legal origins**:

- English common law
- French civil law
- German civil law
- Scandinavian civil law

The French and German civil laws derived from the Roman law, whereas the Scandinavian countries developed their own civil law tradition that is less derivative of Roman law. The civil law tradition, which is the most influential and widely spread, is based on the comprehensive *codification of legal rules*. In contrast, English common law is formed by the *discrete rulings* of independent judges on specific disputes and *judicial precedent*.

These distinct legal systems, especially **English common law** and **French civil law**, spread around the world through conquest, colonization, voluntary adoption, and subtle imitation. The United Kingdom and its former colonies, including Australia, Canada, India, Malaysia, Singapore, South Africa, New Zealand, and the United States, have the English common law system. France and the parts of Europe conquered by Napoleon, such as Belgium, the Netherlands, Italy, Portugal, and Spain, ended up with the French civil law tradition. Further, many former overseas colonies of France, the Netherlands, Portugal, and Spain, such as Algeria, Argentina, Brazil, Chile, Indonesia, Mexico, and the Philippines, also ended up with the French civil law system. The German civil law family comprises Germany and the Germanic countries of Europe, such as Austria and Switzerland, and a few East Asian countries such as Japan and Korea. The Scandinavian civil law family includes four Nordic countries: Denmark, Finland, Norway, and Sweden. Thus, in most countries, the national legal system did not indigenously develop but rather was transplanted from one of several legal origins. Although national legal systems have evolved and adapted to local conditions, it is still possible to classify them into a few distinct families. Such a classification is provided in Exhibit 4.2. The exhibit also provides the indexes for shareholder rights and rule of law for each country as computed by LLSV (1998).

Exhibit 4.2 shows that the average shareholder rights index is 4.00 for English common law countries, 2.33 for both French and German civil law countries, and 3.00 for Scandinavian civil law countries. Thus, English common law countries tend to offer the strongest protection for investors, French and German civil law countries offer the weakest, and Scandinavian civil law countries fall in the middle. The quality of law enforcement, as measured by the rule of law index, is the highest in Scandinavian and German civil law countries, followed by English common law countries; it is lowest in French civil law countries.

Clearly, there is a marked difference in the legal protection of investors between the two most influential legal systems, namely, English common law and French civil law. A logical question is: Why is the English common law system more protective of investors than the French civil law system? According to the prevailing view, the state historically has played a more active role in regulating economic activities and has been less protective of property rights in civil law countries than in common law countries. In England, control of the court passed from the crown to Parliament and property owners in the seventeenth century. English common law thus became more protective of property owners, and this protection was extended to investors over time. This legal tradition in England allows the court to exercise its discretionary judgment or "smell test" over which managerial self-dealings are *unfair* to investors. In France as well as in Germany, parliamentary power was weak and commercial laws were codified by the state, with the role of the court confined to simply determining whether the codified rules were violated or not. Because managers can be creative enough to expropriate investors without obviously violating the codified rules, investors receive low protection in civil law countries.

Glaesser and Shleifer (2002) offer an intriguing explanation of the English and French legal origins based on the divergent political situations prevailing in the Middle Ages. In France, local feudal lords were powerful and there were incessant wars. Under this turbulent situation, there was a need for the protection of adjudicators from local powers, which can only be provided by the king. France came to adopt a royal judge-inquisitor model based on the *Justinian code* of the Roman Empire in the thirteenth century. According to this model, judges appointed by the king collect evidence, prepare written records, and determine the outcome of the case. Understandably, royal judges were mindful of the preferences of the king. The French legal tradition was formalized by the *Code Napoleon*. Napoleon extensively codified legal rules, *bright line rules* in legal terms, and required state-appointed judges to merely apply these rules. In England, in contrast, local lords were less powerful and war was less frequent. In a more peaceful England, which partly reflects the country's geographical isolation, local magnates were mainly afraid of royal power and preferred adjudication by a local jury that was not beholden to the preferences of the crown and was more knowledgeable about local facts and preferences. Initially, the jury consisted of 12 armed knights who were less likely to be intimidated by local bullies or special pressure groups. After the adoption of *Magna Carta* in 1215, local magnates basically paid the crown for the privilege of local, independent adjudication and other rights. The divergent legal developments in England and France came to have lasting effects on the legal systems of many countries.

EXHIBIT 4.2

Classification of Countries by Legal Origins

Legal Origin	Country	Shareholder Rights Index	Rule of Law Index
1. English common law	Australia	4	10.00
	Canada	5	10.00
	Hong Kong	5	8.22
	India	5	4.17
	Ireland	4	7.80
	Israel	3	4.82
	Kenya	3	5.42
	Malaysia	4	6.78
	New Zealand	4	10.00
	Nigeria	3	2.73
	Pakistan	5	3.03
	Singapore	4	8.57
	South Africa	5	4.42
	Sri Lanka	3	1.90
	Thailand	2	6.25
	United Kingdom	5	8.57
	United States	5	10.00
	Zimbabwe	3	3.68
	English-origin average	**4.00**	**6.46**
2. French civil law	Argentina	4	5.35
	Belgium	0	10.00
	Brazil	3	6.32
	Chile	5	7.02
	Colombia	3	2.08
	Ecuador	2	6.67
	Egypt	2	4.17
	France	3	8.98
	Greece	2	6.18
	Indonesia	2	3.98
	Italy	1	8.33
	Jordan	1	4.35
	Mexico	1	5.35
	Netherlands	2	10.00
	Peru	3	2.50
	Philippines	3	2.73
	Portugal	3	8.68
	Spain	4	7.80
	Turkey	2	5.18
	Uruguay	2	5.00
	Venezuela	1	6.37
	French-origin average	**2.33**	**6.05**
3. German civil law	Austria	2	10.00
	Germany	1	9.23
	Japan	4	8.98
	South Korea	2	5.35
	Switzerland	2	10.00
	Taiwan	3	8.52
	German-origin average	**2.33**	**8.68**
4. Scandinavian civil law	Denmark	2	10.00
	Finland	3	10.00
	Norway	4	10.00
	Sweden	3	10.00
	Scandinavian-origin average	**3.00**	**10.00**

Note: Shareholder rights index scales from 0 (lowest) to 6 (highest). Rule of law index scales from 0 (lowest) to 10 (highest).

Source: Rafael La Porta, Florencio Lopez-de-Silanes, Andrei Shleifer, Robert W. Vishny, "Law and Finance," *Journal of Political Economy* 106 (1998), pp. 1113–55.

Consequences of Law

Protection of investors' rights not only has interesting legal origins, but the concept is shown to have major economic consequences on the pattern of corporate ownership and valuation, the development of capital markets, economic growth, and others. To illustrate, let us consider two European countries, Italy and the United Kingdom. As shown in Exhibit 4.3, Italy has a French civil law tradition with weak shareholder protection, whereas the United Kingdom, with its common law tradition, provides strong investor protection. In Italy (U.K.), the three largest shareholders own 58 percent (19 percent) of the company, on average. Company ownership is thus highly concentrated in Italy and more diffused in the United Kingdom. In addition, as of 1999, only 247 companies were listed on the stock exchange in Italy, whereas 2,292 companies were listed in the United Kingdom. In the same year, the stock market capitalization as a proportion of the annual GDP was 71 percent in Italy but 248 percent in the United Kingdom. The stark contrast between the two countries suggests that protection of investors can have significant economic consequences. Concentrated ownership can be viewed as a rational response to weak investor protection, but it may create different conflicts of interest between large controlling shareholders and small outside shareholders. We now discuss some of the issues in detail.

Ownership and Control Pattern

Companies domiciled in countries with weak investor protection may need to have concentrated ownership as a substitute for legal protection. With concentrated ownership, large shareholders can control and monitor managers effectively and solve the agency problem. LLSV (1998) indeed found that corporate ownership tends to be more concentrated in countries with weaker investor protection. As can be seen from Exhibit 4.4, the three largest shareholders own 43 percent of companies on average in English common law countries, and 54 percent of companies on average in French civil law countries.

If large shareholders benefit only from pro-rata cash flows, there will be no conflicts between large shareholders and small shareholders. What is good for large shareholders should be good for small shareholders as well. Since investors may be able to derive private benefits from control, however, they may seek to acquire control rights exceeding cash flow rights. Dominant investors may acquire control through various schemes, such as:

1. Shares with superior voting rights
2. Pyramidal ownership structure
3. Interfirm cross-holdings

Many companies issue shares with differential voting rights, deviating from the one-share one-vote principle. By accumulating superior voting shares, investors can acquire control rights exceeding cash flow rights. In addition, large shareholders, who are often founders and their families, can use a **pyramidal ownership** structure in which they control a holding company that owns a controlling block of another company, which in turn owns controlling interests in yet another company, and so on. Also,

---

EXHIBIT 4.3

Does Law Matter?: Italy versus the U.K.

	Italy	U.K.
Legal origin	French civil law	English common law
Shareholder rights	1 (low)	5 (high)
Ownership by three largest shareholders	58%	19%
Market cap/GDP	71%	248%
Listed stocks	247	2,292

Note: Shareholder rights refer to the antidirector rights index as computed by La Porta, Lopez-de-Silanes, Shleifer, and Vishny (1998). Both the ratio of stock market capitalization to GDP and the number of listed stocks are as of 1999.

Source: Various studies of LLSV and the CIA's *World Factbook*.

EXHIBIT 4.4	Consequences of Law: Ownership and Capital Markets			
Legal Origin	Country	Ownership Concentration	External Cap/GNP	Domestic Firms/Population
1. English common law	Australia	0.28	0.49	63.55
	Canada	0.40	0.39	40.86
	Hong Kong	0.54	1.18	88.16
	India	0.40	0.31	7.79
	Ireland	0.39	0.27	20.00
	Israel	0.51	0.25	127.60
	Kenya	na	na	2.24
	Malaysia	0.54	1.48	25.15
	New Zealand	0.48	0.28	69.00
	Nigeria	0.40	0.27	1.68
	Pakistan	0.37	0.18	5.88
	Singapore	0.49	1.18	80.00
	South Africa	0.52	1.45	16.00
	Sri Lanka	0.60	0.11	11.94
	Thailand	0.47	0.56	6.70
	United Kingdom	0.19	1.00	35.68
	United States	0.20	0.58	30.11
	Zimbabwe	0.55	0.18	5.81
	English-origin average	**0.43**	**0.60**	**35.45**
2. French civil law	Argentina	0.53	0.07	4.58
	Belgium	0.54	0.17	15.50
	Brazil	0.57	0.18	3.48
	Chile	0.45	0.80	19.92
	Colombia	0.63	0.14	3.13
	Ecuador	na	na	13.18
	Egypt	0.62	0.08	3.48
	France	0.34	0.23	8.05
	Greece	0.67	0.07	21.60
	Indonesia	0.58	0.15	1.15
	Italy	0.58	0.08	3.91
	Jordan	na	na	23.75
	Mexico	0.64	0.22	2.28
	Netherlands	0.39	0.52	21.13
	Peru	0.56	0.40	9.47
	Philippines	0.57	0.10	2.90
	Portugal	0.52	0.08	19.50
	Spain	0.51	0.17	9.71
	Turkey	0.59	0.18	2.93
	Uruguay	na	na	7.00
	Venezuela	0.51	0.08	4.28
	French-origin average	**0.54**	**0.21**	**10.00**
3. German civil law	Austria	0.58	0.06	13.87
	Germany	0.48	0.13	5.14
	Japan	0.18	0.62	17.78
	South Korea	0.23	0.44	15.88
	Switzerland	0.41	0.62	33.85
	Taiwan	0.18	0.86	14.22
	German-origin average	**0.34**	**0.46**	**16.79**
4. Scandinavian civil law	Denmark	0.45	0.21	50.40
	Finland	0.37	0.25	13.00
	Norway	0.36	0.22	33.00
	Sweden	0.28	0.51	12.66
	Scandinavian-origin average	**0.37**	**0.30**	**27.26**

Note: Ownership concentration measures the average share ownership by three largest shareholders. External Cap/GNP is the ratio of the stock market capitalization held by minority shareholders (other than three shareholders) to the gross national product for 1994. Domestic Firms/Population is the ratio of the number of domestic firms listed in a given country to its population (million) in 1994.

Source: Various studies of LLSV.

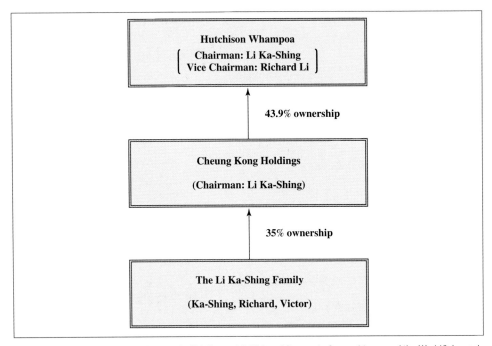

EXHIBIT 4.5

Hutchison Whampoa: The Chain of Control

Source: R. La Porta, F. Lopez-de-Silanes, A. Shleifer, and R. Vishny, "Corporate Ownership around the World," *Journal of Finance* 54 (1999), p. 483.

equity cross-holdings among a group of companies, such as *keiretsu* and *chaebols*, can be used to concentrate and leverage voting rights to acquire control. Obviously, a combination of these schemes may also be used to acquire control.

Hutchison Whampoa, the third most valuable public company in Hong Kong, provides an interesting example of pyramidal control structure. The company is 43.9 percent controlled by another public company, Cheung Kong Holdings, which is the fifth-largest publicly traded company in Hong Kong. Cheung Kong Holdings, in turn, is 35 percent controlled by the Li Ka-Shing family. The cash flow rights of the Li family in Hutchison Whampoa are thus 15.4 percent ($.35 \times .439 = .154$), but the family's control rights in Hutchson Whampoa is 43.9 percent. The chain of control of Hutchison Whampoa is illustrated in Exhibit 4.5. In Korea, the ownership structure can be more complicated. Take Samsung Electronics, Korea's most valuable company. Lee Keun-Hee, the chairman of the Samsung *chaebol* and the son of Samsung's founder, controls 8.3 percent of Samsung Electronics directly. In addition, Lee controls 15 percent of Samsung Life, which controls 8.7 percent of Samsung Electronics and 14.1 percent of Cheil Chedang, which controls 3.2 percent of Samsung Electronics and 11.5 percent of Samsung Life. This byzantine web of cross-holdings enables Lee to exercise an effective control of Samsung Electronics.[10]

As in Asia, concentrated ownership and a significant wedge between control and cash flow rights are widespread in continental Europe. Exhibit 4.6 illustrates the pyramidal ownership structure for Daimler-Benz, a German company, at the beginning of the 1990s.[11] The company has three major block holders: Deutsche Bank (28.3 percent), Mercedes-Automobil Holding AG (25.23 percent), and the Kuwait

---

[10]Examples here are from R. La Porta, F. Lopez-de-Silanes, A. Shleifer, and R. Vishny, "Corporate Ownership around the World," *Journal of Finance* 54 (1999), pp. 471–517. Recently, Samsung group has been reorganized around Samsung C&T, a construction and trading arm, which became the de facto holding company of the group.

[11]This example is from Julian Franks and Colin Mayer, "Ownership and Control of German Corporations," *Review of Financial Studies* 14 (2001), pp. 943–77. Note that the ownership structure of Daimler-Benz has been significantly altered since 1990.

EXHIBIT 4.6 Ownership Structure of Daimler-Benz AG, 1990

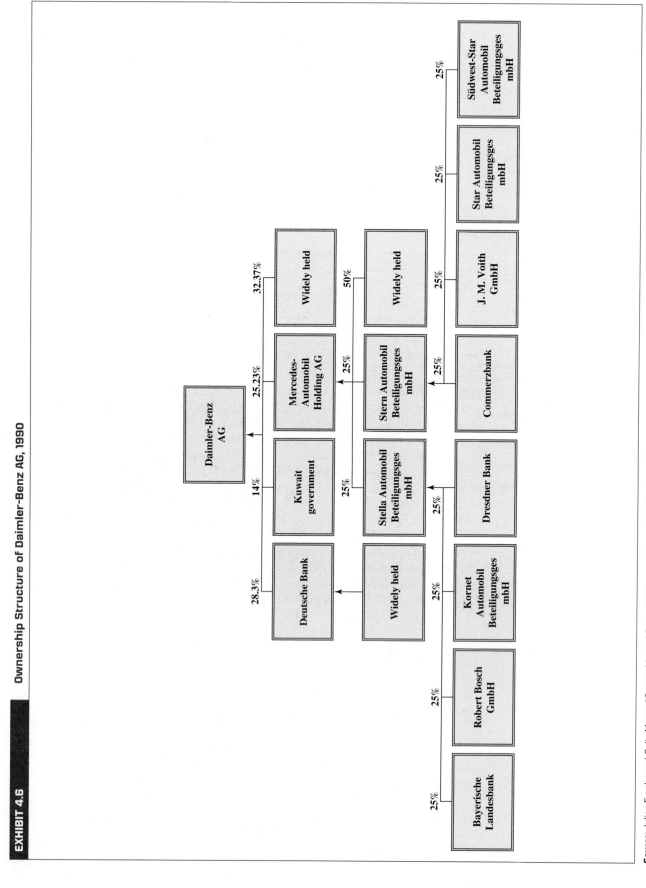

Source: Julian Franks and Colin Mayer, "Ownership and Control of German Corporation," *Review of Financial Studies* 14 (2001), p. 949.

government (14 percent). The remaining 32.37 percent of shares are widely held. The pyramidal ownership structure illustrated in Exhibit 4.6 makes it possible for large investors to acquire significant control rights with relatively small investments. For example, Robert Bosch GmbH controls 25 percent of Stella Automobil, which in turn owns 25 percent of Mercedes-Automobil Holding, which controls 25 percent of Daimler-Benz AG. Robert Bosch can possibly control up to 25 percent of the voting rights of Daimler-Benz AG with only 1.56 percent cash flow rights in the company.

Private Benefits of Control

Once large shareholders acquire control rights exceeding cash flow rights, they may extract **private benefits of control** that are not shared by other shareholders on a pro-rata basis. A few studies document the existence and magnitude of private benefits. Nenova (2001) computed the premium for voting shares relative to nonvoting shares in different countries. The voting premium, defined as the total vote value (value of a vote times the number of votes) as a proportion of the firm's equity market value, is only about 2 percent in the United States and 2.8 percent in Canada. This implies that private benefits of control are not very significant in both countries. In contrast, the voting premium is 23 percent in Brazil, 9.5 percent in Germany, 29 percent in both Italy and Korea, and 36 percent in Mexico, suggesting that in these countries, dominant shareholders extract substantial private benefits of control. Unless investors can derive significant private benefits of control, they will not pay substantial premiums for voting shares over nonvoting shares.

Dyck and Zingales (2004), on the other hand, computed "block premium," that is, the difference between the price per share paid for the control block and the exchange price after the announcement of the control transaction, divided by the exchange price after the control transaction. Obviously, control blocks will command premiums only if block holders can extract private benefits of control. Similar to Nenova's findings, Dyck and Zingales report that during the period 1990–2000, the average block premium was only 1 percent in Canada, the United Kingdom, and the United States, and 2 percent in Australia and Finland. However, the average block premium was much higher in other countries—65 percent in Brazil, 58 percent in the Czech Republic, 27 percent in Israel, 37 percent in Italy, 16 percent in Korea, and 34 percent in Mexico. Clearly, large shareholders extract significant private benefits of control in those countries where the rights of minority shareholders are not well protected.

Capital Markets and Valuation

The legal analysis of corporate governance predicts that investor protection promotes the development of external capital markets. When investors are assured of receiving fair returns on their funds, they will be willing to pay more for securities. To the extent that this induces companies to seek more funds from outside investors, strong investor protection will be conducive to large capital markets. LLSV (1997) empirically document that countries with strong shareholder protection tend to have more valuable stock markets and more companies listed on stock exchanges per capita than countries with weak protection. Also, a few studies report that higher insider cash flow rights are associated with higher valuation of corporate assets, whereas greater insider control rights are associated with lower valuation of corporate assets. Exhibit 4.4 shows that the stock market capitalization held by minority shareholders (excluding the three largest shareholders) as a proportion to the GNP for the year 1994 is 0.60 in English common law countries and 0.21 in French civil law countries. The exhibit also shows that the number of domestic firms listed on stock exchanges per population (million) is about 35 in English common law countries, compared with only 10 in French civil law countries.

Weak investor protection can also be a contributing factor to sharp market declines during a financial crisis. In countries with weak investor protection, insiders may treat outside investors reasonably well as long as business prospects warrant continued external financing. However, once future prospects dim, insiders may start to expropriate the outside investors as the need for external funding dissipates. The accelerated expropriation can induce sharp declines in security prices. Johnson, Boon, Breach, and Friedman (2000) provide evidence that during the Asian financial crisis of 1997–1998, stock markets actually declined more in countries with weaker investor protection.

The existence of well-developed financial markets, promoted by strong investor protection, may stimulate economic growth by making funds readily available for investment at low cost. Earlier, Schumpeter (1934) argued that financial development promotes economic growth. Several studies now document the empirical link between financial development and economic growth, supporting the Schumpeter hypothesis.[12] According to Beck et al. (2000), financial development can contribute to economic growth in three major ways: (i) It enhances savings; (ii) it channels savings toward real investments in productive capacities, thereby fostering capital accumulation; and (iii) it enhances the efficiency of investment allocation through the monitoring and signaling functions of capital markets.

www.oecd.org/daf/da
/corporategovernance
principles/43653645.pdf

This site provides practical guides to corporate governance.

Corporate Governance Reform

In the wake of the Asian financial crisis of 1997–1998 and the spectacular failure of several major companies like Daewoo, Enron, WorldCom, and Parmalat, scandal-weary investors around the world are demanding corporate governance reform. The failure of these companies hurts shareholders as well as other stakeholders, including workers, customers, and suppliers. Many employees who invested heavily in company stock for their retirement were dealt severe financial blows. It is not just the companies' internal governance mechanisms that failed; auditors, regulators, banks, and institutional investors also failed in their respective roles. Failure to reform corporate governance will damage investor confidence, stunt the development of capital markets, raise the cost of capital, distort capital allocation, and even shake confidence in capitalism itself.

Objectives of Reform

During the 1980s, when the economies of Germany and Japan were strong performers, the governance systems of the two countries received much attention and admiration. In both Germany and Japan, banks and a few permanent large shareholders play the central role in corporate governance. This "bank-centered" governance system was seen as guiding corporate managers to pursue long-term performance goals and also as effectively supporting companies when they were in financial distress. In contrast, the "market-centered" governance system of the United States was viewed as inducing short-term-oriented corporate decisions and being ineffectual in many ways. However, as the U.S. economy and its stock market surged ahead in the 1990s, with Germany and Japan lagging behind, the U.S.-style market-centered governance system replaced the German-Japanese system as a subject of admiration. The American market-oriented system seemed the wave of the future. But then, the subsequent slowdown of the U.S. economy and stock market and the shocking corporate scandals again dethroned the U.S. system. It seems fair to say that no country has a perfect system for other countries to emulate.

There is a growing consensus that corporate governance reform should be a matter of global concern. Although some countries face more serious problems than others, existing governance mechanisms have failed to effectively protect outside investors in many countries. What should be the objective of reform? Our discussion in this chapter suggests a simple answer: *Strengthen the protection of outside investors from expropriation by managers and controlling insiders.* Among other things, reform requires: (i) strengthening the independence of boards of directors with more outsiders, (ii) enhancing the transparency and disclosure standard of financial statements, and (iii) energizing the regulatory and monitoring functions of the SEC (in the United States) and stock exchanges. In many developing and transition countries, it may be necessary to first modernize the legal framework.

---

[12]Examples include King and Levine (1993), Rajan and Zingales (1998), and Beck, Levine, and Loayza (2000).

Political Dynamics

However, as we have seen from the experiences of many countries, governance reform is easier said than done. First of all, the existing governance system is a product of the historical evolution of the country's economic, legal, and political infrastructure. It is not easy to change historical legacies. Second, many parties have vested interests in the current system, and they will resist any attempt to change the status quo. For example, Arthur Levitt, chairman of the SEC during much of the 1990s, attempted to reform the accounting industry, but it successfully resisted the attempt through the use of lobbyists and advertising. In Levitt's words (*The Wall Street Journal*, June 17, 2002, p. C7): "The ferocity of the accounting profession's opposition to our attempt to reform the industry a few years ago is no secret. . . . They will do everything possible to protect their franchise, and will do so with little regard for the public interest." This earlier failure to reform the accounting industry contributed to the breakout of corporate scandals in the United States. It is noted that the former executives of WorldCom were indicted for allegedly orchestrating the largest accounting fraud in history, with the help of conniving auditors.[13] In another example, following the Asian financial crisis, the Korean government led efforts to reform the country's *chaebol* system but met with stiff resistance from the founding families, which were basically afraid of losing their private benefits of control. Nevertheless, reform efforts in Korea were partially successful, partly because the weight and prestige of the government were behind them and partly because public opinion was generally in favor of reform.

To be successful, reformers should understand the political dynamics surrounding governance issues and seek help from the media, public opinion, and nongovernmental organizations (NGOs). The role of NGOs and the media can be illustrated by the success of the People's Solidarity for Participatory Democracy (PSPD) in Korea, organized by Hasung Jang of Korea University. The PSPD and Professor Jang have utilized legal pressure and media exposure to create public opinion and to shame corporate executives into changing their practices. For example, PSPD successfully challenged the transfer pricing of SK Telecom. Specifically, SK Telecom transferred huge profits to two subsidiaries, Sunkyung Distribution, which is 94.6 percent owned by SK Group Chairman Choi Jong-Hyun, and Daehan Telecom, fully owned by Choi's son and his son-in-law, thereby expropriating outside shareholders of SK Telecom. The PSPD exposed this practice to the media, and the episode was reported in the *Financial Times* as well as local newspapers and television. Facing unfavorable public opinion, SK Telecom finally agreed to stop the practice.[14]

The Sarbanes-Oxley Act

Facing public uproar following the U.S. corporate scandals, politicians took actions to remedy the problem. The U.S. Congress passed the **Sarbanes-Oxley Act** in July 2002. The key objective of the Act is to protect investors by improving the accuracy and reliability of corporate disclosure, thereby restoring the public's confidence in the integrity of corporate financial reporting. The major components of the Sarbanes-Oxley Act are

- Accounting regulation—The creation of a public accounting oversight board charged with overseeing the auditing of public companies, and restricting the consulting services that auditors can provide to clients.
- Audit committee—The company should appoint independent "financial experts" to its audit committee.
- Internal control assessment—Public companies and their auditors should assess the effectiveness of internal control of financial record keeping and fraud prevention.

---

[13]*New York Times*, September 2, 2002, p. A16.

[14]Alexander Dyck and Luigi Zingales, "The Corporate Governance Role of the Media," working paper (2002).

- Executive responsibility—Chief executive and finance officers (CEO and CFO) must sign off on the company's quarterly and annual financial statements. If fraud causes an overstatement of earnings, these officers must return any bonuses.

The Sarbanes-Oxley Act represents one of the most important securities legislations since the original securities laws of the 1930s. As mandated by the Act, the NYSE and the NASDAQ also strengthened the listing standards by adopting various measures to protect investors. These measures call for, among other things: (i) listed companies to have boards of directors with a majority of independents; (ii) the compensation, nominating, and audit committees to be entirely composed of independent directors; and (iii) the publication of corporate governance guidelines and reporting of annual evaluation of the board and CEO. These measures, if properly implemented, should improve the corporate governance regime in the United States.

Evidences regarding the effect of the Sarbanes-Oxley Act on the corporate disclosure and governance standards are generally positive. For example, Lobo and Zhou (2006) found a marked increase in "conservatism" in financial reporting following the enactment. Specifically, firms began to report lower discretionary accruals (meaning less active earnings management) and recognize losses more quickly than gains when they report income in the post-Act period. It is noted that Enron managed earnings very aggressively by prematurely recognizing revenue and hiding or shifting losses and liabilities to many non-consolidated special purpose entities. These dubious accounting practices, which eventually led to Enron's implosion, declined partly because of the harsh penalties on CEO and CFO imposed by the Sarbanes-Oxley Act (up to a $5 million fine and 20 years in prison) for falsely certifying financial statements that do not satisfy the requirements of the Act. Another study by Linck, Netter, and Yang (2009) found substantial changes in the company boards and directors as well following the Sarbanes-Oxley enactment. Specifically, the study noted that (i) board committees meet more often, (ii) boards become larger and more independent, and (iii) board members are more likely to be lawyers, consultants, or financial experts and less likely to be corporate insiders. These findings indicate that the boards of directors became more proactive for fulfilling their responsibilities and also better qualified for doing their duties. After the passage of the Sarbanes-Oxley Act, firms are also found to be more cautious in their decision making. For instance, Kang, Liu, and Qi (2010) documented that U.S. firms apply a higher discount rate to new investment projects, reflecting greater managerial caution, especially among smaller firms.

The implementation of the Sarbanes-Oxley Act, however, was not free from frictions. Many companies find the compliance with a particular provision of the act, Section 404, onerous, costing millions of dollars. Section 404 requires public companies and their auditors to assess the effectiveness of internal control of financial record keeping and fraud prevention and file reports with the Securities and Exchange Commission (SEC). Clearly, the cost of compliance disproportionately affects smaller companies. In addition, many U.S.-listed foreign firms that have different governance structures at home also find it costly to comply with the Sarbanes-Oxley Act. Since the passage of the act, some foreign firms have chosen to list their shares on the London Stock Exchange and other European exchanges, instead of U.S. exchanges, to avoid the costly compliance.

The Cadbury Code of Best Practice

Like the United States, the United Kingdom was hit by a spate of corporate scandals in the 1980s and early 1990s, resulting in the bankruptcy of such high-profile companies as Ferranti, Colorol Group, BCCI, and Maxwell Group. The "scandalous" collapse of these prominent British companies was popularly attributed to their complete corporate control by a single top executive, weak governance mechanisms, and the failure of their boards of directors. Against this backdrop, the British government appointed the *Cadbury Committee* in 1991 with the broad mandate of addressing corporate governance problems in the United Kingdom. Sir Adrian Cadbury, CEO of Cadbury

Company, chaired the committee.[15] The work of the committee led to successful governance reform in the United Kingdom.

In December 1992, the Cadbury Committee issued its report, including the *Code of Best Practice* in corporate governance. The code recommends that (i) boards of directors of public companies include at least three outside (nonexecutive) directors, and that (ii) the positions of chief executive officer (CEO) and chairman of the board (COB) of these companies be held by two different individuals; boards of directors of most British companies were dominated by insiders, with the positions of CEO and COB often held by the same individuals. Specifically, the code prescribed that:

> The board should meet regularly, retain full and effective control over the company and monitor the executive management. There should be a clearly accepted division of responsibilities at the head of a company, which will ensure a balance of power and authority, such that no one individual has unfettered power of decisions. Where the chairman is also the chief executive, it is essential that there should be a strong and independent element on the board, with a recognized senior member. The board should include non-executive directors of significant calibre and number for their views to carry significant weight in the board's decisions.

The **Cadbury Code** has not been legislated into law, and compliance with the code is voluntary. However, the London Stock Exchange (LSE) currently requires that each listed company show whether the company is in compliance with the code and explain why if it is not. This "comply or explain" approach has apparently persuaded many companies to comply rather than explain; currently, 90 percent of all LSE-listed companies have adopted the Cadbury Code. According to a study by Dahya, McConnell, and Travlos (2002), the proportion of outside directors rose from 26 percent before the adoption to 47 percent afterward among those companies newly complying with the code. On the other hand, joint CEO/COB positions declined from 37 percent of the companies before the adoption to 15 percent afterward. This means that even though the compliance is voluntary, the Cadbury Code has made a significant impact on the internal governance mechanisms of U.K. companies. The Dahya et al. study further shows that the "negative" relationship between CEO turnover and company performance became stronger after the introduction of the Cadbury Code. This means that the job security of chief executives has become more sensitive to company performance, strengthening managerial accountability and weakening its entrenchment.

The Dodd-Frank Act

Following the subprime mortgage crisis and the bailout of large financial institutions with taxpayers' money, the U.S. Congress passed the Dodd-Frank Wall Street Reform and Consumer Protection Act in July 2010. Among other things, the act aims at strengthening government regulation of banking firms and their internal governance mechanisms, thereby preventing similar financial crises in the future. The act represents the most comprehensive overhaul of the rules of finance since the Great Depression and is likely to have a major impact on the way decisions are made within financial firms. The key features of the **Dodd-Frank Act** include

- Volker rule—Deposit-taking banks will be banned from proprietary trading and from owning more than a small fraction of hedge funds and private equity firms. The rule is named after Paul Volker, former Federal Reserve chairman, who argued that banks should not be allowed to engage in casino-like activities that endanger the safety of depositors' money.

- Resolution authority—The government can seize and dismantle a large bank in an orderly manner if the bank faces impending failure and poses a systemic risk to the broader financial system. This authority aims, in part, to reduce the cost and risk associated with the bailing out of banks that are "too big to fail."

---

[15]For a detailed discussion of the Cadbury Committee and its effect on corporate governance in the U.K., refer to Dahya, McConnell, and Travlos (2002).

Banks that are deemed too big to fail can have skewed incentives for excessive risk-taking. Shareholders at big firms get nonbinding votes on executive pay and golden parachutes, to control skewed executive incentives.

- Derivative securities—Derivatives trading in over-the-counter markets will be transferred to electronic exchanges, with contracts settled through central clearing houses, to increase transparency and reduce counter-party risk.

- Systemic risk regulation—A Financial Stability Oversight Council of government regulators chaired by the Treasury secretary will identify systemically important financial firms and monitor their activities and financial conditions. These firms must draw up a "living will" to describe how they would be liquidated if they fail.

- Consumer protection—A new, independent Consumer Financial Protection Bureau will monitor predatory mortgage loans and other loan products.

The Dodd-Frank Act is focused on controlling banks' excessive risk-taking and mitigating the systemic risk in the financial system. If the act is successfully implemented, it would strengthen bank governance and help reduce the probability and cost of financial crises in the future.[16]

Lastly, it is noted that corporate governance reforms would not only strengthen shareholders' cash flow rights but also enhance corporate performance. For instance, in their study of U.S. firms, Gompers, Ishii, and Metrick (2003) found that firms with stronger corporate governance have higher firm value, higher profits, higher sales growth, and lower capital expenditure, and make fewer corporate acquisitions. They also found that an investment strategy based on buying firms with the strongest corporate governance and selling firms with the weakest corporate governance would have earned a large "abnormal return" during their study period. Their study shows that enhancement of corporate governance would improve firm performance, boost firm value, and raise stock returns. In a comparative study of corporate valuation around the world, Chua, Eun, and Lai (2007) found that despite international financial integration in recent years, corporate valuation varies a great deal across countries. Specifically, corporate valuation is directly related to the quality of corporate governance, as well as the economic growth options and the degree of financial openness.

SUMMARY

In the wake of recurrent financial crises and high-profile corporate scandals and failures in the United States and abroad, corporate governance has attracted a lot of attention worldwide. This chapter provides an overview of corporate governance issues, with the emphasis on intercountry differences in the governance mechanisms.

1. The public corporation, which is jointly owned by many shareholders with limited liability, is a major organizational innovation with significant economic consequences. The efficient risk-sharing mechanism allows the public corporation to raise large amounts of capital at low cost and profitably undertake many investment projects, boosting economic growth.

2. The public corporation has a major weakness: the agency problem associated with the conflicts of interest between shareholders and managers. Self-interested managers can take actions to promote their own interests at the expense of shareholders.

---

[16]It is too early to assess the effects of the Dodd-Frank Act. So far, the Consumer Financial Protection Bureau was formally launched, with the clear mandate to protect consumers. It was observed that in part due to the Act, major banks decreased risky trading activities, increased the capital reserves and, according to Dimitrov, Palia, and Tang (2015), the credit rating agencies became more conservative in bond ratings.

The agency problem tends to be more serious for firms with excessive free cash flows but without growth opportunities.

3. To protect shareholder rights, curb managerial excesses, and restore confidence in capital markets, it is important to strengthen corporate governance, defined as the economic, legal, and institutional framework in which corporate control and cash flow rights are distributed among shareholders, managers, and other stakeholders of the company.

4. The central issue in corporate governance is: how to best protect outside investors from expropriation by managers and controlling insiders so that investors can receive fair returns on their funds.

5. The agency problem can be alleviated by various methods, including (a) strengthening the independence of boards of directors; (b) providing managers with incentive contracts, such as stocks and stock options, to better align the interests of managers with those of shareholders; (c) concentrated ownership so that large shareholders can control managers; (d) using debt to induce managers to disgorge free cash flows to investors; (e) listing stocks on the London or New York stock exchange where shareholders are better protected; and (f) inviting hostile takeover bids if the managers waste funds and expropriate shareholders.

6. Legal protection of investor rights systematically varies across countries, depending on the historical origin of the national legal system. English common law countries tend to provide the strongest protection, French civil law countries the weakest. The civil law tradition is based on the comprehensive codification of legal rules, whereas the common law tradition is based on discrete rulings by independent judges on specific disputes and on judicial precedent. The English common law tradition, based on independent judges and local juries, evolved to be more protective of property rights, which were extended to the rights of investors.

7. Protecting the rights of investors has major economic consequences in terms of corporate ownership patterns, the development of capital markets, economic growth, and more. Poor investor protection results in concentrated ownership, excessive private benefits of control, underdeveloped capital markets, and slower economic growth.

8. Outside the United States and the United Kingdom, large shareholders, often founding families, tend to control managers and expropriate small outside shareholders. In other words, large, dominant shareholders tend to extract substantial private benefits of control.

9. Corporate governance reform efforts should be focused on how to better protect outside investors from expropriation by controlling insiders. Often, controlling insiders resist reform efforts, as they do not like to lose their private benefits of control. Reformers should understand political dynamics and mobilize public opinion to their cause.

KEY WORDS

agency problem, *85*
Cadbury Code, *103*
complete contract, *84*
concentrated ownership, *88*
corporate governance, *82*
Dodd-Frank Act, *103*
English common law, *92*

equity cross-holdings, *97*
Free cash flows, *85*
French civil law, *92*
incentive contracts, *87*
legal origins, *92*
managerial entrenchment, *85*

private benefits of control, *99*
public corporation, *83*
pyramidal ownership, *95*
residual control rights, *85*
Sarbanes-Oxley Act, *101*
shareholder rights, *82*

www.mhhe.com/er8e

QUESTIONS

1. The majority of major corporations are franchised as public corporations. Discuss the key strength and weakness of the "public corporation." When do you think the public corporation as an organizational form is unsuitable?

2. The public corporation is owned by a multitude of shareholders but run by professional managers. Managers can take self-interested actions at the expense of shareholders. Discuss the conditions under which the so-called agency problem arises.

3. Following corporate scandals and failures in the United States and abroad, there has been a growing demand for corporate governance reform. What should be the key objectives of corporate governance reform? What kinds of obstacles can thwart reform efforts?

4. Studies show that the legal protection of shareholder rights varies a great deal across countries. Discuss the possible reasons why the English common law tradition provides the strongest protection of investors and the French civil law tradition the weakest.

5. Explain "the wedge" between control and cash flow rights and discuss its implications for corporate governance.

6. Discuss different ways that dominant investors may establish and maintain control of a company with relatively small investments.

7. The *Cadbury Code of Best Practice*, adopted in the United Kingdom, led to a successful reform of corporate governance in the country. Explain the key requirements of the code and discuss how it contributed to the success of reform.

8. Many companies grant stock or stock options to managers. Discuss the benefits and possible costs of using this kind of incentive compensation scheme.

9. It has been shown that foreign companies listed on U.S. stock exchanges are valued more than those from the same countries that are not listed in the United States. Explain why U.S.-listed foreign firms are valued more than those that are not. Also explain why not every foreign firm wants to list stocks in the United States.

10. Explain "free cash flows." Why do managers like to retain free cash flows instead of distributing it to shareholders? Discuss what mechanisms may be used to solve this problem.

11. An epic bribe scandal at Petrobras, a major oil company controlled by the Brazilian government, that broke out in 2015 shocked the economic and political system of Brazil. Put simply, the company insiders, outside suppliers and contractors, and politicians colluded and stole billions of dollars from the company via kickbacks, bid riggings, overcharging for construction projects, and the like. The Petrobras scandal led to a sharp drop of the company share price, laying off thousands of workers, and tilting the national economy toward recession. The scandal also seriously tarnished the image of Brazil as a promising emerging market. Document in detail what happened at Petrobras and then investigate how the company's governance and the country's political culture may have contributed to the scandal.

INTERNET EXERCISES

It is often mentioned that the United States has a "market-centered" corporate governance system, whereas Germany has a "bank-centered" system. Review the website of the OECD, www.oecd.org, or any other relevant websites and answer the following questions:

(a) Compare and contrast the corporate governance systems of the two countries.

(b) How did the two countries come to have the particular governance systems?

(c) What are the consequences of the different governance systems in the two countries?

MINI CASE

Parmalat: Europe's Enron

Following such high-profile corporate scandals as Enron and WorldCom in the United States, European business executives smugly proclaimed that the same could not happen on their side of the Atlantic as Europe does not share America's laissez-faire capitalism. Unfortunately, however, they were proved wrong quickly when Parmalat, a jewel of Italian capitalism, collapsed spectacularly as a result of massive accounting frauds.

Parmalat was founded in 1961 as a dairy company. Calisto Tanzi, the founder, transformed Parmalat into a national player by embarking on an aggressive acquisition program in the 1980s when local governments of Italy privatized their municipal dairies. While solidifying its dominant position in the Italian home market, Parmalat aggressively ventured into international markets during the 1990s, establishing operations in 30 countries throughout the Americas, Asia/Pacific, and Southern Africa. To finance its rapid expansion, the company borrowed heavily from international banks and investors. Worldwide sales of Parmalat reached €7.6 billion in 2002 and its aspiration to become the Coca-Cola of milk seemed within reach. However, things began to unravel in 2003.

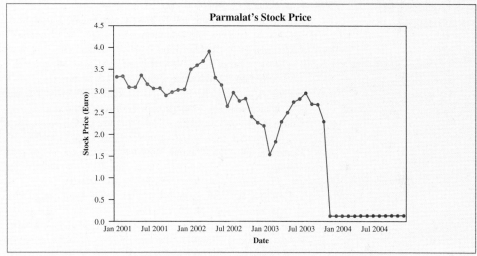

Parmalat's Stock Price

Data Source: DataStream.

Parmalat first defaulted on a $185 million debt payment in November 2003, which prompted a scrutiny of the firm's finances. Auditors and regulators soon found out that a $4.9 billion cash reserve supposedly held in a Bank of America account of the Cayman Island subsidiary of Parmalat actually did not exist, and that the total debt of the company was around €16 billion—more than double the amount (€7.2 billion) shown on the balance sheet. Italian investigators subsequently discovered that Parmalat managers simply "invented assets" to cover the company's debts and falsified accounts over a 15-year period. Following the discovery of massive frauds, Parmalat was forced into bankruptcy in December 2003. Calisto Tanzi, founder and former CEO, was arrested on suspicion of fraud, embezzlement, false accounting, and misleading investors. The Parmalat saga represents the largest and most brazen corporate fraud case in European history and is widely dubbed Europe's Enron.

Enrico Bondi, a new CEO of Parmalat, filed a $10 billion lawsuit against Citigroup, Bank of America, and former auditors Grant Thornton and Deloitte Touche Tohmatsu, for sharing responsibility for the company's collapse. He also filed legal actions against UBS of Switzerland and Deutsche Bank for the transactions that allegedly contributed to the collapse of Parmalat. Bondi has alleged that Parmalat's foreign "enablers," including international banks and auditors, were complicit in the frauds. He maintained that they knew about Parmalat's fraudulent finances and helped the company to disguise them in exchange for fat fees. Bondi effectively declared a war on Parmalat's international bankers and creditors.

www.mhhe.com/er8e

www.mhhe.com/er8e

The accompanying graph illustrates Parmalat's share price behavior. Following a sharp drop in share price, trading of the company's shares was suspended on December 22, 2003.

Discussion Points

1. How was it possible for Parmalat managers to "cook the books" and hide it for so long?

2. Investigate and discuss the role that international banks and auditors might have played in Parmalat's collapse.

3. Study and discuss Italy's corporate governance regime and its role in the failure of Parmalat.

REFERENCES & SUGGESTED READINGS

Beck, T., R. Levine, and N. Loayza. "Finance and the Sources of Growth." *Journal of Financial Economics* 58 (2000), pp. 261–300.

Chua, Choong, C. Eun, and S. Lai. "Corporate Valuation around the World: The Effects of Governance, Growth, and Openness." *Journal of Banking and Finance* 3 (2007), pp. 35–56.

Claessens, S., S. Djankov, and L. H. P. Lang. "The Separation of Ownership and Control in East Asian Corporations." *Journal of Financial Economics* 58 (2000), pp. 81–112.

Coase, Ronald. "The Nature of the Firm." *Economica* 4 (1937), pp. 386–405.

Dahya, Jay, John McConnell, and Nickolaos Travlos. "The Cadbury Committee, Corporate Performance, and Top Management Turnover." *Journal of Finance* 57 (2002), pp. 461–83.

Demsetz, H., and K. Lehn. "The Structure of Corporate Ownership: Causes and Consequences." *Journal of Political Economy* 93 (1985), pp. 1155–77.

Denis, D., and J. McConnell. "International Corporate Governance." Working Paper (2002).

Dimitrov, V., D. Palia, and L. Tang. "Impact of the Dodd-Frank Act on Credit Ratings." *Journal of Financial Economics* 115 (2015), pp. 505–20.

Doidge, C., A. Karolyi, and R. Stulz. "Why Are Foreign Firms Listed in the U.S. Worth More?" Working Paper, NBER (2002).

Dyck, A., and L. Zingales. "The Corporate Governance Role of the Media." Working Paper (2002).

Dyck, A., and L. Zingales. "Private Benefits of Control: An International Comparison." *Journal of Finance* 59 (2004), pp. 537–600.

Eun, C., and Victor Haung. "Asset Pricing in Chinese Domestic Stock Markets: Is There a Logic?" *Pacific-Basin Finance Journal* (2007), pp. 452–80.

Franks, J. R., and C. Mayer. "Ownership and Control of German Corporations." *Review of Financial Studies* 14 (2001), pp. 943–77.

Glaesser, E., and A. Shleifer. "Legal Origin." *Quarterly Journal of Economics* 117 (2002), pp. 1193–1229.

Gompers, Paul, Joy Ishii, and Andrew Metrick. "Corporate Governance and Equity Prices." *Quarterly Journal of Economics* 118 (2003), pp. 107–55.

Gorton, G., and F. A. Schmid. "Universal Banking and the Performance of German Firms." *Journal of Financial Economics* 58 (2000), pp. 28–80.

Holstrom, B., and S. N. Kaplan. "Corporate Governance and Merger Activity in the U.S.: Making Sense of the 1980s and 1990s." Working Paper, NBER (2001).

Jensen, M. "Eclipse of the Public Corporation." *Harvard Business Review* (1989), pp. 61–74.

Jensen, M., and W. Meckling. "Theory of the Firm: Managerial Behavior, Agency Cost, and Ownership Structure." *Journal of Financial Economics* 3 (1976), pp. 305–60.

Jensen, M., and K. Murphy. "Performance Pay and Top Management Incentives." *Journal of Political Economy* 98 (1990), pp. 225–63.

Johnson, S., P. Boon, A. Breach, and E. Friedman. "Corporate Governance in the Asian Financial Crisis." *Journal of Financial Economics* 58 (2000), pp. 141–86.

Johnson, S., R. La Porta, F. Lopez-de-Silanes, and A. Shleifer. "Tunneling." *American Economic Review* 90 (2000), pp. 22–27.

Kang, J., and A. Shivdasani. "Firm Performance, Corporate Governance, and Top Executive Turnover in Japan." *Journal of Financial Economics* 38 (1995), pp. 29–58.

Kang, Qiang, Qiao Liu, and Rong Qi. "The Sarbanes-Oxley Act and Corporate Investment: A Structural Assessment." *Journal of Financial Economics* 96 (2010), pp. 291–305.

King, R., and R. Levine. "Finance and Growth: Schumpeter Might Be Right." *Quarterly Journal of Economics* 108 (1993), pp. 717–38.

La Porta, R., F. Lopez-de-Silanes, A. Shleifer, and R. Vishny. "Legal Determinants of External Finance." *Journal of Finance* 52 (1997), pp. 1131–50.

———. "Law and Finance." *Journal of Political Economy* 106 (1998), pp. 1113–55.

———. "Corporate Ownership around the World." *Journal of Finance* 54 (1999), pp. 471–517.

———. "Investor Protection and Corporate Governance." *Journal of Financial Economics* 58 (2000), pp. 3–27.

———. "Investor Protection and Corporate Valuation." *Journal of Finance* 57 (2002), pp. 1147–69.

Lemmon, M. L., and K. V. Lins. "Ownership Structure, Corporate Governance, and Firm Value: Evidence from the East Asian Financial Crisis." Working Paper (2001).

Linck, J., J. Netter, and T. Yang. "The Effects and Unintended Consequences of the Sarbanes-Oxley Act on the Supply and Demand for Directors," *Review of Financial Studies* 22 (2009), pp. 3287–328.

Lobo, G. and J. Zhou. "Did Conservatism in Financial Reporting Increase after the Sarbanes-Oxley Act? Initial Evidence," *Accounting Horizons* 20 (2006), pp. 57–73.

Morck, R., A. Shleifer, and R. Vishny. "Management Ownership and Market Valuation: An Empirical Analysis." *Journal of Financial Economics* 20 (1988), pp. 293–315.

Nenova, T., "The Value of Corporate Votes and Control Benefits: A Cross-Country Analysis." Working Paper (2001).

Rajan, R., and L. Zingales. "Financial Dependence and Growth." *American Economic Review* 88 (1998), pp. 559–86.

Reese, W. A., Jr., and M. S. Weisbach. "Protection of Minority Shareholder Interests, Cross-listings in the United States, and Subsequent Equity Offerings." Working Paper, NBER (2001).

Schumpeter, J. *The Theory of Economic Development.* Translated by R. Opie. Cambridge, MA: Harvard University Press, 1934.

Shleifer, A., and R. Vishny. "A Survey of Corporate Governance." *Journal of Finance* 52 (1997), pp. 737–83.

Short, H., and K. Keasey. "Managerial Ownership and the Performance of Firms: Evidence from the UK." *Journal of Corporate Finance* 5 (1999), pp. 79–101.

Smith, Adam. *An Inquiry Into the Nature and Causes of the Wealth of Nations.* (1776).

Stulz, R., and R. Williamson. "Culture, Openness, and Finance." *Journal of Financial Economics* 10 (2003), pp. 313–49.

Zingales, L. "The Value of the Voting Right: A Study of the Milan Stock Exchange Experience." *Review of Financial Studies* 7 (1994), pp. 125–48.

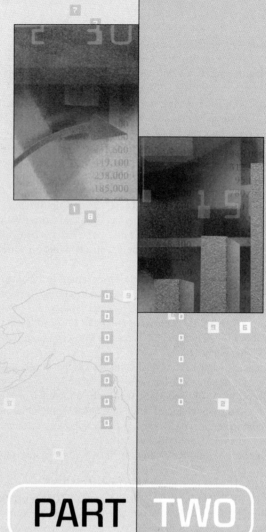

PART TWO

110

The Foreign Exchange Market, Exchange Rate Determination, and Currency Derivatives

PART TWO begins with a discussion of the organization of the market for foreign exchange. Both spot and forward transactions are studied. The next chapter examines exchange rate determination. The discussion focuses on how changes in the exchange rate between two countries' currencies depend on the relative difference between the nominal interest rates and inflation rates between the two countries. The final chapter of this section introduces currency derivative contracts useful for managing foreign currency exposure.

CHAPTER 5 provides an introduction to the organization and operation of the spot and forward foreign exchange market. This chapter describes institutional arrangements of the foreign exchange market and details of how foreign exchange is quoted and traded worldwide.

CHAPTER 6 presents the fundamental international parity relationships among exchange rates, interest rates, and inflation rates. An understanding of these parity relationships is essential for practicing financial management in a global setting.

CHAPTER 7 provides an extensive treatment of exchange-traded currency futures and options contracts. Basic valuation models are developed.

CHAPTER

5 The Market for Foreign Exchange

www.bis.org

This is the website of the Bank for International Settlements. Many interesting reports and statistics can be obtained here. The report titled *Triennial Central Bank Survey* can be downloaded for study.

MONEY REPRESENTS PURCHASING power. Possessing money from your country gives you the power to purchase goods and services produced (or assets held) by other residents of your country. However, to purchase goods and services produced by the residents of another country generally requires first purchasing the other country's currency. This is done by selling one's own currency for the currency of the country with whose residents you desire to transact. More formally, one's own currency has been used to buy *foreign exchange*, and in doing so the buyer has converted his purchasing power into the purchasing power of the seller's country.

The market for foreign exchange is the largest financial market in the world by virtually any standard. It is open somewhere in the world 365 days a year, 24 hours a day. The 2016 triennial central bank survey compiled by the Bank for International Settlements (BIS) places worldwide daily trading of spot and forward foreign exchange at $4.74 trillion. This is equivalent to more than $600 in daily transactions for every person on earth. This represents a 5 percent decrease from 2013 at current exchange rates. The decrease in turnover is largely attributed to exchange rate movements that influence comparison to previous surveys; at constant exchange rates, turnover increased slightly. London remains the world's largest foreign exchange trading center. According to the 2016 triennial survey, daily trading volume in the U.K. is estimated at $2.21 trillion, a 10 percent decrease from 2013. The U.S. daily turnover was $1.19 trillion, the same as in 2013. Exhibit 5.1 presents a pie chart showing the shares of global foreign exchange turnover.

Broadly defined, the **foreign exchange (FX) market** encompasses the conversion of purchasing power from one currency into another, bank deposits of foreign currency, the extension of credit denominated in a foreign currency, foreign trade financing, trading in foreign currency options and futures contracts, and currency swaps. Obviously, one chapter cannot adequately cover all these topics. Consequently, we confine the discussion in this chapter to the spot and forward market for foreign exchange. In Chapter 7, we examine currency futures and options contracts, and in Chapter 14, currency swaps are discussed.

This chapter begins with an overview of the function and structure of the foreign exchange market and the major market participants that trade currencies in this market. Following is a discussion of the spot market for foreign exchange. This section covers how to read spot market quotations, derives cross-rate quotations, and develops the concept of triangular arbitrage as a means of ensuring market efficiency. The chapter concludes with a discussion of the forward market for foreign exchange.

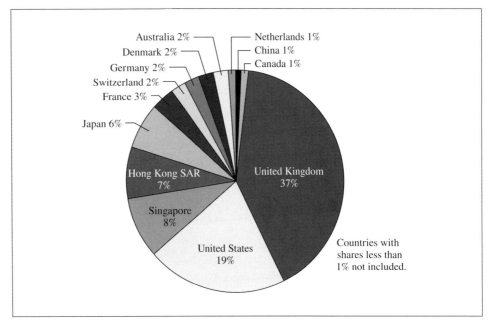

Note: Percent of total reporting foreign exchange turnover, adjusted for local inter-dealer double-counting.

Source: Tabulated from data in Table 6 in the *Triennial Central Bank Survey, Preliminary Results*. Bank for International Settlements, Basle, September 2016.

www.newyorkfed.org

This is the website of the Federal Reserve Bank of New York. The report titled *The Foreign Exchange and Interest Rate Derivatives Markets Survey: Turnover in the United States* can be downloaded for study.

Forward market quotations are presented, the purpose of the market is discussed, and the purpose of swap rate quotations is explained.

This chapter lays the foundation for much of the discussion throughout the remainder of the text. Without a solid understanding of how the foreign exchange market works, international finance cannot be studied in an intelligent manner. As authors, we urge you to read this chapter carefully and thoughtfully.

Function and Structure of the FX Market

The structure of the foreign exchange market is an outgrowth of one of the primary functions of a commercial banker: to assist clients in the conduct of international commerce. For example, a corporate client desiring to import merchandise from abroad would need a source of foreign exchange if the import was invoiced in the exporter's home currency. Alternatively, the exporter might need a way to dispose of foreign exchange if payment for the export was invoiced and received in the importer's home currency. Assisting in foreign exchange transactions of this type is one of the services that commercial banks provide for their clients, and one of the services that bank customers expect from their bank.

thomsonreuters.com

This website explains the various Thomson Reuters spot and forward FX electronic trading systems.

www.icap.com

This website explains ICAP's spot and forward FX electronic dealing systems.

The spot and forward foreign exchange markets are **over-the-counter (OTC) markets**; that is, trading does not take place in a central marketplace where buyers and sellers congregate. Rather, the foreign exchange market is a worldwide linkage of bank currency traders, nonbank dealers, and FX brokers, who assist in trades, connected to one another via a network of telephones, computer terminals, and automated dealing systems. Thomson Reuters and ICAP are the largest vendors of quote screen monitors used in trading currencies. The communications system of the foreign exchange market is second to none, including industry, government, the military, and national security and intelligence operations. The International Finance in Practice box "The Mouse Takes Over the Floor" describes the electronic nature of today's FX trading environment.

Twenty-four-hour-a-day currency trading follows the sun around the globe. Three major market segments can be identified: Australasia, Europe, and North America.

The Mouse Takes Over the Floor

When electronic trading first began to make a significant dent in the foreign exchange market, traders reportedly concerned about the loss of the human factor in dealing were heard to grumble that a computer wasn't going to buy them a beer.

Ten years ago a deal was still done when somebody yelled "done" into one of their telephones amid the background noise of other traders doing the same while voice broker prices were constantly being pumped out via a Tannoy system known as the squawkbox or the "hoot'n holler."

"It was bloody noisy and bloody good fun," reminisced one ex-dealer, who felt the advent of technology had robbed the market of much of its personality.

Today, that roar is more of a steady hum as traders face banks of screens and hold electronic conversations while the "hoot'n holler" is used to spread analyst assessments of the latest economic data. The old noise level has been transplanted to bars where, it seems, plenty of beers are still being bought.

Thomson Reuters' first screen-based trading system was launched in 1982 for the interbank market, where the majority of foreign exchange dealing takes place. The company launched a conversational dealing product in 1989 and an anonymous "matching" platform in 1992, but faced its first stiff competition only in 1993 with the launch of Electronic Broking Services (EBS), a platform owned by a number of the big banks and designed with the express purpose of preventing Thomson Reuters from gaining a monopoly position. [EBS was acquired by ICAP, a British-based interdealer, in 2006.] Now, both platforms still dominate the interbank market but face competition from the Internet, where a number of web-based portals are encouraging new participants to trade directly.

In simple volume terms the online platforms look like minnows. EBS reports average daily volumes worth about $100bn whereas the larger Internet platforms have average volumes between $15bn–$20bn. But Justyn Trenner of Client-Knowledge calculates the combined value of all online trading is now worth $100bn a day and highlights the rapid growth in the sector.

Platforms such as FXAll, Hotspot FXi and e-Speed are quick to dismiss suggestions of direct competition with the giants. Instead, they say they offer different parties, such as corporate treasurers or fund managers, the opportunity to participate directly and trade outside their usual banking relationships.

If electronic technology in the interbank market helped smaller banks access price transparency in the interbank market, the latest generation of Internet platforms is doing the same for those banks' clients.

"We're not going for the interbank market; we live in the space where banks face out to clients," says John Eley, chief executive of Hotspot foreign exchange, who says bank clients, who would previously call three or four dealers for quotes, can get the same range in seconds off a web-based platform, and then deal themselves.

"Multibank portals lower the barriers for third-party foreign exchange trades by cutting costs and reducing risk," adds Mark

www.Fxall.com

This is the website for the Internet FX trading platform discussed in the article "The Mouse Takes Over the Floor." It is a Thomson Reuters Company.

Australasia includes the trading centers of Sydney, Tokyo, Hong Kong, Singapore, and Bahrain; Europe includes Zurich, Frankfurt, Paris, Brussels, Amsterdam, and London; and North America includes New York, Montreal, Toronto, Chicago, San Francisco, and Los Angeles. Most trading rooms operate over a 9- to 12-hour working day, although some banks have experimented with operating three eight-hour shifts in order to trade around the clock. Especially active trading takes place when the trading hours of the Australasia centers and the European centers overlap and when the hours of the European and the North American centers overlap. More than half of the trading in the United States occurs between 8:00 A.M. and noon eastern standard time (1:00 P.M. and 5:00 P.M. Greenwich Mean Time [London]), when the European markets are still open. Certain trading centers have a more dominant effect on the market than others. For example, trading diminishes dramatically in the Australasian market segment when the Tokyo traders are taking their lunch break! Exhibit 5.2 provides a general indication of the participation level in the global FX market by showing average electronic conversations per hour. All conversations do not result in a completed trade.

FX Market Participants

The market for foreign exchange can be viewed as a two-tier market. One tier is the **wholesale** or **interbank market** and the other tier is the **retail** or **client market**. FX market participants can be categorized into five groups: international banks, bank customers, nonbank dealers, FX brokers, and central banks.

Warms, chief marketing officer at FXAll, who says the volumes traded by hedge funds have tripled on the platform.

Rick Sears, head of foreign exchange at the Chicago Mercantile Exchange, says volumes in its foreign exchange products had risen sharply since its electronic Globex platform allowed investors to trade its futures contracts 24 hours a day. Between 40 and 45 percent of CME's foreign exchange participants are commodity trading accounts (CTAs) and hedge funds.

"These groups are a lot more comfortable dealing electronically than before. They used to worry about execution risk but e-trading is increasingly popular," he says.

The considerable growth of online platforms, and the survival of a number of different models has surpassed most observers' expectations. Early predictions were that multibank portals such as FXAll, which offer prices from a wide range of banks, would surpass proprietary platforms owned by a single bank. Instead, both are growing rapidly. A recent survey by Greenwich Associates, the US consultancy group, listed both FXAll and UBS's proprietary platforms as leading online trading volumes.

There were also initial fears that the sudden surge in trading outlets could fragment liquidity, hampering trading, but this does not yet appeared to have happened. "Instead, it is more channels for the same market—a price on one platform or another is virtually the same," says Fabian Shey, global head of foreign exchange distribution at UBS.

Mr. Trenner suggested that overall, the shrinking of foreign exchange trading into a few global centers—Tokyo, London and New York—and banks' reorganization to follow suit had instead consolidated liquidity.

When EBS was first launched, dealers raised concerns about the demise of voice brokers' and dealers' market-making role,

warning that removing the obligation to quote two-way prices could weaken liquidity in times of crisis with dealers happy to take prices and less prepared to quote them.

But 11 years on, the market has not suffered a significant problem and very little evidence of prices lurching through "grapping"—when the new bid-offer spread does not overlap with the last price posted.

The relative smoothness of price moves is proof, says Jack Jeffery, chief executive of EBS, that the marketplace has evolved with the development of trading technologies.

"The market is so liquid with so many diverse views and flows that marketmaking has changed," he said. "It is now about participation. If you participate, you are contributing to liquidity, not just taking it out."

Some still fret, however, that the market's current dependence on technology leaves it at the mercy of computer servers.

Outages are extremely rare, however, and long-time participants are sanguine about the risks posed.

"Yes, there's a risk, but the market is very adaptable," says Nick Beecroft, head of foreign exchange trading at Standard Chartered.

"In the event of a serious IT meltdown, there are plenty of lines from broking houses to dealing floors and it would just be a question of pulling all the ex-spot brokers back on to the phones, from other products. FX is a highly resilient marketplace."

It seems fears about the loss of the human factor are as yet groundless.

EXHIBIT 5.2

Average Electronic FX Conversations per Hour (Monday–Friday, 2001)

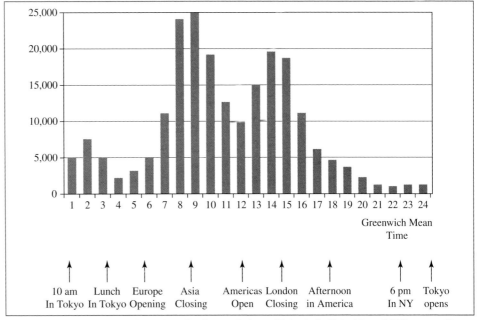

Greenwich Mean Time

10 am In Tokyo	Lunch In Tokyo	Europe Opening	Asia Closing	Americas Open	London Closing	Afternoon in America	6 pm In NY	Tokyo opens

Source: Federal Reserve Bank of New York, "The Foreign Exchange Market in the United States," 2001, www.ny.frb.org.

International banks provide the core of the FX market. Approximately 100 to 200 banks worldwide actively "make a market" in foreign exchange, that is, they stand willing to buy or sell foreign currency for their own account. These international banks serve their retail clients, the *bank customers*, in conducting foreign commerce or making international investment in financial assets that require foreign exchange. Bank customers broadly include MNCs, money managers, and private speculators. According to 2016 BIS statistics, retail or bank client transactions account for approximately 7 percent of FX trading volume. The other 93 percent of trading volume is from interbank trades between international banks or nonbank dealers. *Nonbank dealers* are large nonbank financial institutions such as investment banks, mutual funds, pension funds, and hedge funds, whose size and frequency of trades make it cost-effective to establish their own dealing rooms to trade directly in the interbank market for their foreign exchange needs. In 2016, nonbank dealers accounted for 50 percent of FX trading volume.

Part of the interbank trading among international banks involves adjusting the inventory positions they hold in various foreign currencies. However, most interbank trades are *speculative* or *arbitrage* transactions, where market participants attempt to correctly judge the future direction of price movements in one currency versus another or attempt to profit from temporary price discrepancies in currencies between competing dealers. Market psychology is a key ingredient in currency trading, and a dealer can often infer another's trading intention from the currency position being accumulated.

FX brokers match dealer orders to buy and sell currencies for a fee, but do not take a position themselves. Brokers have knowledge of the quotes offered by many dealers in the market. Today, however, only a few specialized broking firms still exist. The vast majority of interbank trades flows over Thomson Reuters and ICAP platforms. The International Finance in Practice box "Where Money Talks Very Loudly" explains how FX trading has changed over the past several years and how nonbank dealers using electronic trading platforms can compete with bank traders and other non-bank dealers.

One frequently sees or hears news media reports that the *central bank* (national monetary authority) of a particular country has intervened in the foreign exchange market in an attempt to influence the price of its currency against that of a major trading partner, or a country that it "fixes" or "pegs" its currency against. *Intervention* is the process of using foreign currency reserves to buy one's own currency in order to decrease its supply and thus increase its value in the foreign exchange market, or alternatively, selling one's own currency for foreign currency in order to increase its supply and lower its price. For example, intervention that successfully increases the value of one's currency against a trading partner may reduce exports and increase imports, thus alleviating persistent trade deficits of the trading partner. Central bank traders intervening in the currency market often lose bank reserves in attempting to accomplish their goal. There is little evidence that interventions conducted by a single central bank are successful; however, coordinated joint interventions involving several central banks have had more success.

See the following websites that are examples of online FX trading platforms as discussed in the International Finance in Practice box "Where Money Talks Very Loudly."

www.bgcpartners.com

www.currenex.com

www.forexster.com

Correspondent Banking Relationships

The interbank market is a network of **correspondent banking relationships**, with large commercial banks maintaining demand deposit accounts with one another, called correspondent banking accounts. The correspondent bank account network allows for the efficient functioning of the foreign exchange market, as Example 5.1 demonstrates.

EXAMPLE | 5.1: Correspondent Banking Relationship

As an example of how the network of correspondent bank accounts facilitates international foreign exchange transactions, consider U.S. Importer desiring to purchase merchandise from Dutch Exporter invoiced in euros, at a cost of €750,000. U.S. Importer will contact his U.S. Bank and inquire about the $/€ exchange rate. Say U.S. Bank offers a price of $1.3092/€1.00. If U.S. Importer accepts the price, U.S.

continued

EXAMPLE | 5.1: continued

Bank will debit U.S. Importer's demand deposit account $981,900 = €750,000 × 1.3092 for the purchase of the euros. U.S. Bank will instruct its correspondent bank in the euro zone, EZ Bank, to debit its correspondent bank account €750,000 and to credit that amount to Dutch Exporter's bank account. U.S. Bank will then credit its books $981,900, as an offset to the $981,900 debit to U.S. Importer's account, to reflect the decrease in its correspondent bank account balance with EZ Bank.

This rather contrived example assumes that U.S. Bank and Dutch Exporter both have bank accounts at EZ Bank. A more realistic interpretation is to assume that EZ Bank represents the entire euro zone banking system. Additionally, the example implies some type of communication system between U.S. Bank and EZ Bank. The *Society for Worldwide Interbank Financial Telecommunication (SWIFT)* allows international commercial banks to communicate instructions of the type in this example to one another. SWIFT is a private nonprofit message transfer system with headquarters in Brussels, with intercontinental switching centers in the Netherlands and Virginia. *The Clearing House (CHIPS)*, formerly known as the *Clearing House Interbank Payments System*, in cooperation with the U.S. Federal Reserve Bank System, called Fedwire, provides a clearinghouse for the interbank settlement for over 95 percent of U.S. dollar payments between international banks. CHIPS processes an average of $1.5 trillion of payments each day. Returning to our example, suppose U.S. Bank first needed to purchase euros in order to have them for transfer to Dutch Exporter. U.S. Bank can use CHIPS for settling the purchase of euros for dollars from, say, Swiss Bank, with structured invoice information via SWIFT to Swiss Bank to deposit the euros in its account with EZ Bank and to EZ Bank to transfer ownership to Dutch Exporter. The transfer between Swiss Bank and EZ Bank would in turn be accomplished through correspondent bank accounts or through CHIPS multilateral netting capability.

In August 1995, *Exchange Clearing House Limited (ECHO)*, the first global clearinghouse for settling interbank FX transactions, began operation. ECHO was a multilateral netting system that on each settlement date netted a client's payments and receipts in each currency, regardless of whether they are due to or from multiple counterparties. Multilateral netting eliminates the risk and inefficiency of individual settlement. In 1997, ECHO merged with CLS Services Limited and operates currently as part of CLS Group. Eighteen currencies are currently eligible for settlement among 60 members.

www.swift.com

www.theclearinghouse.org

www.cls-group.com

The Spot Market

The **spot market** involves almost the immediate purchase or sale of foreign exchange. Typically, cash settlement is made two business days (excluding holidays of either the buyer or the seller) after the transaction for trades between the U.S. dollar and a non–North American currency. For regular spot trades between the U.S. dollar and the Mexican peso or the Canadian dollar, settlement takes only one business day.[1] According to BIS statistics, spot foreign exchange trading accounted for 35 percent of FX trades in 2016. Exhibit 5.3 provides a detailed analysis of foreign exchange turnover by instrument and counterparty.

Spot Rate Quotations

Spot rate currency quotations can be stated in direct or indirect terms. To understand the difference, let's refer to Exhibit 5.4. The exhibit shows currency quotations by bank dealers from ICAP and other sources as of late afternoon eastern time on Monday, May 16, 2016. The first column provides **direct quotations** from the U.S.

---

[1]The banknote market for converting small amounts of foreign exchange, which travelers are familiar with, is different from the spot market.

Where Money Talks Very Loudly

Foreign exchange is the largest, most dynamic market in the world. About $4.74 trillion worth of currency is traded daily in a market that literally does not sleep. Centered in Tokyo, London and New York, traders deal smoothly across borders and time zones, often in multiples of $1bn, in transactions that take less than a second.

The market's development into its current form has left it virtually unrecognizable from 10 years ago.

Then, banks dealt currencies on behalf of their clients via traders holding multiple telephone conversations or perhaps using the relatively new electronic systems offered by Thomson Reuters and Electronic Broking Services (EBS). Today, clients can deal alongside banks on a number of platforms and the quiet hum of computers has done much to reduce the noise level on trading floors.

Old timers complain that a lot of the "personality" has been drained from trading by the rise of faceless systems. But the marketplace itself is, if anything, more vigorous now than then. Many banks and trading platforms are reporting stiff rises in recent volumes traded and, allowing for some growth in market share, most believe overall trading activity has risen as the transparency of the market, and access to it, has improved.

EBS recently said that half of its top 35 busiest trading days since the launch of the company 10 years ago had been in the first two months of 2004. Thomson Reuters said it saw growth of 35 percent year-on-year in 2003 in spot market transactions and that year-to-date, it estimated spot volumes to be 50 percent higher from a year ago.

"FX has come of age as an asset class over the last five years," says Nick Beecroft, head of foreign exchange trading at Standard Chartered. "There is much more activity, from active hedgers and from asset managers in other classes who tend to worry about FX much more than they did five, let alone 10 years ago."

Then, the market largely consisted of deals between banks and the technologies being introduced were designed to replicate that. Roughly 50 percent of foreign exchange deals were conducted by conversations between two counterparties and a further 35 percent were conducted through voice brokers, who "matched" bids and offers without either side knowing who the counterparty was.

Thomson Reuters had launched its first screen-based system in 1982, and in 1989 followed it up with a conversational platform designed to mimic dealers' telephone trades. In 1992 it went live with a matching system aimed at reproducing the role played by voice brokers. EBS's matching platform was launched in 1993 in a bid by banks to curb Thomson Reuters' development of a monopoly position. [EBS was acquired by ICAP in 2006.]

The advent of electronic broking for the interbank market gave smaller banks, which previously had little access to the best prices, the opportunity to deal alongside the bigger banks on an even basis because of the transparency afforded by electronic price provision.

Foreign Exchange Survey 2015

Overall		Nonfinancial Corporations		Banks	
Company	Market Share %	Company	Market Share %	Company	Market Share %
Citi	16.11	HSBC	8.94	Deutsche Bank	19.29
Deutsche Bank	14.54	Citi	8.80	Citi	16.99
Barclays	8.11	Deutsche Bank	7.67	Barclays	7.16
JPMorgan	7.65	JPMorgan	6.92	Bank of America Merrill Lynch	6.78
UBS	7.30	RBS	6.26		
Bank of America Merrill Lynch	6.22	Societé Générale	6.18	UBS	6.58
		Bank of America Merrill Lynch	6.10	HSBC	5.67
HSBC	5.40			JPMorgan	4.43
BNP Paribas	3.65	Barclays	5.41	RBS	4.13
Goldman Sachs	3.40	BNP Paribas	5.02	Standard Charted	3.69
RBS	3.38	ING Group	3.50	BNP Paribas	3.45

Source: *Euromoney*, May 2015.

Today, only a few specialist voice-broking firms still operate and the bulk of interbank business flows over Thomson Reuters and EBS's platforms.

Since then, however, there has been another seismic shift in the foreign exchange (FX) marketplace; the extension of price transparency to clients outside the banking world.

Through an array of web-based platforms fund managers and hedge funds, for example, can rapidly view a series of quotes for a particular currency pair, and conduct the deal themselves. On some platforms, the counterparty could as easily be another fund manager as a bank.

"The market has changed more in the last three years than the previous seven," says John Nelson, global head of FX markets at ABN Amro. "One stroke of a key will send a trade from the back office of one counterparty and settle in the back of the other almost instantly."

Rapid price dissemination has, to a great extent, now leveled the playing field and extended the reach of FX trading well beyond the core investment bank market.

"What differentiated banks from customers then was that banks could see the real market prices and customers couldn't. Fast-forward to now, and I can see real-time market prices streaming over my desktop," says Justyn Trenner, chief executive of ClientKnowledge, an independent research firm. "This greatly facilitates the more sophisticated fund managers in actively trading FX as an asset class." The near instant dissemination of news, data and price information has led to what market theorists call "efficiency"—an accurate price at any given time. But it has affected the way in which currency pairs move.

"You get more zigs and zags within a trend than you used to see because everybody reacts to every piece of news at the same time," says Chris Furness, senior currencies strategist at 4Cast economic consultancy, who likened today's behaviour to a school of fish that all change direction at the same time. The upshot of more dramatic intraday price movement, particularly over the past two years, is greater overall volatility.

"Having absorbed the uncertainties around the launch of the euro and despite a contraction in the number of traders, this is a very healthy time for the market," says Mark Robson, head of treasury and fixed income at Thomson Reuters.

But although there are new direct players as a result of new trading opportunities and as the price playing field has been leveled, many of the smaller banks have been relegated to the sidelines.

Once more they may specialise in their regional currency but they are more usually clients of the bigger banks because of the expense of the new wave of trading technology.

The few banks with the deepest pockets have developed and operate successful e-trading platforms of their own that add to the volumes they trade and their profits. In turn, they can afford to offer clients the tailormade products that are becoming the norm.

"The intense competition in this space means everyone is trying to distinguish themselves through customisation," says Joe Noviello, chief information officer at e-speed, Cantor Fitzgerald's online platform, which expanded to offer FX trading last year.

Leveraged Funds		E-Trading, Proprietary Platforms	
Company	Market Share %	Company	Market Share %
Citi	21.32	Deutsche Bank	17.50
JPMorgan	16.54	Citi	17.08
Barclays	12.58	Barclays	9.21
Deutsche Bank	10.76	UBS	8.70
UBS	7.44	JPMorgan	7.06
Bank of America Merrill Lynch	5.34	Bank of America Merrill Lynch	6.47
Goldman Sachs	4.65	HSBC	4.14
Standard Charted	3.00	Goldman Sachs	3.51
HSBC	2.96	RBS	3.42
Morgan Stanley	2.43	BNP Paribas	2.29

EXHIBIT 5.3

Average Daily Foreign Exchange Turnover by Instrument and Counterparty

Instrument/Counterparty	Turnover in USD (billion)	Percent
Spot	1,6	35
With reporting dealers	607	13
With other financial institutions	930	20
With nonfinancial customers	117	2
Outright Forwards	700	15
With reporting dealers	189	4
With other financial institutions	431	9
With nonfinancial customers	80	2
Foreign Exchange Swaps	2,3	50
With reporting dealers	1,209	26
With other financial institutions	1,027	22
With nonfinancial customers	147	3
Total	4,7	100

Note: Turnover is net of local and cross-border interdealer double-counting.

Source: Tabulated from data in Table 4 in the *Triennial Central Bank Survey, Preliminary Results*, Bank for International Settlements, Basle, September 2016.

perspective, that is, the price of one unit of the foreign currency in U.S. dollars. For example, the spot quote for one U.K. pound was 1.4402. (Forward quotations for one-, three-, and six-month contracts, which will be discussed in a following section, appear directly under the spot quotations for five currencies.) The second column provides **indirect quotations** from the U.S. perspective, that is, the price of one U.S. dollar in the foreign currency. For example, we see that the spot quote for one dollar in U.K. pound sterling was £0.6944. Obviously, the direct quotation from the U.S. perspective is an indirect quote from the British viewpoint, and the indirect quote from the U.S. perspective is a direct quote from the British viewpoint.

It is common practice among currency traders worldwide to both price and trade currencies against the U.S. dollar. For example, BIS statistics indicate that in 2016, 88 percent of currency trading in the world involved the dollar on one side of the transaction. Additionally, of all currency trading involved the euro on one side of the transaction, 21 percent involved the Japanese yen, 13 percent the British pound, 7 percent the Australian dollar, and 5 percent each the Swiss franc and the Canadian dollar. Exhibit 5.5 provides a detailed analysis of foreign exchange turnover by currency.

Most currencies in the interbank market are quoted in **European terms**, that is, the U.S. dollar is priced in terms of the foreign currency (an indirect quote from the U.S. perspective). By convention, however, it is standard practice to price certain currencies in terms of the U.S. dollar, or in what is referred to as **American terms** (a direct quote from the U.S. perspective). Prior to 1971, the British pound was a nondecimal currency; that is, a pound was not naturally divisible into 10 subcurrency units. Thus, it was cumbersome to price decimal currencies in terms of the pound. By necessity, the practice developed of pricing the British pound, as well as the Australian dollar and New Zealand dollar, in terms of decimal currencies, and this convention continues today. When the common euro currency was introduced, it was decided that it also would be quoted in American terms. To the uninitiated, this can be confusing, and it is something to bear in mind when examining currency quotations.

In this textbook, we will use the following notation for spot rate quotations. In general, $S(j/k)$ will refer to the price of one unit of currency k in terms of currency j. Thus, the American term quote from Exhibit 5.4 for the British (U.K.) pound on Monday, May 16 is $S(\$/\pounds) = 1.4402$. The corresponding European quote is $S(\pounds/\$) = .6944$.

EXHIBIT 5.4		Exchange Rates

Currencies   May 16, 2016

U.S.-dollar foreign-exchange rates in late New York trading

Country/currency	in US$	Per US$
	— Mon —	
Americas		
Argentina peso	.0708	14.134
Brazil real	.2856	3.5014
Canada dollar	.7755	1.2895
Chile peso	.001440	694.28
Colombia peso	.000330	3028.50
Ecuador US dollar	1	1
Mexico peso	.0546	18.306
Peru new sol	.3003	3.330
Uruguay peso	.03242	30.8450
Venezuela b. fuerte	.100125	9.9875
Asia-Pacific		
Australian dollar	.7289	1.3720
1-mos forward	.7280	1.3737
3-mos forward	.7264	1.3767
6-mos forward	.7242	1.3809
China yuan	.1534	6.5205
Hong Kong dollar	.1288	7.7637
India rupee	.01497	66.805
Indonesia rupiah	.0000751	13310
Japan yen	.009172	109.03
1-mos forward	.009179	108.94
3-mos forward	.009198	108.72
6-mos forward	.009230	108.34
Malaysia ringgit	.2483	4.0273
New Zealand dollar	.6759	1.4795
Pakistan rupee	.00956	104.60
Philippines peso	.0215	46.450
Singapore dollar	.7302	1.3695
South Korea won	.0008477	1179.66
Taiwan dollar	.03064	32.642

Country/currency	in US$	Per US$
	— Mon —	
Thailand baht	.02832	35.420
Vietnam dong	.00004500	22220
Europe		
Czech Rep. koruna	.04186	23.889
Denmark krone	.1520	6.5795
Euro area euro	1.1321	.8833
1-mos forward	1.1331	.8825
3-mos forward	1.1353	.8808
6-mos forward	1.1389	.8780
Hungary forint	.003593	278.30
Norway krone	.1224	8.1732
Poland zloty	.2570	3.8915
Russia ruble	.01527	65.482
Sweden krona	.1211	8.2610
Switzerland franc	1.0229	.9776
1-mos forward	1.0242	.9764
3-mos forward	1.0270	.9737
6-mos forward	1.0318	.9692
Turkey lira	.3371	2.9667
UK pound	1.4402	.6944
1-mos forward	1.4403	.6943
3-mos forward	1.4407	.6941
6-mos forward	1.4416	.6937
Middle East/Africa		
Bahrain dinar	2.6523	.3770
Egypt pound	.1133	8.8298
Israel shekel	.2617	3.8210
Jordan dinar	1.4097	.7094
Kuwait dinar	3.3141	.3017
Lebanon pound	.0006636	1507.00
Saudi Arabia riyal	.2666	3.7503
South Africa rand	.0650	15.3900
UAE dirham	.2723	3.6729

Sources: Compiled from Bloomberg data, May 16, 2016, and from using the OANDA online currency converter at www.oanda.com.

When the context is clear as to what terms the quotation is in, the less cumbersome S will be used to denote the spot rate.

It should be intuitive that the American and European term quotes are reciprocals of one another. That is,

$$S(\$/£) = \frac{1}{S(£/\$)} \qquad\qquad (5.1)$$

$$1.4401 = \frac{1}{.6944}$$

where the difference from 1.4402 is due to rounding.

EXHIBIT 5.5

Average Daily Foreign Exchange Turnover by Currency against All Other Currencies

Currency	Turnover Stated in USD (billions)	Percent
U.S. dollar	$4,152	88
Euro	1,505	32
Japanese yen	1,005	21
Pound sterling	609	13
Australian dollar	327	7
Canadian dollar	242	5
Swiss franc	237	5
Other currencies	1,397	29
Total—double-counted	$9,474	200
Total—not double-counted	$4,737	100

Note: Because there are two sides to each transaction, each currency is reported twice. Turnover is net of local and cross-border interdealer double-counting.

Source: Tabulated from data in Table 5 in the *Triennial Central Bank Survey, Preliminary Results*, Bank for International Settlements, Basle, September 2016.

Analogously,

$$S(£/\$) = \frac{1}{S(\$/£)}$$

$$.6943 = \frac{1}{1.4402} \tag{5.2}$$

where the difference from .6944 is due to rounding.

Cross-Exchange Rate Quotations

Let's ignore the transaction costs of trading temporarily while we develop the concept of a cross-rate. A **cross-exchange rate** is an exchange rate between a currency pair where neither currency is the U.S. dollar. The cross-exchange rate can be calculated from the U.S. dollar exchange rates for the two currencies, using either European or American term quotations. For example, the €/£ cross-rate can be calculated from American term quotations as follows:

$$S(€/£) = \frac{S(\$/£)}{S(\$/€)} \tag{5.3}$$

where from Exhibit 5.4,

$$S(€/£) = \frac{1.4402}{1.1321} = 1.2721$$

That is, if £1.00 costs $1.4402 and €1.00 costs $1.1321, the cost of £1.00 in euros is €1.2721. In European terms, the calculation is

$$S(€/£) = \frac{S(€/\$)}{S(£/\$)} \tag{5.4}$$

$$= \frac{.8833}{.6944}$$

$$= 1.2720$$

where the difference from 1.2721 is due to rounding.

Analogously,

$$S(£/€) = \frac{S(\$/€)}{S(\$/£)} \tag{5.5}$$

$$= \frac{1.1321}{1.4402}$$

$$= .7861$$

money.cnn.com/data/currencies

This subsite at the CNN, *Fortune,* and *Money* magazines website provides a currency converter. As an example, use the converter to calculate the current S(€/£) and S(£/€) cross-exchange rates.

EXHIBIT 5.6			Key Cross-Currency Rates								
	USD	EUR	JPY	GBP	CHF	CAD	AUD	NZD	HKD	NOK	SEK
Sweden	8.2619	9.3525	.07577	11.898	8.4503	6.4070	6.0221	5.6098	1.0642	1.0116	—
Norway	8.1675	9.2456	.07491	11.762	8.3538	6.3338	5.9533	5.5457	1.0520	—	.98857
Hong Kong	7.7638	8.7886	.07121	11.181	7.9409	6.0208	5.6590	5.2716	—	.95097	.93971
New Zealand	1.4728	1.6672	.01351	2.1209	1.5063	1.1421	1.0735	—	.18969	.18032	.17826
Australia	1.3719	1.5530	.01258	1.9757	1.4032	1.0639	—	.93154	.17671	.16797	.16606
Canada	1.2895	1.4597	.01183	1.8570	1.3189	—	.93992	.87557	.16609	.15788	.15608
Switzerland	.97770	1.1068	.00897	1.4080	—	.75820	.71265	.66386	12.593	11.971	11.834
UK	.69440	.78606	.00637	—	.71023	.53850	.50615	.47150	.08944	.08502	.08405
Japan	109.03	123.42	—	157.01	111.52	84.552	79.472	74.031	14.043	13.349	13.197
Euro	.88339	—	.00810	1.2722	.90354	.68506	.64390	.59982	.11378	.10816	.10692
U.S.	—	1.1320	.00917	1.4401	1.0228	.77549	.72890	.67900	.12880	.12244	.12104

Source: Composite 4 p.m. ET values on May 16, 2016, from Bloomberg.

and

$$S(\pounds/\text{\euro}) = \frac{S(\pounds/\$)}{S(\text{\euro}/\$)} \tag{5.6}$$

$$= \frac{.6944}{.8833}$$

$$= .7861$$

Equations 5.3 to 5.6 imply that given N currencies, one can calculate a triangular matrix of the $N \times (N-1)/2$ cross-exchange rates. Available on Bloomberg are 55 cross-exchange rates for all pair combinations of eleven key currencies that are stated as $S(j/k)$ and $S(k/j)$. Exhibit 5.6 presents an example of the table for Monday, May 16, 2016.

Alternative Expressions for the Cross-Exchange Rate

For some purposes, it is easier to think of cross-exchange rates calculated as the product of an American term and a European term exchange rate rather than as the quotient of two American term or two European term exchange rates. For example, substituting $S(\text{\euro}/\$)$ for $1/S(\$/\text{\euro})$ allows Equation 5.3 to be rewritten as:

$$S(\text{\euro}/\pounds) = S(\$/\pounds) \times S(\text{\euro}/\$) \tag{5.7}$$

$$= 1.4402 \times .8833$$

$$= 1.2721$$

In general terms,

$$S(j/k) = S(\$/k) \times S(j/\$) \tag{5.8}$$

and taking reciprocals of both sides of Equation 5.8 yields

$$S(k/j) = S(k/\$) \times S(\$/j) \tag{5.9}$$

Note the $ signs cancel one another out in both Equations 5.8 and 5.9.

The Bid-Ask Spread

Up to this point in our discussion, we have ignored the bid-ask spread in FX transactions. Interbank FX traders buy currency for inventory at the **bid price** and sell from inventory at the higher **offer** or **ask price**. Consider the Reuters quotations from Exhibit 5.4. What are they, bid or ask? Most likely they are mid-rates, that is, the average of the bid and ask rates. For ease of discussion, however, and without loss of generality, we will assume that the "per US $" quotations are buying, or bid quotes, and the "in US $" quotations are selling, or ask quotes. Thus the European term quotations are interbank bid prices and the American term quotations are interbank ask prices.

To be more specific about the £/$ quote we have been using as an example, we can specify that it is a bid quote by writing $S^b(£/\$) = .6944$, meaning the bank dealer will bid, or pay, £.6944 for one U.S. dollar. However, if the bank dealer is buying dollars for British pounds, it must be selling British pounds for U.S. dollars. This implies that the $/£ quote we have been using as an example is an ask quote, which we can designate as $S^a(\$/£) = 1.4402$. That is, the bank dealer will sell one British pound for $1.4402.

Returning to the reciprocal relationship between European and American term quotations, the recognition of the bid-ask spread implies:

$$S^a(\$/£) = \frac{1}{S^b(£/\$)} \qquad (5.10)$$

In American terms, the bank dealer is asking $1.4402 for one British pound; that means the bank dealer is willing to pay, or bid, less. Interbank bid-ask spreads are quite small. Let's assume the bid price is $0.0005 less than the ask; thus $S^b(\$/£) = 1.4397$. Similarly, the bank dealer will want an ask price in European terms greater than its bid price.

The reciprocal relationship between European and American term quotes implies:

$$S^a(£/\$) = \frac{1}{S^b(\$/£)} \qquad (5.11)$$
$$= \frac{1}{1.4397}$$
$$= .6946$$

Thus, the bank dealer's ask price of £0.6946 per U.S. dollar is indeed greater than its bid price of £0.6944.

The following table summarizes the reciprocal relationship between American and European bid and ask quotations.

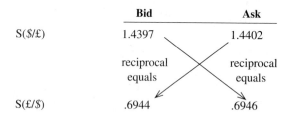

	Bid	**Ask**
S($/£)	1.4397	1.4402
	reciprocal equals	reciprocal equals
S(£/$)	.6944	.6946

Note that in each row the quotations refer to buying or selling one unit of the denominator currency, in the first row £s and in the second row $s.

Spot FX Trading

Examination of Exhibit 5.4 indicates that for most currencies, quotations are carried out to four decimal places in both American and European terms. However, for some currencies (e.g., the Colombian peso, Indian rupee, Indonesian rupiah) quotations in European terms are carried out to zero or only two or three decimal places, but in American terms the quotations may be carried out to as many as seven decimal places (see, for example, the South Korean won).

In the interbank market, the standard-size trade among large banks in the major currencies is for the U.S.-dollar equivalent of $10,000,000, or "ten dollars" in trader jargon. Dealers quote both the bid and the ask, willing to either buy or sell up to $10,000,000 at the quoted prices. Spot quotations are good for only a few seconds. If a trader cannot immediately make up his mind whether to buy or sell at the proffered prices, the quotes are likely to be withdrawn.

In conversation, interbank FX traders use a shorthand abbreviation in expressing spot currency quotations. Consider the $/£ bid-ask quotes from above, $1.4397–$1.4402. The "1.43" is known as the bid quote *big figure*, and it is assumed to be known by all traders. The second two digits to the right of the decimal place are referred to as the *small figure*. Similarly, the "1.44" is the ask *big figure*. Assuming spot bid-ask spreads for the British pound sterling are around 5 "points," it is unambiguous for a trader to respond with "97 to 02" when asked what is his quote for British pound sterling.

The establishment of the bid-ask spread will facilitate acquiring or disposing of inventory. Suppose most $/£ dealers are trading at $1.4397–$1.4402. A trader believing the pound will soon appreciate substantially against the dollar will desire to acquire a larger inventory of British pounds. A quote of "98–03" will encourage some traders to sell at the higher-than-market bid price, but also dissuade other traders from purchasing at the higher offer price. Analogously, a quote of "96–01" will allow a dealer to lower his pound inventory if he thinks the pound is ready to depreciate.

The retail bid-ask spread is wider than the interbank spread; that is, lower bid and higher ask prices apply to the smaller sums traded at the retail level. This is necessary to cover the fixed costs of a transaction that exist regardless of which tier the trade is made in.

Interbank trading rooms are typically organized with individual traders dealing in a particular currency. The dealing rooms of large banks are set up with traders dealing against the U.S. dollar in all the major currencies: the Japanese yen, euro, Canadian dollar, Swiss franc, and British pound, plus the local currency if it is not one of the majors. Individual banks may also specialize by making a market in regional currencies or in the currencies of less-developed countries, again all versus the U.S. dollar. Additionally, banks will usually have a cross-rate desk where trades between two currencies not involving the U.S. dollar are handled. It is not uncommon for a trader for an active currency pair to make as many as 1,500 quotes and 400 trades in a day.[2] In smaller European banks accustomed to more regional trading, dealers will frequently quote and trade versus the euro.

The Cross-Rate Trading Desk

Earlier in the chapter, it was mentioned that most interbank trading goes through the dollar. Suppose a bank customer wants to trade out of British pounds into Swiss francs. In dealer jargon, a nondollar trade such as this is referred to as a **currency against currency** trade. The bank will frequently (or effectively) handle this trade for its customer by selling British pounds for U.S. dollars and then selling U.S. dollars for Swiss francs. At first blush, this might seem ridiculous. Why not just sell the British pounds directly for Swiss francs? To answer this question, let's return to Exhibit 5.6 of the cross-exchange rates. Suppose a bank's home currency was one of the 11 currencies in the exhibit and that it made markets in the other 10 currencies. The bank's trading room would typically be organized with 10 trading desks, each for trading one of the nondollar currencies against the U.S. dollar. A dealer needs to be concerned only with making a market in his nondollar currency against the dollar. However, if each of the 11 currencies was traded directly with the others, the dealing room would need to accommodate 55 trading desks. Or worse, individual traders would be responsible for making a market in several currency pairs, say, the €/$, €/£, and €/SF, instead of just the €/$. As Grabbe (1996) notes, this would entail an informational complexity that would be virtually impossible to handle.

Banks handle currency against currency trades, such as for the bank customer who wants to trade out of British pounds into Swiss francs, at the cross-rate desk. Recall from Equation 5.8 that a $S(SF/£)$ quote can be obtained from the product of $S(\$/£)$ and $S(SF/\$)$. Recognizing transaction costs implies the following restatement of Equation 5.8:

$$S^b(SF/£) = S^b(\$/£) \times S^b(SF/\$) \tag{5.12}$$

The bank will quote its customer a buying (bid) price for the British pounds in terms of Swiss francs determined by multiplying its American term bid price for British pounds and its European term bid price (for U.S. dollars) stated in Swiss francs.

---

[2]These numbers were obtained during a discussion with the manager of the spot trading desk at the New York branch of UBS.

EXAMPLE | 5.2: Calculating the Cross-Exchange Rate Bid-Ask Spread.

Let's assume (as we did earlier) that the $/£ bid-ask prices are $1.4397–$1.4402 and the £/$ bid-ask prices are £0.6944–£0.6946. Let's also assume the $/€ bid-ask prices are $1.1316–$1.1321 and the €/$ bid-ask prices are €0.8833–€0.8837. These bid and ask prices and Equation 5.12 imply that $S^b(\text{€/£}) = 1.4397 \times .8833 = 1.2717$. The reciprocal of $S^b(\text{€/£})$ implies that $S^a(\text{£/€}) = .7863$. Analogously, Equation 5.13 suggests that $S^a(\text{€/£}) = 1.4402 \times .8837 = 1.2727$, and its reciprocal implies that $S^b(\text{£/€}) = .7857$. That is, the €/£ bid-ask prices are €1.12717–€1.2727 and the £/€ bid-ask prices are £0.7857–£0.7863. Note that the cross-rate bid-ask spreads are much larger than the American or European bid-ask spreads. For example, the €/£ bid-ask spread is €0.0010 versus a €/$ spread of €0.0004. The £/€ bid-ask spread is £0.0006 versus the $/€ spread of $0.0005, which is a sizable difference since a British pound is priced at more than 1.4 dollars. The implication is that cross-exchange rates *implicitly* incorporate the bid-ask spreads of the two transactions that are necessary for trading out of one nondollar currency and into another. Hence, even when a bank makes a direct market in one nondollar currency versus another, the trade is *effectively* going through the dollar because the "currency against currency" exchange rate is consistent with a cross-exchange rate calculated from the dollar exchange rates of the two currencies. Exhibit 5.7 provides a more detailed presentation of cross-rate foreign exchange transactions.

Taking reciprocals of Equation 5.12 yields

$$S^a(\text{£/}SF) = S^a(\text{£/\$}) \times S^a(\$/SF) \tag{5.13}$$

which is analogous to Equation 5.9. In terms of our example, Equation 5.13 says the bank could alternatively quote its customer an offer (ask) price for Swiss francs in terms of British pounds determined by multiplying its European term ask price (for U.S. dollars) stated in British pounds by its American term ask price for Swiss francs.

EXHIBIT 5.7

Cross-Rate Foreign Exchange Transactions

Bank Quotations	American Terms Bid	American Terms Ask	European Terms Bid	European Terms Ask
British pounds	1.4397	1.4402	.6944	.6946
Euros	1.1316	1.1321	.8833	.8837

a. Bank Customer wants to sell £1,000,000 for euros. The Bank will sell U.S. dollars (buy British pounds) for $1.4397. The sale yields Bank Customer:
£1,000,000 × 1.4397 = $1,439,700.
The Bank will buy dollars (sell euros) for €0.8833. The sale of dollars yields Bank Customer:
$1,439,700 × €0.8833 = €1,271,687.
Bank Customer has effectively sold British pounds at a €/£ bid price of €1,271,687/£1,000,000 = €1.2717/£1.00.

b. Bank Customer wants to sell €1,000,000 for British pounds. The Bank will sell U.S. dollars (buy euros) for €0.8837. The sale yields Bank Customer:
€1,000,000 ÷ .8837 = $1,131,606.
The Bank will buy dollars (sell British pounds) for $1.4402. The sale of dollars yields Bank Customer:
$1,131,606 ÷ 1.4402 = £785,728.
Bank Customer has effectively bought British pounds at a €/£ ask price of €1,000,000/£785,728 = €1.2727/£1.00.

From parts (a) and (b), we see the currency against currency bid-ask spread for British pounds is €1.2717 – €1.2727.

Triangular Arbitrage

Certain banks specialize in making a direct market between nondollar currencies, pricing at a narrower bid-ask spread than the cross-rate spread. Nevertheless, the implied cross-rate bid-ask quotations impose a discipline on the nondollar market makers. If their direct quotes are not consistent with cross-exchange rates, a triangular arbitrage profit is possible.[3] **Triangular arbitrage** is the process of trading out of the U.S. dollar into a second currency, then trading it for a third currency, which is in turn traded for U.S. dollars. The purpose is to earn an arbitrage profit via trading from the second to the third currency when the direct exchange rate between the two is not in alignment with the cross-exchange rate.

EXAMPLE | 5.3: Taking Advantage of a Triangular Arbitrage Opportunity

To illustrate a triangular arbitrage, assume the cross-rate trader at Deutsche Bank notices that Crédit Lyonnais is buying dollars at $S^b(€/\$) = .8833$ the same as Deutsche Bank's bid price. Similarly, he observes that Barclays is buying British pounds at $S^b(\$/£) = 1.4397$, also the same as Deutsche Bank. He next finds that Crédit Agricole is making a direct market between the euro and the pound, with a current ask price of $S^a(€/£) = 1.2712$. Cross-rate Equation 5.12 implies that the €/£ bid price should be no lower than $S^b(€/£) = 1.4397 \times .8833 = 1.2717$. Yet Crédit Agricole is offering to *sell* British pounds at a rate of only 1.2712!

A triangular arbitrage profit is available if the Deutsche Bank traders are quick enough. A sale of $5,000,000 to Crédit Lyonnais for euros will yield €4,416,500 = $5,000,000 × .8833. The €4,416,500 will be resold to Crédit Agricole for £3,474,276 = €4,416,500/1.2712. Likewise, the British pounds will be resold to Barclays for $5,001,915= £3,474,276 × 1.4397, yielding an arbitrage profit of $1,915. Exhibit 5.8 presents a diagram and a summary of this triangular arbitrage example.

Obviously, Crédit Agricole must raise its asking price above €1.2712/£1.00. The cross-exchange rates (from Exhibit 5.7) gave €/£ bid-ask prices of €1.2717 – €1.2727. These prices imply that Crédit Agricole can deal inside the spread and sell for less than €1.2727, but not less than €1.2717. An ask price of €1.2720, for example, would eliminate profit to the arbitrageur. At that price, the €4,416,500 would be resold for £3,474,091 = €4,416,500/1.2720, which in turn would yield only $4,998,769 = £3,472,091 × 1.4397 or a *loss* of $1,231. In today's "high-tech" FX market, many FX trading rooms around the world have developed in-house software that receives a digital feed of real-time FX prices from the ICAP Spot electronic broking system to explore for triangular arbitrage opportunities. Just a few years ago, prior to the development of computerized dealing systems, the FX market was considered too efficient to yield triangular arbitrage profits!

Spot Foreign Exchange Market Microstructure

Market microstructure refers to the basic mechanics of how a marketplace operates. Five empirical studies on FX market microstructure shed light on the operation of the spot FX marketplace. Huang and Masulis (1999) studied spot FX rates on DM/$ trades over the period from October 1, 1992 to September 29, 1993. They found that bid-ask spreads in the spot FX market increased with FX exchange rate volatility and decreased with dealer competition. These results are consistent with models of market microstructure. They also found that the bid-ask spread decreased when the percentage of large dealers in the marketplace increased. They concluded that dealer competition is a fundamental determinant of the spot FX bid-ask spread.

Lyons (1998) tracked the trading activity of a DM/$ trader at a large New York bank over a period of five trading days. The dealer he tracked was extremely profitable over the study period, averaging profits of $100,000 per day on volume of $1 billion.

---

[3]An arbitrage is a zero-risk, zero-investment strategy from which a profit is guaranteed.

EXHIBIT 5.8

**Triangular Arbitrage
Example**

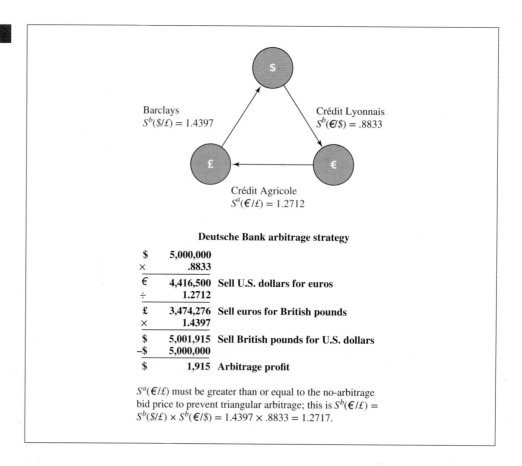

Deutsche Bank arbitrage strategy

$	5,000,000	
×	.8833	
€	4,416,500	Sell U.S. dollars for euros
÷	1.2712	
£	3,474,276	Sell euros for British pounds
×	1.4397	
$	5,001,915	Sell British pounds for U.S. dollars
−$	5,000,000	
$	1,915	Arbitrage profit

$S^a(€/£)$ must be greater than or equal to the no-arbitrage
bid price to prevent triangular arbitrage; this is $S^b(€/£) =$
$S^b(\$/£) \times S^b(€/\$) = 1.4397 \times .8833 = 1.2717.$

Lyons was able to disentangle total trades into those that were speculative and those
that were non-speculative, or where the dealer acted as a financial intermediary for a
retail client. He determined that the dealer's profits came primarily from the dealer's
role as an intermediary. This makes sense, since speculative trading is a zero-sum
game among all speculators, and in the long run it is unlikely that any one trader has a
unique advantage. Interestingly, Lyons found that the half-life of the dealer's position
in nonspeculative trades was only 10 minutes! That is, the dealer typically traded or
swapped out of a nonspeculative position within 20 minutes.

Ito, Lyons, and Melvin (1998) studied the role of private information in the spot FX
market. They examined ¥/$ and DM/$ between September 29, 1994, and March 28, 1995.
Their study provides evidence against the common view that private information is irrelevant, since all market participants are assumed to possess the same set of public information. Their evidence came from the Tokyo foreign exchange market, which prior to
December 21, 1994, closed for lunch between noon and 1:30 P.M. After December 21,
1994, the variance in spot exchange rates increased during the lunch period relative to
the period of closed trading. This was true for both ¥/$ and DM/$ trades, but more so for
the ¥/$ data, which is to be expected since ¥/$ trading is more intensive in the Tokyo FX
market. Ito, Lyons, and Melvin attributed these results to a greater revelation of private
information in trades being allocated to the lunch hour. This suggests that private information is, indeed, an important determinant of spot exchange rates.

Cheung and Chinn (2001) conducted a survey of U.S. foreign exchange traders
and received 142 usable questionnaires. The purpose of their survey was to elicit
information about several aspects of exchange rate dynamics not typically observ-
able in trading data. In particular they were interested in traders' perceptions about
news events—innovations in macroeconomic variables—that cause movements in
exchange rates. The traders they surveyed responded that the bulk of the adjustment to

economic announcements regarding unemployment, trade deficits, inflation, GDP, and the Federal funds rate takes place within one minute. In fact, "about one-third of the respondents claim that full price adjustment takes place in less than 10 seconds"! They also found that central bank intervention does not appear to have a substantial impact on exchange rates, but intervention does increase market volatility. Dominguez (1998) confirmed this latter finding.

The Forward Market

In conjunction with spot trading, there is also a forward foreign exchange market. The **forward market** involves contracting today for the future purchase or sale of foreign exchange. The forward price may be the same as the spot price, but usually it is higher (at a premium) or lower (at a discount) than the spot price. Forward exchange rates are quoted on most major currencies for a variety of maturities. Bank quotes for maturities of 1, 3, 6, 9, and 12 months are readily available. Quotations on nonstandard, or broken-term, maturities are also available. Maturities extending beyond one year are becoming more frequent, and for good bank customers, a maturity extending out to 5, 10, and even as long as 30 years, is possible.

Forward Rate Quotations

To learn how to read forward exchange rate quotations, let's examine Exhibit 5.4. Notice that **forward rate** quotations appear directly under the spot rate quotations for five major currencies (the British pound, Australian dollar, Japanese yen, Swiss franc, and euro) for one-, three-, and six-month maturities. As an example, the settlement date of a three-month forward transaction is three calendar months from the spot settlement date for the currency. That is, if today is Monday, May 16, 2016, and spot settlement is May 18, then the forward settlement date would be August 18, 2016, a period of 92 days from May 18.

In this textbook, we will use the following notation for forward rate quotations. In general, $F_N(j/k)$ will refer to the price of one unit of currency k in terms of currency j for delivery in N months. N equaling 1 denotes a one-month maturity based on a 360-day banker's year. Thus, N equaling 3 denotes a three-month maturity. When the context is clear, the simpler notation F will be used to denote a forward exchange rate.

Forward quotes are either direct or indirect, one being the reciprocal of the other. From the U.S. perspective, a direct forward quote is in American terms. As an example, let's consider the American term Swiss franc forward quotations in relationship to the spot rate quotation for Monday, May 16, 2016. We see that:

$$S(\$/SF) = 1.0229$$
$$F_1(\$/SF) = 1.0242$$
$$F_3(\$/SF) = 1.0270$$
$$F_6(\$/SF) = 1.0318$$

From these quotations, we can see that in American terms the Swiss franc is trading at a *premium* to the dollar, and that the premium increases out to six months, the further the forward maturity date is from May 16. As we will more formally learn in the next chapter, under certain conditions the forward exchange rate is an unbiased predictor of the expected spot exchange rate N months into the future.[4] Thus, according to the forward rate, when the Swiss franc is trading at a premium to the dollar in American terms, we can say the market expects the dollar to **depreciate**, or become less valuable, relative to the Swiss franc. Consequently, it costs more dollars to buy a Swiss franc forward.

---

[4]The forward exchange rate is an unbiased predictor of the expected spot exchange rate under an assumption of risk-neutrality.

European term forward quotations are the reciprocal of the American term quotes. In European terms, the corresponding Swiss franc forward quotes to those stated above are:

$$S(SF/\$) = .9776$$
$$F_1(SF/\$) = .9764$$
$$F_3(SF/\$) = .9737$$
$$F_6(SF/\$) = .9692$$

From these quotations, we can see that in European terms the dollar is trading at a *discount* to the Swiss franc and that the discount increases out to six months, the further the forward maturity date is from May 16. Thus, according to the forward rate, when the dollar is trading at a discount to the Swiss franc in European terms, we can say the market expects the Swiss franc to **appreciate**, or become more valuable, relative to the dollar. Consequently, it costs fewer Swiss francs to buy a dollar forward. This is exactly what we should expect, since the European term quotes are the reciprocals of the corresponding American term quotations.

Long and Short Forward Positions

One can buy (take a long position) or sell (take a short position) foreign exchange forward. Bank customers can contract with their international bank to buy or sell a specific sum of freely traded FX for delivery on a certain date. Likewise, interbank traders can establish a long or short position by dealing with a trader from a competing bank. Exhibit 5.9 graphs both the long and short positions for the three-month Swiss franc contract, using the American quote for May 16, 2016, from Exhibit 5.4. The graph measures profits or losses on the vertical axis. The horizontal axis shows the spot price of foreign exchange on the maturity date of the forward contract, $S_3(\$/SF)$. If one uses the forward contract, he has "locked in" the forward price for forward purchase or sale of foreign exchange. Regardless of what the spot price is on the maturity date of the forward contract, the trader buys (if he is long) or sells (if he is short) at $F_3(\$/SF) = 1.0270$ per unit of FX. Forward contracts can also be used for speculative purposes, as Example 5.4 demonstrates.

Non-Deliverable Forward Contracts

Because of government-instituted capital controls, the currencies of some emerging market countries are not freely traded and thus it is not possible to obtain these currencies offshore in the spot market to settle a forward position. For many of these currencies (such as the Chinese yuan and Russian ruble), trading in *non-deliverable forward* (*NDF*) contracts exists. A non-deliverable forward contract is settled in cash, usually U.S. dollars, at the difference between the spot exchange on the maturity date of the contract and the NDF rate times the notional amount of the contract. For example, a long position in a NDF contract on CNY12,000,000 with a forward price of $F(\$/CNY) = .1653$ would be settled by the long receiving $6,000 = (.1658 - .1653) \times$ CNY12,000,000 from the short if the spot rate at the maturity date of the NDF contract is $S(\$/CNY) = .1658$. This cash settlement is in lieu of the long receiving CNY12,000,000, with a spot dollar value of $1,989,600 = (CNY12,000,000 \times \$0.1658)$, for payment of the forward price $1,983,600 = (CNY12,000,000 \times \$0.1653)$, a $6,000 difference in sums.

Forward Cross-Exchange Rates

Forward cross-exchange rate quotations are calculated in an analogous manner to spot cross-rates, so it is not necessary to provide detailed examples. In generic terms,

$$F_N(j/k) = \frac{F_N(\$/k)}{F_N(\$/j)} \tag{5.14}$$

or

$$F_N(j/k) = \frac{F_N(j/\$)}{F_N(k/\$)} \tag{5.15}$$

and

$$F_N(k/j) = \frac{F_N(\$/j)}{F_N(\$/k)} \tag{5.16}$$

or

$$F_N(k/j) = \frac{F_N(k/\$)}{F_N(j/\$)} \qquad (5.17)$$

For example, using the forward quotations in Exhibit 5.4, the three-month AD/SF cross-exchange forward rate using American term quotes (Equation 5.14) is:

$$F_3(AD/SF) = \frac{F_3(\$/SF)}{F_3(\$/AD)} = \frac{1.0270}{.7264} = 1.4138$$

and using European term quotes (Equation 5.15) is:

$$F_3(AD/SF) = \frac{F_3(AD/\$)}{F_3(SF/\$)} = \frac{1.3767}{.9737} = 1.4139.$$

where the difference from 1.4138 is due to rounding.

EXAMPLE | 5.4: A Speculative Forward Position

It is May 16, 2016. Suppose the $/SF trader has just heard an economic forecast from the bank's head economist that causes him to believe that the dollar will likely appreciate in value against the Swiss franc over the next three months. If he decides to act on this information, the trader will short the three-month $/SF contract. We will assume that he sells SF5,000,000 forward against dollars. Suppose the forecast has proven correct, and on August 16, 2016, spot $/SF is trading at $1.0200. The trader can buy Swiss franc spot at $1.0200 and deliver it under the forward contract at a price of $1.0270. The trader has made a speculative profit of ($1.0270 − $1.0200) = $0.0070 per unit, as Exhibit 5.9 shows. The total profit from the trade is $35,000 = (SF5,000,000 × $0.0070). If the dollar depreciated and S_3 was $1.0300, the speculator would have lost ($1.0270 − $1.0300) = −$0.0030 per unit, for a total loss of −$15,000 = (SF5,000,000)(−$0.0030).

EXHIBIT 5.9

Graph of Long and Short Position in the Three-Month Swiss Franc Contract

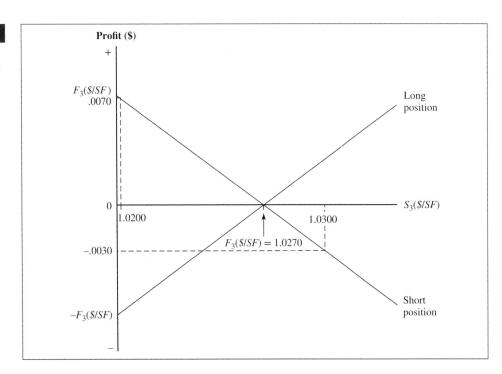

Forward Premium

It is common to express the premium or discount of a forward rate as an annualized percentage deviation from the spot rate. The forward premium (or discount) is useful for comparing against the interest rate differential between two countries, as we will see more clearly in Chapter 6 on international parity relationships. The **forward premium** or **discount** can be calculated using American or European term quotations, as Example 5.5 demonstrates.

> **EXAMPLE | 5.5:** Calculating the Forward Premium/Discount
> The formula for calculating the forward premium or discount for currency j in American terms is:
>
> $$f_{N,j} = \frac{F_N(\$/j) - S(\$/j)}{S(\$/j)} \times 360/days \qquad (5.18)$$
>
> When the context is clear, the forward premium will simply be stated as f.
> As an example of calculating the forward premium, let's use the May 16 quotes from Exhibit 5.4 to calculate the three-month forward premium or discount for the Japanese yen versus the U.S. dollar. The calculation is:
>
> $$f_{3,¥} = \frac{.009198 - .009172}{.009172} \times \frac{360}{92} = .0111$$
>
> We see that the three-month forward premium is .0111, or 1.11 percent. In words, we say that the Japanese yen is trading at a 1.11 percent premium versus the U.S. dollar for delivery in 92 days.
>
> In European terms the forward premium or discount for the U.S. dollar is calculated as:
>
> $$f_{N,\$} = \frac{F_N(j/\$) - S(j/\$)}{S(j/\$)} \times 360/days \qquad (5.19)$$
>
> Using the May 16 three-month European term quotations for the Japanese yen from Exhibit 5.4 yields:
>
> $$f_{3,\$} = \frac{108.72 - 109.03}{109.03} \times \frac{360}{92} = -.0111$$
>
> We see that the three-month forward discount is −.0111, or −1.11 percent. In words, we say that the U.S. dollar is trading versus the Japanese yen at a 1.11 percent discount for delivery in 92 days.

Swap Transactions

Forward swap trades can be classified as outright or swap transactions. In conducting their trading, bank dealers do take speculative positions in the currencies they trade, but more often traders offset the currency exposure inherent in a trade. From the bank's standpoint, an **outright forward transaction** is an uncovered speculative position in a currency, even though it might be part of a currency hedge to the bank customer on the other side of the transaction. **Swap transactions** provide a means for the bank to mitigate the currency exposure in a forward trade. A forward swap transaction is the simultaneous sale (or purchase) of spot foreign exchange against a forward purchase (or sale) of approximately an equal amount of the foreign currency.

Interbank forward swap transactions account for approximately 50 percent of FX trading, whereas outright forward trades are 15 percent. (See Exhibit 5.3.) Both forward swaps and outright forward transactions are exempt from new over-the-counter regulation as "swaps" under the Dodd-Frank Act. Because swap transactions are the more common type of interbank forward trades, bank dealers in conversation among themselves use a shorthand notation to quote bid and ask forward prices in terms of *forward points* that are either added to or subtracted from the spot bid and ask quotations, as Example 5.6 demonstrates.

EXAMPLE | 5.6: Forward Point Quotations

Assume the Swiss franc/U.S. dollar (*SF*/$) bid-ask rates are SF0.9776–SF0.9779. With reference to these rates, forward prices might be displayed as:

Spot	.9776–.9779
One-Month	12–10
Three-Month	39–35
Six-Month	84–78

When the second number in a forward point "pair" is smaller than the first, the dealer "knows" the forward points are subtracted from the spot bid and ask prices to obtain the outright forward rates. For example, the spot bid price of SF0.9776 minus .0012 (or 12 points) equals SF0.9764, the one-month forward bid price. The spot ask price of SF0.9779 minus .0010 (or 10 points) equals SF0.9769, the one-month ask price. Analogously, the three-month outright forward bid-ask rates are SF0.9737–SF0.9744 and the six-month outright forward bid-ask rates are SF0.9692–SF0.9701.[5] The following table summarizes the calculations.

Spot		.9776–.9779
	Forward Point Quotations	Outright Forward Quotations
One-Month	12–10	.9764–.9769
Three-Month	39–35	.9737–.9744
Six-Month	84–78	.9692–.9701

Three things are notable about the outright prices. First, the dollar is trading at a forward discount to the Swiss franc. Second, all bid prices are less than the corresponding ask prices, as they must be for a trader to be willing to make a market. Third, the bid-ask spread increases in time to maturity, as is typical. These three conditions prevail only *because* the forward points were subtracted from the spot prices. As a check, note that in points the spot bid-ask spread is 3 points, the one-month forward bid-ask spread is 5 points, the three-month spread is 7 points, and the six-month spread is 9 points.

If the forward prices were trading at a premium to the spot price, the second number in a forward point pair would be larger than the first, and the trader would know to add the points to the spot bid and ask prices to obtain the outright forward bid and ask rates. For example, if the three-month and six-month swap points were 5–9 and 13–19, the corresponding three-month and six-month bid-ask rates would be SF0.9781–SF0.9788 and SF0.9789–SF0.9798. In points, the three- and six-month bid-ask spreads would be 7 and 9, that is, increasing in term to maturity.

Exhibit 5.10 presents spot and forward point quotations for the euro on May 16, 2016. Forward point quotations are for maturities of one week to 30 years. Note that for each pair the ask number of points is larger than the bid; therefore, they are to be added to the spot quotes. The two-year forward points are 351.61 (bid) and 357.61 (ask). Given that the spot quotes are 1.1330 – 1.1332, the two-year outright forward quotes are 1.168161 – 1.168961.

Quoting forward rates in terms of forward points is convenient for two reasons. First, forward points may remain constant for long periods of time, even if the spot rates fluctuate frequently. Second, in swap transactions where the trader is attempting to minimize currency exposure, the actual spot and outright forward rates are often of no consequence. What is important is the premium or discount differential, measured in forward points. To illustrate, suppose a bank customer wants to sell dollars three months forward against

---

[5]If the one-month forward points quotation were, say, 12–12, further elaboration from the market maker would be needed to determine if the forward points would be added to or subtracted from the spot prices. An electronic dealing system would state forward points as −12−−12 if they were to be subtracted.

	Bid	Ask
Spot	1.1330	1.1332
30Term	Forward	Points
1W FWD	2.20	2.30
2W FWD	4.49	4.59
3W FWD	6.63	6.99
1M FWD	10.60	10.85
2M FWD	21.25	21.47
3M FWD	31.74	32.54
4M FWD	43.02	43.78
5M FWD	56.25	56.50
6M FWD	67.97	69.02
7M FWD	80.63	81.73
8M FWD	96.66	98.31
9M FWD	111.80	113.30
10M FWD	123.63	125.88
11M FWD	139.38	141.18
1Y FWD	153.70	155.70
2Y FWD	351.61	357.61
5Y FWD	1054.50	1074.50
10Y FWD	2030.00	2075.00
15Y FWD	2745.00	2845.00
20Y FWD	3531.00	3681.00
30Y FWD	5259.40	5277.40

Source: www.investing.com, May 16, 2016.

Swiss francs. The bank can handle this trade for its customer and simultaneously neutralize the exchange rate risk in the trade by selling (borrowed) dollars spot against Swiss francs. The bank will lend francs for three months until they are needed to deliver against the dollars it has purchased forward. The dollars received will be used to liquidate the dollar loan. Implicit in this transaction is the interest rate differential between the dollar borrowing rate and the Swiss franc lending rate. The interest rate differential is captured by the forward premium or discount measured in forward points. As a rule, when the interest rate of the quoted (indirect) currency is less than the interest rate of the quoting (direct) currency, the outright forward rate is greater than the spot exchange rate, and vice versa. This will become clear in Chapter 6 on international parity relationships, where in American terms it is shown that the forward premium $(F - S)/S \approx i_\$ - i_f$, the difference between the U.S. dollar and foreign currency interest rates.

As in the spot market, the bid-ask spread in the forward retail market is wider than the interbank spread. In addition to the bid-ask spread, banks will typically require their retail clients to maintain a compensating balance to cover the cost of the bank's advisory services in assisting with forward foreign exchange transactions and for other bank services.

Problems encountered in the OTC derivatives (generically referred to as "swaps") markets that became highlighted during the global financial crisis have resulted in new regulation designed to increase trading stability in financial markets. This regulation includes the creation of a central counterparty for guaranteeing both sides of a trade. On November 16, 2012, however, the Secretary of the U.S. Treasury Department exempted foreign exchange swaps and foreign exchange forward contracts from regulation as "swaps" under the Commodity Exchange Act (CEA), as amended by the Dodd-Frank Act. The Secretary was clearly concerned about the implications of subjecting a market as large as the forward market to the CEA's centralized clearing and trading requirements, which would require massive capital backing much greater than for any other type of derivatives market.

Exchange-Traded Currency Funds

An **exchange-traded fund (ETF)** is a portfolio of financial assets in which shares representing fractional ownership of the fund trade on an organized exchange. In recent years, ETFs have been created representing investment in a number of stock market indices. Like mutual funds, ETFs allow small investors the opportunity to invest in portfolios of financial assets that they would find difficult to construct individually. In 2005, a firm associated with Guggenheim Investments first offered an ETF on the euro common currency named the CurrencyShares Euro Trust. The fund is designed for both institutional and retail investors who desire to take a position in a financial asset that will track the performance of the euro with respect to the U.S. dollar. Upon obtaining dollars from investors, the trust purchases euros that are held in two deposit accounts, one of which earns interest. Guggenheim issues baskets of 50,000 shares for trading, with each share representing 100 euros. Individual shares are denominated in the U.S. dollar and trade on the New York Stock Exchange. The net asset value (NAV) of one share at any point in time will reflect the spot dollar value of 100 euros plus accumulated interest minus expenses. Guggenheim has since created eight additional currency trusts on the Australian dollar, British pound sterling, Canadian dollar, Chinese yuan, Japanese yen, Singapore dollar, Swedish krona, and the Swiss franc. The total NAV of all nine currency trusts stood at over $1 billion in May 2016. Currency is now recognized as a distinct asset class, like stocks and bonds. Guggenheim currency trusts facilitate investing in these nine currencies.

SUMMARY

This chapter presents an introduction to the market for foreign exchange. Broadly defined, the foreign exchange market encompasses the conversion of purchasing power from one currency into another, bank deposits of foreign currency, the extension of credit denominated in a foreign currency, foreign trade financing, and trading in foreign currency options and futures contracts. This chapter limits the discussion to the spot and forward markets for foreign exchange. The other topics are covered in later chapters.

1. The FX market is the largest and most active financial market in the world. It is open somewhere in the world 24 hours a day, 365 days a year. In 2016, average daily trading in spot and forward foreign exchange was $4.74 trillion.

2. The FX market is divided into two tiers: the retail or client market and the wholesale or interbank market. The retail market is where international banks service their customers who need foreign exchange to conduct international commerce or trade in international financial assets. The great majority of FX trading takes place in the interbank market among international banks that are adjusting inventory positions or conducting speculative and arbitrage trades.

3. The FX market participants include international banks, bank customers, nonbank FX dealers, FX brokers, and central banks.

4. In the spot market for FX, nearly immediate purchase and sale of currencies take place. In the chapter, notation for defining a spot rate quotation was developed. Additionally, the concept of a cross-exchange rate was developed. It was determined that nondollar currency transactions must satisfy the bid-ask spread determined from the cross-rate formula or a triangular arbitrage opportunity exists.

5. In the forward market, buyers and sellers can transact today at the forward price for the future purchase and sale of foreign exchange. Notation for forward exchange

rate quotations was developed. The use of forward points as a shorthand method for expressing forward quotes from spot rate quotations was presented. Additionally, the concept of a forward premium was developed.

6. Exchange-traded currency funds were discussed as a means for both institutional and retail traders to easily take positions in nine key currencies.

KEY WORDS

American terms, *120*
appreciate, *130*
ask price, *123*
bid price, *123*
client market, *114*
correspondent banking
  relationships, *116*
cross-exchange rate, *122*
currency against
  currency, *125*
depreciate, *129*
direct quotation, *117*

European terms, *120*
exchange-traded fund
  (ETF), *135*
foreign exchange (FX)
  market, *112*
forward market, *129*
forward premium/
  discount, *132*
forward rate, *129*
indirect quotation, *120*
interbank market, *114*
offer price, *123*

outright forward
  transaction, *132*
over-the-counter (OTC)
  market, *113*
retail market, *114*
spot market, *117*
spot rate, *117*
swap transactions, *132*
triangular arbitrage, *127*
wholesale market, *114*

QUESTIONS

1. Give a full definition of the market for foreign exchange.
2. What is the difference between the retail or client market and the wholesale or interbank market for foreign exchange?
3. Who are the market participants in the foreign exchange market?
4. How are foreign exchange transactions between international banks settled?
5. What is meant by a currency trading at a discount or at a premium in the forward market?
6. Why does most interbank currency trading worldwide involve the U.S. dollar?
7. Banks find it necessary to accommodate their clients' needs to buy or sell FX forward, in many instances for hedging purposes. How can the bank eliminate the currency exposure it has created for itself by accommodating a client's forward transaction?
8. A CAD/$ bank trader is currently quoting a *small figure* bid-ask of 35–40, when the rest of the market is trading at CAD1.3436–CAD1.3441. What is implied about the trader's beliefs by his prices?
9. What is triangular arbitrage? What is a condition that will give rise to a triangular arbitrage opportunity?
10. Over the past five years, the exchange rate between the British pound and the U.S. dollar, $/£, has changed from about 1.90 to about 1.45. Would you agree that over this five-year period, British goods have become cheaper for buyers in the United States?

PROBLEMS

1. Using the American term quotes from Exhibit 5.4, calculate a cross-rate matrix for the euro, Swiss franc, Japanese yen, and British pound so that the resulting triangular matrix is similar to the portion above the diagonal in Exhibit 5.6.
2. Using the American term quotes from Exhibit 5.4, calculate the one-, three-, and six-month forward cross-exchange rates between the Australian dollar and the Swiss franc. State the forward cross-rates in "Australian" terms.

3. A foreign exchange trader with a U.S. bank took a short position of £5,000,000 when the $/£ exchange rate was 1.55. Subsequently, the exchange rate has changed to 1.61. Is this movement in the exchange rate good from the point of view of the position taken by the trader? By how much has the bank's liability changed because of the change in exchange rate?

4. Restate the following one-, three-, and six-month outright forward European term bid-ask quotes in forward points.

Spot	1.3431–1.3436
One-Month	1.3432–1.3442
Three-Month	1.3448–1.3463
Six-Month	1.3488–1.3508

5. Using the spot and outright forward quotes in problem 4, determine the corresponding bid-ask spreads in points.

6. Using Exhibit 5.4, calculate the one-, three-, and six-month forward premium or discount for the Japanese yen versus the U.S. dollar using American term quotations. For simplicity, assume each month has 30 days. What is the interpretation of your results?

7. Using Exhibit 5.4, calculate the one-, three-, and six-month forward premium or discount for the U.S. dollar versus the British pound using European term quotations. For simplicity, assume each month has 30 days. What is the interpretation of your results?

8. A bank is quoting the following exchange rates against the dollar for the Swiss franc and the Australian dollar:

SFr/$ = 1.5960–70

A$/$ = 1.7225–35

An Australian firm asks the bank for an A$/SFr quote. What cross-rate would the bank quote?

9. Given the following information, what are the NZD/SGD currency against currency bid-ask quotations?

| | American Terms | | European Terms | |
Bank Quotations	Bid	Ask	Bid	Ask
New Zealand dollar	.7265	.7272	1.3751	1.3765
Singapore dollar	.6135	.6140	1.6287	1.6300

10. Doug Bernard specializes in cross-rate arbitrage. He notices the following quotes:

Swiss franc/dollar = SFr1.5971/$

Australian dollar/U.S. dollar = A$1.8215/$

Australian dollar/Swiss franc = A$1.1440/SFr

Ignoring transaction costs, does Doug Bernard have an arbitrage opportunity based on these quotes? If there is an arbitrage opportunity, what steps would he take to make an arbitrage profit, and how much would he profit if he has $1,000,000 available for this purpose?

11. Assume you are a trader with Deutsche Bank. From the quote screen on your computer terminal, you notice that Dresdner Bank is quoting €0.7627/$1.00 and Credit Suisse is offering SF1.1806/$1.00. You learn that UBS is making a direct market

between the Swiss franc and the euro, with a current €/SF quote of .6395. Show how you can make a triangular arbitrage profit by trading at these prices. (Ignore bid-ask spreads for this problem.) Assume you have $5,000,000 with which to conduct the arbitrage. What happens if you initially sell dollars for Swiss francs? What €/SF price will eliminate triangular arbitrage?

12. The current spot exchange rate is $1.95/£ and the three-month forward rate is $1.90/£. On the basis of your analysis of the exchange rate, you are pretty confident that the spot exchange rate will be $1.92/£ in three months. Assume that you would like to buy or sell £1,000,000.

a. What actions do you need to take to speculate in the forward market? What is the expected dollar profit from speculation?

b. What would be your speculative profit in dollar terms if the spot exchange rate actually turns out to be $1.86/£?

13. Omni Advisors, an international pension fund manager, plans to sell equities denominated in Swiss francs (CHF) and purchase an equivalent amount of equities denominated in South African rands (ZAR).

Omni will realize net proceeds of 3 million CHF at the end of 30 days and wants to eliminate the risk that the ZAR will appreciate relative to the CHF during this 30-day period. The following exhibit shows current exchange rates between the ZAR, CHF, and the U.S. dollar (USD).

Currency Exchange Rates

| | ZAR/USD | | CHF/USD | |
Maturity	Bid	Ask	Bid	Ask
Spot	6.2681	6.2789	1.5282	1.5343
30-day	6.2538	6.2641	1.5226	1.5285
90-day	6.2104	6.2200	1.5058	1.5115

a. Describe the currency transaction that Omni should undertake to eliminate currency risk over the 30-day period.

b. Calculate the following:
- The CHF/ZAR cross-currency rate Omni would use in valuing the Swiss equity portfolio.
- The current value of Omni's Swiss equity portfolio in ZAR.
- The annualized forward premium or discount at which the ZAR is trading versus the CHF.

1. A currency trader makes a market in a currency and attempts to generate speculative profits from dealing against other currency traders. Today electronic dealing systems are frequently used by currency traders. The most widely used spot trading system is offered by ICAP. Go to their website, www.icap.com to learn more about what they do, what markets they are in, and what products they offer.

2. In addition to the historic currency symbols, such as, $, ¥, £, and €, there is an official three-letter symbol for each currency that is recognized worldwide. These symbols can be found at the Full Universal Currency Converter website: www.xe.com/currencyconverter. Go to this site. What is the currency symbol for the Costa Ricon colon? The Guyanese dollar?

MINI CASE

Shrewsbury Herbal Products, Ltd.

Shrewsbury Herbal Products, located in central England close to the Welsh border, is an old-line producer of herbal teas, seasonings, and medicines. Its products are marketed all over the United Kingdom and in many parts of continental Europe as well.

Shrewsbury Herbal generally invoices in British pound sterling when it sells to foreign customers in order to guard against adverse exchange rate changes. Nevertheless, it has just received an order from a large wholesaler in central France for £320,000 of its products, conditional upon delivery being made in three months' time and the order invoiced in euros.

Shrewsbury's controller, Elton Peters, is concerned with whether the pound will appreciate versus the euro over the next three months, thus eliminating all or most of the profit when the euro receivable is paid. He thinks this an unlikely possibility, but he decides to contact the firm's banker for suggestions about hedging the exchange rate exposure.

Mr. Peters learns from the banker that the current spot exchange rate in €/£ is €1.4537; thus the invoice amount should be €465,184. Mr. Peters also learns that the three-month forward rates for the pound and the euro versus the U.S. dollar are $1.8990/£1.00 and $1.3154/€1.00, respectively. The banker offers to set up a forward hedge for selling the euro receivable for pound sterling based on the €/£ forward cross-exchange rate implicit in the forward rates against the dollar.

What would you do if you were Mr. Peters?

REFERENCES & SUGGESTED READINGS

Bank for International Settlements. *Triennial Central Bank Survey, 2010, Preliminary Results.* Basle, Switzerland: Bank for International Settlements, September 2010.

Cheung, Yin-Wong, and Menzie David Chinn. "Currency Traders and Exchange Rate Dynamics: A Survey of the US Market." *Journal of International Money and Finance* 20 (2001), pp. 439–71.

Dominguez, Kathryn M. "Central Bank Intervention and Exchange Rate Volatility." *Journal of International Money and Finance* 17 (1998), pp. 161–90.

Federal Reserve Bank of New York. *The Foreign Exchange and Interest Rate Derivatives Markets: Turnover in the United States.* New York: Federal Reserve Bank of New York, April 2007.

Grabbe, J. Orlin. *International Financial Markets,* 3rd ed. Upper Saddle River, N.J.: Prentice Hall, 1996.

Huang, Roger D., and Ronald W. Masulis. "FX Spreads and Dealer Competition across the 24-Hour Trading Day." *Review of Financial Studies* 12 (1999) pp. 61–93.

International Monetary Fund. *International Capital Markets: Part I. Exchange Rate Management and International Capital Flows.* Washington, D.C.: International Monetary Fund, 1993.

Ito, Takatoshi, Richard K. Lyons, and Michael T. Melvin. "Is There Private Information in the FX Market? The Tokyo Experiment." *Journal of Finance* 53 (1998), pp. 1111–30.

Lyons, Richard K. "Profits and Position Control: A Week of FX Dealing." *Journal of International Money and Finance* 17 (1998), pp. 97–115.

UBS Investment Bank. *Foreign Exchange and Money Market Transactions.* This book can be found and downloaded at www.ibb.ubs.com/Individuals/files/brochure/booken.pdf.

6 International Parity Relationships and Forecasting Foreign Exchange Rates

FOR COMPANIES AND investors alike, it is important to have a firm understanding of the forces driving exchange rate changes as these changes would affect investment and financing opportunities. To that end, this chapter examines several key international parity relationships, such as interest rate parity and purchasing power parity, that have profound implications for international financial management. Some of these are, in fact, manifestations of the *law of one price* that must hold in *arbitrage equilibrium.*[1] An understanding of these parity relationships provides insights into (i) how foreign exchange rates are determined, and (ii) how to forecast foreign exchange rates.

Because **arbitrage** plays a critical role in the ensuing discussion, we may as well define it upfront. The term *arbitrage* can be defined as *the act of simultaneously buying and selling the same or equivalent assets or commodities for the purpose of making certain, guaranteed profits.* As long as there are profitable arbitrage opportunities, the market cannot be in equilibrium. The market can be said to be in equilibrium when no profitable arbitrage opportunities exist. Such well-known parity relationships as interest rate parity and purchasing power parity, in fact, represent arbitrage equilibrium conditions. Let us begin our discussion with interest rate parity.

Interest Rate Parity

Interest rate parity (IRP) is an arbitrage condition that must hold when international financial markets are in equilibrium. Suppose that you have $1 to invest over, say, a one-year period. Consider two alternative ways of investing your fund: (i) invest domestically at the U.S. interest rate, or, alternatively, (ii) invest in a foreign country, say, the U.K., at the foreign interest rate and hedge the exchange risk by selling the maturity value of the foreign investment forward. It is assumed here that you want to consider only default-free investments.

If you invest $1 domestically at the U.S. interest rate ($i_\$$), the maturity value will be

$$\$1(1 + i_\$)$$

Because you are assumed to invest in a default-free instrument like a U.S. Treasury note, there is no uncertainty about the future maturity value of your investment in dollar terms.

---

[1]The law of one price prevails when the same or equivalent things are trading at the same price across different locations or markets, precluding profitable arbitrage opportunities. As we will see, many equilibrium pricing relationships in finance are obtained from imposing the law of one price, that is, the two things that are equal to each other must be selling for the same price.

To invest in the U.K., on the other hand, you carry out the following sequence of transactions:

1. Exchange $1 for a pound amount, that is, £$(1/S)$, at the prevailing spot exchange rate (S).[2]
2. Invest the pound amount at the U.K. interest rate $(i_£)$, with the maturity value of £$(1/S)(1 + i_£)$.
3. Sell the maturity value of the U.K. investment forward in exchange for a *predetermined dollar amount*, that is, $[(1/S)(1 + i_£)]F$, where F denotes the forward exchange rate.

Note that the exchange rate, S or F, represents the dollar price of one unit of foreign currency, that is, British pound in the above example. When your British investment matures in one year, you will receive the full maturity value, £$(1/S)(1 + i_£)$. But since you have to deliver exactly the same amount of pounds to the counterparty of the forward contract, your net pound position is reduced to zero. In other words, the exchange risk is completely hedged. Because, as with the U.S. investment, you are assured of receiving a predetermined dollar amount, your U.K. investment coupled with forward hedging is a perfect substitute for the domestic U.S. investment. Because you've hedged the exchange risk by a forward contract, you've effectively *redenominated* the U.K. investment in dollar terms. The "effective" dollar interest rate from the U.K. investment alternative is given by

$$\frac{F}{S}(1 + i_£) - 1$$

Arbitrage equilibrium then would dictate that the future dollar proceeds (or, equivalently, the dollar interest rates) from investing in the two equivalent investments must be the same, implying that

$$(1 + i_\$) = \frac{F}{S}(1 + i_£), \text{ or alternatively}$$

$$F = S\left[\frac{1 + i_\$}{1 + i_£}\right] \tag{6.1}$$

which is a formal statement of IRP. It should be clear from the way we arrived at Equation 6.1 that IRP is a manifestation of the **law of one price (LOP)** applied to international money market instruments. The IRP relationship has been known among currency traders since the late 19th century. But it was only during the 1920s that the relationship became widely known to the public from the writings of John M. Keynes and other economists.[3]

Alternatively, IRP can be derived by constructing an **arbitrage portfolio**, which involves (i) no net investment, as well as (ii) no risk, and then requiring that such a portfolio should not generate any net cash flow in equilibrium. Consider an arbitrage portfolio consisting of three separate positions:

1. Borrowing $\$S$ in the United States, which is just enough to buy £1 at the prevailing spot exchange rate (S).
2. Lending £1 in the U.K. at the U.K. interest rate.
3. Selling the maturity value of the U.K. investment forward.

Exhibit 6.1 summarizes the present and future (maturity date) cash flows, CF_0 and CF_1, from investing in the arbitrage portfolio.

Two things are noteworthy in Exhibit 6.1. First, the net cash flow at the time of investment is zero. This, of course, implies that the arbitrage portfolio is indeed fully

---

[2]For notational simplicity, we delete the currency subscripts for the exchange rate notations, S and F. If the exchange rate, S or F, is expressed as the amount of foreign currency per dollar, the IRP formula will become as follows: $(1 + i_\$) = (S/F)(1 + i_£)$.

[3]A systematic exposition of the interest rate parity is generally attributed to Keynes's *Monetary Reform* (1924).

Transactions	CF_0	CF_1
1. Borrow in the U.S.	$\$S$	$-S(1 + i_\$)$
2. Lend in the U.K.	$-\$S$	$S_1(1 + i_£)$
3. Sell the £ receivable forward*	0	$(1 + i_£)(F - S_1)$
Net cash flow	0	$(1 + i_£)F - (1 + i_\$)S$

*Selling the £ receivable "forward" will not result in any cash flow at the present time, that is, $CF_0 = 0$. But at the maturity, the seller will receive $\$(F - S_1)$ for each pound sold forward. S_1 denotes the future spot exchange rate.

self-financing; it doesn't cost any money to hold this portfolio. Second, the net cash flow on the maturity date is known with certainty. That is so because none of the variables involved in the net cash flow, that is, S, F, $i_\$$, and $i_£$, is uncertain. Because no one should be able to make certain profits by holding this arbitrage portfolio, market equilibrium requires that the net cash flow on the maturity date be zero for this portfolio:

$$(1 + i_£)F - (1 + i_\$)S = 0 \tag{6.2}$$

which, upon simple rearrangement, is the same result as Equation 6.1.

The IRP relationship is sometimes approximated as follows:

$$(i_\$ - i_£) = \left[\frac{F - S}{S}\right](1 + i_£) \cong \left[\frac{F - S}{S}\right] \tag{6.3}$$

As can be seen clearly from Equation 6.1, IRP provides a linkage between interest rates in two different countries. Specifically, the interest rate will be higher in the United States than in the U.K. when the dollar is at a forward discount, that is, $F > S$. Recall that the exchange rates, S and F, represent the dollar prices of one unit of foreign currency. When the dollar is at a forward discount, this implies that the dollar is expected to depreciate against the pound. If so, the U.S. interest rate should be higher than the U.K. interest rate to compensate for the expected depreciation of the dollar. Otherwise, nobody would hold dollar-denominated securities. On the other hand, the U.S. interest rate will be lower than the U.K. interest rate when the dollar is at a forward premium, that is, $F < S$. Equation 6.1 indicates that the forward exchange rate will deviate from the spot rate as long as the interest rates of the two countries are not the same.[4]

When IRP holds, you will be indifferent between investing your money in the United States and investing in the U.K. with forward hedging. However, if IRP is violated, you will prefer one to another. You will be better off by investing in the United States (U.K.) if $(1 + i_\$)$ is greater (less) than $(F/S)(1 + i_£)$. When you need to borrow, on the other hand, you will choose to borrow where the dollar interest is lower. When IRP doesn't hold, the situation also gives rise to **covered interest arbitrage** opportunities.

Covered Interest Arbitrage

To understand the covered interest arbitrage (CIA) process, it is best to work with a numerical example.

EXAMPLE | 6.1: Suppose that the annual interest rate is 5 percent in the United States and 8 percent in the U.K., and that the spot exchange rate is $\$1.80/£$ and the forward exchange rate, with one-year maturity, is $\$1.78/£$. In terms of our notation, $i_\$ = 5\%$, $i_£ = 8\%$, $S = \$1.80$, and $F = \$1.78$. Assume that the arbitrager can borrow up to $\$1,000,000$ or £555,556, which is equivalent to $\$1,000,000$ at the current spot exchange rate.

Let us first check if IRP is holding under current market conditions. Substituting the given data, we find,

$$\left[\frac{F}{S}\right](1 + i_£) = \left[\frac{1.78}{1.80}\right](1.08) = 1.068$$

continued

---

[4]To determine if an arbitrage opportunity exists, one should use the exact version of IRP, not the approximate version.

EXAMPLE | 6.1: continued

which is not exactly equal to $(1 + i_\$) = 1.05$. Specifically, we find that the current market condition is characterized by

$$(1 + i_\$) < \left[\frac{F}{S}\right](1 + i_\pounds). \tag{6.4}$$

Clearly, IRP is not holding, implying that a profitable arbitrage opportunity exists. Because the interest rate is lower in the United States than in the U.K. after adjusting for the exchange rates (F/S), an arbitrage transaction should involve borrowing in the United States and lending in the U.K.

The arbitrager can carry out the following transactions:

1. In the United States, borrow $1,000,000. Repayment in one year will be $1,050,000 = $1,000,000 × 1.05.
2. Buy £555,556 spot using $1,000,000.
3. Invest £555,556 in the U.K. The maturity value will be £600,000 = £555,556 × 1.08.
4. Sell £600,000 forward in exchange for $1,068,000 = (£600,000)($1.78/£).

In one year when everything matures, the arbitrager will receive the full maturity value of his U.K. investment, that is, £600,000. The arbitrager then will deliver this pound amount to the counterparty of the forward contract and receive $1,068,000 in return. Out of this dollar amount, the maturity value of the dollar loan, $1,050,000, will be paid. The arbitrager still has $18,000 (= $1,068,000 − $1,050,000) left in his account, which is his arbitrage profit. In making this *certain profit*, the arbitrager neither invested any money out of his pocket nor bore any risk. He indeed carried out "covered interest arbitrage," which means that he borrowed at one interest rate and simultaneously lent at another interest rate, with exchange risk fully covered via forward hedging.[5] Exhibit 6.2 provides a summary of CIA transactions.

How long will this arbitrage opportunity last? A simple answer is: only for a short while. As soon as deviations from IRP are detected, informed traders will immediately carry out CIA transactions. As a result of these arbitrage activities, IRP will be restored quite quickly. To see this, let's get back to our numerical example, which triggered covered interest arbitrage activities. Because every trader will (i) borrow in the United States as much as possible, (ii) lend in the U.K., (iii) buy the pound spot, and, at the same time, (iv) sell the pound forward, the following adjustments will occur to the initial market condition described in Equation 6.4:

1. The interest rate will rise in the United States ($i_\$\uparrow$).
2. The interest rate will fall in the U.K. ($i_\pounds\downarrow$).
3. The pound will appreciate in the spot market ($S\uparrow$).
4. The pound will depreciate in the forward market ($F\downarrow$).

EXHIBIT 6.2

Covered Interest Arbitrage: Cash Flow Analysis

Transactions	CF_0	CF_1
1. Borrow $1,000,000	$1,000,000	−$1,050,000
2. Buy £ spot	−$1,000,000	
	£555,556	
3. Lend £555,556	−£555,556	£600,000
4. Sell £600,000 forward		−£600,000
		$1,068,000
Net cash flow	0	$18,000

---

[5]The arbitrage profit is, in fact, equal to the effective interest rate differential times the amount borrowed, $18,000 = (1.068 − 1.05) ($1,000,000).

EXHIBIT 6.3

**The Interest Rate Parity
Diagram**

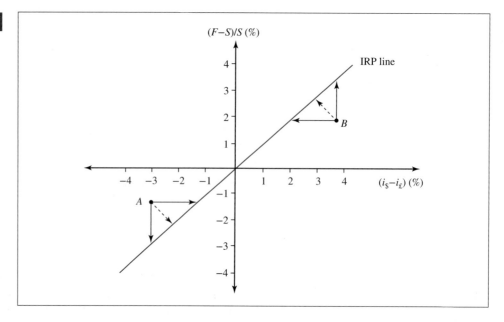

These adjustments will raise the left-hand side of Equation 6.4 and, at the same time, lower the right-hand side until both sides are equalized, restoring IRP.

The adjustment process is depicted in Exhibit 6.3. The initial market condition described by Equation 6.4 is represented by point A in the exhibit, substantially off the IRP line.[6] CIA activities will increase the interest rate differential (as indicated by the horizontal arrow) and, at the same time, lower the forward premium/discount (as indicated by the vertical arrow). Since the foreign exchange and money markets share the burden of adjustments, the actual path of adjustment to IRP can be depicted by the dotted arrow. When the initial market condition is located at point B, IRP will be restored partly by an increase in the forward premium, $(F - S)/S$, and partly by a decrease in the interest rate differential, $i_\$ - i_\pounds$.

EXAMPLE | 6.2: Before we move on, it would be useful to consider another CIA example. Suppose that the market condition is summarized as follows:

Three-month interest rate in the United States: 8.0% per annum.

Three-month interest rate in Germany: 5.0% per annum.

Current spot exchange rate: €0.800/$.

Three-month forward exchange rate: €0.7994/$.

The current example differs from the previous example in that the transaction horizon is three months rather than a year, and the exchange rates are quoted in *European* rather than *American* terms.

If we would like to apply IRP as defined in Equation 6.1, we should convert the exchange rates into American terms and use three-month interest rates, not annualized rates. In other words, we should use the following numerical values to check if IRP is holding:

$i_\$ = 8.0/4 = 2.0\%$ $i_\euro = 5.0/4 = 1.25\%$

$S = 1/0.800 = \$1.250/\euro$ $F = 1/0.7994 = \$1.2510/\euro$

It is important to make sure that both the interest rates and the forward exchange rate have the same maturity.

continued

[6]Note that at point A, the interest rate differential is −3%, i.e., $i_\$ - i_\pounds = 5\% - 8\% = -3\%$, and the forward premium is −1.11%, i.e., $(F - S)/S = (1.78 - 1.80)/1.80 = -0.0111$, or −1.11%.

EXAMPLE | 6.2: continued

Now, we can compute the right-hand side of Equation 6.1:

$$\left[\frac{F}{S}\right](1+i_{\text{€}}) = \left[\frac{1.2510}{1.2500}\right](1.0125) = 1.0133,$$

which is less than $(1 + i_{\$}) = 1.02$. Clearly, IRP is not holding and an arbitrage opportunity thus exists. Since the interest rate is lower in Germany after allowing for exchange rates than in the United States, the arbitrage transaction should involve borrowing in Germany and lending in the United States. Again, we assume that the arbitrager can borrow up to $1,000,000 or the equivalent € amount, €800,000.

The arbitrager can carry out the following transactions:

1. Borrow €800,000 in Germany. Repayment in three months will be €810,000 = €800,000 × 1.0125.

2. Buy $1,000,000 spot using €800,000.

3. Invest $1,000,000 in the United States. The maturity value will be $1,020,000 in three months.

4. Buy €810,000 forward in exchange for $1,013,310 = €810,000($1.2510/€).

In three months, the arbitrager will receive the full maturity value of the U.S. investment, $1,020,000. But then, the arbitrager should deliver $1,013,310 to the counterparty of the forward contract and receive €810,000 in return, which will be used to repay the euro loan. The arbitrage profit will thus be $6,690 (= $1,020,000 − $1,013,310).[7]

Interest Rate Parity and Exchange Rate Determination

Being an arbitrage equilibrium condition involving the (spot) exchange rate, IRP has an immediate implication for exchange rate determination. To see why, let us reformulate the IRP relationship in terms of the spot exchange rate:

$$S = \left[\frac{1 + i_{\text{£}}}{1 + i_{\$}}\right] F \qquad (6.5)$$

Equation 6.5 indicates that given the forward exchange rate, the spot exchange rate depends on relative interest rates. All else equal, an increase in the U.S. interest rate will lead to a higher foreign exchange value of the dollar.[8] This is so because a higher U.S. interest rate will attract capital to the United States, increasing the demand for dollars. In contrast, a decrease in the U.S. interest rate will lower the foreign exchange value of the dollar.

In addition to relative interest rates, the forward exchange rate is an important factor in spot exchange rate determination. Under certain conditions the forward exchange rate can be viewed as the expected future spot exchange rate conditional on all relevant information being available now, that is,

$$F = E(S_{t+1} | I_t) \qquad (6.6)$$

where S_{t+1} is the future spot rate when the forward contract matures, and I_t denotes the set of information currently available.[9] When Equations 6.5 and 6.6 are combined, we obtain

$$S = \left[\frac{1 + i_{\text{£}}}{1 + i_{\$}}\right] E(S_{t+1} | I_t) \qquad (6.7)$$

---

[7]It is left to the readers to figure out how IRP may be restored in this example.

[8]A higher U.S. interest rate ($i_{\$}\uparrow$) will lead to a lower spot exchange rate ($S\downarrow$), which means a stronger dollar. Note that the variable S represents the number of U.S. dollars per pound.

[9]The set of relevant information should include money supplies, interest rates, trade balances, and so on that would influence the exchange rates.

Two things are noteworthy from Equation 6.7. First, "expectation" plays a key role in exchange rate determination. Specifically, the expected future exchange rate is shown to be a major determinant of the current exchange rate; when people "expect" the exchange rate to go up in the future, it goes up now. People's expectations thus become *self-fulfilling*. Second, exchange rate behavior will be driven by news events. People form their expectations based on the set of information (I_t) they possess. As they receive news continuously, they are going to update their expectations continuously. As a result, the exchange rate will tend to exhibit a *dynamic* and *volatile* short-term behavior, responding to various news events. By definition, news events are unpredictable, making forecasting future exchange rates an arduous task.

When the forward exchange rate F is replaced by the expected future spot exchange rate, $E(S_{t+1})$ in Equation 6.3, we obtain:

$$(i_\$ - i_£) \approx E(e) \tag{6.8}$$

where $E(e)$ is the expected rate of change in the exchange rate, that is, $[E(S_{t+1}) - S_t]/S_t$. Equation 6.8 states that the interest rate differential between a pair of countries is (approximately) equal to the expected rate of change in the exchange rate. This relationship is known as the **uncovered interest rate parity**.[10] If, for instance, the annual interest rate is 5 percent in the United States and 8 percent in the U.K., as assumed in our numerical example, the uncovered IRP suggests that the pound is expected to depreciate against the dollar by about 3 percent, that is, $E(e) \approx -3\%$.

Currency Carry Trade

Unlike IRP, the uncovered interest rate parity often doesn't hold, giving rise to uncovered interest arbitrage opportunities. A popular example of such trade is provided by **currency carry trade**. Currency carry trade involves buying a high-yielding currency and funding it with a low-yielding currency, without any hedging. Since the interest rate in Japan has been near zero since the mid-1990s, the yen has been the most popular funding currency for carry trade, followed by the Swiss franc. Due to the low-interest-rate policy of the Federal Reserve to combat the Great Recession, the U.S. dollar has also become a popular funding currency in recent years. Popular investment currencies, on the other hand, include the Australian dollar, New Zealand dollar, and British pound, due to relatively high interest rates prevalent in these countries. Suppose you borrow in Japanese yen and invest in the Australian dollar. Your carry trade then will be profitable as long as the interest rate spread between the Australian dollar and Japanese yen, $i_{A\$} - i_¥$, is greater than the rate of appreciation ($e_{A\$,¥}$) of the yen against the Australian dollar during the carry period, that is, $i_{A\$} - i_¥ > e_{A\$,¥}$.

If many investors carry out the preceding trade on a massive scale, the yen may even depreciate, at least in the short run, against the Australian dollar, which is contrary to the prediction of the uncovered interest rate parity. The yen may depreciate in the short run as investors are selling the yen for the Australian dollar. If the yen depreciates against the Australian dollar by more than the Japanese interest rate, the funding cost for this carry trade would be effectively negative, making the carry trade more profitable.[11] However, if the Japanese yen appreciates against the Australian dollar by more than the interest rate spread, you would lose money from the carry trade. Clearly, currency carry trade is a risky investment, especially when the exchange rate is volatile.

Exhibit 6.4 plots the six-month interest rate spread between the yen and Australian dollar, $i_{A\$} - i_¥$, and the rate of change in the exchange rate between the two currencies, $e_{A\$,¥}$, during the same six-month period. The exhibit shows that for (nonoverlapping)

---

[10]As we will discuss shortly, the same relationship is also known as the international Fisher effect.

[11]Suppose you borrowed in Japanese yen at a 0.50% interest rate and the yen depreciated by 1.25% during the carry period. Then, the effective funding cost for the carry trade would become negative, −0.75% (= 0.50% − 1.25%).

EXHIBIT 6.4

Interest Rate Spreads and Exchange Rate Changes: Six-Month Carry Trade Periods for Australian Dollar–Japanese Yen Pair

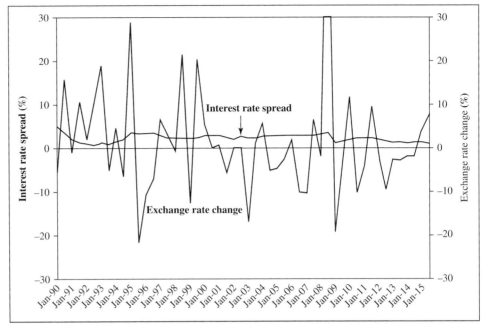

Note: Interest rates and exchange rates are obtained from Datastream. For interest rates, interbank six-month rates are used for both countries. The interest rate spread and the rate of change in the exchange rate are plotted at the start of each six-month carry period.

six-month periods examined, this carry trade was mostly profitable during the periods 2000–2007 and 2009–2013, when the yen often depreciated against the Australian dollar. At other times, the carry trade was often unprofitable due to intermittent, sharp appreciations of the yen. Note that the yen appreciated very sharply in the second half of 2008, reflecting the surging demand for Japanese yen as a safe-haven asset during the recent global financial crisis, generating significant loss for the carry trade.

Reasons for Deviations from Interest Rate Parity

Although IRP tends to hold quite well, it may not hold precisely all the time for at least two reasons: transaction costs and capital controls.

In our previous examples of CIA transactions, we implicitly assumed, among other things, that no transaction costs existed. As a result, in our first CIA example, for each dollar borrowed at the U.S. interest rate ($i_\$$), the arbitrager could realize the following amount of positive profit:

$$(F/S)(1 + i_\pounds) - (1 + i_\$) > 0 \tag{6.9}$$

In reality, transaction costs do exist. The interest rate at which the arbitrager borrows, i^a, tends to be higher than the rate at which he lends, i^b, reflecting the bid-ask spread. Likewise, there exist bid-ask spreads in the foreign exchange market as well. The arbitrager has to buy foreign exchanges at the higher ask price and sell them at the lower bid price. Each of the four variables in Equation 6.9 can be regarded as representing the midpoint of the spread.

Because of spreads, arbitrage profit from each dollar borrowed may become nonpositive:

$$(F^b/S^a)(1 + i_\pounds^{\,b}) - (1 + i_\$^{\,a}) \leq 0 \tag{6.10}$$

where the superscripts a and b to the exchange rates and interest rates denote the ask and bid prices, respectively. This is so because

$$(F^b/S^a) < (F/S)$$
$$(1 + i_\pounds^{\,b}) < (1 + i_\pounds)$$
$$(1 + i_\pounds^{\,a}) > (1 + i_\$)$$

EXHIBIT 6.5

Interest Rate Parity with Transaction Costs

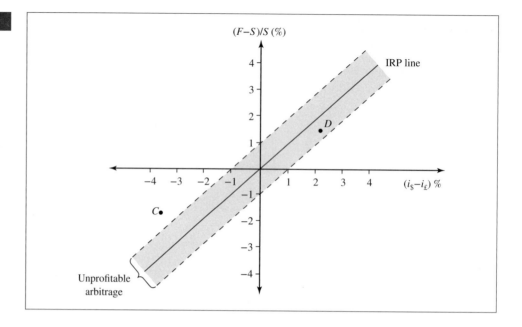

If the arbitrage profit turns negative because of transaction costs, the current deviation from IRP does not represent a profitable arbitrage opportunity. Thus, the IRP line in Exhibit 6.5 can be viewed as included within a band around it, and only IRP deviations outside the band, such as point *C*, represent profitable arbitrage opportunities. IRP deviations within the band, such as point *D*, would not represent profitable arbitrage opportunities. The width of this band will depend on the size of transaction costs.

Another major reason for deviations from IRP is capital controls imposed by governments. For various macroeconomic reasons, governments sometimes restrict capital flows, inbound and/or outbound.[12] Governments achieve this objective by means of jawboning, imposing taxes, or even outright bans on cross-border capital movements. These control measures imposed by governments can effectively impair the arbitrage process, and, as a result, deviations from IRP may persist.

An interesting historical example is provided by Japan, where capital controls were imposed on and off until December 1980, when the Japanese government liberalized international capital flows. Otani and Tiwari (1981) investigated the effect of capital controls on IRP deviations during the period 1978–1981. They computed deviations from interest rate parity (DIRP) as follows:[13]

$$\text{DIRP} = \left[\frac{(1 + i_{\yen})S}{(1 + i_{\$})F} \right] - 1 \tag{6.11}$$

where:

$i_{\yen}$ = interest rate on three-month Gensaki bonds.[14]
$i_{\$}$ = interest rate on three-month Euro-dollar deposits.
S = yen/dollar spot exchange rate in Tokyo.
F = yen/dollar three-month forward exchange rate in Tokyo.

---

[12]Capital controls were often imposed by governments in an effort to improve the balance-of-payments situations and to keep the exchange rate at a desirable level.

[13]Readers can convince themselves that DIRP in Equation 6.11 will be zero if IRP holds exactly.

[14]Gensaki bonds, issued in the Tokyo money market, are sold with a repurchase agreement. While interest rates on Gensaki bonds are determined by market forces, they can still be affected by various market imperfections.

EXHIBIT 6.6

Deviations from Interest Rate Parity: Japan, 1978–1981 (in percent)

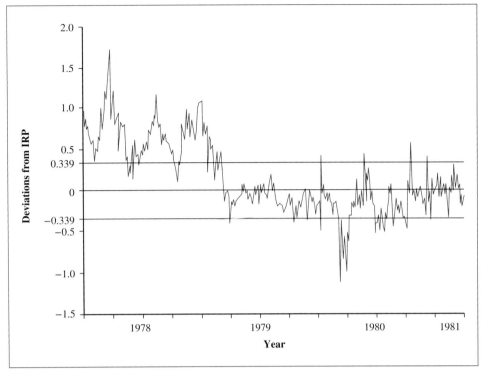

Note: Daily data were used in computing the deviations. The zone bounded by +0.339 and −0.339 represents the average width of the band around the IRP for the sample period.

Source: I. Otani and S. Tiwari, "Capital Controls and Interest Rate Parity: The Japanese Experience, 1978–81" *IMF Staff Papers* 28 (1981), pp. 793–816.

Deviations from IRP computed as above are plotted in Exhibit 6.6. If IRP holds strictly, deviations from it would be randomly distributed, with the expected value of zero.

Exhibit 6.6, however, shows that deviations from IRP hardly hover around zero. The deviations were quite significant at times until near the end of 1980. They were the greatest during 1978. This can be attributed to various measures the Japanese government took to discourage capital inflows, which was done to keep the yen from appreciating. As these measures were removed in 1979, the deviations were reduced. They increased again considerably in 1980, however, reflecting an introduction of capital control; Japanese financial institutions were asked to discourage foreign currency deposits.

In December 1980, Japan adopted the new *Foreign Exchange and Foreign Trade Control Law*, which generally liberalized foreign exchange transactions. Not surprisingly, the deviations hover around zero in the first quarter of 1981. The empirical evidence presented in Exhibit 6.6 closely reflects changes in capital controls during the study period. This implies that deviations from IRP, especially in 1978 and 1980, do not represent unexploited profit opportunities; rather, they reflect the existence of significant barriers to cross-border arbitrage.

Purchasing Power Parity

When the law of one price is applied internationally to a *standard consumption basket,* we obtain the theory of **purchasing power parity** (PPP). This theory states that the exchange rate between currencies of two countries should be equal to the ratio of the countries' price levels. The basic idea of PPP originated with scholars at the University of Salamanca, the oldest University in Spain, in the 16th century. Following the conquest of the Americas, Spain experienced a major influx of gold from the new world, which resulted in domestic inflation and the depreciation of the Spanish escudo against foreign currencies. This new monetary phenomenon served as a backdrop for the birth of PPP theory. The theory was later espoused by classical economists such as David Ricardo in the 19th century. But it is Gustav Cassel, a Swedish economist, who formulated PPP in its modern form and popularized it in the 1920s. In those years, many countries, including Germany, Hungary, and the Soviet Union, experienced hyperinflation. As the purchasing power of the currencies in these countries sharply declined, the same currencies also depreciated sharply against stable currencies like the U.S. dollar. The PPP became popular against this historical backdrop.

Let $P_\$$ be the dollar price of the standard consumption basket in the United States and $P_£$ the pound price of the same basket in the United Kingdom. Formally, PPP states that the exchange rate between the dollar and the pound should be

$$S = P_\$/P_£ \tag{6.12}$$

where S is the dollar price of one pound. PPP implies that if the standard commodity basket costs \$225 in the United States and £150 in the U.K., then the exchange rate should be \$1.50 per pound:

$$\$1.50/£ = \$225/£150$$

If the price of the commodity basket is higher in the United States, say, \$300, then PPP dictates that the exchange rate should be higher, that is, \$2.00/£.

To give an alternative interpretation to PPP, let us rewrite Equation 6.12 as follows:

$$P_\$ = S \times P_£$$

This equation states that the dollar price of the commodity basket in the United States, $P_\$$, must be the same as the dollar price of the basket in the U.K., that is, $P_£$ multiplied by S. In other words, PPP requires that the price of the standard consumption basket be the same across countries when measured in a common currency. Clearly, PPP is the manifestation of the law of one price applied to the standard consumption basket. As discussed in the International Finance in Practice box "McCurrencies," PPP is a way of defining the equilibrium exchange rate.

www.economist.com/content
/big-mac-index

Offers a discussion of exchange rate theory using the Big Mac Index.

As a light-hearted guide to the "correct" level of exchange rate, *The Economist* each year compiles local prices of Big Macs around the world and computes the so-called "Big Mac PPP," the exchange rate that would equalize the hamburger prices between America and elsewhere. Comparing this PPP and the actual exchange rate, a currency may be judged to be either undervalued or overvalued. In July 2016, a Big Mac cost (on average) \$5.04 in America and 19 yuan in China. Thus, the Big Mac PPP would be about 3.77 yuan per dollar. The actual exchange rate, however, is 6.68 yuan per dollar, implying that the yuan is substantially undervalued. In contrast, the Big Mac PPP for Switzerland is 1.39 Swiss francs per dollar, compared with the actual exchange rate of 0.99 francs per dollar. This implies that the Swiss franc is very much overvalued.

The PPP relationship of Equation 6.12 is called the *absolute* version of PPP. When the PPP relationship is presented in the "rate of change" form, we obtain the *relative* version:

$$e = \left[\frac{\pi_\$ - \pi_£}{1 + \pi_£} \right] \approx \pi_\$ - \pi_£ \tag{6.13}$$

where e is the rate of change in the exchange rate and $\pi_\$$ and $\pi_£$ are the inflation rates in the United States and U.K., respectively. For example, if the inflation rate is 6 percent per year in the United States and 4 percent in the U.K., then the pound should appreciate against the dollar by about 2 percent, that is, $e \approx 2$ percent, per year. It is noted that even if absolute PPP does not hold, relative PPP may hold.[15]

---

[15]From Equation 6.12 we obtain $(1 + e) = (1 + \pi_\$)/(1 + \pi_£)$. Rearranging the above expression we obtain $e = (\pi_\$ - \pi_£)/(1 + \pi_£)$, which is approximated by $e = \pi_\$ - \pi_£$ as in Equation 6.13.

PPP Deviations and the Real Exchange Rate

Whether PPP holds or not has important implications for international trade. If PPP holds and thus the differential inflation rates between countries are exactly offset by exchange rate changes, countries' competitive positions in world export markets will not be systematically affected by exchange rate changes. However, if there are deviations from PPP, changes in nominal exchange rates cause changes in the **real exchange rates**, affecting the international competitive positions of countries. This, in turn, would affect countries' trade balances.

The real exchange rate, q, which measures deviations from PPP, can be defined as follows:[16]

$$q = \frac{1 + \pi_\$}{(1 + e)(1 + \pi_£)} \tag{6.14}$$

First, note that if PPP holds, that is, $(1 + e) = (1 + \pi_\$)/(1 + \pi_£)$, the real exchange rate will be unity, $q = 1$. When PPP is violated, however, the real exchange rate will deviate from unity. Suppose, for example, the annual inflation rate is 5 percent in the United States and 3.5 percent in the U.K., and the pound appreciated against the dollar by 4.5 percent. Then the real exchange rate is .97:

$$q = (1.05)/(1.045)(1.035) = .97$$

In the above example, the dollar depreciated by more than is warranted by PPP, strengthening the competitiveness of U.S. industries in the world market. If the dollar depreciates by less than the inflation rate differential, the real exchange rate will be greater than unity, weakening the competitiveness of U.S. industries. To summarize,

$q = 1$: Competitiveness of the domestic country unaltered.
$q < 1$: Competitiveness of the domestic country improves.
$q > 1$: Competitiveness of the domestic country deteriorates.

Exhibit 6.7 plots the real "effective" exchange rates for the U.S. dollar, Japanese yen, Canadian dollar, Germany (euro), Chinese yuan, and British pound since 1980. The rates plotted in Exhibit 6.7 are, however, the real effective exchange rate "indices" computed using 2010 rates as the base, that is, 2010 = 100. The real effective exchange rate is a weighted average of bilateral real exchange rates, with the weight for each foreign currency determined by the country's share in the domestic country's international trade. The real effective exchange rate rises if domestic inflation exceeds inflation abroad and the nominal exchange rate fails to depreciate to compensate for the higher domestic inflation rate. Thus, if the real effective exchange rate rises (falls), the domestic country's competitiveness declines (improves). It is noted that the real effective exchange rate of the Chinese yuan fell sharply in the first half of the 1980s and stayed at a low level until 2006 when it began to rise slowly. Similarly, the real effective exchange rate for Germany generally fell until 2000. It then began to rise until 2009 when it began to steadily decline. On the other hand, the British pound appreciated in real terms from the mid-1990s until 2007, hurting the competitiveness of British companies, but it fell significantly since then until 2009, when it began to appreciate steadily.

Evidence on Purchasing Power Parity

As is clear from the above discussions, whether PPP holds in reality is a question of considerable importance. In view of the fact that PPP is the manifestation of the law of one price applied to a standard commodity basket, it will hold only if the prices of constituent commodities are equalized across countries in a given currency and if the composition of the consumption basket is the same across countries.

The PPP has been the subject of a series of tests, yielding generally negative results. For example, in his study of disaggregated commodity arbitrage between the

---

[16]The real exchange rate measures the degree of deviations from PPP over a certain period of time, assuming that PPP held roughly at a starting point. If PPP holds continuously, the real exchange rate will remain unity.

McCurrencies

When our economics editor invented the Big Mac index in 1986 as a light-hearted introduction to exchange-rate theory, little did she think that 30 years later she would still be munching her way, a little less sylph-like, around the world. As burgernomics enters its third decade, the Big Mac index is widely used and abused around the globe. It is time to take stock of what burgers do and do not tell you about exchange rates.

The Economist's Big Mac index is based on one of the oldest concepts in international economics: the theory of purchasing-power parity (PPP), which argues that in the long run, exchange rates should move towards levels that would equalise the prices of an identical basket of goods and services in any two countries. Our "basket" is a McDonald's Big Mac, produced in around 120 countries. The Big Mac PPP is the exchange rate that would leave burgers costing the same in America as elsewhere. Thus a Big Mac in China costs 19 yuan, against an average price in four American cities of $5.04. To make the two prices equal would require an exchange rate of 3.77 yuan to the dollar, compared with a market rate of 6.68. In other words, the yuan is 45% "undervalued" against the dollar. To put it another way, converted into dollars at market rates the Chinese burger is among the cheapest in the table.

Using the same method, the Japanese yen and sterling are undervalued, by 31% and 22% respectively; the Polish zloty and Russian ruble are much more undervalued. Note that most emerging market currencies also look too cheap. On the other hand, the Swiss franc is substantially overvalued, while the Canadian dollar is somewhat undervalued.

The index was never intended to be a precise predictor of currency movements, simply a take-away guide to whether currencies are at their "correct" long-run level. Curiously, however, burgernomics has an impressive record in predicting exchange rates: currencies that show up as overvalued often tend to weaken in later years. But you must always remember the Big Mac's limitations. Burgers cannot sensibly be traded across borders and prices are distorted by differences in taxes and the cost of non-tradable inputs, such as rents.

Despite our frequent health warnings, some American politicians are fond of citing the Big Mac index rather too freely when it suits their cause—most notably in their demands for a big appreciation of the Chinese currency in order to reduce America's huge trade deficit. But the cheapness of a Big Mac in China does not really prove that the yuan is being held far below its fair-market value. Purchasing-power parity is a long-run concept. It signals where exchange rates are eventually heading, but it says little about today's market-equilibrium exchange rate that would make the prices of tradable goods equal. A burger is a product of both traded and non-traded inputs.

It is quite natural for average prices to be lower in poorer countries than in developed ones. Although the prices of tradable things should be similar, non-tradable services will be cheaper because of lower wages. PPPs are therefore a more reliable way to convert GDP per head into dollars than market exchange rates, because cheaper prices mean that money goes further. This is also why every poor country has an implied PPP exchange rate that is higher than today's market rate, making them all appear undervalued. Both theory and practice show that as countries get richer and their productivity rises, their real exchange rates appreciate. But this does not mean that a currency needs to rise massively today. Jonathan Anderson, chief economist at UBS in Hong Kong, reckons that the yuan is now only 10–15% below its fair-market value.

Even over the long run, adjustment towards PPP need not come from a shift in exchange rates; relative prices can change instead. For example, since 1995, when the yen was overvalued by 100% according to the Big Mac index, the local price of Japanese burgers has dropped by one-third. In the same period, American burgers have become one-third dearer. Similarly, the yuan's future real appreciation could come through faster inflation in China than in the United States.

The Big Mac index is most useful for assessing the exchange rates of countries with similar incomes per head. Thus, among emerging markets, the yuan does indeed look undervalued, while the Brazilian real is much less undervalued. Economists would be unwise to exclude Big Macs from their diet, but Super Size servings would equally be a mistake.

Source: "McCurrencies," © *The Economist Newspaper Limited London*, May 25th 2006, updated with July 2016 figures.

United States and Canada, Richardson (1978) was unable to detect commodity arbitrage for a majority of commodity classes. Richardson reported: "The presence of commodity arbitrage could be rejected with 95 percent confidence for at least 13 out of the 22 commodity groups" (p. 346). Although Richardson did not directly test PPP, his findings can be viewed as highly negative news for PPP. If commodity arbitrage is imperfect between neighboring countries like the United States and Canada that have relatively few trade restrictions, PPP is not likely to hold much better for other pairs of countries.

Exhibit 6.8, "A Guide to World Prices," also provides evidence against commodity price parity. The price of aspirin (20 units) ranges from $0.77 in Mexico City to $7.84 in Tokyo. In general, production and distribution of drugs are tightly regulated by the governments in most countries. These regulations make it difficult to carry out

The Hamburger Standard

	Big Mac prices		Implied PPP of the dollar[a]	Actual dollar exchange rate 07/20/16	Under (−)/over (+) valuation against the dollar, %
	In local currency	In dollars			
United States[b]	$5.04	5.04	1.00	1.00	0
Argentina	Peso 50	3.35	9.92	14.94	−34
Australia	A$ 6	4.30	1.19	1.34	−15
Brazil	Real 16	4.78	3.17	3.24	−5
Britain	Pound 3	3.94	0.60	0.76	−22
Canada	C$ 6	4.60	1.19	1.30	−9
Chile	Peso 2,300	3.53	456.35	651.12	−30
China	Yuan 19	2.79	3.77	6.68	−45
Czech Republic	Koruna75	3.06	14.88	24.55	−39
Denmark	DK 30	4.44	5.95	6.76	−12
Egypt	Pound 23	2.59	4.56	8.88	−49
Euro area[c]	Euro 4	4.21	0.79	0.91	−17
Hong Kong	HK$ 19	2.48	3.77	7.76	−51
Hungary	Forint 900	3.15	178.57	285.64	−38
India	Rupee 162	2.41	32.10	67.2	−52
Indonesia	Rupiah 31,000	2.36	6,150.79	13,112.50	−53
Israel	Shekel 17	4.38	3.40	3.86	−13
Japan	Yen 370	3.47	73.41	106.73	−31
Malaysia	Ringgit 8	1.99	1.59	4.03	−61
Mexico	Peso 44	2.37	8.73	18.54	−53
New Zealand	NZ$ 6	4.22	1.19	1.42	−16
Peru	New Sol 10	3.02	1.98	3.31	−40
Philippines	Peso 133	2.82	26.39	47.12	−44
Poland	Zloty 10	2.42	1.98	3.97	−52
Russia	Ruble 130	2.05	25.79	63.41	−60
Singapore	S$ 5	4.01	0.99	1.36	−20
South Africa	Rand 30	2.10	5.95	14.27	−58
South Korea	Won 4,400	3.86	873.02	1,140.95	−24
Sweden	SKr 45	5.23	8.93	8.59	4
Switzerland	SFr 7	6.59	1.39	0.99	31
Taiwan	NT$ 69	2.15	13.69	32.03	−57
Thailand	Baht 119	3.40	23.61	34.97	−32
Turkey	Lire 11	3.53	2.18	3.04	−30
Ukraine	Hryvnia 39	1.57	7.70	24.80	−69

[a]Purchasing power parity: local price divided by price in United States.

[b]Average of New York, Chicago, Atlanta, and San Francisco.

[c]Weighted average of prices in euro area.

Source: McDonald's; *The Economist,* July 23rd, 2016.

cross-border arbitrage, resulting in a wide price disparity for these products. Likewise, the cost of a man's haircut ranges widely from $23.29 in Madrid to $86.67 in Hong Kong. It costs 272 percent (!) more to have a haircut in Hong Kong than in Madrid. The price differential, however, is likely to persist because haircuts are simply not tradable. In comparison, the price disparity for a hamburger is substantially less. For example, it costs $4.28 in London, $4.90 in Tokyo, and $4.49 in Toronto. The lower price disparity may be attributable to the fact that multinational firms like McDonald's set the prices across countries on a comparable basis.

EXHIBIT 6.7   **Real Effective Exchange Rates for Selected Currencies (index, 2010 = 100)**

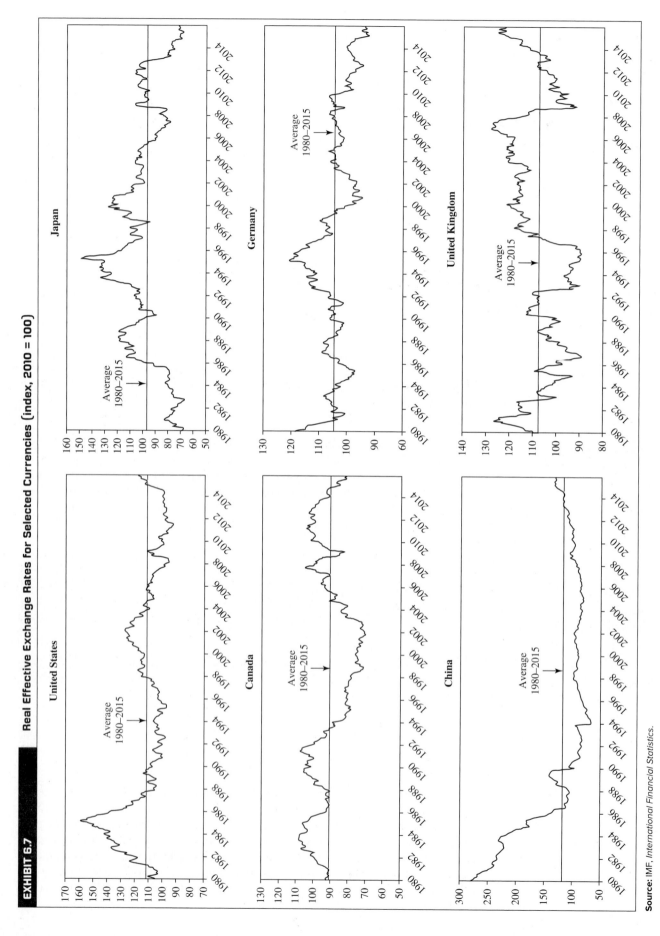

Source: IMF, *International Financial Statistics.*

EXHIBIT 6.8

A Guide to World Prices:
March 2016[a]

Location	Hamburger (1 unit)	Aspirin (20 units)	Man's Haircut (1 unit)	Movie Ticket (1 unit)
Athens	$3.77	$2.03	$40.54	$9.01
Copenhagen	$5.28	$6.26	$57.04	$12.70
Hong Kong	$2.31	$4.61	$86.67	$16.88
London	$4.28	$3.23	$55.48	$20.50
Madrid	$4.17	$5.46	$23.29	$10.11
Mexico City	$2.40	$0.77	$25.00	$4.64
Munich	$4.27	$7.28	$50.68	$10.56
New York City	$3.40	$6.48	$66.22	$10.92
Paris	$4.56	$5.71	$30.48	$13.26
Rio de Janeiro	$4.47	$4.33	$42.79	$8.48
Rome	$4.73	$7.32	$50.41	$12.73
Sydney	$3.83	$2.56	$71.68	$15.23
Tokyo	$4.90	$7.84	$38.29	$15.55
Toronto	$4.49	$2.27	$38.57	$10.04
Vienna	$3.83	$6.48	$60.00	$10.92
Average	$4.05	$4.84	$49.14	$12.10
Standard Deviation	0.84	2.22	17.68	3.86
Coefficient of Variation[b]	0.21	0.46	0.36	0.32

[a]Prices include sales tax and value added tax except in the United States location.

[b]The coefficient of variation is obtained from dividing the standard deviation by the average. It thus provides a measure of dispersion adjusted for the magnitude of the variable.

Source: AIRINC.

Kravis and Lipsey (1978) examined the relationship between inflation rates and exchange rates and found that price levels can move far apart without rapid correction via arbitrage, thus rejecting the notion of integrated international commodity price structure. In a similar vein, Adler and Lehman (1983) found that deviations from PPP follow a random walk, without exhibiting any tendency to revert to PPP.

Frenkel (1981) reported that while PPP did very poorly in explaining the behavior of exchange rates between the U.S. dollar and major European currencies, it performed somewhat better in explaining the exchange rates between a pair of European currencies, such as the British pound versus the German mark, and the French franc versus the German mark. Frenkel's finding may be attributable to the fact that, in addition to the geographical proximity of the European countries, these countries belonged to the European Common Market, with low internal trade barriers and low transportation costs. Even among these European currencies, however, Frenkel found that relative price levels are only one of the many potential factors influencing exchange rates. If PPP holds strictly, relative price levels should be sufficient in explaining the behavior of exchange rates.

Generally unfavorable evidence about PPP suggests that substantial barriers to international commodity arbitrage exist. Obviously, commodity prices can diverge between countries up to the transportation costs without triggering arbitrage. If it costs $50 to ship a ton of rice from Thailand to Korea, the price of rice can diverge by up to $50 in either direction between the two countries. Likewise, deviations from PPP can result from tariffs and quotas imposed on international trade.

As is well recognized, some commodities never enter into international trade. Examples of such **nontradables** include haircuts, housing, and the like. These items are either immovable or inseparable from the providers of these services. Suppose a quality haircut costs $35 in New York City, but the comparable haircut costs only $10 in Mexico City. Obviously, you cannot import haircuts from Mexico. Either you have to travel to Mexico or a Mexican barber must travel to New York City, both of which, of course, are impractical in view of the travel costs and the immigration laws. Consequently, a large price differential for haircuts will persist. As long as there are nontradables, PPP will not hold in its absolute version. If PPP holds for tradables and the relative prices between tradables and nontradables are maintained, then PPP can hold in its relative version. These conditions, however, are not very likely to hold.

Even if PPP may not hold in reality, it can still play a useful role in economic analysis. First, one can use the PPP-determined exchange rate as a benchmark in deciding if a country's currency is undervalued or overvalued against other currencies. Second, one can often make more meaningful international comparisons of economic data using PPP-determined rather than market-determined exchange rates. This point is highlighted in Exhibit 6.9, "How Large Is India's Economy?"

Suppose you want to rank countries in terms of gross domestic product (GDP). If you use market exchange rates, you can either underestimate or overestimate the true GDP values. Exhibit 6.9 provides the GDP values of the major countries in 2014 computed using both PPP and market exchange rates. A country's ranking in terms of GDP value can be quite sensitive to which exchange rate is used. India provides a striking example. When the market exchange rate is used, India ranks ninth, lagging behind such countries as Brazil, the U.K., and Italy. However, when the PPP exchange rate is used, India moves up to the third place after China and the United States, but ahead of Japan, Germany, France, and the U.K. China ranks second only after the United States when the market exchange rate is used, but ranks first ahead of the United States when the PPP rate is used. In contrast, countries like Australia, Canada, France, and the U.K. move down in the GDP ranking when PPP exchange rates are used.

Fisher Effects

Another parity condition we often encounter in the literature is the **Fisher effect**. The Fisher effect holds that *an increase (decrease) in the expected inflation rate in a country will cause a proportionate increase (decrease) in the interest rate in the country.* Formally, the Fisher effect can be written for the United States as follows:

$$i_\$ = \rho_\$ + E(\pi_\$) + \rho_\$ E(\pi_\$) \approx \rho_\$ + E(\pi_\$) \tag{6.15}$$

where $\rho_\$$ denotes the equilibrium expected "real" interest rate in the United States.[17]

For example, suppose the expected real interest rate is 2 percent per year in the United States. Given this, the U.S. (nominal) interest rate will be entirely determined by the expected inflation in the United States. If, for instance, the expected inflation rate is 4.0 percent per year, the interest rate will then be set at about 6 percent. With a 6 percent interest rate, the lender will be fully compensated for the expected erosion of the purchasing power of money while still expecting to realize a 2 percent real return. Of course, the Fisher effect should hold in each country as long as the bond market is efficient.

The Fisher effect implies that the expected inflation rate is the difference between the nominal and real interest rates in each country, that is,

$$E(\pi_\$) = (i_\$ - \rho_\$)/(1 + \rho_\$) \approx i_\$ - \rho_\$$$
$$E(\pi_£) = (i_£ - \rho_£)/(1 + \rho_£) \approx i_£ - \rho_£$$

Now, let us assume that the real interest rate is the same between countries, that is, $\rho_\$ = \rho_£$, because of unrestricted capital flows. When we substitute the above results into the relative PPP in its expectational form in Equation 6.13, that is, $E(e) \approx E(\pi_\$) - E(\pi_£)$, we obtain

$$E(e) \approx i_\$ - i_£ \tag{6.16}$$

---

[17]It is noted that Equation 6.15 obtains from the relationship: $(1 + i_\$) = (1 + \rho_\$)(1 + E(\pi_\$))$.

EXHIBIT 6.9   How Large is India's Economy?

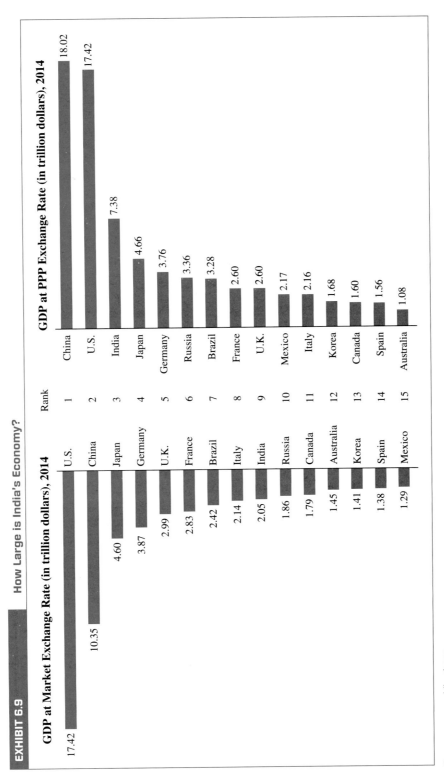

GDP at Market Exchange Rate (in trillion dollars), 2014

U.S.	17.42
China	10.35
Japan	4.60
Germany	3.87
U.K.	2.99
France	2.83
Brazil	2.42
Italy	2.14
India	2.05
Russia	1.86
Canada	1.79
Australia	1.45
Korea	1.41
Spain	1.38
Mexico	1.29

GDP at PPP Exchange Rate (in trillion dollars), 2014

Rank		
1	China	18.02
2	U.S.	17.42
3	India	7.38
4	Japan	4.66
5	Germany	3.76
6	Russia	3.36
7	Brazil	3.28
8	France	2.60
9	U.K.	2.60
10	Mexico	2.17
11	Italy	2.16
12	Korea	1.68
13	Canada	1.60
14	Spain	1.56
15	Australia	1.08

Source: www.worldbank.org.

157

International Parity Relationships among Exchange Rates, Interest Rates, and Inflation Rates

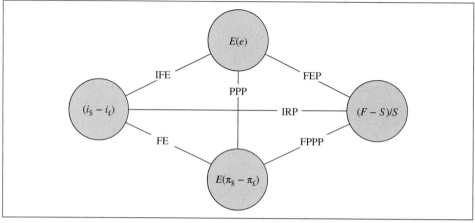

Notes:

1. With the assumption of the same real interest rate, the Fisher effect (FE) implies that the interest rate differential is equal to the expected inflation rate differential.

2. If both purchasing power parity (PPP) and forward expectations parity (FEP) hold, then the forward exchange premium or discount will be equal to the expected inflation rate differential. The latter relationship is denoted by the forward-PPP, i.e., FPPP in the exhibit.

3. IFE stands for the international Fisher effect.

which is known as the **international Fisher effect (IFE)**.[18] IFE suggests that the nominal interest rate differential reflects the expected change in exchange rate. For instance, if the interest rate is 5 percent per year in the United States and 7 percent in the U.K., the dollar is expected to appreciate against the British pound by about 2 percent per year.

Lastly, when the international Fisher effect is combined with IRP, that is, $(F - S)/S = (i_\$ - i_£)/(1 + i_£)$, we obtain

$$(F - S)/S = E(e) \tag{6.17}$$

which is referred to as **forward expectations parity (FEP)**. FEP states that any forward premium or discount is equal to the expected change in the exchange rate. When investors are risk-neutral, forward parity will hold as long as the foreign exchange market is informationally efficient. Otherwise, it need not hold even if the market is efficient. Exhibit 6.10 summarizes the parity relationships discussed so far.[19]

Forecasting Exchange Rates

fx.sauder.ubc.ca

Provides historical time series of exchange rates.

Since the advent of the flexible exchange rate system in 1973, exchange rates have become increasingly more volatile and erratic. At the same time, the scope of business activities has become highly international. Consequently, many business decisions are now made based on forecasts, implicit or explicit, of future exchange rates. Understandably, forecasting exchange rates as accurately as possible is a matter of vital importance for currency traders who are actively engaged in speculating, hedging, and

[18]The international Fisher effect is the same as the uncovered IRP previously discussed. While the Fisher effect should hold in an efficient market, the international Fisher effect need not hold even in an efficient market unless investors are risk-neutral. Generally speaking, the interest rate differential may reflect not only the expected change in the exchange rate but also a risk premium.

[19]Suppose that the Fisher effect holds both in the United States and in the U.K., and that the real interest rate is the same in both the countries. As shown in Exhibit 6.10, the Fisher effect (FE) then implies that the interest rate differential should be equal to the expected inflation differential. Furthermore, when forward parity and PPP are combined, we obtain what might be called "forward-PPP" (FPPP), i.e., the forward premium/discount is equal to the expected inflation differential.

arbitrage in the foreign exchange markets. It is also a vital concern for multinational corporations that are formulating international sourcing, production, financing, and marketing strategies. The quality of these corporate decisions will critically depend on the accuracy of exchange rate forecasts.

Some corporations generate their own forecasts, while others subscribe to outside services for a fee. While forecasters use a wide variety of forecasting techniques, most can be classified into three distinct approaches:

- Efficient market approach
- Fundamental approach
- Technical approach

Let us briefly examine each of these approaches.

Efficient Market Approach

Financial markets are said to be efficient if the current asset prices fully reflect all the available and relevant information. The **efficient market hypothesis** (EMH), which is largely attributable to Professor Eugene Fama of the University of Chicago, has strong implications for forecasting.[20]

Suppose that foreign exchange markets are efficient. This means that the current exchange rate has already reflected all relevant information, such as money supplies, inflation rates, trade balances, and output growth. The exchange rate will then change only when the market receives new information. Since news by definition is unpredictable, the exchange rate will change randomly over time. In a word, incremental changes in the exchange rate will be independent of the past history of the exchange rate. If the exchange rate indeed follows a random walk, the future exchange rate is expected to be the same as the current exchange rate, that is,

$$S_t = E(S_{t+1})$$

In a sense, the **random walk hypothesis** suggests that today's exchange rate is the best predictor of tomorrow's exchange rate.

While researchers found it difficult to reject the random walk hypothesis for exchange rates on empirical grounds, there is no theoretical reason why exchange rates should follow a pure random walk. The parity relationships we discussed previously indicate that the current forward exchange rate can be viewed as the market's consensus forecast of the future exchange rate based on the available information (I_t) if the foreign exchange markets are efficient, that is,

$$F_t = E(S_{t+1} | I_t)$$

To the extent that interest rates are different between two countries, the forward exchange rate will be different from the current spot exchange rate. This means that the future exchange rate should be expected to be different from the current spot exchange rate.

Those who subscribe to the efficient market hypothesis may predict the future exchange rate using either the current spot exchange rate or the current forward exchange rate. But which one is better? Researchers like Agmon and Amihud (1981) compared the performance of the forward exchange rate with that of the random walk model as a predictor of the future spot exchange rate. Their empirical findings indicate that the forward exchange rate failed to outperform the random walk model in predicting the future exchange rate; the two prediction models that are based on the efficient market hypothesis registered largely comparable performances.[21]

---

[20]For a detailed discussion of the efficient market hypothesis, refer to Eugene Fama, "Efficient Capital Markets II," *Journal of Finance* 26 (1991), pp. 1575–1617.

[21]For a detailed discussion, refer to Tamir Agmon and Yakov Amihud, "The Forward Exchange Rate and the Prediction of the Future Spot Rate," *Journal of Banking and Finance* 5 (1981), pp. 425–37.

Predicting the exchange rates using the efficient market approach has two advantages. First, since the efficient market approach is based on market-determined prices, it is costless to generate forecasts. Both the current spot and forward exchange rates are public information. As such, everyone has free access to it. Second, given the efficiency of foreign exchange markets, it is difficult to outperform the market-based forecasts unless the forecaster has access to private information that is not yet reflected in the current exchange rate.

Fundamental Approach

www.oecd.org

Provides macroeconomic data useful for fundamental analysis.

The fundamental approach to exchange rate forecasting uses various models. For example, the monetary approach to exchange rate determination suggests that the exchange rate is determined by three independent (explanatory) variables: (i) relative money supplies, (ii) relative velocity of monies, and (iii) relative national outputs.[22] One can thus formulate the monetary approach in the following empirical form:[23]

$$s = \alpha + \beta_1(m - m^*) + \beta_2(v - v^*) + \beta_3(y^* - y) + u \tag{6.18}$$

where:

s = natural logarithm of the spot exchange rate.
$m - m^*$ = natural logarithm of domestic/foreign money supply.
$v - v^*$ = natural logarithm of domestic/foreign velocity of money.
$y^* - y$ = natural logarithm of foreign/domestic output.
u = random error term, with mean zero.
α, β's = model parameters.

Generating forecasts using the fundamental approach would involve three steps:

Step 1: Estimation of the structural model like Equation 6.18 to determine the numerical values for the parameters such as α and β's.

Step 2: Estimation of future values of the independent variables like $(m - m^*)$, $(v - v^*)$, and $(y^* - y)$.

Step 3: Substituting the estimated values of the independent variables into the estimated structural model to generate the exchange rate forecasts.

If, for example, the forecaster would like to predict the exchange rate one year into the future, he or she has to estimate the values that the independent variables will assume in one year. These values will then be substituted in the structural model that was fitted to historical data.

The fundamental approach to exchange rate forecasting has three main difficulties. First, one has to forecast a set of independent variables to forecast the exchange rates. Forecasting the former will certainly be subject to errors and may not be necessarily easier than forecasting the latter. Second, the parameter values, that is, α and β's, that are estimated using historical data may change over time because of changes in government policies and/or the underlying structure of the economy. Either difficulty can diminish the accuracy of forecasts even if the model is correct. Third, the model itself can be wrong. For example, the model described by Equation 6.18 may be wrong. The forecast generated by a wrong model cannot be very accurate.

Not surprisingly, researchers found that the fundamental models failed to more accurately forecast exchange rates than either the forward rate model or the random walk model. Meese and Rogoff (1983), for example, found that the fundamental models developed based on the monetary approach did worse than the random walk model even if realized (true) values were used for the independent variables. They also

---

[22]For a detailed discussion of the monetary approach, see Appendix 6A.
[23]For notational simplicity, we omit the time subscripts in the following equation.

EXHIBIT 6.11

Moving Average Crossover Rule: Golden Cross vs. Death Cross

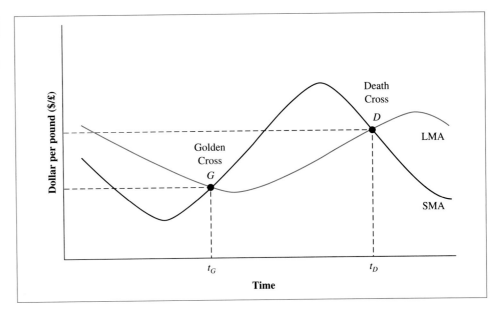

confirmed that the forward rate did not do better than the random walk model. In the words of Meese and Rogoff:

> Ignoring for the present the fact that the spot rate does no worse than the forward rate, the striking feature . . . is that none of the models achieves lower, much less significantly lower, RMSE than the random walk model at any horizon. . . . The structural models in particular fail to improve on the random walk model in spite of the fact that their forecasts are based on realized values of the explanatory variables.[24] (p. 12)

Technical Approach

www.fxstreet.com

Provides information about technical analysis and currency charts.

The technical approach first analyzes the past behavior of exchange rates for the purpose of identifying "patterns" and then projects them into the future to generate forecasts. Clearly, the technical approach is based on the premise that *history repeats itself* (or at least rhymes with itself). The technical approach thus is at odds with the efficient market approach. At the same time, it differs from the fundamental approach in that it does not use the key economic variables such as money supplies or trade balances for the purpose of forecasting. However, technical analysts sometimes consider various transaction data like trading volume, outstanding interests, and bid-ask spreads to aid their analyses. Below, we discuss two examples of technical analysis—the moving average crossover rule and the head-and-shoulders pattern—that are among the most popular tools used by technical analysts.

First, the moving average crossover rule is illustrated in Exhibit 6.11. Many technical analysts or chartists compute moving averages as a way of separating short- and long-term trends from the vicissitudes of daily exchange rates. Exhibit 6.11 illustrates how exchange rates may be forecast based on the movements of short- and long-term moving averages. Because the short-term (such as 50-day) moving average (SMA) weighs recent exchange rate changes more heavily than the long-term (such as 200-day) moving average (LMA), the SMA will lie below (above) the LMA when the British pound is falling (rising) against the dollar. This implies that one may forecast exchange rate movements based on the crossover of the moving averages. According to this rule, a crossover of the SMA above the LMA at point *G* signals that the British pound may continue to appreciate. On the other hand, a crossover of the SMA below the

---

[24]RMSE, which stands for the root mean squared error, is the criterion that Meese and Rogoff used in evaluating the accuracy of forecasts.

EXHIBIT 6.12

**Head-and-Shoulders
Pattern: A Reversal Signal**

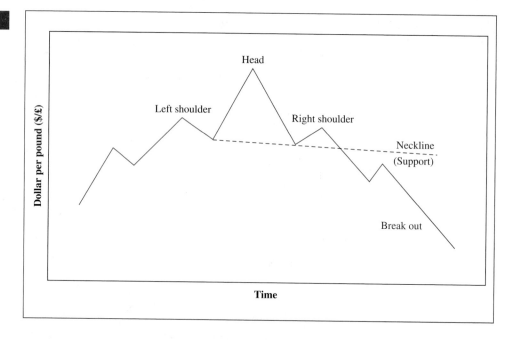

EXHIBIT 6.12

**Head-and-Shoulders
Pattern: A Reversal Signal**

LMA at point *D* signals that the British pound may depreciate for a while. For traders, crossover *G*, called the "golden cross," is a signal to buy, whereas crossover *D*, known as the "death cross," is a signal to sell.

Next, the head-and-shoulders pattern is illustrated in Exhibit 6.12. The head-and-shoulders (HAS) pattern signals a reversal in an upward trending market. The HAS pattern consists of a head, two shoulders, left and right, and the neckline (support level). This pattern is typically viewed as signaling that the British pound is topping out and a major reversal is forthcoming. As the exhibit shows schematically, the left shoulder occurs as the British pound reaches a local high point in a rising market and then falls back to the neckline. The British pound then appreciates to an even higher level, the head, before it falls back again to the neckline. The right shoulder occurs when the British pound appreciates again but to a local high point lower than the head. The HAS pattern is completed when the neckline or the support level is broken. This occurs when the British pound depreciates through the neckline. The completion of the HAS pattern signals that the British pound will depreciate significantly.

While academic studies tend to discredit the validity of **technical analysis**, many traders depend on technical analyses for their trading strategies. If a trader knows that other traders use technical analysis, it can be rational for the trader to use technical analysis too. If enough traders use technical analysis, the predictions based on it can become self-fulfilling to some extent, at least in the short run.

Performance of the Forecasters

Because predicting exchange rates is difficult, many firms and investors subscribe to professional forecasting services for a fee. Since an alternative to subscribing to professional forecasting services is to use a market-determined price such as the forward exchange rate, it is relevant to ask: *Can professional forecasters outperform the market?*

An answer to the above question was provided by Professor Richard Levich of New York University, who evaluated the performances of 13 forecasting services using the forward exchange rate as a benchmark. Under certain conditions, the forward exchange

EXHIBIT 6.13	Performance of Exchange Rate Forecasting Services												
	Forecasting Services												
Currency	1	2	3	4	5	6	7	8	9	10	11	12	13
Canadian dollar	1.29	1.13	1.00	1.59	0.99	1.08	n.a.	1.47	1.17	1.03	1.47	1.74	0.80
British pound	1.11	1.24	0.91	1.44	1.09	0.98	1.05	1.09	1.27	1.69	1.03	1.22	1.01
Belgian franc	0.95	1.07	n.a.	1.33	1.17	n.a.	n.a.	0.99	1.21	n.a.	1.06	1.01	0.77
French franc	0.91	0.98	1.02	1.43	1.27	n.a.	0.98	0.92	1.00	0.96	1.03	1.16	0.70
German mark	1.08	1.13	1.07	1.28	1.19	1.35	1.06	0.83	1.19	1.07	1.13	1.04	0.76
Italian lira	1.07	0.91	1.09	1.45	1.14	n.a.	1.12	1.12	1.00	1.17	1.64	1.54	0.93
Dutch guilder	0.80	1.10	n.a.	1.41	1.06	n.a.	n.a.	0.91	1.26	1.26	1.10	1.01	0.81
Swiss franc	1.01	n.a.	1.08	1.21	1.32	n.a.	n.a.	0.86	1.06	1.04	1.04	0.94	0.63
Japanese yen	1.42	1.05	1.02	1.23	1.08	1.45	1.09	1.24	0.94	0.47	1.31	1.30	1.79

Note: Each entry represents the *R* ratio defined in Equation 6.19. If a forecasting service outperforms (underperforms) the forward exchange rate, the *R* ratio will be less (greater) than unity.

Source: Richard Levich, "Evaluating the Performance of the Forecasters," in Richard Ensor, ed., *The Management of Foreign Exchange Risk,* 2nd ed. (Euromoney Publications, 1982).

rate can be viewed as the market's consensus forecast of the future exchange rate.[25] These services use different methods of forecasting, such as econometric, technical, and judgmental. In evaluating the performance of forecasters, Levich computed the following ratio:

$$R = \frac{\text{MAE(S)}}{\text{MAE(F)}} \tag{6.19}$$

where:

MAE(S) = mean absolute forecast error of a forecasting service.
MAE(F) = mean absolute forecast error of the forward exchange rate as a predictor.[26]

If a professional forecasting service provides more accurate forecasts than the forward exchange rate, that is, MAE(S) < MAE(F), then the ratio *R* will be less than unity for the service. If the service fails to outperform the forward exchange rate, the ratio *R* will be greater than unity.

Exhibit 6.13 provides the *R* ratios for each service for the U.S. dollar exchange rates of nine major foreign currencies for a three-month forecasting horizon. The most striking finding presented in the exhibit is that only 24 percent of the entries, 25 out of 104, are less than unity. This, of course, means that the professional services as a whole clearly failed to outperform the forward exchange rate.[27] In other words, they failed to beat the market.

However, there are substantial variations in the performance records across individual services. In the cases of services 4 and 11, for instance, every entry is greater than unity. In contrast, for service 13, which is Wharton Econometric Forecasting Associates, the majority of entries, seven out of nine, are less than unity. It is also

---

[25]These conditions are: (a) the foreign exchange markets are efficient, and (b) the forward exchange rate does not contain a significant risk premium.

[26]The mean absolute forecast error (MAE) is computed as follows:

MAE = $(1/N) \Sigma_i |P_i - A_i|$

where *P* is the predicted exchange rate, *A* is the actual (realized) exchange rate, and *N* is the number of forecasts made. The MAE criterion penalizes the over- and underestimation equally. If a forecaster has perfect foresight so that *P = A* always, then MAE will be zero.

[27]Levich found that the same qualitative result holds for different horizons like 1 month, 6 months, and 12 months.

clear from the exhibit that the performance record of each service varies substantially across currencies. The R ratio for Wharton, for example, ranges from 0.63 for the Swiss franc to 1.79 for the Japanese yen. Wharton Associates clearly has difficulty in forecasting the dollar/yen exchange rate. Service 10, on the other hand, convincingly beat the market in forecasting the yen exchange rate, with an R ratio of 0.47! This suggests that consumers need to discriminate among forecasting services depending on what currencies they are interested in. Lastly, note that service 12, which is known to use technical analysis, outperformed neither the forward rate nor other services. This result certainly does not add credence to the technical approach to exchange rate forecasting.

In a more recent study, Eun and Sabherwal (2002) evaluated the forecasting performances of 10 major commercial banks from around the world. They used the data from *Risk*, a London-based monthly publication dealing with practical issues related to derivative securities and risk management. During the period April 1989 to February 1993, *Risk* published forecasts provided by the banks for exchange rates 3, 6, 9, and 12 months ahead. These forecasts were made for the U.S. dollar exchange rates of the British pound, German mark, Swiss franc, and Japanese yen on the same day of the month by all the banks. This is a rare case where banks' exchange rate forecasts were made available to the public. Since commercial banks are the market makers as well as key players in foreign exchange markets, they should be in a position to observe the order flows and the market sentiments closely. It is thus interesting to check how these banks perform.

In evaluating the performance of the banks, Eun and Sabherwal used the spot exchange rate as the benchmark. Recall that if you believe the exchange rate follows a random walk, today's spot exchange rate can be taken as the prediction of the future spot exchange rate. They thus computed the forecasting accuracy of each bank and compared it with that of the current spot exchange rate, that is, the rate prevailing on the day the forecast is made. In evaluating the performance of banks, they computed the following ratio:

$$R = \frac{\text{MSE(B)}}{\text{MSE(S)}}$$

where:

MSE(B) = mean squared forecast error of a bank.
MSE(S) = mean squared forecast error of the spot exchange rate.

If a bank provides more accurate forecasts than the spot exchange rate, that is, MSE(B) < MSE(S), then the ratio R will be less than unity, that is, $R < 1$.

Exhibit 6.14 provides the computed R ratios for each of the 10 sample banks as well as the forward exchange rate. Overall, the majority of entries in the exhibit exceed unity, implying that these banks as a whole could not outperform the random walk model. However, some banks significantly outperformed the random walk model, especially in the longer run. For example, in forecasting the British pound exchange rate 12 months into the future, Barclays Bank ($R = 0.60$), Commerzbank ($R = 0.72$), and Industrial Bank of Japan ($R = 0.68$) provided more accurate forecasts, on average, than the random walk model. Likewise, Commerzbank outperformed the random walk model in forecasting the German mark and Swiss franc rates 12 months into the future. But these are more exceptional cases. It is noted that no bank, including the Japanese bank, could beat the random walk model in forecasting the Japanese yen rate at any lead. The last column of Exhibit 6.14 shows that the R-ratio for the forward exchange rate is about unity, implying that the performance of the forward rate is comparable to that of the spot rate.

EXHIBIT 6.14   Forecasting Exchange Rates: Do Banks Know Better?

Currency	Forecast Lead (months)	ANZ Bank (Australia)	Banque-Paribas (France)	Barclays Bank (U.K.)	Chemical Bank (U.S.)	Commerz Bank (Germany)	Generate Bank (France)	Harris Bank (U.S.)	Ind. Bank of Japan (Japan)	Midland-Montagu (U.K.)	Union Bank (Switzerland)	Forward Rate
British Pound	3	2.09	1.31	1.08	1.33	1.31	1.41	1.95	1.10	1.10	0.98	1.02
	6	1.60	1.12	0.92	0.96	1.01	1.17	1.97	0.94	1.11	0.96	1.04
	9	1.42	1.04	0.81	0.88	0.78	0.97	1.65	0.81	0.99	1.09	0.83
	12	1.06	0.84	0.60	1.07	0.72	0.77	1.69	0.68	0.95	1.16	1.02
German Mark	3	1.98	1.39	1.09	1.19	1.59	1.39	1.95	1.14	1.26	1.00	1.01
	6	1.15	1.53	1.16	1.03	1.21	1.21	1.97	1.07	1.27	1.05	1.00
	9	0.92	1.45	1.33	0.99	0.85	0.96	1.71	1.00	1.09	0.93	1.06
	12	0.80	1.19	1.14	1.16	0.62	0.97	1.51	1.00	0.87	1.16	0.96
Swiss Franc	3	2.15	1.47	1.13	1.26	1.66	1.32	1.98	1.05	1.19	1.03	1.02
	6	1.18	1.58	1.30	0.98	1.29	1.35	1.88	1.04	1.24	1.05	1.00
	9	0.88	1.46	1.38	0.84	0.96	1.10	1.66	0.96	1.13	0.87	0.99
	12	0.67	1.16	1.15	0.88	0.74	1.01	1.40	0.91	0.98	1.01	0.94
Japanese Yen	3	3.52	2.31	1.46	1.44	1.73	2.19	2.51	1.52	2.16	1.80	1.08
	6	2.32	2.43	1.55	1.39	1.59	1.62	2.31	1.62	1.68	1.70	1.06
	9	2.54	2.73	1.80	1.57	1.60	1.85	2.22	1.90	1.74	1.97	0.99
	12	2.70	2.61	1.83	1.79	1.44	1.97	1.89	1.93	1.68	2.00	1.10

Source: Cheol Eun and Sanjiv Sabherwal, "Forecasting Exchange Rates: Do Banks Know Better?" *Global Finance Journal*, 2002, pp. 195–215.

SUMMARY

This chapter provides a systematic discussion of the key international parity relationships and two related issues, exchange rate determination and prediction. A thorough understanding of parity relationships is essential for astute financial management.

1. Interest rate parity (IRP) holds that the forward premium or discount should be equal to the interest rate differential between two countries. IRP represents an arbitrage equilibrium condition that should hold in the absence of barriers to international capital flows.

2. If IRP is violated, one can lock in guaranteed profit by borrowing in one currency and lending in another, with exchange risk hedged via forward contract. As a result of this covered interest arbitrage, IRP will be restored.

3. IRP implies that in the short run, the exchange rate depends on (a) the relative interest rates between two countries, and (b) the expected future exchange rate. Other things being equal, a higher (lower) domestic interest rate will lead to appreciation (depreciation) of the domestic currency. People's expectations concerning future exchange rates are self-fulfilling.

4. Purchasing power parity (PPP) states that the exchange rate between two countries' currencies should be equal to the ratio of their price levels. PPP is a manifestation of the law of one price applied internationally to a standard commodity basket. The relative version of PPP states that the rate of change in the exchange rate should be equal to the inflation rate differential between countries. The existing empirical evidence, however, is generally negative on PPP. This implies that substantial barriers to international commodity arbitrage exist.

5. There are three distinct approaches to exchange rate forecasting: (a) the efficient market approach, (b) the fundamental approach, and (c) the technical approach. The efficient market approach uses such market-determined prices as the current exchange rate or the forward exchange rate to forecast the future exchange rate. The fundamental approach uses various formal models of exchange rate determination for forecasting purposes. The technical approach, on the other hand, identifies patterns from the past history of the exchange rate and projects it into the future. The existing empirical evidence indicates that neither the fundamental nor the technical approach outperforms the efficient market approach.

KEY WORDS

arbitrage, *140*
arbitrage portfolio, *141*
covered interest
   arbitrage, 142
currency carry trade, *146*
efficient market
   hypothesis, *159*
Fisher effect, *156*

forward expectations
   parity (FEP), *158*
interest rate parity
   (IRP), *140*
international Fisher effect
   (IFE), *158*
law of one price (LOP), *141*
monetary approach, *172*
nontradables, *155*

purchasing power
   parity (PPP), *149*
quantity theory of money, *172*
random walk
   hypothesis, *159*
real exchange rates, *151*
technical analysis, *162*
uncovered interest rate
   parity, *146*

QUESTIONS

1. Give a full definition of *arbitrage*.

2. Discuss the implications of interest rate parity for exchange rate determination.

3. Explain the conditions under which the forward exchange rate will be an unbiased predictor of the future spot exchange rate.

4. Explain purchasing power parity, both the absolute and relative versions. What causes deviations from purchasing power parity?

5. Discuss the implications of the deviations from purchasing power parity for countries' competitive positions in the world market.

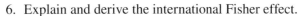

6. Explain and derive the international Fisher effect.

7. Researchers found that it is very difficult to forecast future exchange rates more accurately than the forward exchange rate or the current spot exchange rate. How would you interpret this finding?

8. Explain the random walk model for exchange rate forecasting. Can it be consistent with technical analysis?

9. Derive and explain the monetary approach to exchange rate determination.

10. Explain the following three concepts of purchasing power parity (PPP):

    a. The law of one price.

    b. Absolute PPP.

    c. Relative PPP.

11. Evaluate the usefulness of relative PPP in predicting movements in foreign exchange rates on:

    a. Short-term basis (e.g., three months).

    b. Long-term basis (e.g., six years).

PROBLEMS

1. Suppose that the treasurer of IBM has an extra cash reserve of $100,000,000 to invest for six months. The six-month interest rate is 8 percent per annum in the United States and 7 percent per annum in Germany. Currently, the spot exchange rate is €1.01 per dollar and the six-month forward exchange rate is €0.99 per dollar. The treasurer of IBM does not wish to bear any exchange risk. Where should he or she invest to maximize the return?

2. While you were visiting London, you purchased a Jaguar for £35,000, payable in three months. You have enough cash at your bank in New York City, which pays 0.35 percent interest per month, compounding monthly, to pay for the car. Currently, the spot exchange rate is $1.45/£ and the three-month forward exchange rate is $1.40/£. In London, the money market interest rate is 2.0 percent for a three-month investment. There are two alternative ways of paying for your Jaguar.

    a. Keep the funds at your bank in the United States and buy a £35,000 forward.

    b. Buy a certain pound amount spot today and invest the amount in the U.K. for three months so that the maturity value becomes equal to £35,000. Evaluate each payment method. Which method would you prefer? Why?

3. Currently, the spot exchange rate is $1.50/£ and the three-month forward exchange rate is $1.52/£. The three-month interest rate is 8.0 percent per annum in the U.S. and 5.8 percent per annum in the U.K. Assume that you can borrow as much as $1,500,000 or £1,000,000.

    a. Determine whether interest rate parity is currently holding.

    b. If IRP is not holding, how would you carry out covered interest arbitrage? Show all the steps and determine the arbitrage profit.

    c. Explain how IRP will be restored as a result of covered arbitrage activities.

4. Currently, the spot exchange rate is $0.85/A$ and the one-year forward exchange rate is $0.81/A$. One-year interest is 3.5% in the United States and 4.2% in Australia. You may borrow up to $1,000,000 or A$1,176,471, which is equivalent to $1,000,000 at the current spot rate.

    a. Determine if IRP is holding between Australia and the United States.

    b. If IRP is not holding, explain in detail how you would realize certain profit in U.S. dollar terms.

c. Explain how IRP will be restored as a result of the arbitrage transactions you carry out above.

5. Suppose that the current spot exchange rate is €0.80/$ and the three-month forward exchange rate is €0.7813/$. The three-month interest rate is 5.6 percent per annum in the United States and 5.40 percent per annum in France. Assume that you can borrow up to $1,000,000 or €800,000.

   a. Show how to realize a certain profit via covered interest arbitrage, assuming that you want to realize profit in terms of U.S. dollars. Also determine the size of your arbitrage profit.

   b. Assume that you want to realize profit in terms of euros. Show the covered arbitrage process and determine the arbitrage profit in euros.

6. In the October 23, 1999, issue, *The Economist* reports that the interest rate per annum is 5.93 percent in the United States and 70.0 percent in Turkey. Why do you think the interest rate is so high in Turkey? On the basis of the reported interest rates, how would you predict the change of the exchange rate between the U.S. dollar and the Turkish lira?

CFA® PROBLEMS

7. As of November 1, 1999, the exchange rate between the Brazilian real and U.S. dollar was R$1.95/$. The consensus forecast for the U.S. and Brazil inflation rates for the next one-year period was 2.6 percent and 20.0 percent, respectively. What would you have forecast the exchange rate to be at around November 1, 2000?

8. Omni Advisors, an international pension fund manager, uses the concepts of purchasing power parity (PPP) and the International Fisher Effect (IFE) to forecast spot exchange rates. Omni gathers the financial information as follows:

Base price level	100
Current U.S. price level	105
Current South African price level	111
Base rand spot exchange rate	$0.175
Current rand spot exchange rate	$0.158
Expected annual U.S. inflation	7%
Expected annual South African inflation	5%
Expected U.S. one-year interest rate	10%
Expected South African one-year interest rate	8%

Calculate the following exchange rates (ZAR and USD refer to the South African rand and U.S. dollar, respectively):

   a. The current ZAR spot rate in USD that would have been forecast by PPP.

   b. Using the IFE, the expected ZAR spot rate in USD one year from now.

   c. Using PPP, the expected ZAR spot rate in USD four years from now.

9. Suppose that the current spot exchange rate is €1.50/£ and the one-year forward exchange rate is €1.60/£. The one-year interest rate is 5.4 percent in euros and 5.2 percent in pounds. You can borrow at most €1,000,000 or the equivalent pound amount, that is, £666,667, at the current spot exchange rate.

   a. Show how you can realize a guaranteed profit from covered interest arbitrage. Assume that you are a euro-based investor. Also determine the size of the arbitrage profit.

   b. Discuss how the interest rate parity may be restored as a result of the above transactions.

c. Suppose you are a pound-based investor. Show the covered arbitrage process and determine the pound profit amount.

10. Due to the integrated nature of their capital markets, investors in both the United States and the U.K. require the same real interest rate, 2.5 percent, on their lending. There is a consensus in capital markets that the annual inflation rate is likely to be 3.5 percent in the United States and 1.5 percent in the U.K. for the next three years. The spot exchange rate is currently $1.50/£.

   a. Compute the nominal interest rate per annum in both the United States and the U.K., assuming that the Fisher effect holds.

   b. What is your expected future spot dollar-pound exchange rate in three years from now?

   c. Can you infer the forward dollar-pound exchange rate for one-year maturity?

11. After studying Iris Hamson's credit analysis, George Davies is considering whether he can increase the holding period return on Yucatan Resort's excess cash holdings (which are held in pesos) by investing those cash holdings in the Mexican bond market. Although Davies would be investing in a peso-denominated bond, the investment goal is to achieve the highest holding period return, measured in U.S. dollars, on the investment.

   Davies finds the higher yield on the Mexican one-year bond, which is considered to be free of credit risk, to be attractive but he is concerned that depreciation of the peso will reduce the holding period return, measured in U.S. dollars. Hamson has prepared selected economic and financial data to help Davies make the decision.

Selected Economic and Financial Data for U.S. and Mexico	
Expected U.S. Inflation Rate	2.0% per year
Expected Mexican Inflation Rate	6.0% per year
U.S. One-year Treasury Bond Yield	2.5%
Mexican One-year Bond Yield	6.5%

Nominal Exchange Rates	
Spot	9.5000 Pesos = U.S. $1.00
One-year Forward	9.8707 Pesos = U.S. $1.00

Hamson recommends buying the Mexican one-year bond and hedging the foreign currency exposure using the one-year forward exchange rate. She concludes: "This transaction will result in a U.S. dollar holding period return that is equal to the holding period return of the U.S. one-year bond."

   a. Calculate the U.S. dollar holding period return that would result from the transaction recommended by Hamson. Show your calculations. State whether Hamson's conclusion about the U.S. dollar holding period return resulting from the transaction is correct or incorrect.

After conducting his own analysis of the U.S. and Mexican economies, Davies expects that both the U.S. inflation rate and the real exchange rate will remain constant over the coming year. Because of favorable political developments in Mexico, however, he expects that the Mexican inflation rate (in annual terms) will fall from 6.0 percent to 3.0 percent before the end of the year. As a result, Davies decides to invest Yucatan Resort's cash holdings in the Mexican one-year bond but not to hedge the currency exposure.

b. Calculate the expected exchange rate (pesos per dollar) one year from now. Show your calculations. Note: Your calculations should assume that Davies is correct in his expectations about the real exchange rate and the Mexican and U.S. inflation rates.

c. Calculate the expected U.S. dollar holding period return on the Mexican one-year bond. Show your calculations. Note: Your calculations should assume that Davies is correct in his expectations about the real exchange rate and the Mexican and U.S. inflation rates.

CFA®
PROBLEMS

12. James Clark is a currency trader with Wachovia. He notices the following quotes:

Spot exchange rate	SFr1.2051/$
Six-month forward exchange rate	SFr1.1922/$
Six-month dollar interest rate	2.50% per year
Six-month Swiss franc interest rate	2.0% per year

a. Is the interest rate parity holding? You may ignore transaction costs.

b. Is there an arbitrage opportunity? If yes, show what steps need to be taken to make arbitrage profit. Assuming that James Clark is authorized to work with $1,000,000, compute the arbitrage profit in dollars.

13. Suppose you conduct currency carry trade by borrowing $1,000,000 at the start of each year and investing in the New Zealand dollar for one year. One-year interest rates and the exchange rate between the U.S. dollar ($) and New Zealand dollar (NZ$) are provided below for the period 2000–2009. Note that interest rates are one-year interbank rates on January 1 each year, and that the exchange rate is the amount of New Zealand dollar per U.S. dollar on December 31 each year. The exchange rate was NZ$1.9088/$ on January 1, 2000. Fill out columns 4–7 and compute the total dollar profit from this carry trade over the 10-year period. Also, assess the validity of uncovered interest rate parity based on your solution of this problem. You are encouraged to use the Excel spreadsheet software to tackle this problem.

Year	(1) $i_{NZ\$}(\%)$	(2) $i_{\$}(\%)$	(3) $S_{NZ\$/\$}$	(4) $i_{NZ\$} - i_{\$}$	(5) $e_{NZ\$/\$}$	(6) (4) − (5)	(7) $ Profit
2000	6.53	6.50	2.2599				
2001	6.70	6.00	2.4015				
2002	4.91	2.44	1.9117				
2003	5.94	1.45	1.5230				
2004	5.88	1.46	1.3845				
2005	6.67	3.10	1.4682				
2006	7.28	4.84	1.4182				
2007	8.03	5.33	1.2994				
2008	9.10	4.22	1.7112				
2009	5.10	2.00	1.3742				

Data source: *Datastream.*

INTERNET EXERCISES

1. You provide foreign exchange consulting services based on technical (chartist) analysis. Your client would like to have a good idea about the U.S. dollar and Mexican peso exchange rate six months into the future. First plot the past exchange rates and try to identify patterns that can be projected into the future. What forecast exchange rate would you offer to your client? You may download exchange rate data from fx.sauder.ubc.ca.

MINI CASE

Turkish Lira and Purchasing Power Parity

Veritas Emerging Market Fund specializes in investing in emerging stock markets of the world. Mr. Henry Mobaus, an experienced hand in international investment and your boss, is currently interested in Turkish stock markets. He thinks that Turkey will eventually be invited to negotiate its membership in the European Union. If this happens, it will boost stock prices in Turkey. But, at the same time, he is quite concerned with the volatile exchange rates of the Turkish currency. He would like to understand what drives Turkish exchange rates. Because the inflation rate is much higher in Turkey than in the United States, he thinks that purchasing power parity may be holding at least to some extent. As a research assistant for him, you are assigned to check this out. In other words, you have to study and prepare a report on the following question: Does purchasing power parity hold for the Turkish lira–U.S. dollar exchange rate? Among other things, Mr. Mobaus would like you to do the following:

1. Plot past annual exchange rate changes against the differential inflation rates between Turkey and the United States for the last 20 years.
2. Regress the annual rate of exchange rate changes on the annual inflation rate differential to estimate the intercept and the slope coefficient, and interpret the regression results.

Data sources: You may download the annual inflation rates for Turkey and the United States, as well as the exchange rate between the Turkish lira and the U.S. dollar, from the following source: data.un.org. For the exchange rate, you are advised to use the variable code 186AEZF. You may also obtain the data from other sources.

REFERENCES & SUGGESTED READINGS

Abuaf, N., and P. Jorion. "Purchasing Power Parity in the Long Run." *Journal of Finance* 45 (1990), pp. 157–74.

Adler, Michael, and Bruce Lehman. "Deviations from Purchasing Power Parity in the Long Run." *Journal of Finance* 38 (1983), pp. 1471–87.

Aliber, R. "The Interest Rate Parity: A Reinterpretation." *Journal of Political Economy* (1973), pp. 1451–59.

Eun, Cheol, and Sanjiv Sabherwal. "Forecasting Exchange Rates: Do Banks Know Better?" *Global Finance Journal* (2002), pp. 195–215.

Fisher, Irving. *The Theory of Interest,* rpt. ed. New York: Macmillan, 1980.

Frenkel, Jacob. "Flexible Exchange Rates, Prices and the Role of News: Lessons from the 1970s." *Journal of Political Economy* 89 (1981), pp. 665–705.

Frenkel, Jacob, and Richard Levich. "Covered Interest Arbitrage: Unexploited Profits?" *Journal of Political Economy* 83 (1975), pp. 325–38.

Gande, A, and D. Parsley. "News Spillovers in Sovereign Debt Markets." *Journal of Financial Economics* 75 (2005), pp. 691–734.

Keynes, John M. *Monetary Reform.* New York: Harcourt, Brace, 1924.

Kravis, I., and R. Lipsey. "Price Behavior in the Light of Balance of Payment Theories." *Journal of International Economics* (1978), pp. 193–246.

Larsen, Glen, and Bruce Resnick. "International Party Relationships and Tests for Risk Premia in Forward Foreign Exchange Rates." *Journal of International Financial Markets, Institutions and Money* 3 (1993), pp. 33–56.

Levich, Richard. "Evaluating the Performance of the Forecasters." *The Management of Foreign Exchange Risk.* 2nd ed. In ed. Richard Ensor. Euromoney Publication, 1982, pp. 121–34.

Meese, Richard, and Kenneth Rogoff. "Empirical Exchange Rate Models of the Seventies: Do They Fit Out of Sample?" *Journal of International Economics* 14 (1983), pp. 3–24.

Osler, Carol. "Currency Orders and Exchange Rate Dynamics: Explaining the Success of Technical Analysis." *Journal of Finance* 58 (2003), pp. 1791–1819.

Otani, Ichiro, and Siddharth Tiwari. "Capital Controls and Interest Rate Parity: The Japanese Experience, 1978–81." *International Monetary Fund Staff Papers* 28 (1981), pp. 793–815.

Richardson, J. "Some Empirical Evidence on Commodity Arbitrage and the Law of One Price." *Journal of International Economics* 8 (1978), pp. 341–52.

Taylor, Alan, and Mark Taylor. "The Purchasing Power Parity Debate." *Journal of Economic Perspectives* 18 (2004), pp. 135–158.

www.mhhe.com/er8e

6A

Purchasing Power Parity and Exchange Rate Determination

Although PPP itself can be viewed as a theory of exchange rate determination, it also serves as a foundation for a more complete theory, namely, the **monetary approach**. The monetary approach, associated with the Chicago School of Economics, is based on two basic tenets: purchasing power parity and the quantity theory of money.

From the **quantity theory of money**, we obtain the following identity that must hold in each country:

$$P_\$ = M_\$ V_\$/y_\$ \tag{6A.1A}$$

$$P_\pounds = M_\pounds V_\pounds/y_\pounds \tag{6A.1B}$$

where M denotes the money supply, V the velocity of money, measuring the speed at which money is being circulated in the economy, y the national aggregate output, and P the general price level; the subscripts denote countries. When the above equations are substituted for the price levels in the PPP Equation 6.12, we obtain the following expression for the exchange rate:

$$S = (M_\$/M_\pounds)(V_\$/V_\pounds)(y_\pounds/y_\$) \tag{6A.2}$$

According to the monetary approach, what matters in the exchange rate determination are

1. The relative money supplies.
2. The relative velocities of money.
3. The relative national outputs.

All else equal, an increase in the U.S. money supply will result in a proportionate depreciation of the dollar against the pound. So will an increase in the velocity of the dollar, which has the same effect as an increased supply of dollars. But an increase in U.S. output will result in a proportionate appreciation of the dollar.

The monetary approach, which is based on PPP, can be viewed as a long-run theory, not a short-run theory, of exchange rate determination. This is so because the monetary approach does not allow for price rigidities. It assumes that prices adjust fully and completely, which is unrealistic in the short run. Prices of many commodities and services are often fixed over a certain period of time. A good example of short-term price rigidity is the wage rate set by a labor contract. Despite this apparent shortcoming, the monetary approach remains an influential theory and serves as a benchmark in modern exchange rate economics.

7 Futures and Options on Foreign Exchange

ON JANUARY 24, 2008 it was disclosed by Société Générale, France's second largest bank, that a 31-year-old rogue trader had taken unauthorized positions in European stock index futures contracts totaling $73 billion that resulted in trading losses of $7.2 billion when the stock market turned downward against the trader's positions. The trader was able to hide his positions for months by concealing his bets with a series of offsetting transactions with fictional counterparties. The loss forced Société Générale to raise $8 billion in emergency capital. Similarly, in 1995, another rogue trader brought down Barings PLC by losing $1.3 billion from an unhedged $27 billion position in various exchanged-traded futures and options contracts, primarily the Nikkei 225 stock index futures contract traded on the Singapore International Monetary Exchange. The losses occurred when the market moved unfavorably against the trader's speculative positions. Barings was taken over by ING Group, the Dutch banking and insurance conglomerate. The trader served three years in prison in Singapore for fraudulent trading.

As these stories imply, futures and options contracts can be very risky investments, indeed, when used for speculative purposes. Nevertheless, they are also important risk-management tools. In this chapter, we introduce exchange-traded currency futures contracts, options contracts, and options on currency futures that are useful for both speculating on foreign exchange price movements and hedging exchange rate uncertainty. These contracts make up part of the foreign exchange market that was introduced in Chapter 5, where we discussed spot and forward exchange rates.

The discussion begins by comparing forward and futures contracts, noting similarities and differences between the two. We discuss the markets where futures are traded, the currencies on which contracts are written, and contract specifications for the various currency contracts.

Next, options contracts on foreign exchange are introduced, comparing and contrasting the options and the futures markets. The exchanges where options are traded are identified and contract terms are specified. The over-the-counter options market is also discussed. Basic option-pricing boundary relationships are illustrated using actual market prices. Additionally, illustrations of how a speculator might use currency options are also provided. The chapter closes with the development of a currency option-pricing model. This chapter and the knowledge gained about forward contracts in Chapters 5 and 6 set the stage for Chapters 8, 9, and 10, which explain how these vehicles can be used for hedging foreign exchange risk.

Futures Contracts: Some Preliminaries

In Chapter 5, a *forward contract* was defined as a vehicle for buying or selling a stated amount of foreign exchange at a stated price per unit at a specified time in the future. Both forward and futures contracts are classified as **derivative** or **contingent claim securities** because their values are derived from or contingent upon the value of the underlying security. But while a **futures** contract is similar to a forward contract, there are many distinctions between the two. A forward contract is tailor-made for a client by his international bank. In contrast, a futures contract has **standardized** features and is **exchange-traded**, that is, traded on organized exchanges rather than over the counter. A client desiring a position in futures contracts contacts his broker, who transmits the order to the exchange floor where it is transferred to the trading pit. In the trading pit, the price for the order is negotiated by open outcry between floor brokers or traders.

The main standardized features are the **contract size** specifying the amount of the underlying foreign currency for future purchase or sale and the **maturity date** of the contract. A futures contract is written for a specific amount of foreign currency rather than for a tailor-made sum. Hence, a position in multiple contracts may be necessary to establish a sizable hedge or speculative position. Futures contracts have specific **delivery months** during the year in which contracts mature on a specified day of the month.

An **initial performance bond** (formerly called *margin*) must be deposited into a collateral account to establish a futures position. The initial performance bond is generally equal to about 2 percent of the contract value. Either cash or Treasury bills may be used to meet the performance bond requirement. The account balance will fluctuate through daily settlement, as illustrated by the following discussion. The performance bond put up by the contract holder can be viewed as "good-faith" money that he will fulfill his side of the financial obligation.

The major difference between a forward contract and a futures contract is the way the underlying asset is priced for future purchase or sale. A forward contract states a price for the future transaction. By contrast, a futures contract is **settled-up**, or **marked-to-market**, daily at the settlement price. The **settlement price** is a price representative of futures transaction prices at the close of daily trading on the exchange. It is determined by a settlement committee for the commodity, and it may be somewhat arbitrary if trading volume for the contract has been light for the day. A buyer of a futures contract (one who holds a **long** position) in which the settlement price is higher (lower) than the previous day's settlement price has a positive (negative) settlement for the day. Because a long position entitles the owner to purchase the underlying asset, a higher (lower) settlement price means the futures price of the underlying asset has increased (decreased). Consequently, a long position in the contract is worth more (less). The change in settlement prices from one day to the next determines the settlement amount. That is, the change in settlement prices per unit of the underlying asset, multiplied by the size of the contract, equals the size of the daily settlement to be added to (or subtracted from) the long's performance bond account. Analogously, the seller of the futures contract (**short** position) will have his performance bond account increased (or decreased) by the amount the long's performance bond account is decreased (or increased). Thus, futures trading between the long and the short is a **zero-sum game**; that is, the sum of the long and short's daily settlement is zero. If the investor's performance bond account falls below a **maintenance performance bond** level (roughly equal to 90 percent of the initial performance bond), additional funds must be deposited into the account to bring it back to the initial performance bond level in order to keep the position open. An investor

EXHIBIT 7.1

Differences between Futures and Forward Contracts

Trading Location
Futures: Traded competitively on organized exchanges.
Forward: Traded by bank dealers via a network of telephones and computerized dealing systems.

Contractual Size
Futures: Standardized amount of the underlying asset.
Forward: Tailor-made to the needs of the participant.

Settlement
Futures: Daily settlement, or marking-to-market, done by the futures clearinghouse through the participant's performance bond account.
Forward: Participant buys or sells the contractual amount of the underlying asset from the bank at maturity at the forward (contractual) price.

Expiration Date
Futures: Standardized delivery dates.
Forward: Tailor-made delivery date that meets the needs of the investor.

Delivery
Futures: Delivery of the underlying asset is seldom made. Usually a reversing trade is transacted to exit the market.
Forward: Delivery of the underlying asset is commonly made.

Trading Costs
Futures: Bid-ask spread plus broker's commission.
Forward: Bid-ask spread plus indirect bank charges via compensating balance requirements.

---

who suffers a liquidity crunch and cannot deposit additional funds will have his position liquidated by his broker.

The marking-to-market feature of futures markets means that market participants realize their profits or suffer their losses on a day-to-day basis rather than all at once at maturity as with a forward contract. At the end of daily trading, a futures contract is analogous to a new forward contract on the underlying asset at the new settlement price with a one-day-shorter maturity. Because of the daily marking-to-market, the futures price will converge through time to the spot price on the last day of trading in the contract. That is, the final settlement price at which any transaction in the underlying asset will transpire is the spot price on the last day of trading. The effective price is, nevertheless, the original futures contract price, once the profit or loss in the performance bond account is included. Exhibit 7.1 summarizes the differences between forward and futures contracts.

Two types of market participants are necessary for a derivatives market to operate most efficiently: **speculators** and **hedgers**. A speculator attempts to profit from a change in the futures price. To do this, the speculator will take a long or short position in a futures contract depending upon his expectations of future price movement. A hedger, on the other hand, wants to avoid price variation by locking in a purchase price of the underlying asset through a long position in the futures contract or a sales price through a short position. In effect, the hedger passes off the risk of price variation to the speculator, who is better able, or at least more willing, to bear this risk.

Both forward and futures markets for foreign exchange are very liquid. A **reversing trade** can be made in either market that will close out, or neutralize, a position.[1] In forward markets, approximately 90 percent of all contracts result in the short making

---

[1]In the forward market, the investor holds offsetting positions after a reversing trade; in the futures market the investor actually exits the marketplace.

delivery of the underlying asset to the long. This is natural given the tailor-made terms of forward contracts. By contrast, only about 1 percent of currency futures contracts result in delivery. While futures contracts are useful for speculation and hedging, their standardized delivery dates are unlikely to correspond to the actual future dates when foreign exchange transactions will transpire. Thus, they are generally closed out in a reversing trade. The **commission** that buyers and sellers pay to transact in the futures market is a single amount paid up front that covers the *round-trip* transactions of initiating and closing out the position. These days, through a discount broker, the commission charge can be as little as $15 per currency futures contract.

In futures markets, a **clearinghouse** serves as the third party to all transactions. That is, the buyer of a futures contract effectively buys from the clearinghouse and the seller sells to the clearinghouse. This feature of futures markets facilitates active secondary market trading because the buyer and the seller do not have to evaluate one another's creditworthiness. The clearinghouse is made up of *clearing members*. Individual brokers who are not clearing members must deal through a clearing member to clear a customer's trade. In the event of default of one side of a futures trade, the clearing member stands in for the defaulting party, and then seeks restitution from that party. The clearinghouse's liability is limited because a contractholder's position is marked-to-market daily. Given the organizational structure, it is only logical that the clearinghouse maintains the futures performance bond accounts for the clearing members.

Frequently, a futures exchange may have a **daily price limit** on the futures price, that is, a limit as to how much the settlement price can increase or decrease from the previous day's settlement price. Forward markets do not have this. Obviously, when the price limit is hit, trading will halt as a new market-clearing equilibrium price cannot be obtained. Exchange rules exist for expanding the daily price limit in an orderly fashion until a market-clearing price can be established.

Currency Futures Markets

www.cmegroup.com

This is the website of the CME Group. It provides detailed information about the futures contracts and options contracts traded on it.

www.theice.com

This is the website of the Intercontinental Exchange (ICE). Several FX futures contracts are traded on their electronic trading platform.

On May 16, 1972, trading in currency futures contracts began at the Chicago Mercantile Exchange (CME). Trading activity in currency futures has expanded rapidly at the CME. In 1978, only 2 million contracts were traded; this figure stood at nearly 200 million contracts in 2015. In 2007, the CME Group was formed through a merger between the CME and the Chicago Board of Trade (CBOT). The following year, the CME Group acquired the New York Mercantile Exchange (NYMEX). Most CME currency futures trade in a March, June, September, and December expiration cycle, with the delivery date being the third Wednesday of the expiration month. The last day of trading for most contracts is the second business day prior to the delivery date. Trading in CME currency futures contracts takes place Sunday through Friday on the GLOBEX trading system from 5:00 P.M. to 4:00 P.M. Chicago time the next day. GLOBEX is a worldwide automated order-entry and matching system for futures and options that provides nearly 24-hour trading. Exhibit 7.2 summarizes the basic CME Group currency contract specifications. The International Finance in Practice box "FX Market Volumes Surge" details the popularity of CME Group currency products and the GLOBEX trading platform.

In addition to the CME, currency futures trading takes place on the Intercontinental Exchange (ICE) Futures U.S. (formerly the New York Board of Trade), the Mexican Derivatives Exchange, the BM&F Exchange in Brazil, the Budapest Commodity Exchange, and the Derivatives Market Division of the Korea Exchange.

FX Market Volumes Surge

The FX market is growing at record levels, according to figures released by the CME Group, the largest regulated foreign exchange market in the world.

Last month the CME Group reported average daily notional volume at a record level of $121 billion, up 82 percent compared to a year earlier.

With a number of indicators at play, like the news of Greece's credit concerns and the continued appetite for high-yielding currencies like the Australian dollar and the Canadian dollar, the CME saw record volumes and notional values in the euro and Australian and Canadian dollars. Euro FX futures and options saw total average daily volume of 362,000 contracts with total notional ADV of slightly over $62 billion.

Australian dollar futures and options climbed to nearly 119,000 contracts in average daily volume with almost $11 billion in total notional ADV, and Canadian dollar futures

and options surpassed 88,000 contracts in ADV and $8 billion in total notional ADV.

With foreign currency futures going from strength to strength, the CME Group recently published a white paper outlining the benefits of FX futures.

"These contracts provide an ideal tool to manage currency or FX risks in an uncertain world," it said. "Product innovation, liquidity, and financial surety are the three pillars upon which the CME Group has built its world-class derivatives market. The CME Group provides products based on a wide range of frequently transacted currencies, liquidity offered on the state-of-the-art CME Globex electronic trading platform, and financial sureties afforded by its centralized clearing system."

EXHIBIT 7.2

CME Group Currency Futures Specifications

Currency	Contract Size
Price Quoted in U.S. Dollars	*CME*
Australian dollar	AUD100,000
Brazilian real	BRL100,000
British pound	GBP62,500
Canadian dollar	CAD100,000
Chinese renminbi	CNY1,000,000
Czech koruna	CZK4,000,000
Euro FX	EUR125,000
Hungarian forint	HUF30,000,000
Indian rupee	INR5,000,000
Israeli shekel	ILS1,000,000
Japanese yen	JPY12,500,000
Korean won	KRW125,000,000
Mexican peso	MXN500,000
New Zealand dollar	NZD100,00
Norwegian krone	NOK2,000,000
Polish zloty	PLN500,000
Russian ruble	RUB2,500,000
South African rand	ZAR500,000
Swedish krona	SEK2,000,000
Swiss franc	CHF125,000
Cross-Rate Futures	
(Underlying Currency/Price Currency)	
Euro FX/British pound	EUR125,000
Euro FX/Japanese yen	EUR125,000
Euro FX/Swiss franc	EUR125,000

Source: CME Group, www.cmegroup.com, website.

Basic Currency Futures Relationships

Exhibit 7.3 shows quotations for CME futures contracts. For each delivery month for each currency, we see the opening price quotation, the high and the low quotes for the trading day (in this case May 16, 2016), and the settlement price. Each is presented in American terms, that is, $F(\$/i)$. (We use the same symbol F for futures prices as for forward prices, and explain why shortly.) For each contract, the **open interest** is also presented. This is the total number of short or long contracts outstanding for the particular delivery month. Note that the open interest is greatest for each currency in the **nearby** contract, in this case the June 2016 contract. Few of these contracts will actually result in delivery, so if we were to follow the open interest in the June contracts through time, we would see the number for each different currency decrease as the last day of trading (June 13, 2016) approaches as a result of reversing trades. Additionally, we would note increased open interest in the September 2013 contract as trading interest in the soon-to-be nearby contract picks up. In general, open interest (loosely an indicator of demand) typically decreases with the term-to-maturity of most futures contracts.

EXHIBIT 7.3	CME Group Currency Futures Contract Quotations					
	Open	High	Low	Settle	Change	Open interest
Currency Futures						
Japanese Yen (CME)–¥12,500,000; $ per 100¥						
June	.9210	.9226	.9173	.9182	−.0030	159,608
Sept	.9246	.9255	.9202	.9212	−.0030	1,443
Canadian Dollar (CME)–CAD 100,000; $ per CAD						
June	.7724	.7768	.7714	.7753	.0023	118,862
Sept	.7719	.7766	.7715	.7753	.0023	2,744
British Pound (CME)–£62,500; $ per £						
June	1.4353	1.4416	1.4333	1.4391	.0023	238,280
Sept	1.4356	1.4421	1.4342	1.4398	.0023	1,796
Swiss Franc (CME)–CHF 125,000; $ per CHF						
June	1.0258	1.0271	1.0231	1.0235	−.0032	43,970
Sept	1.0300	1.0300	1.0276	1.0282	−.0032	178
Australian Dollar (CME)–AUD 100,000; $ per AUD						
June	.7246	.7301	.7241	.7280	.0016	119,002
Sept	.7222	.7275	.7217	.7254	.0016	2,404
Mexican Peso (CME)–MXN 500,000; $ per MXN						
June	.05487	.05512	.05440	.05481	−.00006	91,662
Euro (CME)–€125,000; $ per €						
June	1.1312	1.1352	1.1311	1.1327	.0011	339,149
Sept	1.1347	1.1386	1.1347	1.1363	.0011	5,793
Euro/Japanese Yen (ICE-US)–€125,000; ¥ per €						
June	122.66	123.53	122.64	123.36	.51	8,857
Sept	–	–	–	123.35	.51	2
Euro/British Pound (ICE-US)–€125,000; £ per €						
June	.78845	.78995	.78665	.78710	−.00050	28,429
Sept	–	–	–	.78915	−.00055	4
Euro/Swiss Franc (ICE-US)–€125,000; CHF per €						
June	1.1031	1.1069	1.1031	1.1067	.0045	16,149

Sources: The Wall Street Journal, Tuesday, May 17, 2016, p. C7. Euro/JPY, Euro/GBP, and Euro/CHF quotations are May 16, 2016 values from Bloomberg.

EXAMPLE | 7.1: Reading Futures Quotations

As an example of reading futures quotations, let's use the September 2016 Australian dollar contract. From Exhibit 7.3, we see that on Monday, May 16, 2016, the contract opened for trading at a price of $0.7222/AUD, and traded in the range of $0.7217/AUD (low) to $0.7275/AUD (high) throughout the day. The settlement ("closing") price was $0.7254/AUD. The open interest, or the number of September 2016 contracts outstanding, was 2,404.

At the settlement price of $0.7254, the holder of a long position in one contract is committing himself to paying $72,540 for AUD100,000 on the delivery day, September 21, 2016, if he actually takes delivery. Note that the settlement price increased $0.0016 from the previous day. That is, it increased from $0.7238/AUD to $0.7254/AUD. Both the buyer and the seller of the contract would have their accounts marked-to-market by the change in the settlement prices. That is, one holding a long position from the previous day would have $160.00 (=$0.0016 × AUD100,000) added to his performance bond account and the short would have $160.00 subtracted from his account.

Even though marking-to-market is an important economic difference between the operation of the futures market and the forward market, it has little effect on the pricing of futures contracts as opposed to the way forward contracts are priced. To see this, note the pattern of AUD forward prices from the *Exchange Rates* presented in Exhibit 5.4 in Chapter 5. They go from a spot price of $0.7289/AUD to $0.7280 (1-month) to $0.7264 (3-months) to $0.7242 (6-months). To the extent that forward prices are an unbiased predictor of future spot exchange rates, the market is anticipating the U.S. dollar to appreciate over the next six months relative to the Australian dollar. Similarly, we see an appreciating pattern of the U.S. dollar from the pattern of settlement prices for the AUD futures contracts: $0.7280 (June) to $0.7254 (September). It is also noteworthy that both the forward and the futures contracts together display a chronological pattern. For example, the June futures contract price (with a delivery date of June 15) and the September futures contract price (with a delivery date of September 21) surround the 1-month forward contract price (with a value date of June 20) and the 3-month forward contract price (with a value date of August 18); these coupled with the 6-month forward contract price (with a value date of November 18) display an essentially consistent pattern: $0.7289, $0.7280, $0.7280, $0.7264, $0.7254, and $0.7242 appreciating from May to November. Thus, both the forward market and the futures market are useful for **price discovery**, or obtaining the market's forecast of the spot exchange rate at different future dates.

Example 7.1 implies that futures are priced very similarly to forward contracts. In Chapter 6, we developed the interest rate parity (IRP) model, which states that the forward price for delivery at time T is

$$F_T(\$/i) = S_0(\$/i)\frac{(1 + r_\$)^T}{(1 + r_i)^T} \tag{7.1}$$

We will use the same equation to define the futures price. This should work well since the similarities between the forward and the futures markets allow arbitrage opportunities if the prices between the markets are not roughly in accord.[2]

---

[2] As a theoretical proposition, Cox, Ingersoll, and Ross (1981) show that forward and futures prices should not be equal unless interest rates are constant or can be predicted with certainty. For our purposes, it is not necessary to be theoretically specific.

EXAMPLE | 7.2: Speculating and Hedging with Currency Futures

Suppose a trader takes a position on May 16, 2016, in one September 2016 euro futures contract at $1.1363/€. The trader holds the position until the last day of trading when the spot price is $1.1208/€. This will also be the final settlement price because of **price convergence**. The trader's profit or loss depends upon whether he had a long or short position in the September euro contract. If the trader had a long position, and he was a speculator with no underlying position in euros, he would have a cumulative loss of −$1,937.50 [=($1.1208 − $1.1363) × €125,000] from May 16 through September 21. This amount would be subtracted from his margin account as a result of daily marking-to-market. If he takes delivery, he will pay out-of-pocket $142,037.50 for the €125,000 (which have a spot market value of $140,100.00). The effective cost, however, is $142,037.50 (= $140,100.00 + $1,937.50), including the amount subtracted from the margin money. Alternatively, as a hedger desiring to acquire €125,000 on September 21 for $1.1363/€, our trader has locked in a purchase price of $142,037.50 from a long position in the September € futures contract.

If the trader had taken a short position, and he was a speculator with no underlying position in euros, he would have a cumulative profit of $1,937.50 [= ($1.1363 − $1.1208) × €125,000] from May 16 through September 21. This amount would be added to his margin account as a result of daily marking-to-market. If he makes delivery, he will receive $142,037.50 for the €125,000 (which also cost $140,100.00 in the spot market). The effective amount he receives, however, is $142,037.50 (= $140,100.00 + $1,937.50), including the amount added to his margin account. Alternatively, as a hedger desiring to sell €125,000 on September 21 for $1.1363/€, our trader has locked in a sales price of $142,037.50 from a short position in the September € futures contract. Exhibit 7.4 graphs these long and short futures positions.

EXHIBIT 7.4

Graph of Long and Short Positions in the September 2016 Euro Futures Contract

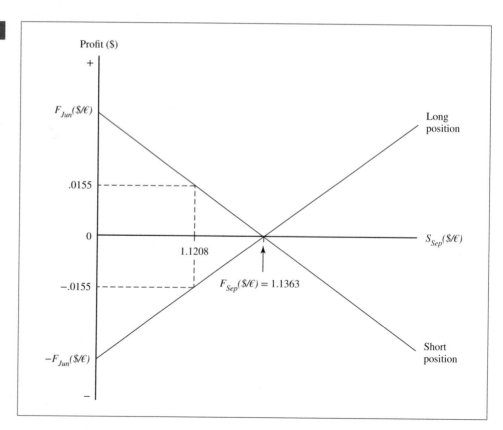

Options Contracts: Some Preliminaries

An **option** is a contract giving the owner the right, but not the obligation, to buy or sell a given quantity of an asset at a specified price at some time in the future. Like a futures or forward contract, an option is a derivative, or contingent claim, security. Its value is derived from its definable relationship with the underlying asset—in this chapter, foreign currency, or some claim on it. An option to buy the underlying asset is a **call**, and an option to sell the underlying asset is a **put**. Buying or selling the underlying asset via the option is known as exercising the option. The stated price paid (or received) is known as the **exercise** or **striking price**. In options terminology, the buyer of an option is frequently referred to as the long and the seller of an option is referred to as the **writer** of the option, or the short.

Because the option owner does not have to exercise the option if it is to his disadvantage, the option has a price, or **premium**. There are two types of options, American and European. The names do not refer to the continents where they are traded, but rather to their exercise characteristics. A **European option** can be exercised only at the maturity or expiration date of the contract, whereas an **American option** can be exercised at any time during the contract. Thus, the American option allows the owner to do everything he can do with a European option, and the right of early exercise.

Currency Options Markets

Prior to 1982, all currency option contracts were over-the-counter options written by international banks, investment banks, and brokerage houses. Over-the-counter options are tailor-made according to the specifications of the buyer in terms of maturity length, exercise price, and the amount of the underlying currency. Generally, these contracts are written for large amounts, at least $1,000,000 of the currency serving as the underlying asset. Frequently, they are written for U.S. dollars, with the euro, British pound, Japanese yen, Canadian dollar, and Swiss franc serving as the underlying currency, though options are also available on less actively traded currencies. Over-the-counter options are typically European style.

In December 1982, the Philadelphia Stock Exchange (PHLX) began trading options on foreign currency. In 2008, the PHLX was acquired by the NASDAQ OMX Group. Currently, the PHLX trades World Currency Options on seven currencies, as shown in Exhibit 7.5, which shows contract specifications. The PHLX currency options contracts are cash settlement contracts in U.S. dollars. Contracts trade in the March, June, September, and December expiration cycle plus two near-term months so that there are six expirations trading at all times. These options are European style and are cash settled on the Saturday (expiration date) following the third Friday (last day of trading) of the expiration month. The trading hours of these contracts are 9:30 A.M. to 4:00 P.M. Philadelphia time.

The volume of OTC currency options trading is much larger than that of organized-exchange option trading. According to the Bank for International Settlements, in 2016

EXHIBIT 7.5		
PHLX World Currency Options Specifications	Currency	Contract Size
	Australian dollar	AUD10,000
	British pound	GBP10,000
	Canadian dollar	CAD10,000
	Euro	EUR10,000
	Japanese yen	JPY1,000,000
	New Zealand dollar	NZD10,000
	Swiss franc	CHF10,000

the average daily OTC options trading volume was $254 billion. By comparison exchange-traded currency option volume is negligible. As an exchange-traded derivative, PHLX options are exempt from regulation as "swaps" under the Dodd-Frank Act, as are currency futures, but OTC currency options are not.

Currency Futures Options

The CME Group trades American style options on most of the currency futures contracts it offers (refer to Exhibit 7.2.) With these options, the underlying asset is a futures contract on the foreign currency instead of the physical currency. One futures contract underlies one options contract. Additionally, European style options recently began trading on the key currency futures contracts.

Most CME futures options trade with expirations in the March, June, September, December expiration cycle of the underlying futures contract and three serial noncycle months. For example, in January, options with expirations in January, February, and March would trade on the March futures contract, options with expirations in April and June would trade on the June futures contract, and options with September and December expirations, would trade on futures with corresponding expirations. Options expire on the second Friday prior to the third Wednesday of the options contract month. Trading takes place Sunday through Friday on the GLOBEX system from 5:00 P.M. to 4:00 P.M. Chicago time the next day.

Options on currency futures behave very similarly to options on the physical currency since the futures price converges to the spot price as the futures contract nears maturity. Exercise of a futures option results in a long futures position for the call buyer or the put writer and a short futures position for the put buyer or the call writer. If the futures position is not offset prior to the futures expiration date, receipt or delivery of the underlying currency will, respectively, result or be required.

Basic Option-Pricing Relationships at Expiration

At expiration, a European option and an American option (which has not been previously exercised), both with the same exercise price, will have the same terminal value. For call options the time T expiration value per unit of foreign currency can be stated as:

$$C_{aT} = C_{eT} = Max \, [S_T - E, \, 0], \tag{7.2}$$

where C_{aT} denotes the value of the American call at expiration, C_{eT} is the value of the European call at expiration, E is the exercise price per unit of foreign currency, S_T is the expiration date spot price, and Max is an abbreviation for denoting the maximum of the arguments within the brackets. A call (put) option with $S_T > E \, (E > S_T)$ expires **in-the-money** and it will be exercised. If $S_T = E$ the option expires **at-the-money**. If $S_T < E \, (E < S_T)$ the call (put) option expires **out-of-the-money** and it will not be exercised.

EXAMPLE | 7.3: Expiration Value of a European Call Option

As an illustration of pricing Equation 7.2, consider the PHLX 112 Sep EUR European call option from Exhibit 7.6. This option has a current premium, C_e, of 2.76 cents per EUR. The exercise price is 112 cents per EUR and September 16, 2016, is the last day of trading. Suppose that on that date the spot rate is $1.1625/EUR. In this event, the call option has an exercise value of 116.25 − 112 = 4.25 cents per each of the

continued

EXAMPLE | 7.3: continued

EUR10,000 of the contract, or $425. That is, the call owner can buy EUR10,000, worth $11,625 (= EUR10,000 × $1.1625) in the spot market, for $11,200 (= EUR10,000 × $1.12). On the other hand, if the spot rate is 1.1007/EUR on the last day of trading, the call option has a negative exercise value, 110.07 − 112 = −1.93 cents per EUR. The call buyer is under no obligation to exercise the option if it is to his disadvantage, so he should not. He should let it expire worthless, or with zero value. His loss is limited to the option premium paid of 2.76 cents per EUR, or $276 [= EUR 10,000 × $0.00276] for the contract.

Exhibit 7.7A graphs the 112 Sep EUR call option from the buyer's perspective and Exhibit 7.7B graphs it from the call writer's perspective at expiration. Note that the two graphs are mirror images of one another. The call buyer can lose no more than the call premium but theoretically has an unlimited profit potential. The call writer can profit by no more than the call premium but theoretically can lose an unlimited amount. At a terminal spot price of $S_T = E + C_e = 112 + 2.76 = 114.76$ cents per EUR, both the call buyer and writer break even, that is, neither earns nor loses anything.

The speculative possibilities of a long position in a call are clearly evident from Exhibit 7.7. Anytime the speculator believes that S_T will be in excess of the breakeven point, he will establish a long position in the call. The speculator who is correct realizes a profit. If the speculator is incorrect in his forecast, the loss will be limited to the premium paid. Alternatively, if the speculator believes that S_T will be less than the breakeven point, a short position in the call will yield a profit, the largest amount being the call premium received from the buyer. If the speculator is incorrect, very large losses can result if S_T is much larger than the breakeven point.

EXHIBIT 7.6

PHLX World Currency Options Quotations

NASDAQ OMX PHLX Options		Calls	Puts	
Japanese Yen				90.94
1,000,000 J.Yen-100ths of a cent per unit.				
89	Jun	2.11	.58	
90	Jun	1.47	.95	
91	Jun	.99	1.46	
92	Jun	.64	2.11	
89	Sep	3.15	1.36	
90	Sep	2.60	1.80	
91	Sep	2.13	2.32	
92	Sep	1.74	2.93	
Euro				112.01
10,000 Euro-cents per unit.				
111	Jun	1.83	.66	
111.5	Jun	1.52	.83	
112	Jun	1.23	1.04	
112.5	Jun	.96	1.28	
113	Jun	.76	1.57	
111	Sep	3.38	1.83	
111.5	Sep	3.05	2.02	
112	Sep	2.76	2.22	
112.5	Sep	2.48	2.44	
113	Sep	2.22	2.68	

Source: Mid-prices compiled from bid and ask quotations obtained from Bloomberg on Friday, May 20, 2016.

EXHIBIT 7.7A

Graph of 112 September
EUR Call Option: Buyer's
Perspective

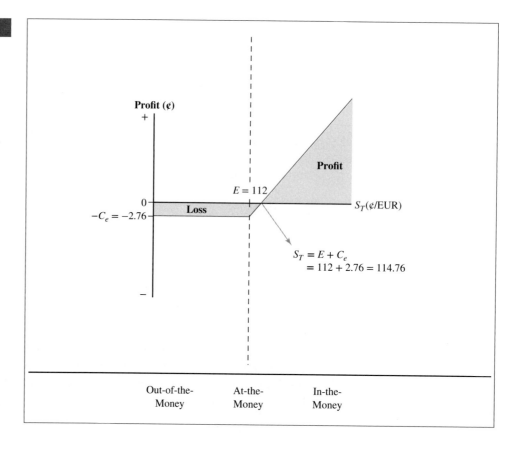

EXHIBIT 7.7B

Graph of 112 September
EUR Call Option: Writer's
Perspective

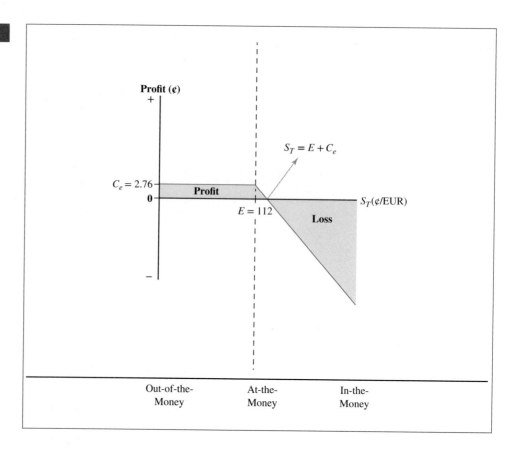

Analogously, at expiration a European put and an American put will have the same value. Algebraically, the expiration value can be stated as:

$$P_{aT} = P_{eT} = Max \ [E - S_T, 0], \tag{7.3}$$

where P denotes the value of the put at expiration.

EXAMPLE | 7.4: Expiration Value of a European Put Option

As an example of pricing Equation 7.3, consider the 112 Sep EUR European put, which has a current premium, P_e, of 2.22 cents per EUR. If S_T is \$1.1007/EUR, the put contract has an exercise value of $112 - 110.07 = 1.93$ cents per EUR for each of the EUR10,000 of the contract, or \$193. That is, the put owner can sell EUR10,000, worth \$11,007 (= EUR10,000 × \$1.1007) in the spot market, for \$11,200 (= EUR10,000 × \$1.12). If $S_T = \$1.1625/EUR$, the exercise value is $112 - 116.25 = -4.25$ cents per EUR. The put buyer would rationally not exercise the put; in other words, he should let it expire worthless with zero value. His loss is limited to the option premium paid of 2.22 cents per EUR, or \$222 [= EUR10,000 × \$0.0222] for the contract.

Exhibit 7.8A graphs the 112 Sep EUR put from the buyer's perspective and Exhibit 7.8B graphs it from the put writer's perspective at expiration. The two graphs are mirror images of one another. The put buyer can lose no more than the put premium and the put writer can profit by no more than the premium. The put buyer can earn a maximum profit of $E - P_e = 112 - 2.22 = 109.78$ cents per EUR if the terminal spot exchange rate is an unrealistic \$0/EUR. The put writer's maximum loss is 109.78 cents per EUR. Additionally, at $S_T = E - P_e = 109.78$ cents per EUR, the put buyer and writer both break even; neither loses nor earns anything.

The speculative possibilities of a long position in a put are clearly evident from Exhibit 7.8. Anytime the speculator believes that S_T will be less than the breakeven point, he will establish a long position in the put. If the speculator is correct, he will realize a profit. If the speculator is incorrect in his forecast, the loss will be limited to the premium paid. Alternatively, if the speculator believes that S_T will be in excess of the breakeven point, a short position in the put will yield a profit, the largest amount being the put premium received from the buyer. If the speculator is incorrect, very large losses can result if S_T is much smaller than the breakeven point.

American Option-Pricing Relationships

An American call or put option can be exercised at any time prior to expiration. Consequently, in a rational marketplace, American options will satisfy the following basic pricing relationships at time t prior to expiration:

$$C_a \geq Max \ [S_t - E, 0] \tag{7.4}$$

and

$$P_a \geq Max \ [E - S_t, 0] \tag{7.5}$$

Verbally, these equations state that the American call and put premiums at time t will be at least as large as the immediate exercise value, or **intrinsic value**, of the call or put option. (The t subscripts are deleted from the call and put premiums to simplify the notation.) Because the owner of a long-maturity American option can exercise it on any date that he could exercise a shorter maturity option, or at some later date after the shorter maturity option expires, it follows that all else remaining the same, the longer-term American option will have a market price at least as large as the shorter-term option.

EXHIBIT 7.8A

Graph of 112 September
EUR Put Option: Buyer's
Perspective

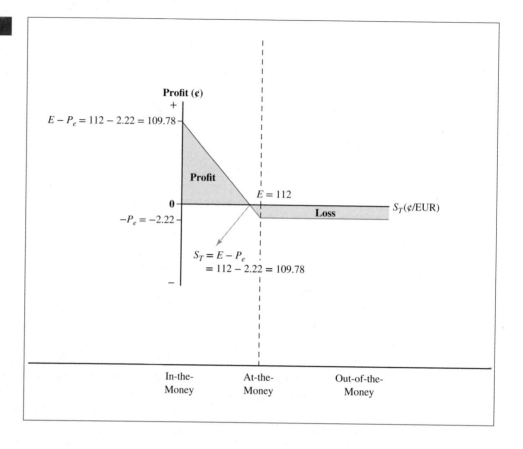

EXHIBIT 7.8B

Graph of 112 September
EUR Put Option: Writer's
Perspective

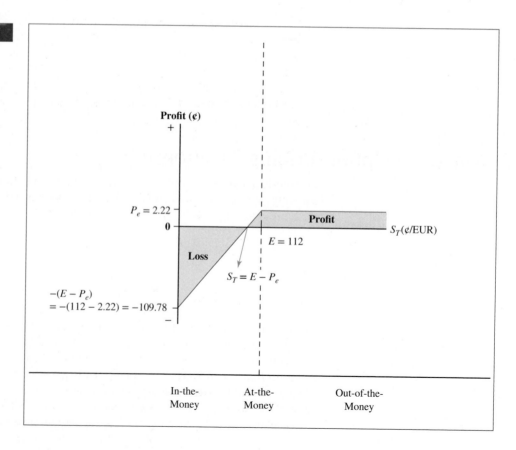

EXHIBIT 7.9

Market Value, Time Value,
and Intrinsic Value of an
American Call Option

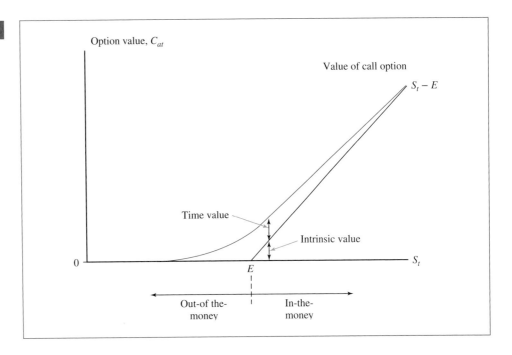

A call (put) option with $S_t > E$ ($E > S_t$) is referred to as trading in-the-money. If $S_t \cong E$ the option is trading at-the-money. If $S_t < E$ ($E < S_t$) the call (put) option is trading out-of-the-money. The difference between the option premium and the option's intrinsic value is nonnegative and is sometimes referred to as the option's **time value**. For example, the time value for an American call is $C_a - Max\,[S_t - E, 0]$. The time value exists, meaning investors are willing to pay more than the immediate exercise value, because the option may move more in-the-money, and thus become more valuable, as time elapses. Exhibit 7.9 graphs the intrinsic value and time value for an American call option.

European Option-Pricing Relationships

The pricing boundaries for European put and call premiums are more complex because they can only be exercised at expiration. Hence, there is a time value element to the boundary expressions. Exhibit 7.10 develops the lower boundary expression for a European call.

Exhibit 7.10 compares the costs and payoffs of two portfolios a U.S. dollar investor could make. Portfolio A involves purchasing a European call option and lending (or investing) an amount equal to the present value of the exercise price, E, at the U.S. interest rate $r_\$$, which we assume corresponds to the length of the investment period. The cost of this investment is $C_e + E/(1 + r_\$)$. If at expiration, S_T is less than or equal to E, the call option will not have a positive exercise value and the call owner will let it expire worthless. If at expiration, S_T is greater than E, it will be to the call owner's advantage to exercise the call; the exercise value will be $S_T - E > 0$. The risk-free loan will pay off the amount E regardless of which state occurs at time T.

By comparison, the U.S. dollar investor could invest in portfolio B, which consists of lending the present value of one unit of foreign currency i at the foreign interest rate r_i, which we assume corresponds to the length of the investment period. In U.S. dollar terms, the cost of this investment is $S_t/(1 + r_i)$. Regardless of which state exists at time T, this investment will pay off one unit of foreign currency, which in U.S. dollar terms will have value S_T.

It is easily seen from Exhibit 7.10 that if $S_T > E$, portfolios A and B pay off the same amount, S_T. However, if $S_T \leq E$, portfolio A has a larger payoff than portfolio B.

EXHIBIT 7.10

Equation for a European Call Option Lower Boundary

	Current Time	Expiration	
		$S_T \leq E$	$S_T > E$
Portfolio A:			
Buy Call	$-C_e$	0	$S_T - E$
Lend PV of E at $r_\$$.	$\dfrac{-E/(1 + r_\$)}{-C_e - E/(1 + r_\$)}$	$\dfrac{E}{E}$	$\dfrac{E}{S_T}$
Portfolio B:			
Lend PV of one unit of currency *i* at rate r_i	$-S_t/(1 + r_i)$	S_T	S_T

It follows that in a rational marketplace, portfolio A will be priced to sell for at least as much as portfolio B, that is, $C_e + E/(1 + r_\$) \geq S_t/(1 + r_i)$. This implies that

$$C_e \geq Max\left[\frac{S_t}{(1 + r_i)} - \frac{E}{(1 + r_\$)}, 0\right] \tag{7.6}$$

since the European call can never sell for a negative amount.

Similarly, it can be shown that the lower boundary pricing relationship for a European put is:

$$P_e \geq Max\left[\frac{E}{(1 + r_\$)} - \frac{S_t}{(1 + r_i)}, 0\right] \tag{7.7}$$

The derivation of this formula is left as an exercise for the reader. (Hint: Portfolio A involves buying a put and lending spot, portfolio B involves lending the present value of the exercise price.)

Note that both C_e and P_e are functions of only five variables: S_t, E, r_i, $r_\$$, and implicitly the term-to-maturity. From Equations 7.6 and 7.7, it can be determined that, when all else remains the same, the call premium C_e (put premium P_e) will increase:

1. The larger (smaller) is S_t,
2. The smaller (larger) is E,
3. The smaller (larger) is r_i,
4. The larger (smaller) is $r_\$$, and
5. The larger (smaller) $r_\$$ is relative to r_i.

Implicitly, both $r_\$$ and r_i will be larger the longer the length of the option period. When $r_\$$ and r_i are not too much different in size, a European FX call and put will increase in price when the option term-to-maturity increases. However, when $r_\$$ is very much larger than r_i, a European FX call will increase in price, but the put premium will decrease, when the option term-to-maturity increases. The opposite is true when r_i is very much greater than $r_\$$.

Recall that IRP implies $F_T = S_t[(1 + r_\$)/(1 + r_i)]$, which in turn implies that $F_T/(1 + r_\$) = S_t/(1 + r_i)$. Hence, European call and put prices on spot foreign exchange, Equations 7.6 and 7.7 can be, respectively, restated as:[3]

$$C_e \geq Max\left[\frac{(F_T - E)}{(1 + r_\$)}, 0\right] \tag{7.8}$$

---

[3]An American option can be exercised at any time during its life. If it is not advantageous for the option owner to exercise it prior to maturity, the owner can let it behave as a European option, which can only be exercised at maturity. It follows from Equations 7.4 and 7.8 (for calls) and 7.5 and 7.9 (for puts) that a more restrictive lower boundary relationship for American call and put options are, respectively:

$C_a \geq Max\ [S_t - E, (F - E)/(1 + r_\$), 0]$ and $P_a \geq Max\ [E - S_t, (E - F)/(1 + r_\$), 0]$

and

$$P_e \geq Max\left[\frac{(E - F_T)}{(1 + r_\$)}, 0\right] \qquad (7.9)$$

EXAMPLE | 7.5: European Option-Pricing Valuation

Let's see if Equations 7.8 and 7.9 actually hold for the 112 Sep EUR European call and the 112 Sep EUR European put options we considered. The last day of trading for both of these options is September 16, 2016, or in 119 days from May 20, 2016, the options quotation date. On that date, the 4-month dollar LIBOR (interest) rate was 0.80 percent. Thus, $(1 + r_\$)$ is $[1 + .0080 (119/360)] = 1.0026$. We will use the September futures price of \$1.1245 on May 20, 2016 for F_T. Thus, for the 112 Sep EUR call,

$$2.76 \geq Max\ [(112.45 - 112)/(1.0026), 0] = Max\ [.45, 0] = .45.$$

Thus, the lower boundary relationship on the European call premium holds. For the 112 Sep EUR put,

$$2.22 \geq Max\ [(112 - 112.45)/(1.0026), 0] = Max\ [-.45, 0] = 0.$$

Thus, the lower boundary relationship on the European put premium holds as well.

In More Depth

Binomial Option-Pricing Model

The option pricing relationships we have discussed to this point have been lower boundaries on the call and put premiums, instead of exact equality expressions for the premiums. The binomial option-pricing model provides an exact pricing formula for a European call or put.[4] We will examine only a simple one-step case of the binomial model to better understand the nature of option pricing.

We want to use the binomial model to value the PHLX 112 Sep EUR European call from Exhibit 7.6. We see from the exhibit that the option is quoted at a premium of 2.76 cents. The current spot price of the EUR in American terms is $S_0 = 112.01$ cents. Our estimate of the option's volatility (annualized standard deviation of the change in the spot rate) is $\sigma = 9.682$ percent, which was obtained from Bloomberg. The last day of trading in the call option is in 119 days on September 16, 2016, or in $T = 119/365 = .3260$ years. The one-step binomial model assumes that at the end of the option period the EUR will have appreciated to $S_{uT} = S_0 \cdot u$ or depreciated to $S_{dT} = S_0 \cdot d$, where $u = e^{\sigma \cdot \sqrt{T}}$ and $d = 1/u$. The spot rate at T will be either $118.37 = 112.01(1.0568)$ or $106.00 = 112.01\ (.9463)$ where $u = e^{.09682 \cdot \sqrt{.3260}} = 1.0568$ and $d = 1/u = .9463$. At the exercise price of $E = 112$, the option will only be exercised at time T if the EUR appreciates; its exercise value would be $C_{uT} = 6.37 = 118.37 - 112$. If the EUR depreciates it would not be rational to exercise the option; its value would be $C_{dT} = 0$.

The binominal option-pricing model only requires that $u > 1 + r_\$ > d$. From Example 7.5 we see that $1 + r_\$ = 1.0026$. Thus, we see that $1.0568 > 1.0026 > .9463$.

The binomial option-pricing model relies on the risk-neutral probabilities of the underlying asset increasing and decreasing in value. For our purposes, the risk-neutral probability of the EUR appreciating is calculated as:

$$q = (F_T - S_0 \cdot d)/S_0(u - d),$$

---

[4]The binomial option-pricing model was independently derived by Sharpe (1978), Rendleman and Bartter (1979), and Cox, Ross, and Rubinstein (1979).

where F_T is the forward (or futures) price that spans the option period. We will use the September EUR futures price on May 20, 2016, as our estimate of $F_T(\$/EUR) = \$1.1245$. Therefore,

$$q = (112.45 - 106.00)/(118.37 - 106.00) = .5214.$$

It follows that the risk-neutral probability of the EUR depreciating is $1 - q = 1 - .5214 = .4786$.

Because the European call option can only be exercised at time T, the binomial call option premium is determined by:

$$C_0 = [qC_{uT} + (1 - q)C_{dT}]/(1 + r_\$)$$ (7.10)
$$= [.5214(6.37) + .4786(0)]/(1.0026)$$
$$= 3.31 \text{ cents per EUR.}$$

A schematic of this binomial options-pricing example is presented in Exhibit 7.11. Alternatively, (if C_{uT} is positive) the binomial call price can be expressed as:

$$C_0 = [F_T \cdot h - E((S_0 \cdot u/E)(h - 1) + 1)]/(1 + r_\$),$$ (7.11)

where $h = (C_{uT} - C_{dT})/S_0(u - d)$ is the risk-free hedge ratio. The *hedge ratio* is the size of the long (short) position the investor must have in the underlying asset per option the investor must write (buy) to have a risk-free offsetting investment that will result in the investor receiving the same terminal value at time T regardless of whether the underlying asset increases or decreases in value. For our example numbers, we see that

$$h = (6.37 - 0)/(118.37 - 106.00) = .5150$$

Thus, the call premium is:

$$C_0 = [112.45(.5150) - 112((118.37/112)(.5150 - 1) + 1)]/(1.0026)$$
$$= 3.31 \text{ cents per EUR.}$$

Equation 7.11 is more intuitive than Equation 7.10 because it is in the same general form as Equation 7.8. In an analogous manner, a binomial put option-pricing model can be developed. Nevertheless, for our example, the binomial call option-pricing model yielded a price that was too large compared to the actual market price of 2.76 cents. This is what we might expect from such a simple model. In the next section, we consider a more refined option-pricing model.

EXHIBIT 7.11

Schematic of Binomial Option-Pricing Example

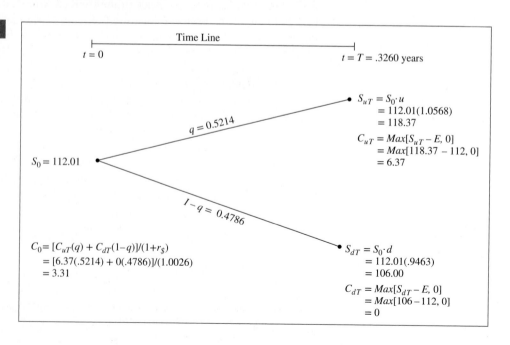

In More Depth

European Option-Pricing Formula

In the last section, we examined a simple one-step version of binomial option-pricing model. Instead, we could have assumed the stock price followed a multiplicative binomial process by subdividing the option period into many subperiods. In this case, S_T and C_T could be many different values. When the number of subperiods into which the option period is subdivided goes to infinity, the European call and put pricing formulas presented in this section are obtained. Exact European call and put pricing formulas are:[5]

$$C_e = S_t e^{-r_i T} N(d_1) - E e^{-r_s T} N(d_2) \tag{7.12}$$

and

$$P_e = E e^{-r_s T} N(-d_2) - S_t e^{-r_i T} N(-d_1) \tag{7.13}$$

The interest rates r_i and $r_\$$ are assumed to be annualized and constant over the term-to-maturity T of the option contract, which is expressed as a fraction of a year.

Invoking IRP, where with continuous compounding $F_T = S_t e^{(r_\$ - r_i)T}$, C_e and P_e in Equations 7.12 and 7.13 can be, respectively, restated as:

$$C_e = [F_T N(d_1) - E N(d_2)] e^{-r_s T} \tag{7.14}$$

and

$$P_e = [E N(-d_2) - F_T N(-d_1)] e^{-r_s T} \tag{7.15}$$

where

$$d_1 = \frac{\ln(F_T/E) + .5\sigma^2 T}{\sigma \sqrt{T}}$$

and

$$d_2 = d_1 - \sigma \sqrt{T}$$

$N(d)$ denotes the cumulative area under the standard normal density function from $-\infty$ to d_1 (or d_2). The variable σ is the annualized volatility of the change in exchange rate $\ln(S_{t+1}/S_t)$. Equations 7.14 and 7.15 indicate that C_e and P_e are functions of only five variables: F_T, E, $r_\$$, T, and σ. It can be shown that both C_e and P_e increase when σ becomes larger.

EXAMPLE | 7.6: The European Option-Pricing Model

As an example of using the European options-pricing model, consider the PHLX 112 Sep EUR European call option from Exhibit 7.6. The option has a premium of 2.76 U.S. cents per EUR on May 20, 2016. The last day of trading in the option will be on September 16, 2016—119 days from the quotation date, or $T = 119/365 = .3260$. We will use the September futures price on May 20, 2016, as our estimate of $F_T(\$/EUR) = \$112.45$. The rate $r_\$$ is estimated as the annualized 4-month dollar LIBOR (interest rate) of 0.80 percent on the same day. The estimated volatility is 9.682 percent and was obtained from Bloomberg.

The values d_1 and d_2 are:

$$d_1 = \frac{\ln(112.45/112) + .5(.09682)^2(.3260)}{(.09682)\sqrt{.3260}} = .1002$$

continued

---

[5]The European option-pricing model was developed by Biger and Hull (1983), Garman and Kohlhagen (1983), and Grabbe (1983). The evolution of the model can be traced back to European option-pricing models developed by Merton (1973) and Black (1976).

EXHIBIT 7.12

European FX Option Pricing Model Output from FXOPM.xls

	A	B	C	D	E	F	G
1							
2	Spot rate(D)=		112.01		Forward rate(D)=		112.45
3							
4	Spot rate(F)=		89.28		Forward rate(F)=		88.93
5							
6	U.S. interest rate=		0.8000%		Foreign interest rate=		−.4000%
7							
8	Exercise price=		112.00		Option volatility=		9.682
9							
10	Days to expiration=		119		Years to expiration(T)=		0.3260
11							
12	d_1=		0.1002		$N(d_1)$=		0.5399
13							
14	d_2=		0.0449		$N(d_2)$=		0.5179
15							
16	Call option premium=		2.70		Put option premium=		2.25
17							

EXAMPLE | 7.6: continued

and

$$d_2 = .1002 - (.09682)\sqrt{.3260} = .0449$$

Consequently, it can be determined that $N(.1002) = .5399$ and $N(.0449) = .5179$. We now have everything we need to compute the model price:

$$C_e = [112.45(.5399) - 112(.5179)]e^{-(.0080)(.3260)}$$

$$= [60.7118 - 58.0048](.9974)$$

$$= 2.70 \text{ cents per EUR vs. the actual market mid-price of 2.76 cents.}$$

As we see, the model has done a good job of valuing the EUR call.

The value $N(d)$ can be calculated using the NORMSDIST function of Microsoft Excel. Equations 7.14 and 7.15 are widely used in practice, especially by international banks in trading OTC options. Exhibit 7.12 shows the output from using the text software spreadsheet FXOPM.xls to solve for the option price for the 112 Sep EUR European call (and put) option using the European options-pricing model presented in Example 7.6.

Empirical Tests of Currency Options

Shastri and Tandon (1985) empirically test the American boundary relationships we developed in this chapter (Equations 7.4, 7.5, 7.6, 7.7, 7.8, and 7.9) using PHLX put and call data. They discover many violations of the boundary relationships, but conclude that nonsimultaneous data could account for most of the violations. Bodurtha and Courtadon (1986) test the immediate exercise boundary relationships (Equations 7.4 and 7.5) for PHLX American put and call options. They also find many violations when using last daily trade data. However, when they use simultaneous price data and incorporate transaction costs, they conclude that the PHLX American currency options are efficiently priced.

Shastri and Tandon (1986) also test the European option-pricing model using PHLX American put and call data. They determine that a nonmember of the PHLX could not earn abnormal profits from the hedging strategies they examine. This implies that the European option-pricing model works well in pricing American currency options.

Barone-Adesi and Whaley (1987) also find that the European option-pricing model works well for pricing American currency options that are *at* or *out-of-the money*, but does not do well in pricing *in-the-money* calls and puts. For *in-the-money* options, their approximate American option-pricing model yields superior results.

SUMMARY

This chapter introduced currency futures and options on foreign exchange. These instruments are useful for speculating and hedging foreign exchange rate movements. In later chapters, it will be shown how to use these vehicles for hedging purposes.

1. Forward, futures, and options contracts are derivative, or contingent claim, securities. That is, their value is derived or contingent upon the value of the asset that underlies these securities.

2. Forward and futures contracts are similar instruments, but there are differences. Both are contracts to buy or sell a certain quantity of a specific underlying asset at some specific price in the future. Futures contracts, however, are exchange-traded, and there are standardized features that distinguish them from the tailor-made terms of forward contracts. The two main standardized features are contract size and maturity date.

3. Additionally, futures contracts are marked-to-market on a daily basis at the new settlement price. Hence, the performance bond account of an individual with a futures position is increased or decreased, reflecting daily realized profits or losses resulting from the change in the futures settlement price from the previous day's settlement price.

4. A futures market requires speculators and hedgers to effectively operate. Hedgers attempt to avoid the risk of price change of the underlying asset, and speculators attempt to profit from anticipating the direction of future price changes.

5. The CME Group and the NASDAQ OMX Futures Exchange are the two largest currency futures exchanges.

6. The pricing equation typically used to price currency futures is the IRP relationship, which is also used to price currency forward contracts.

7. An option is the right, but not the obligation, to buy or sell the underlying asset for a stated price over a stated time period. Call options give the owner the right to buy, put options the right to sell. American options can be exercised at any time during their life; European options can only be exercised at maturity.

8. Exchange-traded options with standardized features are traded on two exchanges. Options on spot foreign exchange are traded at the NASDAQ OMX PHLX, and options on currency futures are traded at the CME.

9. Basic boundary expressions for put and call option prices were developed and examined using actual option-pricing data.

10. A European option-pricing model for put and call options was also presented and explained using actual market data.

KEY WORDS

American option, *181*	delivery months, *174*	initial performance bond, *174*
at-the-money, *182*	derivative security, *174*	
call, *181*	European option, *181*	intrinsic value, *185*
clearinghouse, *176*	exchange-traded, *174*	long, *174*
commission, *176*	exercise price, *181*	maintenance performance bond, *174*
contingent claim security, *174*	futures, *174*	
	hedgers, *175*	marked-to-market, *174*
contract size, *174*	in-the-money, *182*	maturity date, *174*
daily price limit, *176*		nearby, *178*

www.mhhe.com/er8e

open interest, *178*	put, *181*	standardized, *174*
option, *181*	reversing trade, *175*	striking price, *181*
out-of-the-money, *182*	settled-up, *174*	time value, *187*
premium, *181*	settlement price, *174*	writer, *181*
price convergence, *180*	short, *174*	zero-sum game, *174*
price discovery, *179*	speculators, *175*	

QUESTIONS

1. Explain the basic differences between the operation of a currency forward market and a futures market.

2. For a derivatives market to function most efficiently, two types of economic agents are needed: hedgers and speculators. Explain.

3. Why are most futures positions closed out through a reversing trade rather than held to delivery?

4. How can the FX futures market be used for price discovery?

5. What is the major difference in the obligation of one with a long position in a futures (or forward) contract in comparison to an options contract?

6. What is meant by the terminology that an option is in-, at-, or out-of-the-money?

7. List the arguments (variables) of which an FX call or put option model price is a function. How do the call and put premiums change with respect to a change in the arguments?

PROBLEMS

1. Assume today's settlement price on a CME EUR futures contract is $1.3140/EUR. You have a short position in one contract. Your performance bond account currently has a balance of $1,700. The next three days' settlement prices are $1.3126, $1.3133, and $1.3049. Calculate the changes in the performance bond account from daily marking-to-market and the balance of the performance bond account after the third day.

2. Do problem 1 again assuming you have a long position in the futures contract.

3. Using the quotations in Exhibit 7.3, calculate the face value of the open interest in the September 2016 Swiss franc futures contract.

4. Using the quotations in Exhibit 7.3, note that the June 2016 Mexican peso futures contract has a price of $0.05481 per MXN. You believe the spot price in September will be $0.06133 per MXN. What speculative position would you enter into to attempt to profit from your beliefs? Calculate your anticipated profits, assuming you take a position in three contracts. What is the size of your profit (loss) if the futures price is indeed an unbiased predictor of the future spot price and this price materializes?

5. Do problem 4 again assuming you believe the September 2016 spot price will be $0.04829 per MXN.

6. Using the market data in Exhibit 7.6, show the net terminal value of a long position in one 90 Sep Japanese yen European call contract at the following terminal spot prices, cents per yen: 81, 85, 90, 95, and 99. Ignore any time value of money effect.

7. Using the market data in Exhibit 7.6, show the net terminal value of a long position in one 90 Sep Japanese yen European put contract at the following terminal spot prices, cents per yen: 81, 85, 90, 95, and 99. Ignore any time value of money effect.

8. Assume that the Japanese yen is trading at a spot price of 92.04 cents per 100 yen. Further assume that the premium of an American call (put) option with a striking price of 93 is 2.10 (2.20) cents. Calculate the intrinsic value and the time value of the call and put options.

9. Assume the spot Swiss franc is $0.7000 and the six-month forward rate is $0.6950. What is the minimum price that a six-month American call option with a striking price of $0.6800 should sell for in a rational market? Assume the annualized sixmonth Eurodollar rate is 3.5 percent.

10. Do problem 9 again assuming an American put option instead of a call option.

11. Use the European option-pricing models developed in the chapter to value the call of problem 9 and the put of problem 10. Assume the annualized volatility of the Swiss franc is 14.2 percent. This problem can be solved using the FXOPM.xls spreadsheet.

12. Use the binomial option-pricing model developed in the chapter to value the call of problem 9. The volatility of the Swiss franc is 14.2 percent.

INTERNET EXERCISES

1. Data on currency futures can be found at the CME Group website, www.cmegroup .com. Go to the "Delayed quotes" section of this website and see which currency futures contracts have increasing and which have decreasing futures prices in current trading.

MINI CASE

The Options Speculator

A speculator is considering the purchase of five three-month Japanese yen call options with a striking price of 96 cents per 100 yen. The premium is 1.35 cents per 100 yen. The spot price is 95.28 cents per 100 yen and the 90-day forward rate is 95.71 cents. The speculator believes the yen will appreciate to $1.00 per 100 yen over the next three months. As the speculator's assistant, you have been asked to prepare the following:

1. Graph the call option cash flow schedule.
2. Determine the speculator's profit if the yen appreciates to $1.00/100 yen.
3. Determine the speculator's profit if the yen appreciates only to the forward rate.
4. Determine the future spot price at which the speculator will only break even.

REFERENCES & SUGGESTED READINGS

Barone-Adesi, Giovanni, and Robert Whaley. "Efficient Analytic Approximation of American Option Values." *Journal of Finance* 42 (1987), pp. 301–20.

Biger, Nahum, and John Hull. "The Valuation of Currency Options." *Financial Management* 12 (1983), pp. 24–28.

Black, Fischer. "The Pricing of Commodity Contracts." *Journal of Financial Economics* 3 (1976), pp. 167–79.

——— and Myron Scholes. "The Pricing of Options and Corporate Liabilities." *Journal of Political Economy* 81 (1973), pp. 637–54.

Bodurtha, James, Jr., and George Courtadon. "Efficiency Tests of the Foreign Currency Options Market." *Journal of Finance* 41 (1986), pp. 151–62.

Cox, John C., Jonathan E. Ingersoll, and Stephen A. Ross. "The Relation between Forward Prices and Futures Prices." *Journal of Financial Economics* 9 (1981), pp. 321–46.

Cox, John C., Stephen A. Ross, and Mark Rubinstein. "Option Pricing: A Simplified Approach." *Journal of Financial Economics* 7 (1979), pp. 229–63.

Garman, Mark, and Steven Kohlhagen. "Foreign Currency Option Values." *Journal of International Money and Finance* 2 (1983), pp. 231–38.

Grabbe, J. Orlin. "The Pricing of Call and Put Options on Foreign Exchange." *Journal of International Money and Finance* 2 (1983), pp. 239–54.

——— *International Financial Markets,* 3rd ed. Upper Saddle River, N.J.: Prentice Hall, 1996.

Merton, Robert. "Theory of Rational Option Pricing." *The Bell Journal of Economics and Management Science* 4 (1973), pp. 141–83.

Rendleman, Richard J., Jr., and Brit J. Bartter. "Two-State Option Pricing." *Journal of Finance* 34 (1979), pp. 1093–1110.

Sharpe, William F. "Chapter 14." *Investments.* Englewood Cliffs, N.J.: Prentice Hall, 1978.

Shastri, Kuldeep, and Kishore Tandon. "Arbitrage Tests of the Efficiency of the Foreign Currency Options Market." *Journal of International Money and Finance* 4 (1985), pp. 455–68.

——— "Valuation of Foreign Currency Options: Some Empirical Tests." *Journal of Financial and Quantitative Analysis* 21 (1986), pp. 145–60.

www.mhhe.com/er8e

PART THREE

Foreign Exchange Exposure and Management

PART THREE is composed of three chapters covering the topics of transaction, economic, and translation exposure management, respectively.

CHAPTER 8 covers the management of transaction exposure that arises from contractual obligations denominated in a foreign currency. Several methods for hedging this exposure are compared and contrasted. The chapter also includes a discussion of why a MNC should hedge, a debatable subject in the minds of both academics and practitioners.

CHAPTER 9 covers economic exposure, that is, the extent to which the value of the firm will be affected by unexpected changes in exchange rates. The chapter provides a way to measure economic exposure, discusses its determinants, and presents methods for managing and hedging economic exposure.

CHAPTER 10 covers translation exposure or, as it is sometimes called, accounting exposure. Translation exposure refers to the effect that changes in exchange rates will have on the consolidated financial reports of a MNC. The chapter discusses, compares, and contrasts the various methods for translating financial statements denominated in foreign currencies, and includes a discussion of managing translation exposure using funds adjustment and the pros and cons of using balance sheet and derivatives hedges.

www.stern.nyu.edu/~igiddy /fxrisk.htm

Provides an overview of exchange risk management issues.

8 Management of Transaction Exposure

AS THE NATURE of business becomes international, many firms are exposed to the risk of fluctuating exchange rates. Changes in exchange rates may affect the settlement of contracts, cash flows, and the firm valuation. It is thus important for financial managers to know the firm's foreign currency exposure and properly manage the exposure. By doing so, managers can stabilize the firm's cash flows and enhance the firm's value.

Three Types of Exposure

Before we get into the important issue of how to manage transaction exposure, let us briefly discuss different types of exposure. It is conventional to classify foreign currency exposures into three types:

- Transaction exposure
- Economic exposure
- Translation exposure

Transaction exposure, a subject to be discussed in this chapter, can be defined as the sensitivity of "realized" domestic currency values of the firm's contractual cash flows *denominated* in foreign currencies to unexpected exchange rate changes. Since settlements of these contractual cash flows affect the firm's domestic currency cash flows, transaction exposure is sometimes regarded as a short-term economic exposure. Transaction exposure arises from fixed-price contracting in a world where exchange rates are changing randomly.

Economic exposure, a subject to be discussed in Chapter 9, can be defined as the extent to which the value of the firm would be affected by unanticipated changes in exchange rates. Any anticipated changes in exchange rates would have been already discounted and reflected in the firm's value. As we will discuss later, changes in exchange rates can have a profound effect on the firm's competitive position in the world market and thus on its cash flows and market value.

On the other hand, **translation exposure**, which will be discussed in Chapter 10, refers to the potential that the firm's consolidated financial statements can be affected by changes in exchange rates. Consolidation involves translation of subsidiaries' financial statements from local currencies to the home currency. Consider a U.S. multinational firm that has subsidiaries in the United Kingdom and Japan. Each subsidiary will produce financial statements in local currency. To consolidate financial statements worldwide, the firm must translate the subsidiaries' financial statements in local currencies into the U.S. dollar, the home currency. As we will see later, translation involves many controversial issues. Resultant translation gains and losses represent the accounting system's attempt to measure economic exposure *ex post*. It does not provide a good measure of *ex ante* economic exposure. In the remainder of this chapter, we will focus on how to manage transaction exposure.

As discussed before, the firm is subject to transaction exposure when it faces *contractual* cash flows that are fixed in foreign currencies. Suppose that a U.S. firm sold its product to a German client on three-month credit terms and invoiced €1 million. When the U.S. firm receives €1 million in three months, it will have to convert (unless it hedges) the euros into dollars at the spot exchange rate prevailing on the maturity date, which cannot be known in advance. As a result, the dollar receipt from this foreign sale becomes uncertain; should the euro appreciate (depreciate) against the dollar, the dollar receipt will be higher (lower). This situation implies that if the firm does nothing about the exposure, it is effectively speculating on the future course of the exchange rate.

For another example of transaction exposure, consider a Japanese firm entering into a loan contract with a Swiss bank that calls for the payment of SF100 million for principal and interest in one year. To the extent that the yen/Swiss franc exchange rate is uncertain, the Japanese firm does not know how much yen it will take to buy SF100 million spot in one year's time. If the yen appreciates (depreciates) against the Swiss franc, a smaller (larger) yen amount will be needed to pay off the SF-denominated loan.

These examples suggest that whenever the firm has foreign-currency-denominated receivables or payables, it is subject to transaction exposure, and their settlements are likely to affect the firm's cash flow position. Furthermore, in view of the fact that firms are now more frequently entering into commercial and financial contracts denominated in foreign currencies, judicious management of transaction exposure has become an important function of international financial management. Unlike economic exposure, transaction exposure is well defined: The magnitude of transaction exposure is the same as the amount of foreign currency that is receivable or payable. This chapter will thus focus on alternative ways of hedging transaction exposure using various financial contracts and *operational techniques:*

Financial contracts

- Forward market hedge
- Money market hedge
- Option market hedge
- Swap market hedge

Operational techniques

- Choice of the invoice currency
- Lead/lag strategy
- Exposure netting

Before we discuss how to manage transaction exposure, however, it is useful to introduce a particular business situation that gives rise to exposure. Suppose that Boeing Corporation exported a Boeing 737 to British Airways and billed £10 million payable in one year. The money market interest rates and foreign exchange rates are given as follows:

The U.S. interest rate:	6.10% per annum.
The U.K. interest rate:	9.00% per annum.
The spot exchange rate:	$1.50/£.
The forward exchange rate:	$1.46/£ (1-year maturity).

Let us now look at the various techniques for managing this transaction exposure.

Forward Market Hedge

Perhaps the most direct and popular way of hedging transaction exposure is by currency forward contracts. Generally speaking, the firm may sell (buy) its foreign currency receivables (payables) forward to eliminate its exchange risk exposure. In the earlier example, in order to hedge foreign exchange exposure, Boeing may simply sell forward its pounds receivable, £10 million for delivery in one year, in exchange for a given amount of U.S. dollars. On the maturity date of the contract, Boeing will have to deliver £10 million to the bank, which is the counterparty of the contract, and, in return, take delivery of $14.6 million ($1.46 × 10 million), regardless of the spot exchange rate that may prevail on the maturity date. Boeing will, of course, use the £10 million that it is going to receive from British Airways to fulfill the forward contract. Since Boeing's pound receivable is exactly offset by the pound payable (created by the forward contract), the company's net pound exposure becomes zero.

Since Boeing is assured of receiving a given dollar amount, $14.6 million, from the counter-party of the forward contract, the dollar proceeds from this British sale will not be affected at all by future changes in the exchange rate. This point is illustrated in Exhibit 8.1. Once Boeing enters into the forward contract, exchange rate uncertainty becomes irrelevant for Boeing. Exhibit 8.1 also illustrates how the dollar proceeds from the British sale will be affected by the future spot exchange rate when exchange exposure is not hedged. The exhibit shows that the dollar proceeds under the forward hedge will be higher than those under the unhedged position if the future spot exchange rate turns out to be less than the forward rate, that is, $F = $1.46/£, and the opposite will hold if the future spot rate becomes higher than the forward rate. In the latter case, Boeing forgoes an opportunity to benefit from a strong pound.

Suppose that on the maturity date of the forward contract, the spot rate turns out to be $1.40/£, which is less than the forward rate, $1.46/£. In this case, Boeing would have received $14.0 million, rather than $14.6 million, had it not entered into the forward contract. Thus, one can say that Boeing gained $0.6 million from forward hedging. Needless to say, Boeing will not always gain in this manner. If the spot rate is, say, $1.50/£ on the maturity date, then Boeing could have received $15.0 million by remaining unhedged. Thus, one can say *ex post* that forward hedging cost Boeing $0.40 million.

The gains and losses from forward hedging can be illustrated as in Exhibits 8.2 and 8.3. The gain/loss is computed as follows:

$$\text{Gain} = (F - S_T) \times £10 \text{ million} \tag{8.1}$$

Obviously, the gain will be positive as long as the forward exchange rate (F) is greater than the spot rate on the maturity date (S_T), that is, $F > S_T$, and the gain will be negative (that is, a loss will result) if the opposite holds. As Exhibit 8.3 shows, the firm theoretically can gain as much as $14.6 million when the pound becomes worthless, which, of course, is unlikely, whereas there is no limit to possible losses.

It is important, however, to note that the above analysis is *ex post* in nature, and that no one can know for sure what the future spot rate will be beforehand. The firm must decide whether to hedge or not *ex ante*. To help the firm decide, it is useful to consider the following three alternative scenarios:

1. $\bar{S}_T \approx F$
2. $\bar{S}_T < F$
3. $\bar{S}_T > F$

where $\bar{S}_T$ denotes the firm's expected spot exchange rate for the maturity date.

Under the first scenario, where the firm's expected future spot exchange rate, $\bar{S}_T$, is about the same as the forward rate, F, the "expected" gains or losses are approximately zero.

EXHIBIT 8.1

Dollar Proceeds from the British Sale: Forward Hedge versus Unhedged Position

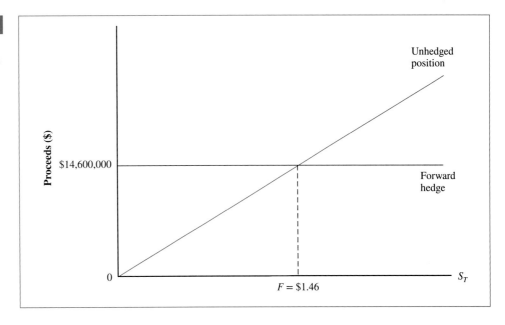

EXHIBIT 8.2

Gains/Losses from Forward Hedge

Spot Exchange Rate on the Maturity Date (S_T)	Receipts from the British Sale		Gains/Losses from Hedge[b]
	Unhedged Position	Forward Hedge	
$1.30	$13,000,000	$14,600,000	$1,600,000
$1.40	$14,000,000	$14,600,000	$ 600,000
$1.46[a]	$14,600,000	$14,600,000	0
$1.50	$15,000,000	$14,600,000	−$ 400,000
$1.60	$16,000,000	$14,600,000	−$1,400,000

[a]The forward exchange rate (F) is $1.46/£ in this example.

[b]The gains/losses are computed as the proceeds under the forward hedge minus the proceeds from the unhedged position at the various spot exchange rates on the maturity date.

EXHIBIT 8.3

Illustration of Gains and Losses from Forward Hedging

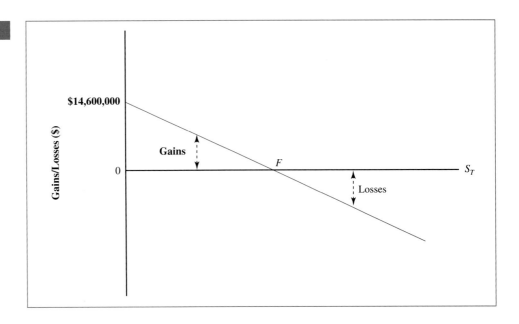

But forward hedging eliminates exchange exposure. In other words, the firm can eliminate foreign exchange exposure without sacrificing any expected dollar proceeds from the foreign sale. Under this scenario the firm would be inclined to hedge as long as it is averse to risk. Note that this scenario becomes valid when the forward exchange rate is an unbiased predictor of the future spot rate.[1]

Under the second scenario, where the firm's expected future spot exchange rate is less than the forward rate, the firm expects a positive gain from forward hedging. Since the firm expects to increase the dollar proceeds while eliminating exchange exposure, it would be even more inclined to hedge under this scenario than under the first scenario. The second scenario, however, implies that the firm's management dissents from the market's consensus forecast of the future spot exchange rate as reflected in the forward rate.

Under the third scenario, on the other hand, where the firm's expected future spot exchange rate is more than the forward rate, the firm can eliminate exchange exposure via the forward contract only at the cost of reduced expected dollar proceeds from the foreign sale. Thus, the firm would be less inclined to hedge under this scenario, other things being equal. Despite lower expected dollar proceeds, however, the firm may still end up hedging. Whether the firm actually hedges or not depends on the degree of risk aversion; the more risk averse the firm is, the more likely it is to hedge. From the perspective of a hedging firm, the reduction in the expected dollar proceeds can be viewed implicitly as an "insurance premium" paid for avoiding the hazard of exchange risk.

The firm can use a currency futures contract, rather than a forward contract, to hedge. However, a futures contract is not as suitable as a forward contract for hedging purpose for two reasons. First, unlike forward contracts that are tailor-made to the firm's specific needs, futures contracts are standardized instruments in terms of contract size, delivery date, and so forth. In most cases, therefore, the firm can only hedge approximately. Second, due to the marking-to-market property, there are interim cash flows prior to the maturity date of the futures contract that may have to be invested at uncertain interest rates. As a result, exact hedging again would be difficult.

Money Market Hedge

Transaction exposure can also be hedged by lending and borrowing in the domestic and foreign money markets. Generally speaking, the firm may borrow (lend) in foreign currency to hedge its foreign currency receivables (payables), thereby matching its assets and liabilities in the same currency. Again using the same example presented above, Boeing can eliminate the exchange exposure arising from the British sale by first borrowing in pounds, then converting the loan proceeds into dollars, which then can be invested at the dollar interest rate. On the maturity date of the loan, Boeing is going to use the pound receivable to pay off the pound loan. If Boeing borrows a particular pound amount so that the maturity value of this loan becomes exactly equal to the pound receivable from the British sale, Boeing's net pound exposure is reduced to zero, and Boeing will receive the future maturity value of the dollar investment.

The first important step in money market hedging is to determine the amount of pounds to borrow. Since the maturity value of borrowing should be the same as the pound receivable, the amount to borrow can be computed as the discounted present value of the pound receivable, that is, £10 million/(1.09) = £9,174,312. When Boeing borrows £9,174,312, it then has to repay £10 million in one year, which is equivalent

---

[1]As mentioned in Chapter 6, the forward exchange rate will be an unbiased predictor of the future spot rate if the exchange market is informationally efficient and the risk premium is not significant. Empirical evidence indicates that the risk premium, if it exists, is generally not very significant. Unless the firm has private information that is not reflected in the forward rate, it would have no reason for disagreeing with the forward rate.

EXHIBIT 8.4

Cash Flow Analysis of a Money Market Hedge

Transaction	Current Cash Flow	Cash Flow at Maturity
1. Borrow pounds	£ 9,174,312	−£10,000,000
2. Buy dollar spot with pounds	$13,761,468 −£ 9,174,312	
3. Invest in the United States	−$13,761,468	$14,600,918
4. Collect pound receivable		£10,000,000
Net cash flow	0	$14,600,918

to its pound receivable. The step-by-step procedure of money market hedging can be illustrated as follows:

Step 1: Borrow £9,174,312.

Step 2: Convert £9,174,312 into $13,761,468 at the current spot exchange rate of $1.50/£.

Step 3: Invest $13,761,468 in the United States.

Step 4: Collect £10 million from British Airways and use it to repay the pound loan.

Step 5: Receive the maturity value of the dollar investment, that is, $14,600,918 = ($13,761,468)(1.061), which is the guaranteed dollar proceeds from the British sale.

Exhibit 8.4 provides a cash flow analysis of money market hedging. The table shows that the net cash flow is zero at the present time, implying that, apart from possible transaction costs, the **money market hedge** is fully self-financing. The table also clearly shows how the 10 million receivable is exactly offset by the 10 million payable (created by borrowing), leaving a net cash flow of $14,600,918 on the maturity date.[2]

The maturity value of the dollar investment from the money market hedge turns out to be nearly identical to the dollar proceeds from forward hedging. This result is no coincidence. Rather, this is due to the fact that the interest rate parity (IRP) condition is approximately holding in our example. If the IRP is not holding, the dollar proceeds from money market hedging will not be the same as those from forward hedging. As a result, one hedging method will dominate another. In a competitive and efficient world financial market, however, any deviations from IRP are not likely to persist.

Options Market Hedge

One possible shortcoming of both forward and money market hedges is that these methods completely eliminate exchange risk exposure. Consequently, the firm has to forgo the opportunity to benefit from favorable exchange rate changes. To elaborate on this point, let us assume that the spot exchange rate turns out to be $1.60 per pound on the maturity date of the forward contract. In this instance, forward hedging would cost the firm $1.4 million in terms of forgone dollar receipts (see Exhibit 8.2). If Boeing had indeed entered into a forward contract, it would regret its decision to do so. With its pound receivable, Boeing ideally would like to protect itself only if the pound weakens, while retaining the opportunity to benefit if the pound strengthens. Currency options provide such a *flexible* "optional" hedge against exchange exposure. Generally speaking, the firm may buy a foreign currency call (put) option to hedge its foreign currency payables (receivables).

---

[2]In the case where the firm has an account payable denominated in pounds, the money market hedge calls for borrowing in dollars, buying pounds spot, and investing at the pound interest rate.

To show how the options hedge works, suppose that in the over-the-counter market Boeing purchased a put option on 10 million British pounds with an exercise price of $1.46 and a one-year expiration. Assume that the option premium (price) was $0.02 per pound. Boeing thus paid $200,000 (= $0.02 × 10 million) for the option. This transaction provides Boeing with the right, but not the obligation, to sell up to £10 million for $1.46/£, regardless of the future spot rate.

Now assume that the spot exchange rate turns out to be $1.30 on the expiration date. Since Boeing has the right to sell each pound for $1.46, it will certainly exercise its put option on the pound and convert £10 million into $14.6 million. The main advantage of options hedging is that the firm can decide whether to exercise the option based on the realized spot exchange rate on the expiration date. Recall that Boeing paid $200,000 upfront for the option. Considering the time value of money, this upfront cost is equivalent to $212,200 (= $200,000 × 1.061) as of the expiration date. This means that under the options hedge, the net dollar proceeds from the British sale become $14,387,800:

$$\$14,387,800 = \$14,600,000 - \$212,200$$

Since Boeing is going to exercise its put option on the pound whenever the future spot exchange rate falls below the exercise rate of $1.46, it is assured of a "minimum" dollar receipt of $14,387,800 from the British sale.

Next, consider an alternative scenario where the pound appreciates against the dollar. Assume that the spot rate turns out to be $1.60 per pound on the expiration date. In this event, Boeing would have no incentive to exercise the option. It will rather let the option expire and convert £10 million into $16 million at the spot rate. Subtracting $212,200 for the option cost, the net dollar proceeds will become $15,787,800 under the option hedge. As suggested by these scenarios, the options hedge allows the firm to *limit the downside risk while preserving the upside potential.* The firm, however, has to pay for this flexibility in terms of the option premium. There rarely exist free lunches in finance! Note that neither the forward nor the money market hedge involves any upfront cost.

Exhibit 8.5 provides the net dollar proceeds from the British sale under options hedging for a range of future spot exchange rates. The same results are illustrated in Exhibit 8.6. As Exhibit 8.6 shows, the options hedge sets a "floor" for the dollar proceeds. The future dollar proceeds will be at least $14,387,800 under the option hedge. Boeing thus can be said to have an insurance policy against the exchange risk hazard; the upfront option cost, $200,000, Boeing incurred can be explicitly regarded as an insurance premium. When a firm has an account payable rather than a receivable, in terms of a foreign currency, the firm can set a "ceiling" for the future dollar cost of buying the foreign currency amount by buying a call option on the foreign currency amount.

Exhibit 8.6 also compares the dollar proceeds from forward and options hedges. As indicated in the exhibit, the options hedge dominates the forward hedge for future spot rates greater than $1.48 per pound, whereas the opposite holds for spot rates lower

EXHIBIT 8.5	Future Spot Exchange Rate (S_T)	Exercise Decision	Gross Dollar Proceeds	Option Cost	Net Dollar Proceeds
Dollar Proceeds from Options Hedge	$1.30	Exercise	$14,600,000	$212,200	$14,387,800
	$1.40	Exercise	$14,600,000	$212,200	$14,387,800
	$1.46	Neutral	$14,600,000	$212,200	$14,387,800
	$1.50	Not exercise	$15,000,000	$212,200	$14,787,800
	$1.60	Not exercise	$16,000,000	$212,200	$15,787,800

Note: The exercise exchange rate (E) is $1.46 in this example.

EXHIBIT 8.6

Dollar Proceeds from the British Sale: Option versus Forward Hedge

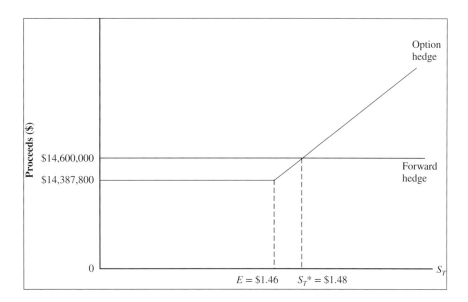

than $1.48 per pound. Boeing will be indifferent between the two hedging methods at the "break-even" spot rate of $1.48 per pound.

The break-even spot rate, which is useful for choosing a hedging method, can be determined as follows:

$$\$(10,000,000)S_T - \$212,200 = \$14,600,000$$

By solving the equation for S_T, we obtain the break-even spot rate, $S_T^* = \$1.48$. The break-even analysis suggests that if the firm's expected future spot rate is greater (less) than the break-even rate, then the options (forward) hedge may be preferred.

Unlike the forward contract, which has only one forward rate for a given maturity, there are multiple exercise exchange rates (prices) for the options contract. In the preceding discussion, we worked with an option with an exercise price of $1.46. Considering that Boeing has a pound receivable, it is tempting to think that it would be a good idea for Boeing to buy a put option with a higher exercise price, thereby increasing the minimum dollar receipt from the British sale. But it becomes immediately clear that the firm has to pay for it in terms of a higher option premium.

Again, there is no free lunch. Choice of the exercise price for the options contract ultimately depends on the extent to which the firm is willing to bear exchange risk. For instance, if the firm's objective is only to avoid very unfavorable exchange rate changes (that is, a major depreciation of the pound in Boeing's example), then it should consider buying an out-of-money put option with a low exercise price, saving option costs. The three alternative hedging strategies are summarized in Exhibit 8.7.

Hedging Foreign Currency Payables

So far, we have discussed how to hedge foreign currency transaction exposure using Boeing's receivable as an example. In this section, we are going to discuss how to hedge foreign currency "payables." Suppose Boeing imported a Rolls-Royce jet engine for £5 million payable in one year. The market condition is summarized as follows:

The U.S. interest rate:	6.00% per annum.
The U.K. interest rate:	6.50% per annum.
The spot exchange rate:	$1.80/£.
The forward exchange rate:	$1.75/£ (1-year maturity)

EXHIBIT 8.7	Boeing's Alternative Hedging Strategies: A Summary	
Strategy	**Transactions**	**Outcomes**
Forward market hedge	1. Sell £10,000,000 forward for U.S. dollars now. 2. In one year, receive £10,000,000 from the British client and deliver it to the counterparty of the forward contract.	Assured of receiving $14,600,000 in one year; future spot exchange becomes irrelevant.
Money market hedge	1. Borrow £9,174,312 and buy $13,761,468 spot now. 2. In one year, collect £10,000,000 from the British client and pay off the pound loan using the amount.	Assured of receiving $13,761,468 now or $14,600,918 in one year; future spot exchange rate becomes irrelevant.
Options market hedge	1. Buy a put option on £10,000,000 for an upfront cost of $200,000. 2. In one year, decide whether to exercise the option upon observing the prevailing spot exchange rate.	Assured of receiving at least $14,387,800 or more if the future spot exchange rate exceeds the exercise exchange rate; Boeing controls the downside risk while retaining the upside potential.

We examine alternative ways of hedging this foreign currency payable using (i) forward contracts, (ii) money market instruments, and (iii) currency options contracts. Facing an account payable, Boeing will have to try to minimize the dollar cost of paying off the payable.

Forward Contracts

If Boeing decides to hedge this payable exposure using a forward contract, it only needs to buy £5 million forward in exchange for the following dollar amount:

$$\$8,750,000 = (£5,000,000)\,(\$1.75/£).$$

On the maturity date of the forward contract, Boeing will receive £5,000,000 from the counter-party of the contract in exchange for $8,750,000. Boeing then can use £5,000,000 to make payment to Rolls-Royce. Since Boeing will have £5,000,000 for sure in exchange for a given dollar amount, that is, $8,750,000, regardless of the spot exchange rate that may prevail in one year, Boeing's foreign currency payable is fully hedged.

Money Market Instruments

If Boeing first computes the present value of its foreign currency payable, that is

$$£4,694,836 = £5,000,000/1.065,$$

and immediately invests exactly the same pound amount at the British interest rate of 6.5 percent per annum, it is assured of having £5,000,000 in one year. Boeing then can use the maturity value of this investment to pay off its pound payable. Under this money market hedging, Boeing has to outlay a certain dollar amount today in order to buy spot the pound amount that needs to be invested:

$$\$8,450,705 = (£4,694,836)\,(\$1.80/£).$$

The future value of this dollar cost of buying the necessary pound amount is computed as follows:

$$\$8,957,747 = (\$8,450,705)\,(1.06),$$

which exceeds the dollar cost of securing £5,000,000 under forward hedging, $8,750,000. Since Boeing will have to try to minimize the dollar cost of securing the pound amount, forward hedge would be preferable to money market hedge.

Currency Options Contracts

If Boeing decides to use a currency options contract to hedge its pound payable, it needs to buy "call" options on £5,000,000. Boeing also will have to decide on the exercise or strike price for the call options. We assume that Boeing chooses the exercise price at $1.80/£ with the premium of $0.018 per pound. The total cost of options as of the maturity date (considering the time value of money) then can be computed as follows:

$$\$95,400 = (\$0.018/\pounds)\ (\pounds5,000,000)\ (1.06).$$

If the British pound appreciates against the dollar beyond $1.80/£, the strike price of the options contract, Boeing will choose to exercise its options and purchase £5,000,000 for $9,000,000 = (£5,000,000) ($1.80/£). If the spot rate on the maturity date turns out to be below the strike price, on the other hand, Boeing will let the option expire and purchase the pound amount in the spot market. Thus, Boeing will be able to secure £5,000,000 for a maximum of $9,095,400 (= $9,000,000 + $95,400), or less.

It would be useful to compare the forward hedge and options hedge. Exhibit 8.8 illustrates the dollar costs of securing £5,000,000 under the two alternative hedging approaches for different levels of spot exchange rate on the maturity date. As can be seen from Exhibit 8.8, options hedge would be preferable if the spot exchange rate turns out to be less than $1.731/£ as the options hedge involves a lower dollar cost. On the other hand, if the spot exchange rate turns out to be higher than $1.731/£, the forward hedge would be preferable. The break-even spot exchange rate, that is, S_T^*, can be computed from the following equation:

$$\$8,750,000 = (5,000,000)\ S_T + \$95,400,$$

where the dollar cost of securing £5,000,00 under the forward hedge is equated to that under the options hedge. When we solve the above equation for S_T, we obtain the break-even spot exchange rate.

EXHIBIT 8.8

Dollar Costs of Securing the Pound Payable: Option versus Forward Hedge

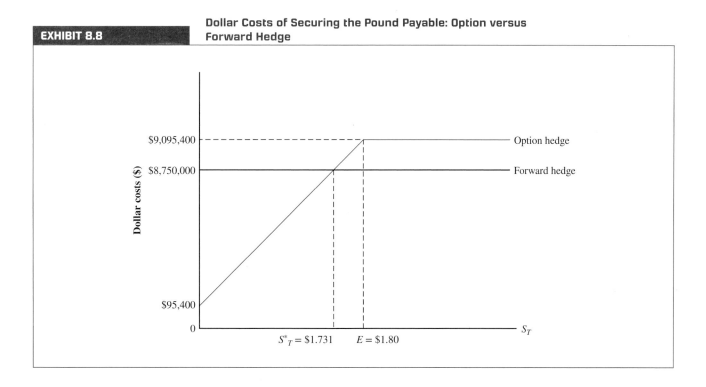

Cross-Hedging Minor Currency Exposure

www.florin.com/v4
/valore4.html

Discusses issues related to
currency risk management.

If a firm has receivables or payables in major currencies such as the British pound, euro, and Japanese yen, it can easily use forward, money market, or options contracts to manage its exchange risk exposure. In contrast, if the firm has positions in less liquid currencies such as the Korean won, Thai bhat, and Czech koruna, it may be either very costly or impossible to use financial contracts in these currencies. This is because financial markets of developing countries are relatively underdeveloped and often highly regulated. Facing this situation, the firm may consider using **cross-hedging** techniques to manage its minor currency exposure. Cross-hedging involves hedging a position in one asset by taking a position in another asset.

Suppose a U.S. firm has an account receivable in Korean won and would like to hedge its won position. If there were a well-functioning forward market in won, the firm would simply sell the won receivable forward. But the firm finds it costly to do so. However, since the won/dollar exchange rate is highly correlated with the yen/dollar exchange rate, the U.S. firm may sell a yen amount, which is equivalent to the won receivable, forward against the dollar thereby cross-hedging its won exposure. Obviously, the effectiveness of this cross-hedging technique would depend on the stability and strength of the won/yen correlation. A study by Aggarwal and Demaskey (1997) indicates that Japanese yen derivative contracts are fairly effective in cross-hedging exposure to minor Asian currencies such as the Indonesian rupiah, Korean won, Philippine peso, and Thai bhat. Likewise, euro derivatives can be effective in cross-hedging exposures in some Central and East European currencies such as the Czech koruna, Hungarian forint, and Romanian leu.

Another study by Benet (1990) suggests that commodity futures contracts may be used effectively to cross-hedge some minor currency exposures. Suppose the dollar price of the Mexican peso is positively correlated to the world oil price. Note that Mexico is a major exporter of oil, accounting for roughly 5 percent of the world market share. Considering this situation, a firm may use oil futures contracts to manage its peso exposure. The firm can sell (buy) oil futures if it has peso receivables (payables). In the same vein, soybean and coffee futures contracts may be used to cross-hedge a Brazilian real exposure. Again, the effectiveness of this cross-hedging technique would depend on the strength and stability of the relationship between the exchange rate and the commodity futures prices.

Hedging Contingent Exposure

In addition to providing a flexible hedge against exchange exposure, options contracts can also provide an effective hedge against what might be called **contingent exposure**. Contingent exposure refers to a situation in which the firm may or may not be subject to exchange exposure. Suppose General Electric (GE) is bidding on a hydroelectric project in Quebec Province, Canada. If the bid is accepted, which will be known in three months, GE is going to receive C$100 million to initiate the project. Since GE may or may not face exchange exposure depending on whether its bid will be accepted, it faces a typical contingent exposure situation.[3]

It is difficult to deal with contingent exposure using traditional hedging tools like forward contracts. Suppose that GE sold C$100 million forward to hedge the contingent exposure. If GE's bid is accepted, then GE will have no problem because it will

---

[3]These days, it is not unusual for the exporter to let the importer choose the currency of payment. For example, Boeing may allow British Airways to pay either $15 million or £10 million. To the extent that Boeing does not know in advance which currency it is going to receive, it faces a contingent exposure. Given the future spot exchange rate, British Airways will choose to pay with a cheaper currency. It is noteworthy that in this example, Boeing provided British Airways with a free option to buy up to $15 million using pounds (which is equivalent to an option to sell pounds for dollars) at the implicit exercise rate of $1.50/£.

EXHIBIT 8.9

Contingent Exposure
Management: The Case of
GE Bidding for a Quebec
Hydroelectric Project

Alternative Strategies	Bid Outcome	
	Bid Accepted	Bid Rejected
Do nothing	An unhedged long position in C$100 million	No exposure
Sell C$ forward	No exposure	An unhedged short position in C$100 million
Buy a put option on C$[a]	If the future spot rate becomes less than the exercise rate, $(S_T < E)$	
	Convert C$100 million at the exercise price	Exercise the option and make a profit
	If the future spot rate becomes greater than the exercise rate, $(S_T > E)$	
	Let the option expire and convert C$100 million at the spot exchange rate	Simply let the option expire

[a]If the future spot rate turns out to be equal to the exercise price, i.e., $S_T = E$, GE will be indifferent between
(i) exercising the option and (ii) letting the option expire and converting C$100 million at the spot rate.

have C$100 million to fulfill the forward contract. However, if the bid is rejected, GE now faces an unhedged short position in Canadian dollars. Clearly, a forward contract does not provide a satisfactory hedge against contingent exposure. A "do-nothing" policy does not guarantee a satisfactory outcome either. The problem with this policy is that if GE's bid is accepted, the firm ends up with an unhedged long position in Canadian dollars.

An alternative approach is to buy a three-month put option on C$100 million. In this case, there are four possible outcomes:

1. The bid is accepted and the spot exchange rate turns out to be less than the exercise rate: In this case, the firm will simply exercise the put option and convert C$100 million at the exercise rate.

2. The bid is accepted and the spot exchange rate turns out to be greater than the exercise rate: In this case, the firm will let the put option expire and convert C$100 million at the spot rate.

3. The bid is rejected and the spot exchange rate turns out to be less than the exercise rate: In this case, although the firm does not have Canadian dollars, it will exercise the put option and make a profit.

4. The bid is rejected and the spot rate turns out to be greater than the exercise rate: In this case, the firm will simply let the put option expire.

The above scenarios indicate that when the put option is purchased, each outcome is adequately covered; the firm will not be left with an unhedged foreign currency position. Again, it is stressed that the firm has to pay the option premium upfront. The preceding discussion is summarized in Exhibit 8.9.

Hedging Recurrent Exposure with Swap Contracts

Firms often have to deal with a "sequence" of accounts payable or receivable in terms of a foreign currency. Such recurrent cash flows in a foreign currency can best be hedged using a currency swap contract, which is an agreement to exchange one currency for another at a predetermined exchange rate, that is, the swap rate, on a sequence of future dates. As such, a swap contract is like a portfolio of forward contracts with different maturities. Swaps are very flexible in terms of amount and maturity; the maturity can range from a few months to 20 years.

Suppose that Boeing is scheduled to deliver an aircraft to British Airways at the beginning of each year for the next five years, starting in 1996. British Airways, in turn, is scheduled to pay £10,000,000 to Boeing on December 1 of each year for five years, starting in 1996. In this case, Boeing faces a sequence of exchange risk exposures. As previously mentioned, Boeing can hedge this type of exposure using a swap agreement by which Boeing delivers £10,000,000 to the counterparty of the contract on December 1 of each year for five years and takes delivery of a predetermined dollar amount each year. If the agreed swap exchange rate is $1.50/£, then Boeing will receive $15 million each year, regardless of the future spot and forward rates. Note that a sequence of five forward contracts would not be priced at a uniform rate, $1.50/£; the forward rates will be different for different maturities. In addition, longer-term forward contracts are not readily available.

Hedging through Invoice Currency

While such financial hedging instruments as forward, money market, swap, and options contracts are well known, hedging through the choice of invoice currency, an operational technique, has not received much attention. The firm can *shift, share,* or *diversify* exchange risk by appropriately choosing the currency of invoice. For instance, if Boeing invoices $15 million rather than £10 million for the sale of the aircraft, then it does not face exchange exposure anymore. Note, however, that the exchange exposure has not disappeared; it has merely shifted to the British importer. British Airways now has an account payable denominated in U.S. dollars.

Instead of shifting the exchange exposure entirely to British Airways, Boeing can share the exposure with British Airways by, for example, invoicing half of the bill in U.S. dollars and the remaining half in British pounds, that is, $7.5 million and £5 million. In this case, the magnitude of Boeing's exchange exposure is reduced by half. As a practical matter, however, the firm may not be able to use risk shifting or sharing as much as it wishes for fear of losing sales to competitors. Only an exporter with substantial market power can use this approach. In addition, if the currencies of both the exporter and the importer are not suitable for settling international trade, neither party can resort to risk shifting/sharing to deal with exchange exposure.

The firm can diversify exchange exposure to some extent by using currency basket units such as the SDR as the invoice currency. Often, multinational corporations and sovereign entities are known to float bonds denominated either in the SDR or in the ECU prior to the introduction of the euro. For example, the Egyptian government charges for the use of the Suez Canal using the SDR. Obviously, these currency baskets are used to reduce exchange exposure. As previously noted, the SDR now comprises four individual currencies, the U.S. dollar, the euro, the Japanese yen, and the British pound. Because the SDR is a portfolio of currencies, its value should be substantially more stable than the value of any individual constituent currency. Currency basket units can be a useful hedging tool especially for long-term exposure for which no forward or options contracts are readily available.

Hedging via Lead and Lag

Another operational technique the firm can use to reduce transaction exposure is leading and lagging foreign currency receipts and payments. To "lead" means to pay or collect early, whereas to "lag" means to pay or collect late. The firm would like to lead soft currency receivables and lag hard currency receivables to avoid the loss from depreciation of the soft currency and benefit from the appreciation of the hard currency. For the same reason, the firm will attempt to lead the hard currency payables and lag soft currency payables.

To the extent that the firm can effectively implement the **lead/lag strategy**, the transaction exposure the firm faces can be reduced. However, a word of caution is in order. Suppose, concerned with the likely depreciation of sterling, Boeing would like British Airways to prepay £10 million. Boeing's attempt to lead the pound receivable may encounter difficulties. First of all, British Airways would like to lag this payment, which is denominated in the soft currency (the pound), and thus has no incentive to prepay unless Boeing offers a substantial discount to compensate for the prepayment. This, of course, reduces the benefits of collecting the pound receivable early. Second, pressing British Airways for prepayment can hamper future sales efforts by Boeing. Third, to the extent that the original invoice price, £10 million, incorporates the expected depreciation of the pound, Boeing is already partially protected against the depreciation of the pound.

The lead/lag strategy can be employed more effectively to deal with intrafirm payables and receivables, such as material costs, rents, royalties, interests, and dividends, among subsidiaries of the same multinational corporation. Since managements of various subsidiaries of the same firm are presumably working for the good of the entire firm, the lead/lag strategy can be applied more aggressively.

Exposure Netting

In 1984, Lufthansa, a German airline, signed a contract to buy $3 billion worth of aircraft from Boeing and entered into a forward contract to purchase $1.5 billion forward for the purpose of hedging against the expected appreciation of the dollar against the German mark. This decision, however, suffered from a major flaw: A significant portion of Lufthansa's cash flows was also dollar-denominated. As a result, Lufthansa's net exposure to the exchange risk might not have been significant. Lufthansa had a so-called "natural hedge." In 1985, the dollar depreciated substantially against the mark and, as a result, Lufthansa experienced a major foreign exchange loss from settling the forward contract. This episode shows that when a firm has both receivables and payables in a given foreign currency, it should consider hedging only its net exposure.

So far, we have discussed exposure management on a currency-by-currency basis. In reality, a typical multinational corporation is likely to have a portfolio of currency positions. For instance, a U.S. firm may have an account payable in euros and, at the same time, an account receivable in Danish krones. Considering that the euro and krone often move against the dollar nearly in lockstep, the firm can just wait until these accounts become due and then buy euros spot with krones. It can be wasteful and unnecessary to buy euros forward and sell krones forward. In other words, if the firm has a portfolio of currency positions, it makes sense to hedge residual exposure rather than hedge each currency position separately.

If the firm would like to apply **exposure netting** aggressively, it helps to centralize the firm's exchange exposure management function in one location. Many multinational corporations are using a **reinvoice center**, a financial subsidiary, as a mechanism for centralizing exposure management functions. All the invoices arising from intrafirm transactions are sent to the reinvoice center, where exposure is netted. Once the residual exposure is determined, then foreign exchange experts at the center determine optimal hedging methods and implement them.

Should the Firm Hedge?

We have discussed how the firm can hedge exchange exposure if it wishes. We have not discussed whether the firm should try to hedge to begin with. There hardly exists a consensus on whether the firm should hedge. Some would argue that exchange

www.sec.gov/info/edgar.shtml

Company files with SEC show
how companies deal with
exchange risk exposure.

exposure management at the corporate level is redundant when stockholders can manage the exposure themselves. Others would argue that what matters in the firm valuation is only systematic risk; corporate risk management may only reduce the total risk. These arguments suggest that corporate exposure management would not necessarily add to the value of the firm.

While the above arguments against corporate risk management may be valid in a "perfect" capital market, one can make a case for it based on various market imperfections:

1. Information asymmetry: Management knows about the firm's exposure position much better than stockholders. Thus, the management of the firm, not its stockholders, should manage exchange exposure.

2. Differential transaction costs: The firm is in a position to acquire low-cost hedges; transaction costs for individual stockholders can be substantial. Also, the firm has hedging tools like the reinvoice center that are not available to stockholders.

3. Default costs: If default costs are significant, corporate hedging would be justifiable because it will reduce the probability of default. Perception of a reduced default risk, in turn, can lead to a better credit rating and lower financing costs.

4. Progressive corporate taxes: Under progressive corporate tax rates, stable before-tax earnings lead to lower corporate taxes than volatile earnings with the same average value. This happens because under progressive tax rates, the firm pays more taxes in high-earning periods than it saves in low-earning periods.

The last point merits elaboration. Suppose the country's corporate income tax system is such that a tax rate of 20 percent applies to the first $10 million of corporate earnings and a 40 percent rate applies to any earnings exceeding $10 million. Firms thus face a simple progressive tax structure. Now consider an exporting firm that expects to earn $15 million if the dollar depreciates, but only $5 million if the dollar appreciates. Let's assume that the dollar may appreciate or depreciate with equal chances. In this case, the firm's expected tax will be $2.5 million:

$$\text{Expected tax} = \tfrac{1}{2}\,[(.20)(\$5,000,000)]$$
$$+ \tfrac{1}{2}\,[(.20)(\$10,000,000) + (.40)(\$5,000,000)]$$
$$= \$2,500,000$$

Now consider another firm, B, that is identical to firm A in every respect except that, unlike firm A, firm B aggressively and successfully hedges its risk exposure and, as a result, it can expect to realize certain earnings of $10,000,000, the same as firm A's expected earnings. Firm B, however, expects to pay only $2 million for taxes. Obviously, hedging results in a $500,000 tax saving. Exhibit 8.10 illustrates this situation.

While not every firm is hedging exchange exposure, many firms are engaged in hedging activities, suggesting that corporate risk management is relevant to maximizing the firm's value. To the extent that for various reasons, stockholders themselves cannot properly manage exchange risk, the firm's managers can do it for them, contributing to the firm's value. Some corporate hedging activities, however, might be motivated by managerial objectives; managers may want to stabilize cash flows so that the risk to their human capital can be reduced.

A study by Allayannis and Weston (2001) provides direct evidence on the important issue of whether hedging actually adds to the value of the firm. Specifically, they examine whether firms with currency exposure that use foreign currency derivative contracts, such as currency forward and options, increase their valuation. The authors find that U.S. firms that face currency risk and use currency derivatives for hedging have, on average, about 5 percent higher value than firms that do not use currency

EXHIBIT 8.10

Tax Savings from Hedging
Exchange Risk Exposure

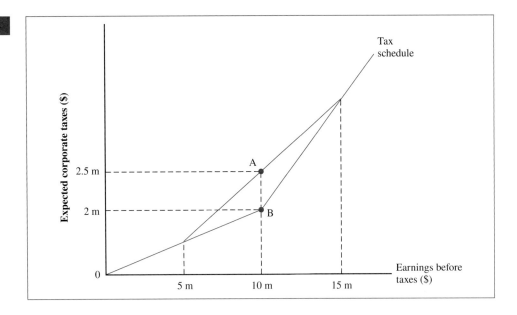

derivatives. For firms that have no direct foreign involvement but may be exposed to exchange rate movements via export/import competition, they find a small hedging valuation premium. In addition, they find that firms that stop hedging experience a decrease in firm valuation compared with those firms that continue to hedge. Their study thus clearly suggests that corporate hedging contributes to firm value.

What Risk Management Products Do Firms Use?

In an extensive survey, Jesswein, Kwok, and Folks (1995) documented the extent of knowledge and use of foreign exchange risk management products by U.S. corporations. On the basis of a survey of *Fortune* 500 firms, they found that the traditional forward contract is the most popular product. As Exhibit 8.11 shows, about 93 percent of respondents of the survey used forward contracts. This old, traditional instrument

EXHIBIT 8.11

A Survey of Knowledge and
Use of Foreign Exchange
Risk Management Products
by U.S. Firms[a]

Type of Product	Heard of (Awareness)	Used (Adoption)
Forward contracts	100.0%	93.1%
Foreign currency swaps	98.8	52.6
Foreign currency futures	98.8	20.1
Exchange-traded currency options	96.4	17.3
Exchange-traded futures options	95.8	8.9
Over-the-counter currency options	93.5	48.8
Cylinder options	91.2	28.7
Synthetic forwards	88.0	22.0
Synthetic options	88.0	18.6
Participating forwards, etc.	83.6	15.8
Forward exchange agreements, etc.	81.7	14.8
Foreign currency warrants	77.7	4.2
Break forwards, etc.	65.3	4.9
Compound options	55.8	3.8
Lookback options, etc.	52.1	5.1
Average across products	84.4%	23.9%

[a]The products are ranked by the percentages of respondents who have heard of products. There are 173 respondents in total.

Source: Kurt Jesswein, Chuck Kwok, and William Folks, Jr., "Corporate Use of Innovative Foreign Exchange Risk Management Products," *Columbia Journal of World Business* (Fall 1995).

EXHIBIT 8.12

Currency Derivative
Contracts Usage by Asian,
U.K., and U.S. Multinational
Firms

Type of Product	Percentage of Firms Used		
	Asia	U.K.	U.S.
Forward contracts	88%	92%	98%
Futures contracts	24	4	4
Futures options	10	8	9
Options	58	46	43
Swaps	52	36	54

Source: Andrew P. Marshall, "Foreign Exchange Risk Management in UK, USA, and Asia Pacific Multinational Companies," *Journal of Multinational Financial Management* 10 (2000).

has not been supplanted by recent "fancy" innovations. The next commonly used instruments are foreign currency swaps (52.6 percent) and over-the-counter currency options (48.8 percent). Such recent innovations as compound options (3.8 percent) and look-back options (5.1 percent) are among the least extensively used instruments. These findings seem to indicate that most U.S. firms meet their exchange risk management needs with forward, swap, and options contracts.

The Jesswein, Kwok, and Folks survey also shows that, among the various industries, the finance/insurance/real estate industry stands out as the most frequent user of exchange risk management products. This finding is not surprising. This industry has more finance experts who are skillful at using derivative securities. In addition, this industry handles mainly financial assets, which tend to be exposed to exchange risk. The survey further shows that the corporate use of foreign exchange risk management products is positively related to the firm's degree of international involvement. This finding is not surprising either. As the firm becomes more internationalized through cross-border trade and investments, it is likely to handle an increasing amount of foreign currencies, giving rise to a greater demand for exchange risk hedging.

In a similar survey covering about 180 multinational firms headquartered in the U.K., United States, and Asia (Australia, Hong Kong, Japan, Korea, and Singapore), Marshall (2000) documented that U.K. and U.S. firms show relatively similar patterns of using various currency derivative contracts to manage transaction exposure. But Asian firms show somewhat different patterns. As can be seen from Exhibit 8.12, most multinational firms use currency forward contracts, regardless of their domiciles. This finding is consistent with the Jesswein, Kwok, and Folks survey. But the use of currency futures and options contracts is substantially more popular among Asian multinationals, especially among the Japanese and Singaporean firms, than among U.K. and U.S. multinationals. The same survey further shows that regardless of the domiciles, multinational firms extensively use such operational techniques as netting, matching, and leading and lagging to manage transaction exposure. The survey suggests that many multinational firms use a combination of operational techniques and financial contracts to deal with transaction exposure.

SUMMARY

1. The firm is subject to a transaction exposure when it faces contractual cash flows denominated in foreign currencies. Transaction exposure can be hedged by financial contracts like forward, money market, and options contracts, as well as by such operational techniques as the choice of invoice currency, lead/lag strategy, and exposure netting.

2. If the firm has a foreign-currency-denominated receivable (payable), it can hedge the exposure by selling (buying) the foreign currency receivable (payable) forward. The firm can *expect* to eliminate the exposure without incurring costs as long as the forward exchange rate is an unbiased predictor of the future spot rate. The firm can achieve equivalent hedging results by lending and borrowing in the domestic and foreign money markets.

3. Unlike forward and money market hedges, currency options provide flexible hedges against exchange exposure. With the options hedge, the firm can limit the downside risk while preserving the upside potential. Currency options also provide the firm with an effective hedge against contingent exposure.

4. The firm can shift, share, and diversify exchange exposure by appropriately choosing the invoice currency. Currency basket units such as the SDR and ECU can be used as invoice currencies to partially hedge long-term exposure for which financial hedges are not readily available.

5. The firm can reduce transaction exposure by leading and lagging foreign currency receipts and payments, especially among its own affiliates.

6. When a firm has a portfolio of foreign currency positions, it makes sense only to hedge the residual exposure rather than hedging each currency position separately. The reinvoice center can help implement the portfolio approach to exposure management.

7. In a perfect capital market where stockholders can hedge exchange exposure as well as the firm, it is difficult to justify exposure management at the corporate level. In reality, capital markets are far from perfect, and the firm often has advantages over the stockholders in implementing hedging strategies. There thus exists room for corporate exposure management to contribute to the firm's value.

KEY WORDS

contingent exposure, *208*
cross-hedging, *208*
economic exposure, *198*
exposure netting, *211*
forward market
  hedge, *200*

hedging through invoice
  currency, *210*
lead/lag strategy, *211*
money market hedge, *203*
options market
  hedge, *203*

reinvoice center, *211*
transaction
  exposure, *198*
translation
  exposure, *198*

QUESTIONS

1. How would you define *transaction exposure*? How is it different from economic exposure?

2. Discuss and compare hedging transaction exposure using the forward contract versus money market instruments. When do alternative hedging approaches produce the same result?

3. Discuss and compare the costs of hedging by forward contracts and options contracts.

4. What are the advantages of a currency options contract as a hedging tool compared with the forward contract?

5. Suppose your company has purchased a put option on the euro to manage exchange exposure associated with an account receivable denominated in that currency. In this case, your company can be said to have an "insurance" policy on its receivable. Explain in what sense this is so.

6. Recent surveys of corporate exchange risk management practices indicate that many U.S. firms simply do not hedge. How would you explain this result?

7. Should a firm hedge? Why or why not?

8. Using an example, discuss the possible effect of hedging on a firm's tax obligations.

9. Explain *contingent exposure* and discuss the advantages of using currency options to manage this type of currency exposure.

10. Explain cross-hedging and discuss the factors determining its effectiveness.

www.mhhe.com/er8e

PROBLEMS

The spreadsheet TRNSEXP.xls may be used in solving parts of problems 2, 3, 4, and 6.

1. Cray Research sold a supercomputer to the Max Planck Institute in Germany on credit and invoiced €10 million payable in six months. Currently, the six-month forward exchange rate is $1.10/€ and the foreign exchange adviser for Cray Research predicts that the spot rate is likely to be $1.05/€ in six months.

   a. What is the expected gain/loss from a forward hedge?

   b. If you were the financial manager of Cray Research, would you recommend hedging this euro receivable? Why or why not?

   c. Suppose the foreign exchange adviser predicts that the future spot rate will be the same as the forward exchange rate quoted today. Would you recommend hedging in this case? Why or why not?

   d. Suppose now that the future spot exchange rate is forecast to be $1.17/€. Would you recommend hedging? Why or why not?

2. IBM purchased computer chips from NEC, a Japanese electronics concern, and was billed ¥250 million payable in three months. Currently, the spot exchange rate is ¥105/$ and the three-month forward rate is ¥100/$. The three-month money market interest rate is 8 percent per annum in the United States and 7 percent per annum in Japan. The management of IBM decided to use a money market hedge to deal with this yen account payable.

   a. Explain the process of a money market hedge and compute the dollar cost of meeting the yen obligation.

   b. Conduct a cash flow analysis of the money market hedge.

3. You plan to visit Geneva, Switzerland, in three months to attend an international business conference. You expect to incur a total cost of SF5,000 for lodging, meals, and transportation during your stay. As of today, the spot exchange rate is $0.60/SF and the three-month forward rate is $0.63/SF. You can buy the three-month call option on SF with an exercise price of $0.64/SF for the premium of $0.05 per SF. Assume that your expected future spot exchange rate is the same as the forward rate. The three-month interest rate is 6 percent per annum in the United States and 4 percent per annum in Switzerland.

   a. Calculate your expected dollar cost of buying SF5,000 if you choose to hedge by a call option on SF.

   b. Calculate the future dollar cost of meeting this SF obligation if you decide to hedge using a forward contract.

   c. At what future spot exchange rate will you be indifferent between the forward and option market hedges?

   d. Illustrate the future dollar cost of meeting the SF payable against the future spot exchange rate under both the options and forward market hedges.

4. Boeing just signed a contract to sell a Boeing 737 aircraft to Air France. Air France will be billed €20 million payable in one year. The current spot exchange rate is $1.05/€ and the one-year forward rate is $1.10/€. The annual interest rate is 6 percent in the United States and 5 percent in France. Boeing is concerned with the volatile exchange rate between the dollar and the euro and would like to hedge exchange exposure.

   a. It is considering two hedging alternatives: sell the euro proceeds from the sale forward or borrow euros from Crédit Lyonnaise against the euro receivable. Which alternative would you recommend? Why?

   b. Other things being equal, at what forward exchange rate would Boeing be indifferent between the two hedging methods?

5. Suppose that Baltimore Machinery sold a drilling machine to a Swiss firm and gave the Swiss client a choice of paying either $10,000 or SF15,000 in three months.

   a. In the example, Baltimore Machinery effectively gave the Swiss client a free option to buy up to $10,000 using Swiss francs. What is the "implied" exercise exchange rate?

   b. If the spot exchange rate turns out to be $0.62/SF, which currency do you think the Swiss client will choose to use for payment? What is the value of this free option for the Swiss client?

   c. What is the best way for Baltimore Machinery to deal with exchange exposure?

6. Princess Cruise Company (PCC) purchased a ship from Mitsubishi Heavy Industry for 500 million yen payable in one year. The current spot rate is ¥124/$ and the one-year forward rate is 110/$. The annual interest rate is 5 percent in Japan and 8 percent in the United States. PCC can also buy a one-year call option on yen at the strike price of $.0081 per yen for a premium of .014 cents per yen.

   a. Compute the future dollar costs of meeting this obligation using the money market and forward hedges.

   b. Assuming that the forward exchange rate is the best predictor of the future spot rate, compute the expected future dollar cost of meeting this obligation when the option hedge is used.

   c. At what future spot rate do you think PCC may be indifferent between the option and forward hedge?

7. Consider a U.S.-based company that exports goods to Switzerland. The U.S. company expects to receive payment on a shipment of goods in three months. Because the payment will be in Swiss francs, the U.S. company wants to hedge against a decline in the value of the Swiss franc over the next three months. The U.S. risk-free rate is 2 percent, and the Swiss risk-free rate is 5 percent. Assume that interest rates are expected to remain fixed over the next six months. The current spot rate is $0.5974.

   a. Indicate whether the U.S. company should use a long or short forward contract to hedge currency risk.

   b. Calculate the no-arbitrage price at which the U.S. company could enter into a forward contract that expires in three months.

   c. It is now 30 days since the U.S. company entered into the forward contract. The spot rate is $0.55. Interest rates are the same as before. Calculate the value of the U.S. company's forward position.

8. Suppose that you are a U.S.-based importer of goods from the United Kingdom. You expect the value of the pound to increase against the U.S. dollar over the next 30 days. You will be making payment on a shipment of imported goods in 30 days and want to hedge your currency exposure. The U.S. risk-free rate is 5.5 percent, and the U.K. risk-free rate is 4.5 percent. These rates are expected to remain unchanged over the next month. The current spot rate is $1.50.

   a. Indicate whether you should use a long or short forward contract to hedge the currency risk.

   b. Calculate the no-arbitrage price at which you could enter into a forward contract that expires in 30 days.

   c. Move forward 10 days. The spot rate is $1.53. Interest rates are unchanged. Calculate the value of your forward position.

   d. Using the text software spreadsheet TRNSEXP, replicate the analysis in Exhibit 8.8.

**INTERNET
EXERCISES**

WWW

Bankware, a Boston-based company specializing in banking-related softwares, exported its software for automatic teller machines (ATM) to Oslo Commerce Bank, which is trying to modernize its operation. Facing competition from European software vendors, Bankware decided to bill the sales in the client's currency, Norwegian krone 500,000, payable in one year. Since there are no active forward currency markets for the Norwegian currency, Bankware is considering selling a euro or British pound amount forward for cross-hedging purpose. Assess the hedging effectiveness of selling the euro versus pound amount forward to cover the company's exposure to the Norwegian currency. In solving this problem, consult exchange rate data available from the following website: www.federalreserve.gov/releases/H10/hist. You may consult other websites.

MINI CASE

Airbus' Dollar Exposure

Airbus sold an A400 aircraft to Delta Airlines, a U.S. company, and billed $30 million payable in six months. Airbus is concerned about the euro proceeds from international sales and would like to control exchange risk. The current spot exchange rate is $1.05/€ and the six-month forward exchange rate is $1.10/€. Airbus can buy a six-month put option on U.S. dollars with a strike price of €0.95/$ for a premium of €0.02 per U.S. dollar. Currently, six-month interest rate is 2.5 percent in the euro zone and 3.0 percent in the United States.

1. Compute the guaranteed euro proceeds from the American sale if Airbus decides to hedge using a forward contract.

2. If Airbus decides to hedge using money market instruments, what action does Airbus need to take? What would be the guaranteed euro proceeds from the American sale in this case?

3. If Airbus decides to hedge using put options on U.S. dollars, what would be the "expected" euro proceeds from the American sale? Assume that Airbus regards the current forward exchange rate as an unbiased predictor of the future spot exchange rate.

4. At what future spot exchange do you think Airbus will be indifferent between the option and money market hedge?

**CASE
APPLICATION**

Richard May's Options

It is Tuesday afternoon, February 14, 2012. Richard May, Assistant Treasurer at American Digital Graphics (ADG), sits in his office on the thirty-fourth floor of the building that dominates Rockefeller Plaza's west perimeter. It's Valentine's Day, and Richard and his wife have dinner reservations with another couple at Balthazar at 7:30. I must get this hedging memo done, thinks May, and get out of here. Foreign exchange options? I had better get the story straight before someone in the Finance Committee starts asking questions. Let's see, there are two ways in which I can envision us using options now. One is to hedge a dividend due on September 15th from ADG Germany. The other is to hedge our upcoming payment to Matsumerda for their spring RAM chip statement. With the yen at 78 and increasing I'm glad we haven't covered the payment so far, but now I'm getting nervous and I would like to protect my posterior. An option to buy yen on June 10 might be just the thing.

Before we delve any further into Richard May's musings, let us learn a bit about ADG and about foreign exchange options. American Digital Graphics is a $12 billion sales company engaged in, among other things, the development, manufacture, and marketing of microprocessor-based equipment. Although 30 percent of the firm's sales are currently abroad, the firm has full-fledged manufacturing facilities in only three foreign countries, Germany, Canada, and Brazil. An assembly plant in Singapore exists primarily to solder Japanese semiconductor chips onto circuit boards and to screw these into Brazilian-made boxes for shipment to the United States, Canada, and Germany. The German subsidiary has developed half of its sales to France, the Netherlands, and the United Kingdom, billing in euros. ADG Germany has accumulated a cash reserve of €900,000, worth $1,178,100 at today's exchange rate. While the Hamburg office has automatic permission to repatriate €3 million, they have been urged to seek authorization to convert another €1 million by September 15th. The firm has an agreement to buy three hundred thousand RAM chips at ¥8000 each semi-annually, and it is this payment that will fall due on June 10th.

The conventional means of hedging exchange risk are forward or future contracts. These, however, are fixed and inviolable agreements. In many practical instances the hedger is uncertain whether foreign currency cash inflow or outflow will materialize. In such cases, what is needed is the right, but not the obligation, to buy or sell a designated quantity of a foreign currency at a specified price (exchange rate). This is precisely what a foreign exchange option provides.

A foreign exchange option gives the holder *the right to buy or sell a designated quantity of a foreign currency* at a specified exchange rate up to or at a stipulated date. The terminal date of the contract is called the expiration date (or maturity date). If the option may be exercised before the expiration date, it is called an American option; if only at the expiration date, a European option.

The party retaining the option is the option buyer; the party giving the option is the option seller (or writer). The exchange rate at which the option can be exercised is called the exercise price or strike price. The buyer of the option must pay the seller some amount, called the option price or the premium, for the rights involved.

The important feature of a foreign exchange option is that the holder of the option has the right, but not the obligation, to exercise it. He will only exercise it if the currency moves in a favorable direction. Thus, once you have paid for an option, you cannot lose, unlike a forward contract, where you are obliged to exchange the currencies and therefore will lose if the movement is unfavorable.

The disadvantage of an option contract, compared to a forward or futures contract is that you have to pay a price for the option, and this price or premium tends to be quite high for certain options. In general, the option's price will be higher the greater the risk to the seller (and the greater the value to the buyer because this is a zero-sum game). The risk of a call option will be greater, and the premium higher, the higher the forward rate relative to the exercise price; after all, one can always lock in a profit by buying at the exercise price and selling at the forward rate. The chance that the option will be exercised profitably is also higher, the more volatile is the currency, and the longer the option has to run before it expires.

Returning to Richard May in his Rockefeller Center office, we find that he has been printing spot, forward and currency options, and futures quotations from the company's Bloomberg terminal.

The option prices are quoted in U.S. cents per euro. Yen are quoted in hundredths of a cent. Looking at these prices, Richard realizes that he can work out how much the euro or yen would have to change to make the option worthwhile. Richard makes a mental note that ADG can typically borrow in the Eurocurrency market at LIBOR + 1% and lend at LIBID.

"I'll attach these numbers to my memo," mutters May, but the truth is he has yet to come to grips with the real question, which is when, if ever, are currency options a better means of hedging exchange risk for an international firm than traditional forward exchange contracts or future's contracts.

Please assist Mr. May in his analysis of currency hedging for his report to ADG's Finance Committee. In doing so, you may consult the following highlighted market quotes.

EXHIBIT 8.13   Spot Exchange Rates

Currency Group										Key Cross Currency Rates – Majors
02/14/12					Rate: Spot		Monitor: Last Price			Source: BGN
										Bloomberg BGN(NY)
	USD	EUR	JPY	GBP	CHF	CAD	AUD	NZD	HKD	NOK	SEK
SEK	6.7062	8.7768	.08545	10.500	7.2701	6.6934	7.1352	5.5546	.86496	1.1662	–
NOK	5.7505	7.5260	.07327	9.0038	6.2341	5.7396	6.1184	4.7631	.74170	–	.85749
HKD	7.7531	10.147	.09879	12.139	8.4052	7.7384	8.2492	6.4218	–	1.3483	1.1561
NZD	1.2073	1.5801	.01538	1.8903	1.3088	1.2050	1.2846	–	.15572	.20995	.18003
AUD	.93987	1.2301	.01198	1.4716	1.0189	.93809	–	.77848	.12122	.16344	.14015
CAD	1.0019	1.3113	.01277	1.5687	1.0862	–	1.0660	.82986	.12923	.17423	.14940
CHF	.92243	1.2072	.01175	1.4443	–	.92068	.98144	.76403	.11897	.16041	.13755
GBP	.63868	.83588	.00814	–	.69239	.63746	.67954	.52901	.08238	.11106	.09524
JPY	78.479	102.71	–	122.88	85.078	78.330	83.500	65.003	10.122	13.647	11.702
EUR	.76408	–	.00974	1.1963	.82834	.76263	.81296	.63288	.09855	.13287	.11394
USD	–	1.3088	.01274	1.5657	1.0841	.99810	1.0640	.82829	.12898	.17390	.14912

EXHIBIT 8.14   Forward Exchange Rates

Currency Group										Key Cross Currency Rates – Majors
02/14/12					Rate: 4 Month		Monitor: Outrights			Source: BGN
										Bloomberg BGN(NY)
	USD	EUR	JPY	GBP	CHF	CAD	AUD	NZD	HKD	NOK	SEK
SEK	6.7042	8.7760	.08542	10.497	7.2692	6.6924	7.1355	5.5526	.86471	1.1661	–
NOK	5.7494	7.5262	.07326	9.0022	6.2339	5.7393	6.1193	4.7618	.74156	–	.85758
HKD	7.7531	10.149	.09879	12.140	8.4065	7.7395	8.2520	6.4214	–	1.3485	1.1565
NZD	1.2074	1.5805	.01538	1.8905	1.3091	1.2053	1.2851	–	.15573	.21000	.18010
AUD	.93955	1.2299	.01197	1.4711	1.0187	.93790	–	.77816	.12118	.16342	.14014
CAD	1.0018	1.3113	.01276	1.5685	1.0862	–	1.0662	.82969	.12921	.17424	.14942
CHF	.92228	1.2073	.01175	1.4441	–	.92066	.98162	.76386	.11896	.16041	.13757
GBP	.63867	.83604	.00814	–	.69249	.63754	.67976	.52896	.08237	.11108	.09526
JPY	78.482	102.74	–	122.88	85.096	78.344	83.532	65.001	10.123	13.650	11.706
EUR	.76392	–	.00973	1.1961	.82830	.76258	.81307	.63270	.09853	.13287	.11395
USD	–	1.3090	.01274	1.5658	1.0843	.99824	1.0643	.82823	.12898	.17393	.14916

Currency Group										Key Cross Currency Rates – Majors
02/14/12					Rate: 7 Month		Monitor: Outrights			Source: BGN
										Bloomberg BGN(NY)
	USD	EUR	JPY	GBP	CHF	CAD	AUD	NZD	HKD	NOK	SEK
SEK	6.7045	8.7761	.08543	10.497	7.2694	6.6926	7.1355	5.5528	.86472	1.1661	–
NOK	5.7495	7.5261	.07326	9.0021	6.2339	5.7394	6.1192	4.7619	.74155	–	.85757
HKD	7.7534	10.149	.09879	12.139	8.4066	7.7397	8.2518	6.4215	–	1.3485	1.1564
NZD	1.2074	1.5805	.01538	1.8904	1.3091	1.2053	1.2850	–	.15573	.21000	.18009
AUD	.93959	1.2299	.01197	1.4711	1.0188	.93794	–	.77820	.12119	.16342	.14014
CAD	1.0018	1.3113	.01276	1.5685	1.0862	–	1.0662	.82969	.12920	.17423	.14942
CHF	.92229	1.2073	.01175	1.4440	–	.92066	.98159	.76387	.11895	.16041	.13756
GBP	.63869	.83604	.00814	–	.69250	.63756	.67975	.52898	.08238	.11109	.09526
JPY	78.484	102.73	–	122.88	85.096	78.345	83.529	65.002	10.123	13.650	11.706
EUR	.76394	–	.00973	1.1961	.82831	.76260	.81306	.63272	.09853	.13287	.11395
USD	–	1.3090	.01274	1.5657	1.0843	.99824	1.0643	.82823	.12898	.17393	.14915

EXHIBIT 8.15   **Money Market Rates**

EURO MONEY RATES							
SECURITY	TIME	BID	ASK	CHANGE	HIGH	LOW	PRV CLS
DEPOSIT RATES							
2) EUDR1T –0/N	17:01	.1000	.3500	+.0750	.4500	.1450	.1500
3) EUDR2T –T/N	13:59	.1500	.4000	—	.2800	.2250	.2750
4) EUDR3T –S/N	20:00	.1500	.4000	+.0250	.3000	.1450	.2500
5) EUDR1Z –1WK	12:32	.3200	.3700	+.0350	.4100	.3000	.3100
6) EUDR2Z –2WK	20:00	.2500	.5000	—	.4450	.2200	.3750
7) EUDR3Z –3WK	20:00	.3000	.5000	—	.5000	.2700	.4000
8) EUDRA –1MO	16:23	.4500	.5700	–.0600	.7200	.5100	.5700
9) EUDRB –2MO	20:00	.6000	.7200	—	.7100	.6550	.6600
10) EUDRC –3MO	19:59	.9500	1.0000	—	1.1000	.9600	.9750
11) EUDRD –4MO	19:59	1.0600	1.1100	–.0200	1.1550	1.0650	1.1050
12) EUDRE –5MO	19:59	1.1800	1.2300	–.0100	1.3500	1.1700	1.2150
13) EUDRF –6MO	19:59	1.2900	1.3400	–.0100	1.3700	1.3000	1.3250
14) EUDRG –7MO	19:59	1.3500	1.4000	–.0100	1.4600	1.3650	1.3850
15) EUDRH –8MO	19:59	1.4200	1.4700	–.0100	1.5250	1.4350	1.4550
16) EUDRI –9MO	19:59	1.4800	1.5300	–.0100	1.6500	1.4900	1.5150
17) EUDRJ –10MO	19:59	1.5400	1.5900	–.0100	1.6400	1.5650	1.5750
18) EUDRK –11MO	19:59	1.5900	1.6500	–.0100	1.6950	1.5900	1.6300
19) EUDR1 –1YR	20:00	1.6500	1.7100	–.0100	1.8000	1.6500	1.6900

JAPANESE YEN MONEY RATES						
SECURITY	LAST	CHANGE	TIME	PREVIOUS	BID	ASK
DEPOSITS						
2) O/N	.0010	—	6:01	.0010	.0010	.0010
3) T/N	.0850	—	19:59	.0850	.0100	.1600
4) S/N	.1550	—	7:28	.1550	.0800	.2300
5) 1 Week	.1050	—	19:59	.1050	.0300	.1800
6) 2 Week	.1050	—	19:59	.1050	.0300	.1800
7) 3 Week	.1300	—	19:58	.1300	.0800	.1800
8) 1 Month	.1050	—	19:59	.1050	.0600	.1500
9) 2 Month	.1300	—	19:59	.1300	.1000	.1600
10) 3 Month	.1700	—	19:59	.1700	.1400	.2000
11) 4 Month	.2100	—	19:59	.2100	.1800	.2400
12) 5 Month	.2600	—	19:59	.2600	.2300	.2900
13) 6 Month	.3100	—	19:59	.3100	.2800	.3400
14) 7 Month	.3600	—	19:59	.3600	.3300	.3900
15) 8 Month	.4000	—	19:59	.4000	.3700	.4300
16) 9 Month	.4500	—	19:59	.4500	.4200	.4800
17) 10 Month	.4800	—	19:59	.4800	.4500	.5100
18) 11 Month	.5000	—	19:59	.5000	.4700	.5300
19) 1 Year	.5300	—	19:59	.5300	.5000	.5600

(continued)

EXHIBIT 8.15 Money Market Rates *(continued)*

USD MONEY MARKET RATES

SECURITY		TIME	BID	ASK	CHANGE	HIGH	LOW	PRV CLS
Fed Funds								
2) FDFD		15:49	.11000	.14000	—	.23000	.09000	.12000
Deposit Rates								
4) O/N		19:59	.0800	.1800	—	.2900	.1300	.1300
5) USD Depo	T/N	14:23	.1300	.2000	−.0500	.2000	.1350	.2500
6) USD Depo	S/N	20:00	.0800	.1800	—	.1600	.1300	.1300
7) USD Depo	1 WK	19:59	.1000	.2000	—	.2300	.1500	.1500
8) USD Depo	2 WK	20:00	.1200	.2200	—	.3000	.1690	.1700
9) USD Depo	3 WK	20:00	.1300	.2300	—	.2450	.1400	.1800
10) USD Depo	1 Mo	20:00	.1700	.2400	—	.3950	.2050	.2050
11) USD Depo	2 Mo	20:00	.3000	.3600	—	.8250	.2800	.3300
12) USD Depo	3 Mo	20:00	.4600	.5100	—	.8750	.3700	.4850
13) USD Depo	4 Mo	20:00	.5700	.6200	—	.7108	.5631	.5950
14) USD Depo	5 Mo	20:00	.6500	.7000	—	.7584	.6203	.6750
15) USD Depo	6 Mo	19:24	.7300	.7800	—	1.3550	.4550	.7550
16) USD Depo	7 Mo	20:03	.7800	.8300	−.0100	1.6300	.7351	1.6300
17) USD Depo	8 Mo	20:00	.8300	.8800	—	.9116	.7919	.8550
18) USD Depo	9 Mo	20:01	.8800	1.8300	−.3750	1.3550	.8548	1.7300
19) USD Depo	10 Mo	20:00	.9300	.9800	—	1.0771	.8706	.9550
20) USD Depo	11 Mo	20:00	.9900	1.0400	—	1.1213	.9222	1.0150

EXHIBIT 8.16 Currency Futures

View: Futures **EURO FX CURR FUT** Chicago Mercantile E Delayed Futures		1) Edit Columns Contracts: 6/6		2) Chart on CCRV Pricing Date: 02/14/12 COMB Aggr Volume: 268379		Contact Table Sort By: Expiration Aggr Open Int: 286579		
Ticker		Last	Change	Time	Bid	Ask	Open Int	Volume	Previous
3) ECH2	Mar12	1.3090	−.0115	20:26	1.3089	1.3090	281213	267388	1.3205
4) ECM2	Jun 12	1.3096	−.0114	20:25	1.3095	1.3097	5261	973	1.3210
5) ECU2	Sep 12	1.3110 s	−.0107	20:10	1.3098	1.3107	81	12	1.3217
6) ECZ2	Dec 12	1.3121 s	−.0103	20:10	1.1800	–	16	6	1.3224
7) ECH3	Mar13	1.3132 s	−.0103	20:10	–	–	8	–	1.3235
8) ECM3	Jun 13	1.3141 s	−.0102	20:10	–	–	–	–	1.3243

View: Futures **JPN YEN CURR FUT** Chicago Mercantile E Delayed Futures		1) Edit Columns Contracts: 6/6		2) Chart on CCRV Pricing Date: 02/14/12 COMB Aggr Volume: 106781		Contact Table Sort By: Expiration Display: Quoted Val. Aggr Open Int: 162112		
Ticker		Last	Change	Time	Bid	Ask	Open Int	Volume	Previous
3) JYH2	Mar 12	127.47	−1.39	20:27	127.46	127.47	160202	106024	128.86
4) JYM2	Jun 12	127.59	−1.40	20:24	127.59	127.62	1882	753	128.99
5) JYU2	Sep 12	127.79 s	−1.38	20:10	127.53	128.08	18	2	129.17
6) JYZ2	Dec 12	128.01 s	−1.38	20:10	125.30	–	10	2	129.39
7) JYH3	Mar 13	128.32 s	−1.39	20:10	–	–	–	–	129.71
8) JYM3	Jun 13	128.64 s	−1.39	20:10	–	–	–	–	130.03

EXHIBIT 8.17   **Currency Options**

XEC Curncy	95) Templates	96) Actions	97) Expiry	Implied Vols (OMON)
ECU SPOT USD STD	↑131.08 −.80 −.61%	Hi 131.80	Lo 131.80	HV 10.21 91) News
Calc Mode	/ Center 131.00	Strike 5	Exch NASDAQ OM	

| | | Calls | | | | | | Strike | | | Puts | | | | | |

Ticker	Bid	Ask	Last	IVM	DM	Volm	QInt	Strike	Ticker	Bid	Ask	Last	IVM	DM	Volm	QInt
16 Jun 12 (123d); CSize 100; R 0.12							5		16 Jun 12 (123d); CSize 100; R 0.12							
11) XEM2C C	4.07	4.33	5.00y	12.03	.56	–	2	130	41) XEM2P C	3.10	3.27	3.10	12.25	−.44	10	953
12) XEM2C C	3.79	4.02	–	11.91	.54	–	–	130.5	42) XEM2P C	3.32	3.47	5.18y	12.15	−.46	–	18
13) XEM2C C	3.51	3.74	4.20y	11.83	.52	–	1	131	43) XEM2P C	3.55	3.69	3.56	12.06	−.48	1	346
14) XEM2C C	3.25	3.47	–	11.73	.49	–	–	131.5	44) XEM2P C	3.78	3.92	4.94y	11.95	−.50	–	8
15) XEM2C C	2.99	3.22	–	11.62	.47	–	–	135	45) XEM2P C	4.02	4.16	5.48y	11.85	−.53	–	7
22 Sep 12 (221d); CSize 100; R 0.12							5		22 Sep 12 (221d); CSize 100; R 0.12							
16) XEU2C C	6.10	6.44	–	12.76	.58	–	–	129	46) XEU2P C	4.03	4.28	–	12.75	−.42	–	–
17) XEU2C C	5.52	5.82	5.88y	12.58	.55	–	5	130	47) XEU2P C	4.44	4.67	4.69y	12.59	−.45	–	242
18) XEU2C C	4.97	5.25	–	12.43	.52	–	–	131	48) XEU2P C	4.89	5.09	5.04y	12.43	−.48	–	35
19) XEU2C C	4.45	4.73	–	12.31	.49	–	–	132	49) XEU2P C	5.35	5.56	7.00y	12.26	−.51	–	123
20) XEU2C C	3.94	4.21	–	12.11	.46	–	–	133	50) XEU2P C	5.84	6.06	–	12.09	−.54	–	–
22 Dec 12 (312d); CSize 100; R 0.12							5		22 Dec 12 (312d); CSize 100; R 0.12							
21) XEZ2C C	7.07	7.54	–	12.88	.58	–	–	129	51) XEZ2P C	4.95	5.44	–	12.97	−.42	–	–
22) XEZ2C C	6.50	6.95	–	12.74	.55	–	–	130	52) XEZ2P C	5.37	5,82	5.55y	12.81	−.45	–	10
23) XEZ2C C	5.96	6.38	–	12.62	.53	–	–	131	53) XEZ2P C	5.82	6.25	–	12.66	−.47	–	–
24) XEZ2C C	5.44	5.85	–	12.48	.50	–	–	132	54) XEZ2P C	6.28	6.71	8.07y	12.51	−.50	–	5
25) XEZ2C C	4.93	5.35	–	12.35	.47	–	–	133	55) XEZ2P C	6.76	7.20	–	12.37	−.53	–	–
18 Feb 12 (4d); CSize 100; R 0.12							5		18 Feb 12 (4d); CSize 100; R 0.12							
26) XEG2C C	1.94	2.12	2.22	7.38	.98	1	1	129	56) XEG2P C	.10	.20	.25y	14.28	−.15	–	15
27) XEG2C C	1.15	1.30	1.33	10.44	.76	1	5	130	57) XEG2P C	.25	.39	.21	13.18	−.20	1	162

XEC Curncy	95) Templates	96) Actions	97) Expiry	Implied Vols (OMON)
JAPAN ¥ SPOT USD STD	↑127.43 −1.48 −1.15%	Hi 128.20	Lo 127.33	HV 6.87 91) News
Calc Mode	/ Center 127.41	Strike 5	Exch NASDAQ OM	

| | | Calls | | | | | | Strike | | | Puts | | | | | |

Ticker	Bid	Ask	Last	IVM	DM	Volm	QInt	Strike	Ticker	Bid	Ask	Last	IVM	DM	Volm	QInt
16 Jun 12 (123d); CSize 100; R 0.12							5		16 Jun 12 (123d); CSize 100; R 0.12							
1) XNM2C C	3.09	3.40	–	9.31	.57	–	–	126.5	31) XNM2P C	2.02	2.25	–	8.78	−.43	–	–
2) XNM2C C	2.82	3.11	–	9.26	.54	–	–	127	32) XNM2P C	2.25	2.47	–	8.77	−.46	–	–
3) XEM2C C	2.57	2.84	–	9.23	.51	–	–	127.5	33) XNM2P C	2.48	2.71	–	8.73	−.49	1	–
4) XEM2C C	2.33	2.57	–	9.17	.48	–	–	128	34) XNM2P C	2.73	3.00	–	8.75	−.52	–	–
5) XEM2C C	2.10	2.35	–	9.16	.45	–	–	128.5	35) XNM2P C	3.00	3.28	–	8.74	−.55	–	–
22 Sep 12 (221d); CSize 100; R 0.12							5		22 Sep 12 (221d); CSize 100; R 0.12							
6) XNU2C C	5.22	5.74	–	10.51	.61	–	–	125	36) XNU2P C	2.47	2.85	3.10y	9.65	−.38	–	10
7) XNU2C C	4.66	5.12	–	10.42	.57	–	–	126	37) XNU2P C	2.89	3.26	2.59y	9.61	−.42	–	10
8) XNU2C C	4.14	4.55	–	10.36	.54	–	–	127	38) XNU2P C	3.35	3.69	–	9.54	−.46	–	–
9) XNU2C C	3.67	4.02	–	10.32	.50	–	–	128	39) XNU2P C	3.85	4.24	–	9.57	−.51	–	–
10) XNU2C C	3.20	3.58	–	10.30	.46	–	–	129	40) XNU2P C	4.40	4.80	–	9.57	−.55	–	–
22 Dec 12 (312d); CSize 100; R 0.12							5		22 Dec 12 (312d); CSize 100; R 0.12							
11) XNZ2C C	6.29	6.90	–	11.24	.60	–	–	125	41) XNZ2P C	3.30	3.04	–	10.17	−.40	–	–
12) XNZ2C C	5.73	6.29	–	11.17	.57	–	–	126	42) XNZ2P C	3.74	4,24	–	10.11	−.43	–	–
13) XNZ2C C	5.21	5.74	–	11.09	.54	–	–	127	43) XNZ2P C	4.20	4.70	–	10.06	−.46	–	–
14) XNZ2C C	4.74	5.24	–	11.08	.51	–	–	128	44) XNZ2P C	4.70	5.19	–	10.01	−.50	–	–
15) XNZ2C C	4.28	4.77	–	11.05	.48	–	–	129	45) XNZ2P C	5.23	5.73	–	9.98	−.53	–	–
18 Feb 12 (4d); CSize 100; R 0.12							5		18 Feb 12 (4d); CSize 100; R 0.12							
16) XNG2C C	2.34	2.60	–	12.79	.92	–	–	125	46) XNG2P C	–	.16	–	16.92	−.14	–	–
17) XNG2C C	1.42	1.66	–	10.97	.84	–	–	126	47) XNG2P C	.01	.25	–	11.02	−.17	–	–

REFERENCES & SUGGESTED READINGS

Aggarwal, R., and A. Demaskey. "Cross-Hedging Currency Risks in Asian Emerging Markets Using Derivatives in Major Currencies." *Journal of Portfolio Management,* Spring (1997), pp. 88–95.

Allayannis, George, and James Weston. "The Use of Foreign Currency Derivatives and Firm Market Value." *Review of Financial Studies* 14 (2001), pp. 243–76.

Aubey, R., and R. Cramer. "Use of International Currency Cocktails in the Reduction of Exchange Rate Risk." *Journal of Economics and Business,* Winter (1977), pp. 128–34.

Beidelman, Carl, John Hillary, and James Greenleaf. "Alternatives in Hedging Long-Date Contractual Foreign Exchange Exposure." *Sloan Management Review,* Summer (1983), pp. 45–54.

Benet, B. "Commodity Futures Cross-Hedging of Foreign Exchange Exposure." *Journal of Futures Markets,* Fall (1990), pp. 287–306.

Dufey, Gunter, and S. Srinivasulu. "The Case for Corporate Management of Foreign Exchange Risk." *Financial Management,* Winter (1983), pp. 54–62.

E-Masry, Ahmed. "Derivatives Use and Risk Management Practices by UK Nonfinancial Companies." *Managerial Finance* 32 (2006), pp. 137–159.

Folks, William. "Decision Analysis for Exchange Risk Management." *Financial Management,* Winter (1972), pp. 101–12.

Giddy, Ian. "The Foreign Exchange Option as a Hedging Tool." *Midland Corporate Finance Journal,* Fall (1983), pp. 32–42.

Jesswein, Kurt, Chuck C. Y. Kwok, and William Folks, Jr. "Corporate Use of Innovative Foreign Exchange Risk Management Products." *Columbia Journal of World Business,* Fall (1995), pp. 70–82.

Khoury, Sarkis, and K. H. Chan. "Hedging Foreign Exchange Risk: Selecting the Optimal Tool." *Midland Corporate Finance Journal,* Winter (1988), pp. 40–52.

Levi, Maurice. *International Finance.* New York: McGraw-Hill, 1990.

Marshall, Andrew. "Foreign Exchange Risk Management in U.K., USA, and Asia Pacific Multinational Companies." *Journal of Multinational Financial Management* 10 (2000), pp. 185–211.

Smithson, Charles. "A LEGO Approach to Financial Engineering: An Introduction to Forwards, Futures, Swaps and Options." *Midland Corporate Finance Journal,* Winter (1987), pp. 16–28.

Stulz, Rene, and Clifford Smith. "The Determinants of Firms' Hedging Policies." *Journal of Financial and Quantitative Analysis,* December 1985, pp. 391–405.

9 Management of Economic Exposure

AS BUSINESS BECOMES increasingly global, more and more firms find it necessary to pay careful attention to foreign exchange exposure and to design and implement appropriate hedging strategies. Suppose, for example, that the U.S. dollar substantially depreciates against the Japanese yen, as it often has since the mid-eighties. This change in the exchange rate can have significant economic consequences for both U.S. and Japanese firms. For example, it can adversely affect the competitive position of Japanese car makers in the highly competitive U.S. market by forcing them to raise dollar prices of their cars by more than their U.S. competitors do. Actually, the recent depreciation of Japanese yen in the wake of the adoption of expansionary monetary policy in Japan has been helping the sales and profits of Japanese multinational firms. The same change in the exchange rate, however, will tend to weaken the competitive position of import-competing U.S. car makers. On the other hand, should the dollar depreciate against the yen, it would bolster the competitive position of U.S. car makers at the expense of Japanese car makers.

Changes in exchange rates can affect not only firms that are directly engaged in international trade but also purely domestic firms. Consider, for example, a U.S. bicycle manufacturer that sources only domestic materials and sells exclusively in the U.S. market, with no foreign-currency receivables or payables in its accounting book. This seemingly purely domestic U.S. firm can be subject to foreign exchange exposure if it competes against imports, say, from a Taiwanese bicycle manufacturer. When the Taiwanese dollar depreciates against the U.S. dollar, this is likely to lead to a lower U.S. dollar price of Taiwanese bicycles, boosting their sales in the United States, thereby hurting the U.S. manufacturer.

Changes in exchange rates may affect not only the operating cash flows of a firm by altering its competitive position but also dollar (home currency) values of the firm's assets and liabilities. Consider a U.S. firm that has borrowed Swiss francs. Since the dollar amount needed to pay off the franc debt depends on the dollar/franc exchange rate, the U.S. firm can gain or lose as the Swiss franc depreciates or appreciates against the dollar. A classic example of the peril of facing currency exposure is provided by Laker Airways, a British firm founded by Sir Freddie Laker, which pioneered the concept of mass-marketed, low-fare air travel. The company heavily borrowed U.S. dollars to finance acquisitions of aircraft while it derived more than half of its revenue in sterling. As the dollar kept appreciating against the British pound (and most major currencies) throughout the first half of the 1980s, the burden of servicing the dollar debts became overwhelming for Laker Airways, forcing it to default.

The preceding examples suggest that exchange rate changes can systematically affect the value of the firm by influencing its operating cash flows as well as the domestic currency values of its assets and liabilities. In a study examining the exposure of U.S. firms to currency risk, Jorion (1990) documented that a significant relationship

EXHIBIT 9.1

Exchange Rate Exposure of U.S. Industry Portfolios[a]

Industry	Market Beta[b]	Forex Beta[c]
1. Aerospace	0.999	0.034
2. Apparel	1.264	0.051
3. Beverage	1.145	−0.437
4. Building materials	1.107	0.604
5. Chemicals	1.074	−0.009
6. Computers, office equipment	0.928	0.248
7. Electronics, electrical equipment	1.202	0.608*
8. Food	1.080	−0.430
9. Forest and paper products	1.117	0.445
10. Furniture	0.901	1.217*
11. Industrial and farm equipment	1.125	0.473
12. Metal products	1.081	−0.440
13. Metals	1.164	0.743*
14. Mining and crude oil	0.310	−0.713
15. Motor vehicles and parts	0.919	1.168*
16. Petroleum refining	0.515	−0.746*
17. Pharmaceuticals	1.124	−1.272*
18. Publishing and printing	1.154	0.567
19. Rubber and plastics	1.357	0.524
20. Science, photo, and control equipment	0.975	−0.437*
21. Cosmetics	1.051	0.417
22. Textiles	1.279	1.831*
23. Tobacco	0.898	−0.768*
24. Toys, sporting goods	1.572	−0.660
25. Transportation equipment	1.613	1.524*

[a]The market and forex (foreign exchange) betas are obtained from regressing the industry portfolio (monthly) returns, constructed from the *Fortune* 500 companies, on the U.S. stock market index returns and the rate of change in the dollar exchange rate index over the sample period 1.1989–12.93.

[b]For every industry portfolio the market beta is statistically significant at the 1% level.

[c]The forex beta is significant for some industry portfolios and insignificant for others. Those forex betas that are significant at 10% or higher are denoted by (*).

Source: Betty Simkins and Paul Laux, "Derivatives Use and the Exchange Rate Risk of Investing in Large U.S. Corporations," Case Western Reserve University Working Paper (1996).

exists between stock returns and the dollar's value. Previous studies, such as Choi and Prasad (1995), Simkins and Laux (1996), and Allayannis and Ofek (2001), also document that U.S. stock returns are sensitive to exchange rate movements.

Exhibit 9.1, which is excerpted from the Simkins and Laux study, provides an estimate of the U.S. industries' market betas as well as the "forex" betas. The market and forex betas measure the sensitivities of an industry portfolio against the U.S. stock market index and the dollar exchange rate index, respectively. As Exhibit 9.1 shows, the forex beta varies greatly across industry lines; it ranges from −1.272 for pharmaceuticals to 1.831 for textiles. A negative (positive) forex beta means that stock returns tend to move down (up) as the dollar appreciates. Out of the 25 total industries studied, 10 were found to have a significant exposure to exchange rate movements.

This chapter is devoted to the management of economic exposure to currency risk. But we need to first discuss how to measure economic exposure. Unlike transaction exposure, economic exposure needs to be estimated first.

How to Measure Economic Exposure

Currency risk or uncertainty, which represents random changes in exchange rates, is not the same as the currency exposure, which measures "what is at risk." Under certain conditions, a firm may not face any exposure at all, that is, nothing is at risk, even if the exchange rates change randomly. Suppose your company maintains a vacation home for employees in the British countryside and the local price of this property is always moving together with the pound price of the U.S. dollar. As a result, whenever the pound depreciates against the dollar, the local currency price of this property goes up by the same proportion. In this case, your company is not exposed to currency risk even if the pound/dollar exchange rate fluctuates randomly. The British asset your company owns has an embedded hedge against exchange risk, rendering the dollar price of the asset *insensitive* to exchange rate changes.

Consider an alternative situation in which the local (pound) price of your company's British asset barely changes. In this case, the dollar value of the asset will be highly *sensitive* to the exchange rate since the former will change as the latter does. To the extent that the dollar price of the British asset exhibits "sensitivity" to exchange rate movements, your company is exposed to currency risk. Similarly, if your company's operating cash flows are sensitive to exchange rate changes, the company is again exposed to currency risk.

Exposure to currency risk thus can be properly measured by the *sensitivities* of (i) the future home currency values of the firm's assets (and liabilities) and (ii) the firm's operating cash flows to random changes in exchange rates. The same point is illustrated by Exhibit 9.2; assets include the tangible assets (property, plant and equipment, inventory) as well as financial assets. Let us first discuss the case of asset exposure. For expositional convenience, assume that dollar inflation is nonrandom. Then, from the perspective of the U.S. firm that owns an asset in Britain, the exposure can be measured by the coefficient (b) in regressing the dollar value (P) of the British asset on the dollar/pound exchange rate (S).[1]

$$P = a + b \times S + e \tag{9.1}$$

where a is the regression constant and e is the random error term with mean zero, that is, $E(e) = 0$; $P = SP^*$, where P^* is the local currency (pound) price of the asset.[2] It is obvious from the above equation that the regression coefficient b measures the sensitivity of the dollar value of the asset (P) to the exchange rate (S). If the regression coefficient is zero, that is, $b = 0$, the dollar value of the asset is independent of exchange

EXHIBIT 9.2

Channels of Economic Exposure

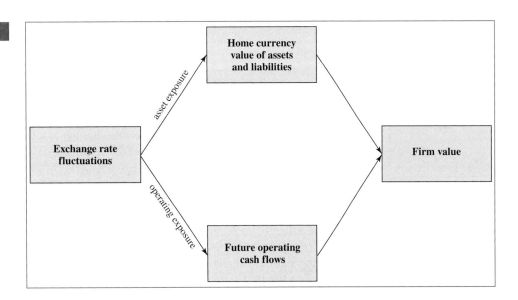

---

[1]Our discussion in this section draws on Adler and Dumas (1984) who clarified the notion of currency exposure.

[2]In addition, the covariance between the random error (residual) term and the exchange rate is zero, i.e., $Cov(S,e) = 0$, by construction.

State	Probability	P*	S	P (=SP*)	Parameters
A. Case 1					
1	1/3	£ 980	$1.40	$1,372	Cov(P,S) = 34/3
2	1/3	£1,000	$1.50	$1,500	Var(S) = .02/3
3	1/3	£1,070	$1.60	$1,712	*b* = £1,700
Mean			$1.50	$1,528	
B. Case 2					
1	1/3	£1,000	$1.40	$1,400	Cov(P,S) = 0
2	1/3	£ 933	$1.50	$1,400	Var(S) = .02/3
3	1/3	£ 875	$1.60	$1,400	*b* = 0
Mean			$1.50	$1,400	
C. Case 3					
1	1/3	£1,000	$1.40	$1,400	Cov(P,S) = 20/3
2	1/3	£1,000	$1.50	$1,500	Var(S) = .02/3
3	1/3	£1,000	$1.60	$1,600	*b* = £1,000
Mean			$1.50	$1,500	

rate movements, implying no exposure. On the basis of the above analysis, one can say that *exposure is the regression coefficient*. Statistically, the **exposure coefficient**, *b*, is defined as follows:

$$b = \frac{\text{Cov}(P, S)}{\text{Var}(S)}$$

where $\text{Cov}(P, S)$ is the covariance between the dollar value of the asset and the exchange rate, and $\text{Var}(S)$ is the variance of the exchange rate.

Next, we show how to apply the exposure measurement technique using numerical examples. Suppose that a U.S. firm has an asset in Britain whose local currency price is random. For simplicity, let us assume that there are three possible states of the world, with each state equally likely to occur. The future local currency price of this British asset as well as the future exchange rate will be determined, depending on the realized state of the world. First, consider Case 1, described in Panel A of Exhibit 9.3. Case 1 indicates that the local currency price of the asset (P^*) and the dollar price of the pound (S) are positively correlated, so that depreciation (appreciation) of the pound against the dollar is associated with a declining (rising) local currency price of the asset. The dollar price of the asset on the future (liquidation) date can be $1,372, or $1,500 or $1,712, depending on the realized state of the world.

When we compute the parameter values for Case 1, we obtain $\text{Cov}(P,S) = 34/3$, $\text{Var}(S) = 0.02/3$, and thus $b = £1,700$. This pound amount, £1,700, represents the sensitivity of the future dollar value of the British asset to random changes in exchange rate. This finding implies that the U.S. firm faces a substantial exposure to currency risk. Note that the magnitude of the exposure is expressed in British pounds. For illustration, the computations of the parameter values for Case 1 are shown in Exhibit 9.4.

Next, consider Case 2. This case indicates that the local currency value of the asset is clearly negatively correlated with the dollar price of the British pound. In fact, the effect of exchange rate changes is exactly offset by movements of the local currency price of the asset, rendering the dollar price of the asset totally insensitive to exchange rate changes. The future dollar price of the asset will be uniformly $1,400 across the three states of the world. One thus can say that the British asset is effectively *denominated* in terms of the dollar. Although this case may be unrealistic, it shows that uncertain exchange rates or exchange risk does not necessarily constitute exchange exposure. Despite the fact that the future exchange rate is uncertain, the U.S. firm has nothing at risk in this case. Since the firm faces no exposure, no hedging will be necessary.

EXHIBIT 9.4

Computations of Regression Parameters: Case 1

1. Computation of Means

$$\bar{P} = \sum_i q_i P_i = \frac{1}{3}(1{,}372 + 1{,}500 + 1{,}712) = 1{,}528$$

$$\bar{S} = \sum_i q_i S_i = \frac{1}{3}(1.40 + 1.50 + 1.60) = 1.50$$

2. Computation of Variance and Covariance

$$\text{Var}(S) = \sum_i q_i (S_i = \bar{S})^2$$
$$= \frac{1}{3}[(1.40 - 1.50)^2 + (1.50 - 1.50)^2 + (1.60 - 1.50)^2]$$
$$= 0.02/3$$

$$\text{Cov}(P,S) = \sum_i q_i (P_i - \bar{P})(S_i - \bar{S})$$
$$= \frac{1}{3}[(1{,}372 - 1{,}528)(1.40 - 1.50) + (1{,}500 - 1{,}528)$$
$$(1.50 - 1.50) + (1{,}712 - 1{,}528)(1.60 - 1.50)]$$
$$= 34/3$$

3. Computation of the Exposure Coefficient

$$b = \text{Cov}(P,S)/\text{Var}(S) = (34/3)/(0.02/3) = 1{,}700$$

Note: q_i denotes the probability for the *i*th state.

We now turn to Case 3, where the local currency price of the asset is fixed at £1,000. In this case, the U.S. firm faces a "contractual" cash flow that is *denominated* in pounds. This case, in fact, represents an example of the special case of economic exposure, transaction exposure. Intuitively, what is at risk is £1,000, that is, the exposure coefficient, b, is £1,000. Readers can confirm this by going through the same kind of computations as shown in Exhibit 9.4. Measurement of transaction exposure is thus very simple. The exposure coefficient, b, is the same as the magnitude of the contractual cash flow fixed in terms of foreign currency.

Once the magnitude of exposure is known, the firm can hedge the exposure by simply selling the exposure forward. In Case 3, where the asset value is fixed in terms of local currency, it is possible to completely eliminate the variability of the future dollar price of the asset by selling £1,000 forward. In Case 1, however, where the local currency price of the asset is random, selling £1,700 forward will not completely eliminate the variability of the future dollar price; there will be a residual variability that is independent of exchange rate changes.

On the basis of regression Equation 9.1, we can decompose the variability of the dollar value of the asset, Var(P), into two separate components: exchange rate-related and residual. Specifically,

$$\text{Var}(P) = b^2\text{Var}(S) + \text{Var}(e) \tag{9.2}$$

The first term in the right-hand side of the equation, $b^2\text{Var}(S)$, represents the part of the variability of the dollar value of the asset that is related to random changes in the exchange rate, whereas the second term, Var(e), captures the residual part of the dollar value variability that is independent of exchange rate movements.

The consequences of hedging the exposure by forward contracts are illustrated in Exhibit 9.5. Consider Case 1, where the firm faces an exposure coefficient (b) of £1,700. If the firm sells £1,700 forward, the dollar proceeds that the firm will receive are given by

$$\$1{,}700(F - S)$$

where F is the forward exchange rate and S is the spot rate realized on the maturity date. Note that for each pound sold forward, the firm will receive a dollar amount

EXHIBIT 9.5

Consequences of Hedging Currency Exposure

Future Quantities	State 1	State 2	State 3	Variance
A. Case 1 ($B_i = £1,700$)				
Local currency asset price (P^*)	980	1,000	1,070	
Exchange rate (S)	1.40	1.50	1.60	
Dollar value ($P = SP^*$)	1,372	1,500	1,712	19,659
Proceeds from forward contract	170	0	−170	
Dollar value of hedged position (HP)	1,542	1,500	1,542	392
B. Case 3 ($b = £1,000$)				
Local currency asset price (P^*)	1,000	1,000	1,000	
Exchange rate (S)	1.40	1.50	1.60	
Dollar value ($P = SP^*$)	1,400	1,500	1,600	6,667
Proceeds from forward contract	100	0	−100	
Dollar value of hedged position (HP)	1,500	1,500	1,500	0

Note: In both cases, the forward exchange rate (F) is assumed to be \$1.50/£. Proceeds from the forward contract are computed as $b(F − S)$. Recall that each of the three states is equally likely to happen, i.e., $q_i = 1/3$ for each state.

equal to ($F − S$). In Exhibit 9.5, the forward exchange rate is assumed to be \$1.50, which is the same as the expected future spot rate. Thus, if the future spot rate turns out to be \$1.40 under state 1, the dollar proceed from the forward contract will be \$170 = 1,700(1.50 − 1.40). Since the dollar value (P) of the asset is \$1,372 under state 1, the dollar value of the hedged position (HP) will be \$1,542 (= \$1,372 + \$170) under state 1.

As shown in part A of Exhibit 9.5, the variance of the dollar value of the hedged position is only 392(\$)², whereas that of the unhedged position is 19,659(\$)². This result implies that much of the uncertainty regarding the future dollar value of the asset is associated with exchange rate uncertainty. As a result, once the exchange exposure is hedged, most of the variability of the dollar value of the asset is eliminated. The residual variability of the dollar value of the asset that is independent of exchange rate changes, Var(e), is equal to 392(\$)².

Let us now turn to Case 3 where the local currency price of the asset is fixed. In this case, complete hedging is possible in the specific sense that there will be no residual variability. As shown in part B of Exhibit 9.5, the future dollar value of the asset, which is totally dependent upon the exchange rate, has a variance of 6,667(\$)². Once the firm hedges the exposure by selling £1,000 forward, the dollar value of the hedged position (HP) becomes nonrandom, and is \$1,500 across the three states of the world. Since the asset now has a constant dollar value, it is effectively *redenominated* in terms of the dollar.

Operating Exposure: Definition

While many managers understand the effects of random exchange rate changes on the dollar value of their firms' assets and liabilities denominated in foreign currencies, they often do not fully understand the effect of volatile exchange rates on operating cash flows. As the economy becomes increasingly globalized, more firms are subject to international competition. Fluctuating exchange rates can seriously alter the relative competitive positions of such firms in domestic and foreign markets, affecting their operating cash flows.

Unlike the exposure of assets and liabilities (such as accounts payable and receivable, loans denominated in foreign currencies, and so forth) that are listed in accounting statements, the exposure of operating cash flows depends on the effect of random exchange rate changes on the firm's competitive position, which is not readily measurable. This difficulty notwithstanding, it is important for the firm to properly manage **operating exposure** as well as **asset exposure**. In many cases, operating exposure may account for a larger portion of the firm's total exposure than contractual exposure. Formally, operating exposure can be defined as the *extent to which the firm's operating cash flows would be affected by random changes in exchange rates.*

Illustration of Operating Exposure

Before we discuss what determines operating exposure and how to manage it, it is useful to illustrate the exposure using a simple example. Suppose that a U.S. computer company has a wholly owned British subsidiary, Albion Computers PLC, that manufactures and sells personal computers in the U.K. market. Albion Computers imports microprocessors from Intel, which sells them for $512 per unit. At the current exchange rate of $1.60 per pound, each Intel microprocessor costs £320. Albion Computers hires British workers and sources all the other inputs locally. Albion faces a 50 percent income tax rate in the U.K.

Exhibit 9.6 summarizes projected operations for Albion Computers, assuming that the exchange rate will remain unchanged at $1.60 per pound. The company expects to sell 50,000 units of personal computers per year at a selling price of £1,000 per unit. The unit variable cost is £650, which comprises £320 for the imported input and £330 for the locally sourced inputs. Needless to say, the pound price of the imported input will change as the exchange rate changes, which, in turn, can affect the selling price in the U.K. market. Each year, Albion incurs fixed overhead costs of £4 million for rents, property taxes, and the like, regardless of output level. As the exhibit shows, the projected operating cash flow is £7,250,000 per year, which is equivalent to $11,600,000 at the current exchange rate of $1.60 per pound.

Now, consider the possible effect of a depreciation of the pound on the projected dollar operating cash flow of Albion Computers. Assume that the pound may depreciate from $1.60 to $1.40 per pound. The dollar operating cash flow may change following a pound depreciation due to:

1. The **competitive effect**: A pound depreciation may affect operating cash flow in pounds by altering the firm's competitive position in the marketplace.

2. The **conversion effect**: A given operating cash flow in pounds will be converted into a lower dollar amount after the pound depreciation.

To get a feel of how the dollar operating cash flow may change as the exchange rate changes, consider the following cases with varying degrees of realism:

Case 1: No variables change, except the price of the imported input.

Case 2: The selling price as well as the price of the imported input changes, with no other changes.

Case 3: All the variables change.

EXHIBIT 9.6

Projected Operations for Albion Computers PLC: Benchmark Case ($1.60/£)

Sales (50,000 units at £1,000/unit)	£50,000,000
Variable costs (50,000 units at £650/unit)[a]	32,500,000
Fixed overhead costs	4,000,000
Depreciation allowances	1,000,000
Net profit before tax	£12,500,000
Income tax (at 50%)	6,250,000
Profit after tax	6,250,000
Add back depreciation	1,000,000
Operating cash flow in pounds	£ 7,250,000
Operating cash flow in dollars	$ 11,600,000

[a]The unit variable cost, £650, comprises £330 for the locally sourced inputs and £320 for the imported input, which is priced in dollars, i.e., $512. At the exchange rate of $1.60/£, the imported part costs £320.

EXHIBIT 9.7

Projected Operations for Albion Computers PLC: Case 1 ($1.40/£)

Sales (50,000 units at £1,000/unit)	£50,000,000
Variable costs (50,000 units at £696/unit)	34,800,000
Fixed overhead costs	4,000,000
Depreciation allowances	1,000,000
Net profit before tax	£10,200,000
Income tax (at 50%)	5,100,000
Profit after tax	5,100,000
Add back depreciation	1,000,000
Operating cash flow in pounds	£ 6,100,000
Operating cash flow in dollars	$ 8,540,000

EXHIBIT 9.8

Projected Operations for Albion Computers PLC: Case 2 ($1.40/£)

Sales (50,000 units at £1,143/unit)	£57,150,000
Variable costs (50,000 units at £696/unit)	34,800,000
Fixed overhead costs	4,000,000
Depreciation allowances	1,000,000
Net profit before tax	£17,350,000
Income tax (at 50%)	8,675,000
Profit after tax	8,675,000
Add back depreciation	1,000,000
Operating cash flow in pounds	£ 9,675,000
Operating cash flow in dollars	$ 13,545,000

In Case 1, which is illustrated in Exhibit 9.7, the unit variable cost of the imported input rises to £366 (= $512/$1.40) following the pound depreciation, with no other changes. Following the depreciation, the total variable costs become £34.8 million, lowering the firm's before-tax profit from £12.5 million (for the benchmark case) to £10.2 million. Considering that the firm faces a 50 percent income tax rate, depreciation of the pound will lower the net operating cash flow from £7.25 million (for the benchmark case) to £6.1 million. In terms of dollars, Albion's projected net operating cash flow changes from $11.6 million to $8.54 million as the exchange rate changes from $1.60 per pound to $1.40 per pound. Albion may be forced not to raise the pound selling price because it faces a British competitor that manufactures similar products using only locally sourced inputs. An increase in selling price can potentially lead to a sharp decline in unit sales volume. Under this kind of competitive environment, Albion's costs are responsive to exchange rate changes, but the selling price is not. This asymmetry makes the firm's operating cash flow sensitive to exchange rate changes, giving rise to operating exposure.

In Case 2, which is analyzed in Exhibit 9.8, the selling price as well as the price of the imported input increases following the pound depreciation. In this case, Albion Computers does not face any serious competition in the British market and faces a highly inelastic demand for its products. Thus, Albion can raise the selling price to £1,143 (to keep the dollar selling price at $1,600 after the pound depreciation) and still maintain the sales volume at 50,000 units. Computations presented in Exhibit 9.8 indicate that the projected operating cash flow actually increases to £9,675,000, which is equivalent to $13,545,000. Compared with the benchmark case, the dollar operating cash flow is higher when the pound depreciates. This case shows that a pound depreciation need not always lead to a lower dollar operating cash flow.

We now turn to Case 3 where the selling price, sales volume, and the prices of both locally sourced and imported inputs change following the pound depreciation. In particular, we assume that both the selling price and the price of locally sourced inputs increase at the rate of 8 percent, reflecting the underlying inflation rate in

EXHIBIT 9.9

Projected Operations for Albion Computers PLC: Case 3 ($1.40/£)

Sales (40,000 units at £1,080/unit)	£43,200,000
Variable costs (40,000 units at £722/unit)	28,880,000
Fixed overhead costs	4,000,000
Depreciation allowances	1,000,000
Net profit before tax	£ 9,320,000
Income tax (at 50%)	4,660,000
Profit after tax	4,660,000
Add back depreciation	1,000,000
Operating cash flow in pounds	£ 5,660,000
Operating cash flow in dollars	$ 7,924,000

EXHIBIT 9.10

Summary of Operating Exposure Effect of Pound Depreciation on Albion Computers PLC

Variables	Benchmark Case	Case 1	Case 2	Case 3
Exchange rate ($/£)	1.60	1.40	1.40	1.40
Unit variable cost (£)	650	696	696	722
Unit sales price (£)	1,000	1,000	1,143	1,080
Sales volume (units)	50,000	50,000	50,000	40,000
Annual cash flow (£)	7,250,000	6,100,000	9,675,000	5,660,000
Annual cash flow ($)	11,600,000	8,540,000	13,545,000	7,924,000
Four-year present value ($)[a]	33,118,000	24,382,000	38,671,000	22,623,000
Operating gains/losses ($)[b]		−8,736,000	5,553,000	−10,495,000

[a]The discounted present value of dollar cash flows was computed over a four-year period using a 15 percent discount rate. A constant cash flow is assumed for each of four years.

[b]Operating gains or losses represent the present value of change in cash flows, which is due to pound depreciation, from the benchmark case.

the U.K. As a result, the selling price will be £1,080 per unit and the unit variable cost of locally sourced inputs will be £356. Since the price of the imported input is £366, the combined unit variable cost will be £722. Facing an **elastic demand** for its products, sales volume declines to 40,000 units per year after the price increase. As Exhibit 9.9 shows, Albion's projected operating cash flow is £5.66 million, which is equivalent to $7.924 million. The projected dollar cash flow under Case 3 is lower than that of the benchmark case by $3.676 million.

Exhibit 9.10 summarizes the projected operating exposure effect of the pound depreciation on Albion Computers PLC. For expositional purposes it is assumed here that a change in exchange rate will have effects on the firm's operating cash flow for four years. The exhibit provides, among other things, the four-year present values of operating cash flows for each of the three cases as well as for the benchmark case. The proper discount rate for Albion's cash flow is assumed to be 15 percent. The exhibit also shows the operating gains or losses computed as the present value of changes in operating cash flows (over a four-year period) from the benchmark case that are due to the exchange rate change. In Case 3, for instance, the firm expects to experience an operating loss of $10,495,000 due to the pound depreciation.

Determinants of Operating Exposure

Unlike contractual (i.e., transaction) exposure, which can readily be determined from the firm's accounting statements, operating exposure cannot be determined in the same manner. A firm's operating exposure is determined by (i) the structure of the markets in which the firm sources its inputs, such as labor and materials, and sells its products, and (ii) the firm's ability to mitigate the effect of exchange rate changes by adjusting its markets, product mix, and sourcing.

To highlight the importance of market structure in determining operating exposure, consider a hypothetical company, Ford Mexicana, a subsidiary of Ford, which imports cars from the parent and distributes them in Mexico. If the dollar appreciates against the Mexican peso, Ford Mexicana's costs go up in peso terms. Whether this creates operating exposure for Ford critically depends on the structure of the car market in Mexico. For example, if Ford Mexicana faces competition from Mexican car makers whose peso costs did not rise, it will not be able to raise the peso price of imported Ford cars without risking a major reduction in sales. Facing a highly elastic demand for its products, Ford Mexicana cannot afford to let the **exchange rate pass-through** into the peso price. As a result, an appreciation of the dollar will squeeze the profit of Ford Mexicana, subjecting the parent firm to a high degree of operating exposure.

In contrast, consider the case in which Ford Mexicana faces import competition only from other U.S. car makers like General Motors and Chrysler rather than from local producers. Since peso costs of those other imported U.S. cars will be affected by a dollar appreciation in the same manner, the competitive position of Ford Mexicana will not be adversely affected. Under this market structure, the dollar appreciation is likely to be reflected in higher peso prices of imported U.S. cars pretty quickly. As a result, Ford will be able to better maintain its dollar profit, without being subject to a major operating exposure.

Generally speaking, a firm is subject to high degrees of operating exposure when *either* its cost *or* its price is sensitive to exchange rate changes. On the other hand, when *both* the cost *and* the price are sensitive or insensitive to exchange rate changes, the firm has no major operating exposure.

Given the market structure, however, the extent to which a firm is subject to operating exposure depends on the firm's ability to stabilize cash flows in the face of exchange rate changes. Even if Ford faces competition from local car makers in Mexico, for example, it can reduce exposure by starting to source Mexican parts and materials, which would be cheaper in dollar terms after the dollar appreciation. Ford can even start to produce cars in Mexico by hiring local workers and sourcing local inputs, thereby making peso costs relatively insensitive to changes in the dollar/peso exchange rate. In other words, the firm's flexibility regarding production locations, sourcing, and financial hedging strategy is an important determinant of its operating exposure to exchange risk.

Before we discuss how to hedge operating exposure, it is important to recognize that changes in nominal exchange rates may not always affect the firm's competitive position. This is the case when a change in exchange rate is exactly offset by the inflation differential. To show this point, let us again use the example of Ford Mexicana competing against local car makers. Suppose that the annual inflation rate is 4 percent in the United States and 15 percent in Mexico. For simplicity, we assume that car prices appreciate at the same pace as the general domestic inflation rate in both the United States and Mexico. Now, suppose that the dollar appreciates about 11 percent against the peso, offsetting the inflation rate differential between the two countries. This, of course, implies that purchasing power parity is holding.

Under this situation the peso price of Ford cars appreciates by about 15 percent, which reflects a 4 percent increase in the dollar price of cars and an 11 percent appreciation of the dollar against the peso. Since the peso prices of both Ford and locally produced cars rise by the same 15 percent, the 11 percent appreciation of the dollar will not affect the competitive position of Ford vis-à-vis local car makers. Ford thus does not have operating exposure.

If, however, the dollar appreciates by more than 11 percent against the peso, Ford cars will become relatively more expensive than locally produced cars, adversely affecting Ford's competitive position. Ford is thus exposed to exchange risk. Since purchasing power parity does not hold very well, especially in the short run, exchange rate changes are likely to affect the competitive positions of firms that are sourcing from different locations but selling in the same markets.

EXHIBIT 9.11

Exchange Rate
Pass-Through Coefficients
for U.S. Manufacturing
Industries

Industry Code (SIC)	Industry	Pass-Through Coefficient
20	Food and kindred products	0.2485
22	Textile mill products	0.3124
23	Apparels	0.1068
24	Lumber and wood products	0.0812
25	Furniture and fixtures	0.3576
28	Chemicals and allied products	0.5312
30	Rubber and plastic products	0.5318
31	Leather products	0.3144
32	Stone, glass, concrete products	0.8843
33	Primary metal industries	0.2123
34	Fabricated metal products	0.3138
35	Machinery, except electrical	0.7559
36	Electrical and electronic machinery	0.3914
37	Transportation equipment	0.3583
38	Measurement instruments	0.7256
39	Miscellaneous manufacturing	0.2765
Average		0.4205

Source: Jiawen Yang. "Exchange Rate Pass-Through in U.S. Manufacturing Industries," *Review of Economics and Statistics* 79 (1997), pp. 95–104.

Before we move on, it would be useful to examine the relationship between exchange rate changes and the price adjustments of goods. Facing exchange rate changes, a firm may choose one of the following three pricing strategies: (i) pass the cost shock fully to its selling prices (complete pass-through), (ii) fully absorb the shock to keep its selling prices unaltered (no pass-through), or (iii) do some combination of the two strategies described above (partial pass-through). Import prices in the United States do not fully reflect exchange rate changes, exhibiting a partial pass-through phenomenon.

In a comprehensive study, Yang (1997) investigated exchange rate pass-through in U.S. manufacturing industries during the sample period 1980–1991 and found that the pricing behavior of foreign exporting firms is generally consistent with partial pass-through. Exhibit 9.11, constructed based on the Yang study, provides the pass-through coefficients for different industries; the coefficient would be 1 for complete pass-through and 0 for no pass-through. As can be seen from the exhibit, the pass-through coefficient ranges from 0.0812 for SIC 24 (lumber and wood products) to 0.8843 for SIC 32 (stone, glass, and concrete products). The average coefficient is 0.4205, implying that when the U.S. dollar appreciates or depreciates by 1 percent, import prices of foreign products change, on average, by about 0.42 percent. This means that foreign exporting firms are substantially exposed to exchange risk. It is noteworthy that partial pass-through is common but varies a great deal across industries. Import prices would be affected relatively little by exchange rate changes in industries with low product differentiation and thus high demand elasticities. In contrast, in industries with a high degree of product differentiation and thus low demand elasticities, import prices will tend to change more as the exchange rates change, limiting exposure to exchange risk. In a more recent study, Gopinath and Rigobon (2008) found that the pass-through coefficient is only 0.22 on average. The reduced pass-through coefficient may imply that international trade has become more competitive, reducing the pricing power of exporting firms.

Managing Operating Exposure

As the economy becomes increasingly globalized, many firms are engaged in international activities such as exports, cross-border sourcing, joint ventures with foreign partners, and establishing production and sales affiliates abroad. The cash flows of such firms can be quite sensitive to exchange rate changes. The objective of managing operating exposure is to stabilize cash flows in the face of fluctuating exchange rates.

Since a firm is exposed to exchange risk mainly through the effect of exchange rate changes on its competitive position, it is important to consider exchange exposure management in the context of the firm's long-term strategic planning. For example, in making such strategic decisions as choosing where to locate production facilities, where to purchase materials and components, and where to sell products, the firm should consider the currency effect on its overall future cash flows. Managing operating exposure is thus not a short-term tactical issue. The firm can use the following strategies for managing operating exposure:

1. Selecting low-cost production sites.
2. Flexible sourcing policy.
3. Diversification of the market.
4. Product differentiation and R&D efforts.
5. Financial hedging.

Selecting Low-Cost Production Sites

When the domestic currency is strong or expected to become strong, eroding the competitive position of the firm, it can choose to locate production facilities in a foreign country where costs are low due to either the undervalued currency or underpriced factors of production. In recent decades, Japanese car makers, including Nissan and Toyota, have shifted production to U.S. manufacturing facilities in order to mitigate the negative effects of the strong yen and volatile exchange rate on U.S. sales. German car makers such as Daimler Benz and BMW also chose to establish manufacturing facilities in the United States for the same reason.

Also, the firm can choose to establish and maintain production facilities in multiple countries to deal with the effect of exchange rate changes. Consider Nissan, which has manufacturing facilities in the United States, United Kingdom, and Mexico, as well as in Japan. Multiple manufacturing sites provide Nissan with a great deal of flexibility regarding where to produce, given the prevailing exchange rates. While the yen appreciated substantially against the dollar, the Mexican peso depreciated against the dollar in recent years. Under this sort of exchange rate development, Nissan may choose to increase production in the United States, and especially in Mexico, in order to serve the U.S. market. This is, in fact, how Nissan has reacted to the rising yen in recent years. Maintaining multiple manufacturing sites, however, may prevent the firm from taking advantage of economies of scale, raising its cost of production. The resultant higher cost can partially offset the advantages of maintaining multiple production sites.

Flexible Sourcing Policy

Even if the firm has manufacturing facilities only in the domestic country, it can substantially lessen the effect of exchange rate changes by sourcing from where input costs are low. In the early 1980s when the dollar was very strong against most major currencies, U.S. multinational firms often purchased materials and components from low-cost foreign suppliers in order to keep themselves from being priced out of the market.

Facing the strong yen in recent years, many Japanese firms are adopting the same practices. It is well known that Japanese manufacturers, especially in the car and consumer electronics industries, depend heavily on parts and intermediate products from such low-cost countries as Thailand, Malaysia, and China. A **flexible sourcing policy** need not be confined just to materials and parts. Firms can also hire low-cost guest workers from foreign countries instead of high-cost domestic workers in order to be competitive. For example, Japan Airlines is known to heavily hire foreign crews to stay competitive in international routes in the face of a strong yen.

In a recent study, Holberg and Moon (2014) argued how operational hedge can be particularly effective for firms with overseas activities. Consider a U.S. firm, say, Boeing, that is selling its products, such as Boeing 787, to Japan. Boeing then is exposed to currency risk as the exchange rate between the dollar and the Japanese yen fluctuates. However, if Boeing purchases inputs such as aircraft landing gear, fuselage, and the like, in Japan where it sells outputs, it doesn't need to convert its yen receivables to dollars, thus avoiding exchange risk exposure. In addition, in the event that the Japanese demand for Boeing aircraft declines due to recession, Boeing can simply reduce its purchase of inputs from Japan, allowing the firm to better adjust to the declining sales in Japan. As a result, Boeing will be able to protect itself not only from the price risk associated with exchange rate changes but also from the quantity risk associated with the changing demand.

Diversification of the Market

Another way of dealing with exchange exposure is to diversify the market for the firm's products as much as possible. Suppose that General Electric (GE) is selling power generators in Mexico as well as in Germany. Reduced sales in Mexico due to the dollar appreciation against the peso can be compensated by increased sales in Germany due to the dollar depreciation against the euro. As a result, GE's overall cash flows will be much more stable than would be the case if GE sold only in one foreign market, either Mexico or Germany. As long as exchange rates do not always move in the same direction, the firm can stabilize its operating cash flows by diversifying its export market.

It is sometimes argued that the firm can reduce currency exposure by diversifying across different business lines. The idea is that although each individual business may be exposed to exchange risk to some degree, the firm as a whole may not face a significant exposure. It is pointed out, however, that the firm should not get into new lines of business solely to diversify exchange risk because conglomerate expansion can bring about inefficiency and losses. Expansion into a new business should be justified on its own right.

On January 15, 2015, the Swiss central bank scrapped its policy of limiting the value of the franc at 1.20 francs per euro, letting the franc sharply appreciate against the euro. This sudden policy change immediately made Swiss goods nearly 20 percent more expensive to euro-based customers, hurting exports to the euro zone. But the U.S. dollar had been rising against most currencies, including the Swiss franc, at the same time, making Swiss goods less expensive in the United States (and also in those countries whose currencies are tied to the dollar). This situation helped offset the reduced sales in the euro zone. Given that not all major currencies would move against the Swiss franc in the same direction at the same time, it certainly helps to have diversified markets for Swiss goods. It is also noted that following this policy change, many Swiss firms moved some of their operations to low-cost countries, especially in Eastern Europe, to further mitigate the adverse effect of the rising Swiss franc.

R&D Efforts and Product Differentiation

Investment in R&D activities can allow the firm to maintain and strengthen its competitive position in the face of adverse exchange rate movements. Successful R&D efforts allow the firm to cut costs and enhance productivity. In addition, R&D efforts can lead to the introduction of new and unique products for which competitors offer no close substitutes. Since the demand for unique products tends to be highly inelastic (i.e., price insensitive), the firm would be less exposed to exchange risk. At the same time, the firm can strive to create a perception among consumers that its product is indeed different from those offered by competitors. Once the firm's product acquires a unique identity, its demand is less likely to be price-sensitive.

Volvo, a Swedish automobile manufacturer, provides a good example here. The company has invested heavily in strengthening safety features of its cars and successfully established its reputation as the producer of safe cars. This reputation, reinforced by a focused marketing campaign, "Volvo for Life," helped the company to carve out a niche among safety-minded consumers in highly competitive world automobile markets.[3]

---

[3]Volvo was acquired by the Chinese carmaker Geely Holding Group in 2010.

Financial Hedging

While not a substitute for the long-term, **operational hedging** approaches discussed earlier, **financial hedging** can be used to stabilize the firm's cash flows. For example, the firm can lend or borrow foreign currencies on a long-term basis. Or, the firm can use currency forward or options contracts and roll them over if necessary. It is noted that existing financial contracts are designed to hedge against nominal, rather than real, changes in exchange rates. Since the firm's competitive position is affected by real changes in exchange rates, financial contracts can at best provide an approximate hedge against the firm's operating exposure. However, if operational hedges, which involve redeployment of resources, are costly or impractical, financial contracts can provide the firm with a flexible and economical way of dealing with exchange exposure.

CASE APPLICATION

Exchange Risk Management at Merck[4]

To further examine how companies actually manage exchange risk exposure, we choose Merck & Co. Incorporated, a major U.S. pharmaceutical company, and study its approach to overall exchange exposure management. While Merck's actual hedging decision reflects its own particular business situation, the basic framework for dealing with currency exposure can be informative for other firms.

Merck & Co. primarily develops, produces, and markets health care pharmaceuticals. As a multinational company that operates in more than 100 countries, Merck had worldwide sales of $6.6 billion in 1989, and it controlled about a 4.7 percent market share worldwide. Merck's major foreign competitors are European firms and emerging Japanese firms. Merck is among the most internationally oriented U.S. pharmaceutical companies, with overseas assets accounting for about 40 percent of the firm's total and with roughly 50 percent of its sales overseas.

As is typical in the pharmaceutical industry, Merck established overseas subsidiaries. These subsidiaries number about 70 and are responsible for finishing imported products and marketing in the local markets of incorporation. Sales are denominated in local currencies, and thus the company is directly affected by exchange rate fluctuations. Costs are incurred partly in the U.S. dollar for basic manufacturing and research and partly in terms of local currency for finishing, marketing, distribution, and so on. Merck found that costs and revenues were not matched in individual currencies mainly because of the concentration of research, manufacturing, and headquarters operations in the United States.

To reduce the currency mismatch, Merck first considered the possibility of redeploying resources in order to shift dollar costs to other currencies. The company, however, decided that relocating employees and manufacturing and research sites was not a practical and cost-effective way of dealing with exchange exposure. Having decided that operational hedging was not appropriate, Merck considered the alternative of financial hedging. Merck developed a five-step procedure for financial hedging:

1. Exchange forecasting.
2. Assessing strategic plan impact.
3. Hedging rationale.
4. Financial instruments.
5. Hedging program.

Step 1: Exchange Forecasting

The first step involves reviewing the likelihood of adverse exchange movements. The treasury staff estimates possible ranges for dollar strength or weakness over the five-year planning horizon. In doing so, the major factors expected to influence exchange rates, such as the U.S. trade deficit, capital flows, the U.S. budget deficit, and government policies regarding exchange rates, are considered. Outside forecasters are also polled on the outlook for the dollar over the planning horizon.

---

[4]This case is adopted from Lewent and Kearney (1990).

Step 2: Assessing Strategic Plan Impact

Once the future exchange rate ranges are estimated, cash flows and earnings are projected and compared under the alternative exchange rate scenarios, such as strong dollar and weak dollar. These projections are made on a five-year cumulative basis rather than on a year-to-year basis because cumulative results provide more useful information concerning the magnitude of exchange exposure associated with the company's long-range plan.

Step 3: Deciding Whether to Hedge

In deciding whether to hedge exchange exposure, Merck focused on the objective of maximizing long-term cash flows and on the potential effect of exchange rate movements on the firm's ability to meet its strategic objectives. This focus is ultimately intended to maximize shareholder wealth. Merck decided to hedge for two main reasons. First, the company has a large portion of earnings generated overseas while a disproportionate share of costs is incurred in dollars. Second, volatile cash flows can adversely affect the firm's ability to implement the strategic plan, especially investments in R&D that form the basis for future growth. To succeed in a highly competitive industry, the company needs to make a long-term commitment to a high level of research funding. But the cash flow uncertainty caused by volatile exchange rates makes it difficult to justify a high level of research spending. Management decided to hedge in order to reduce the potential effect of volatile exchange rates on future cash flows.

Step 4: Selecting the Hedging Instruments

The objective was to select the most cost-effective hedging tool that accommodated the company's risk preference. Among various hedging tools, such as forward currency contracts, foreign currency borrowing, and currency options, Merck chose currency options because it was not willing to forgo the potential gains if the dollar depreciated against foreign currencies as it has been doing against major currencies since the mid-eighties. Merck regarded option costs as premiums for the insurance policy designed to preserve its ability to implement the strategic plan.

Step 5: Constructing a Hedging Program

Having selected currency options as the key hedging vehicle, the company still had to formulate an implementation strategy regarding the term of the hedge, the strike price of the currency options, and the percentage of income to be covered. After simulating the outcomes of alternative implementation strategies under various exchange rate scenarios, Merck decided to (i) hedge for a multiyear period using long-dated options contracts, rather than hedge year-by-year, to protect the firm's strategic cash flows, (ii) not use far out-of-money options to save costs, and (iii) hedge only on a partial basis, with the remainder self-insured.

To help formulate the most cost-effective hedging program, Merck developed a computer-based model that simulates the effectiveness of various hedging strategies. Exhibit 9.12

EXHIBIT 9.12

Cash Flows Unhedged versus Hedged

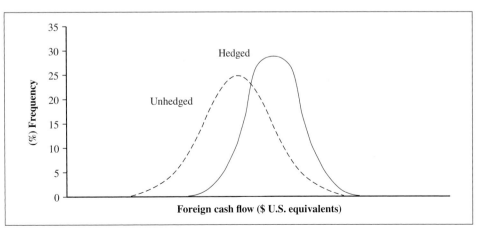

Source: J. Lewent and J. Kearney, "Identifying, Measuring, and Hedging Currency Risk at Merck," Bank of America Journal of Applied Corporate Finance, Winter 1990.

provides an example of simulation results, comparing distributions of hedged and unhedged cash flows. Obviously, the hedged cash flow distribution has a higher mean and a lower standard deviation than the unhedged cash flow distribution. As we discuss in Chapter 8, hedging may not only reduce risk but also increase cash flows if a reduced risk lowers the firm's cost of capital and tax liabilities. In this scenario, hedging is preferred to no hedging.

SUMMARY

In this chapter, we discussed how to measure and manage economic exposure to exchange risk. We also examined how companies manage currency risk in the real world.

1. Exchange rate changes can systematically affect the value of the firm by influencing the firm's operating cash flows as well as the domestic currency values of its assets and liabilities.

2. It is conventional to classify foreign currency exposure into three classes: economic exposure, transaction exposure, and translation exposure.

3. Economic exposure can be defined as the extent to which the value of the firm would be affected by unexpected changes in exchange rates. Transaction exposure is defined as the sensitivity of realized domestic currency values of the firm's contractual cash flows denominated in foreign currencies to unexpected exchange rate changes. Translation exposure, on the other hand, refers to the potential that the firm's consolidated financial statements can be affected by changes in exchange rates.

4. If the firm has an asset in a foreign country, its exposure to currency risk can be properly measured by the coefficient in regressing the dollar value of the foreign asset on the exchange rate. Once the magnitude of exposure is known, the firm can hedge the exposure simply by selling the exposure forward.

5. Unlike the exposure of assets and liabilities that are listed in accounting statements, operating exposure depends on the effect of random exchange rate changes on the firm's future cash flows, which are not readily measurable. Despite this difficulty, it is important to properly manage operating exposure since operating exposure may account for a larger portion of the firm's total exposure than contractual exposure.

6. A firm's operating exposure is determined by (a) the structure of the markets in which the firm sources its inputs and sells its products, and (b) the firm's ability to mitigate the effect of exchange rate changes on its competitive position by adjusting markets, product mix, and sourcing.

7. Since a firm is exposed to exchange risk mainly via the effect of exchange rate changes on its competitive position, it is important to consider exchange exposure management in the context of the firm's overall long-term strategic plan. The objective of exposure management is to stabilize cash flow in the face of fluctuating exchange rates.

8. To manage operating exposure, the firm can use various strategies, such as (a) choosing low-cost production sites, (b) maintaining flexible sourcing policy, (c) diversification of the market, (d) product differentiation, and (e) financial hedging using currency options and forward contracts.

KEY WORDS

asset exposure, *230*
competitive effect, *231*
conversion effect, *231*
elastic demand, *233*

exchange rate
   pass-through, *234*
exposure coefficient, *228*
financial hedging, *238*

flexible sourcing
   policy, *236*
operating exposure, *230*
operational hedging, *238*

QUESTIONS

1. How would you define economic exposure to exchange risk?

2. Explain the following statement: "Exposure is the regression coefficient."

3. Suppose that your company has an equity position in a French firm. Discuss the condition under which dollar/euro exchange rate uncertainty does not constitute exchange exposure for your company.

4. Explain the competitive and conversion effects of exchange rate changes on the firm's operating cash flow.

5. Discuss the determinants of operating exposure.

6. Discuss the implications of purchasing power parity for operating exposure.

7. General Motors exports cars to Spain, but the strong dollar against the euro hurts sales of GM cars in Spain. In the Spanish market, GM faces competition from Italian and French car makers, such as Fiat and Renault, whose operating currencies are the euro. What kind of measures would you recommend so that GM can maintain its market share in Spain?

8. What are the advantages and disadvantages to a firm of financial hedging of its operating exposure compared to operational hedges (such as relocating its manufacturing site)?

9. Discuss the advantages and disadvantages of maintaining multiple manufacturing sites as a hedge against exchange rate exposure.

10. Evaluate the following statement: "A firm can reduce its currency exposure by diversifying across different business lines."

11. Exchange rate uncertainty may not necessarily mean that firms face exchange risk exposure. Explain why this may be the case.

PROBLEMS

1. Suppose that you hold a piece of land in the city of London that you may want to sell in one year. As a U.S. resident, you are concerned with the dollar value of the land. Assume that if the British economy booms in the future, the land will be worth £2,000, and one British pound will be worth $1.40. If the British economy slows down, on the other hand, the land will be worth less, say, £1,500, but the pound will be stronger, say, $1.50/£. You feel that the British economy will experience a boom with a 60 percent probability and a slowdown with a 40 percent probability.

   a. Estimate your exposure (b) to the exchange risk.

   b. Compute the variance of the dollar value of your property that is attributable to exchange rate uncertainty.

   c. Discuss how you can hedge your exchange risk exposure and also examine the consequences of hedging.

2. A U.S. firm holds an asset in France and faces the following scenario:

	State 1	State 2	State 3	State 4
Probability	25%	25%	25%	25%
Spot rate	$1.20/€	$1.10/€	$1.00/€	$0.90/€
P^*	€1,500	€1,400	€1,300	€1,200
P	$1,800	$1,540	$1,300	$1,080

   In the above table, P^* is the euro price of the asset held by the U.S. firm and P is the dollar price of the asset.

   a. Compute the exchange exposure faced by the U.S. firm.

   b. What is the variance of the dollar price of this asset if the U.S. firm remains unhedged against this exposure?

    c. If the U.S. firm hedges against this exposure using a forward contract, what is the variance of the dollar value of the hedged position?

3. Suppose you are a British venture capitalist holding a major stake in an e-commerce start-up in Silicon Valley. As a British resident, you are concerned with the pound value of your U.S. equity position. Assume that if the American economy booms in the future, your equity stake will be worth $1,000,000, and the exchange rate will be $1.40/£. If the American economy experiences a recession, on the other hand, your American equity stake will be worth $500,000, and the exchange rate will be $1.60/£. You assess that the American economy will experience a boom with a 70 percent probability and a recession with a 30 percent probability.

    a. Estimate your exposure to the exchange risk.

    b. Compute the variance of the pound value of your American equity position that is attributable to the exchange rate uncertainty.

    c. How would you hedge this exposure? If you hedge, what is the variance of the pound value of the hedged position?

INTERNET EXERCISES

Coca-Cola, a well-known U.S. multinational company, derives about three-quarters of its revenue from overseas markets. It is thus highly likely that the company is exposed to currency risks. Investigate the company's exchange risk management policies and practices from its Annual Report (10-K) filed with the Securities and Exchange Commission (SEC) of the United States, especially the "Financial Risk Management" section, which are available from the following website: www.sec.gov/edgar.shtml

How would you evaluate Coca-Cola's approach to exchange risk management?

MINI CASE

Economic Exposure of Albion Computers PLC

Consider Case 3 of Albion Computers PLC discussed in the chapter. Now, assume that the pound is expected to depreciate to $1.50 from the current level of $1.60 per pound. This implies that the pound cost of the imported part, that is, Intel's microprocessors, is £341 (=$512/$1.50). Other variables, such as the unit sales volume and the U.K. inflation rate, remain the same as in Case 3.

    a. Compute the projected annual cash flow in dollars.

    b. Compute the projected operating gains/losses over the four-year horizon as the discounted present value of change in cash flows, which is due to the pound depreciation, from the benchmark case presented in Exhibit 9.6.

    c. What actions, if any, can Albion take to mitigate the projected operating losses due to the pound depreciation?

REFERENCES & SUGGESTED READINGS

Adler, Michael, and Bernard Dumas. "Exposure to Currency Risk: Definition and Measurement." *Financial Management*, Spring (1984), pp. 41–50.

Allayannis, George, and Eli Ofek. "Exchange Rate Exposure, Hedging, and the Use of Foreign Currency Derivatives." *Journal of International Money and Finance* 20 (2001), pp. 273–96.

Bartov, Eli, and Gordon Bodnar. "Firm Valuation, Earnings Expectations, and the Exchange-Rate Exposure Effect." *Journal of Finance* 49, 1994, pp. 1755–85.

Choi, Jongmoo, and Anita Prasad. "Exchange Rate Sensitivity and Its Determinants: A Firm and Industry Analysis of U.S. Multinationals." *Financial Management* 23 (1995), pp. 77–88.

Dornbusch, Rudiger "Exchange Rates and Prices." *American Economic Review* 77, 1987, pp. 93–106.

Dufey, Gunter, and S. L. Srinivasulu. "The Case for Corporate Management of Foreign Exchange Risk." *Financial Management*, Winter (1983), pp. 54–62.

Eaker, Mark. "The Numeraire Problem and Foreign Exchange Risk." *Journal of Finance*, May 1981, pp. 419–27.

Flood, Eugene, and Donald Lessard. "On the Measurement of Operating Exposure to Exchange Rates: A Conceptual Approach." *Financial Management* 15, Spring (1986), pp. 25–36.

Glaum, M., M. Brunner, and H. Himmel. "The DAX and the Dollar: The Economic Exchange Rate Exposure of German Corporations." Working Paper, Europa-Universitat Viadrina, 1998.

Gopinath, Gita, and Roberto Rigobon. "Sticky Borders." *Quarterly Journal of Economics* (2008), pp. 531–75.

Hekman, Christine R. "Don't Blame Currency Values for Strategic Errors." *Midland Corporate Finance Journal,* Fall (1986), pp. 45–55.

Holberg, Gerard, and Katie Moon. "Offshore Activities and Financial vs. Operational Hedging." Working Paper (2014).

Jacque, Laurent. "Management of Foreign Exchange Risk: A Review Article." *Journal of International Business Studies,* Spring (1981), pp. 81–100.

Jorion, Philippe. "The Exchange-Rate Exposure of U.S. Multinationals." *Journal of Business* 63 (1990), pp. 331–45.

Lessard, Donald, and S. B. Lightstone. "Volatile Exchange Rates Can Put Operations at Risk." *Harvard Business Review,* July/August 1986, pp. 107–14.

Lewent, Judy, and John Kearney. "Identifying, Measuring and Hedging Currency Risk at Merck." *Journal of Applied Corporate Finance,* Winter (1990), pp. 19–28.

Pringle, John, and Robert Connolly. "The Nature and Causes of Foreign Currency Exposure." *Journal of Applied Corporate Finance,* Fall (1993), pp. 61–72.

Simkins, Berry, and Paul Laux. "Derivatives Use and the Exchange Rate Risk of Investing in Large U.S. Corporations." Case Western Reserve University Working Paper (1996).

Wihlborg, Clas. "Economics of Exposure Management of Foreign Subsidiaries of Multinational Corporations." *Journal of International Business Studies,* Winter (1980), pp. 9–18.

Williamson, Rohan. "Exchange Rate Exposure and Competition: Evidence from the Automotive Industry." *Journal of Financial Economics* 59 (2001), pp. 441–75.

Yang, Jiawen. "Exchange Rate Pass-through in U.S. Manufacturing Industries." *Review of Economics and Statistics* 79 (1997), pp. 95–104.

10 Management of Translation Exposure

THIS CHAPTER CONCLUDES our discussion of foreign exchange exposure and management. In it we discuss translation exposure. **Translation exposure**, also frequently called *accounting exposure,* refers to the effect that an unanticipated change in exchange rates will have on the consolidated financial reports of a MNC. When exchange rates change, the value of a foreign subsidiary's assets and liabilities denominated in a foreign currency change when they are viewed from the perspective of the parent firm. Consequently, there must be a mechanical means for handling the consolidation process for MNCs that logically deals with exchange rate changes.

This chapter presents the basic methods of handling translation adjustments. We present an example of a simple consolidation using the different methods for handling translation adjustments so that the effects of the various methods can be compared. Special consideration is given to recently prescribed methods of the Financial Accounting Standards Board (FASB), the authoritative body in the United States that specifies accounting policy for U.S. business firms and certified public accounting firms. However, translation methods used in other major developed countries are also briefly examined.

We use a case application to explore at length the impact of exchange rate changes on the consolidation process according to the currently prescribed FASB statement. Following this, the relationships between translation exposure and economic exposure and translation exposure and transaction exposure are addressed. Next, the need for, and methods for, managing translation exposure are examined. The chapter concludes with a discussion of an empirical analysis of the effect of a change in translation methods on firm value.

Translation Methods

Four methods of foreign currency translation have been used in recent years: the current/noncurrent method, the monetary/nonmonetary method, the temporal method, and the current rate method.

Current/Noncurrent Method

The **current/noncurrent method** of foreign currency translation was generally accepted in the United States from the 1930s until 1975, when FASB 8 became effective. The underlying principle of this method is that assets and liabilities should be translated based on their maturity. Current assets and liabilities, which by definition have a maturity of one year or less, are converted at the current exchange rate. Noncurrent assets and liabilities are translated at the historical exchange rate in

www.fasb.org

This is the website of the Financial Accounting Standards Board. Information about FASB and FASB statements can be found here.

effect at the time the asset or liability was first recorded on the books. Under this method, a foreign subsidiary with current assets in excess of current liabilities will cause a translation gain (loss) if the local currency appreciates (depreciates). The opposite will happen if there is negative net working capital in local terms in the foreign subsidiary.

Most income statement items under this method are translated at the average exchange rate for the accounting period. However, revenue and expense items that are associated with noncurrent assets or liabilities, such as depreciation expense, are translated at the historical rate that applies to the applicable balance sheet item.

Monetary/Nonmonetary Method

According to the **monetary/nonmonetary method**, all monetary balance sheet accounts (for example, cash, marketable securities, accounts receivable, notes payable, accounts payable) of a foreign subsidiary are translated at the current exchange rate. All other (nonmonetary) balance sheet accounts, including stockholders' equity, are translated at the historical exchange rate in effect when the account was first recorded. In comparison to the current/noncurrent method, this method differs substantially with respect to accounts such as inventory, long-term receivables, and long-term debt. The underlying philosophy of the monetary/nonmonetary method is that monetary accounts have a similarity because their value represents a sum of money whose currency equivalent after translation changes each time the exchange rate changes. This method classifies accounts on the basis of similarity of attributes rather than similarity of maturities.

Under this method, most income statement accounts are translated at the average exchange rate for the period. However, revenue and expense items associated with nonmonetary accounts, such as cost of goods sold and depreciation, are translated at the historical rate associated with the balance sheet account.

Temporal Method

Under the **temporal method**, monetary accounts such as cash, receivables, and payables (both current and noncurrent) are translated at the current exchange rate. Other balance sheet accounts are translated at the current rate, if they are carried on the books at current value; if they are carried at historical costs, they are translated at the rate of exchange on the date the item was placed on the books. Since fixed assets and inventory are usually carried at historical costs, the temporal method and the monetary/nonmonetary method will typically provide the same translation. Nevertheless, the underlying philosophies of the two methods are entirely different. Under current value accounting, all balance sheet accounts are translated at the current exchange rate.

Under the temporal method, most income statement items are translated at the average exchange rate for the period. Depreciation and cost of goods sold, however, are translated at historical rates if the associated balance sheet accounts are carried at historical costs.

Current Rate Method

reports.duni.com /en/corporate/investors /reports/2014

This website illustrates translation and transaction exposure as reported in the 2014 annual report of a Swedish multinational firm.

Under the **current rate method**, all balance sheet accounts are translated at the current exchange rate, except for stockholders' equity. This is the simplest of all translation methods to apply. The common stock account and any additional paid-in capital are carried at the exchange rates in effect on the respective dates of issuance. Year-end retained earnings equal the beginning balance of retained earnings plus any additions for the year. A "plug" equity account named **cumulative translation adjustment (CTA)** is used to make the balance sheet balance, since translation gains or losses do not go through the income statement according to this method.

Under the current rate method, income statement items are to be translated at the exchange rate at the dates the items are recognized. Since this is generally impractical, an appropriately weighted average exchange rate for the period may be used for the translation.

EXAMPLE |10.1: Comparison of Translation Methods

Exhibits 10.1A and 10.1B use examples to present a comparison of the effects of the different translation methods on financial statement preparation. The examples assume that the balance sheet and income statement of a Swiss subsidiary, which keeps its books in Swiss francs, is translated into U.S. dollars, the reporting currency of the MNC.

Exhibit 10.1A first presents the balance sheet and income statement in Swiss francs, from which it can be seen that both additions to retained earnings and accumulated retained earnings are SF900,000. (The example assumes that the subsidiary is at the end of its first year of operation.) The historical exchange rate is SF3.00/$1.00. The next four columns show the translated statements after an assumed appreciation of the Swiss franc to SF2.00/$1.00. The average exchange for the period is thus SF2.50/$1.00. As one can see from the exhibit, total assets vary from $2,550,000 under the monetary/nonmonetary method, which has a foreign exchange loss of $550,000 passed through the income statement, to $3,300,000 under the current rate method, which has an effective foreign exchange gain of $540,000 carried in the cumulative translation adjustment (CTA) account.

Under the temporal method, it is assumed that the firm carries its inventory at the current market value of SF1,800,000 instead of at the historical value of SF1,500,000. Note that the temporal method and the monetary/nonmonetary methods would both translate inventory to a value of $500,000 if the subsidiary was assumed to carry inventory at its historical value under the temporal method.

Exhibit 10.1B also shows the translated balance sheet and income statements after an assumed depreciation of the Swiss franc from SF3.00/$1.00 to SF4.00/$1.00. The average exchange rate for the period is thus SF3.50/$1.00. As the exhibit shows, total assets vary from $1,650,000 under the current rate method, which has an effective foreign exchange loss of $257,000 carried in the CTA account, to $2,025,000 under the monetary/nonmonetary method, which has a foreign exchange gain of $361,000.

Financial Accounting Standards Board Statement 8

FASB 8 became effective on January 1, 1976. Its objective was to measure in dollars an enterprise's assets, liabilities, revenues, or expenses that are denominated in a foreign currency according to generally accepted accounting principles. FASB 8 is essentially the temporal method of translation as previously defined, but there are some subtleties. For example, according to the temporal method, revenues and expenses are to be measured at the average exchange rate for the period. In practice, MNCs prepare monthly statements. What is done is to cumulate the monthly figures to obtain the total for the year.

FASB 8 ran into acceptance problems from the accounting profession and MNCs from the very beginning. The temporal method requires taking foreign exchange gains or losses through the income statement, as was demonstrated in Example 10.1. Consequently, reported earnings could, and did, fluctuate substantially from year to year, which was irritating to corporate executives.

Additionally, many MNCs did not like translating inventory at historical rates, which was required if the firm carried the inventory at historical values, as most did, and do. It was felt that it would be much simpler to translate at the current rate.

Financial Accounting Standards Board Statement 52

Given the controversy surrounding FASB 8, a proposal was put on the agenda of the FASB in January 1979 to consider all features of FASB 8. Subsequently, in February 1979, a task force was established with representatives of the board, the International

Comparison of Effects of Translation Methods on Financial Statement Preparation after Appreciation from SF 3.00 to SF 2.00 = $1.00
(in 000 currency units)

EXHIBIT 10.1A

	Local Currency	Current/ Noncurrent	Monetary/ Nonmonetary	Temporal	Current Rate
Balance Sheet					
Cash	SF 2,100	$1,050	$1,050	$1,050	$1,050
Inventory					
(Current value = SF1,800)	1,500	750	500	900	750
Net fixed assets	3,000	1,000	1,000	1,000	1,500
Total assets	SF 6,600	$2,800	$2,550	$2,950	$3,300
Current liabilities	SF 1,200	$ 600	$ 600	$ 600	$ 600
Long-term debt	1,800	600	900	900	900
Common stock	2,700	900	900	900	900
Retained earnings	900	700	150	550	360
CTA	—	—	—	—	540
Total liabilities and equity	SF 6,600	$2,800	$2,550	$2,950	$3,300
Income Statement					
Sales revenue	SF10,000	$4,000	$4,000	$4,000	$4,000
COGS	7,500	3,000	2,500	3,000	3,000
Depreciation	1,000	333	333	333	400
Net operating income	1,500	667	1,167	667	600
Income tax (40%)	600	267	467	267	240
Profit after tax	900	400	700	400	360
Foreign exchange gain (loss)	—	300	(550)	150	—
Net income	900	700	150	550	360
Dividends	0	0	0	0	0
Addition to retained earnings	SF 900	$ 700	$ 150	$ 550	$ 360

Comparison of Effects of Translation Methods on Financial Statement Preparation after Depreciation from SF 3.00 to SF 4.00 = $1.00
(in 000 currency units)

EXHIBIT 10.1B

	Local Currency	Current/ Noncurrent	Monetary/ Nonmonetary	Temporal	Current Rate
Balance Sheet					
Cash	SF 2,100	$ 525	$ 525	$ 525	$ 525
Inventory					
(Current value = SF1,800)	1,500	375	500	450	375
Net fixed assets	3,000	1,000	1,000	1,000	750
Total assets	SF 6,600	$ 1,900	$ 2,025	$ 1,975	$ 1,650
Current liabilities	SF 1,200	$ 300	$ 300	$ 300	$ 300
Long-term debt	1,800	600	450	450	450
Common stock	2,700	900	900	900	900
Retained earnings	900	100	375	325	257
CTA	—	—	—	—	(257)
Total liabilities and equity	SF 6,600	$ 1,900	$ 2,025	$ 1,975	$ 1,650
Income Statement					
Sales revenue	SF 10,000	$2,857	$ 2,857	$ 2,857	$ 2,857
COGS	7,500	2,143	2,500	2,143	2,143
Depreciation	1,000	333	333	333	286
Net operating income	1,500	381	24	381	428
Income tax (40%)	600	152	10	152	171
Profit after tax	900	229	14	229	257
Foreign exchange gain (loss)	—	(129)	361	96	—
Net income	900	100	375	325	257
Dividends	0	0	0	0	0
Addition to retained earnings	SF 900	$ 100	$ 375	$ 325	$ 257

Accounting Standards Committee (now the International Accounting Standards Board), and the accounting standards bodies from Canada and the United Kingdom. After many meetings and hearings, FASB 52 was issued in December 1981, and all U.S. MNCs were required to adopt the statement for fiscal years beginning on or after December 15, 1982.

The stated objectives of FASB 52 are to:

a. Provide information that is generally compatible with the expected economic effects of a rate change on an enterprise's cash flows and equity; and
b. Reflect in consolidated statements the financial results and relationships of the individual consolidated entities as measured in their functional currencies in conformity with U.S. generally accepted accounting principles.[1]

Many discussions of FASB 52 claim that it is a current rate method of translation. This, however, is a misnomer, as FASB 52 requires the current rate method of translation in some circumstances and the temporal method in others. Which method of translation is prescribed by FASB 52 depends upon the functional currency used by the foreign subsidiary whose statements are to be translated. The **functional currency** is defined in FASB 52 as "the currency of the primary economic environment in which the entity operates."[2] Normally, that is the local currency of the country in which the entity conducts most of its business. However, under certain circumstances, the functional currency may be the parent firm's home country currency or some third-country currency. Exhibit 10.2 summarizes the method for determining the functional currency.

EXHIBIT 10.2	
Salient Economic Factors for Determining the Functional Currency	*Cash Flow Indicators* Foreign Currency: Foreign entity's cash flows are primarily in foreign currency and they do not directly affect the parent firm's cash flows. Parent's Currency: Foreign entity's cash flows directly affect the parent's cash flows and are readily available for remittance to the parent firm. *Sales Price Indicators* Foreign Currency: Sales prices for the foreign entity's products are generally not responsive on a short-term basis to exchange rate changes, but are determined more by local competition and government regulation. Parent's Currency: Sales prices for the foreign entity's products are responsive on a short-term basis to exchange rate changes, where sales prices are determined through worldwide competition. *Sales Market Indicators* Foreign Currency: There is an active local sales market for the foreign entity's products. Parent's Currency: The sales market is primarily located in the parent's country or sales contracts are denominated in the parent's currency. *Expense Indicators* Foreign Currency: Factor of production costs of the foreign entity are primarily local costs. Parent's Currency: Factor of production costs of the foreign entity are primarily, and on a continuing basis, costs for components obtained from the parent's country. *Financing Indicators* Foreign Currency: Financing of the foreign entity is primarily denominated in the foreign currency and the debt service obligations are normally handled by the foreign entity. Parent's Currency: Financing of the foreign entity is primarily from the parent, with debt service obligations met by the parent, or the debt service obligations incurred by the foreign entity are primarily made by the parent. *(continued)*

[1]See FASB 52, paragraph 4.
[2]See FASB 52, paragraph 5.

EXHIBIT 10.2

Salient Economic Factors for Determining the Functional Currency (continued)

Intercompany Transactions and Arrangements Indicators
Foreign Currency: There is a low volume of intercompany transactions and a minor interrelationship of operations between the foreign entity and the parent. However, the foreign entity may benefit from competitive advantages of the parent, such as patents or trademarks.
Parent's Currency: There is a large volume of intercompany transactions and an extensive interrelationship of operations between the foreign entity and the parent. Moreover, if the foreign entity is only a shell company for carrying accounts that could be carried on the parent's books, the functional currency would generally be the parent's currency.

Source: Excerpted from *Foreign Currency Translation, Statement of Financial Accounting Standards No. 52,* Paragraph 42, Financial Accounting Standards Board, Stamford, CT, December 1981.

The **reporting currency** is defined as the currency in which the MNC prepares its consolidated financial statements. That currency is usually the currency in which the parent firm keeps its books, which in turn is usually the currency of the country in which the parent is located and conducts most of its business. However, the reporting currency could be some third currency. For our purposes in this chapter, the terms reporting currency and parent currency will be used synonymously, and will be assumed to be the U.S. dollar.

The Mechanics of the FASB 52 Translation Process

The actual translation process prescribed by FASB 52 is a two-stage process. First, it is necessary to determine in which currency the foreign entity keeps its books. If the local currency in which the foreign entity keeps its books is not the functional currency (and, as shown in Exhibit 10.3, it does not have to be), remeasurement into the functional currency is required. *Remeasurement* is intended "to produce the same result as if the entity's books had been maintained in the functional

EXHIBIT 10.3

FASB 52 Two-Stage Translation Process[a]

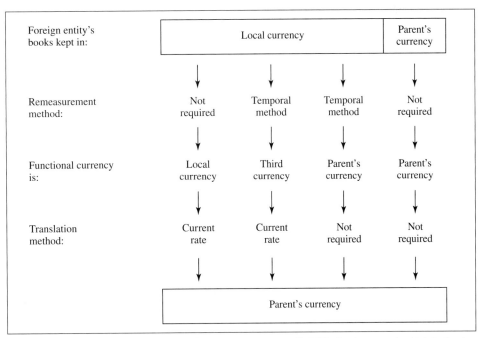

[a]The translation process prescribed by FASB 52 is a two-stage process. First, if the local currency in which the foreign entity keeps its books is not the functional currency, remeasurement by the temporal method is required. Second, when the foreign entity's functional currency is not the same as the parent's currency, the foreign entity's books are translated from the functional currency into the reporting currency using the current rate method. If the foreign entity is in a highly inflationary economy, FASB 52 requires that the local currency be remeasured into the parent's currency.

Source: Derived from J. S. Arpan and L. H. Radenbaugh, *International Accounting and Multinational Enterprises,* 2nd ed. (New York: Wiley, 1985), Exhibit 5.2, p. 136, and Andrew A. Haried, Leroy F. Imdieke, and Ralph E. Smith, *Advanced Accounting,* 6th ed. (New York: Wiley, 1994), Illustration 15-3, p. 562.

currency."[3] The temporal method of translation is used to accomplish the remeasurement. Second, when the foreign entity's functional currency is not the same as the parent's currency, the foreign entity's books are *translated* from the functional currency into the reporting currency using the current rate method. Obviously, translation is not required if the foreign entity's functional currency is the same as the reporting currency.

Highly Inflationary Economies

In highly inflationary economies, FASB 52 requires that the foreign entity's financial statements be remeasured from the local currency "as if the functional currency were the reporting currency" using the temporal translation method.[4] A highly inflationary economy is defined as "one that has cumulative inflation of approximately 100 percent or more over a 3-year period."[5] The purpose of this requirement is to prevent large important balance sheet accounts, carried at historical values, from having insignificant values once translated into the reporting currency at the current rate. We know that according to relative purchasing power parity a currency from a higher inflationary economy will depreciate relative to the currency of a lower inflationary economy by approximately the differential of the two countries' inflation rates. Hence, for example, the fixed asset account of a foreign entity in a highly inflationary economy, carried on the books in the local currency, would soon lose value relative to the reporting currency, and translate into a relatively insignificant amount in comparison to its true book value.

International Accounting Standards

As markets have become more integrated as a result of cross-border investing and financing, international accounting standards that provide a common accounting language are gaining acceptance. In fact, since January 2005, all companies doing business in the European Union have to use the accounting standards promulgated by the International Accounting Standards Board (IASB). Since investors desire a means to easily compare financial statements of companies incorporated in many countries, this achievement should eventually have a major effect on harmonizing accounting standards around the world.

In April 2001, the IASB assumed accounting standard-setting responsibilities from its predecessor body, the International Accounting Standards Committee (IASC). Similar to the FASB, the ISAB publishes its standards in a series of pronouncements called International Financial Reporting Standards. It also adopted and maintains the pronouncements of the IASC, called International Accounting Standards (IAS). IAS 21, *The Effects of Changes in Foreign Exchange Rates*, is the standard for handling foreign currency translation. IAS 21 most closely resembles the monetary/nonmonetary translation method discussed earlier in the chapter. Thus, in the European Union, a different translation method is currently used than in the United States. However, a common set of high-quality global standards is a priority of the IASB and FASB. In 2009, the two boards issued a further statement to a previously issued memorandum of understanding to achieve substantial convergence of accounting standards by 2011. This effort is currently behind schedule, but it appears that most countries may soon follow a common standard for foreign currency translation.

www.ifrs.org

This is the website of the IFRS Foundation. The IASB is the independent standard-setting body of the IFRS Foundation. Information about the organization and its objectives can be found at this site.

CASE APPLICATION

Consolidation of Accounts according to FASB 52: The Centralia Corporation

We use a case application to illustrate consolidating the balance sheet of a MNC according to FASB 52. The basic information is provided in Exhibit 10.4, which shows the unconsolidated balance sheets for Centralia Corporation, a U.S. parent firm, and its two wholly

---

[3]See FASB 52, paragraph 10.

[4]See FASB 52, paragraph 11.

[5]See FASB 52, paragraph 11.

EXHIBIT 10.4

Nonconsolidated Balance Sheet for Centralia Corporation and Its Mexican and Spanish Affiliates, December 31, 2016 (in 000 currency units)

	Centralia Corp. (Parent)	Mexican Affiliate	Spanish Affiliate
Assets			
Cash	$ 950[a]	Ps 6,000	€ 825
Accounts receivable	1,750[b]	9,000	1,045
Inventory	3,000	15,000	1,650
Investment in Mexican affiliate	2,200[c]	—	—
Investment in Spanish affiliate	1,660[d]	—	—
Net fixed assets	9,000	46,000	4,400
Total assets	$18,560	Ps 76,000	€ 7,920
Liabilities and Net Worth			
Accounts payable	$ 1,800	Ps 10,000[b]	€ 1,364
Notes payable	2,200	17,000	1,210[e]
Long-term debt	7,110	27,000	3,520
Common stock	3,500	16,000[c]	1,320[d]
Retained earnings	3,950	6,000[c]	506[d]
Total liabilities and net worth	$18,560	Ps 76,000	€ 7,920

[a]The parent firm has a deposit of CD200,000 in a Canadian bank. This sum is carried on the parent firm's books at $150,000, translated at CD1.3333/$1.00.

[b]The parent firm is owed Ps3,000,000 by the Mexican affiliate. This sum is included in the parent's accounts receivable as $300,000. The remainder of the parent's (Mexican affiliate's) accounts receivable (payable) is denominated in dollars (pesos).

[c]The Mexican affiliate is wholly owned by the parent firm. It is carried on the parent firm's books at $2,200,000. This represents the sum of the common stock (Ps16,000,000) and retained earnings (Ps6,000,000) on the Mexican affiliate's books, translated at Ps10.00/$1.00.

[d]The Spanish affiliate is wholly owned by the parent firm. It is carried on the parent firm's books at $1,660,000. This represents the sum of the common stock (€1,320,000) and the retained earnings (€506,000) on the Spanish affiliate's books, translated at €1.10/$1.00.

[e]The Spanish affiliate has outstanding notes payable of SF375,000 (÷ SF1.3636/€1.00 = €275,000) from a Swiss bank. This loan is carried on the Spanish affiliate's books as part of the €1,210,000 = €275,000 + €935,000.

owned affiliates located in Mexico and Spain. Centralia Corporation is a midwestern manufacturer of small kitchen electrical appliances. The Mexican manufacturing affiliate has been established to cater to the Mexican market, which is expected to expand rapidly under NAFTA. Similarly, the Spanish manufacturing affiliate was established to handle demand in the European Union. The functional currency of the Mexican affiliate is the peso, and the euro is the functional currency for the Spanish affiliate. The reporting currency is the U.S. dollar. The initial exchange rates assumed in the example are: $1.00 = CD1.3333 = Ps10.00 = €1.10 = SF1.50.

The nonconsolidated balance sheets and the footnotes to the statements indicate that the Mexican affiliate owes the parent firm Ps3,000,000, which is carried on the parent's books as a $300,000 accounts receivable at the current exchange rate of Ps10.00/$1.00. Additionally, the $2,200,000 investment of the parent firm in the Mexican affiliate is the translated amount of Ps22,000,000 of equity on the Mexican affiliate's books. Similarly, the $1,660,000 investment of the parent in the Spanish affiliate is the translated amount of €1,826,000 of equity on the Spanish affiliate's books. The footnotes also show that the parent firm has CD200,000 deposited in a Canadian bank, carried as $150,000 in the cash account, and the Spanish affiliate has a SF375,000 loan outstanding from a Swiss bank, translated at SF1.3636/€1.00, and carried at €275,000 as part of its €1,210,000 of notes payable.

Exhibit 10.5 shows the process of consolidating the balance sheets for Centralia Corp. and its affiliates. Of importance is to note that *both* intracompany debt *and* investment net out in the consolidation. That is, the Ps3,000,000 owed by the Mexican affiliate to the parent is not reflected in the consolidated accounts receivable nor in the accounts payable. When this debt is eventually paid, in effect it will be the same as taking money out of one company pocket and putting it into another. In a similar vein, the investment of the parent in each

EXHIBIT 10.5	Consolidated Balance Sheet for Centralia Corporation and Its Mexican and Spanish Affiliates, December 31, 2016: Pre-Exchange Rate Change (in 000 dollars)			
	Centralia Corp. (Parent)	Mexican Affiliate	Spanish Affiliate	Consolidated Balance Sheet
Assets				
Cash	$ 950[a]	$ 600	$ 750	$ 2,300
Accounts receivable	1,450[b]	900	950	3,300
Inventory	3,000	1,500	1,500	6,000
Investment in Mexican affiliation	—[c]	—	—	—
Investment in Spanish affiliation	—[d]	—	—	—
Net fixed assets	9,000	4,600	4,000	17,600
Total assets				$29,200
Liabilities and Net Worth				
Accounts payable	$ 1,800	$ 700[b]	$ 1,240	$ 3,740
Notes payable	2,200	1,700	1,100[e]	5,000
Long-term debt	7,110	2,700	3,200	13,010
Common stock	3,500	—[c]	—[d]	3,500
Retained earnings	3,950	—[c]	—[d]	3,950
Total liabilities and net worth				$29,200

[a]This sum includes CD200,000 the parent firm has on deposit in a Canadian bank, carried on the books as $150,000. CD200,000/(CD1.3333/$1.00) = $150,000.

[b]$1,750,000 − $300,000 (= Ps3,000,000/(Ps10.00/$1.00)) intracompany loan = $1,450,000.

[c,d]The investment in the affiliates cancels with the net worth of the affiliates in the consolidation.

[e]The Spanish affiliate owes a Swiss bank SF375,000 (÷ SF1.3636/€1.00 = €275,000). This is carried on the books as part of the €1,210,000 = €275,000 + €935,000. €1,210,000/(€1.10/$1.00) = $1,100,000.

affiliate cancels with the net worth of each affiliate. The parent owns the affiliates, and, in turn, the shareholders' investment represents ownership of the parent firm. In this manner, the shareholders own the entire MNC.

The consolidation presented in Exhibit 10.5 is rather simplistic. It is nice and neat from the standpoint that the consolidated balance sheet, in fact, balances. That is, total assets equal total liabilities and net worth. Implicit in the example are that the current exchange rates used are the same as those used when the affiliates were originally established; that is, they have not changed from that time. Thus, the example is not very realistic even though it properly presents the mechanics of the consolidation process under FASB 52. After all, the central purpose of a translation method is to deal in some systematic way with exchange rate *changes*.

To determine the effect that exchange rate changes will have on the consolidated balance sheet of a MNC, it is useful to prepare a translation exposure report. A **translation exposure report** shows, for each account that is included in the consolidated balance sheet, the amount of foreign exchange exposure that exists for each foreign currency in which the MNC has exposure. Continuing with our example of Centralia Corporation and its affiliates, we know from Exhibit 10.4 that the MNC has foreign exchange exposure from the Mexican peso, euro, Canadian dollar, and Swiss franc. A change in any one of these currency exchange rates versus the reporting currency will have an effect on the consolidated balance sheet if there exists a net translation exposure for that currency.

Exhibit 10.6 presents the translation exposure report for Centralia. The report shows, for each exposure currency, the amount of exposed assets and exposed liabilities denominated in that currency, and the net difference, or net exposure. For the Canadian dollar the net exposure is a positive CD200,000; for the Mexican peso a positive Ps25,000,000; for the euro a positive €2,101,000; and for the Swiss franc a negative SF375,000. A positive net exposure means there are more exposed assets than liabilities, and vice versa for negative net exposure. When the exchange rate of an exposure currency depreciates against the reporting currency, exposed assets fall in translated value by a greater (smaller) amount than exposed liabilities if there is positive (negative) net exposure. Analogously, when an

EXHIBIT 10.6	Translation Exposure Report for Centralia Corporation and Its Mexican and Spanish Affiliates, December 31, 2016 (in 000 currency units)			
	Canadian Dollar	Mexican Peso	Euro	Swiss Franc
Assets				
Cash	CD200	Ps 6,000	€ 825	SF 0
Accounts receivable	0	9,000	1,045	0
Inventory	0	15,000	1,650	0
Net fixed assets	0	46,000	4,400	0
Exposed assets	CD200	Ps 76,000	€ 7,920	SF 0
Liabilities				
Accounts payable	CD 0	Ps 7,000	€ 1,364	SF 0
Notes payable	0	17,000	935	375
Long-term debt	0	27,000	3,520	0
Exposed liabilities	CD 0	Ps 51,000	€ 5,819	SF 375
Net exposure	CD200	Ps 25,000	€ 2,101	(SF 375)

exposure currency appreciates against the reporting currency, exposed assets increase in translated value by a smaller (greater) amount than exposed liabilities if there is negative (positive) net exposure. Consequently, the consolidation process will not result in a consolidated balance sheet that balances after an exchange rate change.

To show the effect on the consolidation process after an exchange rate change, let's perform the consolidation of the nonconsolidated balance sheets from Exhibit 10.4 once again, assuming this time that exchange rates have changed from $1.00 = CD1.3333 = Ps10.00 = €1.10 = SF1.50 to $1.00 = CD1.3333 = Ps10.00 = €1.1786 = SF1.50. We are assuming that only the euro has changed (depreciated) versus all other currencies in order to keep the example simple so as to better decipher the effect of an exchange rate change.

To get an overview of the effect of the exchange rate change, recall from Exhibit 10.6 that there is a positive net exposure of €2,101,000. This implies that after the 7.145 percent depreciation from €1.1000/$1.00 to €1.1786/$1.00, the exposed assets denominated in euros will fall in translated value by $127,377 more than the exposed liabilities denominated in euros. This can be calculated as follows:

$$\frac{\text{Net exposure currency } i}{S_{new}[i/\text{reporting}]} - \frac{\text{Net exposure currency } i}{S_{old}[i/\text{reporting}]}$$

= Reporting currency imbalance.

For our example,

$$\frac{€2,101,000}{€1.1786/\$1.00} - \frac{€2,101,000}{€1.1000/\$1.00} = -\$127,377$$

In other words, the net translation exposure of €2,101,000 in dollars is $1,910,000 when translated at the exchange rate of €1.1000/$1.00. A 7.145 percent depreciation of the euro to €1.1786/$1.00 will result in a translation loss of $127,377 = €2,101,000 ÷ 1.1786 × .07145.

Exhibit 10.7 shows the consolidation process and consolidated balance sheet for Centralia Corporation and its two foreign affiliates after the depreciation of the euro. Note that the values for the accounts are the same as in Exhibit 10.5 for the parent firm and the Mexican affiliate. However, the values of the accounts of the Spanish affiliate are different because of the exchange rate change. In order for the consolidated balance sheet to now balance, it is necessary to have a "plug" equity account with a balance of −$127,377. As before, we referred to this special equity account as the cumulative translation adjustment account, or CTA account. The balance of this account at any time represents the accumulated total of all past translation adjustments. FASB 52 handles the effect of exchange rate changes as

EXHIBIT 10.7	Consolidated Balance Sheet for Centralia Corporation and Its Mexican and Spanish Affiliates, December 31, 2016: Post-Exchange Rate Change (in 000 dollars)			
	Centralia Corp. (Parent)	Mexican Affiliate	Spanish Affiliate	Consolidated Balance Sheet
Assets				
Cash	$ 950ᵃ	$ 600	$ 700	$ 2,250
Accounts receivable	1,450ᵇ	900	887	3,237
Inventory	3,000	1,500	1,400	5,900
Investment in Mexican affiliate	—ᶜ	—	—	—
Investment in Spanish affiliate	—ᵈ	—	—	—
Net fixed assets	9,000	4,600	3,733	17,333
Total Assets				$ 28,720
Liabilities and Net Worth				
Accounts payable	$ 1,800	$ 700ᵇ	$ 1,157	$ 3,657
Notes payable	2,200	1,700	1,043ᵉ	4,943
Long-term debt	7,110	2,700	2,987	12,797
Common stock	3,500	—ᶜ	—ᵈ	3,500
Retained earnings	3,950	—ᶜ	—ᵈ	3,950
CTA	—	—	—	(127)
Total liabilities and net worth				$ 28,720

ᵃThis includes CD200,000 the parent firm has in a Canadian bank, carried as $150,000 CD200,000/ (CD1.3333/$1.00) = $150,000.

ᵇ$1,750,000 − $300,000 (= Ps3,000,000/(Ps10.00/$1.00)) intracompany loan = $1,450,000.

ᶜ,ᵈInvestment in affiliates cancels with the net worth of the affiliates in the consolidation.

ᵉThe Spanish affiliate owes a Swiss bank SF375,000 (÷ SF1.2727/€1.00 = €294,649). This is carried on the books, after the exchange rate change, as part of €1,229,649 = €294,649 + €935,000. €1,229,649/(€1.1786/$1.00) = $1,043,313.

an adjustment to equity rather than as an adjustment to net income because "exchange rate changes have an indirect effect on the net investment that may be realized upon sale or liquidation, but . . . prior to sale or liquidation, that effect is so uncertain and remote as to require that translation adjustments arising currently should not be reported as part of operating results."[6]

Management of Translation Exposure

Translation Exposure versus Transaction Exposure

In Chapter 8, we discussed transaction exposure and ways to manage it. It is interesting to note that some items that are a source of transaction exposure are also a source of translation exposure, and some are not. Exhibit 10.8 presents a transaction exposure report for Centralia Corporation and its two affiliates. Items that create transaction exposure are receivables or payables that are denominated in a currency other than the currency in which the unit transacts its business, or cash holdings denominated in a foreign currency. From the exhibit, it can be seen that the parent firm has two sources of transaction exposure. One is the CD200,000 deposit that it has in a Canadian bank. Obviously, if the Canadian dollar depreciates, the deposit will be worth less to Centralia Corporation once converted to U.S. dollars. Previously, it was noted that this deposit was also a translation exposure; it is, in fact, for the same reason that it is a transaction exposure. The Ps3,000,000 accounts receivable the parent holds on the Mexican affiliate is also a transaction exposure, but it is not a translation exposure because of the netting of intracompany payables and receivables. The SF375,000 notes payable the Spanish affiliate owes the Swiss bank is both a transaction and a translation exposure.

---
[6]See FASB 52, paragraph 111.

EXHIBIT 10.8

Transaction Exposure Report for Centralia Corporation and Its Mexican and Spanish Affiliates, December 31, 2016

Affiliate	Amount	Account	Translation Exposure
Parent	CD200,000	Cash	Yes
Parent	Ps3,000,000	Accounts receivable	No
Spanish	SF375,000	Notes payable	Yes

It is, generally, not possible to eliminate both translation and transaction exposure. In some cases, the elimination of one exposure will also eliminate the other. But in other cases, the elimination of one exposure actually creates the other. Since transaction exposure involves real cash flows, we believe it should be considered the more important of the two. That is, the financial manager would not want to legitimately create transaction exposure at the expense of minimizing or eliminating translation exposure. As previously noted, the translation process has no direct effect on reporting currency cash flows, and will only have a realizable effect on net investment upon the sale or liquidation of the assets. Actual practitioners appear to concur. In a recent survey of exchange risk management practices of U.K., U.S., and Asia Pacific multinational firms, Marshall (2000) found that 83 percent placed a "significant" or the "most" amount of emphasis on managing transaction exposure, whereas only 37 percent placed that much emphasis on managing translation exposure.

Centralia Corporation and its affiliates can take certain measures to reduce its transaction exposure and to simultaneously reduce its translation exposure. One step the parent firm can take is to convert its Canadian dollar cash deposits into U.S. dollar deposits. Secondly, the parent firm can request payment of the Ps3,000,000 owed to it by the Mexican affiliate. Third, the Spanish affiliate has enough cash to pay off the SF375,000 loan to the Swiss bank. If these three steps are taken, all transaction exposure for the MNC will be eliminated. Moreover, translation exposure will be reduced. This can be seen from Exhibit 10.9, which presents a revision of Exhibit 10.6, the translation exposure report for Centralia Corporation and its affiliates. Exhibit 10.9 shows that there is no longer any translation exposure associated with the Canadian dollar or the Swiss franc. Additionally, the exhibit shows that the net exposure has been reduced from Ps25,000,000 to Ps22,000,000 for the peso and from €2,101,000 to €1,826,000 for the euro.

Hedging Translation Exposure

Exhibit 10.9 indicates that there is still considerable translation exposure with respect to changes in the exchange rate of the Mexican peso and the euro against the U.S. dollar. There are two methods for dealing with this remaining exposure, if one desires to attempt to control accounting changes in the historical value of net investment. These methods are a balance sheet hedge or a derivatives hedge.

Balance Sheet Hedge

Note that translation exposure is not entity specific; rather, it is currency specific. Its source is a mismatch of net assets and net liabilities denominated in the same currency. A **balance sheet hedge** eliminates the mismatch. Using the euro as an example, Exhibit 10.9 shows that there are €1,826,000 more exposed assets than liabilities. If the Spanish affiliate, or more practicably the parent firm or the Mexican affiliate, had €1,826,000 more liabilities, or less assets, denominated in euros, there would not be any translation exposure with respect to the euro. A perfect balance sheet hedge would have been created. A change in the €/$ exchange rate would no longer have any effect on the consolidated balance sheet since the change in value of the assets denominated in euros would completely offset the change in value of the liabilities denominated in euros. Nevertheless, if the parent firm or the Mexican affiliate increased its liabilities through, say, euro-denominated borrowings to affect the balance sheet hedge, it would simultaneously be creating transaction exposure in the euro, if the new liability could not be covered from euro cash flows generated by the Spanish affiliate.

	Canadian Dollar	Mexican Peso	Euro	Swiss Franc
Assets				
Cash	CD0	Ps 3,000	€ 550	SF0
Accounts receivable	0	9,000	1,045	0
Inventory	0	15,000	1,650	0
Net fixed assets	0	46,000	4,400	0
Exposed assets	CD0	Ps 73,000	€ 7,645	SF0
Liabilities				
Accounts payable	CD0	Ps 7,000	€ 1,364	SF0
Notes payable	0	17,000	935	0
Long-term debt	0	27,000	3,520	0
Exposed liabilities	CD0	Ps 51,000	€ 5,819	SF0
Net exposure	CD0	Ps 22,000	€ 1,826	SF0

Derivatives Hedge

According to Exhibit 10.6, we determined that when the net exposure for the euro was €2,101,000, a depreciation from €1.1000/$1.00 to €1.1786/$1.00 would create a paper loss of stockholders' equity equal to $127,377. According to the revised translation exposure report shown as Exhibit 10.9, the same depreciation in the euro will result in an equity loss of $110,704, still a sizable amount. (The calculation of this amount is left as an exercise for the reader.) If one desires, a derivative product, such as a forward contract, can be used to attempt to hedge this potential loss. We use the word "attempt" because as the following example demonstrates, using a **derivatives hedge** to control translation exposure really involves speculation about foreign exchange rate changes.

EXAMPLE | 10.2: Hedging Translation Exposure with a Forward Contract

To see how a forward contract can be used to hedge the $110,704 potential translation loss in equity, assume that the forward rate coinciding with the date of the consolidation is €1.1393/$1.00. If the expected spot rate on the consolidation date is forecast to be €1.1786/$1.00, a forward sale of €3,782,468 will "hedge" the risk:

$$\frac{\text{Potential translation loss}}{F \text{ (reporting/functional)} - \text{Expected}[S \text{ (reporting/functional)}]}$$

$$= \text{forward contract position in functional currency,}$$

$$\frac{\$110,704}{1/(€ 1.1393/\$1.00) - 1/(€ 1.1786/\$1.00)} = €3,782,468$$

The purchase of €3,782,468 at the expected spot price will cost $3,209,289. The delivery of €3,782,468 under the forward contract will yield $3,319,993, for a profit of $110,704. If everything goes as expected, the $110,704 profit from the forward hedge will offset the equity loss from the translation adjustment. Note, however, that the hedge will not provide a certain outcome because the size of the forward position is based on the expected future spot rate. Consequently, the forward position taken in euros is actually a speculative position. If the realized spot rate turns out to be less than €1.1393/$1.00, a loss from the forward position will result. Moreover, the hedging procedure violates the hypothesis of the forward rate being the market's unbiased predictor of the future spot rate.

In 1998, FASB 133 was issued. This statement establishes accounting and reporting standards for derivative instruments and hedging activities. To qualify for hedge accounting under FASB 133, a company must identify a clear link between an exposure and a derivative instrument. FASB 133 clarifies which transactions qualify as an acceptable hedge and how to treat an unexpected gain or loss if the hedge is not effective. Under FASB 133, the firm must document the effectiveness of its hedge transactions. Large gains or losses resulting from ineffective hedging are recorded in current income, whereas small gains or losses due to a lack of perfect (but nevertheless effective) hedging are posted to other comprehensive income (OCI), which is an equity account on the balance sheet. Under FASB 52, and prior to FASB 133, a company with an imprecise hedge might be allowed to post all gains or losses from an ineffective translation exposure hedge to the CTA account. However, under FASB 133 this process is modified: Effective hedge results are consolidated along with the CTA in OCI, but differences between total hedge results and the translation exposure being hedged (ineffective hedge results) flow first through current earnings on the income statement. Consequently, as in Example 10.2, if everything goes as expected (i.e., the "hedge" produces effective results), the gain from the derivatives hedge will fully offset the translation loss, resulting in a cumulative translation adjustment of zero.

Translation Exposure versus Operating Exposure

As noted, an unhedged depreciation in the euro will result in an equity loss. Such a loss, however, would only be a paper loss. It would not have any direct effect on reporting currency cash flows. Moreover, it would only have a realizable effect on net investment in the MNC if the affiliate's assets were sold or liquidated. However, as was discussed in Chapter 9, the depreciation of the local currency may, under certain circumstances, have a favorable operating effect. A currency depreciation may, for example, allow the affiliate to raise its sales price because the prices of imported competitive goods are now relatively higher. If costs do not rise proportionately and unit demand remains the same, the affiliate would realize an operating profit as a result of the currency depreciation. It is substantive issues such as these, which result in realizable changes in operating profit, that management should concern itself with.

Empirical Analysis of the Change from FASB 8 to FASB 52

Garlicki, Fabozzi, and Fonfeder (1987) empirically tested a sample of MNCs to determine if there was a change in value when the firms were required to switch from FASB 8 to FASB 52. FASB 8 calls for recognizing translation gains or losses immediately in net income. FASB 52 calls for recognizing translation gains or losses in the cumulative translation adjustment account on the balance sheet. Consequently, the change in the translation process had an effect on reported earnings. "Despite the impact of the change . . . on reported earnings, the actual cash flow of multinationals would not be affected *if managers were not making suboptimal decisions based on accounting rather than economic considerations under Statement 8.* In such circumstances, the mandated switch . . . should not change the value of the firm."[7]

The researchers tested their hypothesis concerning a change in value on the initial exposure draft date and on the date FASB 52 was adopted. They found that there was no significant positive reaction to the change or perceived change in the foreign currency translation process. The results suggest that market agents do not react to cosmetic earnings changes that do not affect value. Other researchers have found similar results when investigating other accounting changes that had only a cosmetic effect on earnings. The results of Garlicki, Fabozzi, and Fonfeder also underline the futility of attempting to manage translation gains and losses.

---

[7]Garlicki, Fabozzi, and Fonfeder (1987).

SUMMARY

In this chapter, we have discussed the nature and management of translation exposure. Translation exposure relates to the effect that an unanticipated change in exchange rates will have on the consolidated financial reports of a MNC.

1. The four recognized methods for consolidating the financial reports of a MNC include the current/noncurrent method, the monetary/nonmonetary method, the temporal method, and the current rate method.

2. An example comparing and contrasting the four translation methods was presented under the assumptions that the foreign currency had appreciated and depreciated. It was noted that under the current rate method the gain or loss due to translation adjustment does not affect reported cash flows, as it does with the other three translation methods.

3. The old translation method prescribed by the Financial Accounting Standards Board, FASB 8, was discussed and compared with the present prescribed process, FASB 52.

4. In implementing FASB 52, the functional currency of the foreign entity must be translated into the reporting currency in which the consolidated statements are reported. The local currency of a foreign entity may not always be its functional currency. If it is not, the temporal method of translation is used to remeasure the foreign entity's books into the functional currency. The current rate method is used to translate from the functional currency to the reporting currency. In some cases, a foreign entity's functional currency may be the same as the reporting currency, in which case translation is not necessary.

5. It was noted that the European Union follows IAS 21, a monetary/nonmonetary translation method promulgated by the International Accounting Standards Board.

6. A case application illustrating the translation process of the balance sheet of a parent firm with two foreign wholly owned affiliates according to FASB 52 was presented. This was done assuming the foreign exchange rates had not changed since the inception of the businesses, and again after an assumed change, to more thoroughly show the effects of balance sheet consolidation under FASB 52. When a net translation exposure exists, a cumulative translation adjustment account is necessary to bring balance to the consolidated balance sheet after an exchange rate change.

7. Two ways to control translation risk were presented: a balance sheet hedge and a derivatives "hedge." Since translation exposure does not have an immediate direct effect on operating cash flows, its control is relatively unimportant in comparison to transaction exposure, which involves potential real cash flow losses. Since it is, generally, not possible to eliminate both translation and transaction exposure, it is more logical to effectively manage transaction exposure, even at the expense of translation exposure.

KEY WORDS

balance sheet hedge, *255*
cumulative translation
  adjustment (CTA), *245*
current/noncurrent
  method, *244*

current rate method, *245*
derivatives hedge, *256*
functional currency, *248*
monetary/nonmonetary
  method, *245*

reporting currency, *249*
temporal method, *245*
translation exposure, *244*
translation exposure
  report, *252*

QUESTIONS

1. Explain the difference in the translation process between the monetary/nonmonetary method and the temporal method.

2. How are translation gains and losses handled differently according to the current rate method in comparison to the other three methods, that is, the current/noncurrent method, the monetary/nonmonetary method, and the temporal method?

3. Identify some instances under FASB 52 when a foreign entity's functional currency would be the same as the parent firm's currency.

4. Describe the remeasurement and translation process under FASB 52 of a wholly owned affiliate that keeps its books in the local currency of the country in which it operates, which is different than its functional currency.

5. It is, generally, not possible to completely eliminate both translation exposure and transaction exposure. In some cases, the elimination of one exposure will also eliminate the other. But in other cases, the elimination of one exposure actually creates the other. Discuss which exposure might be viewed as the most important to effectively manage, if a conflict between controlling both arises. Also, discuss and critique the common methods for controlling translation exposure.

PROBLEMS

1. Assume that FASB 8 is still in effect instead of FASB 52. Construct a translation exposure report for Centralia Corporation and its affiliates that is the counterpart to Exhibit 10.6 in the text. Centralia and its affiliates carry inventory and fixed assets on the books at historical values.

2. Assume that FASB 8 is still in effect instead of FASB 52. Construct a consolidated balance sheet for Centralia Corporation and its affiliates after a depreciation of the euro from €1.1000/$1.00 to €1.1786/$1.00 that is the counterpart to Exhibit 10.7 in the text. Centralia and its affiliates carry inventory and fixed assets on the books at historical values.

3. In Example 10.2, a forward contract was used to establish a derivatives "hedge" to protect Centralia from a translation loss if the euro depreciated from €1.1000/ $1.00 to €1.1786/$1.00. Assume that an over-the-counter put option on the euro with a strike price of €1.1393/$1.00 (or $0.8777/€1.00) can be purchased for $0.0088 per euro. Show how the potential translation loss can be "hedged" with an option contract.

INTERNET EXERCISES

WWW

Ford Motor Company manufactures and sells motor vehicles worldwide. Through their worldwide operations they are exposed to all types of foreign currency risk. Their website is www.ford.com. Go to this website and access their 2015 annual report. Scroll through the report until you find the section "Quantitative and Qualitative Disclosures about Market Risk" on page 87. In the subsections titled "Automotive Market and Counterparty Risk" and "Foreign Currency Risk" is a discussion of how Ford hedges economic and transaction exposure, but no mention is made about translation exposure. This is consistent with the discussion in the chapter mentioning that the translation process does not have a direct effect on reporting currency cash flows, and will only have a realizable effect on net investment upon the sale or liquidation of exposed assets.

MINI CASE

Sundance Sporting Goods, Inc.

Sundance Sporting Goods, Inc., is a U.S. manufacturer of high-quality sporting goods—principally golf, tennis, and other racquet equipment, and also lawn sports, such as croquet and badminton—with administrative offices and manufacturing facilities in Chicago, Illinois. Sundance has two wholly owned manufacturing affiliates, one in Mexico and the other in Canada. The Mexican affiliate is located in Mexico City and services all of Latin America. The Canadian affiliate is in Toronto and serves only Canada. Each affiliate keeps its books in its local currency, which is also the functional currency for the affiliate. The current exchange rates are: $1.00 = CD1.25 = Ps3.30 = A1.00 = ¥105 = W800. The nonconsolidated balance sheets for Sundance and its two affiliates appear in the accompanying table.

You joined the International Treasury division of Sundance six months ago after spending the last two years receiving your MBA degree. The corporate treasurer has asked you to prepare a report analyzing all aspects of the translation exposure faced by Sundance as a MNC. She has also asked you to address in your analysis the relationship between the firm's translation exposure and its transaction exposure. After performing a forecast of future spot rates of exchange, you decide that you must do the following before any sensible report can be written.

a. Using the current exchange rates and the nonconsolidated balance sheets for Sundance and its affiliates, prepare a consolidated balance sheet for the MNC according to FASB 52.

b. i. Prepare a translation exposure report for Sundance Sporting Goods, Inc., and its two affiliates.

   ii. Using the translation exposure report you have prepared, determine if any reporting currency imbalance will result from a change in exchange rates to which the firm has currency exposure. Your forecast is that exchange rates will change from $1.00 = CD1.25 = Ps3.30 = A1.00 = ¥105 = W800 to $1.00 = CD1.30 = Ps3.30 = A1.03 = ¥105 = W800.

c. Prepare a second consolidated balance sheet for the MNC using the exchange rates you expect in the future. Determine how any reporting currency imbalance will affect the new consolidated balance sheet for the MNC.

d. i. Prepare a transaction exposure report for Sundance and its affiliates. Determine if any transaction exposures are also translation exposures.

   ii. Investigate what Sundance and its affiliates can do to control its transaction and translation exposures. Determine if any of the translation exposure should be hedged.

Nonconsolidated Balance Sheet for Sundance Sporting Goods, Inc. and Its Mexican and Canadian Affiliates, December 31, 2016 (in 000 currency units)

	Sundance, Inc. (Parent)	Mexican Affiliate	Canadian Affiliate
Assets			
Cash	$ 1,500	Ps 1,420	CD 1,200
Accounts receivable	2,500[a]	2,800[e]	1,500[f]
Inventory	5,000	6,200	2,500
Investment in Mexican affiliate	2,400[b]	—	—
Investment in Canadian affiliate	3,600[c]	—	—
Net fixed assets	12,000	11,200	5,600
Total assets	$27,000	Ps 21,620	CD 10,800
Liabilities and Net Worth			
Accounts payable	$ 3,000	Ps 2,500[a]	CD 1,700
Notes payable	4,000[d]	4,200	2,300
Long-term debt	9,000	7,000	2,300
Common stock	5,000	4,500[b]	2,900[c]
Retained earnings	6,000	3,420[b]	1,600[c]
Total liabilities and net worth	$27,000	Ps 21,620	CD 10,800

[a]The parent firm is owed Ps1,320,000 by the Mexican affiliate. This sum is included in the parent's accounts receivable as $400,000, translated at Ps3.30/$1.00. The remainder of the parent's (Mexican affiliate's) accounts receivable (payable) is denominated in dollars (pesos).

[b]The Mexican affiliate is wholly owned by the parent firm. It is carried on the parent firm's books at $2,400,000. This represents the sum of the common stock (Ps4,500,000) and retained earnings (Ps3,420,000) on the Mexican affiliate's books, translated at Ps3.30/$1.00.

[c]The Canadian affiliate is wholly owned by the parent firm. It is carried on the parent firm's books at $3,600,000. This represents the sum of the common stock (CD2,900,000) and the retained earnings (CD1,600,000) on the Canadian affiliate's books, translated at CD1.25/$1.00.

[d]The parent firm has outstanding notes payable of ¥126,000,000 due a Japanese bank. This sum is carried on the parent firm's books as $1,200,000, translated at ¥105/$1.00. Other notes payable are denominated in U.S. dollars.

[e]The Mexican affiliate has sold on account A120,000 of merchandise to an Argentine import house. This sum is carried on the Mexican affiliate's books as Ps396,000, translated at A1.00/Ps3.30. Other accounts receivable are denominated in Mexican pesos.

[f]The Canadian affiliate has sold on account W192,000,000 of merchandise to a Korean importer. This sum is carried on the Canadian affiliate's books as CD300,000, translated at W800/CD1.25. Other accounts receivable are denominated in Canadian dollars.

**REFERENCES
& SUGGESTED
READINGS**

Arpan, J. S., and L. H. Radenbaugh. *International Accounting and Multinational Enterprises,* 2nd ed. New York: Wiley, 1985.

Financial Accounting Standards Board. *Accounting for the Translation of Foreign Currency Transactions and Foreign Currency Financial Statements, Statement of Financial Accounting Standards No. 8.* Stamford, CT: Financial Accounting Standards Board, October 1975.

Financial Accounting Standards Board. *Foreign Currency Translation, Statement of Financial Accounting Standards No. 52.* Stamford, Conn.: Financial Accounting Standards Board, December 1981.

Financial Accounting Standards Board. "Summary of Statement No. 133." www.fasb.org.

Garlicki, T. Dessa, Frank J. Fabozzi, and Robert Fonfeder. "The Impact of Earnings under FASB 52 on Equity Returns." *Financial Management* 16 (1987), pp. 36–44.

Haried, Andrew A., Leroy F. Imdieke, and Ralph E. Smith. *Advanced Accounting,* 6th ed. New York: Wiley, 1994.

Kawaller, Ira G. "What Analysts Need to Know about Accounting for Derivatives." *Financial Analysts Journal* 60 (2004), pp. 24–30.

Marshall, Andrew P. "Foreign Exchange Risk Management in UK, USA, and Asia Pacific Multinational Companies." *Journal of Multinational Financial Management* 10 (2000), pp. 185–211.

PART FOUR

World Financial Markets and Institutions

PART FOUR PROVIDES a thorough discussion of international financial institutions, assets, and marketplaces, and develops the tools necessary to manage exchange rate uncertainty.

CHAPTER 11 differentiates between international bank and domestic bank operations and examines the institutional differences of various types of international banking offices. International banks and their clients constitute the Eurocurrency market and form the core of the international money market.

CHAPTER 12 distinguishes between foreign bonds and Eurobonds, which together make up the international bond market. The advantages of sourcing funds from the international bond market as opposed to raising funds domestically are discussed. A discussion of the major types of international bonds is included in the chapter.

CHAPTER 13 covers international equity markets. The chapter begins with a statistical documentation of the size of equity markets in both developed and developing countries. Various methods of trading equity shares in the secondary markets are discussed. Additionally, the chapter provides a discussion of the advantages to the firm of cross-listing equity shares in more than one country.

CHAPTER 14 covers interest rate and currency swaps, useful tools for hedging long-term interest rate and currency risk.

CHAPTER 15 covers international portfolio investment. It documents that the potential benefits from international diversification are available to all national investors.

11 International Banking and Money Market

WE BEGIN OUR discussion of world financial markets and institutions in this chapter, which takes up four major topics: international banking; international money market operations, in which banks are dominant players; the international debt crisis; and the global financial crisis. The chapter starts with a discussion of the services international banks provide to their clients. This is appropriate since international banks and domestic banks are characterized by different service mixes. Statistics that show the size and financial strength of the world's largest international banks are presented next. The first part of the chapter concludes with a discussion of the different types of bank operations that encompass international banking. The second part begins with an analysis of the Eurocurrency market, the creation of Eurocurrency deposits by international banks, and the Eurocredit loans they make. These form the foundation of the international money market. Euronotes, Eurocommercial paper, and forward rate agreements are other important money market instruments that are discussed. The third part of the chapter offers a history of the severe international debt crisis of only a few years ago and the dangers of private bank lending to sovereign governments. The chapter concludes with a lengthy discussion of the ongoing global financial crisis.

International Banking Services

International banks can be characterized by the types of services they provide that distinguish them from domestic banks. Foremost, international banks facilitate the imports and exports of their clients by arranging trade financing. Additionally, they serve their clients by arranging for foreign exchange necessary to conduct cross-border transactions and make foreign investments. In conducting foreign exchange transactions, banks often assist their clients in hedging exchange rate risk in foreign currency receivables and payables through forward and options contracts. Since international banks have the facilities to trade foreign exchange, they generally also trade foreign exchange products for their own account.

The major features that distinguish international banks from domestic banks are the types of deposits they accept and the loans and investments they make. Large international banks both borrow and lend in the Eurocurrency market. Additionally, they are frequently members of international loan syndicates, participating with other international banks to lend large sums to MNCs needing project financing and sovereign governments needing funds for economic development. Moreover, depending on the regulations of the country in which it operates and its organizational type, an international bank may participate in the underwriting of Eurobonds and foreign bonds. Today banks are frequently structured as bank holding companies so that they can perform both traditional commercial banking functions, the subject of this chapter, and also engage in investment banking activities.

International banks frequently provide consulting services and advice to their clients. Areas in which international banks typically have expertise are foreign exchange hedging strategies, interest rate and currency swap financing, and international cash management services. All of these international banking services and operations are covered in depth in this and other chapters of the text. Not all international banks provide all services, however. Banks that do provide a majority of these services are commonly known as **universal banks** or **full service banks**.

The World's Largest Banks

Exhibit 11.1 lists the world's 30 largest banks ranked by total assets. The exhibit shows total assets, net income, and market value in billions of U.S. dollars. The exhibit indicates that 8 of the world's 30 largest banks are from the U.S.; 4 each are from Australia, Canada, and the UK; 3 each are from China and France; and 1 each is from Germany, Japan, the Netherlands, and Spain.

From Exhibit 11.1, one might correctly surmise that the world's major international finance centers are New York, London, Tokyo, Paris, and increasingly Sydney, Beijing,

EXHIBIT 11.1	**The World's 30 Largest Banks** (in billions of U.S. dollars, as of April 2016)				
Rank	Bank	Country	Total Assets	Net Income	Market Value
1	ICBC	China	3,420.3	44.2	198.0
2	Bank of China	China	2,589.6	27.2	143.0
3	JPMorgan Chase	USA	2,423.8	23.5	234.2
4	HSBC Holdings	United Kingdom	2,409.7	13.5	133.0
5	Bank of America	USA	2,185.5	15.8	156.0
6	BNP Paribas	France	2,166.3	7.4	66.8
7	Wells Fargo	USA	1,849.2	22.7	256.0
8	Citigroup	USA	1,801.0	15.8	138.1
9	Deutsche Bank	Germany	1,779.7	−7.5	26.4
10	Barclays	United Kingdom	1,650.8	−0.5	41.8
11	Mizuho Financial	Japan	1,625.5	5.0	40.7
12	Banco Santander	Spain	1,455.9	6.6	72.5
13	Société Générale	France	1,449.6	4.4	32.5
14	Royal Bank of Scotland	United Kingdom	1,201.8	−2.4	42.4
15	Lloyds Banking Group	United Kingdom	1,189.0	0.8	70.0
16	ING Group	Netherlands	914.4	5.5	49.9
17	Royal Bank of Canada	Canada	853.0	7.7	90.7
18	TD Bank	Canada	834.0	6.2	81.8
19	National Australia Bank	Australia	671.6	5.0	56.5
20	Commonwealth Bank	Australia	657.0	6.9	99.2
21	Bank of Nova Scotia	Canada	653.5	5.5	61.7
22	ANZ	Australia	625.8	5.9	54.9
23	Westpac Banking Group	Australia	571.0	6.3	80.6
24	Natixis	France	543.4	1.5	17.2
25	Bank of Montreal	Canada	496.9	3.4	41.8
26	US Bancorp	USA	428.6	5.8	75.0
27	Bank of New York Mellon	USA	372.9	3.2	44.2
28	PNC Financial Services	USA	361.0	4.0	44.0
29	BB&T	USA	212.4	2.1	29.1
30	China Huarong Asset Mgt.	China	118.5	2.3	14.3

Source: Compiled from *The Global 2000,* www.forbes.com.

and Shanghai. London, New York, and Tokyo, however, are by far the most important international finance centers because of the relatively liberal banking regulations of their respective countries, the size of their economies, and the importance of their currencies in international transactions. These three financial centers are frequently referred to as *full service centers* because the major banks that operate in them usually provide a full range of services.

Reasons for International Banking

The opening discussion on the services international banks provide implied some of the reasons why a bank may establish multinational operations. Rugman and Kamath (1987) provide a more formal list:

1. *Low marginal costs*—Managerial and marketing knowledge developed at home can be used abroad with low marginal costs.

2. *Knowledge advantage*—The foreign bank subsidiary can draw on the parent bank's knowledge of personal contacts and credit investigations for use in that foreign market.

3. *Home country information services*—Local firms may be able to obtain from a foreign subsidiary bank operating in their country more complete trade and financial market information about the subsidiary's home country than they can obtain from their own domestic banks.

4. *Prestige*—Very large multinational banks have high perceived prestige, liquidity, and deposit safety that can be used to attract clients abroad.

5. *Regulation advantage*—Multinational banks are often not subject to the same regulations as domestic banks. There may be reduced need to publish adequate financial information, lack of required deposit insurance and reserve requirements on foreign currency deposits, and the absence of territorial restrictions.

6. *Wholesale defensive strategy*—Banks follow their multinational customers abroad to prevent the erosion of their clientele to foreign banks seeking to service the multinational's foreign subsidiaries.

7. *Retail defensive strategy*—Multinational banking operations help a bank prevent the erosion of its traveler's check, tourist, and foreign business markets from foreign bank competition.

8. *Transaction costs*—By maintaining foreign branches and foreign currency balances, banks may reduce transaction costs and foreign exchange risk on currency conversion if government controls can be circumvented.

9. *Growth*—Growth prospects in a home nation may be limited by a market largely saturated with the services offered by domestic banks.

10. *Risk reduction*—Greater stability of earnings is possible with international diversification. Offsetting business and monetary policy cycles across nations reduces the country-specific risk a bank faces if it operates in a single nation.

Types of International Banking Offices

The services and operations of international banks are a function of the regulatory environment in which the bank operates and the type of banking facility established. Following is a discussion of the major types of international banking offices, detailing the purpose of each and the regulatory rationale for its existence. The discussion moves from correspondent bank relationships, through which minimal service can be provided to a bank's customers, to a description of offices providing a fuller array of services, to those that have been established by regulatory change for the purpose of leveling the worldwide competitive playing field.[1]

Correspondent Bank

The large banks in the world will generally have a correspondent relationship with other banks in all the major financial centers in which they do not have their own banking operation. A **correspondent bank relationship** is established when two banks maintain a correspondent bank account with one another. For example, a large New York bank will have a correspondent bank account in a London bank, and the London bank will maintain one with the New York bank.

The correspondent banking system enables a bank's MNC client to conduct business worldwide through his local bank or its contacts. Correspondent banking services center around foreign exchange conversions that arise through the international transactions the MNC makes. However, correspondent bank services also include assistance with trade financing, such as honoring letters of credit and accepting drafts drawn on the correspondent bank. Additionally, a MNC needing foreign local financing for one of its subsidiaries may rely on its local bank to provide it with a letter of introduction to the correspondent bank in the foreign country.

The correspondent bank relationship is beneficial because a bank can service its MNC clients at a very low cost and without the need of having bank personnel physically located in many countries. A disadvantage is that the bank's clients may not receive the level of service through the correspondent bank that they would if the bank had its own foreign facilities to service its clients.

Representative Offices

A **representative office** is a small service facility staffed by parent bank personnel that is designed to assist MNC clients of the parent bank in dealings with the bank's correspondents. It is a way for the parent bank to provide its MNC clients with a level of service greater than that provided through merely a correspondent relationship. The parent bank may open a representative office in a country in which it has many MNC clients or at least an important client. Representative offices also assist MNC clients with information about local business practices, economic information, and credit evaluation of the MNC's foreign customers.

Foreign Branches

A **foreign branch bank** operates like a local bank, but legally it is a part of the parent bank. As such, a branch bank is subject to both the banking regulations of its home country and the country in which it operates. U.S. branch banks in foreign countries are regulated from the United States by the Federal Reserve Act and Federal Reserve Regulation K: International Banking Operations, which covers most of the regulations relating to U.S. banks operating in foreign countries and foreign banks operating within the United States.

There are several reasons why a parent bank might establish a branch bank. The primary one is that the bank organization can provide a much fuller range of services for its MNC customers through a branch office than it can through a representative office. For example, branch bank loan limits are based on the capital of the parent bank, not the branch bank. Consequently, a branch bank will likely be able to extend a larger loan to a customer than a locally chartered subsidiary bank of the parent. Additionally, the books of a foreign branch are part of the parent bank's books. Thus, a branch bank system allows customers much faster check clearing than does a correspondent bank network because the debit and credit procedure is handled internally within one organization.

Another reason a U.S. parent bank may establish a foreign branch bank is to compete on a local level with the banks of the host country. Branches of U.S. banks are not subject to U.S. reserve requirements on deposits and are not required to have Federal

---

[1]Much of the discussion in this section follows Hultman (1990).

Deposit Insurance Corporation (FDIC) insurance on deposits. Consequently, branch banks are on the same competitive level as local banks in terms of their cost structure in making loans.

Branch banking is the most popular way for U.S. banks to expand operations overseas. Most branch banks are located in Europe, in particular the United Kingdom. Many branch banks are operated as "shell" branches in offshore banking centers, a topic covered later in this section.

The most important piece of legislation affecting the operation of foreign banks in the United States is the International Banking Act of 1978 (IBA). In general, the act specifies that foreign branch banks operating in the United States must comply with U.S. banking regulations just like U.S. banks. In particular, the IBA specifies that foreign branch banks must meet the Fed reserve requirements on deposits and make FDIC insurance available for customer deposits.

Subsidiary and Affiliate Banks

A **subsidiary bank** is a locally incorporated bank that is either wholly owned or owned in major part by a foreign parent. An **affiliate bank** is one that is only partially owned but not controlled by its foreign parent. Both subsidiary and affiliate banks operate under the banking laws of the country in which they are incorporated. U.S. parent banks find subsidiary and affiliate banking structures desirable because they are allowed to underwrite securities.

Foreign-owned subsidiary banks in the United States tend to locate in the states that are major centers of financial activity, as do U.S. branches of foreign parent banks. In the United States, foreign bank offices tend to locate in the highly populous states of New York, California, Illinois, Florida, Georgia, and Texas.[2]

Edge Act Banks

Edge Act banks are federally chartered subsidiaries of U.S. banks that are physically located in the United States and are allowed to engage in a full range of international banking activities. Senator Walter E. Edge of New Jersey sponsored the 1919 amendment to Section 25 of the Federal Reserve Act to allow U.S. banks to be competitive with the services foreign banks could supply their customers. Federal Reserve Regulation K allows Edge Act banks to accept foreign deposits, extend trade credit, finance foreign projects abroad, trade foreign currencies, and engage in investment banking activities with U.S. citizens involving foreign securities. As such, Edge Act banks do not compete directly with the services provided by U.S. commercial banks.

An Edge Act bank is typically located in a state different from that of its parent in order to get around the prohibition on interstate branch banking. However, since 1979, the Federal Reserve has permitted interstate banking by Edge Act banks. Moreover, the IBA permits foreign banks operating in the United States to establish Edge Act banks. Thus, both U.S. and foreign Edge Act banks operate on an equally competitive basis.

Edge Act banks are not prohibited from owning equity in business corporations, unlike domestic commercial banks. Thus, it is *through* the Edge Act that U.S. parent banks have historically owned foreign banking subsidiaries and held ownership positions in foreign banking affiliates. Since 1966, however, U.S. banks can invest directly in foreign banks, and since 1970, U.S. bank holding companies have been permitted to invest in foreign companies.

Offshore Banking Centers

A significant portion of the external banking activity takes place through offshore banking centers. An **offshore banking center** is a country whose banking system is organized to permit external accounts beyond the normal economic activity of the country. The International Monetary Fund recognizes the Bahamas, Bahrain, the Cayman Islands, Hong Kong, Sint Maarten, Panama, and Singapore as major offshore banking centers.

---

[2]See Goldberg and Grosse (1994).

Offshore banks operate as branches or subsidiaries of the parent bank. The principal features that make a country attractive for establishing an offshore banking operation are virtually total freedom from host-country governmental banking regulations—for example, low reserve requirements and no deposit insurance, low taxes, a favorable time zone that facilitates international banking transactions, and, to a minor extent, strict banking secrecy laws. It should not be inferred that offshore host governments tolerate or encourage poor banking practices, as entry is usually confined to the largest and most reputable international banks.

The primary activities of offshore banks are to seek deposits and grant loans in currencies other than the currency of the host government. Offshore banking was spawned in the late 1960s when the Federal Reserve authorized U.S. banks to establish "shell" branches, which needs to be nothing more than a post office box in the host country. The actual banking transactions were conducted by the parent bank. The purpose was to allow smaller U.S. banks the opportunity to participate in the growing Eurodollar market without having to bear the expense of setting up operations in a major European money center. Today there are hundreds of offshore bank branches and subsidiaries, about one-third operated by U.S. parent banks.[3] Most offshore banking centers continue to serve as locations for shell branches, but Hong Kong and Singapore have developed into full service banking centers that now rival London, New York, and Tokyo.

International Banking Facilities

In 1981, the Federal Reserve authorized the establishment of **International Banking Facilities (IBF)**. An IBF is a separate set of asset and liability accounts that are segregated on the parent bank's books; it is not a unique physical or legal entity. Any U.S.-chartered depository institution, a U.S. branch or subsidiary of a foreign bank, or a U.S. office of an Edge Act bank may operate an IBF. IBFs operate as foreign banks in the United States. They are not subject to domestic reserve requirements on deposits, nor is FDIC insurance required on deposits. IBFs seek deposits from non-U.S. citizens and can make loans only to foreigners. All nonbank deposits must be nonnegotiable time deposits with a maturity of at least two business days and be of a size of at least $100,000.

IBFs were established largely as a result of the success of offshore banking. The Federal Reserve desired to return a large share of the deposit and loan business of U.S. branches and subsidiaries to the United States. IBFs have been successful in capturing a large portion of the Eurodollar business that was previously handled offshore. However, offshore banking will never be completely eliminated because IBFs are restricted from lending to U.S. citizens, while offshore banks are not.

Exhibit 11.2 summarizes the organizational structure and characteristics of international banking offices from the perspective of the United States.

Capital Adequacy Standards

A concern of bank regulators worldwide and of bank depositors is the safety of bank deposits. **Bank capital adequacy** refers to the amount of equity capital and other securities a bank holds as reserves against risky assets to reduce the probability of a bank failure. In a 1988 agreement known as the **Basel Accord**, after the Swiss city in which it is headquartered, the Bank for International Settlements (BIS) established a framework for measuring bank capital adequacy for banks in the Group of Ten (G-10) countries and Luxembourg. The BIS is the central bank for clearing international transactions between national central banks, and also serves as a facilitator in reaching international banking agreements among its members.

---

[3]See Chapter 10 of Hultman (1990) for an excellent discussion of the development of offshore banking and international banking facilities.

EXHIBIT 11.2		Organizational Structure of International Banking Offices from the U.S. Perspective				
Type of Bank	Physical Location	Accept Foreign Deposits	Make Loans to Foreigners	Subject to Fed Reserve Requirements	FDIC Insured Deposits	Separate Legal Equity from Parent
Domestic bank	U.S.	No	No	Yes	Yes	No
Correspondent bank	Foreign	N/A	N/A	No	No	N/A
Representative office	Foreign	No	No	Yes	Yes	No
Foreign branch	Foreign	Yes	Yes	No	No	No
Subsidiary bank	Foreign	Yes	Yes	No	No	Yes
Affiliate bank	Foreign	Yes	Yes	No	No	Yes
Edge Act bank	U.S.	Yes	Yes	No	No	Yes
Offshore banking center	Technically Foreign	Yes	Yes	No	No	No
International banking facility	U.S.	Yes	Yes	No	No	No

www.bis.org

This is the official website of the Bank for International Settlements. It is quite extensive. One can download many papers on international bank policies and reports containing statistics on international banks, capital markets, and derivative securities markets. There is also a link to the websites of most central banks in the world.

The Basel Accord called for a minimum bank capital adequacy ratio of 8 percent of risk-weighted assets for internationally active banks. The accord divides bank capital into two categories: Tier I Core capital, which consists of shareholder equity and retained earnings, and Tier II Supplemental capital, which consists of internationally recognized nonequity items such as preferred stock and subordinated bonds. Supplemental capital could count for no more than 50 percent of total bank capital, or no more than 4 percent of risk-weighted assets. In determining risk-weighted assets, four categories of risky assets are each weighted differently. More risky assets receive a higher weight. Government obligations are weighted at zero percent, short-term interbank assets are weighted at 20 percent, residential mortgages at 50 percent, and other assets at 100 percent. Thus, a bank with $100 million in each of the four asset categories would have the equivalent of $170 million in risk-weighted assets. It would need to maintain $13.6 million in capital against these investments, of which no more than one-half, or $6.8 million, could be Tier II capital.

The 1988 Basel Capital Accord primarily addressed banking in the context of deposit gathering and lending. Thus, its focus was on *credit* risk. The accord was widely adopted throughout the world by national bank regulators. Nevertheless, it had its problems and its critics. One major criticism concerned the arbitrary nature in which the accord was implemented. The 8 percent minimum capital requirement assigned to risk-weighted assets was unchanging regardless of whether the degree of credit risk fluctuated throughout the business cycle, regardless of whether the bank was located in a developed or a developing country, and regardless of the types of risks in which banks were engaged. Bank trading in equity, interest rate, and exchange rate derivative products escalated throughout the 1990s. Many of these products were not even in existence when the Basel Accord was drafted. Consequently, even if the accord was satisfactory in safeguarding bank depositors from traditional credit risks, the capital adequacy requirements were not sufficient to safeguard against the *market* risk from derivatives trading. For example, Barings Bank, which collapsed in 1995 due in part to the activities of a rogue derivatives trader, was considered to be a safe bank by the Basel capital adequacy standards.

Given the shortcomings of the 1988 accord, the Basel Committee concluded in the early 1990s that an updated capital accord was needed. A 1996 amendment, which went into effect in 1998, required commercial banks engaging in significant trading activity to set aside additional capital under the 8 percent rule to cover the market risks inherent in their trading accounts. A new Tier III capital composed of short-term subordinated debt could be used to satisfy the capital requirement on market risk. By this time additional shortcomings of the original accord were becoming evident.

Operational risk, which includes such matters as computer failure, poor documentation, and fraud, was becoming evident as a significant risk. This expanded view of risk reflects the type of business in which banks now engage and the business environment in which banks operate. In 1999, the Basel Committee proposed a new capital accord. In June 2004, after an extensive consultative process, the new capital adequacy framework commonly referred to as Basel II was endorsed by central bank governors and bank supervisors in the G-10 countries. The committee issued an updated version in November 2005, which is currently available for implementation.

Basel II is based on three mutually reinforcing pillars: minimum capital requirements, a supervisory review process, and the effective use of market discipline. The new framework sets out the details for adopting more risk-sensitive minimum capital requirements that are extended up to the holding company level of diversified bank groups. With respect to the first pillar, bank capital is defined as per the 1988 accord, but the minimum 8 percent capital ratio is calculated on the sum of the bank's credit, market, and operational risks. In determining adequate capital, the new framework provides a range of options open to banks for valuing credit risk and operational risk. Banks are encouraged to move along the spectrum of approaches as they develop more sophisticated risk measurement systems. Market risk is determined by marking-to-market the value of the bank's trading account, or if that is not possible, marking to a model determined value.

The second pillar is designed to ensure that each bank has a sound internal process in place to properly assess the adequacy of its capital based on a thorough evaluation of its risks. For example, banks are required to conduct meaningful stress tests designed to estimate the extent to which capital requirements could increase in an adverse economic scenario. Banks and supervisors are to use the results of these tests to ensure that banks hold sufficient capital. The third pillar is designed to complement the other two. It is believed that public disclosure of key information will bring greater market discipline to bear on banks and supervisors to better manage risk and improve bank stability.[4]

Throughout the global financial crisis that began in mid-2007, many banks struggled to maintain adequate liquidity.[5] The crisis illustrated how quickly and severely liquidity can crystallize and certain sources of funding can evaporate, compounding concern related to the valuation of assets and capital adequacy. Prior to the onset of the financial crisis, banks built up significant exposures to off-balance-sheet market risks that were not adequately reflected in the capital requirements of Basel II. A number of banking organizations have experienced large losses, most of which were sustained in the banks' trading accounts. These losses have not arisen from actual defaults, but rather from credit agency downgrades, widening credit spreads, and the loss of liquidity.

In July 2009, the Basel Committee on Banking Supervision finalized a package of proposed enhancements to Basel II to strengthen the regulation and supervision of internationally active banks. This package of enhancements is referred to as Basel 2.5. The proposed enhancement to Pillar 1 calls for increasing the minimum capital requirement to cover illiquid credit products in the trading account; complex securitizations, such as asset-backed securities and collateralized debt obligations; and exposures to off-balance-sheet vehicles.[6] Pillar 2 proposals call for more rigorous supervision and risk management; more specifically, the proposals call for clear expectations for the board of directors and senior management to understand firm-wide risk exposure. Pillar 3 proposals call for enhanced disclosure requirements for securitizations and off-balance-sheet vehicles to allow market participants to better assess the firm's risk exposure. Basel 2.5 was due to be implemented by year-end 2011 and at this time has been adopted by most Basel Committee member jurisdictions.

---

[4]The information in this section is from *International Convergence of Capital Measurement and Capital Standards: A Revised Framework*, Bank for International Settlements, June 2004.

[5]See the section titled "Global Financial Crisis" for an in-depth discussion of the crisis.

[6]See Appendix 11B for an explanation of asset-backed securities and collateralized debt obligations.

Building on Basel 2.5, the Basel Committee on September 12, 2010 announced a third accord, Basel III, which is designed to substantially strengthen the regulatory capital framework and increase the quality of bank capital. Under the committee's reforms, Tier I capital is redefined to include only common equity and retained earnings (i.e., eliminating non-redeemable, non-cumulative preferred stock). Further, Tier I capital is to be increased from 4 to 6 percent. Additionally, the committee introduced a 2.5 percent capital buffer that can be drawn down in periods of financial stress. The 2.5 percent buffer brings Tier I capital to 8.5 percent and total capital to 10.5. These reforms are to be fully in place by January 1, 2019. At the time of this writing, implementation has largely been completed in the Basel Committee member jurisdictions.

International Money Market

Eurocurrency Market

The core of the international money market is the Eurocurrency market. A **Eurocurrency** is a *time* deposit of money in an international bank located in a country different from the country that issued the currency. For example, Eurodollars are deposits of U.S. dollars in banks located outside of the United States, Eurosterling are deposits of British pound sterling in banks outside of the United Kingdom, and Euroyen are deposits of Japanese yen in banks outside of Japan. The prefix *Euro* is somewhat of a misnomer, since the bank in which the deposit is made does not have to be located in Europe. The depository bank could be located in Europe, the Caribbean, or Asia. Indeed, as we saw in the previous section, Eurodollar deposits can be made in offshore shell branches or IBFs, where the physical dollar deposits are actually with the U.S. parent bank. An "Asian dollar" market exists, with headquarters in Singapore, but it can be viewed as a major division of the Eurocurrency market.

The origin of the Eurocurrency market can be traced back to the 1950s and early 1960s, when the former Soviet Union and Soviet-bloc countries sold gold and commodities to raise hard currency. Because of anti-Soviet sentiment, these Communist countries were afraid of depositing their U.S. dollars in U.S. banks for fear that the deposits could be frozen or taken. Instead they deposited their dollars in a French bank whose telex address was EURO-BANK. Since that time, dollar deposits outside the United States have been called Eurodollars and banks accepting Eurocurrency deposits have been called **Eurobanks**.[7]

The Eurocurrency market is an *external* banking system that runs parallel to the *domestic* banking system of the country that issued the currency. Both banking systems seek deposits and make loans to customers from the deposited funds. In the United States, banks are subject to the Federal Reserve Regulation D, specifying reserve requirements on bank time deposits. Additionally, U.S. banks must pay FDIC insurance premiums on deposited funds. Eurodollar deposits, on the other hand, are not subject to these arbitrary reserve requirements or deposit insurance; hence the cost of operations is less. Because of the reduced cost structure, the Eurocurrency market, and in particular the Eurodollar market, has grown spectacularly since its inception.

The Eurocurrency market operates at the *interbank* and/or *wholesale* level. The majority of Eurocurrency transactions are interbank transactions, representing sums of $1,000,000 or more. Eurobanks with surplus funds and no retail customers to lend to will lend to Eurobanks that have borrowers but need loanable funds. The rate charged by banks with excess funds is referred to as the *interbank offered rate*; they will accept interbank deposits at the *interbank bid rate*. The spread is generally 10–12 basis points for most major Eurocurrencies; however, it has been somewhat higher during the ongoing global economic crisis. Rates on Eurocurrency deposits are quoted for maturities

---

[7]See Rivera-Batiz and Rivera-Batiz (1994) for an account of the historical origin of the Eurocurrency market.

EXHIBIT 11.3	Eurocurrency Interest Rate Quotations: May 20, 2016					
	Overnight	One Week	One Month	Three Months	Six Months	One Year
Euro	−0.45 to −0.35	−0.39 to −0.31	−0.47 to −0.21	−0.31 to −0.21	−0.22 to −0.12	−0.09 to 0.01
Danish Krone	−1.00 to 0.00	−0.51 to −0.26	−0.48 to −0.23	−0.46 to −0.21	−0.41 to −0.16	−0.32 to −0.07
Sterling	0.30 to 0.45	0.45 to 0.55	0.46 to 0.56	0.60 to 0.70	0.72 to 0.82	1.00 to 1.03
Swiss Franc	−0.85 to −0.77	−0.90 to −0.65	−0.89 to −0.64	−0.85 to −0.60	−0.80 to −0.55	−0.66 to −0.41
Canadian Dollar	0.45 to 0.55	0.56 to 0.76	0.58 to 0.68	0.76 to 0.86	0.94 to 1.04	1.21 to 1.31
U.S. Dollar	0.38 to 0.39	0.52 to 0.62	0.45 to 0.49	0.44 to 0.67	1.13 to 1.20	1.31 to 1.51
Japanese Yen	−0.30 to 0.10	−0.30 to −0.10	−0.28 to −0.20	−0.22 to −0.02	−0.24 to −0.04	−0.19 to 0.12
Singapore Dollar	0.03 to 0.06	0.63 to 0.75	0.63 to 0.75	0.88 to 1.00	1.13 to 1.25	1.25 to 1.38

Source: Collected from Bloomberg, May 20, 2016.

ranging from one day to one year; however, more standard maturities are for 1, 2, 3, 6, 9, and 12 months. Exhibit 11.3 shows sample Eurocurrency interest rates. Appendix 11A illustrates the creation of the Eurocurrency.

London has historically been, and remains, the major Eurocurrency financial center. These days, most people have heard of the **London Interbank Offered Rate (LIBOR)**, the reference rate in London for Eurocurrency deposits. To be clear, there is a LIBOR for Eurodollars, Euro–Canadian dollars, Euroyen, and even euros. In other financial centers, other reference rates are used. For example, *SIBOR* is the Singapore Interbank Offered Rate, and *TIBOR* is the Tokyo Interbank Offered Rate. Obviously, competition forces the various interbank rates for a particular Eurocurrency to be close to one another.

The advent of the common euro currency on January 1, 1999, among the 11 countries of the European Union making up the Economic and Monetary Union created a need for a new interbank offered rate designation. It also creates some confusion as to whether one is referring to the common euro currency or another Eurocurrency, such as Eurodollars. Because of this, it is starting to become common practice to refer to *international* currencies instead of Eurocurrencies and *prime* banks instead of Eurobanks. **Euro Interbank Offered Rate (EURIBOR)** is the rate at which interbank deposits of the euro are offered by one prime bank to another in the euro zone.

In the wholesale money market, Eurobanks accept Eurocurrency fixed time deposits and issue **negotiable certificates of deposit (NCDs)**. In fact, these are the preferable ways for Eurobanks to raise loanable funds, as the deposits tend to be for a lengthier period and the acquiring rate is often slightly less than the interbank rate. Denominations are at least $500,000, but sizes of $1,000,000 or larger are more typical.

Exhibit 11.4 shows the year-end values of international bank external liabilities (Eurodeposits and other Euro liabilities) in billions of U.S. dollars for the years 2011–2015. The 2015 column shows that total external liabilities were $21,078.7 billion and that interbank liabilities accounted for $13,956.1 billion of this amount, whereas nonbank deposits were $7,122.6 billion. The 2015 statistics point to a slowdown in international banking activity that began early that year. The major currencies denominating these were the U.S. dollar, the euro, and the British pound sterling.

www.euribor.org

This website provides a discussion of EURIBOR and related rates.

EXHIBIT 11.4		2011	2012	2013	2014	2015
International Bank External Liabilities (at year-end in billions of U.S. dollars)	*Type Liability*					
	To banks	18,720.1	17,494.4	17,822.4	17,444.9	13,956.1
	To nonbanks	7,182.8	7,630.9	8,051.8	7,736.1	7,122.6
	Total	25,902.9	25,125.3	25,874.3	25,181.1	21,078.7

Source: Compiled from various issues of *International Banking and Financial Market Developments*, Bank for International Settlements.

Approximately 90 percent of wholesale Eurobank external liabilities come from fixed time deposits, the remainder from NCDs. There is an interest penalty for the early withdrawal of funds from a fixed time deposit. NCDs, on the other hand, being negotiable, can be sold in the secondary market if the depositor suddenly needs his funds prior to scheduled maturity. The NCD market began in 1967 in London for Eurodollars. NCDs for currencies other than the U.S. dollar are offered by banks in London and in other financial centers, but the secondary market for nondollar NCDs is not very liquid.

ICE LIBOR

www.theice.com/iba/libor

This is the website of ICE Benchmark Administration, the administrator of LIBOR. Historic LIBOR rates can be obtained from this site.

At 11:00 A.M. every trading day in London, the ICE Benchmark Administration (IBA), an independently capitalized unit of the Intercontinental Exchange (ICE), *fixes* the London Interbank Offered Rate (LIBOR) for five Eurocurrencies (USD, GBP, EUR, CHF, JPY) for seven different maturities. ICE LIBOR serves as the primary daily benchmark used by banks, securities houses, and investors to set payments on at least $350 trillion in the international money, derivatives, and capital markets around the world.[8] The IBA fixes LIBOR for each Eurocurrency it tracks by averaging the middle two quartiles of rates at which a panel of Eurobanks active in the London Eurocurrency market believes they can borrow money from other London prime banks. Hence, the panel banks are estimating their LIBID (London Interbank Bid Rate), or the lending banks' LIBOR. A small variation of the daily fixing represents a substantial amount of money. For example, one basis point of the $350 trillion-worth of financial instruments fixed by ICE LIBOR represents $35 billion on an annual basis. Consequently, a small manipulation of LIBOR could have serious consequences and implications. The IBA took over operation of LIBOR in 2014 from NYSE Euronext after ICE acquired NYSE Euronext in November 2013. In turn, NYSE Euronext had recently taken over the administration of LIBOR from the British Bankers Association (BBA) after scandals during its administration.

The International Finance in Practice box "The Rotten Heart of Finance" discusses two LIBOR scandals that have come to light in recent years. One has to do with BBA LIBOR panel banks understating the rates at which they could borrow during the depths of Global Financial Crisis (see the section later in this chapter) so as not to signal to the market any financial weakness implied by the true rate at which they would have to pay to borrow Eurocurrency. During this time Eurobanks did not trust the financial strength of one another and were afraid of what unknown toxic assets may be on a counterparty's balance sheet. As a result, little trading actually took place in the Eurocurrency market. The second scandal has to do with the recently discovered massive collusion among panel banks to manipulate the daily rate fixing in their favor in order to earn excess profit from their financial positions indexed to BBA LIBOR. Barclays was the first international bank to admit wrongdoing and to be penalized in this ongoing scandal. In June 2012, it paid a fine of £250 ($450) million and in July its chairman and CEO was dismissed by the board. In all, probes into rate rigging by bank regulators have ensnarled at least 18 of the world's largest financial institutions and dozens of bank traders and brokers. In total, U.K. and U.S. regulators have imposed more than $6 billion in penalties on banks, and one trader was sentenced to a 14-year prison term while others have yet to learn their fates.

Eurocredits

Eurocredits are short- to medium-term loans of Eurocurrency extended by Eurobanks to corporations, sovereign governments, nonprime banks, or international organizations. The loans are denominated in currencies other than the home currency of the Eurobank. Because these loans are frequently too large for a single bank to handle, Eurobanks will band together to form a bank lending **syndicate** to share the risk.

---

[8]Similarly, the Japanese Bankers Association fixes the JBA TIBOR, the Association of Banks in Singapore fixes ABS SIBOR for Eurodollars, and the European Banking Federation fixes EBF EURIBOR.

The credit risk on these loans is greater than on loans to other banks in the interbank market. Thus, the interest rate on Eurocredits must compensate the bank, or banking syndicate, for the added credit risk. On Eurocredits originating in London the base lending rate is LIBOR. The lending rate on these credits is stated as LIBOR +X percent, where X is the lending margin charged depending upon the creditworthiness of the borrower. Additionally, rollover pricing was created on Eurocredits so that Eurobanks do not end up paying more on Eurocurrency time deposits than they earn from the loans. Thus, a Eurocredit may be viewed as a series of shorter-term loans, where at the end of each time period (generally three or six months), the loan is rolled over and the base lending rate is repriced to current LIBOR over the next time interval of the loan.

Exhibit 11.5 shows the relationship among the various interest rates we have discussed in this section. The numbers come from Exhibit 11.3. On May 20, 2016, U.S. domestic banks were paying 0.875 percent for six-month NCDs and the prime lending rate, the base rate charged the bank's most creditworthy corporate clients, was 3.50 percent. This appears to represent a spread of 2.625 percent for the bank to cover operating costs and earn a profit. By comparison, Eurobanks will accept six-month Eurodollar time deposits, say, Eurodollar NCDs, at a LIBID rate of 1.13 percent. The rate charged for Eurodollar credits is LIBOR + X percent, where any lending margin less than 2.30 percent appears to make the Eurodollar loan more attractive than the prime rate loan. Since lending margins typically fall in the range of 0.25 percent to 3 percent, with the median rate being 0.50 percent to 1.50 percent, the exhibit shows the narrow borrowing-lending spreads of Eurobankers in the Eurodollar credit market. This analysis seems to suggest that borrowers can obtain funds somewhat more cheaply in the Eurodollar market. However, international competition in recent years has forced U.S. commercial banks to lend domestically at rates below prime.

EXAMPLE | 11.1: Rollover Pricing of a Eurocredit

Teltrex International can borrow $3,000,000 at LIBOR plus a lending margin of 0.75 percent per annum on a three-month rollover basis from Barclays in London. Suppose that three-month LIBOR is currently 5.53 percent. Further suppose that over the second three-month interval LIBOR falls to 5.12 percent. How much will Teltrex pay in interest to Barclays over the six-month period for the Eurodollar loan?

Solution: $3,000,000 × (.0553 + .0075)/4 + $3,000,000 ×
(.0512 + .0075)/4 = $47,100 + $44,025
= $91,125

EXHIBIT 11.5

Comparison of U.S. Lending and Borrowing Rates with Eurodollar Rates on May 20, 2016

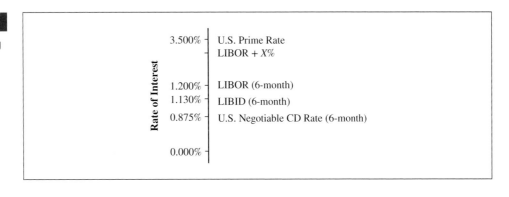

The Rotten Heart of Finance

The most memorable incidents in earth-changing events are sometimes the most banal. In the rapidly spreading scandal of LIBOR (the London inter-bank offered rate) it is the very every-dayness with which bank traders set about manipulating the most important figure in finance. They joked, or offered small favours. "Coffees will be coming your way," promised one trader in exchange for a fiddled number. "Dude. I owe you big time!. . . I'm opening a bottle of Bollinger," wrote another. One trader posted diary notes to himself so that he wouldn't forget to fiddle the numbers the next week. "Ask for High 6M Fix," he entered in his calendar, as he might have put "Buy milk".

What may still seem to many to be a parochial affair involving Barclays, a 300-year-old British bank, rigging an obscure number, is beginning to assume global significance. The number that the traders were toying with determines the prices that people and corporations around the world pay for loans or receive for their savings. It is used as a benchmark to set payments on about $800 trillion-worth of financial instruments, ranging from complex interest-rate derivatives to simple mortgages. The number determines the global flow of billions of dollars each year. Yet it turns out to have been flawed.

Over the past week damning evidence has emerged, in documents detailing a settlement between Barclays and regulators in America and Britain, that employees at the bank and at several other unnamed banks tried to rig the number time and again over a period of at least five years. And worse is likely to emerge. Investigations by regulators in several countries, including Canada, America, Japan, the EU, Switzerland and Britain, are looking into allegations that LIBOR and similar rates were rigged by large numbers of banks. Corporations and lawyers, too, are examining whether they can sue Barclays or other banks for harm they have suffered. That could cost the banking industry tens of billions of dollars. "This is the banking industry's tobacco moment," says the chief executive of a multinational bank, referring to the lawsuits and settlements that cost America's tobacco industry more than $200 billion in 1998. "It's that big," he says.

As many as 20 big banks have been named in various investigations or lawsuits alleging that LIBOR was rigged. The scandal also corrodes further what little remains of public trust in banks and those who run them.

Like many of the City's ways, LIBOR is something of an anachronism, a throwback to a time when many bankers within the Square Mile knew one another and when trust was more important than contract. For LIBOR, a borrowing rate is set daily by a panel of banks for ten currencies and for 15 maturities. The most important of these, three-month dollar LIBOR, is supposed to indicate what a bank would pay to borrow dollars for three months from other banks at 11AM on the day it is set. The dollar rate is fixed each day by taking estimates from a panel, currently comprising 18 banks, of what they think they would have to pay to borrow if they needed money. The top four and bottom four estimates are then discarded, and LIBOR is the average of those left. The submissions of all the participants are published, along with each day's LIBOR fix.

In theory, LIBOR is supposed to be a pretty honest number because it is assumed, for a start, that banks play by the rules and give truthful estimates. The market is also sufficiently small that most banks are presumed to know what the others are doing. In reality, the system is rotten. First, it is based on banks' estimates, rather than the actual prices at which banks have lent to or borrowed from one another. "There is no reporting of transactions, no one really knows what's going on in the market," says a former senior trader closely involved in setting LIBOR at a large bank. "You have this vast overhang of financial instruments that hang their own fixes off a rate that doesn't actually exist."

Forward Rate Agreements

A major risk Eurobanks face in accepting Eurodeposits and in extending Eurocredits is interest rate risk resulting from a mismatch in the maturities of the deposits and credits. For example, if deposit maturities are longer than credit maturities, and interest rates fall, the credit rates will be adjusted downward while the bank is still paying a higher rate on deposits. Conversely, if deposit maturities are shorter than credit maturities, and interest rates rise, deposit rates will be adjusted upward while the bank is still receiving a lower rate on credits. Only when deposit and credit maturities are perfectly matched will the rollover feature of Eurocredits allow the bank to earn the desired deposit-loan rate spread.

A **forward rate agreement (FRA)** is an interbank contract that allows the Euro-bank to hedge the interest rate risk in mismatched deposits and credits. The size of the market is enormous. In December 2015, the notional value of FRAs outstanding was $58,326 billion. An FRA involves two parties, a buyer and a seller, where:

1. the buyer agrees to pay the seller the increased interest cost on a notional amount if interest rates fall below an agreement rate, or

2. the seller agrees to pay the buyer the increased interest cost if interest rates increase above the agreement rate.

A second problem is that those involved in setting the rates have often had every incentive to lie, since their banks stood to profit or lose money depending on the level at which LIBOR was set each day. Worse still, transparency in the mechanism of setting rates may well have exacerbated the tendency to lie, rather than suppressed it. Banks that were weak would not have wanted to signal that fact widely in markets by submitting honest estimates of the high price they would have to pay to borrow, if they could borrow at all.

In the case of Barclays, two very different sorts of rate fiddling have emerged. The first sort, and the one that has raised the most ire, involved groups of derivatives traders at Barclays and several other unnamed banks trying to influence the final LIBOR fixing to increase profits (or reduce losses) on their derivative exposures. The sums involved might have been huge. Barclays was a leading trader of these sorts of derivatives, and even relatively small moves in the final value of LIBOR could have resulted in daily profits or losses worth millions of dollars. In 2007, for instance, the loss (or gain) that Barclays stood to make from normal moves in interest rates over any given day was £20m ($40m at the time). In settlements with the Financial Services Authority (FSA) in Britain and America's Department of Justice, Barclays accepted that its traders had manipulated rates on hundreds of occasions.

Galling as the revelations are of traders trying to manipulate rates for personal gain, the actual harm done would probably have paled in comparison with the subsequent misconduct of the banks. Traders acting at one bank, or even with the clubby co-operation of counterparts at rival banks, would have been able to move the final LIBOR rate by only one or two hundredths of a percentage point (or one to two basis points). For the decade or so before the financial crisis in 2007, LIBOR traded in a relatively tight band with alternative market measures of funding costs. Moreover, this was a period in which banks and the global economy were awash with money, and borrowing costs for banks and companies were low.

Yet a second sort of LIBOR-rigging has also emerged in the Barclays settlement. Barclays and, apparently, many other banks submitted dishonestly low estimates of bank borrowing costs over at least two years, including during the depths of the financial crisis. In terms of the scale of manipulation, this appears to have been far more egregious—at least in terms of the numbers. Almost all the banks in the LIBOR panels were submitting rates that may have been 30–40 basis points too low on average. That could create the biggest liabilities for the banks involved.

Regulators around the world have woken up, however belatedly, to the possibility that these vital markets may have been rigged by a large number of banks. The list of institutions that have said they are either co-operating with investigations or being questioned includes many of the world's biggest banks. Among those that have disclosed their involvement are Citigroup, Deutsche Bank, HSBC, JPMorgan Chase, RBS and UBS.

Last October, European Commission officials raided the offices of banks and other companies involved in trading derivatives based on EURIBOR (the euro inter-bank offered rate). The Swiss competition commission launched an investigation in February, prompted by an "application for leniency" by UBS, into possible adverse effects on Swiss clients and companies of alleged manipulation of LIBOR and TIBOR (the Tokyo inter-bank offered rate) by the two Swiss and ten other international banks and "other financial intermediaries".

Two big changes are needed. The first is to base the rate on actual lending data where possible. Some markets are thinly traded, though, and so some hypothetical or expected rates may need to be used to create a complete set of benchmarks. So a second big change is needed. Because banks have an incentive to influence LIBOR, a new system needs to explicitly promote truth-telling and reduce the possibilities for co-ordination of quotes. Adding a calendar note to "Fix LIBOR" just won't do.

Source: Excerpted from *The Economist*, July 7, 2012, pp. 25–27.

Exhibit 11.6 graphs the payoff profile of an FRA. *SR* denotes the settlement rate and *AR* denotes the agreement rate.

FRAs are structured to capture the maturity mismatch in standard-length Eurodeposits and credits. For example, the FRA might be on a six-month interest rate for a six-month period beginning three months from today and ending nine months from today; this would be a "three against nine" FRA. The following time line depicts this FRA example.

| Start | Agreement Period (3 Months) | Cash Settlement | FRA Period (6 Months) | End |

The payment amount under an FRA is calculated as the absolute value of:

$$\frac{\text{Notional Amount} \times (SR - AR) \times days/360}{1 + (SR \times days/360)}$$

where *days* denotes the length of the FRA period.

EXHIBIT 11.6

Forward Rate Agreement Payoff Profile

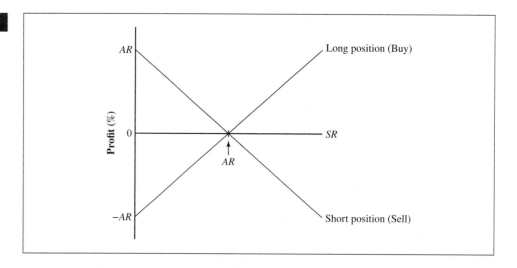

EXAMPLE | 11.2: Three against Six Forward Rate Agreement

As an example, consider a bank that has made a three-month Eurodollar loan of $3,000,000 against an offsetting six-month Eurodollar deposit. The bank's concern is that three-month LIBOR will fall below expectations and the Eurocredit is rolled over at the new lower base rate, making the six-month deposit unprofitable.[9] To protect itself, the bank could sell a $3,000,000 "three against six" FRA. The FRA will be priced such that the agreement rate is the expected three-month dollar LIBOR in three months.

Assume *AR* is 6 percent and the actual number of days in the three-month FRA period is 91. Thus, the bank expects to receive $45,500 (= $3,000,000 × .06 × 91/360) as the base amount of interest when the Eurodollar loan is rolled over for a second three-month period. If *SR* (i.e., three-month market LIBOR) is 5⅛ percent, the bank will receive only $38,864.58 in base interest, or a shortfall of $6,635.42. Since *SR* is less than *AR*, the bank will profit from the FRA it sold. It will receive from the buyer in three months a cash settlement at the beginning of the 91-day FRA period equaling the present value of the *absolute* value of [$3,000,000 × (.05125 − .06) × 91/360] = $6,635.42. This *absolute* present value is:

$$\frac{\$3{,}000{,}000 \times (.05125 - .06) \times 91/360}{1 + (.05125 \times 91/360)}$$

$$= \frac{\$6{,}635.42}{1.01295}$$

$$= \$6{,}550.59$$

The sum, $6,550.59, equals the present value as of the *beginning* of the 91-day FRA period of the shortfall of $6,635.42 from the expected Eurodollar loan proceeds that are needed to meet the interest on the Eurodollar deposit. Had *SR* been greater than *AR*, the bank would have paid the buyer the present value of the excess amount of interest above what was expected from rolling over the Eurodollar credit. In this event, the bank would have effectively received the agreement rate on its three-month Eurodollar loan, which would have made the loan a profitable transaction.

---

[9]Consistent with the Unbiased Expectations Hypothesis (UEH), the agreement rate *AR* is the expected rate at the beginning of the FRA period. For example, in a "three against six" FRA, the *AR* can be calculated as the annualized forward rate that ties together current three-month LIBOR and six-month LIBOR:

$$([1 + (6 \text{ mth LIBOR})(T_2/360)]/[1 + (3 \text{ mth LIBOR})(T_1/360)] - 1) \times 360/(T_2 - T_1) = f = AR,$$

where T_2 and T_1 are, respectively, the actual number of days to maturity of the six-month and three-month Eurocurrency periods and f is the annualized forward rate. See Chapter 15 of Bodie, Kane, and Marcus (2011) for an in-depth discussion of the UEH.

EXHIBIT 11.7

Size of the Euronote Market
(in billions of U.S. dollars)

Instrument	2011	2012	2013	2014	2015 (1Q)
Euronotes	317.2	338.1	385.1	361.8	357.6
Eurocommercial Paper	578.4	502.4	484.8	521.6	530.3
Total	895.7	840.5	869.9	883.4	887.9

Source: Compiled from various issues of *International Banking and Financial Market Developments*, Bank for International Settlements.

FRAs can be used for speculative purposes also. If one believes rates will be less than the AR, the sale of an FRA is the suitable position. In contrast, the purchase of an FRA is the suitable position if one believes rates will be greater than the AR.

Euronotes

Euronotes are short-term notes underwritten by a group of international investment or commercial banks called a "facility." A client-borrower makes an agreement with a facility to issue Euronotes in its own name for a period of time, generally 3 to 10 years. Euronotes are sold at a discount from face value and pay back the full face value at maturity. Euronotes typically have maturities from three to six months. Borrowers find Euronotes attractive because the interest expense is usually slightly less—typically LIBOR plus 1/8 percent—in comparison to syndicated Eurobank loans. The banks find them attractive to issue because they earn a small fee from the underwriting or supply the funds and earn the interest return.

Eurocommercial Paper

Eurocommercial paper, like domestic commercial paper, is an unsecured short-term promissory note issued by a corporation or a bank and placed directly with the investment public through a dealer. Like Euronotes, Eurocommercial paper is sold at a discount from face value. Maturities typically range from one to six months.

The vast majority of Eurocommercial paper is denominated in the euro and the U.S. dollar. There are, however, a number of differences between the U.S. and Eurocommercial paper markets. The maturity of Eurocommercial paper tends to be about twice as long as U.S. commercial paper. For this reason, the secondary market is more active than for U.S. paper. Additionally, Eurocommercial paper issuers tend to be of much lower quality than their U.S. counterparts; consequently, yields tend to be higher.[10]

Exhibit 11.7 shows the value of the Euronote and Eurocommercial paper market in billions of U.S. dollars from year-end 2011 through the first quarter of 2015.

Eurodollar Interest Rate Futures Contracts

In Chapter 7, we focused on futures contracts on foreign exchange. Nevertheless, future contracts are traded on many different underlying assets. One particularly important contract is the Eurodollar interest rate futures traded on the CME Group of exchanges and the Singapore Exchange. The Eurodollar contract has become the most widely used futures contract for hedging short-term U.S. dollar interest rate risk. Other Eurocurrency futures contracts that trade are the Euroyen, EuroSwiss, and the EURIBOR contract, which began trading after the introduction of the euro.

The CME Eurodollar futures contract is written on a hypothetical $1,000,000 90-day deposit of Eurodollars. The contract trades in the March, June, September, and December cycle and the four nearest noncycle months. The hypothetical delivery date is the third Wednesday of the delivery month. The last day of trading is two business days prior to the delivery date. The contract is a cash settlement contract. That is, the delivery of a $1,000,000 Eurodollar deposit is not actually made or received. Instead, final settlement is made through realizing profits or losses in the performance bond account on the delivery date based on the final settlement price on the last day

www.sgx.com

This is the website of the Singapore Exchange. It provides detailed information about the securities and derivatives traded on it.

---

[10]See Dufey and Giddy (1994) for a list of the differences between the U.S. and Eurocommercial paper markets.

EXHIBIT 11.8

CME Group Eurodollar
Futures Contract
Quotations

	Settle	Change	Open Interest	Volume
Eurodollar (CME)-$1,000,000; pts of 100%				
Jun 16	99.350	−.010	1,189,501	111,055
Sep	99.240	−.020	1,128,870	98,386
Dec	99.145	−.025	1,435,860	122,756
Mar 17	99.080	−.035	903,812	83,536
Jun	99.020	−.040	904,486	76,193
Sep	98.960	−.045	726,280	73,261
Dec	98.895	−.045	1,054,382	114,417
Mar 18	98.845	−.050	505,537	53,941
Jun	98.790	−.050	454,557	45,773
Sep	98.735	−.055	370,422	40,984
Dec	98.675	−.055	522,255	52,614
Mar 19	98.630	−.055	303,790	28,733
Jun	98.580	−.055	264,054	19,403
Sep	98.525	−.055	184,347	15,927
Dec	98.465	−.055	210,475	14,977
Mar 20	98.415	−.055	118,741	14,029
Jun	98.355	−.055	62,903	10,952
Sep	98.300	−.055	58,922	10,787
Dec	98.240	−.055	80,188	9,435
Mar 21	98.190	−.050	42,073	7,027
Jun	98.130	−.050	33,253	526
Sep	98.075	−.050	18,157	452
Dec	98.020	−.050	14,362	773
Mar 22	97.975	−.050	7,901	366
Jun	97,930	−.045	5,470	34
Sep	97.890	−.040	5,358	59

Source: Closing Values on Monday, May 16, 2016, from Bloomberg.

of trading. Exhibit 11.8 presents an example of CME Eurodollar futures quotations. Contracts trade out 10 years into the future.

EXAMPLE | 11.3: Reading Eurodollar Futures Quotations

Eurodollar futures prices are stated as an index number of three-month LIBOR, calculated as: $F = 100 - \text{LIBOR}$. For example, from Exhibit 11.8 we see that the December 2016 contract (with hypothetical delivery on December 21, 2016) had a settlement price of 99.145 on Monday, May 16, 2016. The implied three-month LIBOR yield is thus 0.855 percent. The minimum price change is one-half basis point (bp). On $1,000,000 of face value, a one-basis-point change represents $100 on an annual basis. Since the contract is for a 90-day deposit, one-half basis point corresponds to a $12.50 price change.

EXAMPLE | 11.4: Eurodollar Futures Hedge

As an example of how this contract can be used to hedge interest rate risk, consider the treasurer of a MNC, who on Monday, May 16, 2016, learns that his firm expects to receive $20,000,000 in cash from a large sale of merchandise on December 18, 2016. The money will not be needed for a period of 90 days. Thus, the treasurer should invest the excess funds for this period in a money market instrument such as a Eurodollar deposit.

EXAMPLE | 11.4: continued

The treasurer notes that three-month LIBOR is currently 0.62760 percent. The implied three-month LIBOR rate in the December 2016 contract is higher at 0.855 percent. Additionally, the treasurer notes that the pattern of future expected three-month LIBOR rates implied by the pattern of Eurodollar futures prices suggests that three-month LIBOR is expected to increase through September 2022. The treasurer believes that a 90-day rate of return of 0.855 percent is a decent rate to "lock in," so he decides to hedge against lower three-month LIBOR in December 2016. By hedging, the treasurer is locking in a certain return of $42,750 (=$20,000,000 × .00855 × 90/360) for the 90-day period the MNC has $20,000,000 in excess funds.

To construct the hedge, the treasurer will need to buy, or take a long position, in Eurodollar futures contracts. At first it may seem counterintuitive that a long position is needed, but remember, a decrease in the implied three-month LIBOR yield causes the Eurodollar futures price to increase. To hedge the interest rate risk in a $20,000,000 deposit, the treasurer will need to buy 20 December 2016 contracts.

Assume that on the last day of trading in the December 2016 contract three-month LIBOR is 0.70 percent. The treasurer is indeed fortunate that he chose to hedge. At 0.70 percent, a 90-day Eurodollar deposit of $20,000,000 will generate only $35,000 of interest income, or $7,750 less than at a rate of 0.855 percent. In fact, the treasurer will have to deposit the excess funds at a rate of 0.70 percent. But the shortfall will be made up by profits from the long futures position. At a rate of 0.70 percent, the final settlement price on the December 2016 contract is 99.30 (=100 − 0.70). The profit earned on the futures position is calculated as: [99.30 − 99.145] × 100 bp × 2 × $12.50 × 20 contracts = $7,750. This is precisely the amount of the shortfall.

International Debt Crisis

Certain principles define sound banking behavior. "At least five of these principles—namely, avoid an undue concentration of loans to single activities, individuals, or groups; expand cautiously into unfamiliar activities; know your counterparty; control mismatches between assets and liabilities; and beware that your collateral is not vulnerable to the same shocks that weaken the borrower—remain as relevant today as in earlier times."[11] Nevertheless, violation of the first two of these principles by some of the largest international banks in the world was responsible for the **international debt crisis** (sometimes called the Third World debt crisis), which was caused by lending to the sovereign governments of some **less-developed countries (LDCs)**.

History

The international debt crisis began on August 20, 1982, when Mexico asked more than 100 U.S. and foreign banks to forgive its $68 billion in loans. Soon Brazil, Argentina, and more than 20 other developing countries announced similar problems in making the debt service on their bank loans. At the height of the crisis, Third World countries owed $1.2 trillion!

For years it appeared as if the crisis might bring down some of the world's largest banks. On average in 1989, the World Bank estimated that 19 LDCs had debt outstanding equivalent to 53.6 percent of their GNP. Interest payments alone amounted to 22.3 percent of export income. The international banking community was obviously shaken. As an indication of the magnitude of the involvement of some of the banks in LDC loans at the height of the crisis, Exhibit 11.9 lists the 10 largest U.S. bank lenders *just* to Mexico.

---

[11]The quotation is from *International Capital Markets: Part II. Systematic Issues in International Finance* (International Monetary Fund, Washington, D.C.), August 1993, p. 2.

EXHIBIT 11.9

Ten Biggest U.S. Bank Lenders to Mexico
(in billions of U.S. dollars as of September 30, 1987)

Bank	Outstanding Loans to Mexico	Loan Loss Reserves for Developing Country Loans
Citicorp	$2.900	$3.432
BankAmerica Corp.	2.407	1.808
Manufacturers Hanover Corp.	1.883	1.833*
Chemical New York Corp.	1.733	1.505*
Chase Manhattan Corp.	1.660	1.970
Bankers Trust New York Corp.	1.277	1.000
J. P. Morgan & Co.	1.137	1.317
First Chicago Corp.	0.898	0.930
First Interstate Bancorp.	0.689	0.500
Wells Fargo & Co.	0.587	0.760

*As of June 30, 1987.

Source: The Wall Street Journal, December 30, 1987.

The source of the international debt crisis was oil. In the early 1970s, the Organization of Petroleum Exporting Countries (OPEC) became the dominant supplier of oil worldwide. Throughout this time period, OPEC raised oil prices dramatically. As a result of these price increases, OPEC amassed a tremendous amount of U.S. dollars, which was the currency generally demanded as payment from the oil-importing countries.

OPEC deposited billions in Eurodollar deposits; by 1976 the deposits amounted to nearly $100 billion. Eurobanks were faced with a huge problem of lending these funds in order to generate interest income to pay the interest on the deposits. Third World countries were only too eager to assist the eager Eurobankers in accepting Eurodollar loans that could be used for economic development *and* for payment of oil imports. The lending process became circular and known as *petrodollar recycling*: Eurodollar loan proceeds were used to pay for new oil imports; some of the oil revenues from developed and LDCs were redeposited, and the deposits were re-lent to Third World borrowers.

OPEC raised oil prices again in the late 1970s. The high oil prices were accompanied by high inflation and high unemployment in the industrialized countries. Tight monetary policies instituted in a number of the major industrialized countries led to a global recession and a decline in the demand for commodities, such as oil, and in commodity prices. The same economic policies led to higher real interest rates, which increased the borrowing costs of the LDCs, since most of the bank borrowing was denominated in U.S. dollars and had been made on a floating-rate basis. The collapse of commodity prices and the resultant loss of income made it impossible for the LDCs to meet their debt service obligations.

Why would the international banks make such risky loans to LDC sovereign governments in the first place? One reason obviously was that they held vast sums of money in Eurodollar deposits that needed to be quickly placed to start producing interest income. Banks were simply too eager and not careful enough in analyzing the risks they were undertaking in lending to unfamiliar borrowers. Additionally, many U.S. banks claim that there was official *arm-twisting* from Washington to assist the economic development of the Third World countries.

Debt-for-Equity Swaps

In the midst of the LDC debt crisis, a secondary market developed for LDC debt at prices discounted significantly from face value. The secondary market consisted of approximately 50 creditor banks, investment banks, and boutique market makers. The LDC debt was purchased for use in **debt-for-equity swaps**. As part of debt rescheduling agreements among the bank lending syndicates and the debtor nations, creditor

EXHIBIT 11.10

**Debt-for-Equity Swap
Illustration**

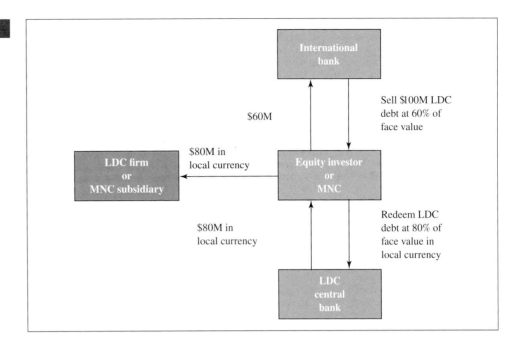

banks would sell their loans for U.S. dollars at discounts from face value to MNCs desiring to make equity investment in subsidiaries or local firms in the LDCs. An LDC central bank would buy the bank debt from a MNC at a smaller discount than the MNC paid, but in local currency. The MNC would use the local currency to make preapproved new investment in the LDC that was economically or socially beneficial to the LDC and its populace.

Exhibit 11.10 diagrams a hypothetical debt-for-equity swap. The exhibit shows a MNC purchasing $100 million of Mexican debt (either directly or through a market maker) from a creditor bank for $60 million, that is, at a 40 percent discount from face value. The MNC then redeems the $100 million note from the Mexican central bank for the equivalent of $80 million in Mexican pesos at the current exchange rate. The Mexican pesos are invested in a Mexican subsidiary of the MNC or in an equity position in an LDC firm. The MNC has paid $60 million for $80 million in Mexican pesos.

During the midst of the LDC debt crisis, Latin American debt was going at an average discount of approximately 70 percent. The September 10, 1990, issue of *Barron's* quotes Brazilian sovereign debt at 21.75 cents per dollar, Mexican debt at 43.12 cents, and Argentinean debt at only 14.25 cents.

Real-life examples of debt-for-equity swaps abound. Chrysler invested $100 million in pesos in Chrysler de Mexico from money obtained from buying Mexican debt at a 56 percent discount. Volkswagen paid $170 million for $283 million in Mexican debt, which it swapped for the equivalent of $260 million of pesos. In a more complicated deal, CitiBank, acting as a market maker, paid $40 million to another bank for $60 million of Mexican debt, which was swapped with Banco de Mexico, the Mexican central bank, for $54 million worth of pesos later used by Nissan to expand a truck plant outside of Mexico City.

Who benefits from a debt-for-equity swap? All parties are presumed to, or else the swap would not have taken place. The creditor bank benefits from getting an unproductive loan off its books and at least a portion of the principal repaid. The market maker obviously benefits from earning the bid-ask spread on the discounted loan amount. The LDC benefits in two ways. The first benefit comes from being able to pay off a "hard" currency loan (generally at a discount from face value) on which it cannot meet the debt service with its own local currency. The second benefit comes from the new productive investment made in the country, which was designed to foster economic growth. The equity investor benefits from the purchase of LDC local currency needed to make the investment at a discount from the current exchange rate.

Third World countries have only been open to allowing debt-for-equity swaps for certain types of investment. The LDC obtains the local currency to redeem the hard currency loan by printing it. This obviously increases the country's money supply and is inflationary. Thus, LDCs have only allowed swaps where the benefits of the new equity investment were expected to be greater than the harm caused to the economy by increased inflation. Acceptable types of investments have been in:

1. Export-oriented industries, such as automobiles, that will bring in hard currency.
2. High-technology industries that will lead to larger exports, improve the technological base of the country, and develop the skills of its people.
3. Tourist industry, such as resort hotels, that will increase tourism and visitors bringing hard currency.
4. Low-income housing developments that will improve the standard of living of some of the populace.

The Solution: Brady Bonds

Today, most debtor nations and creditor banks would agree that the international debt crisis is effectively over. U.S. Treasury Secretary Nicholas F. Brady of the first Bush administration is largely credited with designing a strategy in the spring of 1989 to resolve the problem. Brady's solution was to offer creditor banks one of three alternatives: (i) convert their loans to marketable bonds with a face value equal to 65 percent of the original loan amount; (ii) convert the loans into collateralized bonds with a reduced interest rate of 6.5 percent; or, (iii) lend additional funds to allow the debtor nations to get on their feet. As one can imagine, few banks chose the third alternative. The second alternative called for extending the debt maturities by 25 to 30 years and the purchase by the debtor nation of zero-coupon U.S. Treasury bonds with a corresponding maturity to guarantee the bonds and make them marketable. These bonds have come to be called **Brady bonds**.

By 1992, Brady bond agreements had been negotiated in many countries, including Argentina, Brazil, Mexico, Uruguay, Venezuela, Nigeria, and the Philippines. By August of 1992, 12 of 16 major debtor nations had reached refinancing agreements accounting for 92 percent of their outstanding private bank debt. In total, over $100 billion in bank debt has been converted to Brady bonds.

The Asian Crisis

As noted in Chapter 2, the Asian crisis began in mid-1997 when Thailand devalued the baht. Subsequently other Asian countries devalued their currencies by letting them float—ending their pegged value with the U.S. dollar. Not since the LDC debt crisis have international financial markets experienced such widespread turbulence. The troubles, which began in Thailand, soon affected other countries in the region and also emerging markets in other regions.[12]

Interestingly, the Asian crisis followed a period of economic expansion in the region financed by record private capital inflows. Bankers from the G-10 countries actively sought to finance the growth opportunities in Asia by providing businesses

---

[12]The discussion in this section closely follows the discussion on the Asian crisis found in *International Capital Markets: Developments, Prospects, and Key Policy Issues* (International Monetary Fund, Washington, D.C.), September 1998, pp. 1–6 and the Bank for International Settlements working paper titled "Supervisory Lessons to Be Drawn from the Asian Crisis," June 1999.

in the region with a full assortment of products and services. Domestic price bubbles in East Asia, particularly in real estate, were fostered by these capital inflows. The simultaneous liberalization of financial markets contributed to bubbles in financial asset prices as well. Additionally, the close interrelationships common among commercial firms and financial institutions in Asia resulted in poor investment decision making.

The risk exposure of the lending banks in East Asia was primarily to local banks and commercial firms, and not to sovereignties, as in the LDC debt crisis. It may have been implicitly assumed, however, that the governments would come to the rescue of their private banks should financial problems develop. The history of managed growth in the region at least suggested that the economic and financial system, as an integral unit, could be managed in an economic downturn. This did not turn out to be the case.

Global Financial Crisis

On December 1, 2008, the National Bureau of Economic Research officially announced that the U.S. economy was in a recession that began a year earlier in December 2007. This announcement merely confirmed what many had suspected for months. During the previous month, Japan, Hong Kong, and most of Europe also announced that they were in recessions. What, at least symptomatically, started as a credit crunch in the United States during the summer of 2007, had turned into a global economic downturn that some feared could rival the Great Depression of 1929–1933, which officially lasted for 43 months in the United States. June 2009 marked the trough in the United States. In the seven years since, the world economy has been slowly recovering but remains fragile.

To gain a deeper understanding of the financial crisis, this section starts with a discussion of the credit crunch and how it escalated into a financial crisis. The changing landscape in banking, which has seen the end of independent investment banking firms as a viable business model, is also covered. This is followed with a discussion of the economic stimulus packages the U.S. Treasury and the Federal Reserve Board devised to alleviate the economic turmoil in the United States and the coordinated efforts made by the worlds' central bankers as the situation turned global. The section concludes with a discussion on financial regulatory reform being enacted to prevent and mitigate future crises.

The Credit Crunch

The credit crunch, or the inability of borrowers to easily obtain credit, began in the United States in the summer of 2007. The origin of the credit crunch can be traced back to three key contributing factors: liberalization of banking and securities regulation, a global savings glut, and the low interest rate environment created by the Federal Reserve in the early part of this decade.

Liberalization of Banking and Securities Regulation   The U.S. Glass-Steagall Act of 1933 mandated a separation of commercial banking from other financial services firms—such as securities, insurance, and real estate. Under the act, commercial banks could sell new offerings of government securities, but they could not operate as an investment bank and underwrite corporate securities or engage in brokerage operations. Because commercial banks viewed themselves at a disadvantage relative to foreign banks that were not restricted from investment banking functions, pressure on Congress increased to repeal the act. Through various steps, erosion of the basic intent of the act started in 1987, with its official repeal coming in 1999 with the passage of the Financial Services Modernization Act. The repeal of Glass-Steagall caused a blurring of the functioning of commercial banks, investment banks, insurance companies, and real estate mortgage banking firms. Money market funds collected uninsured deposits that were lent to financial firms, investment banks began performing commercial banking functions and vice versa, and a variety of derivative and securitized products providing liquidity to previously illiquid loans became available. As a result, a weakly regulated **shadow banking system** whose operations were both opaque and highly levered developed in parallel to the operation of regulated banks. Its evolution contributed to the credit crunch.

Global Savings Glut   As was discussed in Chapter 3, a country's current account balance is the difference between the sum of its exports and imports of goods and services with the rest of the world. When a country runs a current account deficit, it gives a financial claim to foreigners of an amount greater than it has received against them. Countries with current account surpluses are able to spend or invest their surpluses in deficit countries. China and Japan generate current account surpluses because their economies are oriented towards exports of consumer goods. OPEC generates surpluses through the sale of petroleum to the rest of the world, which is typically denominated in U.S. dollars. The People's Bank of China and the Bank of Japan, the central banks of these two countries, hold vast sums as foreign currency reserves. At year-end 2008, it was estimated that China held $1.955 trillion in foreign currency reserves, with as much as 70 percent of it denominated in U.S. dollars. In order to earn interest, countries typically hold their U.S. dollar reserves in U.S. Treasury securities or U.S. government agency securities. It is estimated that at the end of June 2008, China held $1.2 trillion in U.S. securities. OPEC members too have huge investment in U.S. securities and also make investments through sovereign wealth funds. Against this backdrop, it is clear that the world was awash in liquidity in recent years, much of it denominated in U.S. dollars, awaiting investment. The bottom line is that the United States has been able to maintain domestic investment at a rate that otherwise would have required higher domestic savings (or reduced consumption) and also found a ready market with central banks for U.S. Treasury and government agency securities, helping keep U.S. interest rates low.

Low Interest Rate Environment   The fed funds target rate fell from 6.5 percent set on May 16, 2000 to 1.0 percent on June 25, 2003, and stayed below 3.0 percent until May 3, 2005. The decrease in the fed funds rate was the Fed's response to the financial turmoil created by the fall in stock market prices in 2000 as the high-tech, dot-com, boom came to an end. Low interest rates created the means for first-time homeowners to afford mortgage financing and also created the means for existing homeowners to trade up to more expensive homes. Low interest rate mortgages created an excess demand for homes, driving prices up substantially in most parts of the country. Many homeowners refinanced and withdrew equity from their homes, which was frequently used for the consumption of consumer good. Much of these consumer goods were produced abroad, thus contributing to U.S. current account deficits.

During this time, many banks and mortgage financers lowered their credit standards to attract new home buyers who could afford to make mortgage payments at current low interest rates, or at "teaser" rates that were temporarily set at a low level during the early years of an adjustable-rate mortgage, but would likely be reset to a higher rate later on. Many of these home buyers would not have qualified for mortgage financing under more stringent credit standards, nor would they have been able to afford mortgage payments at more conventional rates of interest. These so-called subprime mortgages were typically not held by the originating bank making the loan, but instead were re-packaged into **mortgage-backed securities (MBSs)** to be sold to investors. (See the In More Depth section for a discussion of the MBS.) As a result of the global savings glut, investors were readily available to purchase these MBS. The excessive demand for this type of securities, coupled with the fact that most originating banks simply rolled the mortgages into MBS instead of holding the paper, created the environment for lax credit standards and the growth in the subprime mortgage market.

To cool the growth of the economy, the Fed steadily increased the fed funds target rate at meetings of the Federal Open Market Committee, from a low of 1.0 percent on June 25, 2003 to 5.25 percent on June 29, 2006. In turn, mortgage rates increased and home prices stopped increasing, thus stalling new housing starts and precluding mortgage refinancing to draw out paper capital gains. Many subprime borrowers found it difficult, if not impossible, to make mortgage payments in this economic environment, especially when their adjustable-rate mortgages were reset at higher rates. As matters unfolded, it was discovered that the amounts of subprime MBS debt in **structured investment vehicles (SIVs)** and **collateralized debt obligations (CDOs)**, and who exactly owned it, were essentially unknown, or at least unappreciated. (See the In Depth Section for an in-depth discussion of SIVs and CDOs.) While it was thought SIVs and CDOs would spread MBS risk worldwide to investors best able to bear it, it turned out that many banks that did not hold mortgage debt directly, held it indirectly through MBS in SIVs they sponsored. To make matters worse, the diversification the investors in MBS, SIVs and CDOs thought they had was only illusory. MBS, SIVs and CDOs, however, were diversified over a single asset class—poor quality residential mortgages! When subprime debtors began defaulting on their mortgages, commercial paper investors were unwilling to finance SIVs and trading in the interbank Eurocurrency market essentially ceased as traders became fearful of the counterparty risk of placing funds with even the strongest international banks. Liquidity worldwide essentially dried up.

In More Depth

A derivative security is one whose value derives from the value of some other asset. Frequently, derivatives are used as risk management tools to hedge, or neutralize, risky positions in the underlying assets. However, derivative securities can also be used for speculative purposes, resulting in extremely risky positions. Four types of derivative securities played prominent roles in the subprime credit crisis: mortgage-backed securities (MBS), structured investment vehicles (SIVs), collateralized debt obligations (CDOs), and credit default swaps (CDSs).

Mortgage-Backed Securities and Structured Investment Vehicles

A mortgage-backed security is a derivative security because its value is derived from the value of the underlying mortgages (assets) that secure it. Conceptually, mortgage-backed securities seem to make sense. Each MBS represents a portfolio of mortgages, thus diversifying the credit risk that the investor holds. Structured investment vehicles (SIVs) have been one large investor in MBS. An SIV is a virtual bank, frequently operated by a commercial bank or an investment bank, but which operates off the balance sheet. Typically, an SIV raises short-term funds in the commercial paper market to finance longer-term investment in MBS and other asset-backed securities. SIVs are frequently highly levered, with ratios of 10 to 15 (and in some cases more) times the amount of equity raised. Since yield curves are typically upward sloping, the SIV might normally earn 25 basis points by doing this. Obviously, SIVs are subject to the interest rate risk of the yield curve inverting, that is, short-term rates rising above long-term rates, thus necessitating the SIV to refinance the MBS investment at short-term rates in excess of the rate being earned on the MBS. Default risk is another risk with which SIVs must contend. If the underlying mortgage borrowers default on their home loans, the SIV will lose investment value. Nevertheless, SIVs predominately invest only in high-grade Aaa/AAA MBS. By investing in a variety of MBS, an SIV further diversifies the credit risk of MBS investment. The SIV's value obviously derives from the value of the portfolio of MBS it represents.

Collateralized Debt Obligations

Collateralized debt obligations (CDOs) have been other big investors in MBS. A CDO is a corporate entity constructed to hold a portfolio of fixed-income assets as collateral. The portfolio of fixed-income assets is divided into different tranches, each representing a different risk class: AAA, AA-BB, or unrated. CDOs serve as an important funding source for fixed-income securities. An investor in a CDO is taking a position in the cash flows of a particular tranche, not in the fixed-income securities directly. The investment is dependent on the metrics used to define the risk and reward of the tranche. Investors include insurance companies, mutual funds, hedge funds, other CDOs, and even SIVs. MBS and other asset-backed securities have served as collateral for many CDOs.

Credit Defaults Swaps

A **credit default swap (CDS)** is the most popular credit derivative. It is a contract that provides insurance against the risk of default of a particular company or sovereignty, known as the *reference entity*. Default is referred to as a *credit event*. For an annual payment, known as the *spread*, the insurance buyer has the right under the terms of the CDS contract to sell bonds issued by the reference entity for full face value to the insurance seller if a credit event occurs. The total face value of bonds that can be sold is the CDS's *notional value*. Consider a 5-year CDS on a notional value of $100 million with a spread of 80 basis points. The buyer pays the seller $800,000 [= .008 × $100 million] per year each and every year if a credit event does not occur. If one does occur, the buyer provides physical delivery of the bonds to the insurance seller in return for $100 million and does not make any further annual payments. Some CDSs require cash settlement, in which case the seller pays the buyer the difference between the face value and the market value in the event of a default.

CDSs allow the buyer of a risky bond the ability to convert it into a risk free bond. Ignoring a difference in liquidity, a long position in a 5-year risky bond plus a long position in a 5-year CDS on the same bond should equal a position in a 5-year risk-free bond. Consequently, it is clear the CDS spread should equal the difference in the yield spread between the 5-year risky bond and a corresponding 5-year risk-free bond. Various financial institutions make a market in CDS in the over-the-counter market, taking either side of the contract. As this example illustrates, a CDS has the characteristics of a put option. However, CDSs were not regulated by the CFTC because they trade in the OTC market. Moreover, since they are classified as a swap instead of an insurance contract, they were not regulated by state insurance commissions either even though insurance companies are frequently market makers. In essence, the CDS market, which grew from virtually nothing into a $58 trillion market in just a few years, was an unregulated market. CDS can be used by bond investors to hedge the credit default risk in their portfolios. Alternatively, speculators without an underlying position in the bond can use CDSs for speculating on the default of a particular reference entity. Prudent risk management suggests that derivative dealers would hold a risk neutral position, but that has not been the case for CDS market makers. As providers of "insurance," they typically carry a large net short position.

From Credit Crunch to Financial Crisis   As the credit crunch escalated, many CDOs found themselves stuck with various tranches of MBS debt, especially the highest risk tranches, which they had not yet placed or were unable to place as subprime foreclosure rates around the country escalated. Commercial and investment banks were forced to write down billions of subprime debt. As the U.S. economy slipped into recession, banks also started to set aside billions for credit-card debt and other consumer loans they feared would go bad. The credit rating firms—Moody's, S&P, and Fitch—lowered their ratings on many CDOs after recognizing that the models they had used to evaluate the risk of the various tranches were mis-specified. Additionally, the credit rating firms downgraded many MBS, especially those containing subprime mortgages, as foreclosures around the country increased. An unsustainable problem arose for bond insurers who sold credit default swap (CDS) contracts and the banks that purchased this credit insurance. As the bond insurers got hit with claims from bank-sponsored SIVs as the MBS debt in their portfolios defaulted, downgrades of the bond insurers by the credit rating agencies required the insurers to put up more collateral with the counterparties who had purchased the CDSs, which put stress on their capital base and prompted additional credit-rating downgrades, which in turn triggered more margin calls. If big bond insurers, such as American International Group (AIG) failed, the banks that relied on the insurance protection would be forced to write down even more mortgage-backed debt which would further erode their Tier I Core capital bases. By September 2008, a worldwide flight to quality investments—primarily short term U.S. Treasury Securities—ensued. On October 10, 2008, the spread between the three-month Eurodollar rate and the three-month U.S. Treasury bill (the TED spread), frequently used as measure of credit risk, reached a record level of 543 basis points. Exhibit 11.11 graphs the TED spread from January 2007 through mid-December 2008. The demand for safety was so great, at one point in November 2008, the one-month U.S. Treasury bill was yielding only one basis point. Investors were essentially willing to accept zero return for a safe place to put their funds! They were not willing to invest in money market funds that invested in commercial paper that banks and industrial corporations needed for survival. The modern day equivalent of a "bank run" was operating in full force and many financial institutions could not survive.

Impact of the Financial Crisis

The financial crisis has had a pronounced effect on the world economy. As a result, dramatic changes have taken place in the financial services industry, the auto industry, and in financial markets worldwide. Some of the most significant changes are detailed here.

Financial Services Industry

- Northern Rock, a British bank, was nationalized as a result of a liquidity crisis.
- Bear Stearns was sold to JPMorgan Chase in a forced sale for $1.2 billion.

EXHIBIT 11.11

TED Spread (%)

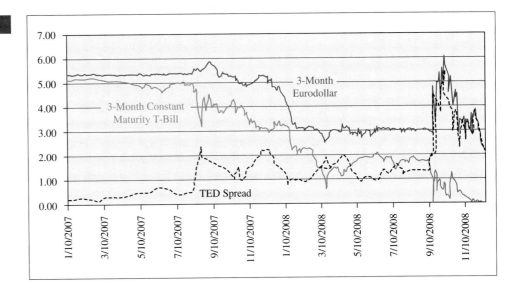

- On September 7, 2008, the Federal National Mortgage Association (Fannie Mae) and the Federal Home Loan Mortgage Corporation (Freddie Mac) were placed under conservatorship by the Federal Housing Finance Agency, where they remain. The U.S. Treasury holds senior preferred stock and common stock warrants amounting to 79.9 percent of each government-sponsored enterprise. Since then, they have drawn about $188 billion in taxpayer funds to stay afloat, while paying about $246 billion to the Treasury in preferred stock dividends.

- Bank of America acquired Merrill Lynch after it reported large CDO losses.

- Lehman Brothers, a 158-year old firm, was allowed to fail, after suffering unprecedented losses from holdings of subprime mortgage debt and other low-rated tranches of mortgages.

- AIG was rescued by the Fed in September 2008 in a $182 billion bailout. Remarkably, in just four years, it has gone from being publicly owned back to the private sector. Whether AIG would have actually failed without the government bailout is a debatable topic and will likely never be known for sure. But one thing is certain, if it had failed there would have been unpredictable ripples throughout the world's financial markets, thus making the bailout a necessary precaution.

- Fearing a loss of confidence among counterparties and facing a liquidity crisis, Goldman Sachs and Morgan Stanley, the last two remaining "bulge bracket" investment banking firms, restructured themselves into commercial bank holding companies.[13]

- Washington Mutual, the largest U.S. savings and loan association, was put into receivership and sold to JPMorgan Chase by the Fed after a 10-day bank run.

- Wachovia was acquired by Wells Fargo. Wachovia's problems began with its 2006 purchase of Golden West Financial Corp., a savings and loan association that built its business making adjustable-rate mortgage loans.

- Citigroup, after suffering a liquidity crisis, was rescued by the Treasury and the Fed, which viewed it as too big and too important to fail. In December 2010, the Treasury completed the sale of its ownership position in Citigroup, earning $12 billion on its $45 billion cash bailout.

Housing and Unemployment

- At mid-year 2008, over 9 percent of the mortgages on single-family homes in the United States were at least one month late in payment or in some stage of foreclosure. Approximately 30 percent of subprime loans were overdue as were over 5 percent of prime loans.

- In September 2008, the S&P Case-Shiller Composite House Price Index of 20 U.S. Cities indicated that house prices were down over 20 percent from its high in June 2006. This decrease put the market values of 10 million homes below the amount of their mortgage balances. New home construction came to a virtual standstill, further weakening the economy. The Case-Shiller index reached a subsequent low in April 2009—down 33 percent. At the time of this writing it is still down 10 percent from its peak.

- In November 2008, the U.S. Department of Labor reported that the unemployment rate was 6.7 percent—the highest rate in 15 years. By October the following year it stood at 10.1 percent. Presently it stands at 4.9 percent, which is considered within policy makers' normal range of full employment.

---

[13]The term "bulge bracket" is an old Wall Street term for referring to the former major investment banking firms. It derives from the fact that in print announcements of new security issues, known as tombstones, the names of the prominent investment banking firms underwriting an issue were printed in bold font that appeared to "bulge" out from the page.

Auto Industry   Problems for the Detroit auto makers started when the lack of liquidity caused by the credit crunch made it difficult for consumers to finance new car purchases. Matters only worsened during the summer of 2008 when gasoline prices hit $4 per gallon—Americans then questioned the practicality of owning the gas guzzling big cars and SUVs they so favored and the Detroit firms manufactured. Auto sales plummeted as the economic downturn escalated and employees in many industries were laid off. On April 30, 2009 Chrysler filed for bankruptcy. A month later, the bankruptcy judge approved a plan whereby Fiat would own 20 percent of the "new" Chrysler, the autoworker's union retirement health care trust would own 55 percent, and the U.S. and Canadian governments would be minority stakeholders. On June 1, 2009, GM filed for bankruptcy and subsequently received a $49.5 billion bailout from the Treasury. Since then it has slimmed down its business model by shedding auto models and dealerships. In 2010, the "new" GM was reoffered to stockholders in an IPO that raised $20.1 billion and reduced the U.S. government's ownership position from 61 to 33 percent. In December 2013, the Treasury sold its remaining shares in GM, realizing a total loss of $11.2 billion.

Financial Markets   The financial crisis has had a devastating effect on financial markets and on investments that depend on their returns. In the United States, stock prices fell to levels once thought unimaginable, although they have since come back. As of March 2013, both the Dow Jones Industrial Average and the Standard & Poor's 500 are marginally up from their previous peaks in October 2007. Foreign stock markets in U.S. dollar terms are down, however. Over the same time period, the MSCI World Index is still down more than 14 percent.

The global financial crisis brought the **sovereign debt crisis** of the euro zone to a head. The debt crisis can be traced back to the formation of the European Monetary Union when each of the member states pledged to harmonize their economies by limiting deficit spending to 3 percent and total sovereign debt to 60 percent of GDP. In the early 2000s, a number of states were failing to stay within the criteria and increased debt levels over the following years, in some cases in ways that were not immediately transparent. From late 2009, fears of a sovereign debt crisis developed among investors as a result of the rising debt levels around the globe and the downgrading of the credit rating of several euro zone countries. European banks own a substantial amount of this sovereign debt, which causes concerns about the solvency of the banking system in the European Union. Concerns intensified in early 2010, leading the EU, the ECB, and the IMF to implement a series of financial bailouts. Specifically, the sovereign debt of Greece, Ireland, Portugal, and Cyprus has been downgraded to "junk" status and each of these countries has received financial support after agreeing to a variety of austerity measures. Other euro zone countries are relatively financially strong. (At present, the 10-year yield on Greek debt is 8.5 percent higher than on German debt.) Fear of contagion spreading to Italy and Spain (other euro-zone countries with big budget deficits), however, continues to be a worry. A flight to quality investments denominated in the U.S. dollar has resulted in an appreciation of the dollar. For example, in April 2008, the $/€ spot exchange rate was $1.60/€ and it presently trades at $1.11/€, the corresponding $/£ rate went from $2.00/£ to $1.25/£. The great advantage of the United States is that the dollar is the major reserve currency. Nevertheless, the financing of the nearly $3.5 trillion of U.S. budget deficits projected over the next 10 years is worrisome. There simply is no precedent for this scale of chronic deficits.

Economic Stimulus

Perhaps the credit crunch could not have been precisely predicted, but at some level the factors that contributed to it did not make sense. Even when the Fed was lowering the Fed Funds rate, Fed Chairman Alan Greenspan said, "I don't know what it is, but we're doing some damage because this is not the way credit markets should operate."[14] Lowering interest rates to such a low level and keeping them there for such a long period of time was a mistake. In retrospect, the global savings glut likely would have supplied a good deal of the liquidity needed by the U.S. and world economies after the dot-com bubble burst. It is difficult to understand how the Fed did not recognize this given the economic data available to it for analysis. Lowering the fed funds rate only added additional liquidity to the U.S. economy and exacerbated Americans' unsustainable buying binge. When the Fed started increasing interest rates, the party came to an end. In testimony before Congress on October 13, 2008, former Fed Chairman Greenspan admitted that he made a mistake with the hands-off regulatory environment he helped foster and further acknowledged that he made a critical forecasting error in his assumption about the resilience of home prices and never anticipated that they could fall so much.

Many new initiatives were made in 2008 to spur U.S. and world economic activity:

- Under the guidance of current Federal Reserve Chairman Ben Bernanke, the Fed began reducing the fed funds rate from the recent high of 5¼ percent at its meeting on September 18, 2007 to 0–25 basis points on December 16, 2008, where it remains. Obviously, the Fed had run out of ammo in this pouch as a means of increasing the money supply and stimulating the economy through normal open market operations. As a consequence, the Fed began a massive program of *quantitative easing*, that is, buying long-term Treasuries and mortgage-backed-securities. Purchases were halted in October 2014 after accumulating $4.5 trillion in assets.

- Similarly, central banks around the world have reduced their short-term rates. A coordinated effort of rate cuts involving the Fed, European Central Bank, Bank of England, and the People's Bank of China took place on October 8, 2008. And, on December 17, 2008, central banks in Norway, the Czech Republic, Hong Kong, Saudi Arabia, Oman, and Kuwait cut interest rates. Quantitative easing programs have also been implemented in the U.K., the euro zone, and in Japan.

- As a result of frozen credit markets, corporations encountered problems obtaining working capital. In an effort to provide credit, the Fed established the Commercial Paper Facility to buy $1.3 trillion in commercial paper directly from U.S. companies.

- The Fed established the $540 billion Money Market Investor Funding Facility to buy commercial paper and certificates of deposit from money market funds to restore the public's confidence in these funds.

- Congress authorized the Federal Deposit Insurance Corporation (FDIC) to increase the level of bank deposit insurance from $100,000 to $250,000, which will likely be made permanent.

- The $700 billion Troubled Assets Relief Program (TARP), spearheaded by former U.S. Treasury Secretary Henry (Hank) Paulson to purchase poor performing mortgages and MBS from financial institutions, was signed into law in October 3, 2008. The idea behind the bailout plan was to get poor performing assets off of banks' books to alleviate the fears of depositors. In a startling change in tactics, Secretary Paulson announced on November 12 that the government would no longer use TARP funds to buy distressed mortgage-related assets from banks, but instead it would concentrate on direct capital injections into banks. In total, $426.40 billion of the TARP funds were eventually disbursed. The program was concluded in December 2014, returning a total of $441.7 billion; hence, it was modestly profitable.

---

[14]Greg Ip and Jon E. Hilsenrath, "How Credit Got So Easy and Why It's Tightening." *The Wall Street Journal*, August 7, 2007, pp. A1 and A7.

The Aftermath

The global economic crisis is ongoing. At this stage, virtually every economic entity has experienced a downturn. Many lessons should be learned from these experiences. One lesson is that bankers seem not to scrutinize credit risk as closely when they serve only as mortgage originators and then pass it on to MBS investors rather than hold the paper themselves. As things have turned out, when the subprime mortgage crisis hit, commercial and investment banks found themselves exposed, in one fashion or another, to more mortgage debt than they realized they held. This outcome is partially a result of the repeal of the Glass-Steagall Act, which allowed commercial banks to engage in investment banking functions. As we have seen, the market has spoken with respect to investment banking as a viable business model—the bulge bracket Wall Street firms no longer exist. It remains doubtful, however, if the subprime credit crunch has taught commercial bankers a lasting lesson. As during the international debt crisis in the 1980s or the Asian crisis in the 1990s, for some reason, bankers always seem willing to lend huge amounts to borrowers with a limited potential to repay. There is no excuse for bankers not properly evaluating the potential risks of an investment or loan. In lending to a sovereign government or making loans to private parties in distant parts of the world, the risks are unique and proper analysis is warranted.

The decision to allow the CDS market to operate without supervision of the CFTC or some other regulatory agency was a serious error in judgment. CDSs are a potentially useful vehicle for offsetting credit risk, but the market is in need of more transparency with respect to OTC derivatives, and market makers need to fully understand the extent of the risk of their positions. Another lesson is that credit rating agencies need to refine their models for evaluating esoteric credit risk in securities such as MBS and CDOs and borrowers must be more wary of putting complete faith in credit ratings.

As anyone would expect, more political and regulatory scrutiny of banking operations and the functioning of financial markets was a virtual certainty in the aftermath of the crisis. In this regard, as previously mentioned, a package of enhancements known as Basel 2.5 proposed by the Basel Committee on Banking Supervision to strengthen the regulation and supervision of internationally active banks has been largely adopted. Additionally, a new accord, named Basel III, aims to strengthen the regulatory capital framework of international banks. At the country level, in the U.K., the Financial Services Act of 2012 created two new financial regulatory bodies that began operation on April 1, 2013. The Financial Policy Committee is charged with a primary objective of identifying, monitoring and taking action to remove or reduce systemic risks and the Prudential Regulation Authority is responsible for the supervision of banks, depository financial institutions, insurers, and major investment firms. In the European Union, existing supervisory architecture was replaced with a system of three European Supervisory Authorities that have been mandated to implement a single rulebook. These three authorities are the European Banking Authority, the European Securities and Markets Authority, and the European Insurance and Occupational Authority. They will operate in conjunction with the European Systemic Risk Board to regulate all financial markets, products, and institutions.

In the United States, on July 21, 2010, President Barack Obama signed into law the Dodd-Frank Wall Street Reform and Consumer Protection Act. This legislation institutes new broad financial regulations that rewrite the rules covering all aspects of finance and expands the power of the government over banking and financial markets. Such sweeping new regulation has not been seen since the Great Depression. A committee of regulators, the Financial Stability Oversight Council, is made responsible for monitoring systemic risk and taking measures to address it. Specifically, the Act gives the FDIC power to seize and break up troubled big financial service firms whose collapse would be a systemic risk to the economy—no longer will banks be viewed as too big to fail. Additionally, the CFTC has expansive new power to regulate derivatives that hopefully will prevent the misuse of OTC derivatives, such as CDSs, in the future. Moreover, advisers to hedge funds and private equity funds must now register with the SEC. And market makers must maintain an investment stake in MBSs, rather than merely create and sell to others. A special provision of the Act is the Volcker Rule (named after former Federal Reserve chairman Paul Volcker), which places limits on commercial bank proprietary trading and their sponsorship of hedge funds and private equity funds. Further, a new consumer protection agency will be established to write new consumer finance rules regulating home mortgages and credit cards that will require banks to provide more transparent disclosure to borrowers and to ensure that borrowers have the means to repay loans. And a new Office of Credit Ratings will watch over the credit rating agencies. In the area of corporate governance, shareholders will have nonbinding votes on executive compensation and golden parachutes. It should be clear that these new financial regulations have been carefully crafted to address the weaknesses we noted that led to the financial crisis. While some doubt the usefulness of financial regulations, and believe that financial crises cannot be prevented, we believe that financial regulations serve as a useful benchmark to guide financial behavior and establish what is appropriate. When no rules are present, anything seems to go.

SUMMARY

In this chapter, the topics of international banking, the international money market, the Third World debt crisis, and the recent global financial crisis were discussed. This chapter begins the textbook's five-chapter sequence on world financial markets and institutions.

1. International banks can be characterized by the types of services they provide. International banks facilitate the imports and exports of their clients by arranging trade financing. They also arrange foreign currency exchange, assist in hedging exchange rate exposure, trade foreign exchange for their own account, and make a market in currency derivative products. Some international banks seek deposits of foreign currencies and make foreign currency loans to nondomestic bank customers. Additionally, some international banks may participate in the underwriting of international bonds if banking regulations allow.

2. Various types of international banking offices include correspondent bank relationships, representative offices, foreign branches, subsidiaries and affiliates, Edge Act banks, offshore banking centers, and International Banking Facilities. The reasons for the various types of international banking offices and the services they provide vary considerably.

3. The core of the international money market is the Eurocurrency market. A Eurocurrency is a time deposit of money in an international bank located in a country different from the country that issued the currency. For example, Eurodollars, which make up the largest part of the market, are deposits of U.S. dollars in banks outside of the United States. The Eurocurrency market is headquartered in London. Eurobanks are international banks that seek Eurocurrency deposits and make Eurocurrency loans. The chapter illustrated the creation of Eurocurrency and discussed the nature of Eurocredits, or Eurocurrency loans.

4. Other main international money market instruments include forward rate agreements, Euronotes, Eurocommercial paper, and Eurodollar interest rate futures.

5. Capital adequacy refers to the amount of equity capital and other securities a bank holds as reserves against risky assets to reduce the probability of a bank failure.

The 1988 Basel Capital Accord established a framework for determining capital adequacy requirements for internationally active banks. The Basel Accord primarily addressed banking in the context of deposit gathering and lending. Thus, its focus was on credit risk. The accord has been widely adopted throughout the world by national bank regulators. Bank trading in equity, interest rate, and exchange rate derivative products escalated throughout the 1990s. The original capital adequacy requirements were not sufficient to safeguard against the market risk from trading in these instruments. Additionally, operational risk, which includes such matters as computer failure, poor documentation, and fraud, was not covered by the original accord. In 2004, a new capital adequacy framework commonly referred to as Basel II was endorsed by central bank governors and bank supervisors in the G-10 countries. It requires 8 percent minimum capital to be held against a bank's credit, market, and operational risk.

The global financial crisis that began in mid-2007 illustrated how quickly and severely liquidity risks can crystallize and certain sources of funding can evaporate, compounding concerns about the valuation of assets and capital adequacy. A number of banking organizations have experienced large losses, most of which were sustained in the banks' trading accounts. These losses have not arisen from actual defaults, but rather from credit agency downgrades, widening credit spreads, and the loss of liquidity. In July 2009, the Basel Committee finalized a package of proposed enhancements to Basel II to strengthen the regulation and supervision of internationally active banks. And in September 2010, the committee announced a third accord, named Basel III, designed to strengthen the regulatory capital framework. The new program aims to build up capital buffers that can be drawn down in periods of stress, strengthen the quality of bank capital, and introduce a leverage ratio requirement to contain the use of excess leverage.

6. The international debt crisis was caused by international banks lending more to Third World sovereign governments than they should have. The crisis began during the 1970s when OPEC countries flooded banks with huge sums of Eurodollars that needed to be lent to cover the interest being paid on the deposits. Because of a subsequent collapse in oil prices, high unemployment, and high inflation, many less-developed countries could not afford to meet the debt service on their loans. The huge sums involved jeopardized some of the world's largest banks, in particular, U.S. banks that had lent most of the money. Debt-for-equity swaps were one means by which some banks shed themselves of Third World problem debt. But the main solution was collateralized Brady bonds, which allowed the less-developed countries to reduce the debt service on their loans and extend the maturities far into the future.

7. The Asian crisis began in mid-1997. The troubles, which began in Thailand, soon affected other countries in the region and also emerging markets in other regions. Not since the LDC debt crisis had international financial markets experienced such widespread turbulence. The crisis followed a period of economic expansion in the region financed by record private capital inflows. Bankers from industrialized countries actively sought to finance the growth opportunities. The risk exposure of the lending banks in East Asia was primarily to local banks and commercial firms, and not to sovereignties, as in the LDC debt crisis. Nevertheless, the political and economic risks were not correctly assessed.

8. The global financial crisis began in the United States in the summer of 2007 as a credit crunch, or the inability of borrowers to easily obtain credit. The origin of the credit crunch can be traced back to three key contributing factors: liberalization of banking and securities regulation, a global savings glut, and the low interest rate environment created by the Federal Reserve in the earlier part of the decade. Low interest rates created the means for first-time homeowners to afford

mortgage financing and for existing homeowners to trade up to more expensive homes. During this time, many banks and mortgage financers lowered their credit standards to attract new home buyers who could afford to make mortgage payments at current low interest rates. These so-called subprime mortgages were typically not held by the originating bank making the loan, but instead were resold for packaging into mortgage-backed securities (MBSs) to be sold to investors. As the economy cooled, many subprime borrowers found it difficult, if not impossible, to make mortgage payments, especially when their adjustable-rate mortgages were reset at higher rates. As matters unfolded, it was discovered that the amount of subprime debt held in exotic investment vehicles, and who exactly held it, was essentially unknown. When subprime debtors began defaulting on their mortgages, liquidity worldwide essentially dried up. Commercial and investment banks suffered huge losses, and many were forced into mergers with stronger banks or had to receive government bailout funds to stay in business. A deep, worldwide recession resulted. At this stage, virtually every economic entity has experienced a downturn. Many lessons should be learned from these experiences. One lesson is that bankers seem not to scrutinize credit risk as closely when they serve only as mortgage originators and then pass it on to MBS investors rather than hold the paper themselves. New banking regulations and financial regulations are currently being implemented to try and prevent or mitigate future financial crises.

KEY WORDS

affiliate bank, *268*
bank capital
   adequacy, *269*
Basel Accord, *269*
Brady bonds, *284*
collateraliged debt
   obligations (CDOs), *287*
correspondent bank
   relationship, *267*
credit default swap
   (CDS), *288*
debt-for-equity swap, *282*
Edge Act bank, *268*
Eurobank, *272*
Eurocommercial paper, *279*
Eurocredit, *274*

Eurocurrency, *272*
Euronote, *279*
Euro Interbank Offered
   Rate (EURIBOR), *273*
foreign branch bank, *267*
forward rate agreement
   (FRA), *276*
full service bank, *265*
International Banking
   Facility (IBF), *269*
international debt
   crisis, *281*
less-developed countries
   (LDCs), *281*
London Interbank Offered
   Rate (LIBOR), *273*

mortgage-backed
   securities (MBSs), *286*
negotiable certificate of
   deposit (NCD), *273*
offshore banking
   center, *268*
representative office, *267*
shadow banking
   system, *286*
sovereign debt crisis, *291*
structured investment
   vechicles (SIVs), *287*
subsidiary bank, *268*
syndicate, *274*
universal bank, *265*

QUESTIONS

1. Briefly discuss some of the services that international banks provide their customers and the marketplace.

2. Briefly discuss the various types of international banking offices.

3. How does the deposit-loan rate spread in the Eurodollar market compare with the deposit-loan rate spread in the domestic U.S. banking system? Why?

4. What is the difference between the Euronote market and the Eurocommercial paper market?

5. Briefly discuss the cause and the solution(s) to the international bank crisis involving less-developed countries.

6. What were the weaknesses of Basel II that became apparent during the global financial crisis that began in mid-2007?

7. Discuss the regulatory and macroeconomic factors that contributed to the credit crunch of 2007–2008.

8. How did the credit crunch become a global financial crisis?

9. What is a structured investment vehicle and what effect did they have on the credit crunch?

10. What is a collateralized debt obligation and what effect did they have on the credit crunch?

11. What is a credit default swap and what effect did they have on the credit crunch?

PROBLEMS

1. Grecian Tile Manufacturing of Athens, Georgia, borrows $1,500,000 at LIBOR plus a lending margin of 1.25 percent per annum on a six-month rollover basis from a London bank. If six-month LIBOR is 4.5 percent over the first six-month interval and 5.375 percent over the second six-month interval, how much will Grecian Tile pay in interest over the first year of its Eurodollar loan?

2. A bank sells a "three against six" $3,000,000 FRA for a three-month period beginning three months from today and ending six months from today. The purpose of the FRA is to cover the interest rate risk caused by the maturity mismatch from having made a three-month Eurodollar loan and having accepted a six-month Eurodollar deposit. The agreement rate with the buyer is 5.50 percent. There are actually 92 days in the three-month FRA period. Assume that three months from today the settlement rate is 4.875 percent. Determine how much the FRA is worth and who pays who—the buyer pays the seller or the seller pays the buyer.

3. Assume the settlement rate in problem 2 is 6.125 percent. What is the solution now?

4. A "three against nine" FRA has an agreement rate of 4.75 percent. You believe six-month LIBOR in three months will be 5.125 percent. You decide to take a speculative position in a FRA with a $1,000,000 notional value. There are 183 days in the FRA period. Determine whether you should buy or sell the FRA and what your expected profit will be if your forecast is correct about the six-month LIBOR rate.

5. Recall the FRA problem presented as Example 11.2. Show how the bank can alternatively use a position in Eurodollar futures contracts to hedge the interest rate risk created by the maturity mismatch it has with the $3,000,000 six-month Eurodollar deposit and rollover Eurocredit position indexed to three-month LIBOR. Assume that the bank can take a position in Eurodollar futures contracts that mature in three months and have a futures price of 94.00.

6. The Fisher effect (Chapter 6) suggests that nominal interest rates differ between countries because of differences in the respective rates of inflation. According to the Fisher effect and your examination of the one-year Eurocurrency interest rates presented in Exhibit 11.3, order the currencies from the eight countries from highest to lowest in terms of the size of the inflation premium embedded in the nominal ask interest rates for May 16, 2016.

CFA®
PROBLEMS

7. George Johnson is considering a possible six-month $100 million LIBOR-based, floating-rate bank loan to fund a project at terms shown in the table below. Johnson fears a possible rise in the LIBOR rate by December and wants to use the December Eurodollar futures contract to hedge this risk. The contract expires December 20, 2009, has a US$1 million contract size, and a discount yield of 7.3 percent. Johnson will ignore the cash flow implications of marking-to-market, initial performance bond requirements, and any timing mismatch between exchange-traded futures contract cash flows and the interest payments due in March.

Loan Terms

September 20, 2009	December 20, 2009	March 20, 2010
• Borrow $100 million at September 20 LIBOR + 200 basis points (bps) • September 20 LIBOR = 7%	• Pay interest for first three months • Roll loan over at December 20 LIBOR + 200 bps	• Pay back principal plus interest

```
                              First loan payment (9%)      Second payment
      Loan initiated          and futures contract expires  and principal
          ↓                          ↓                          ↓
          •                          •                          •
        9/20/09                   12/20/09                   3/20/10
```

a. Formulate Johnson's September 20 floating-to-fixed-rate strategy using the Eurodollar future contracts discussed in the text above. Show that this strategy would result in a fixed-rate loan, assuming an increase in the LIBOR rate to 7.8 percent by December 20, which remains at 7.8 percent through March 20. Show all calculations.

Johnson is considering a 12-month loan as an alternative. This approach will result in two additional uncertain cash flows, as follows:

```
   Loan          First          Second        Third        Fourth payment
  initiated    payment (9%)     payment      payment       and principal
     ↓             ↓              ↓             ↓                ↓
     •             •              •             •                •
   9/20/09      12/20/09       3/20/10       6/20/10          9/20/10
```

b. Describe the strip hedge that Johnson could use and explain how it hedges the 12-month loan (specify number of contracts.) No calculations are needed.

8. Jacob Bower has a liability that:

- has a principal balance of $100 million on June 30, 2008,
- accrues interest quarterly starting on June 30, 2008,
- pays interest quarterly,
- has a one-year term to maturity, and
- calculates interest due based on 90-day LIBOR (the London Interbank Offered Rate).

Bower wishes to hedge his remaining interest payments against changes in interest rates. Bower has correctly calculated that he needs to sell (short) 300 Eurodollar futures contracts to accomplish the hedge. He is considering the alternative hedging strategies outlined in the following table.

Initial Position (6/30/08) in 90-Day LIBOR Eurodollar Contracts

Contract Month	Strategy A (contracts)	Strategy B (contracts)
September 2008	300	100
December 2008	0	100
March 2009	0	100

a. Explain why strategy B is a more effective hedge than strategy A when the yield curve undergoes an instantaneous nonparallel shift.

b. Discuss an interest rate scenario in which strategy A would be superior to strategy B.

INTERNET EXERCISES

1. Exhibit 11.5 compares the spread between the prime borrowing rate and dollar LIBOR. Go to the Bankrate website www.bankrate.com, and search for the input to calculate the current spread and the spread for three months and one year ago.

2. In this chapter, we noted that universal banks provide a host of services to corporate clients. Wells Fargo, one of the world's largest banks, is an example of a universal bank. Go to its website www.wellsfargo.com/biz/international to view the global services it provides.

MINI CASE

Detroit Motors' Latin American Expansion

It is September 1990 and Detroit Motors of Detroit, Michigan, is considering establishing an assembly plant in Latin America for a new utility vehicle it has just designed. The cost of the capital expenditures has been estimated at $65,000,000. There is not much of a sales market in Latin America, and virtually all output would be exported to the United States for sale. Nevertheless, an assembly plant in Latin America is attractive for at least two reasons. First, labor costs are expected to be half what Detroit Motors would have to pay in the United States to union workers. Since the assembly plant will be a new facility for a newly designed vehicle, Detroit Motors does not expect any hassle from its U.S. union in establishing the plant in Latin America. Secondly, the chief financial officer (CFO) of Detroit Motors believes that a debt-for-equity swap can be arranged with at least one of the Latin American countries that has not been able to meet its debt service on its sovereign debt with some of the major U.S. banks.

The September 10, 1990, issue of *Barron's* indicated the following prices (cents on the dollar) on Latin American bank debt:

Brazil	21.75
Mexico	43.12
Argentina	14.25
Venezuela	46.25
Chile	70.25

The CFO is not comfortable with the level of political risk in Brazil and Argentina, and has decided to eliminate them from consideration. After some preliminary discussions with the central banks of Mexico, Venezuela, and Chile, the CFO has learned that all three countries would be interested in hearing a detailed presentation about the type of facility Detroit Motors would construct, how long it would take, the number of locals that would be employed, and the number of units that would be manufactured per year. Since it is time-consuming to prepare and make these presentations, the CFO would like to approach the most attractive candidate first. He has learned that the central bank of Mexico will redeem its debt at 80 percent of face value in a debt-for-equity swap, Venezuela at 75 percent, and Chile 100 percent. As a first step, the CFO decides an analysis based purely on financial considerations is necessary to determine which country looks like the most viable candidate. You are asked to assist in the analysis. What do you advise?

REFERENCES & SUGGESTED READINGS

Acharya, Viral V., Thomas F. Cooley, Matthew P. Richardson, and Ingo Walter. *Regulating Wall Street: The Dodd-Frank Act and the New Architecture of Global Finance.* Hoboken, N.J.: John Wiley & Sons, 2011.

Bank for International Settlements. "Supervisory Lessons to Be Drawn from the Asian Crisis." Basel: Bank for International Settlements, June 1999.

Bank for International Settlements. *International Convergence of Capital Measurement and Capital Standards: A Revised Framework.* Basel: Bank for International Settlements, July 2004.

www.mhhe.com/er8e

www.mhhe.com/er8e

Bodie, Zvi, Alex Kane, and Alan J. Marcus. *Investments*, 9th ed. New York: McGraw-Hill/Irwin, 2011.

Dufey, Gunter, and Ian Giddy. *The International Money Market*, 2nd ed. Upper Saddle River, N.J.: Prentice Hall, 1994.

Goldberg, Lawrence G., and Robert Grosse. "Location Choice of Foreign Banks in the United States." *Journal of Economics and Business* 46 (1994), pp. 367–79.

Hultman, Charles W. *The Environment of International Banking*. Englewood Cliffs, N.J.: Prentice Hall, 1990.

International Monetary Fund. *International Capital Markets*: *Part II. Systemic Issues in International Finance*. Washington, D.C.: International Monetary Fund, August 1993.

International Monetary Fund. *International Capital Markets*: *Developments, Prospects, and Key Policy Issues*. Washington, D.C.: International Monetary Fund, September 1998.

Ip, Greg, and Jan E. Hilsenrath, "How Credit Got So Easy and Why It's Tightening," *The Wall Street Journal*, August 7, 2007, pp. A1 and A7.

Resnick, Bruce G., and Gary L. Shoesmith. "Information Transmission in the World Money Markets." *European Financial Management* 17 (2011), pp. 183–200.

Rivera-Batiz, Francisco L., and Luis Rivera-Batiz. *International Finance and Open Economy Macroeconomics*, 2nd ed. Upper Saddle River, N.J.: Prentice Hall, 1994.

Rugman, Alan M., and Shyan J. Kamath. "International Diversification and Multinational Banking." In Sarkis J. Khoury and Alo Ghosh, eds., *Recent Developments in International Banking and Finance*. Lexington, Mass.: Lexington Books, 1987.

11A Eurocurrency Creation

As an illustration, consider the following simplified example of the creation of Euro-dollars. Assume a U.S. Importer purchases $100 of merchandise from a German Exporter and pays for the purchase by drawing a $100 check on his U.S. checking account (demand deposit). Further assume the German Exporter deposits the $100 check received as payment in a demand deposit in the U.S. bank (which in actuality represents the entire U.S. commercial banking system). This transaction can be represented by T accounts, where changes in assets are on the left and changes in liabilities are on the right side of the T, as follows:

U.S. Commercial Bank		
	Demand Deposits	
	U.S. Importer	−$100
	German Exporter	+$100

At this point, all that has changed in the U.S. banking system is that ownership of $100 of demand deposits has been transferred from domestic to foreign control.

The German Exporter is not likely to leave his deposit in the form of a demand deposit for long, as no interest is being earned on this type of account. If the funds are not needed for the operation of the business, the German Exporter can deposit the $100 in a time deposit in a bank outside the United States and receive a greater rate of interest than if the funds were put in a U.S. time deposit. Assume the German Exporter closes out his demand deposit in the U.S. Bank and redeposits the funds in a London Eurobank. The London Eurobank credits the German Exporter with a $100 time deposit and deposits the $100 into its correspondent bank account (demand deposit) with the U.S. Bank (banking system). These transactions are represented as follows by T accounts:

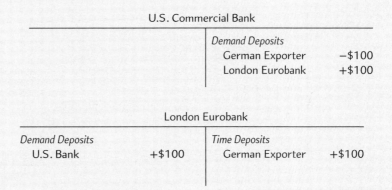

U.S. Commercial Bank		
	Demand Deposits	
	German Exporter	−$100
	London Eurobank	+$100

London Eurobank			
Demand Deposits		*Time Deposits*	
U.S. Bank	+$100	German Exporter	+$100

Two points are noteworthy from these transactions. First, ownership of $100 of demand deposits has again been transferred (from the German Exporter to the London

Eurobank), but the entire $100 still remains on deposit in the U.S. Bank. Second, the $100 time deposit of the German Exporter in the London Eurobank represents the creation of Eurodollars. This deposit exists in *addition* to the dollars deposited in the United States. Hence, no dollars have flowed out of the U.S. banking system in the creation of Eurodollars.

The London Eurobank will soon lend out the dollars, as it cannot afford to pay interest on a time deposit on which it is not earning a return. To whom will the London Eurobank lend the dollars? Most obviously to a party needing dollars for a dollar-denominated business transaction or to an investor desiring to invest in the United States. Let's assume that a Dutch Importer borrows $100 from the London Eurobank for the purpose of purchasing merchandise from a U.S. Exporter for resale in the Netherlands. The T accounts representing these transactions are as follows:

London Eurobank

Demand Deposits			
U.S. Bank	−$100		
Loans			
Dutch Importer	+$100		

U.S. Commercial Bank

		Demand Deposits	
		London Eurobank	−$100
		Dutch Importer	+$100

Dutch Importer

Demand Deposits		*Loan from*	
in U.S. Bank	+$100	London Eurobank	+$100

Note from these transactions that the London Eurobank transfers ownership of $100 of its demand deposits held in the U.S. Commercial Bank to the Dutch Exporter in exchange for the $100 loan.

The Dutch Exporter will draw a check on its demand deposit in the U.S. Bank to pay the U.S. Exporter for the merchandise shipment. The U.S. Exporter will deposit the check in his U.S. Bank demand deposit. These transactions are represented as follows:

Dutch Importer

Demand Deposit		
in U.S. Bank	−$100	
Inventory	+$100	

U.S. Exporter

Inventory	−$100	
Demand Deposit		
in U.S. Bank	+$100	

U.S. Commercial Bank

		Demand Deposit	
		Dutch Importer	−$100
		U.S. Exporte	+$100

The T accounts show that $100 of demand deposits in the U.S. Bank have changed ownership, going from the control of the Dutch Importer to the U.S. Exporter—or from foreign to U.S. ownership. The original $100, however, never left the U.S. banking system.

QUESTION

Explain how Eurocurrency is created.

12 International Bond Market

THIS CHAPTER CONTINUES the discussion of international capital markets and institutions, focusing on the international bond market. The chapter is designed to be useful for the financial officer of a MNC interested in sourcing new debt capital in the international bond market, as well as for the international investor interested in international fixed-income securities.

The chapter opens with a brief statistical presentation showing the size of the world's bond markets and the major currencies in which bonds are denominated. The next section presents some useful definitions that describe exactly what is meant by the international bond market. The accompanying discussion elaborates on the features that distinguish these market segments and the various types of bond instruments traded in them. Included in the discussion is a decomposition of the international bond market by currency denomination, nationality of issuer, and the type of borrower. Trading practices in the Eurobond market are discussed next. The chapter concludes with a discussion of international bond credit ratings and bond market indexes that are useful for performance analysis.

The World's Bond Markets: A Statistical Perspective

Exhibit 12.1 presents an overview of the world's bond markets. It shows the amounts of domestic and international bonds outstanding denominated in the major currencies. The exhibit shows that at year-end 2014 the face value of bonds and (long-term original maturity notes) outstanding in the world was approximately $95,244 billion. Domestic bonds account for the largest share of outstanding bonds, equaling $74,249.4 billion, or 78 percent, of the total. The remaining $20,944.6 billion, 22 percent, are international bonds.

Exhibit 12.1 shows that the U.S. dollar, the euro, the pound sterling, and the yen are the four currencies in which the majority of domestic and international bonds are denominated. Proportionately more domestic bonds than international bonds are denominated in the dollar (44.0 percent versus 40.4 percent) and the yen (14.1 percent versus 2 percent) while more international bonds than domestic bonds are denominated in the euro (41.5 percent versus 14.7 percent), and the pound sterling (9.3 percent versus 5.6 percent).

EXHIBIT 12.1

Amounts of Domestic and International Bonds Outstanding
(at year-end 2014 in billions of U.S. dollars)

Currency	Domestic	Percent	International	Percent	Total	Percent
U.S. dollar	32,653.2	44.0	8,475.9	40.4	41,129.1	43.2
Euro	10,931.4	14.7	8,708.4	41.5	19,639.8	20.6
Pound sterling	4,174.9	5.6	1,947.3	9.3	6,122.2	6.4
Yen	10,457.3	14.1	417.7	2.0	10,875.0	11.4
Other	16,032.6	21.6	1,445.3	6.9	17,477.9	18.4
Total	74,249.4	100.0	20,994.6	100.0	95,244.0	100.0

Source: Derived from data in *International Banking and Financial Market Developments,* Bank for International Settlements, June 2016.

Foreign Bonds and Eurobonds

The international bond market encompasses two basic market segments: foreign bonds and Eurobonds. A **foreign bond** issue is one offered by a foreign borrower to the investors in a national capital market and denominated in that nation's currency. An example is a German MNC issuing dollar-denominated bonds to U.S. investors. A **Eurobond** issue is one denominated in a particular currency but sold to investors in national capital markets other than the country that issued the denominating currency. An example is a Dutch borrower issuing dollar-denominated bonds to investors in the U.K., Switzerland, and the Netherlands. The markets for foreign bonds and Eurobonds operate in parallel with the domestic national bond markets, and all three market groups compete with one another.[1] A "Dragon bond" market exists where non-Japanese Asian issuers sell bonds typically denominated in the U.S. dollar through Asian syndication. This market can be viewed as a segment of the Eurobond market.

Exhibit 12.2 presents the year-end amounts of international bonds outstanding for 2011 through the first quarter of 2015. The exhibit classifies the amounts by type of issue. As the exhibit shows, the amounts of international bonds outstanding have remained rather stable in recent years.

In any given year, roughly 80 percent of new international bonds are likely to be Eurobonds rather than foreign bonds. Eurobonds are known by the currency in which they are denominated, for example, U.S. dollar Eurobonds, yen Eurobonds, and Swiss franc Eurobonds, or, correspondingly, Eurodollar bonds, Euroyen bonds, and EuroSF bonds. Foreign bonds, on the other hand, frequently have colorful names that designate the country in which they are issued. For example, *Yankee* bonds are dollar–denominated foreign bonds originally sold to U.S. investors, *Samurai* bonds are yen-denominated foreign bonds sold in Japan, and *Bulldogs* are pound sterling–denominated foreign bonds sold in the U.K.

Bearer Bonds and Registered Bonds

Eurobonds are usually bearer bonds. With a **bearer bond**, possession is evidence of ownership. The issuer does not keep any records indicating who is the current owner of a bond. With **registered bonds**, the owner's name is on the bond and it is also recorded by the issuer, or else the owner's name is assigned to a bond serial number recorded by the issuer. When a registered bond is sold, a new bond certificate is issued with the new owner's name, or the new owner's name is assigned to the bond serial number.

U.S. security regulations require Yankee bonds and U.S. corporate bonds sold to U.S. citizens to be registered. Bearer bonds are very attractive to investors desiring privacy and anonymity. One reason for this is that they enable tax evasion. Consequently, investors will generally accept a lower yield on bearer bonds than on registered bonds of comparable terms, making them a less costly source of funds for the issuer to service.

---

[1]In this chapter the terms *market segment, market group,* and *market* are used interchangeably when referring to the foreign bond and Eurobond divisions of the international bond market.

EXHIBIT 12.2	2011	2012	2013	2014	2015 (1Q)
International Bonds Amounts Outstanding Classified by Major Instruments (in billions of U.S. dollars)					
Instrument					
Straight fixed-rate	13,541.5	14,824.0	15,545.9	15,140.1	14,569.6
Floating-rate notes	6,339.0	5,959.4	5,975.6	5,450.6	5,037.2
Convertible issues	325.5	318.1	377.0	403.9	395.4
With equity warrants	1.0	0.9	0.0	0.0	0.0
Total	20,207.0	21,102.3	21,898.5	20,994.6	20,002.2

Source: Compiled from various issues of *International Banking and Financial Market Developments*, Bank for International Settlements.

National Security Regulations

Foreign bonds must meet the security regulations of the country in which they are issued. This means that publicly traded Yankee bonds must meet the same regulations as U.S. domestic bonds. The U.S. Securities Act of 1933 requires full disclosure of relevant information relating to a security issue. The U.S. Securities Exchange Act of 1934 established the Securities and Exchange Commission (SEC) to administer the 1933 Act. According to the 1933 Act, securities sold in the United States to public investors must be registered with the SEC, and a prospectus disclosing detailed financial information about the issuer must be provided and made available to prospective investors. The expense of the registration process, the time delay it creates in bringing a new issue to market (four additional weeks), and the disclosure of information that many foreign borrowers consider private have historically made it more desirable for foreign borrowers to raise U.S. dollars in the Eurobond market, which, in general, is not subject to registration under the 1933 Act. The shorter length of time in bringing a Eurodollar bond issue to market, coupled with the lower rate of interest that borrowers pay for Eurodollar bond financing in comparison to Yankee bond financing, are two major reasons why the Eurobond segment of the international bond market is roughly four times the size of the foreign bond segment. Because Eurobonds do not have to meet national security regulations, name recognition of the issuer is an extremely important factor in being able to source funds in the international capital market.

Transactional restrictions prohibit offers and sales of Eurobonds in the United States or to U.S. investors during a 40-day restriction period that allows for the security to become seasoned in the secondary market. The purpose of the restriction period is to protect U.S. investors from investing in unregistered bonds where little investment information is known until "the market" has had the opportunity to evaluate them rather than to prevent U.S. investors from investing in bearer bonds which may facilitate tax avoidance or evasion through the bearer feature.

Withholding Taxes

Prior to 1984, the United States required a 30 percent withholding tax on interest paid to nonresidents who held U.S. government or corporate bonds. Moreover, U.S. firms issuing Eurodollar bonds from the United States were required to withhold the tax on interest paid to foreigners. In 1984, the withholding tax law was repealed. Additionally, U.S. corporations were allowed to issue domestic bearer bonds to nonresidents, but Congress would not grant this privilege to the Treasury.

The repeal of the withholding tax law caused a substantial shift in the relative yields on U.S. government and Eurodollar bonds. Prior to 1984, top-quality Eurodollar bonds sold overseas traded at lower yields than U.S. Treasury bonds of similar maturities that were subject to the withholding tax. Afterward the situation was reversed; foreign investors found the safety of registered U.S. Treasury bonds without the withholding tax more attractive than higher yields on corporate Eurodollar bond issues.

Security Regulations that Ease Bond Issuance

Two other U.S. security regulations have had an effect on the international bond market. One is *Rule 415,* which the SEC instituted in 1982 to allow shelf registration. **Shelf registration** allows an issuer to preregister a securities issue, and then shelve the securities for later sale when financing is actually needed. Shelf registration has thus eliminated the time delay in bringing a foreign bond issue to market in the United States, but it has not eliminated the information disclosure that many foreign borrowers find too expensive and/or objectionable. In 1990, the SEC instituted *Rule 144A,* which allows *qualified institutional buyers (QIBs)* in the United States to trade in private placement issues that do not have to meet the strict information disclosure requirements of publicly traded issues. Rule 144A was designed to make the U.S. capital markets more competitive with the Eurobond market. Rule 144A issues are non-registered and may only trade among QIBs. A large portion of the 144A market is composed of Yankee bonds. The International Finance in Practice box, "SOX and Bonds," discusses how international companies are starting to prefer issuing Yankee bonds in the private placement market in the United States to avoid costly information disclosure required of registered bonds by the Sarbanes-Oxley Act.

Global Bonds

Global bond issues were first offered in 1989. A **global bond** issue is a very large bond issue that would be difficult to sell in any one country or region of the world. Consequently, it is simultaneously sold and subsequently traded in major markets worldwide. Global bonds are fully fungible because the identical instrument trades in all markets without restriction. The average size of global bond issues has been about one billion dollars. Most have been denominated in the U.S. dollar. The portion of a U.S. dollar global bond sold by a U.S. (foreign) borrower in the United States is classified as a domestic (Yankee) bond and the portion sold elsewhere is a Eurodollar bond. If the larger issue size and the worldwide marketability of a global bond issue enhances its liquidity, investors might, ceteris paribus, be willing to accept a lower yield than they would require from smaller issues of domestic, foreign or Eurobonds. This does not appear to be the case, however. In a recent study, Resnick (2012) shows that, ceteris paribus, investors demand an equivalent yield from dollar denominated domestic, Yankee, Eurodollar, and global bonds. Hence, global bond investors demand a competitive yield with other bond market segments. On the other hand, Resnick does find that the gross underwriting spread, a common measure of the costs of bond issuance paid to underwriters, is, ceteris paribus, lower for a global issue in comparison to smaller domestic, Yankee, or Eurodollar bond issues. These cost savings are attributed entirely to economies of scale that result from the large size of the global issue. Miller and Puthenpurackal (2005) also document a cost savings from issuing global bonds. The largest corporate global bond issue to date is the $14.6 billion Deutsche Telekom multicurrency offering. The issue includes three U.S. dollar tranches with 5-, 10-, and 30-year maturities totaling $9.5 billion, two euro tranches with 5- and 10-year maturities totaling €3 billion, two British pound sterling tranches with 5- and 30-year maturities totaling £950 million, and one 5-year Japanese yen tranche of ¥90 billion. Another large global bond issue is the AT&T package of $2 billion of 5.625 percent notes due 2004, $3 billion of 6.000 percent notes due 2009, and $3 billion of 6.500 percent notes due 2029 issued in March 1999. The Republic of Italy issued one of the largest sovereign global bond issues in September 1993, a package of $2 billion of 6.000 percent notes due 2003 and $3.5 billion of 6.875 percent debentures due 2023. One of the largest emerging markets global bond issues to date is the Republic of Korea package issued April 1998 of $1 billion of 8.750 percent notes due 2003 and $3 billion of 8.875 percent bonds due 2008. SEC Rule 415 and Rule 144A have likely facilitated global bond offerings, and more offerings in the future can be expected.

Types of Instruments

The international bond market has been much more innovative than the domestic bond market in the types of instruments offered to investors. In this section, we examine the major types of international bonds. We begin with a discussion of the more standard types of instruments and conclude with the more exotic innovations that have appeared in recent years.

SOX and Bonds

The Sarbanes-Oxley Act (SOX) of 2002 is the U.S. law designed to eliminate corporate fraud. SOX was named for Michael Oxley, the former House Financial Services Committee Chairman, and former Maryland Democratic Senator Paul Sarbanes of Maryland. It was passed after the collapse of Enron and WorldCom.

A recent article by Bloomberg News* reports that its existence is prompting more companies to issue unregistered bonds. "At least 100 . . . companies are selling bonds that aren't registered with the Securities and Exchange Commission instead of debt that requires more disclosure." The sale of unregistered bonds " . . . increased 50 percent in the past two years, five times faster than the rest of the U.S. market."

According to Bloomberg News, private bond placements are surging because companies face little penalty for keeping their finances away from the public. Investors demand only 11 basis points more in yield to buy unregistered securities, whereas it costs millions of dollars to comply with the Sarbanes-Oxley.

SOX compliance costs can easily erase any yield savings from issuing public debt. SOX requires companies to hire external auditors to evaluate their financial reports. The law also applies to foreign borrowers desiring to sell so-called Yankee bonds to the American public. According to Bloomberg News, "international companies that used to sell public debt in the U.S. are staying away to avoid Sarbanes-Oxley."

SOX is consistent with attempts to make the bond market more transparent. Unregistered bonds can only trade between institutions. These trades are not reported on the NASD's Trade Reporting and Compliance Engine.

However, according to Bloomberg News, investors are willing to trade more yield for additional documentation or registration requirements. The market value of unregistered bonds has risen 28 percent a year since 2004, compared with only a 5 percent increase for all corporate debt.

Sellers of unregistered bonds need only to disclose information to owners of their securities. According to Bloomberg News, companies selling unregistered bonds include closely held issuers that have traditionally used private placements to borrow.

For example, "Cargill Inc., the largest U.S. agricultural company, has at least $8.3 billion in unregistered securities. The closely held company only sells debt in private placements or through an SEC exemption known as Rule 144a." A Cargill spokesperson notes "'we have access to a limited pool of investors because we're not selling regi-stered debt. We pay a slightly higher interest rate, and our disclosure goes only to those *qualified institutional buyers* that purchase the debt.'"

*Mark Pittman, "Sarbanes-Oxley Backfires in Unregistered Bond Sales," Bloomberg News, February 14, 2007.

Straight Fixed-Rate Issues

Straight fixed-rate bond issues have a designated maturity date at which the principal of the bond issue is promised to be repaid. During the life of the bond, fixed coupon payments, which are a percentage of the face value, are paid as interest to the bondholders. In contrast to many domestic bonds, which make semiannual coupon payments, coupon interest on Eurobonds is typically paid annually. The reason is that the Eurobonds are usually bearer bonds, and annual coupon redemption is more convenient for the bondholders and less costly for the bond issuer because the bondholders are scattered geographically. Exhibit 12.2 shows that the vast majority of new international bond offerings in any year are straight fixed-rate issues. The euro, U.S. dollar, British pound sterling, and Japanese yen have been the most common currencies denominating straight fixed-rate bonds in recent years.

Euro-Medium-Term Notes

Euro-Medium-Term Notes (Euro-MTNs) are (typically) fixed-rate notes issued by a corporation with maturities ranging from less than a year to about 10 years. Like fixed-rate bonds, Euro-MTNs have a fixed maturity and pay coupon interest on periodic dates. Unlike a bond issue, in which the entire issue is brought to market at once, a Euro-MTN issue is partially sold on a continuous basis through an issuance facility that allows the borrower to obtain funds only as needed on a flexible basis. This feature is very attractive to issuers. Euro-MTNs have become a very popular means of raising medium-term funds since they were first introduced in 1986. All the statistical exhibits in this chapter include the amounts outstanding of MTNs.

An example of straight fixed-rate Euro-MTNs is the $600,000,000 of 5.15 percent notes due January 2013, issued in December 2007 by BT Group Plc of the United Kingdom.

Floating-Rate Notes

The first floating-rate notes were introduced in 1970. **Floating-rate notes (FRNs)** are typically medium-term bonds with coupon payments indexed to some reference rate. Common reference rates are either three-month or six-month U.S. dollar LIBOR. Coupon payments on FRNs are usually quarterly or semiannual and in accord with the reference rate. For example, consider a five-year FRN with coupons referenced to six-month dollar LIBOR paying coupon interest semiannually. At the beginning of every six-month period, the next semiannual coupon payment is *reset* to be .5 × (LIBOR + X percent) of face value, where X represents the default risk premium above LIBOR the issuer must pay based on its creditworthiness. The premium is typically no larger than 1/8 percent for top-quality issuers. As an example, if X equals 1/8 percent and the current six-month LIBOR is 6.6 percent, the next period's coupon rate on a $1,000 face value FRN will be .5 × (.066 + .00125) × $1,000 = $33.625. If on the next reset date six-month LIBOR is 5.7 percent, the following semiannual coupon will be set at $29.125.

Obviously, FRNs behave differently in response to interest rate risk than straight fixed-rate bonds. All bonds experience an inverse price change when the market rate of interest changes. Accordingly, the price of straight fixed-rate bonds may vary significantly if interest rates are extremely volatile. FRNs, on the other hand, experience only mild price changes between reset dates, over which time the next period's coupon payment is fixed (assuming, of course, that the reference rate corresponds to the market rate applicable to the issuer). On the reset date, the market price will gravitate back close to par value when the next period's coupon payment is reset to the new market value of the reference rate, and subsequent coupon payments are repriced to market expectations of future values of the reference rate. (The actual FRN market price may deviate somewhat from exact par value because the default risk premium portion of the coupon payment is fixed at inception, whereas the credit quality of the borrower may change through time.) FRNs make attractive investments for investors with a strong need to preserve the principal value of the investment should they need to liquidate the investment prior to the maturity of the bonds. Exhibit 12.2 shows that FRNs are the second most common type of international bond issue. The euro and the U.S. dollar are the two currencies denominating most outstanding FRNs.

As an example of fixed/FRNs, in May 2006 General Electric Capital Corporation issued $500,000 of four-year notes with interest paid at the fixed rate of 5.464 percent the first year and indexed to three-month LIBOR plus 6 basis points the last three years.

Equity-Related Bonds

There are two types of **equity-related bonds**: convertible bonds and bonds with equity warrants. A **convertible bond** issue allows the investor to exchange the bond for a predetermined number of equity shares of the issuer. The *floor-value* of a convertible bond is its straight fixed-rate bond value. Convertibles usually sell at a premium above the larger of their straight debt value and their conversion value. Additionally, investors are usually willing to accept a lower coupon rate of interest than the comparable straight fixed coupon bond rate because they find the conversion feature attractive. **Bonds with equity warrants** can be viewed as straight fixed-rate bonds with the addition of a call option (or warrant) feature. The warrant entitles the bondholder to purchase a certain number of equity shares in the issuer at a prestated price over a predetermined period of time.

Dual-Currency Bonds

Dual-currency bonds became popular in the mid-1980s. A **dual-currency bond** is a straight fixed-rate bond issued in one currency, say, Swiss francs, that pays coupon interest in that same currency. At maturity, the principal is repaid in another currency, say, U.S. dollars. Coupon interest is frequently at a higher rate than comparable straight fixed-rate bonds. The amount of the dollar principal repayment at maturity is set at inception; frequently, the amount allows for some appreciation in the exchange rate of the stronger currency. From the investor's perspective, a dual-currency bond includes a long-term forward contract. If the dollar appreciates over the life of the bond, the principal repayment will be worth more than a return of principal in Swiss

Instrument	Frequency of Interest Payment	Size of Coupon Payment	Payoff at Maturity
Straight fixed-rate	Annual	Fixed	Currency of issue
Floating-rate note	Quarterly or semiannual	Variable	Currency of issue
Convertible bond	Annual	Fixed	Currency of issue or conversion to equity shares
Straight fixed-rate with equity warrants	Annual	Fixed	Currency of issue plus equity shares from exercised warrants
Dual-currency bond	Annual	Fixed	Dual currency

francs. The market value of a dual-currency bond in Swiss francs should equal the sum of the present value of the Swiss franc coupon stream discounted at the Swiss market rate of interest plus the dollar principal repayment, converted to Swiss francs at the expected future exchange rate, and discounted at the Swiss market rate of interest.

Japanese firms have been large issuers of dual-currency bonds. These bonds were issued and pay coupon interest in yen with the principal reimbursement in U.S. dollars. Yen/dollar dual-currency bonds could be an attractive financing method for Japanese MNCs desiring to establish or expand U.S. subsidiaries. The yen proceeds can be converted to dollars to finance the capital investment in the United States, and during the early years the coupon payments can be made by the parent firm in yen. At maturity, the dollar principal repayment can be made from dollar profits earned by the subsidiary.

Exhibit 12.3 summarizes the typical characteristics of the international bond market instruments discussed in this section.

Currency Distribution, Nationality, and Type of Issuer

Exhibit 12.4 provides the distribution of the amounts of international bond notes outstanding by currency from year-end 2011 through the first quarter of 2015. The exhibit shows that the euro, U.S. dollar, British pound sterling, yen, Swiss franc, and Canadian dollar have been the most frequently used currencies to denominate issues.

Exhibit 12.5 is divided into two panels that show the nationality and type of issuer of international bonds. The top panel indicates that France, Germany, the Netherlands, the United Kingdom, and the United States have been major issuers of international

	2011	2012	2013	2014	2015 (1Q)
Currency					
Euro	9,331.8	9,620.0	9,907.3	8,708.4	7,763.5
U.S. dollar	6,640.5	7,223.8	7,860.7	8,475.9	8,628.1
Pound sterling	1,905.5	1,921.3	2,045.6	1,947.3	1,850.3
Yen	741.9	646.2	485.2	417.7	413.3
Swiss franc	380.8	380.9	352.8	300.9	291.4
Canadian dollar	311.5	287.6	261.6	207.5	179.8
Other	895.0	1,022.5	985.3	936.9	875.8
Total	20,207.0	21,102.3	21,898.5	20,994.6	20,002.2

Source: Compiled from various issues of *International Banking and Financial Market Developments,* Bank for International Settlements.

International Bond Amounts Outstanding Classified by Nationality and Type of Issuer (in billions of U.S. dollars)

	2011	2012	2013	2014	2015 (1Q)
Nationality					
Australia	530.9	570.4	601.2	595.7	581.3
Canada	643.8	684.5	732.8	737.3	739.6
France	1,637.1	1,715.1	1,758.4	1,603.3	1,469.0
Germany	1,869.1	1,921.6	1,902.7	1,743.0	1,598.6
Italy	1,142.2	1,094.9	1,154.9	988.2	889.1
Japan	335.8	329.5	344.1	358.7	364.5
Netherlands	1,265.6	1,307.5	1,337.3	1,244.1	1,143.1
United Kingdom	2,771.9	2,744.2	2,785.3	2,595.8	2,448.9
United States	2,991.5	2,938.5	2,943.6	2,986.9	2,988.9
Other developed countries	4,373.6	4,111.6	4,213.1	3,725.9	3,425.7
Off-shore centers	261.8	316.7	325.8	333.3	338.1
Developing countries	1,691.5	2,042.9	2,379.4	2,628.4	2,639.1
International organizations	1,028.0	1,324.9	1,453.5	1,465.2	1,384.2
Total	20,207.0	21,102.3	21,898.5	20,994.6	20,002.2
Type					
Financial corporations	15,506.3	15,723.4	15,921.4	14,964.2	14,210.8
General Government	1,542.8	1,578.0	1,655.3	1,612.4	1,539.1
International organizations	1,028.1	1,324.9	1,455.3	1,465.7	1,384.6
Non-financial corporations	2,129.8	2,476.0	2,866.7	2,952.4	2,867.6
Total	20,207.0	21,102.3	21,898.5	20,994.6	20,002.2

Source: Compiled from various issues of *International Banking and Financial Market Developments*, Bank for International Settlements.

bonds during the past several years. In terms of type of issuer, the bottom panel of Exhibit 12.5 shows that financial corporations have been the largest issuers of international bonds.

The International Finance in Practice box, "Heineken Refreshes Euromarket with Spectacular Unrated Bonds," discusses a Eurobond offering issued by Heineken.

International Bond Market Credit Ratings

www.fitchratings.com

This is the website of Fitch Ratings, an international bond rating service. Information about Fitch and its services can be found here.

www.moodys.com

This is the website of Moody's Corporation. Information about the bond credit ratings that Moody's Investors Service provides can be found here.

www.standardandpoors.com

This is the website of S&P Global Ratings, a provider of investment information, such as bond ratings. Information about S&P Global Ratings can be found here.

Fitch Ratings, Moody's Investors Service, and S&P Global Ratings (S&P) have for years provided credit ratings on domestic and international bonds and their issuers. These three credit-rating organizations classify bond issues into categories based upon the creditworthiness of the borrower. The ratings are based on an analysis of current information regarding the likelihood of default and the specifics of the debt obligation. The ratings reflect both creditworthiness and exchange rate uncertainty.

Moody's rates bond issues (and issuers) into nine categories, from Aaa, Aa, A, Baa, and Ba down to C. Ratings of Aaa to Baa are known as *investment grade* ratings. These issues are judged not to have any speculative elements; interest payments and principal safety appear adequate at present. The future prospects of lower-rated issues cannot be considered as well assured. Within categories Aa through Caa, Moody's has three numeric modifiers, 1, 2, or 3, to place an issue, respectively, at the upper, middle, or lower end of the category.

S&P Global Ratings rates bond issues (and issuers) into 10 categories. For bond issuers, the categories are AAA, AA, A, BBB, and BB down to CC and R, SD, and D. Categories AAA to BBB are investment grade ratings. An obligor rated R is under regulatory supervision owing to its financial condition. An obligor rated SD or D has failed to pay one or more of its financial obligations when due. Ratings for Categories AA to CCC may be modified with a plus (+) or minus (−) to reflect the relative standing of an issue to others in the category. Fitch uses ratings symbols and definitions similar to S&P's.

Heineken Refreshes Euromarket with Spectacular Unrated Bonds

Heineken launched the euro market's largest unrated bond this week with a spectacular two tranche Eu1.1bn debut transaction. The deal, in 6- and 10-year tranches, was more than four times oversubscribed and priced well inside price guidance. Heineken's success demonstrates the depth of demand for unrated credits in the Eurobond market, despite the growing prevalence of ratings and well publicized investor calls for borrowers to have at least two ratings. The major factor in Heineken's favour was the global reach of its brand—the brewer has operations in over 170 countries.

The 10-year bond—the first from an unrated corporate— was five times oversubscribed, enabling bookrunners Barclays Capital, Citigroup, Credit Suisse First Boston and JP Morgan to increase it from Eu500m to Eu600m. "There was no clear guidance in the market about what we could achieve for Heineken or where they could be positioned as a credit—we had to convince people," said Chris Tuffey, head of corporate syndicate at CSFB in London. "Unrated issues are typically tough to sell investors on, but the Heineken transaction was exactly the opposite— both tranches were heavily oversubscribed." Although the lead managers looked at brand names such as Louis Vuitton Moet Hennessy, McDonald's and Carlsberg in pricing the transaction, the price was decided by investors' perception of the credit. Heineken was priced as a single-A credit, although it paid a small premium for the absence of a rating.

Rene Hooft Graafland, a member of Heineken's executive board, said the Heineken family retains a controlling interest in the company and maintains a very conservative approach in running it. He said the diversity of the company's cashflows and profit sources made Heineken an attractive credit. Explaining why Heineken is not rated, Hooft Graafland said the bond was a one-off issue to partially finance the Eu1.9bn acquisition of Brau-Beteiligung AG, Austria's largest brewer, which was completed on October 15. Heineken does not intend to become a regular bond issuer. "The decision not to obtain a rating was not taken lightly but there were clear indications that there was demand among investors for the Heineken name on an unrated basis," said Hooft Graafland. "The Heineken business model is relatively straightforward and there is high transparency in the way the company is run."

The acquisition of BBAG makes Heineken the leading regional player in central eastern Europe, with a market share of 27%. Besides its lack of a rating, investors were concerned by the level of subsidiary indebtedness and the possibility that the new bonds would be subordinated to the company's outstanding debt. Both issues were tackled by management on the five-day roadshow— and successfully so, judging by the level of oversubscription.

The reason that Heineken's previous debt had been concentrated in the operating subsidiaries rather than the holding company was simply that it was more cost effective under Dutch tax law, which has changed in the last month. "However, we made it clear that the debt level is modest and is historically concentrated in the three big operating companies," said Hooft Graafland. "In addition to the standard covenant package, the bond has a covenant that limits the level of subsidiary indebtedness at 35% of the total consolidated group assets." The main buyers of the 2010s were investors in Switzerland taking 25%, the UK with 22%, and France and the Benelux each with 17%. There was a large retail bid for the shorter maturity at 38%, while fund managers and insurance companies took 32% and 26% respectively. UK investors were by far the largest players in the 2013s, accounting for 36%, followed by French accounts with 14%, while Switzerland and Austria each took 10%. Fund managers predominated by taking 39% of the book, the retail bid was strong at 31%, and insurance companies followed closely with 28%.

Source: Excerpted from *Euroweek*. London: October 26, 2003, p. 1.

It has been noted that a disproportionate share of Eurobonds have high credit ratings in comparison to domestic and foreign bonds. For example, Claes, DeCeuster, and Polfliet (2002) report that approximately 40 percent of Eurobond issues are rated AAA and 30 percent are AA. One explanation is that the issuers receiving low credit ratings invoke their publication rights and have had them withdrawn prior to dissemination. Kim and Stulz (1988) suggest another explanation that we believe is more likely. That is, the Eurobond market is accessible only to firms that have good credit ratings and name recognition to begin with; hence, they are rated highly. Regardless, it is beneficial to know about the ratings Fitch, Moody's, and S&P assign to international bond issues.

Gande and Parsley (2005) study cross-border financial market linkages by examining changes in foreign U.S. dollar denominated sovereign debt yield spreads (i.e., sovereign yield above comparable U.S. Treasury yield) associated with ratings events abroad. They find an asymmetrical relationship. They find that positive ratings events in one country have no impact on sovereign spreads in other countries; however, negative ratings events are associated with a significant increase in spreads. On average, a one-notch downgrade of a sovereign bond is associated with a 12 basis point increase in spreads of sovereign bonds of other countries. They attribute the spillover among countries to highly positively correlated capital and trade flows.

Exhibit 12.6 presents a guide to S&P's Long-Term Issuer Credit Ratings for sovereigns, municipalities, corporations, utilities, and supranationals. As noted in

---

EXHIBIT 12.6   **Long-Term Issuer Credit Rating Definitions**

A S&P Global Ratings issuer credit rating is a forward-looking opinion about an obligor's overall creditworthiness in order to pay its financial obligations. This opinion focuses on the obligor's capacity and willingness to meet its financial commitments as they come due. It does not apply to any specific financial obligation, as it does not take into account the nature of and provisions of the obligation, its standing in bankruptcy or liquidation, statutory preferences, or the legality and enforceability of the obligation.

Counterparty credit ratings, corporate credit ratings and sovereign credit ratings are all forms of issuer credit ratings.

Issuer credit ratings can be either long-term or short-term. Short-term issuer credit ratings reflect the obligor's creditworthiness over a short-term time horizon.

Long-Term Issuer Credit Ratings

AAA: An obligor rated "AAA" has extremely strong capacity to meet its financial commitments. "AAA" is the highest issuer credit rating assigned by S&P Global Ratings.

AA: An obligor rated "AA" has very strong capacity to meet its financial commitments. It differs from the highest-rated obligors only to a small degree.

A: An obligor rated "A" has strong capacity to meet its financial commitments but is somewhat more susceptible to the adverse effects of changes in circumstances and economic conditions than obligors in higher-rated categories.

BBB: An obligor rated "BBB" has adequate capacity to meet its financial commitments. However, adverse economic conditions or changing circumstances are more likely to lead to a weakened capacity of the obligor to meet its financial commitments.

BB; B; CCC; and CC: Obligors rated "BB", "B", "CCC", and "CC" are regarded as having significant speculative characteristics. "BB" indicates the least degree of speculation and "CC" the highest. While such obligors will likely have some quality and protective characteristics, these may be outweighed by large uncertainties or major exposures to adverse conditions.

BB: An obligor rated "BB" is less vulnerable in the near term than other lower-rated obligors. However, it faces major ongoing uncertainties and exposure to adverse business, financial, or economic conditions which could lead to the obligor's inadequate capacity to meet its financial commitments.

B: An obligor rated "B" is more vulnerable than the obligors rated "BB", but the obligor currently has the capacity to meet its financial commitments. Adverse business, financial, or economic conditions will likely impair the obligor's capacity or willingness to meet its financial commitments.

CCC: An obligor rated "CCC" is currently vulnerable, and is dependent upon favorable business, financial, and economic conditions to meet its financial commitments.

CC: An obligor rated "CC" is currently highly vulnerable. The 'CC' rating is used when a default has not yet occurred, but S&P Global Ratings expects default to be a virtual certainty, regardless of the anticipated time to default.

R: An obligor rated "R" is under regulatory supervision owing to its financial condition. During the pendency of the regulatory supervision the regulators may have the power to favor one class of obligations over others or pay some obligations and not others. Please see Standard & Poor's issue credit ratings for a more detailed description of the effects of regulatory supervision on specific issues or classes of obligations.

SD and D: An obligor rated "SD" (selective default) or "D" is in payment default on one or more of its financial obligations (rated or unrated) unless Standard & Poor's believes that such payments will be made within five business days, irrespective of any grace period. The "D" rating also will be used upon the filing of a bankruptcy petition or the taking of similar action if payments on a financial obligation are jeopardized. A "D" rating is assigned when Standard & Poor's believes that the default will be a general default and that the obligor will fail to pay all or substantially all of its obligations as they come due. An "SD" rating is assigned when Standard & Poor's believe that the obligor has selectively defaulted on a specific issue or class of obligations, but it will continue to meet its payment obligations on other issues or classes of obligations in a timely manner. A selective default includes the completion of a distressed exchange offer, whereby one or more financial obligation is either repurchased for an amount of cash or replaced by other instruments having a total value that is less than par.

NR: An issuer designated "NR" is not rated.

The ratings from "AA" to "CCC" may be modified by the addition of a plus (+) or minus (−) sign to show relative standing within the major rating categories.

Local Currency and Foreign Currency Ratings

S&P Global Ratings issuer credit ratings make a distinction between foreign currency ratings and local currency ratings. An issuer's foreign currency rating will differ from its local currency rating when the obligor has a different capacity to meet its obligations denominated in its local currency, vs. obligations denominated in a foreign currency.

Source: www.globalcreditportal.com. June 6, 2016.

Exhibit 12.5, sovereigns issue a sizable portion of all international bonds. In rating a sovereign government, S&P's analysis centers around an assessment of five factors profiled in Exhibit 12.7. The rating assigned to a sovereign is particularly important because it frequently represents the ceiling for ratings S&P will assign to an obligation of an entity domiciled within that country. When the entity has a superior rating in comparison to the sovereign, it generally is not more than one rating grade.

Eurobond Market Structure and Practices

Given that in any year the Eurobond segment of the international bond market accounts for approximately 80 percent of new offerings, it is beneficial to know something about the Eurobond market structure and practices.

Primary Market

A borrower desiring to raise funds by issuing Eurobonds to the investing public will contact an investment banker and ask it to serve as the **lead manager** of an underwriting syndicate that will bring the bonds to market. The **underwriting syndicate** is a group of investment banks, merchant banks, and the merchant banking arms of commercial banks that specialize in some phase of a public issuance. The lead manager will sometimes invite comanagers to form a **managing group** to help negotiate terms with the borrower, ascertain market conditions, and manage the issuance. Exhibit 12.8 lists the top global and regional debt underwriters of international bonds and other debt products for 2015 as determined by the publication *Euromoney*.

The managing group, along with other banks, will serve as **underwriters** for the issue, that is, they will commit their own capital to buy the issue from the borrower at a discount from the issue price. The discount, or **underwriting spread**, is typically in the 2 to 2.5 percent range. By comparison, the spread averages about 1 percent for domestic issues. Most of the underwriters, along with other banks, will be part of a **selling group** that sells the bonds to the investing public. The various members of the underwriting syndicate receive a portion of the spread, depending on the number and type of functions they perform. The lead manager will obviously receive the full spread, but a bank serving as only a member of the selling group will receive a smaller portion. The total elapsed time from the decision date of the borrower to issue Eurobonds until the net proceeds from the sale are received is typically five to six weeks. Exhibit 12.9 presents a tombstone (announcement) for a dollar-denominated Euro-medium-term note issue and the underwriting syndicate that brought the issue to market.

Secondary Market

Eurobonds initially purchased in the **primary market** from a member of the selling group may be resold prior to their maturities to other investors in the secondary market. The **secondary market** for Eurobonds is an over-the-counter market with principal trading in London. However, important trading is also done in other major European money centers, such as Zurich, Luxembourg, Frankfurt, and Amsterdam.

The secondary market comprises market makers and brokers connected by an array of telecommunications equipment. **Market makers** stand ready to buy or sell for their own account by quoting two-way **bid** and **ask prices**. Market makers trade directly with one another, through a broker, or with retail customers. The bid-ask spread represents their only profit; no other commission is charged. New electronic trading platforms, however, allow asset managers to trade directly with one another, cutting out the market maker.

Eurobond market makers and dealers are members of the International Capital Market Association (ICMA), a self-regulatory body based in Zurich. Market makers tend to be the same investment banks, merchant banks, and commercial banks that serve as lead managers in the underwriting process. **Brokers**, on the other hand, accept buy or sell orders from market makers and then attempt to find a matching

www.icmagroup.org

This is the website of the International Capital Market Association. See the Education section of this site for course offerings in financial markets.

EXHIBIT 12.7   Standard and Poor's Sovereign Rating Framework

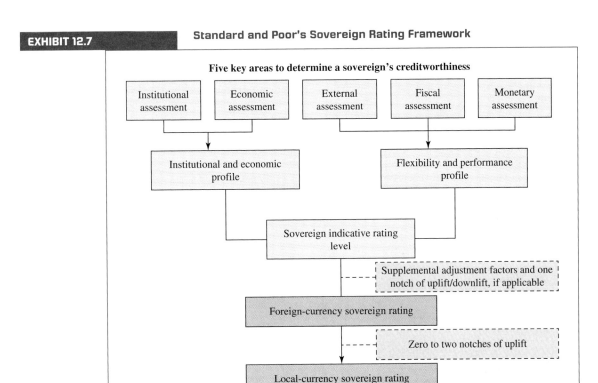

Assessing the Five Main Sovereign Rating Factors

The analysis of each of the five key factors consists of quantitative and qualitative elements. Some factors, such as the robustness of political institutions, are primarily qualitative, while others—such as those relating to the real economy, debt, and external liquidity—use mostly quantitative indicators.

1. Institutional Assessment

The institutional assessment comprises an analysis of how a government's institutions and policymaking affect a sovereign's credit fundamentals by delivering sustainable public finances, promoting balanced economic growth, and responding to economic or political shocks.

2. Economic Assessment

The history of sovereign defaults suggests that a wealthy, diversified, resilient, market-oriented, and adaptable economy—coupled with a track record of sustained economic growth—provides a sovereign with a strong revenue base, enhances its fiscal and monetary policy flexibility, and ultimately boosts its debt-bearing capacity. We observe that market-oriented economies tend to produce higher wealth levels because these economies enable more efficient allocation of resources to promote sustainable, long-term economic growth.

The key drivers of a sovereign's economic assessment are:

- Income levels,

- Growth prospects, and

- Economic diversity and volatility.

The combination of these three factors determines a sovereign's economic assessment. The criteria derive an initial assessment based on a country's income level, as measured by its GDP per capita. Then, the initial assessment receives a positive or negative adjustment by up to two categories based on the economy's growth prospects and its potential concentration or volatility.

3. External Assessment

The external assessment reflects a country's ability to obtain funds from abroad necessary to meet its public- and private-sector obligations to nonresidents. The external assessment refers to the transactions and positions of all residents (public- and private-sector entities) vis-à-vis those of nonresidents because it is the totality of these flows and stocks that affects a country's competitiveness, exchange rate developments, foreign investor sentiment, and, ultimately, the country's international purchasing and repayment power.

(continued)

EXHIBIT 12.7   Standard and Poor's Sovereign Rating Framework (continued)

4. Fiscal Assessment

The fiscal assessment reflects the sustainability of a sovereign's deficits and debt burden. This measure considers fiscal flexibility, long-term fiscal trends and vulnerabilities, debt structure and funding access, and potential risks arising from contingent liabilities.

5. Monetary Assessment

A sovereign's monetary assessment reflects the extent to which its monetary authority can fulfill its mandate while supporting sustainable economic growth and attenuating major economic or financial shocks. Monetary policy can be an important stabilization tool for sovereigns, helping to ease credit conditions when economic growth is below potential and to tighten credit conditions when the economy overheats. Accordingly, a flexible monetary policy could be a significant factor in slowing or preventing a deterioration of sovereign creditworthiness in times of stress.

Source: From S&P Global Ratings, *Sovereign Rating Methodology,* June 7, 2016, www.standardandpoors.com.

EXHIBIT 12.8

Best Global and Regional Debt Capital Markets Houses, 2015

	Overall
Region	**Bank**
Global	Barclays
North America	Bank of America Merrill Lynch
Western Europe	HSBC
Middle East	HSBC
Africa	Barclays
Asia	HSBC
Central and Eastern Europe	UniCredit
Nordics and Baltics	Deutsche Bank
Latin America	Citi
Emerging Markets	HSBC

Source: www.euromoney.com.

party for the other side of the trade; they may also trade for their own account. Brokers charge a small commission for their services to the market maker that engaged them. They do not deal directly with retail clients.

Clearing Procedures

Originally, Eurobond investors found the bearer status and its associated anonymity attractive (perhaps as a vehicle for avoiding or evading income taxes) and were willing to accept a lower yield in comparison to similar-risk domestic or foreign bonds. In recent years, however, increased institutional ownership of Eurobonds has resulted in a growing integration of the euro, domestic, and foreign bond market segments, causing the anonymity feature of bearer bonds to be less valued. Institutional investors are unwilling to pay a premium for a feature lacking value.

Eurobond transactions in the secondary market (in particular institutional transactions) require a system for transferring ownership and payment from one party to another. Two major clearing systems, Euroclear and Clearstream International, have been established to handle most Eurobond trades. Euroclear is based in Brussels and is operated by Euroclear Bank. Clearstream, located in Luxembourg, was established in 2000 through a merger of Deutsche Börse Clearing and Cedel International, two other clearing firms.

Both clearing systems operate in a similar manner. Each clearing system has a group of depository banks that physically store bond certificates. Members of either system hold cash and bond accounts. When a transaction is conducted, electronic book entries are made that transfer book ownership of the bond certificates from the seller to the buyer and transfer funds from the purchaser's cash account to the seller's. Physical transfer of the bonds seldom takes place.

www.euroclear.com

www.clearstream.com

EXHIBIT 12.9

Eurobond Tombstone

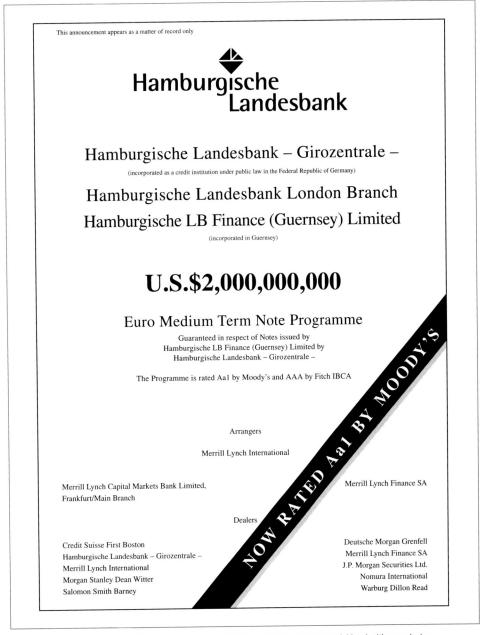

Euroclear and Clearstream perform other functions associated with the efficient operation of the Eurobond market. (1) The clearing systems will finance up to 90 percent of the inventory that a Eurobond market maker has deposited within the system. (2) The clearing systems will assist in the distribution of a new bond issue. The clearing systems will take physical possession of the newly printed bond certificates in the depository, collect subscription payments from the purchasers, and record ownership of the bonds. (3) The clearing systems will also distribute coupon payments. The borrower pays to the clearing system the coupon interest due on the portion of the issue held in the depository, which in turn credits the appropriate amounts to the bond owners' cash accounts.

International Bond Market Indexes

There are several international market indexes. Some of the best known are the indexes produced by J.P. Morgan. Their developed market indexes include the J.P. Morgan Government Bond Index series and the Economic and Monetary Union (EMU) Government Bond Index. These indexes track fixed-income issues from high-income countries. They also produce the Government Bond Index-Emerging Markets and the Corporate Emerging Markets Bond Index that track bond issuance in emerging market countries. The J.P. Morgan Global Aggregate Bond Index U.S. is a dollar-denominated invest-grade index spanning nine asset classes that tracks over 3,200 fixed-income issues from over 50 developed and emerging countries. The Global Aggregate Index extends the U.S. index to include over 5,500 instruments from over 60 countries denominated in over 25 currencies.

Exhibit 12.10 shows that *The Wall Street Journal* publishes daily values of yields to maturity for U.S., Australian, Canadian, German, Japanese, Swedish, Swiss, and British Government Bonds of two-year and 10-year terms to maturity. These data allow for a comparison of the term structures of interest rates of these major industrial countries with one another. Another source of international bond data is the coupon rates, prices, and yields to maturity found in the daily "Benchmark Government Bonds" table in the *Financial Times*. Exhibit 12.11 provides an example.

EXHIBIT 12.10   **Global Government Bonds: Mapping Yields**

Yields and spreads over or under U.S. Treasurys on benchmark two-year and 10-year government bonds in selected other countries; arrows indicate whether the yield rose (▲) or fell (▼) in the latest session

Coupon (%)	Country/ Maturity, in years	Latest (●)	Yield (%) 0 20 40 60 80 100 120	Previous	Month ago	Year ago	Spread Under/Over U.S. Treasurys, in basis points — Latest	Prev	Year ago
0.750	**U.S. 2**	**0.774** ▲		0.746	0.738	0.540			
1.625	10	**1.749** ▲		1.700	1.754	2.146			
3.250	**Australia 2**	**1.573** ▼		1.590	1.999	2.012	79.9	84.5	147.2
4.250	10	**2.241** ▼		2.286	2.571	2.906	49.2	58.6	76.0
1.000	**France 2**	**−0.421** ▼		−0.416	−0.469	−0.140	−119.5	−116.2	−68.1
0.500	10	**0.487** ▲		0.477	0.481	0.916	−126.3	−122.3	−123.0
0.000	**Germany 2**	**−0.501** ▲		−0.505	−0.513	−0.195	−127.5	−125.1	−73.5
0.500	10	**0.147** ▲		0.128	0.131	0.628	−160.2	−157.2	−151.8
4.500	**Italy 2**	**−0.051** ▲		−0.058	0.017	0.146	−82.6	−80.4	−39.5
2.000	10	**1.484** ▲		1.480	1.350	1.791	−26.5	−22.0	−35.5
0.100	**Japan 2**	**−0.249** ▼		−0.247	−0.250	−0.009	−102.4	−99.3	−54.9
0.100	10	**−0.111** ▼		−0.110	−0.111	0.393	−186.0	−181.0	−175.3
4.500	**Spain 2**	**−0.069** ▲		−0.080	−0.038	0.027	−84.3	−82.6	−51.3
1.950	10	**1.613** ▲		1.608	1.497	1.742	−13.7	−9.3	−40.4
1.250	**U.K. 2**	**0.387** ▲		0.369	0.422	0.631	−38.7	−37.7	9.1
2.000	10	**1.396** ▲		1.379	1.417	1.890	−35.3	−32.1	−25.6

Source: *The Wall Street Journal*, May 17, 2016, p. C6.

| EXHIBIT 12.11 | International Government Bond Market Data Provided Daily in the *Financial Times* |

BONDS: BENCHMARK GOVERNMENT

May 16	Redemption	Coupon	Bid Price	Bid Yield	Day Chg Yield	Wk Chg Yield	Month Chg Yld	Year Chg Yld
Australia	10/18	3.25	103.98	1.57	0.02	0.01	−0.43	−0.54
	11/27	2.75	103.88	2.36	0.02	−0.06	−0.32	0.00
Austria	10/19	0.25	99.98	0.26	0.00	0.00	0.00	0.00
	10/26	0.75	102.39	1.51	0.00	0.00	0.00	0.00
Belgium	05/18	0.75	101.74	−0.10	0.00	0.00	0.00	0.00
	06/26	1.00	104.59	0.53	0.02	−0.01	−0.02	0.00
Canada	05/18	0.25	99.39	0.56	0.01	0.04	−0.03	0.00
	06/26	1.50	101.90	1.30	0.02	−0.02	−0.10	0.00
Denmark	11/18	0.25	101.68	−0.42	0.00	0.00	0.00	0.00
	11/25	1.75	112.64	0.39	0.01	0.03	0.02	0.00
Finland	05/18	1.00	99.99	1.01	0.00	0.06	0.00	0.00
	04/26	0.50	100.88	0.41	0.00	0.00	0.00	0.00
France	05/19	1.00	104.20	−0.38	0.00	0.00	0.00	0.00
	11/20	0.25	102.20	−0.23	0.00	0.00	0.00	0.00
	05/26	0.50	100.13	0.49	0.01	−0.01	−0.02	0.00
	05/45	3.25	142.20	1.46	0.02	0.00	0.01	0.00
Germany	04/19	0.50	102.97	−0.51	0.00	0.00	0.00	0.00
	10/20	0.25	103.02	−0.43	0.00	0.00	0.00	0.00
	02/25	0.50	103.42	0.15	0.02	0.02	−0.02	0.00
	08/46	2.50	143.85	0.85	0.02	0.03	0.01	0.00
Greece	07/17	3.38	94.32	8.70	0.02	−0.31	−2.28	0.00
	02/26	3.00	74.89	7.30	−0.04	−0.90	−1.60	0.00
Ireland	10/17	5.50	108.35	−0.36	0.00	0.00	0.00	0.00
	05/26	1.00	101.92	0.80	−0.01	−0.08	−0.06	0.00
Italy	04/19	0.10	100.03	0.09	−0.01	0.02	0.00	0.00
	06/21	0.45	99.68	0.51	0.02	0.02	0.04	0.00
	06/26	1.60	100.47	1.56	0.00	0.02	0.13	0.00
	03/47	2.70	100.28	2.70	0.00	0.01	0.19	0.00
Japan	05/18	0.10	100.70	−0.25	0.00	0.00	0.00	0.00
	05/21	0.05	101.34	−0.22	0.00	0.00	0.00	0.00
	03/26	0.10	102.10	−0.11	0.00	0.00	0.00	0.00
	03/46	0.80	111.84	0.36	0.01	0.08	−0.01	0.00
Netherlands	01/19	1.25	104.60	−0.46	0.00	0.00	0.00	0.00
	07/25	0.25	100.15	0.23	0.01	0.00	−0.02	0.00
New Zealand	03/19	5.00	107.97	2.08	0.01	0.07	−0.04	−1.03
	04/27	4.50	117.92	2.60	0.00	0.00	−0.23	−1.06
Norway	05/19	4.50	111.62	0.59	0.00	0.01	0.10	0.00
	02/26	1.50	101.28	1.36	0.00	0.02	0.09	0.00
Portugal	06/19	4.75	110.90	1.12	0.02	−0.04	−0.13	0.00
	02/26	3.30	101.28	3.14	0.00	−0.12	0.03	0.00
Spain	01/19	0.25	100.60	0.03	0.00	0.00	−0.08	0.00
	04/26	1.95	103.08	1.61	0.01	0.04	0.12	0.00
Sweden	10/18	1.00	99.91	1.04	0.00	0.06	0.01	0.00
	05/25	2.50	117.51	0.50	0.02	−0.01	−0.02	0.00
Switzerland	05/19	3.00	111.83	−0.90	0.00	0.00	0.00	0.00
	05/26	1.25	116.14	−0.33	0.00	0.00	0.00	0.00
United Kingdom	07/18	1.25	101.87	0.39	0.02	−0.03	−0.09	0.00
	01/21	1.50	103.13	0.82	0.02	−0.01	−0.06	0.00
	07/26	1.50	99.74	1.53	0.02	−0.02	−0.09	0.00
	12/46	4.25	144.59	2.23	0.01	0.02	−0.08	0.00
United States	04/18	0.75	99.95	0.78	0.02	0.07	0.00	0.00
	04/21	1.38	100.59	1.25	0.04	0.06	0.00	0.00
	02/26	1.63	98.83	1.76	0.05	0.00	−0.03	0.00
	02/46	2.50	99.07	2.59	0.04	−0.02	0.00	0.00

Source: *Financial Times*, May 17, 2016, p. 19.

SUMMARY

This chapter introduces and discusses the international bond market. The chapter presents a statistical perspective of the market, noting its size, an analysis of the market segments, the types of instruments issued, the major currencies used to denominate international bonds, and the major borrowers by nationality and type. Trading practices of the Eurobond market are examined, as are credit ratings for international bonds and international bond market indexes.

1. At year-end 2014, there were $74.2 trillion in domestic bonds outstanding and $21.0 trillion in international bonds. The four major currencies that are used to denominate bonds are the euro, U.S. dollar, British pound sterling, and Japanese yen.

2. A foreign bond issue is one offered by a foreign borrower to investors in a national capital market and denominated in that nation's currency. A Eurobond issue is one denominated in a particular currency but sold to investors in national capital markets other than the country that issues the denominating currency.

3. The Eurobond segment of the international bond market is roughly four times the size of the foreign bond segment. The two major reasons for this stem from the fact that the U.S. dollar is the currency most frequently sought in international bond financing. First, Eurodollar bonds can be brought to market more quickly than Yankee bonds because they are not offered to U.S. investors and thus do not have to meet the strict SEC registration requirements. Second, Eurobonds are typically bearer bonds that provide anonymity to the owner and thus allow a means for avoiding taxes on the interest received. Because of this feature, investors are generally willing to accept a lower yield on Eurodollar bonds in comparison to registered Yankee bonds of comparable terms, where ownership is recorded. For borrowers, the lower yield means a lower cost of debt service.

4. Straight fixed-rate bonds are the most frequent type of international bond issue, and floating-rate notes are the second. Other types of issues found in the international bond market are convertible bonds, bonds with equity warrants, and dual-currency bonds.

5. Fitch Ratings, Moody's Investors Service, and S&P Global Ratings provide credit ratings on most international bond issues. It has been noted that a disproportionate share of Eurobonds have high credit ratings. The evidence suggests that a logical reason for this is that the Eurobond market is accessible only to firms that have good credit ratings to begin with. An entity's credit rating is seldom higher than the rating assigned to the sovereign government of the country in which it resides. S&P's analysis of a sovereign includes an institutional and economic assessment.

6. New Eurobond issues are offered in the primary market through an underwriting syndicate hired by the borrower to bring the bonds to market. The secondary market for Eurobonds is an over-the-counter arrangement with principal trading done in London.

7. The investment banking firm of J.P. Morgan and Company provides some of the best international bond market indexes that are frequently used for performance evaluations. J.P. Morgan publishes Developed Markets Indexes, Emerging Markets Indexes, and a Global Aggregate Bond Index.

KEY WORDS

ask price, *314*
bearer bond, *305*
bid price, *314*
bonds with equity
   warrants, *309*
brokers, *314*
convertible bond, *309*

dual-currency bond, *309*
equity-related bonds, *309*
Eurobond, *305*
Euro-Medium-Term Notes
   (Euro-MTNs), *308*
floating-rate notes
   (FRNs), *309*

foreign bond, *305*
global bond, *307*
lead manager, *314*
managing group, *314*
market makers, *314*
primary market, *314*
registered bonds, *305*

secondary market, *314*   straight fixed-rate   underwriting spread, *314*
selling group, *314*   bond, *308*   underwriting
shelf registration, *306*   underwriters, *314*   syndicate, *314*

QUESTIONS

1. Describe the differences between foreign bonds and Eurobonds. Also discuss why Eurobonds make up the lion's share of the international bond market.
2. Briefly define each of the major types of international bond market instruments, noting their distinguishing characteristics.
3. Why do most international bonds have high Moody's or Standard & Poor's credit ratings?
4. What factors does S&P Global Ratings analyze in determining the credit rating it assigns to a sovereign government?
5. Discuss the process of bringing a new international bond issue to market.
6. You are an investment banker advising a Eurobank about a new international bond offering it is considering. The proceeds are to be used to fund Eurodollar loans to bank clients. What type of bond instrument would you recommend that the bank consider issuing? Why?
7. What should a borrower consider before issuing dual-currency bonds? What should an investor consider before investing in dual-currency bonds?

PROBLEMS

1. Your firm has just issued five-year floating-rate notes indexed to six-month U.S. dollar LIBOR plus 1/4 percent. What is the amount of the first coupon payment your firm will pay per U.S. $1,000 of face value, if six-month LIBOR is currently 7.2 percent?
2. Consider 8.5 percent Swiss franc/U.S. dollar dual-currency bonds that pay $666.67 at maturity per SF1,000 of par value. It sells at par. What is the implicit SF/$ exchange rate at maturity? Will the investor be better or worse off at maturity if the actual SF/$ exchange rate is SF1.35/$1.00?
3. A five-year, 4 percent Euroyen bond sells at par. A comparable risk five-year, 5.5 percent yen/dollar dual-currency bond pays $833.44 at maturity. It sells for ¥110,000. What is the implied ¥/$ exchange rate at maturity? Hint: The dual-currency bond pays 5.5 percent on a notional value of ¥100,000, whereas the par value of the bond is not necessarily equivalent to ¥100,000.

INTERNET EXERCISES

The Association for Financial Markets in Europe is a trade association representing the world bond market. A newsletter can be found at the website. Go to the website www.afme.eu to see what current topics are of concern in European financial markets.

MINI CASE

Sara Lee Corporation's Eurobonds

Sara Lee Corp. is serving up a brand name and a shorter maturity than other recent corporate borrowers to entice buyers to its first-ever dollar Eurobonds. The U.S. maker of consumer products, from Sara Lee cheesecake to Hanes pantyhose and Hillshire Farm meats, is selling $100 million in bonds with a 6 percent coupon. These are three-year bonds; other corporate bond sellers including Coca-Cola Co., Unilever NV, and Wal-Mart Stores, Inc., have concentrated on their five-year maturities.

"It is a well-known name and it is bringing paper to a part of the maturity curve where there is not much there," said Noel Dunn of Goldman Sachs International. Goldman Sachs expects to find most buyers in the Swiss retail market, where "high-quality American corporate paper is their favorite buy," Dunn said.

These are the first bonds out of a $500 million Eurobond program that Sara Lee announced in August, 1995, and the proceeds will be used for general corporate purposes, said Jeffrey Smith, a spokesman for the company.

The bond is fairly priced, according to Bloomberg Fair Value analysis, which compared a bond with similar issues available in the market. The bond offers investors a yield of 5.881 percent annually or 5.797 percent semiannually. That is 22 basis points more than they can get on the benchmark five-year U.S. Treasury note.

BFV analysis calculates that the bond is worth $100,145 on a $100,000 bond, compared with the re-offer price of $100,320. Anything within a $500 range on a $100,000 bond more or less than its BFV price is deemed fairly priced. Sara Lee is rated "AA–" by S&P Global Ratings and "A1," one notch lower, by Moody's Investors Service.

In July 1994, Sara Lee's Netherlands division sold 200 million Dutch guilders ($127 million) of three-year bonds at 35 basis points over comparable Netherlands government bonds. In January, its Australian division sold 51 million British pounds ($78 million) of bonds maturing in 2004, to yield 9.43 percent.

What thoughts do you have about Sara Lee's debt-financing strategy?

Source: Excerpted from Bloomberg News.

REFERENCES & SUGGESTED READINGS

Claes, A., Marc J. K. DeCeuster, and R. Polfliet. "Anatomy of the Eurobond Market." *European Financial Management* 8, no. 3 (2002).

Gande, Amar, and David C. Parsley. "News Spillovers in the Sovereign Debt Market." *Journal of Financial Economics* 75 (2005), pp. 691–734.

Kim, Yong Cheol, and Rene M. Stultz. "The Eurobond Market and Corporate Financial Policy: A Test of the Clientele Hypothesis." *Journal of Financial Economics* 22 (1988), pp. 189–205.

Miller, Darius P., and John J. Puthenpurackal. "Security Fungibility and the Cost of Capital: Evidence from Global Bonds." *Journal of Financial and Quantitative Analysis* 40 (2005), pp. 849–72.

Resnick, Bruce G. "Investor Yield and Gross Underwriting Spread Comparisons among U.S. Dollar, Yankee, Eurodollar, and Global Bonds." *Journal of International Money and Finance* 31 (2012), pp. 445–63.

13 International Equity Markets

THIS CHAPTER FOCUSES on equity markets, or how ownership in publicly owned corporations is traded throughout the world. It discusses both the *primary* sale of new common stock by corporations to initial investors and how previously issued common stock is traded between investors in the *secondary* markets. This chapter is useful for understanding how companies source new equity capital and provides useful institutional information for investors interested in diversifying their portfolio internationally.

The chapter begins with an overview of the world's equity markets. Statistics are provided that show the comparative sizes and trading opportunities in various secondary equity marketplaces in both developed and developing countries. Differences in market structures are also explored, and comparative transaction costs of equity trading are presented. Following this, the discussion moves to the benefits of multiple listing of a corporation's stock on more than one national stock exchange. The related issue of sourcing new equity capital from primary investors in more than the home national market is also examined. The chapter concludes with a discussion of the factors that affect equity valuation. An examination of the historical market performances and the risks of investing in foreign national equity markets is not presented here, but rather in Chapter 15, where a strong case is made for international diversification of investment funds.

A Statistical Perspective

Before we can intelligently discuss international equity markets, it is helpful to understand where the major national equity markets are located, some information about their relative sizes, and the opportunities for trading and ownership. This section provides these background data, along with a statistical summary of equity markets in the Americas, Asia-Pacific, and Europe-Africa-Middle East regions.

Market Capitalization

At year-end 2015, total market capitalization of the 80 organized stock exchanges tracked by the World Federation of Exchanges stood at $67,125 billion. Exhibit 13.1 shows the market capitalizations for these exchanges for 2011 through 2015. As the exhibit indicates, their total market capitalization increased nearly 39 percent over the five-year period. This increase is a result of most countries recovering from the global financial crisis, although 2015 was a down year for many countries.

The change in market capitalization was somewhat unevenly spread among the regions. For example, the five-year increase in the Americas was 41 percent (largely attributable to the United States), whereas the increase in the Asia-Pacific region was 58 percent (largely-attributable to Hong Kong, Japan, and China), and the Europe-Africa-Middle East was only 15 percent.

EXHIBIT 13.1

Market Capitalization
(in billions of U.S. dollars)

Exchange	2011	2012	2013	2014	2015
Americas					
Barbados Stock Exchange	NA	NA	NA	3	3
Bermuda Stock Exchange	1	1	1	2	2
BM&FBOVESPA	1,229	1,227	1,020	844	491
Bolsa de Comercio de Buenos Aires	44	34	53	60	56
Bolsa de Comercio de Santiago	270	313	265	233	190
Bolsa de Valores de Colombia	201	262	203	147	86
Bolsa de Valores de Lima	82	103	81	79	57
Bolsa de Valores de Panama	NA	NA	NA	14	13
Bolsa Mexicana de Valores	409	525	526	480	402
Bolsa Nacional de Valores	NA	NA	NA	3	2
Canadian Securities Exchange	NA	NA	NA	2	NA
Jamaica Stock Exchange	NA	NA	NA	3	6
Nasdaq–US	3,845	4,582	6,085	6,979	7,281
NYSE	11,796	14,086	17,950	19,351	17,787
TMX Group	1,912	2,059	2,114	2,094	1,592
Total Region	**19,789**	**23,193**	**28,299**	**30,293**	**27,967**
Asia-Pacific					
Australian Securities Exchange	1,198	1,387	1,366	1,289	1,187
BSE India Limited	1,007	1,263	1,139	1,558	1,516
Bursa Malaysia	396	467	500	459	383
Chittagong SE	NA	NA	NA	34	32
Colombo Stock Exchange	19	17	19	24	21
Dhaka Stock Exchange	NA	NA	NA	35	34
Hanoi Stock Exchange	NA	NA	NA	6	7
Hochiminh Stock Exchange	NA	NA	40	46	52
Hong Kong Exchanges and Clearing	2,258	2,832	3,101	3,233	3,185
Indonesia Stock Exchange	390	428	347	422	353
Japan Exchange Group	3,541	3,681	4,543	4,378	4,895
Korea Exchange	996	1,179	1,235	1,213	1,231
National Stock Exchange of India	985	1,234	1,113	1,521	1,485
NZX Limited	0	53	66	74	74
Philippine Stock Exchange	165	229	217	262	239
Port Moresby Stock Exchange	NA	NA	NA	3	2
Shanghai Stock Exchange	2,357	2,547	2,497	NA	4,549
Shenzhen Stock Exchange	1,055	1,150	1,452	2,072	3,639
Singapore Exchange	598	765	744	753	640
Stock Exchange of Thailand	268	390	354	430	349
Sydney Stock Exchange	NA	NA	NA	0	0
Taipei Exchange	NA	60	78	85	83
Taiwan Stock Exchange Corp.	636	735	823	851	745
Total Region	**14,670**	**16,982**	**18,521**	**21,160**	**23,215**

(continued)

EXHIBIT 13.1

Market Capitalization
(in billions of U.S. dollars)
(continued)

Europe–Africa–Middle East	0	0	0	0	0
Abu Dhabi Securities Exchange	63	68	110	114	112
Amman Stock Exchange	27	27	26	26	25
Athens Stock Exchange	34	45	83	55	42
Bahrain Bourse	NA	NA	NA	NA	19
Beirut Stock Exchange	NA	NA	NA	11	11
BME Spanish Exchanges	1,031	995	1,117	993	787
Borsa Istanbul	197	315	196	220	189
Bourse de Casablanca	60	52	54	53	46
Bourse de Valeurs Mobilieres de Tunis	NA	NA	NA	9	9
BRVM	NA	NA	NA	12	12
Bucharest Stock Exchange	NA	NA	NA	22	19
Budapest Stock Exchange	19	21	20	15	18
Cyprus Stock Exchange	3	2	2	4	3
Deutsche Boerse	1,185	1,486	1,936	1,739	1,716
Dubai Financial Market	NA	NA	NA	88	84
Egyptian Exchange	49	59	62	70	55
Euronext	2,447	2,832	3,584	3,319	NA
Irish Stock Exchange	108	NA	170	143	128
Johannesburg Stock Exchange	789	908	943	934	736
Kazakhstan Stock Exchange	23	NA	26	23	35
Ljubljana Stock Exchange	6	6	7	8	6
London SE Group	3,266	3,397	4,429	4,013	3,879
Luxembourg Stock Exchange	68	70	79	63	47
Malta Stock Exchange	3	4	NA	4	4
Moscow Exchange	1,554	825	771	386	393
Muscat Securities Market	NA	NA	NA	38	41
Nairobi Securities Exchange	NA	NA	NA	26	20
Namibian Stock Exchange	NA	NA	NA	2	2
NASDAQ OMX Nordic Exchange	842	996	1,269	1,197	1,268
Nigerian Stock Exchange	NA	NA	NA	63	50
Oslo Bors	221	243	265	219	194
Palestine Exchange	NA	NA	NA	3	3
Qatar Stock Exchange	NA	NA	153	186	143
Saudi Stock Exchange (Tadawul)	339	373	467	483	421
SIX Swiss Exchange	1,090	1,233	1,541	1,495	1,519
Stock Exchange of Mauritius	8	7	9	9	7
Tehran Stock Exchange	107	NA	346	117	89
Tel-Aviv Stock Exchange	157	162	203	201	244
Ukrainian Exchange	NA	NA	NA	12	6
Warsaw Stock Exchange	138	177	205	169	138
Wiener Borse	85	106	118	97	96
Zagreb SE	NA	NA	NA	20	18
Total Region	**13,919**	**14,520**	**18,188**	**16,658**	**15,942**
WFE Total	**48,377**	**54,695**	**65,007**	**68,110**	**67,125**

Source: From various year-end issues of World Federation of Exchanges' *Monthly Report.*

Measure of Liquidity

A liquid stock market is one in which investors can buy and sell stocks quickly at close to the current quoted prices. A measure of **liquidity** for a stock market is the turnover ratio; that is, the ratio of stock market transactions over a period of time divided by the size, or market capitalization, of the stock market. Generally, the higher the turnover ratio, the more liquid the secondary stock market, indicating ease in trading.

Exhibit 13.2 presents the share turnover velocity percentages for 75 of the stock exchanges listed in Exhibit 13.1 for the five years beginning with 2011. The turnover percentages are presented for December of each year as being representative of monthly turnover. The table indicates that turnover ratios are relatively stable over time for most national stock exchanges. The table also indicates that many national stock exchanges had relatively high turnover ratios, with over 40 percent of the exchanges in most years in excess of 30 percent turnover per month.

Exhibit 13.2 also indicates a considerable difference in turnover ratios among the developing countries. Many of the small equity markets in each region (e.g., Argentina, Peru, Sri Lanka, Croatia, Lebanon, Nigeria, and Slovenia) have relatively low turnover ratios, indicating poor liquidity at present. Nevertheless, the larger emerging equity markets (China, India, and Taiwan) demonstrate fairly strong liquidity.

Market Structure, Trading Practices, and Costs

The secondary equity markets of the world serve two major purposes. They provide *marketability* and *share valuation*.[1] Investors or traders who buy shares from the issuing firm in the **primary market** may not want to hold them indefinitely. The **secondary market** allows share owners to reduce their holdings of unwanted shares and purchasers to acquire the stock. Firms would have a difficult time attracting buyers in the primary market without the marketability provided through the secondary market. Additionally, competitive trading between buyers and sellers in the secondary market establishes fair market prices for existing issues.

In conducting a trade in a secondary market, public buyers and sellers are represented by an agent, known as a **broker**. The order submitted to the broker may be a market order or a limit order. A **market order** is executed at the best price available in the market when the order is received, that is, the *market price*. A **limit order** is an order *away from the market* price that is held in a **limit order book** until it can be executed at the desired price.

There are many different designs for secondary markets that allow for efficient trading of shares between buyers and sellers. Generally, however, a secondary market is structured as a dealer or agency market. In a **dealer market**, the broker takes the trade through the dealer, who participates in trades as a principal by buying and selling the security for his own account. Public traders do not trade directly with one another in a dealer market. In an **agency market**, the broker takes the client's order through the agent, who matches it with another public order. The agent can be viewed as a *broker's broker*. Other names for the agent are *official broker* and *central broker*.

Both dealer and agency structures exist in the United States. The **over-the-counter (OTC)** market is a dealer market. OTC stocks are generally unlisted stocks. The National Association of Security Dealers Automated Quotation System (NASDAQ) is a computer-linked system that shows the **bid** (buy) and **ask** (sell) **prices** of all dealers in a security. NASDAQ, however, is generally not classified as an OTC market,

---

[1]Much of the discussion in this section follows from Chapter 2 of Schwartz (1988).

EXHIBIT 13.2

Share Turnover Velocity
(for December in percent)*

Exchange	2011 (in %)	2012 (in %)	2013 (in %)	2014 (in %)	2015 (in %)
Americas					
Barbados Stock Exchange	NA	NA	NA	0.2	30.8
Bermuda Stock Exchange	0.9	3.2	NA	2.5	0.7
BM&FBOVESPA	65.5	64.5	56.8	81.6	80.9
Bolsa de Comercio de Buenos Aires	3.1	5.3	5.2	4.8	5.2
Bolsa de Comercio de Santiago	21.3	16.8	17.4	10.5	8.1
Bolsa de Valores de Colombia	13.3	7.2	7.9	11.1	11.1
Bolsa de Valores de Lima	4.7	25.7	NA	5.5	1.6
Bolsa de Valores de Panama	NA	NA	4.0	2.0	1.4
Bolsa Mexicana de Valores	18.4	21.9	32.2	26.2	24.7
Jamaica Stock Exchange	NA	NA	NA	6.4	6.1
TMX Group	66.4	68.2	56.0	85.1	85.1
Asia-Pacific					
Australian Securities Exchange	68.6	49.3	50.8	57.7	58.2
BSE India Limited	8.6	8.6	7.2	8.0	7.2
Bursa Malaysia	24.2	21.2	22.7	29.1	27.1
Chittagong SE	NA	NA	NA	3.3	3.0
Colombo Stock Exchange	9.7	6.8	6.3	9.4	8.4
Dhaka Stock Exchange	NA	NA	NA	26.7	42.2
Hochiminh Stock Exchange	NA	NA	41.6	47.2	35.1
Hong Kong Exchanges and Clearing	37.8	38.1	39.6	62.0	38.2
Indonesia Stock Exchange	19.0	21.3	18.0	20.2	15.1
Japan Exchange Group	75.0	108.9	132.2	125.0	107.0
Korea Exchange	174.8	97.3	80.7	106.7	121.3
National Stock Exchange of India	42.9	42.4	40.0	44.1	40.6
NZX Limited	NA	12.9	15.1	11.5	13.2
Philippine Stock Exchange	20.9	15.9	12.9	15.8	10.4
Port Moresby Stock Exchange	NA	NA	NA	69221.1	0.6
Shanghai Stock Exchange	82.7	129.9	143.5	565.6	295.0
Shenzhen Stock Exchange	174.5	239.8	287.5	615.7	558.9
Singapore Exchange	24.8	39.4	32.8	35.1	30.7
Stock Exchange of Thailand	57.7	63.7	47.5	85.8	70.2
Taipei Exchange	NA	174.7	215.8	221.6	258.1
Taiwan Stock Exchange Corp.	85.3	84.6	69.7	75.4	69.1
Europe–Africa–Middle East					
Abu Dhabi Securities Exchange	8.1	8.8	44.2	25.0	15.4
Amman Stock Exchange	11.1	11.7	11.5	17.5	12.1
Athens Stock Exchange	23.5	30.6	35.1	46.6	96.3
Beirut Stock Exchange	NA	NA	NA	7.0	3.4

(continued)

EXHIBIT 13.2

Share Turnover Velocity (for December in percent) *
(continued)

Exchange	2011 (in %)	2012 (in %)	2013 (in %)	2014 (in %)	2015 (in %)
Belarusian Currency and Stock Exchange	NA	NA	NA	4.6	1.6
BME Spanish Exchanges	80.7	83.5	81.3	108.8	104.7
Borsa Istanbul	115.8	132.5	192.3	222.7	211.9
Bourse de Casablanca	19.1	22.4	10.6	25.9	23.5
Bourse de Valeurs Mobilieres de Tunis	NA	NA	NA	16.1	9.1
BRVM	NA	NA	NA	5.8	5.1
Bucharest Stock Exchange	NA	NA	NA	20.6	7.4
Budapest Stock Exchange	65.0	33.6	45.9	42.8	34.7
Cyprus Stock Exchange	8.8	5.9	1.2	4.1	4.6
Deutsche Boerse	92.9	58.3	58.3	71.3	73.8
Dubai Financial Market	NA	NA	NA	86.1	26.1
Egyptian Exchange	16.3	27.4	25.1	39.6	28.7
Euronext	52.2	40.4	43.2	55.1	54.7
Irish Stock Exchange	8.9	7.1	10.6	9.2	16.1
Johannesburg Stock Exchange	31.8	29.6	26.5	35.6	47.4
Kazakhstan Stock Exchange	6.4	1.8	1.1	17.0	1.1
Ljubljana Stock Exchange	5.1	5.7	8.6	7.6	6.8
London SE Group	44.7	42.5	38.3	56.4	49.2
Luxembourg Stock Exchange	0.4	0.1	0.1	0.1	0.2
Malta Stock Exchange	0.5	1.1	NA	1.5	2.6
Moscow Exchange	57.3	24.9	32.3	58.7	28.0
Muscat Securities Market	NA	NA	NA	14.7	13.1
Nairobi Securities Exchange	NA	NA	NA	11.1	3.8
Namibian Stock Exchange	NA	NA	NA	1.7	2.4
NASDAQ OMX Nordic Exchange	60.5	38.8	42.0	47.7	53.3
Nigerian Stock Exchange	NA	NA	NA	13.5	6.7
Oslo Bors	53.2	29.6	34.3	55.7	43.0
Palestine Exchange	NA	NA	NA	8.5	31.9
Qatar Stock Exchange	NA	NA	15.9	29.5	12.7
Saudi Stock Exchange (Tadawul)	111.7	104.9	78.9	131.8	95.3
SIX Swiss Exchange	51.2	35.9	41.2	54.1	55.4
Stock Exchange of Mauritius	3.9	4.6	2.6	3.7	3.8
Tehran Stock Exchange	8.0	27.5	27.2	10.7	6.0
Tel-Aviv Stock Exchange	37.0	37.2	34.3	34.9	32.9
Trop-X (Seychelles) Limited	NA	NA	26.4	0.0	0.3
Ukrainian Exchange	NA	NA	NA	0.9	0.5
Warsaw Stock Exchange	37.5	31.2	31.8	32.2	36.6
Wiener Borse	28.1	20.7	21.4	30.7	30.6
Zagreb SE	NA	NA	NA	2.5	3.0

*Monthly share turnover as represented by December values.

Source: Various year-end issues of World Federation of Exchanges' *Monthly Report*.

but rather as a listed stock exchange. On average 14 dealers make a market in the NASDAQ traded issues.

In the United States, firms must meet certain listing requirements in order to have their stock traded on one of several organized stock exchanges. Historically, the two largest of these exchanges were the New York Stock Exchange (NYSE) and the American Stock Exchange (AMEX). In these national exchanges the stocks of some of the largest companies of the most interest to investors were bought and sold on their trading floors. Shares of firms of regional interest once traded on several regional exchanges.

The exchange markets in the United States are agency/auction markets. Each stock traded on the exchange is represented by a **specialist**, who makes a market by holding an inventory of the security. Each specialist has a designated station (desk) on the exchange trading floor where trades in his stock are conducted. Floor brokers bring the flow of public market orders for a security to the specialist's desk for execution. Serving as a dealer, the specialist is obligated to post bid and ask prices for the stock he represents and to stand willing to buy or sell for his own account at these prices. Through an auction process, the "crowd" of floor brokers may arrive at a more favorable market price for their clients between the specialist's bid and ask prices and thus transact among themselves. The specialist also holds the limit order book. In executing these orders, the specialist serves as an agent. Limit order prices receive preference in establishing the posted bid and ask prices if they are more favorable than the specialist's, and he must fill a limit order, if possible, from the flow of public orders before trading for his own account. Both the OTC and the exchange markets in the United States are **continuous markets** where market and limit orders can be executed at any time during business hours.

In recent years, most national stock markets have become automated for at least some of the issues traded on them. The first was the Toronto Stock Exchange (TMX), which in 1977 instituted the Computer Assisted Trading System (CATS). An automated trading system electronically stores and displays public orders on a continuous basis, and allows public traders to cross orders with one another to execute a trade without the assistance of exchange personnel. Automated systems are successful largely because orders can be filled faster and fewer exchange personnel are needed. Indeed, automated trading that bypasses the specialist system now accounts for over 80 percent of NYSE transactions. In some countries the exchange trading floor has been completely eliminated.

Not all stock market systems provide continuous trading. For example, the Paris Bourse was traditionally a call market. In a **call market**, an agent of the exchange accumulates, over a period of time, a batch of orders that are periodically executed by written or verbal auction throughout the trading day. Both market and limit orders are handled in this way. The major disadvantage of a call market is that traders are not certain about the price at which their orders will transact because bid and ask quotations are not available prior to the call. On September 22, 2000, the Paris Bourse merged with the Brussels and Amsterdam exchanges to form Euronext, discussed in a later section in this chapter.

A second type of noncontinuous exchange trading system is **crowd trading**. Typically, crowd trading is organized as follows: In a trading ring, an agent of the exchange periodically calls out the name of the issue. At this point, traders announce their bid and ask prices for the issue, and seek counterparts to a trade. Between counterparts a deal may be struck and a trade executed. Unlike a call market in which there is a common price for all trades, several bilateral trades may take place at different prices. Crowd trading was once the system of trading on the Zurich Stock Exchange, but the Swiss exchange moved to an automated system in August 1996. At present, crowd trading is practiced at the Madrid Stock Exchange for a small percentage of trading.

Continuous trading systems are desirable for actively traded issues, whereas call markets and crowd trading offer advantages for thinly traded issues because they mitigate the possibility of sparse order flow over short time periods. Exhibit 13.3 provides a summary of the major equity trading systems found worldwide.

www.nyse.com

This is the website of the New York Stock Exchange. Information about the NYSE, its operation, membership, and listed companies is provided here. U.S. stock price quotations are available at this site.

www.tmx.com

This is the website of TMX Group, which operates the Toronto Stock Exchange. Information about the exchange, its operation, membership, and listed companies is provided here. Canadian stock and mutual fund prices are available at this site.

EXHIBIT 13.3

Characteristics of Major
Equity Trading Systems

Equity Trading System	Market Characteristics		
	Public Orders	Order Flow	Example
Dealer	Trade with dealer	Continuous	NASDAQ/OTC
Agency	Agent assists with matching of public orders	Continuous or periodic	NYSE specialist system[a] (continuous) Old Paris Bourse (noncontinuous)
Fully automated	Electronic matching of public orders	Continuous	Toronto Stock Exchange

[a]As noted in the text, a specialist may at times also serve as a dealer.

Market Consolidations and Mergers

www.euronext.com

This is the official website of Euronext.

There are approximately 80 major national stock markets. Western and Eastern Europe once had more than 20 national stock exchanges where at least 15 different languages were spoken. Today, stock markets around the world are under pressure from clients to combine or buy stakes in one another to trade shares of companies anywhere, at a faster pace. To satisfy investors' needs, several combinations and trading arrangements have been formed. One of the most promising arrangements is Euronext. Euronext was formed on September 22, 2000, as a result of a merger of the Amsterdam Exchanges, Brussels Exchanges, and the Paris Bourse. Euronext creates a single trading platform serving all members at each of the three subsidiary exchanges. Access to all shares and products is provided. Additionally, a single order book exists for each stock, allowing for transparency and liquidity. A single clearinghouse and payment and delivery system facilitates trading. In June 2001, the Lisbon stock exchange merged with Euronext. Possibly, over time a European stock exchange will develop. However, a lack of common securities regulations, even among the countries of the European Union, hinders this development. Nevertheless, the April 4, 2007, merger of Euronext with the New York Stock Exchange, to form NYSE Euronext, creates the potential for internationalizing trading arrangements in the future. Additionally, on October 1, 2008, NYSE Euronext acquired the American Stock Exchange to form NYSE AMEX. On November 13, 2013, Intercontinental Exchange (ICE), the 12-year-old energy and commodities futures exchange, acquired NYSE Euronext for $11 billion. On March 20, 2014, ICE spun off Euronext in a $1.2 billion IPO. In March 2016, the London Stock Exchange (LSE) and Deutsche Boerse, the German exchange, agreed to merge, which together will have a combined market value in excess of $30 billion.

www.nasdaqomx.com

This is the official website of NASDAQ OMX.

Another noteworthy European trading arrangement is Norex. Norex is an alliance among the Nordic and Baltic exchanges in Denmark, Estonia, Finland, Latvia, Lithuania, Sweden (all owned and operated by OMX, the largest integrated securities market in Northern Europe), Iceland, and Norway. Trading on Norex exchanges is carried out through the Stockholm Automated Exchange (SAXESS), a state-of-the-art computerized and electronic trading system capable of handling 2,000 orders per second. On February 27, 2008, NASDAQ acquired OMX to form NASDAQ OMX, and on July 24, 2008, NASDAQ OMX acquired the Philadelphia Stock Exchange.

Trading in International Equities

During the 1980s world capital markets began a trend toward greater global integration. Several factors account for this movement. First, investors began to realize the benefits of international portfolio diversification. Second, major capital markets became more liberalized through the elimination of fixed trading commissions, the reduction in governmental regulation, and measures taken by the European Union to integrate their capital markets. Third, new computer and communications technology facilitated efficient and fair securities trading through order routing and execution, information dissemination, and clearance and settlement. Fourth, MNCs realized the benefits of sourcing new capital internationally. In this section, we explore some of the major effects that greater global integration has had on the world's equity markets. We begin by examining the cross-listing of shares.

Cross-Listing of Shares

Cross-listing refers to a firm having its equity shares listed on one or more foreign exchanges, in addition to the home country stock exchange. Cross-listing is not a new concept; however, with the increased globalization of world equity markets, the amount of cross-listing has exploded in recent years. In particular, MNCs often cross-list their shares, but non-MNCs also cross-list.

Exhibit 13.4 presents the total number of companies listed on various national stock exchanges in the world and the breakdown of the listings between domestic and foreign for 2015. The exhibit shows that there are some foreign companies listed on virtually all national stock exchanges from developed countries. Several exchanges have a large proportion of foreign listings. In fact, the Luxembourg Stock Exchange has more foreign than domestic listings, while on the Singapore Exchange foreign listings represent 37 percent of the total.

A firm may decide to cross-list its shares for many reasons:

1. Cross-listing provides a means for expanding the investor base for a firm's stock, thus potentially increasing its demand. Increased demand for a company's stock may increase the market price. Additionally, greater market demand and a broader investor base improve the price liquidity of the security.

2. Cross-listing establishes name recognition of the company in a new capital market, thus paving the way for the firm to source new equity or debt capital from local investors as demands dictate. This is an especially important reason for firms from emerging market countries with limited capital markets to cross-list their shares on exchanges in developed countries with enhanced capital market access.

3. Cross-listing brings the firm's name before more investor and consumer groups. Local consumers (investors) may more likely become investors in (consumers of) the company's stock (products) if the company's stock is (products are) locally available. International portfolio diversification is facilitated for investors if they can trade the security on their own stock exchange.

4. Cross-listing into developed capital markets with strict securities regulations and information disclosure requirements may be seen as a signal to investors that improved corporate governance is forthcoming.

5. Cross-listing may mitigate the possibility of a hostile takeover of the firm through the broader investor base created for the firm's shares.

Cross-listing of a firm's stock obligates the firm to adhere to the securities regulations of its home country as well as the regulations of the countries in which it is cross-listed. Cross-listing in the United States means the firm must meet the reporting and disclosure requirements of the U.S. Securities and Exchange Commission. According to the **bonding theory**, a U.S. cross-listing both restricts the ability of corporate insiders of the cross-listed firm from consuming private benefits and also publicly benefits the firm by allowing it to finance new growth opportunities at more advantageous terms. Reconciliation of a company's financial statements to U.S. standards can be a laborious process, and some foreign firms are reluctant to disclose hidden reserves.

EXHIBIT 13.4

Total, Domestic, and Foreign
Company Listings on Major
National Stock Exchanges
for 2015

Exchange	Total	Domestic	Foreign
Americas			
Barbados Stock Exchange	24	20	4
Bermuda Stock Exchange	67	14	53
BM&FBOVESPA	359	345	14
Bolsa de Comercio de Buenos Aires	99	93	6
Bolsa de Comercio de Santiago	310	223	87
Bolsa de Valores de Lima	310	212	98
Bolsa de Valores de Panama	31	30	1
Bolsa Mexicana de Valores	143	136	7
Bolsa Nacional de Valores	10	10	0
Jamaica Stock Exchange	60	59	1
Nasdaq - US	2,859	2,471	388
NYSE	2,424	1,910	514
TMX Group	3,559	3,501	58
Total Region	**10,255**	**9,024**	**1,231**
Asia-Pacific			
Australian Securities Exchange	2,108	1,989	119
BSE India Limited	5,836	5,835	1
Bursa Malaysia	902	892	10
Chittagong SE	256	256	0
Colombo Stock Exchange	294	294	0
Dhaka Stock Exchange	287	287	0
Hanoi Stock Exchange	377	377	0
Hochiminh Stock Exchange	307	307	0
Hong Kong Exchanges and Clearing	1,866	1,770	96
Indonesia Stock Exchange	521	521	0
Japan Exchange Group	3,513	3,504	9
Korea Exchange	1,961	1,948	13
National Stock Exchange of India	1,794	1,793	1
NZX Limited	191	171	20
Philippine Stock Exchange	265	262	3
Port Moresby Stock Exchange	17	6	11
Shanghai Stock Exchange	1,081	1,081	0
Shenzhen Stock Exchange	1,746	1,746	0
Singapore Exchange	769	483	286
Stock Exchange of Thailand	639	639	0
Sydney Stock Exchange	4	4	0
Taipei Exchange	712	681	31
Taiwan Stock Exchange Corp.	896	824	72
Total Region	**26,342**	**25,670**	**672**
Europe-Africa-Middle East			
Abu Dhabi Securities Exchange	68	65	3
Amman Stock Exchange	228	228	0
Athens Stock Exchange	240	236	4
Bahrain Bourse	46	44	2
Beirut Stock Exchange	10	10	0
Belarusian Currency and Stock Exchange	62	62	0
BME Spanish Exchanges	3,651	3,623	28

(continued)

EXHIBIT 13.4

Total, Domestic, and Foreign Company Listings on Major National Stock Exchanges for 2015 (continued)

Borsa Istanbul	393	392	1
Bourse de Casablanca	75	74	1
Bourse de Valeurs Mobilieres de Tunis	78	78	0
BRVM	39	39	0
Bucharest Stock Exchange	84	82	2
Budapest Stock Exchange	45	45	0
Cyprus Stock Exchange	84	84	0
Deutsche Boerse	619	555	64
Dubai Financial Market	60	60	0
Egyptian Exchange	252	250	2
Euronext	1,068	944	124
Irish Stock Exchange	53	43	10
Johannesburg Stock Exchange	382	316	66
Kazakhstan Stock Exchange	85	78	7
Ljubljana Stock Exchange	46	46	0
London SE Group	2,685	2,167	518
Luxembourg Stock Exchange	192	27	165
Malta Stock Exchange	23	23	0
Moscow Exchange	254	251	3
Muscat Securities Market	116	116	0
Nairobi Securities Exchange	64	64	NA
Namibian Stock Exchange	41	8	33
NASDAQ OMX Nordic Exchange	832	800	32
Nigerian Stock Exchange	184	183	1
Oslo Bors	214	171	43
Palestine Exchange	49	49	NA
Qatar Stock Exchange	43	43	0
Saudi Stock Exchange (Tadawul)	171	171	0
SIX Swiss Exchange	270	234	36
Stock Exchange of Mauritius	72	71	1
Tehran Stock Exchange	318	318	0
Tel-Aviv Stock Exchange	461	440	21
Trop-X (Seychelles) Limited	4	3	1
Ukrainian Exchange	160	158	2
Warsaw Stock Exchange	905	872	33
Wiener Borse	92	79	13
Zagreb SE	186	186	0
Total Region	**14,764**	**13,552**	**1,212**
WFE Total	**51,361**	**48,246**	**3,115**

Source: Table 1.2 *Monthly Report,* December 2015. World Federation of Exchanges.

For foreign firms desiring to have their shares traded only among large institutional investors rather than listed on an exchange, less rigorous accounting and disclosure requirements apply under SEC Rule 144A. Rule 144A share sales are often acceptable to family-owned companies, which for privacy or tax reasons operate their businesses with more lax accounting standards.

Yankee Stock Offerings

The introduction to this section indicated that in recent years U.S. investors have bought and sold a large amount of foreign stock. Since the beginning of the 1990s, many foreign companies, Latin American in particular, have listed their stocks on U.S. exchanges to prime the U.S. equity market for future **Yankee stock** offerings, that is,

CIB

COMMERCIAL INTERNATIONAL BANK (EGYPT) S.A.E.

International Offering of
9,999,000 Global Depository Receipts

corresponding to
999,900 Shares (nominal Value of E£100 per Share)

at an
Offer price of US$11.875 per Global Depository Receipt

Seller
National Bank of Egypt

Global Co-ordinator
Co Lead Managers
Robert Fleming & Co. Limited Salomon Brothers International Limited
UBS Limited

Domestic Advisor
Commercial International Investment Company S.A.E.

ING BARINGS

July 1996

Source: "Global Depository Receipt Tombstone," *Euromoney,* October 1998, p. 127. All rights reserved. Used with permission.

the direct sale of new equity capital to U.S. public investors. This was a break from the past for the Latin American companies, which typically sold restricted 144A shares to large investors. Three factors appear to be fueling the sale of Yankee stocks. One is the push for privatization by many Latin American and Eastern European government-owned companies. A second factor is the rapid growth in the economies of the developing countries. The third reason is the large demand for new capital by Mexican companies following approval of the North American Free Trade Agreement.

American Depository Receipts

Foreign stocks can be traded directly on a national stock market, but frequently they are traded in the form of a *depository receipt.* For example, Yankee stock issues often trade on the U.S. exchanges as **American Depository Receipts (ADRs)**. An ADR is a receipt representing a number of foreign shares that remain on deposit with the U.S. depository's custodian in the issuer's home market. The bank serves as the transfer agent for the ADRs, which are traded on the listed exchanges in the United States or in the OTC market. The first ADRs began trading in 1927 as a means of eliminating some of the risks, delays, inconveniences, and expenses of trading the actual shares. At year-end 2015, 390 ADRs traded on U.S. listed exchanges. Several hundred more ADRs trade on the U.S. OTC market. Similarly, *Singapore Depository Receipts* trade on the Singapore Stock Exchange. *Global Depository Receipts (GDRs)* allow a foreign firm to simultaneously cross-list on several national exchanges. Many GDRs are traded on the London and Luxembourg stock exchanges. The DR market has grown significantly over the years; at year-end 2015, there were 3,602 DR programs, representing issuers from 79 countries, trading on the world's exchanges. Exhibit 13.5 shows a tombstone for a Global Depository Receipt.

ADRs offer the U.S. investor many advantages over trading directly in the underlying stock on the foreign exchange. Non-U.S. investors can also invest in ADRs, and

Types of ADRs

	LEVEL I	LEVEL II	LEVEL III	RULE 144A
Description	Unlisted program in the U.S.	Listed on a U.S. exchange	Shares offered and listed on a U.S. exchange	Private placement to Qualified Institutional Buyers
Trading	OTC	NASDAQ, AMEX, NYSE	NASDAQ, AMEX, NYSE	U.S. private placement
SEC Registration	Form F-6	Form F-6	Forms F-1 and F-6	None
U.S. Reporting Requirements	Exempt under Rule 12g3-2(b)	Form 20-F*	Form 20-F*	Exempt under Rule 12g3-2(b)

*Financial statements must be partially reconciled to U.S. GAAP.

Level I: The most basic type of ADR program.
The issuer is not seeking to raise new equity capital in the U.S. and/or cannot list on NASDAQ.
Level II: The issuer is not seeking to raise new equity capital in the U.S. and ADRs can be listed on NASDAQ, AMEX, or NYSE.
Level III: The issuer floats a public offering of new equity in the U.S. and lists the ADRs on NASDAQ, AMEX, or NYSE.
Rule 144A: This type of ADR program is a private placement of equity to Qualified Institutional Buyers (QIBs).
It can only be traded among QIBs.

Source: Excerpted from www.adr.com.

frequently do so rather than invest in the underlying stock because of the investment advantages. These advantages include:

1. ADRs are denominated in dollars, trade on a U.S. stock exchange, and can be purchased through the investor's regular broker. By contrast, trading in the underlying shares would likely require the investor to: set up an account with a broker from the country where the company issuing the stock is located; make a currency exchange; and arrange for the shipment of the stock certificates or the establishment of a custodial account.

2. Dividends received on the underlying shares are collected and converted to dollars by the custodian and paid to the ADR investor, whereas investment in the underlying shares requires the investor to collect the foreign dividends and make a currency conversion. Moreover, tax treaties between the United States and some countries lower the dividend tax rate paid by nonresident investors. Consequently, U.S. investors in the underlying shares need to file a form to get a refund on the tax difference withheld. ADR investors, however, receive the full dollar equivalent dividend, less only the applicable taxes.

3. ADR trades clear in three business days as do U.S. equities, whereas settlement practices for the underlying stock vary in foreign countries.

4. ADR price quotes are in U.S. dollars.

5. ADRs (except Rule 144A issues) are registered securities that provide for the protection of ownership rights, whereas most underlying stocks are bearer securities. Exhibit 13.6 describes the various types of ADR programs.

6. An ADR investment can be sold by trading the depository receipt to another investor in the U.S. stock market, or the underlying shares can be sold in the local stock market. In this case the ADR is delivered for cancellation to the bank depository, which delivers the underlying shares to the buyer. Exhibit 13.7 charts the mechanics of issuance and cancellation of ADRs.

7. ADRs frequently represent a multiple of the underlying shares, rather than a one-for-one correspondence, to allow the ADR to trade in a price range customary for U.S. investors. A single ADR may represent more or less than one underlying share, depending upon the underlying share value.

EXHIBIT 13.7 **Mechanics of Issuance and Cancellation of ADRs**

A broker-dealer can purchase existing ADRs in the United States or purchase underlying shares in an issuer's home market and have new ADRs created, or issued, by the depository bank. While the pool of available ADRs is constantly changing, the broker-dealer decides whether to purchase existing ADRs or have new ones issued, depending on such factors as availability, pricing, and market conditions in the United States and the issuer's home market.

To create new ADRs, underlying shares are deposited with a custodian bank in the issuer's home market. The depository then issues ADRs representing those shares. The process for canceling ADRs is similar to the issuance process, but the steps are reversed. The following chart and description provide a more detailed explanation, including the parties and steps involved.

The ADR purchase and issuance process: two scenarios

EXISTING ADRs

A1 Investor places order with broker in the United States.

A2 Broker in the United States purchases ADRs in the applicable market.

A3 Settlement and delivery of the ADRs (in book-entry or certificate form).

NEW ADRs

B1 Investor places order with broker in the United States.

B2 Broker in the United States places order with local broker (outside U.S.) for equivalent shares.

B3 Local broker purchases shares in local market.

B4 Local shares are deposited with the depository's custodian.

B5 Depository receives confirmation of share deposit.

B6 Depository issues new ADRs and delivers them to broker in the U.S.

B7 Settlement and delivery of the ADRs (in book-entry or certificate form).

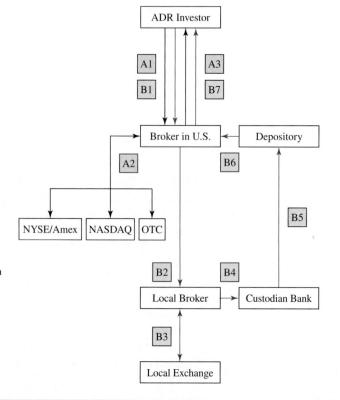

Source: Excerpted from www.adr.com.

8. ADR holders give instructions to the depository bank as to how to vote the rights associated with the underlying shares. Voting rights are not exercised by the depository bank in the absence of specific instructions from the ADR holders.

There are two types of ADRs: sponsored and unsponsored. *Sponsored* ADRs are created by a bank at the request of the foreign company that issued the underlying security. The sponsoring bank often offers ADR holders an assortment of services, including investment information and portions of the annual report translated into English. Sponsored ADRs are the only ones that can be listed on the U.S. stock markets. All new ADR programs must be sponsored. *Unsponsored* ADRs—some dating back prior to 1980 still exist—were usually created at the request of a U.S. investment banking firm without direct involvement by the foreign issuing firm. Consequently, the foreign company may not provide investment information or financial reports to the depository on a regular basis or in a timely manner. The depository fees of sponsored ADRs are paid by the foreign company. ADR investors pay the depository fees on unsponsored ADRs. Unsponsored ADRs may have several issuing banks, with the terms of the offering varying from bank to bank. In general, only sponsored ADRs trade on NASDAQ or the major stock exchanges.

The 390 sponsored ADRs that traded on U.S. listed exchanges at year-end 2015 represent a net increase from 385 a year earlier, but a decline from 392 at year-end 2013. Many of the issuers that have delisted in recent years have continued to offer their depository receipts to investors by converting them to a Level I OTC-traded ADR program. After delisting, the cross-listed firm can apply for deregistration of its securities with the U.S. SEC and the termination of all the reporting requirements under the Securities Exchange Act of 1934. Delisting was facilitated by the March 21, 2007, adoption by the SEC of the Exchange Act Rule 12h-6, which makes it much easier for foreign firms to deregister. It has been widely debated whether the recent surge in delisting indicates that foreign listed firms no longer see benefits from cross-listing in the United States or that U.S. markets have lost their competitiveness because of new regulation such as the Sarbanes-Oxley Act of 2002 (SOX), which instituted a broad set of new reforms regarding corporate governance of publicly held corporations.

There has been much anecdotal evidence that compliance with SOX has been particularly onerous and expensive. Additionally, a particular concern for the United States is the fact that new initial public offerings (IPOs) by Chinese firms, the major source of new IPOs, have been cross-listed in Hong Kong rather than in the United States. For example, in 2005 nine of the ten largest Chinese IPOs were cross-listed in Hong Kong, and in 2006 the $9.7 billion Bank of China IPO was cross-listed there. Again, the anecdotal evidence is that company executives find the burden of compliance with U.S. regulation to be responsible. Alternatively, the reason may simply be that the Chinese government prefers to promote its own stock exchanges. Cross-listed firms that trade in the United States as Level I ADRs are exempt from the reporting requirements of the Securities Exchange Act of 1934 and from the accountability requirements under SOX. Thus, the fact that in recent years the majority of cross-listed firms that delisted from U.S. exchanges continue to trade on the U.S. OTC market suggests that these firms do find the burden of complying with U.S. regulation onerous and expensive, but nevertheless value U.S. markets as a venue for cross-listing.

Global Registered Shares

The merger of Daimler Benz AG and Chrysler Corporation in November 1998 created DaimlerChrysler AG, a German firm. The merger was hailed as a landmark event for global equity markets because it simultaneously created a new type of equity share called Global Registered Shares (GRSs). GRSs are shares that are traded globally, unlike ADRs, which are receipts for bank deposits of home-market shares and traded on foreign markets. The primary exchanges for DaimlerChrysler GRSs were the Frankfurt Stock Exchange and the NYSE; however, they were traded on a total of 20 exchanges worldwide. GRSs are fully fungible—a GRS purchased on one exchange can be sold on another. DaimlerChrysler GRSs traded in both euros and U.S. dollars. A global share registrar that linked the German and U.S. transfer agents and registrars facilitated clearing. In October 2007, the company was renamed Daimler AG, when it spun off Chrysler. Daimler AG continued to trade as a GRS. In May 2010, Daimler decided to delist from the NYSE and submitted a request to that effect with the U.S. SEC. The delisting became effective on June 7, 2010, and Daimler GRSs began trading on the OTC market. As a result, Daimler is no longer subject to the reporting requirements under the U.S. Securities Exchange Act of 1934 or the accountability requirements of the Sarbanes-Oxley Act of 2002, thus saving it millions of euros per year. Daimler reasoned that in today's global marketplace, with high-volume trading platforms, it no longer made sense to be listed on a large number of stock exchanges. On September 23, 2010, Daimler established a Level I ADR program in the OTC market in the U.S., with one ADR equaling one GRS. The main advantages of GRSs over ADRs appear to be that all shareholders have equal status and direct voting rights. The main disadvantage of GRSs appears to be the greater expense in establishing the global registrar and clearing facility. GRSs have met with limited success; many companies that considered them opted for ADRs.[2] Deutsche Bank and UBS also trade as GRSs.

EXAMPLE | 13.1: Daimler AG

Stock in Daimler AG, the famous German automobile manufacturer, trades on both the Frankfurt Stock Exchange in Germany and as a Level I ADR on the OTC market in the United States. On the Frankfurt bourse, Daimler closed at a price of EUR59.50 on Monday, June 6, 2016. On the same day, Daimler closed in the United States at $67.60 per share. To prevent arbitrage trading between the two markets, the securities have to trade at the same price when adjusted for the exchange rate. We see that this is true. The $/EUR exchange rate on June 6 was $1.1355/EUR1.00. Thus, EUR59.50 × $1.1355 = $67.56, an amount very close to the closing price in the United States of $67.60. The difference is easily explainable by the fact that the U.S. OTC market closes several hours after the Frankfurt exchange, and thus market prices had changed slightly.

Empirical Findings on Cross-Listing and ADRs

Several empirical studies document important findings on cross-listing in general and on ADRs in particular.

Park (1990) found that a substantial portion of the variability in (i.e., change in) ADR returns is accounted for by variation in the share price of the underlying security in the home market. However, information observed in the U.S. market is also an important factor in the ADR return generating process.

Kao, Wenchi, Wei, and Vu (1991) examined ADRs as vehicles for constructing diversified equity portfolios. They used 10 years of monthly return data covering the period 1979 through 1989 for ADRs with underlying shares in the U.K., Australia, Japan, the Netherlands, and Sweden. They found that an internationally diversified portfolio of ADRs outperforms both a U.S. stock market and a world stock market benchmark on a risk-adjusted basis.

Jayaraman, Shastri, and Tandon (1993) examined the effect of the listing of ADRs on the risk and return of the underlying stock. They found positive abnormal performance (i.e., return in excess of the expected equilibrium return) of the underlying security on the initial listing date. They interpreted this as evidence that an ADR listing provides the issuing firm with another market from which to source new equity capital. Additionally, they found an increase in the volatility of (i.e., change in) returns of the underlying stock. They interpreted this as consistent with the theory that traders with proprietary information will attempt to profit from their knowledge by taking advantage of price discrepancies caused by information differentials between the ADR and underlying security markets.

Gagnon and Karolyi (2004) compared synchronous intraday prices of ADRs and other types of cross-listed shares in U.S. markets relative to home-market prices after currency adjustment for 581 companies from 39 countries. They discovered that for most stocks, prices of cross-listed shares are within 20 to 85 basis points of the home-market shares, thus limiting arbitrage opportunities after transaction costs. However, when institutional barriers that limit arbitrage exist, prices can deviate by as much as a 66 percent premium and an 87 percent discount. Large deviations seldom exist for more than a day. They also discovered that cross-listed shares trading in the United States are relatively more (less) correlated with the U.S. market index than with the home market when there is proportionately more (less) trading in the U.S. market.

Berkman and Nguyen (2010) studied the impact of cross-listing in the United States on domestic liquidity for a sample of 277 firms from 30 countries over the period 1996 through 2005. Their results indicate that cross-listed firms from countries with poor corporate governance and/or weak accounting standards gain from improvements

---

[2]Much of the information in this section is from the 2003 clinical study by G. Andrew Karolyi.

in domestic liquidity in the first two years after cross-listing but tend to diminish later on. In general, they found little evidence that cross-listing results in significant improvements in domestic liquidity. Their results are seemingly inconsistent with the bonding theory, which predicts that firms from countries with weak investor protection should experience permanent improvements in domestic liquidity.

Abdallah and Ioannidis (2010) reexamined prior work. They found that firms cross-list in a period of good performance in their local market to take advantage of an overvaluation of share prices to raise new capital in the cross-listed country. Additionally, they found that abnormal return exhibits a significant decline after cross-listing, which is more pronounced the higher the level of the pre-cross-listing abnormal return. Their results support earlier findings that local market beta (risk) declines after cross-listing, but that the decrease diminishes over time. These findings are consistent for firms that cross-list on either regulated U.S. exchanges or on the OTC market and for firms from both civil and common law countries. Overall, their results do not support the bonding theory's prediction that cross-listing signals the firm's commitment to protect minority shareholders' interests and thus increase the value of the firm by reducing the required rate of return.

Doidge, Karolyi, and Stulz (2010) studied why foreign cross-listed firms choose to delist from a U.S. exchange. The Exchange Act Rule 12h-6 adopted by the SEC on March 21, 2007, facilitates foreign firms delisting from U.S. exchanges. Two theories present predictions why a firm might choose to delist. The bonding theory predicts that firms with poor growth opportunities, who have little need for new external capital, and those which perform poorly might be likely candidates for delisting. The loss of competitiveness theory predicts that the compliance costs of SOX and possibly other regulatory developments so reduced the net benefits of a U.S. listing that for some firms the value of the cross-listing became negative. The strongest evidence they found concluded that firms that delist and leave U.S. markets (i.e., are not subsequently traded on the U.S. OTC market) do so because they do not foresee the need to raise new external funds. They did not find that SOX is a major determinant in decisions to leave U.S. markets.

International Equity Market Benchmarks

As a benchmark of activity or performance of a given national equity market, an index of the stocks traded on the secondary exchange (or exchanges) of a country is used. Several national equity indexes are available for use by investors.

www.msci.com

This website provides detailed information about the construction of MSCI international stock market indexes.

The indexes constructed and published by MSCI are an excellent source of national stock market performance. MSCI presents return and price level data for 23 national stock market indexes from developed countries, 24 emerging market countries, and 32 frontier markets that cover investment opportunities beyond traditional developed and emerging markets. In constructing each of these indexes, an attempt is made to include equity issues representing at least 85 percent of the free-float market capitalization of each industry within the country. The stocks in each country index are market-value weighted, that is, the proportion of the index a stock represents is determined by its proportion of the total market capitalization of all stocks in the index. Additionally, MSCI publishes a market-value-weighted World Index comprising 23 of its country indexes. The World Index includes approximately 2,600 stock issues of major corporations in the world. MSCI also publishes several regional indexes: the European, Australasia, Far East (EAFE) Index comprising approximately 1,000 stocks from 21 countries; the North American Index composed of the United States and Canada; the Far East Index (three countries); several Europe Indexes (depending upon whether individual constituent countries are included); the Nordic Countries Index (four countries); the Pacific Index (five countries); and the Emerging Markets Index (23 countries). The EAFE Index is widely followed, and it is representative of World Index excluding North American stock market performance. MSCI also publishes dozens of industry indexes, each of which includes equity issues from the respective industry from the countries it follows. Most recently, MSCI introduced two new indexes: the All Country World Investable Market

Index (ACW) and the All Country World ex U.S.A. Investable Market Index (ACW ex US) provide a better representation of the stock market. The ACW Index includes more than 9,000 stock issues represented by the 46 MSCI developed and emerging market country indexes and the ACW ex US includes more than 6,000 issues, which covers 98 percent of the world's non-U.S. markets.

The *Financial Times* reports values in local currency of the major stock market indexes of the national exchanges or markets from various countries in the world. Many of these indexes are prepared by the stock markets themselves or well-known investment advisory firms. Exhibit 13.8 presents a list of the indexes that appear daily in the *Financial Times*.

Standard & Poor's publishes the S&P ADR Index, an investable index designed to allow investors to benchmark international stock performance traded on U.S. stock exchanges. The S&P ADR index includes foreign firms that are members of the S&P Global 1200 Index that trade as Level II or Level III ADRs, global shares, or ordinary shares, in the case of Canadian equities. The index is market-value weighted and includes about 260 securities from 29 countries.

iShares MSCI

BlackRock, Inc., an international investment management firm, operates iShares MSCI as vehicles to facilitate investment in country, regional, and world funds. iShares MSCI are baskets of stocks designed to replicate various MSCI stock indexes. Currently there are dozens of iShares MSCI, of which several are country-specific funds and others replicate aggregate MSCI indexes, such as the World, EAFE, and Emerging Markets Index. iShares are exchange-traded funds; most trade on NYSE AMEX.

www.ishares.com

This website describes the iShares MSCI operated by BlackRock.

iShares that trade on U.S. exchanges are subject to U.S. SEC and Internal Revenue Service diversification requirements. These requirements prohibit the investment of more than 50 percent of the fund in five or fewer securities, or 25 percent of the fund in a single security. Thus, some funds may not perfectly replicate their respective MSCI index. Nevertheless, iShares are a low-cost, convenient way for investors to hold diversified investments in several different countries. Daily values of the 100 longest exchange-traded funds can be found in *The Wall Street Journal*.

The International Finance in Practice box "Foreign Interest in South Africa Takes Off" discusses investing in South Africa via the iShares MSCI South Africa exchange-traded fund.

Factors Affecting International Equity Returns

Before closing this chapter, it is beneficial to explore some of the empirical evidence about which factors influence equity returns. After all, to construct an efficiently diversified international portfolio of stocks, one must estimate the expected return and the variance of returns for each security in the investment set plus the pairwise correlation structure. It may be easier to accurately estimate these parameters if a common set of factors affect equity returns. Some likely candidates are: macroeconomic variables that influence the overall economic environment in which the firm issuing the security conducts its business; exchange rate changes between the currency of the country issuing the stock and the currency of other countries where suppliers, customers, and investors of the firm reside; and the industrial structure of the country in which the firm operates.

Macroeconomic Factors

Two studies have tested the influence of various macroeconomic variables on stock returns. Solnik (1984) examined the effect of exchange rate changes, interest rate differentials, the level of the domestic interest rate, and changes in domestic inflation expectations. He found that international monetary variables had only weak influence on equity returns in comparison to domestic variables. In another study, Asprem

EXHIBIT 13.8		Major National Stock Market Indexes			
Country	Index	Country	Index	Country	Index
Argentina	Merval	Italy	FTSE MIB	Taiwan	Weighted Pr
Australia	All Ordinaries		FTSE Italia Mid Cap	Thailand	Bangkok SET
	S&P/ASX 200 Res		FTSE Italia All-Sh	Turkey	BIST 100
	S&P/ASX 200	Japan	Nikkei 225	UAE	Abu Dhabi General
Austria	ATX		Topix		Index
Belgium	BEL 20		S&P Topix 150	UK	FTSE 100
	BEL Mid		2nd Section		FT 30
Brazil	Bovespa	Jordan	Amman SE		FTSE All Share
Canada	S&P/TSX Met & Min	Kenya	NSE 20		FTSE techMARK 100
	S&P/TSX 60	Kuwait	KSX Market Index		FTSE4Good UK
	S&P/TSX Comp	Latvia	OMX Riga	USA	S&P 500
Chile	IGPA Gen	Lithuania	OMX Vilnlus		FTSE NASDAQ 500
China	Shanghai A	Luxembourg	LuxX		NASDAQ Cmp
	Shanghai B	Malaysia	FTSE Bursa KLCI		NASDAQ 100
	Shanghai Comp	Mexico	IPC		Russell 2000
	Shenzhen A	Morocco	MASI		NYSE Comp.
	Shenzhen B	Netherlands	AEX		Wilshire 5000
	FTSE A200		AEX All Share		DJ Industrial
	FTSE B35	New Zealand	NZX 50		DJ Composite
Colombia	COLCAP	Nigeria	SE All Share		DJ Transport
Creatia	CROBEX	Norway	Oslo All Share		DJ Utilities
Cyprus	CSE M&P Gen	Pakistan	KSE 100	Venezuela	IBC
Czech Republic	PX	Philippines	Manila Comp	Vietnam	VNI
Denmark	OMX Copenhagen			CROSS-	Stoxx 50 €
	20	Poland	Wig	BORDER	Euro Stoxx 50 €
Egypt	EGX 30	Portugal	PSI General		DJ Global Titans $
Estonia	OMX Tallinn		PSI 20		Euronext 100 ID
Finland	OMX Helsinki	Romania	BET Index		FTSE Multinatts $
	General	Russia	RTS		FTSE Global 100 $
France	CAC 40		MICEX Comp.		FTSE 4Good Glob $
	SBF 120	Saudi-Arabia	TADAWUL All Share		FTSE E300
Germany	M-DAX		Index		FTSEurofirst 80 €
	XETRA Dax	Singapore	FTSE Straits Times		FTSEurofirst 100 €
	TecDAX	Slovakia	SAX		FTSE Lattbex Top €
Greece	Athens Gen	Slovenia	SBI TOP		FTSE Eurotop 100
	FTSE/ASE 20	South Africa	FTSE/JSE All Share		FTSE Gold Min $
Hong Kong	Hang Seng		FTSE/JSE Top 40		FTSE All World
	HS China		FTSE/JSE Res 20		FTSE World $
	Enterprise	South Korea	Kospi		MSCI All World $
	HSCC Red Chip		Kospi 200		MSCI ACWI Fr $
Hungary	Bux	Spain	Madrid SE		MSCI Europe €
India	BSE Sens		IBEX 35		MSCI Pacific $
	S&P CNX 500	Sri Lanka	CSE All Share		S&P Global 1200 $
Indonesia	Jakarta Comp	Sweden	OMX Stockholm 30		S&P Europe 350 €
Ireland	ISEQ Overall		OMX Stockholm AS		S&P Euro €
Israel	Tel Aviv 100	Switzerland	SMI Index		

Source: *Financial Times*, May 17, 2016, p. 218.

(1989) found that changes in industrial production, employment, and imports, the level of interest rates, and an inflation measure explained only a small portion of the variability of equity returns for 10 European countries, but that substantially more of the variation was explained by an international market index.

Foreign Interest in South Africa Takes Off

For the past three years South Africa's equity market has been among the world's strongest performers, with returns to foreign investors boosted substantially by a strengthening currency. For most of this period, however, foreign interest was modest, and it is only during the last quarter of 2004 that this began to change as net foreign purchases of South African shares on the Johannesburg Securities Exchange (JSE) soared to ZAR21 billion ($3.74 billion), the highest quarterly level ever.

Fourth quarter net equity purchases were up from a five-year average of ZAR3.7 billion per quarter, or $895 million at the average exchange rate over the period. Andre Roux, Investec's chief economist in South Africa, says: "There appears to be a concerted move by foreign investors to reduce what has been a protracted period of holding an under-weight position in South Africa [SA] equity."

Unlike past foreign buying, this time it is not confined to resource stocks. "They are buying into a buoyant domestic economic story and are including banks, local industrials and telecoms in their buying programmes," says Roux. "In a global context, SA shares offer reasonable value and buyers also appear satisfied that the country is in a period of higher growth with more currency and interest rate stability."

Unfortunately, scope is limited for investment in pure South African-asset mutual funds denominated in dollars, euros or sterling. Currently, the two largest investment vehicles are Barclays Global Investor's $127 million iShares MSCI South Africa Index (iShares SA), an exchange-traded fund (ETF) listed on the American Stock Exchange, and Old Mutual's Bermuda-based £65 million South Africa Trust (SAT), an investment company listed on the London Stock Exchange.

As an ETF, iShares SA is an index tracking product; SAT is actively managed and has as its benchmark the FTSE/JSE All Share Index. Portfolios of both products are dominated by big-cap, blue-chip stocks, but SAT has a lower exposure to resources at 41.3 percent and to financials at 24.6 percent than does iShares SA (48.1 percent and 27.0 percent, respectively). By contrast, SAT has a considerably higher exposure to industrials at 34.1 percent (versus 24.9 percent).

Lower exposure to resources, which suffered in 2004 as a result of the rand's strength, and a higher industrial content which includes top-performing retailers such as Truworths and Massmart, gave SAT the performance edge in 2004. SAT ended the year with a 49.9 percent gain, while iShares SA advanced 43.6 percent in sterling terms. However, in dollar terms iShares SA was ahead with a gain of 55.4 percent.

Source: Excerpted from *Funds International*. London: VRL Publishing, Ltd., January 2005, p. P1.

Exchange Rates

Adler and Simon (1986) examined the exposure of a sample of foreign equity and bond index returns to exchange rate changes. They found that changes in exchange rates generally explained a larger portion of the variability of foreign bond indexes than foreign equity indexes, but that some foreign equity markets were more exposed to exchange rate changes than were the respective foreign bond markets. Additionally, their results suggest that it would likely be beneficial to hedge (i.e., protect) foreign stock investment against exchange rate uncertainty.

In another study, Eun and Resnick (1988) found that the cross-correlations among major stock markets and exchange markets are relatively low, but positive. This result implies that the exchange rate changes in a given country reinforce the stock market movements in that country as well as in the other countries examined. More recently, Gupta and Finnerty (1992), using principal components analysis on 15 years of monthly data on 30 stocks each from five countries, concluded that exchange risk is generally not priced.

Industrial Structure

Studies examining the influence of industrial structure on foreign equity returns are inconclusive. In a study examining the correlation structure of national equity markets, Roll (1992) concluded that the industrial structure of a country was important in explaining a significant part of the correlation structure of international equity index returns. He also found that industry factors explained a larger portion of stock market variability than did exchange rate changes.

In contrast, Eun and Resnick (1984) found for a sample of 160 stocks from eight countries and 12 industries that the pairwise correlation structure of international security returns could be better estimated from models that recognized country factors rather than industry factors. Similarly, using individual stock return data for 829 firms, from 12 countries, and representing seven broad industry groups, Heston and Rouwenhorst (1994) concluded "that industrial structure explains very little of the cross-sectional difference in country return volatility, and that the low correlation between country indexes is almost completely due to country specific sources of variation."

Both Rouwenhorst (1999) and Beckers (1999) examined the effect of the EMU on European equity markets and come up with opposite conclusions. Rouwenhorst concluded that country effects in stock returns have been larger than industry effects in Western Europe since 1982 and that this situation continued throughout the 1993–98 period when interest rates were converging and fiscal and monetary policies were being harmonized in the countries entering the EMU. On the other hand, Beckers found an increase in correlations between markets and between the same sector in different markets arising from the European integration of fiscal, monetary, and economic policies. He concluded that the increase in pairwise correlations in these countries represents a reduction in the diversification benefits from investing in the euro zone.

Griffin and Karolyi (1998) examined the effect of industrial structure on covariances by studying whether a difference exists in the effect between traded-goods industries and nontraded-goods industries. They found that the cross-country covariances are larger for firms within a given industry than the cross-country covariances across firms in different industries in traded-goods industries. In contrast, for nontraded-goods industries, there is little difference in cross-country covariances between firms in the same industry and those in different industries.

Phylaktis and Xia (2006) examined the roles of country and industry effects on international equity returns using a database covering 50 industry groups from 34 countries over the period 1992 to 2001. Their study focuses on the evolving process of those effects over time and on geographical differences. Their main results are that country effects dominate industry effects over the full study period, but since 1999 there has been a shift toward industry effects. The degree of the shift varies across regions and is more pronounced in Europe and North America, whereas country effects dominate in Asia Pacific and Latin America.

SUMMARY

This chapter provides an overview of international equity markets. The material is designed to provide an understanding of how MNCs source new equity capital outside of their own domestic primary market and to provide useful institutional information to investors interested in diversifying their portfolios internationally.

1. The chapter began with a statistical perspective of the major equity markets in developed countries and of emerging equity markets in developing countries. Market capitalization and turnover figures were provided for each marketplace. Examination of Exhibit 13.1 reveals that the market capitalization of a most national equity markets increased from 2011 to 2015 as a result of countries recovering from the global financial crisis. Additionally, it was noted that turnover ratios in many developing countries remained low, indicating that liquidity in these markets has not been improving.

2. A considerable amount of discussion was devoted to differences in secondary equity market structures. Secondary markets have historically been structured as dealer or agency markets. Both of these types of market structure can provide for continuous market trading, but noncontinuous markets tend to be agency markets. Over-the-counter trading, specialist markets, and automated markets allow for

continuous market trading. Call markets and crowd trading are each types of non-continuous trading market systems. It was noted that most national stock markets are now automated for at least some of the issues traded on them.

3. Cross-listing of a company's shares on foreign exchanges was extensively discussed. A firm may cross-list its shares to: establish a broader investor base for its stock; establish name recognition in foreign capital markets; and pave the way for sourcing new equity and debt capital from investors in these markets. Yankee stock offerings, or sale of foreign stock to U.S. investors, was also discussed. Yankee shares trade on U.S. markets as American depository receipts (ADRs), which are bank receipts representing a multiple of foreign shares deposited in a foreign bank. ADRs eliminate some of the risks, delays, inconveniences, and expenses of trading actual shares.

4. A variety of international equity benchmarks was also presented. Knowledge of where to find comparative equity market performance data is useful. Specifically, MSCI indexes were discussed. Also, a list of the major national stock market indexes prepared by the national exchanges or major investment advisory services was presented.

5. Several empirical studies that tested for factors that might influence equity returns indicate that domestic factors, such as the level of domestic interest rates and expected changes in domestic inflation, as opposed to international monetary variables, had the greatest effect on national equity returns. Industrial structure did not appear to be of primary importance. Equity returns were also found to be sensitive to own-currency exchange rate changes.

KEY WORDS

agency market, *326*	call market, *329*	liquidity, *326*
American Depository Receipts (ADRs), *334*	continuous markets, *329*	market order, *326*
	cross-listing, *331*	over-the-counter (OTC), *326*
ask price, *326*	crowd trading, *329*	primary market, *326*
bid price, *326*	dealer market, *326*	secondary market, *326*
bonding theory, *331*	limit order, *326*	specialist, *329*
broker, *326*	limit order book, *326*	Yankee stock, *333*

QUESTIONS

1. Exhibit 13.8 presents a listing of major national stock market indexes as displayed daily in the print edition of the *Financial Times*. At www.ft.com, you can find an online tracking of these national stock market indexes that shows performance over the past day, month, and year. Go to this website and compare the performance for several stock market indexes from various regions of the world. How does the performance compare? What do you think accounts for differences?

2. As an investor, what factors would you consider before investing in the emerging stock market of a developing country?

3. Compare and contrast the various types of secondary market trading structures.

4. Discuss any benefits you can think of for a company to (a) cross-list its equity shares on more than one national exchange, and (b) to source new equity capital from foreign investors as well as domestic investors.

5. Why might it be easier for an investor desiring to diversify his portfolio internationally to buy depository receipts rather than the actual shares of the company?

6. Why do you think the empirical studies about factors affecting equity returns basically showed that domestic factors were more important than international factors, and, secondly, that industrial membership of a firm was of little importance in forecasting the international correlation structure of a set of international stocks?

PROBLEMS

1. On the Tokyo Stock Exchange, Honda Motor Company stock closed at ¥2,907 per share on Monday, June 6, 2016. Honda trades as an ADR on the NYSE. One underlying Honda share equals one ADR. On June 6, 2016, the ¥/$ exchange rate was ¥107.57/$1.00.

   a. At this exchange rate, what is the no-arbitrage U.S. dollar price of one ADR?

   b. By comparison, Honda ADRs traded at $27.18. Do you think an arbitrage opportunity exists?

2. If Honda ADRs were trading at $31 when the underlying shares were trading in Tokyo at ¥2,907, what could you do to earn a trading profit? Use the information in problem 1 to help you, and assume that transaction costs are negligible.

INTERNET EXERCISES

1. Bloomberg provides current values of many of the international stock indexes presented in Exhibit 13.8 at the website www.bloomberg.com. Go to this website and determine what country's stock markets are trading higher and lower today. Is there any current news event that might influence the way different national markets are trading today?

2. The J.P. Morgan website www.adr.com provides online data on trading in ADRs. From this website, what are the top three most widely held ADRs by institutional investment in Asia? In Europe? Does there appear to be a similarity in industry (such as telecom) represented by the top ADRs held by institutional investors in these two regions, or are they from a variety of different industries? Recall from the chapter that the effect of industrial structure on international stock returns is an unresolved issue.

MINI CASE

San Pico's New Stock Exchange

San Pico is a rapidly growing Latin American developing country. The country is blessed with miles of scenic beaches that have attracted tourists by the thousands in recent years to new resort hotels financed by joint ventures of San Pico businessmen and moneymen from the Middle East, Japan, and the United States. Additionally, San Pico has good natural harbors that are conducive to receiving imported merchandise from abroad and exporting merchandise produced in San Pico and other surrounding countries that lack access to the sea. Because of these advantages, many new businesses are being started in San Pico.

Presently, stock is traded in a cramped building in La Cobijio, the nation's capital. Admittedly, the San Pico Stock Exchange system is rather archaic. Twice a day an official of the exchange will call out the name of each of the 43 companies whose stock trades on the exchange. Brokers wanting to buy or sell shares for their clients then attempt to make a trade with one another. This crowd trading system has worked well for over one hundred years, but the government desires to replace it with a new modern system that will allow greater and more frequent opportunities for trading in each company, and will allow for trading the shares of the many new start-up companies that are expected to trade in the secondary market. Additionally, the government administration is rapidly privatizing many state-owned businesses in an attempt to foster their efficiency, obtain foreign exchange from the sale, and convert the country to a more capitalist economy. The government believes that it could conduct this privatization faster and perhaps at more attractive prices if it had a modern stock exchange facility where the shares of the newly privatized companies will eventually trade.

You are an expert in the operation of secondary stock markets and have been retained as a consultant to the San Pico Stock Exchange to offer your expertise in modernizing the stock market. What would you advise?

www.mhhe.com/er8e

www.mhhe.com/er8e

REFERENCES & SUGGESTED READINGS

Abdallah, Abed Al-Nasser, and Christos Ioannidis. "Why Do Firms Cross-List? Evidence from the U.S. Market." *Quarterly Review of Economics and Finance* 50 (2010), pp. 202–13.

Adler, Michael, and David Simon. "Exchange Rate Surprises in International Portfolios." *The Journal of Portfolio Management* 12 (1986), pp. 44–53.

Asprem, Mads. "Stock Prices, Assets Portfolios and Macroeconomic Variables in Ten European Countries." *Journal of Banking and Finance* 13 (1989), pp. 589–612.

Beckers, Stan. "Investment Implications of a Single European Capital Market." *Journal of Portfolio Management*, Spring (1999), pp. 9–17.

Berkman, Henk, and Nhut H. Nguyen. "Domestic Liquidity and Cross-Listing in the United States." *Journal of Banking and Finance* 34 (2010), pp. 1139–51.

Doidge, Craig, G. Andrew Karolyi, and Rene M. Stulz. "Why Do Foreign Firms Leave U.S. Equity Markets?" *Journal of Finance* 65 (2010), pp. 1507–53.

Eun, Cheol S., and Bruce G. Resnick. "Estimating the Correlation Structure of International Share Prices." *Journal of Finance* 39 (1984), pp. 1311–24.

Eun, Cheol S., and Bruce G. Resnick. "Exchange Rate Uncertainty, Forward Contracts, and International Portfolio Selection." *Journal of Finance* 43 (1988), pp. 197–215.

Gagnon, Louis, and G. Andrew Karolyi. "Multi-Market Trading and Arbitrage." Ohio State University working paper (July 2004).

Griffin, John M., and G. Andrew Karolyi. "Another Look at the Role of the Industrial Structure of Markets for International Diversification Strategies." *Journal of Financial Economics* 50 (1998), pp. 351–73.

Gupta, Manoj, and Joseph E. Finnerty. "The Currency Risk Factor in International Equity Pricing." *Review of Quantitative Finance and Account* 2 (1992), pp. 245–57.

Heston, Steven L., and K. Geert Rouwenhorst. "Does Industrial Structure Explain the Benefits of International Diversification?" *Journal of Financial Economics* 36 (1994), pp. 3–27.

Jayaraman, Narayanan, Kuldeep Shastri, and Kishore Tandon. "The Impact of International Cross-Listings on Risk and Return: The Evidence from American Depository Receipts." *Journal of Banking and Finance* 17 (1993), pp. 91–103.

Kao, G., K. C. Wenchi, John Wei, and Joseph Vu. "Risk-Return Characteristics of the American Depository Receipts," unpublished working paper, 1991.

Karolyi, G. Andrew. "DaimlerChrysler AG, The First Truly Global Share." *Journal of Corporate Finance* 9 (2003), pp. 409–30.

Miller, Darius P. "The Market Reaction to International Cross-Listings: Evidence from Depository Receipts." *Journal of Financial Economics* 51 (1999), pp. 103–23.

Park, Jinwoo. *The Impact of Information on ADR Returns and Variances: Some Implications,* unpublished Ph.D. dissertation from The University of Iowa, 1990.

Phylaktis, Kate, and Lichuan Xia. "The Changing Roles of Industry and Country Effects in the Global Equity Markets." *European Journal of Finance* 12 (2006), pp. 627–48.

Roll, Richard. "Industrial Structure and the Comparative Behavior of International Stock Market Indexes." *Journal of Finance* 47 (1992), pp. 3–42.

Rouwenhorst, K. Geert. "European Equity Markets and the EMU." *Financial Analysts Journal*, May/June (1999), pp. 57–64.

Schwartz, Robert A. *Equity Markets.* New York: Harper and Row, 1988.

Solnik, Bruno. "Capital Markets and International Monetary Variables." *Financial Analysts Journal* 40 (1984), pp. 69–73.

14 Interest Rate and Currency Swaps

CHAPTER 5 INTRODUCED forward contracts as a vehicle for hedging exchange rate risk; Chapter 7 introduced futures and options contracts on foreign exchange as alternative tools to hedge foreign exchange exposure. These types of instruments seldom have terms longer than a few years, however. Chapter 7 also discussed Eurodollar futures contracts for hedging short-term U.S.-dollar-denominated interest rate risk. In this chapter, we examine interest rate swaps, both single-currency and cross-currency, which are techniques for hedging long-term interest rate risk and foreign exchange risk.

The chapter begins with some useful definitions that define and distinguish between interest rate and currency swaps. Data on the size of the interest rate and currency swap markets are presented. The next section illustrates the usefulness of interest rate swaps. The following section illustrates the construction of currency swaps. The chapter also details the risks confronting a swap dealer in maintaining a portfolio of interest rate and currency swaps and shows how swaps are priced.

Types of Swaps

In interest rate swap financing, two parties, called **counterparties**, make a contractual agreement to exchange cash flows at periodic intervals. There are two types of interest rate swaps. One is a **single-currency interest rate swap**. The name of this type is typically shortened to *interest rate swap*. The other type can be called a **cross-currency interest rate swap**. This type is usually just called a *currency swap*.

In the basic ("plain vanilla") *fixed-for-floating rate* interest rate swap, one counterparty exchanges the interest payments of a floating-rate debt obligation for the fixed-rate interest payments of the other counterparty. Both debt obligations are denominated in the same currency. Some reasons for using an interest rate swap are to better match cash inflows and outflows and/or to obtain a cost savings. There are many variants of the basic interest rate swap, some of which are discussed below.

In a **currency swap**, one counterparty exchanges the debt service obligations of a bond denominated in one currency for the debt service obligations of the other counterparty denominated in another currency. The basic currency swap involves the exchange of *fixed-for-fixed rate* debt service. Some reasons for using currency swaps are to obtain debt financing in the swapped denomination at a cost savings and/or to hedge long-term foreign exchange rate risk. The International Finance in Practice box "The World Bank's First Currency Swap" discusses the first currency swap.

INTERNATIONAL FINANCE IN PRACTICE

The World Bank's First Currency Swap

The World Bank frequently borrows in the national capital markets around the world and in the Eurobond market. It prefers to borrow currencies with low nominal interest rates, such as the (former) deutsche mark and the Swiss franc. In 1981, the World Bank was near the official borrowing limits in these currencies but desired to borrow more. By coincidence, IBM had a large amount of deutsche mark and Swiss franc debt that it had incurred a few years earlier. The proceeds of these borrowings had been converted to dollars for corporate use. Salomon Brothers convinced the World Bank to issue Eurodollar debt with maturities matching the IBM debt in order to enter into

a currency swap with IBM. IBM agreed to pay the debt service (interest and principal) on the World Bank's Eurodollar bonds, and in turn the World Bank agreed to pay the debt service on IBM's deutsche mark and Swiss franc debt. While the details of the swap were not made public, both counter-parties benefited through a lower all-in cost (interest expense, transaction costs, and service charges) than they otherwise would have had. Additionally, the World Bank benefited by developing an indirect way to obtain desired currencies without going directly to the German and Swiss capital markets.

Size of the Swap Market

www.isda.org

This is the website of the International Swaps and Derivatives Association, Inc. The ISDA's mission is to foster safe and efficient derivatives markets to facilitate effective risk management for all users of derivative products. This site describes the activities of the ISDA and provides information about education webinars the ISDA sponsors about derivative products, risk management techniques, and trading practices.

As the International Finance in Practice box suggests, the market for currency swaps developed first. Today, however, the interest rate swap market is larger. Exhibit 14.1 provides some statistics on the size and growth in the OTC interest rate and currency swap markets. Size is measured by **notional principal**, a reference amount of principal for determining interest payments. The exhibit indicates that the interest rate swap markets has contracted since 2007. The total amount of interest rate swaps outstanding decreased from $310 trillion at year-end 2007 to $289 trillion at year-end 2015, a decrease of 7 percent. This contraction is due to the new tighter regulation of this market discussed in the next section and to the creation of new exchange-traded interest rate futures contracts that offer competition to the OTC interest rate swap market. Total outstanding currency swaps increased 59 percent, from $14.3 trillion at year-end 2007 to over $22.7 trillion by year-end 2015.

While not shown in Exhibit 14.1, the four most common currencies used to denominate interest rate and currency swaps were the euro, U.S. dollar, Japanese yen, and the British pound sterling, with the fifth most common currency being the Canadian dollar for interest rate swaps and the Swiss franc for currency swaps.

EXHIBIT 14.1		

Size of OTC Interest Rate and Currency Swap Markets: Total Notional Principal Outstanding Amounts in Billions of U.S. Dollars*

Year	Interest Rate Swaps	Currency Swaps
2007	309,588	14,347
2008	309,760	13,322
2009	349,236	16,509
2010	364,377	19,271
2011	402,611	22,791
2012	370,002	25,420
2013	456,725	25,448
2014	381,129	24,042
2015	288,634	22,750

*Notional principal is used only as a reference measure to which interest rates are applied for determining interest payments. In an interest rate swap, principal does not actually change hands. At the inception date of a swap, the market value of both sides of the swap are of equivalent value. As interest rates change, the value of the cash flows will change, and both sides may no longer be equal. This is interest rate risk. The deviation can amount to 2 to 4 percent of notional principal. Only this small fraction is subject to credit (or default) risk. Notional principal for interest rate swaps is adjusted to account for the effects of double counting resulting from central clearing and compression resulting from the netting of offsetting transactions.

Sources: Interest rate swap notional values are compiled from various issues of *International Banking and Financial Market Developments*, Bank for International Settlements.

The Swap Bank

A **swap bank** is a generic term to describe a financial institution that facilitates swaps between counterparties. A swap bank can be an international commercial bank, an investment bank, a merchant bank, or an independent operator. The swap bank serves as either a **swap broker** or **swap dealer**. As a broker, the swap bank matches counterparties but does not assume any risk of the swap. The swap broker receives a commission for this service. Today, most swap banks serve as dealers or market makers. As a market maker, the swap bank stands willing to accept either side of a currency swap, and then later lay it off, or match it with a counterparty. In this capacity, the swap bank assumes a position in the swap and therefore assumes certain risks. The dealer capacity is obviously more risky, and the swap bank would receive a portion of the cash flows passed through it to compensate it for bearing this risk.

Problems encountered in the OTC derivatives markets that became highlighted during the global financial crisis have resulted in new regulation designed to increase trading stability in financial markets. With respect to interest rate and currency swaps trading, two new pieces of regulation have specific impact. In the United States, the Commodity Futures Trading Commission has new authority under the Commodities Exchange Act, as amended by the Dodd-Frank Act, to prescribe standards for swap dealers and major swap participants related to the timely and accurate confirmation, reconciliation, compression, and documentation of swaps. In the European Union, the European Securities and Markets Authority adopted new European Market Infrastructure Regulation specifying central counterparties and trade repositories requiring counterparties to have appropriate procedures and arrangements to measure, monitor, and mitigate operational risk and counterparty credit risk for interest rate swaps. Central clearing is not currently required for currency swaps. Additionally, collateral in the form of initial margin must be deposited. With these changes, the swap markets now operate similarly to futures markets as described in Chapter 7. The International Finance in Practice box "Double-Crossed" discusses issues in the implementation of central clearing-houses under new regulation.

Swap Market Quotations

www.bis.org

This is the website of the Bank for International Settlements. This site describes the activities and purpose of the BIS. Many online publications about foreign exchange and OTC derivatives are available at this site.

Swap banks will tailor the terms of interest rate and currency swaps to customers' needs. They also make a market in generic "plain vanilla" swaps and provide current market quotations applicable to counterparties with Aa or Aaa credit ratings. Consider a basic U.S. dollar fixed-for-floating interest rate swap indexed to dollar LIBOR. A swap bank will typically quote a fixed-rate bid-ask spread (either semiannual or annual) versus three-month or six-month dollar LIBOR flat, that is, no credit premium. Suppose the quote for a five-year swap with semiannual payments is 8.50–8.60 percent against six-month LIBOR flat. This means the swap bank will pay semiannual fixed-rate dollar payments of 8.50 percent against receiving six-month dollar LIBOR, or it will receive semiannual fixed-rate dollar payments at 8.60 percent against paying six-month dollar LIBOR.

It is convention for swap banks to quote interest rate swap rates for a currency against a local standard reference in the same currency and currency swap rates against dollar LIBOR. For example, for a five-year swap with semiannual payments in Swiss francs, suppose the bid-ask swap quotation is 6.60–6.70 percent against six-month LIBOR flat. This means the swap bank will pay semiannual fixed-rate SF payments at 6.60 percent against receiving six-month SF (dollar) LIBOR in an interest rate (a currency) swap, or it will receive semiannual fixed-rate SF payments at 6.70 percent against paying six-month SF (dollar) LIBOR in an interest rate (a currency) swap.

It follows that if the swap bank is quoting 8.50–8.60 percent in dollars and 6.60–6.70 percent in SF against six-month dollar LIBOR, it will enter into a currency

Double-Crossed

Bigger May Not Be Better When It Comes To Clearing-Houses

The bookmaker on Aldgate High Street, on the fringes of London's financial district, attracts its fair share of risk-takers. But across the road, at the offices of LCH.Clearnet, part of the London Stock Exchange Group (LSE), the really big bets are handled. It and other clearing-houses now occupy a central position in high finance. They ensure that trillions of dollars are paid out on derivatives contracts each day. A decade of deal-making has created five big beasts of clearing: LSE, Deutsche Börse, CME Group, ICE and HKEX. A planned merger between LSE and the Germans would reduce that to four.

LSE and Deutsche Börse take their names from their respective bourses. But they now make more money from their clearing-houses, LCH.Clearnet and Eurex Clearing. That is because the clearing of derivatives has become central to the modern financial system.

Imagine two banks want to hedge against interest-rate movements, but in opposite directions. They sign a contract that will lead to a payment from one to the other if rates rise, and the reverse if they fall. The potential loss or gain is theoretically unlimited, since there is no ceiling (or floor, as the world is fast learning) to rates. To make sure the other party is able to pay up, the two will often work through a middleman—the clearing-house. For a fee, the clearing-house signs two offsetting but technically separate derivatives contracts with the two parties. As long as both know that it is good for the money, they know their bets are solid.

But the clearing-house is now left with the risk that the losing party fails to stump up. So it asks the two parties to post collateral, or margin, which it can keep if one of them defaults. That way the clearing-house only suffers if the defaulting party owes more than the margin it has posted.

In theory, this system makes bank failures less contagious and the financial system more resilient. In 2009 the G20, a club of big economies, decided that simple derivatives contracts should all be put through clearing-houses, rather than settled directly between the two parties. As a result, clearing-houses, also known as central counterparties, now handle trades with a notional worth of hundreds of trillions of dollars.

The more margin the clearing-houses take, the safer they are. The required margin is calculated using sophisticated actuarial models, and is heavily regulated. The riskier a trade, naturally, the more margin is needed. LCH.Clearnet and Eurex Clearing

hold some €150 billion ($170 billion) in collateral between them. Deutsche Börse notes that its large margin pool helps to ensure the "safety, resiliency and transparency of global financial markets". But having to put up more collateral is expensive for customers. Clearing-houses, which compete for customers, therefore have an incentive not to take too much.

Banks don't just bet on interest rates, of course. They may also buy derivatives tied to bond yields or currency movements, say. Some of those prices move in relation to one another in predictable ways. Gains on an interest-rate future may offset losses on a bond-price future, for example. Clearing-houses take such correlations into account when setting the overall amount of collateral they demand from their customers, a technique called "cross-margining" or "portfolio margining". CME Group boasts that its portfolio-margining service can cut margin requirements by 54–80%. LCH.Clearnet's "Spider" and Eurex's "Prisma" services do something similar.

All of which gives clearing-houses an incentive to merge. Some clients use LCH.Clearnet and Eurex Clearing to make correlated wagers. If the two entities combined, they could use cross-margining to reduce the amount of collateral such customers needed, gaining an advantage over the competition. (The pair say that initially, at least, they would limit such offsetting to perfectly matching derivatives.)

There is a downside, though. The exchange industry is already highly concentrated. Regardless of who gobbles up LSE (ICE may yet enter the fray), the five big groups will soon become four. As they consolidate, the amount of collateral in the system is likely to be reduced.

That could prove risky. Correlations between different asset classes sometimes break down during crises. Such unpredictable movements caused the clearing-house of the Hong Kong Futures Exchange to blow up after the stockmarket crash of 1987, forcing the city's capital markets to close. Such events suggest that models that rely on correlations to trim margin requirements must be ultraconservative.

There is no evidence that any big clearing-house holds too little collateral. Their models are designed to withstand the simultaneous failure of their two biggest customers. They can also tap big default funds if things go wrong. Regulators are untroubled. But it is a worry, nonetheless, that the logic of competition seems to be ever-bigger clearing-houses with ever less collateral.

Source: © The Economist Newspaper Limited, London, April 2, 2016.

swap in which it would pay semiannual fixed-rate dollar payments of 8.50 percent in return for receiving semiannual fixed-rate SF payments at 6.70 percent, or it will receive semiannual fixed-rate dollar payments at 8.60 percent against paying semiannual fixed-rate SF payments at 6.60 percent.

Exhibit 14.2 provides an illustration of interest rate swap quotations. Swap banks typically build swap yield curves such as this from the 90-day LIBOR rates implied in the Eurodollar interest rate futures contracts we discussed in Chapter 7.

EXHIBIT 14.2					Interest Rate Swap Quotations								
	Euro-€		£ Stlg.		SwFr		US $		Yen				
Jun 5	Bid	Ask	Bid	Ask	Bid	Ask	Bid	Ask	Bid	Ask			
1 year	−0.16	−0.13	0.72	0.74	−0.73	−0.65	0.801	0.805	−0.08	−0.06			
2 year	−0.16	−0.14	0.76	0.77	−0.73	−0.70	0.943	0.948	−0.14	−0.13			
3 year	−0.14	−0.10	0.82	0.84	−0.72	−0.68	1.052	1.054	−0.16	−0.14			
4 year	−0.08	−0.04	0.89	0.91	−0.67	−0.64	1.146	1.149	−0.14	−0.12			
5 year	−0.01	0.03	0.97	0.99	−0.60	−0.57	1.236	1.238	−0.11	−0.09			
6 year	0.09	0.12	1.06	1.08	−0.52	−0.49	1.326	1.331	−0.08	−0.04			
7 year	0.20	0.23	1.16	1.17	−0.43	−0.40	1.410	1.415	−0.04	0.00			
8 year	0.32	0.35	1.24	1.26	−0.35	−0.31	1.489	1.449	0.00	0.04			
9 year	0.43	0.46	1.32	1.34	−0.25	−0.23	1.558	1.563	0.04	0.08			
10 year	0.53	0.55	1.39	1.40	−0.17	−0.14	1.625	1.626	0.07	0.11			
12 year	0.70	0.73	1.50	1.52	−0.07	−0.02	NA	NA	0.15	0.17			
15 year	0.88	0.92	1.61	1.63	0.06	0.11	1.870	1.870	0.28	0.31			
20 year	1.04	1.06	1.67	1.68	0.18	0.23	2.002	2.004	0.42	0.45			
25 year	1.06	1.10	1.66	1.67	NA	NA	2.067	2.070	NA	NA			
30 year	1.08	1.09	1.65	1.66	0.29	0.34	2.104	2.106	0.48	0.50			

Bid and Ask rates as of close of London business. £ and Yen quoted on a semi-annual actual/365 basis against 6 month Libor with the exception of the 1 Year GBP rate which is quoted annual actual against 3M Libor. Euro/Swiss Franc/Dollar-quoted on an annual bond 30/360 basis against 6 month Euribor/Libor/Libor.

Source: *Bloomberg*, May 17, 2016.

Interest Rate Swaps

Basic Interest Rate Swap

As an example of a basic, often called "plain vanilla," interest rate swap, consider the following example of a fixed-for-floating rate swap. Bank A is a AAA-rated international bank located in the United Kingdom. The bank needs $10,000,000 to finance floating-rate Eurodollar term loans to its clients. It is considering issuing five-year floating-rate notes indexed to LIBOR. Alternatively, the bank could issue five-year fixed-rate Eurodollar bonds at 10 percent. The FRNs make the most sense for Bank A, since it would be using a floating-rate liability to finance a floating-rate asset. In this manner, the bank avoids the interest rate risk associated with a fixed-rate issue. Without this hedge, Bank A could end up paying a higher rate than it is receiving on its loans should LIBOR fall substantially.

Company B is a BBB-rated U.S. company. It needs $10,000,000 to finance a capital expenditure with a five-year economic life. It can issue five-year fixed-rate bonds at a rate of 11.25 percent in the U.S. bond market. Alternatively, it can issue five-year FRNs at LIBOR plus .50 percent. The fixed-rate debt makes the most sense for Company B because it locks in a financing cost. The FRN alternative could prove very unwise should LIBOR increase substantially over the life of the note, and could possibly result in the project being unprofitable.

A swap bank familiar with the financing needs of Bank A and Company B has the opportunity to set up a fixed-for-floating interest rate swap that will benefit each counterparty and the swap bank. Assume that the swap bank is quoting five-year U.S. dollar interest rate swaps at 10.375–10.50 percent against LIBOR flat. The key, or necessary condition, giving rise to the swap is that a **quality spread differential (QSD)** exists. A QSD is the difference between the default-risk premium differential on the fixed-rate debt and the default-risk premium differential on the floating-rate debt. In general, the former is greater than the latter. The reason for this is that the yield curve for lower-quality debt tends to be steeper than the yield curve for higher-rated debt. Financial theorists have offered a variety of explanations for this phenomenon, none of which is completely satisfactory. Exhibit 14.3 shows the calculation of the QSD.

EXHIBIT 14.3

Calculation of Quality
Spread Differential

	Company B	Bank A	Differential
Fixed-rate	11.25%	10.00%	1.25%
Floating-rate	LIBOR + .50%	LIBOR	.50%
			QSD = .75%

EXHIBIT 14.4

Fixed-for-Floating Interest
Rate Swap*

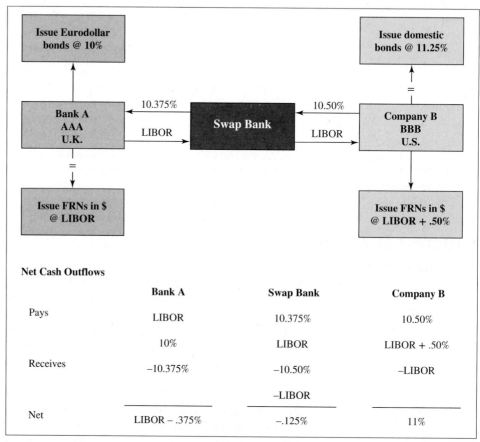

Net Cash Outflows

	Bank A	Swap Bank	Company B
Pays	LIBOR	10.375%	10.50%
	10%	LIBOR	LIBOR + .50%
Receives	−10.375%	−10.50%	−LIBOR
		−LIBOR	
Net	LIBOR − .375%	−.125%	11%

*Debt service expressed as a percentage of $10,000,000 notional value.

Given that a QSD exists, it is possible for each counterparty to issue the debt alternative that is least advantageous for it (given its financing needs), then swap interest payments, such that each counterparty ends up with the type of interest payment desired, but at a lower all-in cost than it could arrange on its own. Exhibit 14.4 diagrams a possible scenario the swap bank could arrange for the two counterparties. The interest rates used in Exhibit 14.4 refer to the percentage rate paid per annum on the notional principal of $10,000,000.

From Exhibit 14.4, we see that the swap bank has instructed Company B to issue FRNs at LIBOR plus .50 percent rather than the more suitable fixed-rate debt at 11.25 percent. Company B passes through to the swap bank 10.50 percent (on the notional principal of $10,000,000) and receives LIBOR in return. In total, Company B pays 10.50 percent (to the swap bank) plus LIBOR + .50 percent (to the floating-rate bondholders) and receives LIBOR percent (from the swap bank) for an **all-in cost** (interest expense, transaction costs, and service charges) of 11 percent.

Thus, through the swap, Company B has converted floating-rate debt into fixed-rate debt at an all-in cost .25 percent lower than the 11.25 percent fixed rate it could arrange on its own.

Similarly, Bank A was instructed to issue fixed-rate debt at 10 percent rather than the more suitable FRNs. Bank A passes through to the swap bank LIBOR percent and receives 10.375 percent in return. In total, Bank A pays 10 percent (to the fixed-rate Eurodollar bondholders) plus LIBOR percent (to the swap bank) and receives 10.375 percent (from the swap bank) for an all-in cost of LIBOR −.375 percent. Through the swap, Bank A has converted fixed-rate debt into floating-rate debt at an all-in cost .375 percent lower than the floating rate of LIBOR it could arrange on its own.

The swap bank also benefits because it pays out less than it receives from each counterparty to the other counterparty. Note from Exhibit 14.4 that it receives 10.50 percent (from Company B) plus LIBOR percent (from Bank A) and pays 10.375 percent (to Bank A) and LIBOR percent (to Company B). The net inflow to the swap bank is .125 percent per annum on the notional principal of $10,000,000. In sum, Bank A has saved .375 percent, Company B has saved .25 percent, and the swap bank has earned .125 percent. This totals .75 percent, which equals the QSD. Thus, if a QSD exists, it can be split in some fashion among the swap parties resulting in lower all-in costs for the counterparties.

In an interest rate swap, the principal sums the two counterparties raise are not exchanged, since both counterparties have borrowed in the same currency. The amount of interest payments that are exchanged are based on a notional sum, which may not equal the exact amount actually borrowed by each counterparty. Moreover, while Exhibit 14.4 portrays a gross exchange of interest payments based on the notional principal, in practice only the net difference is actually exchanged. For example, Company B would pay to the swap bank the net difference between 10.50 percent and LIBOR percent on the notional value of $10,000,000.

In More Depth

Pricing the Basic Interest Rate Swap

After the inception of an interest rate swap, it may become desirable for one and/or the other counterparty to unwind or reverse the swap. The value of an interest rate swap to a counterparty should be the difference in the present values of the payment streams the counterparty will receive and pay on the notional principal. As an example, consider Company B from our previous example. Company B pays 10.50 percent to the swap bank and receives LIBOR percent from the swap bank on a notional value of $10,000,000. It has an all-in cost of 11 percent because it has issued FRNs at LIBOR + .50 percent.

Assume that one year later, the swap bank is quoting four-year dollar swaps at 9.00–9.125 percent versus LIBOR flat. This will also be a reset date for the FRNs. On any reset date, the present value of the future floating-rate payments paid or received at LIBOR on the notional value will always be $10,000,000. The present value of a hypothetical bond issue of $10,000,000 with four remaining 10.50 percent coupon payments at the new swap bid rate of 9 percent is $10,485,958 = $1,050,000 × $PVIFA_{9\%,4}$ + $10,000,000 × $PVIF_{9\%,4}$. The value of the swap is $10,000,000 − $10,485,958 = −$485,958. Thus, Company B should be willing to pay $485,958 to the swap bank to unwind or reverse the original swap. In essence, the market value of the swap is the present value of the difference between paying 10.50 percent and receiving 9 percent on the $10,000,000 notional value discounted at the new swap bid rate of 9 percent. That is: −$150,000 × $PVIFA_{9\%,4}$ = −$485,958.

Currency Swaps

Basic Currency Swap

As an example of a basic currency swap, consider the following example. A U.S. MNC desires to finance a capital expenditure of its German subsidiary. The project has an economic life of five years. The cost of the project is €40,000,000. At the current exchange rate of $1.30/€1.00, the parent firm could raise $52,000,000 in the U.S. capital market by issuing five-year bonds at 8 percent. The parent would then convert the dollars to euros to pay the project cost. The German subsidiary would be expected to earn enough on the project to meet the annual dollar debt service and to repay the principal in five years. The only problem with this situation is that a long-term transaction exposure is created. If the dollar appreciates substantially against the euro over the loan period, it may be difficult for the German subsidiary to earn enough in euros to service the dollar loan.

An alternative is for the U.S. parent to raise €40,000,000 in the international bond market by issuing euro-denominated Eurobonds. (The U.S. parent might instead issue euro-denominated foreign bonds in the German capital market.) However, if the U.S. MNC is not well known, it will have difficulty borrowing at a favorable rate of interest. Suppose the U.S. parent can borrow €40,000,000 for a term of five years at a fixed rate of 7 percent. The current normal borrowing rate for a well-known firm of equivalent creditworthiness is 6 percent.

Assume a German MNC of equivalent creditworthiness has a mirror-image financing need. It has a U.S. subsidiary in need of $52,000,000 to finance a capital expenditure with an economic life of five years. The German parent could raise €40,000,000 in the German bond market at a fixed rate of 6 percent and convert the funds to dollars to finance the expenditure. Transaction exposure is created, however, if the euro appreciates substantially against the dollar. In this event, the U.S. subsidiary might have difficulty earning enough in dollars to meet the debt service. The German parent could issue Eurodollar bonds (or alternatively, Yankee bonds in the U.S. capital market), but since it is not well known its borrowing cost would be, say, a fixed rate of 9 percent.

A swap bank familiar with the financing needs of the two MNCs could arrange a currency swap that would solve the double problem of each MNC, that is, be confronted with long-term transaction exposure or borrow at a disadvantageous rate. (In order not to complicate this example any more than is necessary, it is assumed that the bid and ask swap rates charged by the swap bank are the same; that is, there is no bid-ask spread. This assumption is relaxed in a later example.) The swap bank would instruct each parent firm to raise funds in its national capital market where it is well known and has a **comparative advantage** because of name or brand recognition. Then the principal sums would be exchanged through the swap bank. Annually, the German subsidiary would remit to its U.S. parent €2,400,000 in interest (6 percent of €40,000,000) to be passed through the swap bank to the German MNC to meet the euro debt service. The U.S. subsidiary of the German MNC would annually remit $4,160,000 in interest (8 percent of $52,000,000) to be passed through the swap bank to the U.S. MNC to meet the dollar debt service. At the debt retirement date, the subsidiaries would remit the principal sums to their respective parents to be exchanged through the swap bank in order to pay off the bond issues in the national capital markets. The structure of this currency swap is diagrammed in Exhibit 14.5.

Exhibit 14.5 demonstrates that there is a cost savings for each counterparty because of their relative comparative advantage in their respective national capital markets. The U.S. MNC borrows euros at an all-in-cost (AIC) of 6 percent through the currency swap instead of the 7 percent it would have to pay in the Eurobond market. The German MNC borrows dollars at an AIC of 8 percent through the swap instead of the 9 percent rate it would have to pay in the Eurobond market. The currency swap also serves to contractually lock in a series of future foreign exchange rates for the debt service obligations of each counterparty. At inception, the principal sums are exchanged

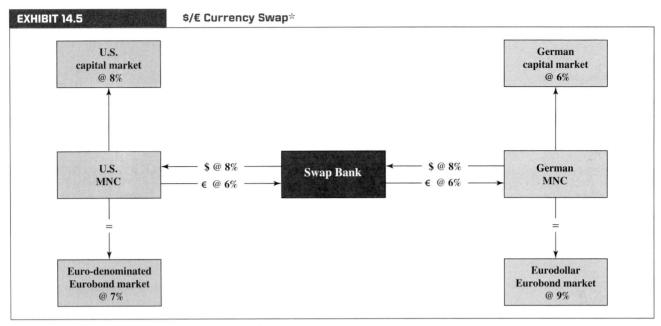

EXHIBIT 14.5 $/€ Currency Swap*

*Debt service in dollars (euros) expressed as a percentage of $52,000,000 (€40,000,000) notional value.

at the current exchange rate of $1.30/€1.00 = $52,000,000/€40,000,000. Each year prior to debt retirement, the swap agreement calls for the counterparties to exchange $4,160,000 of interest on the dollar debt for €2,400,000 of interest on the euro debt; this is a contractual rate of $1.7333/€1.00. At the maturity date, a final exchange, including the last interest payments and the reexchange of the principal sums, would take place: $56,160,000 for €42,400,000. The contractual exchange rate at year five is thus $1.3245/€1.00. Clearly, the swap locks in foreign exchange rates for each counterparty to meet its debt service obligations over the term of the swap.

In More Depth

Equivalency of Currency Swap Debt Service Obligations

To continue with our dollar–euro currency swap example, it superficially appears that the German counterparty is not getting as good a deal from the currency swap as the U.S. counterparty. The reasoning is that the German counterparty is borrowing at a rate of 6 percent (€2,400,000 per year) but paying 8 percent ($4,160,000). The U.S. counterparty receives the $4,160,000 and pays €2,400,000. This reasoning is fraught with an ill appreciation for international parity relationships, as Exhibit 14.6 is designed to show. In short, the exhibit shows that borrowing euros at 6 percent is equivalent to borrowing dollars at 8 percent.

Line 1 of Exhibit 14.6 shows the cash flows of the euro debt in millions. Line 2 shows the cash flows of the dollar debt in millions. The all-in-cost (AIC) for each cash flow stream is also shown for each currency. Line 3 shows the contractual foreign exchange rates between the two counterparties that are locked in by the swap agreement. Line 4 shows the foreign exchange rate that each counterparty and the market should expect based on covered interest rate parity and the forward rate being an unbiased predictor of the expected spot rate, if we can assume that IRP holds between the 6 percent euro rate and the 8 percent dollar rate. This appears reasonable since these rates are, respectively, the best rates available for each counterparty who is well known in its national market. According to this parity relationship: $\bar{S}_t(\$/€) = S_0[1.08/1.06]^t$. For example, from the exhibit $1.350/€1.00 = $1.30[1.08/1.06]^2$.

EXHIBIT 14.6	Equivalency of Currency Swap Cash Flows						
	Time of Cash Flow						
	0	1	2	3	4	5	AIC
1. Euro debt cash flow	40	−2.40	−2.40	−2.40	−2.40	−42.40	6%
2. $ debt cash flow	52	−4.16	−4.16	−4.16	−4.16	−56.16	8%
3. Contractual FX rate	1.300	1.7333	1.7333	1.7333	1.7333	1.3245	NA
4. Implicit FX rate	1.300	1.325	1.350	1.375	1.401	1.427	NA
5. Indifference euro cash flow	40	−3.14	−3.08	−3.03	−2.97	−39.35	6%
6. Indifference $ cash flow	52	−3.18	−3.24	−3.30	−3.36	−60.50	8%

Note: Lines 1 and 5 present alternative cash flows in euros that have present values of €40,000,000 at a 6 percent discount rate. The cash flows in Line 1 are free of exchange risk if the swap is undertaken, whereas the implicit cash flows of Line 5 are not if the swap is forgone. The certain cash flows are preferable. The uncertain euro cash flows of Line 5 are obtained by dividing the dollar cash flows of Line 2 by the corresponding implicit FX rate of Line 4. Analogously, Lines 2 and 6 present alternative cash flows in U.S. dollars that have present values of $52,000,000 at an 8 percent discount rate. The cash flows in Line 2 are free of exchange risk if the swap is undertaken, whereas the implicit cash flows of Line 6 are not if the swap is forgone. The certain cash flows are preferable. The uncertain dollar cash flows of Line 6 are obtained by multiplying the euro cash flows of Line 1 by the corresponding implicit FX rate of Line 4.

Line 5 shows the equivalent cash flows in euros that have a present value of €40,000,000 at a rate of 6 percent. Without the currency swap, the German MNC would have to convert dollars into euros to meet the euro debt service. The expected rate at which the conversion would take place in each year is given by the implicit foreign exchange rates in Line 4. Line 5 can be viewed as a conversion of the cash flows of Line 2 via the implicit exchange rates of Line 4. That is, for year one, $4,160,000 has an expected value of €3,140,000 at the expected exchange rate of $1.325/€1.00. For year two, $4,160,000 has an expected value of €3,080,000 at an exchange rate of $1.350/€1.00. Note that the conversion at the implicit exchange rates converts *8 percent cash flows* into *6 percent cash flows.*

The lender of €40,000,000 should be indifferent between receiving the cash flows of Line 1 or the cash flows of Line 5 from the borrower. From the borrower's standpoint, however, the cash flows of Line 1 are free of foreign exchange risk because of the currency swap, whereas the cash flows of Line 5 are not. Thus, the borrower prefers the certainty of the swap, regardless of the equivalency.

Line 6 shows in dollar terms the cash flows based on the implicit foreign exchange rates of Line 4 that have a present value of $52,000,000. Line 6 can be viewed as a conversion of the 6 percent cash flows of Line 1 into the 8 percent cash flows of Line 6 via these expected exchange rates. A lender should be indifferent between these and the cash flow stream of Line 2. The borrower will prefer to pay the cash flows of Line 2, however, because they are free of foreign exchange risk.

Pricing the Basic Currency Swap

Suppose that a year after the U.S. dollar–euro swap was arranged, interest rates have decreased in the United States from 8 percent to 6.75 percent and in the euro zone from 6 percent to 5 percent. Further assume that because the U.S. rate decreased proportionately more than the euro zone rate, the dollar appreciated versus the euro. Instead of being $1.325/€1.00 as expected, it is $1.310/€1.00. One or both counterparties might be induced to sell their position in the swap to a swap dealer in order to refinance at the new lower rate.

The market value of the U.S. dollar debt is $54,214,170; this is the present value of the four remaining coupon payments of $4,160,000 and the principal of $52,000,000 discounted at 6.75 percent. Similarly, the market value of the euro debt at the new rate of 5 percent is €41,418,380. The U.S. counterparty should be willing to buy its interest in the currency swap for $54,214,170 − €41,418,380 × 1.310 = −$43,908. That is, the U.S. counterparty should be willing to pay $43,908 to give up the stream of dollars it would receive under the swap agreement in return for not having to pay the euro stream. The U.S. MNC is then free to refinance the $52,000,000 8 percent debt at 6.75 percent, and perhaps enter into a new currency swap.

From the German counterparty's perspective, the swap has a value of €41,418,380 − $54,214,170/1.310 = €33,517. The German counterparty should be willing to accept €33,517 to sell the swap, that is, give up the stream of euros in return for not having to pay the dollar stream. The German MNC i`s then in a position to refinance the €40,000,000 6 percent debt at the new rate of 5 percent. The German firm might also enter into a new currency swap.

A Basic Currency Swap Reconsidered

As a more realistic example of a basic currency swap, it is necessary to recognize the bid-ask spread that the swap bank charges for making a market in currency swaps. To extend our earlier example, assume that the swap bank is quoting five-year U.S. dollar (euro) currency swaps at 8.00–8.15 (6.00–6.10) percent against dollar LIBOR flat. Additionally, and more realistically, assume that the swap bank can deal with the U.S. MNC and the German MNC separately. Then the principal sums raised in the national capital markets by the U.S. MNC ($52,000,000) and the German MNC (€40,000,000) would be sold to the swap bank at the current spot rate of $1.30/€1.00 to obtain the desired currency, €40,000,000 for the U.S. MNC and $52,000,000 for the German MNC. The German subsidiary would annually remit €2,440,000 in interest (6.10 percent of €40,000,000) to its U.S. parent to be passed through to the swap bank. The swap bank, in turn, annually remits €2,400,000 (6 percent of €40,000,000) to the German MNC in order for it to meet the euro debt service. The U.S. subsidiary would annually remit $4,238,000 in interest (8.15 percent of $52,000,000) to its German parent to be passed through to the swap bank. The swap bank, in turn, annually remits $4,160,000 (8 percent of $52,000,000) to the U.S. MNC in order for it to meet the annual dollar debt service. At the debt retirement date, the subsidiaries would additionally remit the principal sums to their respective parents (dollars from the U.S. subsidiary of the German MNC and euros from the German subsidiary of the U.S. MNC) to be exchanged through the swap bank in order to pay off the bond issues in the national capital markets. The net result is that the U.S. MNC borrows euros at an AIC of 6.10 percent through the currency swap instead of the 7 percent rate it would have to pay in the Eurobond market. The German MNC borrows dollars at an AIC of 8.15 percent through the swap instead of the 9 percent rate it would have to pay in the Eurobond market. Exhibit 14.7 diagrams this swap.

EXHIBIT 14.7	$/€ Currency Swap with Bid-Ask Spreads

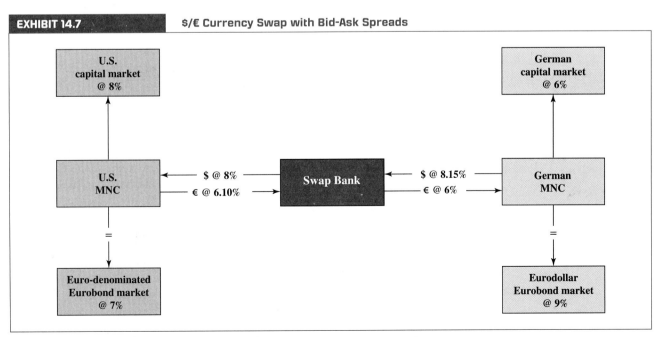

Debt service in dollars (euros) expressed as a percentage of $52,000,000 (€40,000,000) notional value.

EXHIBIT 14.8

Cross-Currency Swap Analyzer, CURSWAP.xls Output

	A	B	C	D	E	F	G
1							
2							
3			FC Bond	FC	$	Actual	
4			Cash Flow	Received	Paid	$ Cash Flow	
5							
6		0	40,000,000	–40,000,000	30,769,231	30,769,231	
7		1	–2,400,000	2,400,000	–2,507,692	–2,507,692	
8		2	–2,400,000	2,400,000	–2,507,692	–2,507,692	
9		3	–2,400,000	2,400,000	–2,507,692	–2,507,692	
10		4	–2,400,000	2,400,000	–2,507,692	–2,507,692	
11		5	–42,400,000	42,400,000	–33,276,923	–33,276,923	
12							
13		AIC	6.00%	6.00%	8.15%	8.15%	
14							
15		Face value:	40,000,000				
16						Bid	Ask
17		Coupon rate:	6.000%		Spot FX rate:	1.30000	1.30000
18							
19		OP as % of par:	100.000%		FC swap rate:	6.00%	6.10%
20							
21		Underwriting fee:	0.000%		$ swap rate:	8.00%	8.15%

Exhibit 14.8 presents a printout of the results from using the text software spreadsheet CURSWAP to solve for the AIC from the perspective of the German MNC. The spreadsheet shows the actual dollar cash flows the German MNC pays under the swap at the AIC of 8.15 percent and the euro cash flows received at 6 percent. (Note that for simplicity the coupon rate on the euro bond is the same as the swap bank's bid rate for five-year euro currency swaps, the FX bid-ask spread on the euro is ignored, there is no underwriting fee, and the euro bond is assumed to sell at par.)

Variations of Basic Interest Rate and Currency Swaps

There are several variants of the basic interest rate and currency swaps we have discussed. For example, a fixed-for-floating interest rate swap does not require a fixed-rate coupon bond. A variant is a *zero-coupon-for-floating* rate swap where the floating-rate payer makes the standard periodic floating-rate payments over the life of the swap, but the fixed-rate payer makes a single payment at the end of the swap. Another variation is the *floating-for-floating* interest rate swap. In this swap, each side is tied to a different floating rate index (e.g., LIBOR and Treasury bills) or a different frequency of the same index (such as three-month and six-month LIBOR). For a swap to be possible, a QSD must still exist. Additionally, interest rate swaps can be established on an amortizing basis, where the debt service exchanges decrease periodically through time as the hypothetical notional principal is amortized. Currency swaps need not involve the swap of fixed-rate debt. *Fixed-for-floating* and *floating-for-floating* currency rate swaps are also frequently arranged. Additionally, *amortizing* currency swaps incorporate an amortization feature in which periodically the amortized portions of the notional principals are reexchanged.

Risks of Interest Rate and Currency Swaps

Some of the major risks that a swap dealer confronts are discussed here.

Interest-rate risk refers to the risk of interest rates changing unfavorably before the swap bank can lay off on an opposing counterparty the other side of an interest rate swap entered into with a counterparty. As an illustration, reconsider the interest rate swap example outlined in Exhibit 14.4. To recap, in that example, the swap bank earns a spread of .125 percent. Company B passes through to the swap bank 10.50 percent per annum (on the notional principal of $10,000,000) and receives LIBOR percent in return. Bank A passes through to the swap bank LIBOR percent and receives 10.375 percent in return. Suppose the swap bank entered into the position with Company B first. If fixed rates increase substantially, say, by .50 percent, Bank A will not be willing to enter into the opposite side of the swap unless it receives, say, 10.875 percent. This would make the swap unprofitable for the swap bank.

Basis risk refers to a situation in which the floating rates of the two counterparties are not pegged to the same index. Any difference in the indexes is known as the basis. For example, one counterparty could have its FRNs pegged to LIBOR, while the other counterparty has its FRNs pegged to the U.S. Treasury bill rate. In this event, the indexes are not perfectly positively correlated and the swap may periodically be unprofitable for the swap bank. In our example, this would occur if the Treasury bill rate was substantially larger than LIBOR and the swap bank receives LIBOR from one counterparty and pays the Treasury bill rate to the other.

Exchange-rate risk refers to the risk the swap bank faces from fluctuating exchange rates during the time it takes for the bank to lay off a swap it undertakes with one counterparty with an opposing counterparty.

Credit risk refers to the probability that a counterparty, or even the swap bank, will default. These days a central clearing party stands between the swap dealer and each counterparty, guaranteeing fulfillment of both sides of an interest rate swap but not a currency swap.

Mismatch risk refers to the difficulty of finding an exact opposite match for a swap the bank has agreed to take. The mismatch may be with respect to the size of the principal sums the counterparties need, the maturity dates of the individual debt issues, or the debt service dates. Textbook illustrations typically ignore these real-life problems.

Sovereign risk refers to the probability that a country will impose exchange restrictions on a currency involved in a swap. This may make it very costly, or perhaps impossible, for a counterparty to fulfill its obligation to the dealer. In this event, provisions exist for terminating the swap, which results in a loss of revenue for the swap bank.

Is the Swap Market Efficient?

The two primary reasons for a counterparty to use a currency swap are to obtain debt financing in the swapped currency at an interest cost reduction brought about through comparative advantages each counterparty has in its national capital market, and/or the benefit of hedging long-run exchange rate exposure. These reasons seem straightforward and difficult to argue with, especially to the extent that name recognition is truly important in raising funds in the international bond market.

The two primary reasons for swapping interest rates are to better match maturities of assets and liabilities and/or to obtain a cost savings via the quality spread differential. In an efficient market without barriers to capital flows, the cost-savings argument through a QSD is difficult to accept. It implies that an arbitrage opportunity exists because of some mispricing of the default risk premiums on different types of debt instruments. If the QSD is one of the primary reasons for the existence of interest rate swaps, one would expect arbitrage to eliminate it over time and that the growth of the swap market would decrease. Quite the contrary has happened as Exhibit 14.1 shows; growth in interest rate swaps has been extremely large in recent years. Thus, the arbitrage argument does not seem to have much merit. Consequently, one must rely on an argument of **market completeness** for the existence and growth of interest rate swaps. That is, all types of debt instruments are not regularly available for all borrowers. Thus, the interest rate swap market assists in tailoring financing to the type desired by a particular borrower. Both counterparties can benefit (as well as the swap dealer) through financing that is more suitable for their asset maturity structures.

SUMMARY

This chapter provides a presentation of currency and interest rate swaps. The discussion details how swaps might be used and the risks associated with each.

1. The chapter opened with definitions of an interest rate swap and a currency swap. The basic interest rate swap is a fixed-for-floating rate swap in which one counterparty exchanges the interest payments of a fixed-rate debt obligation for the floating-interest payments of the other counterparty. Both debt obligations are denominated in the same currency. In a currency swap, one counterparty exchanges the debt service obligations of a bond denominated in one currency for the debt service obligations of the other counterparty, which are denominated in another currency.

2. The function of a swap bank was discussed. A swap bank is a generic term to describe a financial institution that facilitates the swap between counterparties. The swap bank serves as either a broker or a dealer. When serving as a broker, the swap bank matches counterparties, but does not assume any risk of the swap. When serving as a dealer, the swap bank stands willing to accept either side of a currency swap.

3. An example of a basic interest rate swap was presented. It was noted that a necessary condition for a swap to be feasible was the existence of a quality spread differential between the default-risk premiums on the fixed-rate and floating-rate interest rates of the two counterparties. Additionally, it was noted that there was not an exchange of principal sums between the counterparties to an interest rate swap because both debt issues were denominated in the same currency. Interest rate exchanges were based on a notional principal.

4. Pricing an interest rate swap after inception was illustrated. It was shown that after inception, the value of an interest rate swap to a counterparty should be the difference in the present values of the payment streams the counterparty will receive and pay on the notional principal.

5. A detailed example of a basic currency swap was presented. It was shown that the debt service obligations of the counterparties in a currency swap are effectively equivalent to one another in cost. Nominal differences can be explained by the set of international parity relationships.

6. Pricing a currency swap after inception was illustrated. It was shown that after inception, the value of a currency swap to a counterparty should be the difference in the present values of the payment stream the counterparty will receive in one currency and pay in the other currency, converted to one or the other currency denomination.

7. In addition to the basic fixed-for-floating interest rate swap and fixed-for-fixed currency swap, many other variants exist. One variant is the amortizing swap, which incorporates an amortization of the notional principles. Another variant is a zero-coupon-for-floating rate swap in which the floating-rate payer makes the standard periodic floating-rate payments over the life of the swap, but the fixed-rate payer makes a single payment at the end of the swap. Another is the floating-for-floating rate swap. In this type of swap, each side is tied to a different floating-rate index or a different frequency of the same index.

8. Reasons for the development and growth of the swap market were critically examined. It was argued that one must rely on an argument of market completeness for the existence and growth of interest rate swaps. That is, the interest rate swap market assists in tailoring financing to the type desired by a particular borrower when all types of debt instruments are not regularly available to all borrowers.

KEY WORDS

all-in cost, *352*
comparative
    advantage, *354*
counterparties, *347*
cross-currency interest
    rate swap, *347*

currency swap, *347*
market completeness,
    360
notional principal, *348*
quality spread differential
    (QSD), *351*

single-currency interest
    rate swap, *347*
swap bank, *349*
swap broker, *349*
swap dealer, *349*

QUESTIONS

1. Describe the difference between a swap broker and a swap dealer.
2. What is the necessary condition for a fixed-for-floating interest rate swap to be possible?
3. Discuss the basic motivations for a counterparty to enter into a currency swap.
4. How does the theory of comparative advantage relate to the currency swap market?
5. Discuss the risks confronting an interest rate and currency swap dealer.
6. Briefly discuss some variants of the basic interest rate and currency swaps diagrammed in the chapter.
7. If the cost advantage of interest rate swaps would likely be arbitraged away in competitive markets, what other explanations exist to explain the rapid development of the interest rate swap market?
8. Suppose Morgan Guaranty, Ltd. is quoting swap rates as follows: 7.75–8.10 percent annually against six-month dollar LIBOR for dollars and 11.25–11.65 percent annually against six-month dollar LIBOR for British pound sterling. At what rates will Morgan Guaranty enter into a $/£ currency swap?
9. A U.S. company needs to raise €50,000,000. It plans to raise this money by issuing dollar-denominated bonds and using a currency swap to convert the dollars to euros. The company expects interest rates in both the United States and the euro zone to fall.

    a. Should the swap be structured with interest paid at a fixed or a floating rate?
    b. Should the swap be structured with interest received at a fixed or a floating rate?

PROBLEMS

10. Assume a currency swap in which two counterparties of comparable credit risk each borrow at the best rate available, yet the nominal rate of one counterparty is higher than the other. After the initial principal exchange, is the counterparty that is required to make interest payments at the higher nominal rate at a financial disadvantage to the other in the swap agreement? Explain your thinking.

1. Alpha and Beta Companies can borrow for a five-year term at the following rates:

	Alpha	Beta
Moody's credit rating	Aa	Baa
Fixed-rate borrowing cost	10.5%	12.0%
Floating-rate borrowing cost	LIBOR	LIBOR + 1%

    a. Calculate the quality spread differential (QSD).
    b. Develop an interest rate swap in which both Alpha and Beta have an equal cost savings in their borrowing costs. Assume Alpha desires floating-rate debt and Beta desires fixed-rate debt. No swap bank is involved in this transaction.

2. Do problem 1 over again, this time assuming more realistically that a swap bank is involved as an intermediary. Assume the swap bank is quoting five-year dollar interest rate swaps at 10.7–10.8 percent against LIBOR flat.

3. Company A is an AAA-rated firm desiring to issue five-year FRNs. It finds that it can issue FRNs at six-month LIBOR + .125 percent or at three-month LIBOR + .125 percent. Given its asset structure, three-month LIBOR is the preferred index. Company B is an A-rated firm that also desires to issue five-year FRNs. It finds it can issue at six-month LIBOR + 1.0 percent or at three-month LIBOR + .625 percent. Given its asset structure, six-month LIBOR is the preferred index. Assume a notional principal of $15,000,000. Determine the QSD and set up a floating-for-floating rate swap where the swap bank receives .125 percent and the two counterparties share the remaining savings equally.

4. A corporation enters into a five-year interest rate swap with a swap bank in which it agrees to pay the swap bank a fixed rate of 9.75 percent annually on a notional amount of €15,000,000 and receive LIBOR. As of the second reset date, determine the price of the swap from the corporation's viewpoint assuming that the fixed-rate side of the swap has increased to 10.25 percent.

5. DVR, Inc. can borrow dollars for five years at a coupon rate of 2.75 percent. Alternatively, it can borrow yen for five years at a rate of .85 percent. The five-year yen swap rates are 0.64–0.70 percent and the dollar swap rates are 2.41–2.44 percent. The currency ¥/$ exchange rate is 87.575. Determine the dollar AIC and the dollar cash flow that DVR would have to pay under a currency swap where it borrows ¥1,750,000,000 and swaps the debt service into dollars. This problem can be solved using the Excel spreadsheet CURSWAP.xls.

6. Karla Ferris, a fixed income manager at Mangus Capital Management, expects the current positively sloped U.S. Treasury yield curve to shift parallel upward.

   Ferris owns two $1,000,000 corporate bonds maturing on June 15, 2017, one with a variable rate based on six-month U.S. dollar LIBOR and one with a fixed rate. Both yield 50 basis points over comparable U.S. Treasury market rates, have very similar credit quality, and pay interest semiannually.

   Ferris wishes to execute a swap to take advantage of her expectation of a yield curve shift and believes that any difference in credit spread between LIBOR and U.S. Treasury market rates will remain constant.

   a. Describe a six-month U.S. dollar LIBOR-based swap that would allow Ferris to take advantage of her expectation. Discuss, assuming Ferris's expectation is correct, the change in the swap's value and how that change would affect the value of her portfolio. [No calculations required to answer part a.]

   Instead of the swap described in part a, Ferris would use the following alternative derivative strategy to achieve the same result.

   b. Explain, assuming Ferris's expectation is correct, how the following *strategy* achieves the same result in response to the yield curve shift. [No calculations required to answer part b.]

Settlement Date	Nominal Eurodollar Futures Contract Value
12-15-15	$1,000,000
03-15-16	$1,000,000
06-15-16	$1,000,000
09-15-16	$1,000,000
12-15-16	$1,000,000
03-15-17	$1,000,000

   c. Discuss *one* reason why these two derivative strategies provide the same result.

7. Rone Company asks Paula Scott, a treasury analyst, to recommend a flexible way to manage the company's financial risks.

   Two years ago, Rone issued a $25 million (U.S.$), five-year floating-rate note (FRN). The FRN pays an annual coupon equal to one-year LIBOR plus 75 basis points. The FRN is noncallable and will be repaid at par at maturity.

   Scott expects interest rates to increase, and she recognizes that Rone could protect itself against the increase by using a pay-fixed swap. However, Rone's board of directors prohibits both short sales of securities and swap transactions. Scott decides to replicate a pay-fixed swap using a combination of capital market instruments.

   a. Identify the instruments needed by Scott to replicate a pay-fixed swap and describe the required transactions.

   b. Explain how the transactions in part a are equivalent to using a pay-fixed swap.

8. A company based in the United Kingdom has an Italian subsidiary. The subsidiary generates €25,000,000 a year, received in equivalent semiannual installments of €12,500,000. The British company wishes to convert the euro cash flows to pounds twice a year. It plans to engage in a currency swap in order to lock in the exchange rate at which it can convert the euros to pounds. The current exchange rate is €1.5/£. The fixed rate on a plain vanilla currency swap in pounds is 7.5 percent per year, and the fixed rate on a plain vanilla currency swap in euros is 6.5 percent per year.

   a. Determine the notional principals in euros and pounds for a swap with semiannual payments that will help achieve the objective.

   b. Determine the semiannual cash flows from this swap.

9. Ashton Bishop is the debt manager for World Telephone, which needs €3.33 billion Euro financing for its operations. Bishop is considering the choice between issuance of debt denominated in:

   - Euros (€), or
   - U.S. dollars, accompanied by a combined interest rate and currency swap.

   a. Explain *one* risk World would assume by entering into the combined interest rate and currency swap.

   Bishop believes that issuing the U.S.-dollar debt and entering into the swap can lower World's cost of debt by 45 basis points. Immediately after selling the debt issue, World would swap the U.S. dollar payments for Euro payments throughout the maturity of the debt. She assumes a constant currency exchange rate throughout the tenor of the swap.

   Exhibit 1 gives details for the two alternative debt issues. Exhibit 2 provides current information about spot currency exchange rates and the 3-year tenor Euro/U.S. Dollar currency and interest rate swap.

EXHIBIT 1

World Telephone Debt Details

Characteristic	Euro Currency Debt	U.S. Dollar Currency Debt
Par value	€3.33 billion	$3 billion
Term to maturity	3 years	3 years
Fixed interest rate	6.25%	7.75%
Interest payment	Annual	Annual

EXHIBIT 2

Currency Exchange Rate and Swap Information

Spot currency exchange rate	$0.90 per Euro ($0.90/€1.00)
3-year tenor Euro/U.S. Dollar fixed interest rates	5.80% Euro/7.30% U.S. Dollar

b. Show the notional principal and interest payment cash flows of the combined interest rate and currency swap.

Note: Your response should show both the correct currency ($ or €) and amount for *each* cash flow.

Answer problem b in the template provided.

Template for problem b

Cash Flows of the Swap				
World pays				
Notional principal				
Interest payment				
World receives				
Notional principal				
Interest payment				

c. State whether or not World would reduce its borrowing cost by issuing the debt denominated in U.S. dollars, accompanied by the combined interest rate and currency swap. Justify your response with *one* reason.

The website www.finpipe.com/interest-rate-swaps provides a brief description of interest rate swaps. Links at the bottom of the screen lead to other descriptions of derivative products, including currency swaps and other types of swaps that you will find interesting. It is a good idea to bookmark this site for future reference. Use it now to see how well you understand interest rate and currency swaps. If you cannot follow the discussions, go back and reread Chapter 14.

INTERNET EXERCISES

WWW

MINI CASE

The Centralia Corporation's Currency Swap

The Centralia Corporation is a U.S. manufacturer of small kitchen electrical appliances. It has decided to construct a wholly owned manufacturing facility in Zaragoza, Spain, to manufacture microwave ovens for sale in the European Union. The plant is expected to cost €5,500,000, and to take about one year to complete. The plant is to be financed over its economic life of eight years. The borrowing capacity created by this capital expenditure is $2,900,000; the remainder of the plant will be equity financed. Centralia is not well known in the Spanish or international bond market; consequently, it would have to pay 7 percent per annum to borrow euros, whereas the normal borrowing rate in the euro zone for well-known firms of equivalent risk is 6 percent. Alternatively, Centralia can borrow dollars in the United States at a rate of 8 percent.

Study Questions

1. Suppose a Spanish MNC has a mirror-image situation and needs $2,900,000 to finance a capital expenditure of one of its U.S. subsidiaries. It finds that it must pay a 9 percent fixed rate in the United States for dollars, whereas it can borrow euros at 6 percent. The exchange rate has been forecast to be $1.33/€1.00 in one year. Set up a currency swap that will benefit each counterparty.

2. Suppose that one year after the inception of the currency swap between Centralia and the Spanish MNC, the U.S. dollar fixed rate has fallen from 8 to 6 percent and the euro zone fixed rate for euros has fallen from 6 to 5.5 percent. In both dollars and euros, determine the market value of the swap if the exchange rate is $1.3343/€1.00.

CHAPTER

15 International Portfolio Investment

IN RECENT YEARS, portfolio investments by individual and institutional investors in international stocks, bonds, and other financial securities have grown at a phenomenal pace, surpassing in dollar volume foreign direct investments by corporations. As Exhibit 15.1 shows, for instance, the dollar value invested in international equities (ADRs and local shares) by U.S. investors has grown from a rather negligible level in the early 1980s to $200 billion in 1990 and $6,700 billion at the end of 2015. Exhibit 15.1 also shows that foreign equities as a proportion of U.S. investors' portfolio wealth rose from about 1 percent in the early 1980s to about 27 percent by 2015.[1] Considering that U.S. equities account for less than 40 percent of the world equity market capitalization, the volume of international investment may further increase. It is noted that due to the global financial crisis, international portfolio investment fell temporarily in 2008.

The rapid growth in international portfolio investments in recent years reflects the globalization of financial markets. The impetus for globalized financial markets initially came from the governments of major countries that began to deregulate foreign exchange and capital markets in the late 1970s. For instance, the United Kingdom dismantled the investment dollar premium system in 1979, while Japan liberalized its foreign exchange market in 1980, allowing its residents, for the first time, to freely invest in foreign securities.[2] Even developing countries such as Brazil, China, India, Korea, and Mexico took measures to allow foreigners to invest in their capital markets by offering country funds or directly listing local stocks on international stock exchanges. In addition, recent advances in telecommunication and computer technologies have contributed to the globalization of investments by facilitating cross-border transactions and rapid dissemination of information across national borders.

In this chapter, we are going to focus on the following issues: (i) why investors diversify their portfolios internationally, (ii) how much investors can gain from international diversification, (iii) the effects of fluctuating exchange rates on international portfolio investments, (iv) whether and how much investors can benefit from investing in U.S.-based international mutual funds and country funds, and (v) the possible

---

[1]During the period 2000–2002, the dollar value of foreign equity holdings declined somewhat, reflecting the worldwide market slump.

[2]Under the investment dollar premium system, U.K. residents had to pay a premium over the prevailing commercial exchange rate when they bought foreign currencies to invest in foreign securities. Since the premium increased the cost of cross-border portfolio investments, U.K. investors were discouraged from investing overseas.

EXHIBIT 15.1 U.S. Investment in Foreign Equities

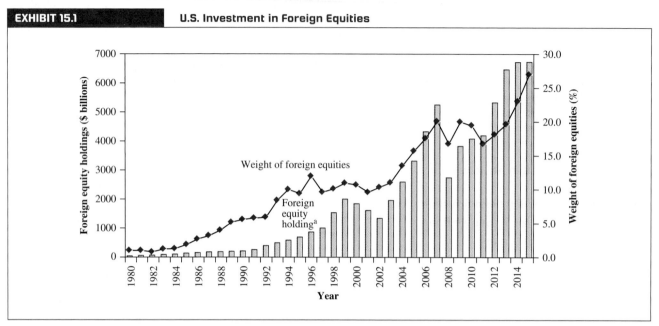

[a]Holding of foreign issues, including American Depository Receipts (ADRs), by U.S. residents.

Source: The Federal Reserve Board, *Flow of Funds Accounts of the United States*, various issues.

reasons for "home bias" in actual portfolio holdings. This chapter provides a self-contained discussion of international portfolio investment; no prior knowledge of portfolio investment theory is assumed.

International Correlation Structure and Risk Diversification

It is clear even from casual observations that security prices in different countries don't always move together closely. This suggests that investors may be able to achieve a given return on their investments at a reduced risk when they diversify their investments internationally rather than domestically. Investors diversify their portfolio holdings internationally for the same reason they may diversify domestically—to reduce risk as much as possible. As is suggested by the time-honored adage "Don't put all your eggs in one basket," most people are averse to risk and would like to diversify it away. Investors can reduce portfolio risk by holding securities that are less than perfectly correlated. In fact, the less correlated the securities in the portfolio, the lower the portfolio risk.

International diversification has a special dimension regarding **portfolio risk diversification**: Security returns are substantially less correlated across countries than within a country. Intuitively, this is so because economic, political, institutional, and even psychological factors affecting security returns tend to vary a great deal across countries, resulting in relatively low correlations among international securities. For instance, economic and political news in China may very well influence returns on most stocks in Hong Kong, but it may have relatively little impact on stock returns in, say, Finland. On the other hand, such news in Russia may affect Finnish stock returns (due to the geographic proximity and the economic ties between the two countries), with relatively little effect on Hong Kong stock returns. In addition, business cycles are often asynchronous among countries, further contributing to low international correlations.

Relatively low international correlations imply that investors should be able to reduce portfolio risk more if they diversify internationally rather than domestically. Since the magnitude of **gains from international diversification** in terms of risk reduction depends on the **international correlation structure**, it is useful to examine it empirically.

EXHIBIT 15.2	Correlations among International Stock Returns* (in U.S. dollars)							
Stock Market	AU	FR	GM	JP	NL	SW	UK	US
Australia (AU)	0.586							
France (FR)	0.286	0.576						
Germany (GM)	0.183	0.312	0.653					
Japan (JP)	0.152	0.238	0.300	0.416				
Netherlands (NL)	0.241	0.344	0.509	0.282	0.624			
Switzerland (SW)	0.358	0.368	0.475	0.281	0.517	0.664		
United Kingdom (UK)	0.315	0.378	0.299	0.209	0.393	0.431	0.698	
United States (US)	0.304	0.225	0.170	0.137	0.271	0.272	0.279	0.439

*The exhibit provides the average pairwise correlations of individual stock returns within each country in the diagonal cells and the average pairwise correlations between countries in the off-diagonal cells. The correlations were computed using the weekly returns from the period 1973–1982.

Source: C. Eun and B. Resnick, "Estimating the Correlation Structure of International Share Prices," *Journal of Finance,* December 1984, p. 1314.

Exhibit 15.2 provides historical data on the international correlation structure. Specifically, the table provides the average pairwise correlations of individual stock returns within each country in the diagonal entries, and the average pairwise correlations of stock returns between countries in the off-diagonal entries. The correlations are in terms of U.S. dollars and computed using the weekly return data from the period 1973–1982. As can be seen from the table, the average *intracountry* correlation is 0.653 for Germany, 0.416 for Japan, 0.698 for the United Kingdom, and 0.439 for the United States. In contrast, the average *intercountry* correlation of the United States is 0.170 with Germany, 0.137 with Japan, and 0.279 with the United Kingdom. The average correlation of the United Kingdom, on the other hand, is 0.299 with Germany and 0.209 with Japan. Clearly, stock returns tend to be much less correlated between countries than within a country.

The international correlation structure documented in Exhibit 15.2 suggests that international diversification can sharply reduce risk. According to Solnik (1974), that is indeed the case. Exhibit 15.3, adopted from the Solnik study, first shows that as the portfolio holds more and more stocks, the risk of the portfolio steadily declines, and eventually converges to the **systematic** (or nondiversifiable) **risk**. Systematic

EXHIBIT 15.3	Risk Reduction: Domestic versus International Diversification*

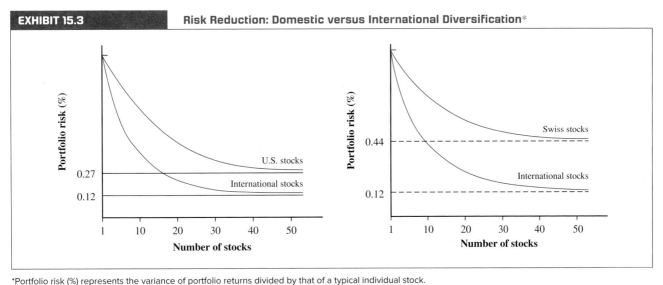

*Portfolio risk (%) represents the variance of portfolio returns divided by that of a typical individual stock.

Source: *Financial Analysts Journal,* July/August 1974.

risk refers to the risk that remains even after investors fully diversify their portfolio holdings. Exhibit 15.3 shows that while a fully diversified U.S. portfolio is about 27 percent as risky as a typical individual stock, a fully diversified international portfolio is only about 12 percent as risky as a typical individual stock. This implies that when fully diversified, an international portfolio can be less than half as risky as a purely U.S. portfolio.

Exhibit 15.3 also illustrates the situation from the Swiss perspective. The figure shows that a fully diversified Swiss portfolio is about 44 percent as risky as a typical individual stock. However, this Swiss portfolio is more than three times as risky as a well-diversified international portfolio. This implies that much of the Swiss systematic risk is, in fact, unsystematic (diversifiable) risk when looked at in terms of international investment. In addition, compared with U.S. investors, Swiss investors have a lot more to gain from international diversification. In sum, Exhibit 15.3 provides rather striking evidence supporting international, as opposed to purely domestic, diversification.[3]

A cautionary note is in order here. A few studies, for example, Roll (1988) and Longin and Solnik (1995), found that international stock markets tend to move more closely together when the market volatility is higher. As was observed during the October 1987 market crash, most developed markets declined together. Considering that investors need risk diversification most precisely when markets are turbulent, this finding casts some doubt on the benefits of international diversification. However, one may say that unless investors liquidate their portfolio holdings during the turbulent period, they can still benefit from international risk diversification. Further, Solnik and Roulet (2000) found that the average correlation of 15 major stock markets with the world market increased by about 10 percent during the period 1971–1998. Although the correlation among international markets may have increased in recent years, securities are still less correlated across countries than within a country.

Optimal International Portfolio Selection

www.msci.com/equity
/index.html

Provides an extensive coverage of world stock markets, including historical time series of major stock market indexes around the world.

Rational investors would select portfolios by considering returns as well as risk. Investors may be willing to assume additional risk if they are sufficiently compensated by a higher expected return. So we now expand our analysis to cover both risk and return. We are going to first examine the risk-return characteristics of major world stock markets and then evaluate the potential gains from holding **optimal international portfolios (OIPs)**.

Exhibit 15.4 provides summary statistics of the monthly returns, in U.S. dollars, for 12 major stock markets during the period 1980–2015.[4] Let us first examine the correlation coefficients among these markets. The correlation of the U.S. stock market with a foreign market varies from 0.38 with Japan to 0.77 with Canada. Apart from Canada, the Dutch and U.K. markets have relatively high correlations, 0.73 and 0.69, respectively, with the U.S. market. The Dutch market, in fact, has relatively high correlations with many markets: for example, 0.81 with Germany, 0.79 with France, and 0.80 with the U.K. This is likely due to a high degree of internationalization of the Dutch economy. In contrast, the Italian and Japanese markets tend to have relatively low correlations with other markets. Generally speaking, neighboring countries, such as Canada and the United States, and Germany and the Netherlands,

---

[3]In Solnik's study, international portfolios were fully hedged against exchange risk and, as a result, both U.S. and Swiss investors faced the same risk in international portfolios, which was essentially determined by local stock market risks. The Solnik study also compared international diversification across countries versus across industries and found the former to be a superior strategy.

[4]All the statistics in Exhibit 15.4 were computed using returns to the Morgan Stanley Capital International (MSCI) stock market indexes rather than individual stocks.

EXHIBIT 15.4   Summary Statistics of the Monthly Returns for 12 Major Stock Markets: 1980.1–2015.12 (all statistics in U.S. dollars)

Stock Market	Correlation Coefficients											Mean (%)	SD (%)	β[a]	SHP[b]	(Rank)
	AU	CN	FR	GM	HK	IT	JP	NL	SD	SW	UK					
Australia (AU)												1.067	6.89	1.07	0.100	(8)
Canada (CN)	0.68											0.895	5.48	0.99	0.094	(9)
France (FR)	0.55	0.58										1.046	6.25	1.11	0.107	(7)
Germany (GM)	0.51	0.57	0.79									0.922	6.57	1.14	0.083	(11)
Hong Kong (HK)	0.55	0.54	0.44	0.47								1.280	8.21	1.07	0.110	(5)
Italy (IT)	0.42	0.50	0.65	0.60	0.38							1.022	7.39	1.06	0.087	(10)
Japan (JP)	0.39	0.38	0.45	0.38	0.31	0.40						0.728	6.10	0.96	0.057	(12)
Netherlands (NL)	0.60	0.70	0.79	0.81	0.54	0.63	0.47					1.076	5.53	1.08	0.126	(3)
Sweden (SD)	0.58	0.59	0.65	0.69	0.51	0.59	0.44	0.71				1.097	6.67	1.13	0.107	(6)
Switzerland (SW)	0.53	0.55	0.72	0.74	0.44	0.51	0.48	0.77	0.63			1.047	4.97	0.85	0.134	(2)
United Kingdom (UK)	0.66	0.69	0.70	0.66	0.57	0.57	0.48	0.80	0.66	0.69		1.029	5.32	1.02	0.122	(4)
United States (US)	0.58	0.77	0.63	0.63	0.50	0.46	0.38	0.73	0.61	0.59	0.69	1.043	4.36	0.88	0.152	(1)

[a]β denotes the systematic risk (beta) of a country's stock market index measured against the world stock market index.

[b]SHP denotes the Sharpe performance measure, which is $(\overline{R}_i - R_f)/\sigma_i$ where $\overline{R}_i$ and σ_i are, respectively, the mean and standard deviation of returns for the ith market. Ranking of each market in terms of the Sharpe performance measure is provided in parentheses. The monthly risk-free interest rate R_f, 0.380%, is the average one-month U.S. Treasury bill rate during the sample period. The average risk-free rate is used here to help evaluate historical performance of stock markets during the sample period.

Source: Returns on MSCI international stock market indexes are from *Datastream*.

tend to exhibit the highest pairwise correlations, most likely due to a high degree of economic interdependence.

Exhibit 15.4 also provides the mean and standard deviation (SD) of monthly returns and the world beta measure for each market. The **world beta** measures the sensitivity of a national market to world market movements.[5] National stock markets have rather distinct risk-return characteristics. The mean return per month ranges from 0.73 percent (8.76 percent per year) for Japan to 1.28 percent (15.36 percent per year) for Hong Kong, whereas the standard deviation ranges from 4.36 percent for the United States to 8.21 percent for Hong Kong. Germany has the highest world beta measure, 1.14, while Switzerland has the lowest, 0.85. This means that the German stock market is the most sensitive to world market movements and the Swiss market the least sensitive.

Lastly, Exhibit 15.4 presents the historical performance measures for national stock markets, that is,

$$\text{SHP}_i = \frac{\overline{R}_i - R_f}{\sigma_i} \tag{15.1}$$

where $\overline{R}_i$ and σ_i are, respectively, the mean and standard deviation of returns, and R_f is the risk-free interest rate. The above expression, known as the **Sharpe performance measure (SHP)**, provides a "risk-adjusted" performance measure. It represents the excess return (above and beyond the risk-free interest rate) per standard deviation risk. In Exhibit 15.4, the Sharpe performance measure is computed by using the average monthly U.S. Treasury bill rate during the sample period as a proxy for the risk-free interest rate.

The Sharpe performance measure computed over our sample period 1980–2015 ranges from 0.057 for Japan to 0.152 for the United States. The U.S. market performed the best, followed by Switzerland and the Netherlands. The strong performance of the United States is mainly due to its low risk, whereas the weak performance of Japan is due to its low return. In computing the Sharpe ratio here, we use the "average" monthly risk-free rate to evaluate the historical performances of stock markets over a sample period. Hong Kong has the highest return among our sample markets but ranks fifth in terms of the Sharpe measure due to its high risk.

Using the historical stock market performance data represented in Exhibit 15.4, we can solve for the composition of the optimal international portfolio from the perspective of U.S. (or U.S. dollar-based) investors.[6] Exhibit 15.5 illustrates the choice of the optimal international portfolio (OIP). The result is presented in Exhibit 15.6. Note that OIP has the highest possible Sharpe ratio (SHP). As can be seen from the next-to-last column of the table, U.S. investors' optimal international portfolio comprises

Hong Kong market	=	10.45%
Italian market	=	0.01%
Swiss market	=	31.15%
U.S. market	=	58.39%
Total	=	100.00%

---

[5]Formally, the world beta is defined as $\beta_i = \sigma_{iW}/\sigma_W^2$, where σ_{iW} is the covariance between returns to the ith market and the world market index, and σ_W^2 is the variance of the world market return. If, for example, the world beta of a market is 1.2, it means that as the world market moves up and down by 1 percent, the market goes up and down by 1.2 percent.

[6]The optimal international portfolio can be solved by maximizing the Sharpe ratio, i.e., $\text{SHP} = [E(R_p) - R_f]/\sigma_p$, with respect to the portfolio weights. Refer to Appendix 15B for a detailed discussion.

EXHIBIT 15.5   **Selection of the Optimal International Portfolio**

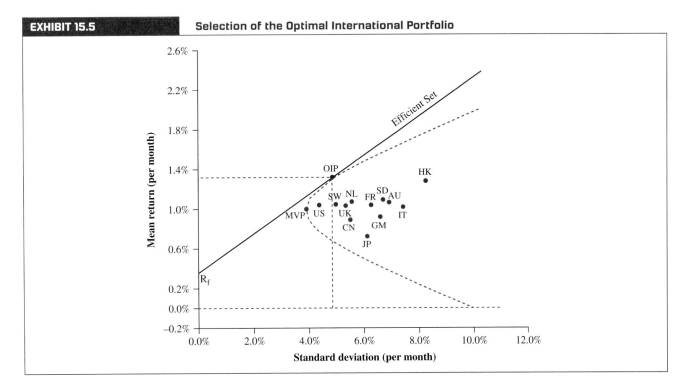

In their optimal international portfolio, U.S. investors allocate the largest share, 58.39 percent, of funds to the U.S. home market, followed by the Swiss (31.15%), Hong Kong (10.45%), and Italian (0.01%) markets. Obviously, the Italian market receives a very tiny fraction of funds in the U.S. investor's OIP. Other markets are not included in U.S. investors' OIP[7]. Apart from OIP, Exhibit 15.5 also shows the minimum variance portfolio (MVP), which is the portfolio with the lowest possible risk among all risky portfolios.[8]

Similarly, we can solve for the composition of the optimal international portfolio from the perspective of each of the national investors. Since the risk-return characteristics of international stock markets vary depending on the numeraire currency used to measure returns, the composition of the optimal international portfolio will also vary across national investors using different numeraire currencies. Exhibit 15.6 presents the composition of the optimal international portfolio from the currency perspective of each national investor. In Exhibit 15.6, we use the stock market parameters computed over the period 1980–2015 and the average risk-free rate during the study period.

For instance, the U.K. (or British pound-based) investor's optimal international portfolio comprises Hong Kong (7.23%), Sweden (13.27%), Switzerland (33.04%), the United Kingdom (19.46%), and the United States (27.0%). It is clear from Exhibit 15.6 that three markets (i.e., Hong Kong, Switzerland, and the United States) are included in every national investor's optimal international portfolio. The Swedish market is also similarly included in every national investor's OIP, with the sole exception of the U.S. investor's OIP. In contrast, the Canadian, French, German, Japanese, and Dutch markets are not

---

[7]It is noted that in Exhibit 15.6, short sales are not allowed in any market and that optimal international portfolios are solved based on the historical (ex post) parameter values. We conduct our portfolio analysis here in order to estimate the "potential gains" from international portfolio diversification. It is noted that when we want to construct an "ex ante" optimal international portfolio to hold for a future period, we need to use estimated (predicted) parameter values.

[8] During the period 1980–2015, U.S. investors' MVP consists of Japan (17.67%), Switzerland (23.84%), and the United States (58.49%). By comparison, Australian MVP consists of Australia (27.58%), Canada (9.97%), Japan (10.86%), Switzerland (26.35%), and the United States (25.24%).

EXHIBIT 15.6 Composition of the Optimal International Portfolio by Investor's Domicile (holding period: 1980–2015)

Stock Market	From the Perspective of Investors Domiciled in												
	AU	CN	FR	GM	HK	IT	JP	NL	SD	SW	UK	US	LC[a]
Australia (AU)	0.2006												0.1320
Canada (CN)		0.0270											
France (FR)													
Germany (GM)													
Hong Kong (HK)	0.0841	0.0790	0.0557	0.0538	0.1103	0.1297	0.1176	0.0584	0.0797	0.0725	0.0723	0.1045	0.0796
Italy (IT)		0.0118	0.0748	0.0713		0.0584		0.0746	0.0236			0.0001	0.0593
Japan (JP)													
Netherlands (NL)													
Sweden (SD)	0.1622	0.0790	0.0208	0.0252	0.0425	0.1350	0.2257	0.0293	0.1055	0.1191	0.1327		0.2714
Switzerland (SW)	0.2355	0.2477	0.5366	0.5155	0.3268	0.4008	0.3515	0.5324	0.4756	0.5992	0.3304	0.3115	
United Kingdom (UK)			0.0322	0.0649				0.0233	0.0648		0.1946		0.1958
United States (US)	0.3176	0.5555	0.2798	0.2693	0.5204	0.2761	0.3052	0.2822	0.2508	0.2092	0.2700	0.5839	0.2619
Total	1.0000	1.0000	1.0000	1.0000	1.0000	1.0000	1.0000	1.0000	1.0000	1.0000	1.0000	1.0000	1.0000
Risk-free rate (%)[b]	0.5125	0.2374	0.3351	0.3576	0.3023	0.6730	0.1666	0.3718	0.3782	0.2368	0.4794	0.3802	

[a]LC column provides the composition of the optimal international portfolio without considering exchange rate changes.

[b]The risk-free rate denotes the average risk-free interest rate faced by investors domiciled in the corresponding country over holding period 1980–2015. The risk-free rate is proxied by the one-month Treasury bill rate or eurocurrency interest rate.

included in any optimal portfolios, including those of domestic investors. It is noted that the Australian market is included in only two optimal portfolios, those of the Australian and Canadian investors.

The last column of Exhibit 15.6 provides the composition of the optimal international portfolio in terms of the local currency (LC), constructed ignoring exchange rate changes. It is the optimal international portfolio that would have been obtained if exchange rates had not changed. As such, it can tell us the effect of currency movements on the compositions of international portfolios.

The LC optimal international portfolio comprises Australia (13.20 percent), Hong Kong (7.96 percent), Italy (5.93 percent), Sweden (27.14 percent), the United Kingdom (19.58 percent), and the United States (26.19 percent). It is interesting to note that the U.K. is included in the LC optimal portfolio but not in the U.S. dollar-based investors' optimal portfolio. This implies that the weak performance of the British pound against the U.S. dollar should be responsible for the exclusion of the British market from the U.S. investors' optimal portfolio. The same holds for the Swedish market. In contrast, the Swiss market is not included in the LC optimal international portfolio but is included in every national investor's optimal portfolio. This inclusion must be due to a strong performance of the Swiss franc rather than the Swiss stock market.

Having obtained optimal international portfolios, we can now evaluate the gains from holding these portfolios over purely domestic portfolios. We can measure the gains from holding international portfolios in two different ways: (i) the increase in the Sharpe performance measure, and (ii) the increase in the portfolio return at the domestic-equivalent risk level. The increase in the Sharpe performance measure, ΔSHP, is given by the difference in the Sharpe ratio between the optimal international portfolio and the domestic portfolio (DP), that is,

$$\Delta\text{SHP} = \text{SHP(OIP)} - \text{SHP(DP)} \tag{15.2}$$

ΔSHP represents the extra return per standard deviation risk accruing from international investment. On the other hand, the increase in the portfolio return at the "domestic-equivalent" risk level is measured by the difference in return between the domestic portfolio and the international portfolio (IP) that has the same risk as the domestic portfolio. This extra return, ΔR, accruing from international investment at the domestic-equivalent risk level, can be computed by multiplying ΔSHP by the standard deviation of the domestic portfolio, that is,

$$\Delta R = (\Delta\text{SHP})(\sigma_{DP}) \tag{15.3}$$

Exhibit 15.7 presents both measures of the gains from international investment from the perspective of each national investor. Let us first examine the results for U.S. investors. As can be seen from the last row of the table, the optimal international portfolio has a mean return of 1.07 percent per month and a standard deviation of 4.20 percent, whereas the U.S. domestic portfolio has a mean return of 1.04 percent and a standard deviation of 4.36 percent. The optimal international portfolio thus has a marginally higher return and a somewhat lower risk than the domestic portfolio. As a result, the Sharpe performance measure increases from 0.152 to 0.164, a 7.9 percent increase. Alternately, U.S. investors can capture an extra return of 0.05 percent per month, or 0.60 percent per year, by holding an international portfolio at the domestic equivalent-risk, that is, at the standard deviation of 4.36 percent. During the sample period, the possible gains for U.S. investors are rather modest.

The gains from international portfolio diversification (IPD) are much larger for some national investors, especially for Australian, Canadian, Italian, German, Hong Kong, and Japanese investors. Each of these national investors can increase the Sharpe ratio by more than 50 percent. Japanese investors, for instance, can increase the Sharpe ratio by 139 percent, or can capture an extra return of 6.0 percent per year at the Japan-equivalent risk level by holding their optimal international portfolio. Similarly, German investors can

EXHIBIT 15.7

Gains from International Diversification by Investor's Domicile (monthly returns: 1980–2015)

Investor's Domicile	Domestic Portfolio			Optimal International Portfolio			Gains from International Investment			
	Mean (%)	SD (%)	SHP	Mean (%)	SD (%)	SHP	ΔSHP	(Δ%)[a]	ΔR(%)[b]	(%p.a.)[c]
Australia (AU)	1.06	5.13	0.106	1.18	3.95	0.169	0.063	(59.4)	0.32	(3.84)
Canada (CN)	0.88	4.34	0.148	1.10	3.77	0.230	0.082	(55.4)	0.36	(4.32)
France (FR)	1.10	5.58	0.137	1.16	4.15	0.200	0.063	(46.0)	0.35	(4.20)
Germany (GM)	0.89	5.96	0.090	1.17	4.16	0.196	0.106	(117.8)	0.63	(7.56)
Hong Kong (HK)	1.37	8.02	0.133	1.19	4.24	0.208	0.075	(56.4)	0.60	(7.20)
Italy (IT)	1.17	6.93	0.072	1.21	4.44	0.121	0.049	(68.1)	0.34	(4.08)
Japan (JP)	0.53	5.35	0.067	1.01	5.29	0.160	0.093	(138.8)	0.50	(6.00)
Netherlands (NL)	1.06	5.06	0.137	1.17	4.17	0.191	0.054	(39.4)	0.27	(3.24)
Sweden (SD)	1.37	6.41	0.155	1.23	4.09	0.209	0.054	(34.8)	0.35	(4.20)
Switzerland (SW)	0.91	4.37	0.155	0.98	4.54	0.165	0.010	(6.5)	0.04	(0.48)
United Kingdom (UK)	1.09	4.57	0.134	1.18	4.42	0.159	0.025	(18.7)	0.11	(1.32)
United States (US)	1.04	4.36	0.152	1.07	4.20	0.164	0.012	(7.9)	0.05	(0.60)

[a]The number provided in parentheses represents the percentage increase in the Sharpe performance measure relative to that of the domestic portfolio, i.e., [ΔSHP/SHP(DP)] × 100, where ΔSHP denotes the difference in the Sharpe ratio between the optimal international portfolio and the domestic portfolio.

[b]This column provides the extra return (ΔR) accruing to the optimal international portfolio at the domestic-equivalent risk level. The extra return is equal to ΔSHP × SD(DP).

[c]This column provides the annualized extra return accruing to the optimal international portfolio.

increase the Sharpe ratio by 118 percent or can capture an extra return of 7.56 percent per year at the Germany-equivalent risk level. Exhibit 15.7 indicates that the gains from international portfolio diversification are relatively modest for investors from the U.K., Switzerland, and the United States. Overall, the data presented in Exhibit 15.7 suggest that, regardless of domicile and numeraire currency, investors can potentially benefit from IPD to a varying degree.[9]

Effects of Changes in the Exchange Rate

The realized dollar returns for a U.S. resident investing in a foreign market will depend not only on the return in the foreign market but also on the change in the exchange rate between the dollar and the local (foreign) currency. Thus, the success of foreign investment rests on the performances of both the foreign security market and the foreign currency.

Formally, the rate of return in dollar terms from investing in the ith foreign market, $R_{i\$}$, is given by

$$R_{i\$} = (1 + R_i)(1 + e_i) - 1$$
$$= R_i + e_i + R_i e_i \qquad (15.4)$$

where R_i is the local currency rate of return from the ith foreign market and e_i is the rate of change in the exchange rate between the local currency and the dollar; e_i will be positive (negative) if the foreign currency appreciates (depreciates) against the dollar. Suppose that a U.S. resident just sold shares of British Petroleum (BP) she had purchased a year ago, and that the share price of BP rose 15 percent in terms of the British pound (i.e., $R = .15$), whereas the British pound depreciated 5 percent against the dollar over the one-year period (i.e., $e = -.05$). Then the rate of return, in dollar terms, from this investment will be calculated as: $R_{i\$} = (1 + .15)(1 - .05) - 1 = .0925$, or 9.25 percent.

The above expression suggests that exchange rate changes affect the risk of foreign investment as follows:

$$\text{Var}(R_{i\$}) = \text{Var}(R_i) + \text{Var}(e_i) + 2\text{Cov}(R_i, e_i) + \Delta\text{Var} \qquad (15.5)$$

where the ΔVar term represents the contribution of the cross-product term, $R_i e_i$, to the risk of foreign investment. Should the exchange rate be certain, only one term, $\text{Var}(R_i)$, would remain in the right-hand side of the equation. Equation 15.5 demonstrates that exchange rate fluctuations contribute to the risk of foreign investment through three possible channels:

1. Its own volatility, $\text{Var}(e_i)$.
2. Its covariance with the local market returns, $\text{Cov}(R_i, e_i)$.
3. The contribution of the cross-product term, ΔVar.

Exhibit 15.8 provides the breakdown of the variance of dollar returns into different components for both the bond and stock markets of six major foreign countries during the period 1990–2015: Australia, Canada, Germany, Japan, Switzerland, and the United Kingdom. Let us first examine the case of bond markets. The exhibit clearly indicates that a large portion of the risk associated with investing in foreign bonds arises from the exchange rate uncertainty. Consider investing in a German bond. As can be seen

---

[9]In analyzing the gains from international investments, it was implicitly assumed that investors fully bear exchange risk. As will be discussed later, investors can hedge exchange risk using, say, forward contracts, therefore enhancing the gains. It is also pointed out that the preceding analyses are strictly "ex-post" in the sense that the risk-return characteristics of securities are assumed to be known to investors. In reality, of course, investors will have to estimate these characteristics, and estimation errors may lead to an inefficient allocation of funds.

EXHIBIT 15.8	Decomposition of the Variance of International Security Returns in U.S. Dollars[a] (monthly data: 1990.1–2015.12)				
		Components of Var($R_{i\$}$)[b]			
	Var($R_{i\$}$)	Var(R_i)	Var(e_i)	2Cov(R_i, e_i)	ΔVar
Bonds					
Australia	13.81	4.57 (33.09%)	11.20 (81.10%)	−2.08 (−15.06%)	0.12 (0.87%)
Canada	7.60	3.47 (45.66%)	4.90 (64.47%)	−0.79 (−10.39%)	0.02 (0.26%)
Germany	10.97	2.86 (26.07)%	9.19 (83.77%)	−1.22 (−11.12%)	0.14 (1.28%)
Japan	12.73	1.98 (15.55%)	9.93 (78.00%)	0.69 (5.42%)	0.13 (1.03%)
Switzerland	12.55	2.07 (16.49%)	10.82 (86.22%)	−0.57 (−4.54%)	0.23 (1.83%)
U.K.	9.91	4.17 (42.08%)	7.57 (76.39%)	−2.02 (−20.38%)	0.19 (1.92%)
U.S.	4.55	4.55 (100%)	0.00 (n.a.)	0.00 (n.a.)	0.00 (n.a.)
Stocks					
Australia	37.75	16.36 (43.34%)	11.20 (29.67%)	10.39 (27.52%)	−0.20 (−0.53%)
Canada	31.35	18.25 (58.21%)	4.90 (15.61%)	8.51 (27.14%)	−0.31 (−0.96%)
Germany	44.44	37.58 (84.56%)	9.19 (20.67%)	−2.54 (−5.72%)	0.21 (0.49%)
Japan	39.85	34.45 (86.46%)	9.93 (24.91%)	−5.07 (−12.72%)	0.54 (1.35%)
Switzerland	24.54	20.75 (84.58%)	10.82 (44.08%)	−7.27 (−29.65%)	0.24 (0.99%)
U.K.	25.77	18.88 (73.28%)	7.57 (29.36%)	−0.86 (−3.34%)	0.18 (0.70%)
U.S.	20.27	20.27 (100%)	0.00 (n.a.)	0.00 (n.a.)	0.00 (n.a.)

[a]The portfolio variances are computed using the monthly percentage returns.

[b]The relative contributions of individual components to the total risk appear in parentheses.

Source: Monthly stock and bond returns data are obtained from the *Datastream* database. Specifically, Morgan Stanley Capital International (MSCI) stock market indexes and *Datastream* benchmark 10-year government bond indexes are used.

from the exhibit, the variance of German bond returns is only 2.86 percent squared in terms of the local currency, but jumps to 10.97 percent squared when measured in dollar terms. This change in volatility is due to the volatility of the exchange rate, Var(e_i) = 9.19, as well as its covariance with the local bond market returns, that is 2Cov(R_i, e_i) = −1.22. As can be expected, the cross-product term contributes relatively little. In the case of investing in the Swiss bond, the local bond market returns account for only 16.49 percent of the volatility of returns in dollar terms. This means that investing in Swiss bonds largely amounts to investing in the Swiss currency.

Without exception, exchange rate volatility is much greater than bond market volatility. And exchange rate changes may covary positively or negatively with local bond market returns. Empirical evidence regarding bond markets suggests that it is essential to control exchange risk to enhance the efficiency of international bond portfolios.

Compared with bond markets, the risk of investing in foreign stock markets is, to a lesser degree, attributable to exchange rate uncertainty. Again, consider investing in the German market. The variance of the German stock market is 37.58 percent squared in terms of the local currency, but it increases to 44.44 percent squared when measured in terms of the U.S. dollar. The local market return volatility accounts for 84.56 percent of the volatility of German stock market returns in dollar terms. In comparison, exchange rate volatility accounts for 20.67 percent of the dollar return variance, still a significant portion. Interestingly, the exchange rate covaries negatively with local stock market returns, partially offsetting the effect of exchange rate volatility. In the case of investing in the Swiss stock market, the local market variance, 20.75, is only modestly less than the dollar return variance, 24.54. In other words, U.S. and Swiss investors face similar risk when they invest in the Swiss stock market. This result is due to the fact that the exchange rate volatility is largely offset by a significantly negative comovement between the local market return and exchange rate change. In the case of Australian stocks, the exchange rate contributes to the dollar return variance through its strongly positive comovement with the local stock market return, as well as through its own volatility. The same largely holds for Canadian stocks.

International Bond Investment

Although the world bond market is comparable in terms of capitalization value to the world stock market, so far it has not received as much attention in international investment literature. This may reflect, at least in part, the perception that exchange risk makes it difficult to realize significant gains from international bond diversification. It is worthwhile to explore this issue and determine if this perception has merit.

Exhibit 15.9 provides summary statistics of monthly returns, in U.S. dollar terms, on long-term government bond indexes from seven major countries: Australia, Canada, Germany, Japan, Switzerland, the United Kingdom, and the United States. It also presents the composition of the optimal international portfolio for U.S. (dollar-based) investors. Note that European bond markets have relatively high correlations. For instance, the correlation of the German bond market is 0.80 with the Swiss bond market and 0.70 with the U.K. bond market. These high correlations reflect the fact that as a group these European currencies tend to float against the U.S. dollar. Similarly, two "commodity currency" bonds, i.e., the Australian bond and the Canadian bond, exhibit a relatively high correlation, 0.69. In contrast, the Japanese bond tends to have relatively low correlations with other bonds. For example, its correlation is 0.29 with the Australian bond, 0.22 with the Canadian bond, and 0.38 with the U.S. bond. Exhibit 15.9 further shows that the mean return ranges from 0.48 percent for Japan to 0.81 percent for Australia, whereas the standard deviation of return ranges from 2.13 percent for the U.S. to 3.71 percent for Australia during 1990–2015. Australia has the highest Sharpe ratio (0.152), followed by the United Kingdom (0.144), Canada (0.138), and the United States (0.135).

In the optimal international portfolio, the U.S. bond receives the most positive weight (44.16%), followed by the U.K. (29.07%), Switzerland (28.88%), Australia (25.59%), and Canada (13.09%) during the study period. In contrast, German and Japanese bonds receive negative weights, –34.0% and –6.79%, respectively, implying that U.S. investors optimally should have borrowed in German and Japanese currencies. The optimal portfolio has a monthly mean return of 0.68 percent and a standard deviation of 2.24 percent, resulting in a Sharpe performance measure of 0.194. Considering that the U.S. bond has a mean return of 0.53 percent, a standard deviation of 2.13 percent, and a Sharpe measure of 0.135, U.S. investors could have benefited substantially from holding the optimal international bond portfolio.

The preponderance of exchange risk in foreign bond investment suggests that investors may be able to increase their gains from international bond diversification if

EXHIBIT 15.9	Summary Statistics of the Monthly Returns to Bonds and the Composition of the Optimal International Bond Portfolio (in U.S. dollars, 1990.1–2015.12)									
	Correlation Coefficients									Optimal International Portfolio[a]
Bond Market	AU	CN	GM	JP	SW	UK	Mean (%)	SD (%)	SHP	(Weight)
Australia (AU)							0.81	3.71	0.152	0.2559
Canada (CN)	0.69						0.62	2.76	0.138	0.1309
Germany (GM)	0.51	0.44					0.61	3.31	0.112	−0.3400
Japan (JP)	0.29	0.22	0.44				0.48	3.56	0.067	−0.0679
Switzerland (SW)	0.42	0.32	0.80	0.49			0.67	3.54	0.122	0.2888
United Kingdom (UK)	0.47	0.50	0.70	0.33	0.59		0.70	3.15	0.144	0.2907
United States (US)	0.35	0.36	0.45	0.38	0.37	0.41	0.53	2.13	0.135	0.4416
Optimal International Portfolio:							0.68	2.24	0.194	

[a]The optimal international bond portfolio is solved allowing for short sales and using one-month U.S. Treasury-bill rate as the monthly risk-free interest rate. The average risk-free interest rate is 0.243% over the sample period. Benchmark 10-year *Datastream* government bond indexes are used.

Source: Bond returns data are obtained from *Datastream*.

they can properly control the exchange risk. Existing studies indeed show that when investors control exchange risk by using currency forward contracts, they can substantially enhance the efficiency of international bond portfolios. Eun and Resnick (1994), for instance, show that when exchange risk is hedged, international bond portfolios tend to dominate international stock portfolios in terms of risk-return efficiency.[10]

The advent of the *euro,* the common European currency, altered the risk-return characteristics of the affected markets. Before the euro was introduced, for instance, the Italian and German bonds had quite different characteristics; the former was generally viewed as a high-risk and high-return investment, whereas the latter a low-risk and low-return investment, largely because the German mark was a hard currency while the Italian lira was a weak one. In the post-euro period, however, both German and Italian bonds (and all the other euro zone bonds) became denominated and transacted in the common currency, rendering nationality of bonds a somewhat less significant factor. Although euro zone bonds differ in terms of credit risk, their risk-return characteristics converged to a certain extent. This implies that non-euro currency bonds like British bonds would play an enhanced role in international diversification strategies as they would retain their unique risk-return characteristics.

International Mutual Funds: A Performance Evaluation

Currently, U.S. investors can achieve international diversification at home simply by investing in U.S.-based international mutual funds, which have proliferated in recent years. By investing in international mutual funds, investors can (i) save any extra transaction and/or information costs they may have to incur when they attempt to invest directly in foreign markets, (ii) circumvent many legal and institutional barriers to direct portfolio investments in foreign markets, and (iii) potentially benefit from the expertise of professional fund managers.

These advantages of international mutual funds should be particularly appealing to small individual investors who would like to diversify internationally but have neither the necessary expertise nor the direct access to foreign markets. It is thus relevant to ask the following question: Can investors benefit from international diversification by investing in existing U.S.-based international mutual funds? To provide an answer to the above question, we are going to examine the historical performance of international mutual funds that invest a substantial portion of their assets in foreign markets.

Exhibit 15.10 provides the risk-return profiles of a sample of U.S.-based international mutual funds that have sufficient track records. Three funds—the ASA (which invests in South African gold-mining stocks), the Canadian Fund, and the Japan Fund—are single-country funds. Other funds invest more broadly. The table shows that all but one fund have a higher mean return than the U.S. stock market index, proxied by the Standard & Poor 500 Index, during the period of 1977.1–1986.12. The average mean return of the international mutual funds is 1.58 percent per month (18.96 percent per year). In comparison, the mean return on the S&P 500 is 1.17 percent per month (14.04 percent per year). The standard deviation of the international mutual funds ranges from 3.36 percent to 11.88 percent, with an average of 5.78 percent. In comparison, the S&P has a standard deviation of 4.25 percent.[11]

Exhibit 15.10 also provides the U.S. beta measures of the international funds and the associated coefficient of determination (R^2) values.[12] Note that most funds have a U.S. beta value that is much less than unity. On average, U.S. stock market movements

---

[10]For further discussion of exchange risk hedging, readers are referred to Appendix 15A.

[11]It is noted that no existing studies provide current, comprehensive evaluation of international mutual fund performances.

[12]The U.S. beta measures the sensitivity of the fund returns to the U.S. stock market returns. The coefficient of determination (R^2) measures the fraction of the variance of fund returns that can be explained by the U.S. market returns.

EXHIBIT 15.10

International Mutual Funds: A Performance Evaluation (monthly returns: 1977.1–1986.12)

Fund	Mean (%)	SD (%)	β_{US}	R^2	SHP[a]
ASA	1.75	11.88	0.80	0.08	0.084
Canadian Fund	0.91	4.64	0.75	0.47	0.035
International Investors	2.34	10.09	0.72	0.09	0.157
Japan Fund	1.72	7.02	0.59	0.13	0.138
Keystone International	1.14	4.29	0.69	0.47	0.091
Merrill Lynch Pacific	1.82	5.45	0.32	0.06	0.196
New Perspective	1.47	3.99	0.80	0.73	0.179
Oppenheimer Global	1.94	6.35	1.02	0.47	0.186
Putnam International	1.64	5.91	0.62	0.20	0.150
Scudder International	1.46	4.23	0.50	0.26	0.168
Sogen International	1.48	3.36	0.70	0.78	0.217
Templeton Growth	1.48	4.13	0.84	0.74	0.176
United International Growth	1.41	3.86	0.71	0.61	0.172
Average	1.58	5.78	0.69	0.39	0.150
U.S. MNC Index	1.34	4.38	0.98	0.90	0.135
S&P 500	1.17	4.25	1.00	1.00	0.099
MSCI World Index	1.46	3.80	0.70	0.61	0.186

[a]The Sharpe measure is computed using the risk-free rate of 0.752%, which is the average monthly Treasury bill rate during the sample period.

Source: Eun, C.; Kolodny, R.; Resnick, B., "U.S.-Based International Mutual Funds: A Performance Evaluation."

account for less than 40 percent of the fluctuations in the international fund returns. In contrast, U.S. stock market movements are known to account for about 90 percent of the fluctuations in U.S. domestic stock fund returns.[13] These results show that the sample funds provided U.S. investors with a valuable opportunity to diversify internationally. In contrast, the U.S. MNC Index, which comprises 60 U.S. multinational corporations with the highest proportions of international revenue, has a U.S. beta value of 0.98 and an R^2 value of 90 percent. This means that the share prices of MNCs behave much like those of domestic firms, without providing effective international diversification.[14]

Lastly, Exhibit 15.10 provides the Sharpe performance measures of international mutual funds. As the table shows, 10 out of 13 international funds outperformed the U.S. stock market index based on the Sharpe measure. The same point is illustrated in Exhibit 15.11, showing that only three international funds lie below the U.S. capital market line (CML).[15] This is in sharp contrast to the findings of previous studies showing that the majority of U.S. domestic mutual funds lie below the U.S. capital market line. Against the alternative benchmark of the World Index, however, the sample funds performed rather poorly. The average SHP value for the international funds, 0.15, is substantially less than the value for the World Index, 0.186. This seems to suggest that it is desirable to invest in a world index fund if available.[16]

---

[13]See, for example, Sharpe (1966), pp. 127–28.

[14]This result is consistent with Jacquillat and Solnik's study (1978), showing that multinational corporations of various countries have very low exposure (beta) to foreign stock market indexes.

[15]The capital market line (CML) is the straight line obtained by connecting the risk-free interest rate and the market portfolio.

[16]The capital asset pricing model (CAPM) suggests that if the world market portfolio is indeed mean-variance efficient, then the expected return on a portfolio will be determined by its world beta. This, in turn, implies that if investors hold parochial portfolios that are less than fully diversified globally, they are bearing some diversifiable risk for which there will be no compensation in terms of extra returns. Under this situation it would be optimal for investors to hold the world market portfolio, proxied by a world index fund, together with the risk-free asset, to achieve the desired combination of risk and return.

EXHIBIT 15.11

Performance of
International Mutual Funds:
1977.1–1986.12

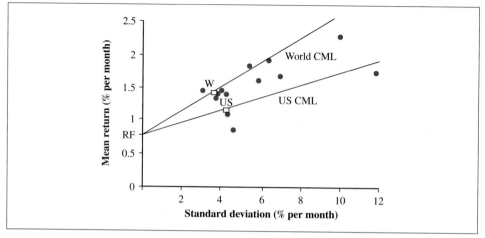

Note: Each international fund is denoted by a round dot (•). The risk-free rate (RF) is .752%, which is the average T-bill rate during the sample period. W and US, respectively, denote the MSCI World Index and the S&P 500.

In More Depth

In addition to international mutual funds, investors may achieve international portfolio diversification "at home" by investing in (i) country funds, (ii) American depository receipts (ADRs), (iii) exchange-traded funds (ETFs), or (iv) hedge funds without having to invest directly in foreign stock markets. In the next section, we discuss each of these instruments.

International Diversification through Country Funds

Recently, country funds have emerged as one of the most popular means of international investment in the United States as well as in other developed countries. As the name suggests, a country fund invests exclusively in stocks of a single country. Using country funds, investors can

1. Speculate in a single foreign market with minimum costs.
2. Construct their own *personal* international portfolios using country funds as building blocks.
3. Diversify into *emerging markets* that are otherwise practically inaccessible.

Many emerging markets, such as India, China, and Russia, still remain substantially segmented. As a result, country funds often provide international investors with the most practical, if not the only, way of diversifying into these foreign markets.

The majority of country funds available, however, have a *closed-end* status. Like other closed-end funds, a **closed-end country fund (CECF)** issues a given number of shares that trade on the stock exchange of the host country as if the fund were an individual stock by itself. Unlike shares of open-end mutual funds, shares of a closed-end country fund cannot be redeemed at the underlying net asset value set at the home market of the fund. Currently, about 30 countries offer CECFs, a partial list of which is provided in Exhibit 15.12. In the United States, the majority of CECFs are listed on the New York Stock Exchange, with a few listed on the American Stock Exchange.

Since the share value of a fund is set on a U.S. stock exchange, it may very well diverge from the underlying net asset value (NAV) set in the fund's home market. The difference is known as a *premium* if the fund share value exceeds the NAV, or a *discount* in the opposite case. Exhibit 15.12 provides the magnitude of premiums/discounts for

EXHIBIT 15.12			U.S. and Home Market Betas of Closed-End Country Funds and Their Net Asset Values					
	Average Fund Premium (%)	Fund Share Value			Net Asset Value			Sample Period
Country		β_{US}	β_{HM}	R^2	β_{US}	β_{HM}	R^2	
Australia	−14.77	0.62	0.48	0.13	0.25	0.81	0.60	1986.1–90.12
Brazil	−24.72	0.11	0.16	0.02	0.32	0.65	0.60	1988.4–90.12
Canada	−6.29	0.04	0.47	0.03	−0.19	0.29	0.11	1986.6–90.12
Germany	1.80	0.73	0.53	0.11	0.15	0.69	0.40	1986.7–90.12
India	−2.66	0.87	0.26	0.04	−0.27	0.66	0.40	1988.8–90.12
Italy	−12.49	0.89	0.68	0.21	0.13	0.57	0.28	1986.3–90.12
Korea	63.17	1.00	0.63	0.19	0.24	0.76	0.62	1985.1–90.12
Malaysia	−0.36	1.34	0.60	0.24	0.58	0.68	0.79	1987.6–90.12
Mexico	−21.14	0.99	0.53	0.13	0.33	0.75	0.62	1985.1–90.12
Spain	−1.57	1.56	0.28	0.14	0.39	0.75	0.65	1988.7–90.12
South Africa	12.16	0.00	0.35	0.13	0.08	0.85	0.59	1985.1–90.12
Switzerland	−7.65	0.79	0.47	0.25	0.33	0.65	0.75	1987.8–90.12
Taiwan	37.89	1.46	0.39	0.26	0.19	0.40	0.13	1987.2–90.12
Thailand	−6.86	1.20	0.44	0.14	0.63	0.85	0.75	1988.2–90.12
U.K.	−16.55	1.04	0.62	0.36	0.55	0.73	0.37	1987.8–90.12
Average		0.84	0.46	0.16	0.25	0.67	0.51	

Source: Chang, E.; Eun, C.; Kolodny, R., "International Diversification through Closed-End Country Funds," *Journal of Banking and Finance*, October 1995.

the sample CECFs. As indicated in the table, the average premium varies a great deal across funds, ranging from 63.17 percent (for the Korea Fund) to −24 percent (for the Brazil Fund). Like the Korea Fund, the Taiwan and Spain funds commanded large premiums, 37.89 percent and 21.57 percent, respectively. Like the Brazil Fund, the Mexico Fund traded at a steep discount, −21.14 percent on average. It was also observed that the fund premium/discount fluctuates widely over time. For instance, the Taiwan Fund premium varied between −25.27 percent and 205.39 percent. Most funds have traded at both a premium and a discount since their inception.[17] The behavior of the fund premium/discount implies that the risk-return characteristics of a CECF can be quite different from those of the underlying NAV.

Cash flows from CECFs are generated by the underlying assets held outside the United States. But CECFs are traded in the United States and their market values, determined in the United States, often diverge from the NAVs. This "hybrid" nature of CECFs suggests that they may behave partly like U.S. securities and partly like securities of the home market. To investigate this issue, consider the following "two-factor" market model:[18]

$$R_i = \alpha_i + \beta^{US}_i R_{US} + \beta^{HM}_i R_{HM} + e_i \tag{15.6}$$

where:

R_i = the return on the ith country fund,

R_{US} = the return on the U.S. market index proxied by the Standard & Poor's 500 Index,

---

[17]A study by Bonser-Neal, Brauer, Neal, and Wheatley (1990) suggests that the country fund premium/discount reflects the barriers to direct portfolio investment in the home countries of the funds. They found that whenever these barriers were lowered, the fund premium declined.

[18]The returns to the home market, R_{HM}, employed in Equation 15.6 is, in fact, the "residual" obtained from regressing the home market returns on the U.S. market returns. U.S. investors who wish to diversify risk internationally will value exposure to the "pure" (or, orthogonal) foreign market risk, i.e., β^{HM}.

R_{HM} = the return on the home market of the country fund,

β^{US}_i = the U.S. beta of the ith country fund, measuring the sensitivity of the fund returns to the U.S. market returns,

β^{HM}_i = the home market beta of the ith country fund, measuring the sensitivity of the fund returns to the home market returns, and

e_i = the residual error term.

Equation 15.6 is estimated for both the CECFs and their underlying net assets; that is, we run two regressions for each fund. In the first regression, the left-hand side (dependent) variable, R_i, is the return that U.S. investors receive on the CECF share itself. In the second regression, the left-hand side variable is the return on the NAV. The estimation results are provided in Exhibit 15.12.

Exhibit 15.12 shows that CECFs tend to have substantially higher U.S. beta values than their underlying NAVs. The average U.S. beta value is 0.84 for CECFs, but is only 0.25 for the NAVs. On the other hand, the average home market beta is 0.46 for CECFs, which is compared with 0.67 for the NAVs. In the case of Korea, for example, the fund (underlying net assets) has a U.S. beta of 1.00 (0.24) and a home market beta of 0.63 (0.76). In the case of Thailand, the fund (underlying net assets) has a U.S. beta of 1.20 (0.63) and a home market beta of 0.44 (0.85). In other words, CECF returns are substantially more sensitive to the U.S. market factor and less so to the home market factor than their corresponding NAVs. This implies that CECFs behave more like U.S. securities in comparison with the NAVs.[19] However, the majority of CECFs retain significant home market betas, allowing U.S. investors to achieve international diversification to a certain extent. Also noteworthy from the table is the fact that the coefficients of determination, R^2, tend to be quite low, 0.16 on average, for CECFs. This implies that CECFs are subject to significant *idiosyncratic* (or unique) risks that are related to neither the U.S. nor home market movements.

While CECFs behave more like U.S. securities, they provide U.S. investors with the opportunity to achieve international diversification at home without incurring excessive transaction costs. We now estimate the potential gains from international diversification using CECFs. Exhibit 15.13 provides the risk-return characteristics of 15 sample funds, as well as the U.S. stock market index, during the sample period 1989.1–1990.12. It also presents the composition of the optimal international portfolio comprising CECFs and, for comparison purposes, the composition of the corresponding optimal portfolio comprising the NAVs.

The optimal portfolio consisting of CECFs dominates the U.S. index in terms of risk-return efficiency; the Sharpe performance measure is 0.233 for the former and 0.087 for the latter. This point can be seen clearly from Exhibit 15.14, which traces out the efficient sets, separately, for CECFs and NAVs.

The figure shows that the NAVs offer superior diversification opportunities compared to the CECFs. Consequently, those who can invest directly in foreign markets without incurring excessive costs are advised to do so. However, for the majority of investors without such opportunities, CECFs still offer a cost-effective way of diversifying internationally. Lastly, note that country funds from emerging markets receive significant weights in the optimal portfolio of CECFs. Specifically, the weight is 12.71 percent for the Brazil Fund, 7.50 percent for the India Fund, and 24.27 percent for the Mexico Fund. These emerging market funds as a whole receive about a 45 percent weight in the optimal CECF portfolio. This implies that CECFs from emerging markets can play an important role in expanding the investment opportunity set for international investors.

---

[19]This finding is consistent with the Bailey and Lim (1992) study showing that CECFs act more like U.S. securities than foreign stock market indexes.

EXHIBIT 15.13	Summary Statistics of the Weekly Returns for Closed-End Country Funds and Their Net Asset Values and the Compositions of Optimal Portfolios (in U.S. dollar terms: 1989.1–1990.12)							
	Country Fund Share			**Net Asset Value**			**Optimal Portfolio**	
Country	Mean (%)	SD (%)	Correlation with U.S.	Mean (%)	SD (%)	Correlation with U.S.	CECF (Weight)	NAV (Weight)
Australia	0.46	5.64	0.12	0.01	1.78	0.25	0.0033	0.0000
Brazil	0.73	6.31	−0.01	0.29	7.55	−0.02	0.1271	0.0023
Canada	0.14	4.91	−0.31	−0.19	1.98	−0.19	0.0660	0.0000
Germany	0.78	9.70	0.22	0.38	4.67	−0.11	0.0253	0.0000
India	0.36	5.93	0.18	0.15	3.92	−0.21	0.0750	0.0882
Italy	0.44	7.00	0.22	0.39	2.20	0.25	0.0000	0.1044
Korea	−0.37	6.79	0.25	0.00	2.91	0.08	0.0000	0.0000
Malaysia	0.72	7.89	0.35	0.37	3.21	0.29	0.0000	0.0000
Mexico	1.11	6.07	0.50	0.77	2.63	0.24	0.2427	0.6026
Spain	0.39	8.76	0.40	0.03	3.08	0.29	0.0000	0.0000
South Africa	0.43	4.00	−0.13	0.36	5.06	−0.03	0.2993	0.0954
Switzerland	0.27	4.50	0.46	0.20	2.48	0.36	0.0000	0.0000
Taiwan	0.57	7.42	0.31	−0.06	7.95	0.05	0.0000	0.0000
Thailand	0.71	8.42	0.29	0.50	5.14	0.23	0.0424	0.0616
U.K.	0.35	4.01	0.44	0.27	4.08	0.23	0.1189	0.0454
U.S. Index	0.18	2.06	1.00	0.18	2.06	1.00		
						Total =	1.0000	1.0000
						Mean =	0.58%	0.58%
						SD =	2.49%	1.81%
						SHP =	0.233	0.320

Source: Chang, E.; Eun, C.; Kolodny, R., "International Diversification through Closed-End Country Funds," *Journal of Banking and Finance*, October 1995.

EXHIBIT 15.14	
Efficient Sets: Country Funds versus Net Assets: 1989.1–1990.12	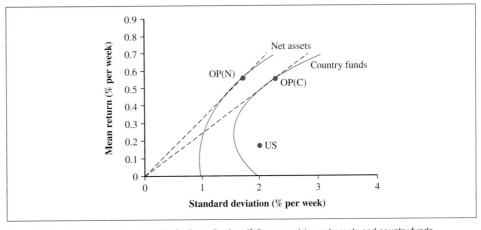

Note: OP(N) and OP(C) denote, respectively, the optimal portfolios comprising net assets and country funds. The efficient sets are illustrated by the dotted lines.

International Diversification with ADRs

U.S. investors can achieve international diversification at home using American depository receipts (ADRs), as well as country funds. As explained in Chapter 13, ADRs represent receipts for foreign shares held in the U.S. (depository) banks' foreign branches or custodians. Like closed-end country funds, ADRs are traded on U.S. exchanges like domestic American securities. Consequently, U.S. investors can save transaction costs and also benefit from speedy and dependable disclosures, settlements, and custody services. It is noted that like American investors, British and European investors may achieve international diversification at home using global depository receipts (GDRs), which represent ownership claims on those foreign shares that are listed on the London Stock Exchange.

A few studies examined the potential benefits of international diversification with ADRs. Officer and Hoffmeister (1987) found that adding ADRs to a domestic portfolio had substantial risk reduction benefits. Including as few as four ADRs in a representative U.S. stock portfolio reduced risk, measured by the standard deviation of returns, by as much as 25 percent without reducing the expected return. They also found that ADRs tend to have very low beta exposure to the U.S. stock market. During the sample period 1973–1983, ADRs were found to have an average U.S. beta of only 0.264.

Wahab and Khandwala (1993) found similar results. They reported that when investors hold an equally weighted portfolio of seven ADRs and the S&P 500, the annualized standard deviation of daily returns drops from 30.2 percent (for a purely domestic portfolio) to 17.5 percent. They also reported that most of the nonsystematic risk of the portfolio is eliminated by adding only seven ADRs to the S&P 500. Adding ADRs beyond seven did not reduce the portfolio risk materially, regardless of portfolio weights.

Considering that the majority of ADRs are from such developed countries as Australia, Japan, and the United Kingdom, U.S. investors have a limited opportunity to diversify into emerging markets using ADRs. However, in a few emerging markets like Mexico, investors can choose from several ADRs. In this situation, investors should consider the relative advantages and disadvantages of ADRs and CECFs as a means of international diversification. Compared with ADRs, CECFs are likely to provide more complete diversification. As shown previously, however, the potential gains from investing in them tend to be reduced by premiums/discounts.

International Diversification with Exchange-Traded Funds

In April 1996, the American Stock Exchange (AMEX) introduced a class of securities called **World Equity Benchmark Shares (WEBS)**, originally designed and managed by Barclays Global Investors. In essence, WEBS are **exchange-traded funds (ETFs)** that are designed to closely track foreign stock market indexes. Currently, there are WEBS tracking the Morgan Stanley Capital International (MSCI) indexes for the following individual countries: Australia, Austria, Belgium, Brazil, Canada, Chile, China, France, Germany, Hong Kong, Indonesia, Ireland, Israel, Italy, Japan, Korea, Malaysia, Mexico, the Netherlands, Peru, Poland, Singapore, South Africa, Spain, Sweden, Switzerland, Taiwan, Thailand, Turkey, and the United Kingdom. The AMEX had previously introduced a similar security for the U.S. market, Standard & Poor's Depository Receipts (SPDRs), known as "spiders," that is designed to track the S&P 500 Index. Using exchange-traded funds (ETFs) like WEBS and spiders, investors can trade a whole stock market index as if it were a single stock. Being open-end funds, WEBS trade at prices that are very close to their net asset values. In addition to single-country index funds, investors can achieve global diversification instantaneously just by holding shares of the S&P Global 100 Index Fund that is also trading on the AMEX with other WEBS. WEBS were later re-named as iShares, which are listed on multiple exchanges, including the New York Stock Exchange, London Stock Exchange, and Hong Kong Stock Exchange.

A study by Khorana, Nelling, and Trester (1998) found that WEBS indeed track the underlying MSCI country indexes very closely. For example, the average correlation of daily returns between WEBS and the underlying country indexes is 0.97. They also found that the average correlation of WEBS with the S&P 500 Index is quite low, 0.22, which makes WEBS an excellent tool for international risk diversification. For those investors who desire international equity exposure, WEBS may well serve as a major alternative to such traditional tools as international mutual funds, ADRs, and closed-end country funds.

International Diversification with Hedge Funds

Hedge funds that represent privately pooled investment funds have experienced a phenomenal growth in recent years. This growth of hedge funds has been mainly driven by the desire of institutional investors, such as pension plans, endowments, and private foundations, to achieve positive or absolute returns, regardless of whether markets are rising or falling. Unlike traditional mutual funds that generally depend on "buy and hold" investment strategies, hedge funds may adopt flexible, dynamic trading strategies, often aggressively using leverages, short positions, and derivative contracts, in order to achieve their investment objectives. These funds may invest in a wide spectrum of securities, such as currencies, domestic and foreign bonds and stocks, commodities, real estate, and so forth. Many hedge funds aim to realize positive returns, regardless of market conditions.

Legally, hedge funds are private investment partnerships. As such, these funds generally do not register as investment companies under the Investment Company Act and are not subject to any reporting or disclosure requirements. As a result, many hedge funds operate in rather opaque environments. Hedge fund advisors typically receive a management fee, often 1–2 percent of the fund asset value as compensation, plus performance fee that can be 20–25 percent of capital appreciation. Investors may not be allowed to liquidate their investments during a certain lock-up period. In the United States, only institutional investors and wealthy individuals are allowed to invest in hedge funds. In many European countries, however, retail investors are also allowed to invest in these funds.

Hedge funds tend to have relatively low correlations with various stock market benchmarks and thus allow investors to diversify their portfolio risk. In addition, hedge funds allow investors to access foreign markets that are not easily accessible. For example, J.P. Morgan provides access to the Jayhawk China Fund, a hedge fund investing in Chinese stocks not readily available in U.S. markets. Also, hedge funds may allow investors to benefit from certain global macroeconomic events. In fact, many hedge funds are classified as "global/macro" funds. Examples of global/macro funds include such well-known names as George Soros' Quantum Fund, Julian Robertson's Jaguar Fund, and Louis Bacon's Moore Global Fund. Some hedge funds were active during the British pound crisis of 1992 and Asian financial crisis of 1997. As is well known, George Soros correctly anticipated the withdrawal of the British pound from the European Monetary System (EMS) and bet on the pound depreciation upon the withdrawal. His funds reportedly took a $10 billion short position on the British pound and made about $1 billion profit during September 1992. Soros funds also had short positions in the Thai baht and Malaysian ringgit during the Asian currency crisis of 1997. This touched off a series of acrimonious exchanges between the Malaysian Prime Minister Mahatir Mohamad and George Soros on whether hedge funds were responsible for the currency crisis.

While investors may benefit from hedge funds, they need to be aware of the associated risk as well. Hedge funds may make wrong bets based on the incorrect prediction of future events and wrong models. The failure of Long Term Capital Management (LTCM) provides an example of the risk associated with hedge fund investing. John Meriwether, a former fixed income trader at Salomon Brothers, founded LTCM in 1993. Teamed up with a group of veteran Wall Street traders and two Nobel laureates, Myron Scholes and Robert Merton, LTCM enjoyed a solid credibility and respectability among the investment community. Using its good name, LTCM pursued highly leveraged fixed income arbitrage strategies. Among other things, LTCM borrowed heavily and bet on international interest convergence between high- and low-quality debts. For example, LTCM bought Italian government bonds and sold German Bund futures. Initially, LTCM did well, realizing about 40 percent annual returns on equity in the first few years. But following the Asian and Russian currency crises, gradual convergence turned into a dramatic divergence. As a result, LTCM's debts increased and its capital base depleted, eventually leading to its downfall. Investors lost large sums of money.

Why Home Bias in Portfolio Holdings?

As previously documented, investors can potentially benefit a great deal from international diversification. The actual portfolios that investors hold, however, are quite different from those predicted by the theory of international portfolio investment. Recently, various researchers, such as French and Poterba (1991), Cooper and Kaplanis (1994), Tesar and Werner (1993), Glassman and Riddick (1993), and Chan, Covrig, and Ng (2005), documented the extent to which portfolio investments are concentrated in domestic equities.

Exhibit 15.15, which is adopted from Lau, Ng, and Zhang (2010), shows the extent of **home bias in portfolio holdings**. U.S. mutual funds, for instance, invested about 87 percent of their funds in domestic equities on average during 1998–2007, when the U.S. stock market accounted for about 45 percent of the world market capitalization value during the period. Relatively speaking, German mutual funds seem to invest more internationally—they put 71 percent of their funds in foreign equities and 29 percent in domestic equities. Considering, however, that the German share in the world market value is only 3.2 percent, German funds also display a striking degree of home bias in their portfolio holdings. It is noted that Brazilian mutual funds invested exclusively in domestic equities, probably due to regulatory restrictions. In recent years, investors have begun to invest in foreign securities in earnest. But, most investors still exhibit a strong home bias in portfolio holdings.

This home bias in actual portfolio holdings obviously runs counter to the strand of literature, including Grubel (1968), Levy and Sarnat (1970), Solnik (1974), Lessard (1976), and Eun and Resnick (1988), that collectively established a strong case for international diversification. This points to the following possibilities. First, domestic securities may provide investors with certain extra services, such as hedging against domestic inflation, that foreign securities do not. Second, there may be barriers, formal or informal, to investing in foreign securities that keep investors from realizing gains from international diversification. In what follows, we are going to examine possible reasons for the home bias in portfolio holdings.[20]

EXHIBIT 15.15

The Home Bias in Equity Portfolios: Selected Countries, 1998–2007

Country	Share in the World Market Value (%)	Proportion of Local Equities in Domestic Mutual Funds (%)
Australia	1.70	78.91
Brazil	0.71	100.00
Canada	2.67	28.67
France	4.13	55.48
Germany	3.21	29.35
Japan	9.29	98.50
Sweden	1.00	48.56
United Kingdom	7.64	42.95
United States	44.86	86.88

Source: Adopted from S.T. Lau et al., "The World Price of Home Bias," *Journal of Financial Economics* 97 (2010), pp. 191–217.

[20]For a survey of this issue, readers are referred to Uppal (1992).

First, consider the possibility that investors face country-specific inflation risk due to the violations of purchasing power parity and that domestic equities may provide a hedging service against domestic inflation risk. In this case, investors who would like to hedge domestic inflation risk may allocate a disproportionate share of their investment funds to domestic equities, resulting in home bias. This, however, is not a likely scenario. Those investors who are averse to inflation risk are likely to invest in domestic risk-free bonds rather than domestic equities, as the latter tends to be a poor hedge against inflation.[21] In addition, a study by Cooper and Kaplanis (1994) rules out inflation hedging as a primary cause for home bias.

Second, the observed home bias may reflect institutional and legal restrictions on foreign investments. For example, many countries used to restrict foreigners' ownership share of domestic firms. In Finland, foreigners could own at most 30 percent of the shares outstanding of any Finnish firm. In Korea, foreigners' ownership proportion was restricted to 20 percent of any Korean firm. As a result, foreigners had to pay premiums for local shares, which may reduce the gains from investing in those restricted markets. At the same time, some institutional investors may not invest more than a certain fraction of their funds overseas under the so-called *prudent man rule*. For example, Japanese insurance companies and Spanish pension funds may invest at most 30 percent of their funds in foreign securities. These inflow and outflow restrictions may contribute to the home bias in actual portfolio holdings.

Third, extra taxes and transaction/information costs for foreign securities can inhibit cross-border investments, giving rise to home bias. Investors often have to pay withholding taxes on dividends from foreign securities for which they may or may not receive tax credits in their home country. Transaction costs can be higher for foreign securities partly because many foreign markets are relatively thin and illiquid and partly because investment in foreign securities often involves transactions in foreign exchange markets. What's more, as argued by Merton (1987), investors tend not to hold securities with which they do not feel familiar. To the extent that investors feel familiar with domestic securities, but not with foreign securities, they are going to allocate funds to domestic, but not to foreign, securities. Consistent with the familiarity bias, Chan, Covrig, and Ng (2005) found that when a country is more remote from the rest of the world and has an uncommon language, domestic (foreign) investors tend to invest more (less) in the country's market. It is even possible that some investors may not be fully aware of the potential gains from international investments. Bailey, Kumar, and Ng (2004) found that the degree of home bias varies across investors. Using brokerage records of tens of thousands of U.S. individual investors, they examined ownership and trading of U.S.-listed foreign stocks and closed-end country funds. They found that wealthier, more experienced, and sophisticated investors are more likely to invest in foreign securities.

The observed home bias in asset holdings is likely to reflect a combination of some of the factors mentioned above. Considering the ongoing integration of international financial markets, coupled with the active financial innovations introducing new financial products such as country funds and international mutual funds, home bias may be substantially mitigated in the near future.

International Diversification with Small-Cap Stocks

To the extent that investors diversify internationally, well-known, large-cap stocks receive the dominant share of fund allocation. There is no doubt "large-cap bias" as well as home bias in international investment. These biases are broadly consistent with

---

[21]Fama and Schwert (1975) showed that common stocks are a perverse hedge against domestic inflation in that returns to common stocks are significantly negatively correlated with the inflation rate. In comparison, bond returns are positively correlated with the inflation rate.

EXHIBIT 15.16

The Average Return
Correlation among 10 Major
International Stock Markets
over Time, 1981–2015[a]

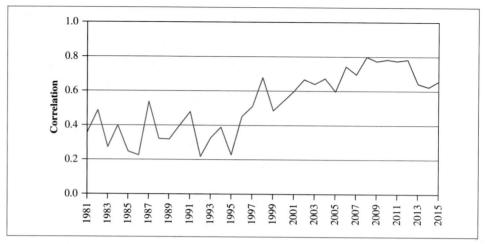

[a]The 10 markets are Australia, Canada, France, Germany, Hong Kong, Italy, Japan, the Netherlands, the United
Kingdom, and the United States. Weekly stock market index returns, in U.S. dollars, are used to compute the
correlations for each year of the study period.
Source: *Datastream.*

the proposition that "familiarity breeds investment."[22] Increasingly, however, returns to
large-cap stocks or stock market indexes that are dominated by large-cap stocks tend
to comove, mitigating the benefit from international diversification. This point is illustrated in Exhibit 15.16, which plots the average return correlation among 10 major
international stock markets over time. As can be seen in the exhibit, the average correlation among international stock market returns was fluctuating around 0.37 until the
mid-1990s, but it has been generally increasing since then. It is noted that the average correlation reached nearly 0.80 in 2009, when the global financial crisis was at its
height. The rising tendency of international correlations in recent years led many investors to become doubtful about the benefit and wisdom of international diversification.

Many well-known large-cap stocks that are popular among international investors
are likely to be those of multinational firms with a substantial foreign customer and
investor base. In contrast, small-cap firms are likely to be locally oriented with a limited international exposure. As a result, returns on large-cap stocks would be substantially driven by common "global factors," whereas returns on small-cap stocks
are likely to be primarily driven by "local factors." This implies that locally oriented,
small-cap stocks may be an effective vehicle for international diversification. In a
recent study, Eun, Huang, and Lai (2008) confirmed that this is indeed the case.

Exhibit 15.17, which is based on the aforementioned study, provides a summary of
the risk-return characteristics of large-cap versus small-cap funds of 10 major markets
during the study period 1980–1999. For each fund, the exhibit provides the annualized
mean return (Mean), standard deviation of return (SD), the Sharpe performance measure (SHP), and the correlation with the U.S. stock market index [Cor(US)]. As can be
seen from the last row of the exhibit, small-cap funds, on average, have a much higher
mean return (21.1%) than large-cap funds (16.6%). This confirms the existence of the
so-called "small-cap premium" in most countries, with the exception of two countries:
the Netherlands and the United States. As expected, the standard deviation of returns
is, on average, higher for small-cap funds (25.3%) than for large-cap funds (22.3%).
The Sharpe performance measure indicates that the small-cap fund outperformed
the large-cap counterpart in each country, except for the same two countries: the
Netherlands and the United States.

---

[22]This proposition is due to Huberman (2001). In a similar vein, Leuz, Lins, and Warnock (2009) show that
foreigners tend to invest less in firms with poor disclosure (less reliable information) and governance standards.

EXHIBIT 15.17	Large- versus Small-Cap Funds: Risk-Return Characteristics							
	Large-Cap Funds				**Small-Cap Funds**			
Countries	Mean	SD	SHP	Cor (US)	Mean	SD	SHP	Cor (US)
Australia	14.9%	25.7%	0.32	0.45	24.9%	33.1%	0.55	0.22
Canada	10.9%	17.9%	0.24	0.71	24.6%	22.5%	0.80	0.45
France	15.3%	21.9%	0.40	0.46	17.2%	21.9%	0.48	0.27
Germany	14.4%	20.1%	0.39	0.41	14.6%	16.5%	0.48	0.19
Hong Kong	22.1%	34.3%	0.45	0.38	27.6%	39.7%	0.53	0.26
Italy	20.0%	27.7%	0.48	0.26	23.2%	27.2%	0.61	0.21
Japan	15.6%	24.2%	0.37	0.22	23.1%	27.8%	0.59	0.13
Netherlands	18.4%	16.2%	0.73	0.61	16.3%	18.4%	0.52	0.20
U.K.	17.3%	19.1%	0.56	0.54	24.0%	23.7%	0.73	0.31
U.S.	17.4%	15.1%	0.71	0.99	15.9%	21.7%	0.43	0.55
Average	16.6%	22.2%	0.46	0.50	21.1%	25.3%	0.57	0.28

Source: Cheol Eun, Victor Huang, and Sandy Lai, "International Diversification with Large- and Small-Cap Stocks," *Journal of Financial and Quantitative Analysis* 43 (2008), pp. 489–524.

Importantly, the small-cap fund is much less correlated with the U.S. stock market index than its large-cap counterpart in each of the 10 countries examined, without exception. For instance, the correlation of the Netherlands small-cap (large-cap) fund with the U.S. market index is 0.20 (0.61). Although not shown in the exhibit, small-cap funds have low correlations not only with large-cap funds but also with each other. For instance, the correlation of the Netherlands small-cap fund with the U.S. small-cap fund is only 0.17. In contrast, large-cap funds tend to have relatively high correlations with each other, reflecting their common exposure to global factors. Thus, small-cap stocks can potentially be a very effective vehicle for international diversification.

Against this backdrop, investment companies recently have introduced many small-cap-oriented international mutual funds, allowing investors to diversify into foreign small-cap stocks without incurring excessive transaction costs. Investment companies, including Fidelity, ING, Lazard, Merrill Lynch, Morgan Stanley, Oppenheimer, and Templeton, currently offer a variety of small-cap-focused international funds. In terms of geographical coverage, some funds are global and international, such as Templeton Global Smaller Companies Fund and Fidelity International Small Cap Fund, while others are regional and national, such as AIM Europe Small Company Fund and DFA Japanese Small Company Fund. To conclude, investors can clearly enhance the gains from international investment by augmenting their portfolios with foreign small-cap stocks.

SUMMARY

This chapter discusses the gains from international portfolio diversification, which emerged as a major form of cross-border investment in the 1980s, rivaling foreign direct investment by firms.

1. International portfolio investment (IPI) has been growing rapidly in recent years due to (a) the deregulation of financial markets, and (b) the introduction of such investment vehicles as international mutual funds, country funds, and internationally cross-listed stocks, which allow investors to achieve international diversification without incurring excessive costs.

2. Investors diversify to reduce risk; the extent to which the risk is reduced by diversification depends on the covariances among individual securities making up the portfolio. Since security returns tend to covary much less across countries than

within a country, investors can reduce portfolio risk more by diversifying internationally than purely domestically.

3. In a full-fledged risk-return analysis, investors can gain from international diversification in terms of "extra" returns at the "domestic-equivalent" risk level. Empirical evidence indicates that regardless of domicile and the numeraire currency used to measure returns, investors can capture extra returns when they hold their optimal international portfolios.

4. Foreign exchange rate uncertainty contributes to the risk of foreign investment through its own volatility as well as through its covariance with local market returns. Generally speaking, exchange rates are substantially more volatile than bond market returns but less so than stock market returns. This suggests that investors can enhance their gains from international diversification, especially in the case of bond investment, when they hedge exchange risk using, say, forward contracts.

5. U.S.-based international mutual funds that investors actually held did provide investors with an effective global risk diversification. In addition, the majority of them outperformed the U.S. stock market index in terms of the Sharpe performance measure. Closed-end country funds (CECFs) also provided U.S. investors with an opportunity to achieve international diversification at home. CECFs, however, were found to behave more like U.S. securities in comparison with their underlying net asset values (NAVs).

6. Despite sizable potential gains from international diversification, investors allocate a disproportionate share of their funds to domestic securities, displaying so-called home bias. Home bias is likely to reflect imperfections in the international financial markets such as excessive transaction/information costs, discriminatory taxes for foreigners, and legal/institutional barriers to international investments.

KEY WORDS

closed-end country fund (CECF), *380*
exchange-traded funds (ETFs), *384*
gains from international diversification, *366*
home bias in portfolio holdings, *386*

international correlation structure, *366*
optimal international portfolios (OIPs), *368*
portfolio risk diversification, *366*
Sharpe performance measure (SHP), *370*

systematic risk, *367*
world beta, *370*
World Equity Benchmark Shares (WEBS), *384*

QUESTIONS

1. What factors are responsible for the recent surge in international portfolio investment?

2. Security returns are found to be less correlated across countries than within a country. Why can this be?

3. Explain the concept of the world beta of a security.

4. Explain the concept of the Sharpe performance measure.

5. Explain how exchange rate fluctuations affect the return from a foreign market, measured in dollar terms. Discuss the empirical evidence for the effect of exchange rate uncertainty on the risk of foreign investment.

6. Would exchange rate changes always increase the risk of foreign investment? Discuss the condition under which exchange rate changes may actually reduce the risk of foreign investment.

7. Evaluate a home country's multinational corporations as a tool for international diversification.

8. Discuss the advantages and disadvantages of closed-end country funds (CECFs) relative to American depository receipts (ADRs) as a means of international diversification.

9. Why do you think closed-end country funds often trade at a premium or discount?

10. Why do investors invest the lion's share of their funds in domestic securities?

11. What are the advantages of investing via international mutual funds?

12. Discuss how the advent of the euro would affect international diversification strategies.

PROBLEMS

1. Suppose you are a euro-based investor who just sold Microsoft shares that you had bought six months ago. You had invested 10,000 euros to buy Microsoft shares for $120 per share; the exchange rate was $1.15 per euro. You sold the stock for $135 per share and converted the dollar proceeds into euro at the exchange rate of $1.06 per euro. First, determine the profit from this investment in euro terms. Second, compute the rate of return on your investment in euro terms. How much of the return is due to the exchange rate movement?

2. Mr. James K. Silber, an avid international investor, just sold a share of Nestlé, a Swiss firm, for SF5,080. The share was bought for SF4,600 a year ago. The exchange rate is SF1.60 per U.S. dollar now and was SF1.78 per dollar a year ago. Mr. Silber received SF120 as a cash dividend immediately before the share was sold. Compute the rate of return on this investment in terms of U.S. dollars.

3. In problem 2, suppose that Mr. Silber sold SF4,600, his principal investment amount, forward at the forward exchange rate of SF1.62 per dollar. How would this affect the dollar rate of return on this Swiss stock investment? In hindsight, should Mr. Silber have sold the Swiss franc amount forward or not? Why or why not?

4. Japan Life Insurance Company invested $10,000,000 in pure-discount U.S. bonds in May 1995 when the exchange rate was 80 yen per dollar. The company liquidated the investment one year later for $10,650,000. The exchange rate turned out to be 110 yen per dollar at the time of liquidation. What rate of return did Japan Life realize on this investment in yen terms?

5. At the start of 1996, the annual interest rate was 6 percent in the United States and 2.8 percent in Japan. The exchange rate was 95 yen per dollar at the time. Mr. Jorus, who is the manager of a Bermuda-based hedge fund, thought that the substantial interest advantage associated with investing in the United States relative to investing in Japan was not likely to be offset by the decline of the dollar against the yen. He thus concluded that it might be a good idea to borrow in Japan and invest in the United States. At the start of 1996, in fact, he borrowed ¥1,000 million for one year and invested in the United States. At the end of 1996, the exchange rate became 105 yen per dollar. How much profit did Mr. Jorus make in dollar terms?

6. Suppose we obtain the following data in dollar terms:

Stock Market	Return (Mean)	Risk (SD)
United States	1.26% per month	4.43%
United Kingdom	1.23% per month	5.55%

The correlation coefficient between the two markets is 0.58. Suppose that you invest equally, that is, 50 percent in each of the two markets. Determine the

expected return and standard deviation risk of the resulting international portfolio.[23] This problem can be solved using the spreadsheet MPTSolver.xls.

7. Suppose you are interested in investing in the stock markets of seven countries—i.e., Australia, Canada, Germany, Japan, Switzerland, the United Kingdom, and the United States—the same seven countries that appear in Exhibit 15.9. Specifically, you would like to solve for the optimal (tangency) portfolio comprising the above seven stock markets. In solving the optimal portfolio, use the input data (i.e., correlation coefficients, means, and standard deviations) provided in Exhibit 15.4. The risk-free interest rate is assumed to be 0.2 percent per month and you can take a short position in any stock market. What are the optimal weights for each of the seven stock markets? What are the risk and return of the optimal portfolio? This problem can be solved using the MPTSolver.xls spreadsheet.

8. The HFS Trustees have solicited input from three consultants concerning the risks and rewards of an allocation to international equities. Two of them strongly favor such action, while the third consultant commented as follows:

"The risk reduction benefits of international investing have been significantly overstated. Recent studies relating to the cross-country correlation structure of equity returns during different market phases cast serious doubt on the ability of international investing to reduce risk, especially in situations when risk reduction is needed the most."

a. Describe the behavior of cross-country equity return correlations to which the consultant is referring. Explain how that behavior may diminish the ability of international investing to reduce risk in the short run.

Assume the consultant's assertion is correct.

b. Explain why it might still be more efficient on a risk/reward basis to invest internationally rather than only domestically in the long run.

The HFS Trustees have decided to invest in non-U.S. equity markets and have hired Jacob Hind, a specialist manager, to implement this decision. He has recommended that an unhedged equities position be taken in Japan, providing the following comment and the table data to support his views:

"Appreciation of a foreign currency increases the returns to a U.S. dollar investor. Since appreciation of the Yen from 100¥/$U.S. to 98¥/$U.S. is expected, the Japanese stock position should not be hedged."

Market Rates and Hind's Expectations

	U.S.	Japan
Spot rate (yen per $U.S.)	n/a	100
Hind's 12-month currency forecast (yen per $U.S.)	n/a	98
1-year Eurocurrency rate (% per annum)	6.00	0.80
Hind's 1-year inflation forecast (% per annum)	3.00	0.50

Assume that the investment horizon is one year and that there are no costs associated with currency hedging.

---

[23]The mean return on the portfolio is simply the weighted average of the returns on the individual securities that are included in the portfolio. The portfolio variance, on the other hand, can be computed using the following formula:

$$\text{Var}(R_p) = \Sigma_i \Sigma_j x_i x_j \sigma_{ij}$$

where x_i represents an investment weight for the ith security, and σ_{ij} denotes the variances and covariances among individual securities. In the case where the portfolio is composed of two securities, its variance is computed as follows:

$$\text{Var}(R_p) = x_1^2 \sigma_1^2 + x_2^2 \sigma_2^2 + 2x_1 x_2 \sigma_{12}$$

The standard deviation, of course, is the square root of the variance. It is also noted that the covariance σ_{ij} is related to the correlation coefficient ρ_{ij} via $\sigma_{ij} = \rho_{ij} \sigma_i \sigma_j$, where σ_i is the standard deviation of returns on the ith security.

c. State and justify whether Hind's recommendation (not to hedge) should be followed. Show any calculations.

9. Rebecca Taylor, an international equity portfolio manager, recognizes that an optimal country allocation strategy combined with an optimal currency strategy should produce optimal portfolio performance. To develop her strategies, Taylor produced the following table, which provides expected return data for the three countries and three currencies in which she may invest. The table contains the information she needs to make market strategy (country allocation) decisions and currency strategy (currency allocation) decisions.

Expected Returns for a U.S.-Based Investor

Country	Local Currency Equity Returns	Exchange Rate Returns	Local Currency Eurodeposit Returns
Japan	7.0%	1.0%	5.0%
United Kingdom	10.5	−3.0	11.0
United States	8.4	0.0	7.5

a. Prepare a ranking of the three countries in terms of expected equity-market return premiums. Show your calculations.

b. Prepare a ranking of the three countries in terms of expected currency return premiums from the perspective of a U.S. investor. Show your calculations.

c. Explain *one* advantage a portfolio manager obtains, in formulating a global investment strategy, by calculating both expected market premiums and expected currency premiums.

10. The Glover Scholastic Aid Foundation has received a €20 million global government bond portfolio from a Greek donor. This bond portfolio will be held in euros and managed separately from Glover's existing U.S. dollar-denominated assets. Although the bond portfolio is currently unhedged, the portfolio manager, Raine Sofia, is investigating various alternatives to hedge the currency risk of the portfolio. The bond portfolio's current allocation and the relevant country performance data are given in Exhibits 1 and 2. Historical correlations for the currencies being considered by Sofia are given in Exhibit 3. Sofia expects that future returns and correlations will be approximately equal to those given in Exhibits 2 and 3.

Exhibit 1. Glover Scholastic Aid Foundation Current Allocation Global Government Bond Portfolio

Country	Allocation (%)	Maturity (years)
Greece	25	5
A	40	5
B	10	10
C	10	5
D	15	10

Exhibit 2. Country Performance Data (in local currency)

Country	Cash Return (%)	5-year Excess Bond Return (%)	10-year Excess Bond Return (%)	Unhedged Currency Return (%)	Liquidity of 90-day Currency Forward Contracts
Greece	2.0	1.5	2.0	—	Good
A	1.0	2.0	3.0	−4.0	Good
B	4.0	0.5	1.0	2.0	Fair
C	3.0	1.0	2.0	−2.0	Fair
D	2.6	1.4	2.4	−3.0	Good

www.mhhe.com/er8e

Exhibit 3. Historical Currency Correlation Table (1998–2003, weekly observations)

Currency	€ (Greece)	A	B	C	D
€ (Greece)	1.00	−0.77	0.45	−0.57	0.77
A	—	1.00	−0.61	0.56	−0.70
B	—	—	1.00	−0.79	0.88
C	—	—	—	1.00	−0.59
D	—	—	—	—	1.00

a. Calculate the expected total annual return (euro-based) of the current bond portfolio if Sofia decides to leave the currency risk unhedged. Show your calculations.

b. Explain, with respect to currency exposure and forward rates, the circumstance in which Sofia should use a currency forward contact to hedge the current bond portfolio's exposure to a given currency.

c. Determine which *one* of the currencies being considered by Sofia should be the *best* proxy hedge for Country B bonds. Justify your response with *two* reasons.

Sofia has been disappointed with the low returns on the current bond portfolio relative to the benchmark—a diversified global bond index—and is exploring general strategies to generate excess returns on the portfolio. She has already researched two such strategies: duration management and investing in markets outside the benchmark index.

d. Identify *three* general strategies (other than duration management and investing in markets outside the benchmark index) that Sofia could use to generate excess returns on the current bond portfolio. Give, for *each* of the three strategies, a potential benefit specific to the current bond portfolio.

INTERNET EXERCISES

WWW

1. You would like to invest in the Mexican stock market and consider two alternative ways of investing in Mexico: (i) the Mexican closed-end country fund trading on the New York Stock Exchange (NYSE) and (ii) the iShares MSCI Mexico ETF trading on the NYSE/Arca. Their websites are,

   www.themexicofund.com

   us.ishares.com/product_info/fund/overview/EWW.htm

   Study all the relevant information from the websites and evaluate the relative merits and demerits of the two securities for your Mexican investment. Which one would you prefer?

MINI CASE

Solving for the Optimal International Portfolio

Suppose you are a financial adviser and your client, who is currently investing only in the U.S. stock market, is considering diversifying into the U.K. stock market. At the moment, there are neither particular barriers nor restrictions on investing in the U.K. stock market. Your client would like to know what kinds of benefits can be expected from doing so. Using the data provided in problem 6, solve the following problems:

1. Graphically illustrate various combinations of portfolio risk and return that can be generated by investing in the U.S. and U.K. stock markets with different proportions. Two extreme proportions are (a) investing 100 percent in the United States with no position in the U.K. market, and (b) investing 100 percent in the U.K. market with no position in the U.S. market.

2. Solve for the optimal international portfolio comprising the U.S. and U.K. markets. Assume that the monthly risk-free interest rate is 0.5 percent and that investors can take a short (negative) position in either market. This problem can be solved using the spreadsheet MPTSolver.xls.

3. What is the extra return that U.S. investors can expect to capture at the U.S.-equivalent risk level? Also trace out the efficient set. Appendix 15.B provides an example.

REFERENCES & SUGGESTED READINGS

Adler, Michael, and Bernard Dumas. "International Portfolio Choice and Corporation Finance: A Synthesis." *Journal of Finance* 38 (1983), pp. 925–84.

Bailey, Warren, and J. Lim. "Evaluating the Diversification Benefits of the New Country Funds." *Journal of Portfolio Management* 18 (1992), pp. 74–80.

Bailey, Warren, Alok Kumar, and David Ng. "Venturing Abroad: Foreign Investments of U.S. Individual Investors." Working Paper (2004).

Bonser-Neal, C., G. Brauer, R. Neal, and S. Wheatley. "International Investment Restriction and Closed-End Country Fund Prices." *Journal of Finance* 45 (1990), pp. 523–47.

Chan, Kalok, Vicentiu Covrig, and Lilian Ng. "What Determines the Domestic Bias and Foreign Bias? Evidence from Mutual Fund Equity Allocations Worldwide." *Journal of Finance* 60 (2005), pp. 1495–1534.

Chuppe, T., H. Haworth, and M. Watkins. "Global Finance: Causes, Consequences and Prospects for the Future." *Global Finance Journal* 1 (1989), pp. 1–20.

Cooper, Ian, and Evi Kaplanis. "Home Bias in Equity Portfolios, Inflation Hedging, and International Capital Market Equilibrium." *Review of Financial Studies* 7 (1994), pp. 45–60.

Cumby, R., and J. Glen. "Evaluating the Performance of International Mutual Funds." *Journal of Finance* 45 (1990), pp. 497–521.

Errunza, Vihang, Ked Hogan, and Mao-Wei Hung. "Can the Gains from International Diversification Be Achieved without Trading Abroad?" *Journal of Finance* (1999), 2075–2107.

Eun, Cheol, and Bruce Resnick. "Exchange Rate Uncertainty, Forward Contracts and International Portfolio Selection." *Journal of Finance* 43 (1988), pp. 197–215.

Eun, Cheol, and Bruce Resnick. "International Diversification of Investment Portfolios: U.S. and Japanese Perspectives." *Management Science* 40 (1994), pp. 140–61.

Eun, Cheol, and Bruce Resnick. "International Equity Investments with Selective Hedging Strategies." *Journal of International Financial Markets,* Institutions and Money 7 (1997), pp. 21–42.

Eun, Cheol, Richard Kolodny, and Bruce Resnick. "Performance of U.S.-Based International Mutual Funds." *Journal of Portfolio Management* 17 (1991), pp. 88–94.

Eun, Cheol, Victor Huang, and Sandy Lai. "International Diversification with Large- and Small-Cap Stocks." *Journal of Financial and Quantitative Analysis* 43 (2008), pp. 489–524.

Fama, Eugene, and W. G. Schwert. "Asset Returns and Inflation." *Journal of Financial Economics* 5 (1975), pp. 115–46.

French, K., and J. Poterba. "Investor Diversification and International Equity Markets." *American Economic Review* 81 (1991), pp. 222–26.

Fung, William, and David Hsieh. "A Primer on Hedge Funds." *Journal of Empirical Finance* 6 (1999), pp. 309–31.

Glassman, Debra, and Leigh Riddick. "Why Empirical Portfolio Models Fail: Evidence That Model Misspecification Creates Home Asset Bias." Unpublished manuscript, 1993.

Grubel, H. G. "Internationally Diversified Portfolios." *American Economic Review* 58 (1968), pp. 1299–1314.

Huberman, G. "Familiarity Breeds Investment." *Review of Financial Studies* 14 (2001), pp. 659–80.

Jacquillat, B., and B. Solnik. "Multinationals Are Poor Tools for Diversification." *Journal of Portfolio Management* 4 (1978), pp. 8–12.

Jorion, Philippe. "Asset Allocation with Hedged and Unhedged Foreign Stocks and Bonds." *Journal of Portfolio Management* 15 (Summer 1989), pp. 49–54.

Khorana, A., E. Nelling, and J. Trester. "The Emergence of Country Index Funds." *Journal of Portfolio Management* (Summer 1998), pp. 78–84.

Larsen, Glen, Jr., and Bruce Resnick. "Universal Currency Hedging for International Equity Portfolios under Parameter Uncertainty." *International Journal of Business* 4 (1999), pp. 1–17.

Larsen, Glen, Jr., and Bruce Resnick. "The Optimal Construction of Internationally Diversified Equity Portfolios Hedged against Exchange Rate Uncertainty." *European Financial Management* 6 (2000), pp. 479–514.

Lessard, D. "World, Country and Industry Relationship in Equity Returns: Implications for Risk Reduction through International Diversification." *Financial Analyst Journal* 32 (1976), pp. 22–28.

Leuz, C., Karl Lins, and Francis Warnock. "Do Foreigners Invest Less in Poorly Governed Firms?" *Reivew of Financial Studies* 22 (2009), pp. 3245–85.

Levy, H., and L. Sarnat. "International Diversification of Investment Portfolios." *American Economic Review* 60 (1970), pp. 668–75.

Longin, Francois, and Bruneo Solnik. "Is the Correlation in International Equity Returns Constant?: 1960–1990." *Journal of International Money and Finance* 14 (1995), pp. 3–26.

Merton, R. "A Simple Model of Capital Market Equilibrium with Incomplete Information." *Journal of Finance* 42 (1987), pp. 483–510.

Officer, Dennis, and Ronald Hoffmeister. "ADRs: A Substitute for the Real Thing?" *Journal of Portfolio Management* (Winter 1987), pp. 61–65.

Roll, Richard. "The International Crash of 1987." *Financial Analyst Journal* 44 (1988), pp. 19–35.

Sener, T. "Objectives of Hedging and Optimal Hedge Ratios: U.S. vs. Japanese Investors." *Journal of Multinational Financial Management* 8 (1998), pp. 137–53.

Sharpe, W. "Mutual Fund Performance." *Journal of Business,* A Supplement, No. 1, Part 2 (1966), pp. 119–38.

Solnik, Bruno. "Why Not Diversify Internationally?" *Financial Analyst Journal* 20 (1974), pp. 48–54.

Solnik, Bruno, and J. Roulet. "Dispersion as Cross-sectional, Correlation." *Financial Analyst Journal* 56 (2000), pp. 54–61.

Tesar, L., and I. Werner. "Home Bias and High Turnover." Unpublished manuscript, 1993.

Uppal, Raman. "The Economic Determinants of the Home Country Bias in Investors' Portfolios: A Survey." *Journal of International Financial Management and Accounting* 4 (1992), pp. 171–89.

Wahab, Mahmood, and Amit Khandwala. "Why Not Diversify Internationally with ADRs?" *Journal of Portfolio Management* (Winter 1993), pp. 75–82.

15A International Investment with Exchange Risk Hedging

In this appendix we show how hedging the exchange rate risk in an international portfolio can enhance the risk-return efficiency of an internationally diversified portfolio of financial assets. We begin by restating Equations 15.4 and 15.5 from the text that state the return and variance of return to a U.S. dollar investor from investing in individual foreign security i:

$$R_{i\$} = (1 + R_i)(1 + e_i) - 1 \tag{15A.1a}$$

$$= R_i + e_i + R_i e_i \tag{15A.1b}$$

$$\approx R_i + e_i. \tag{15A.1c}$$

In Equation 15A.1c, we ignore the cross-product term, $R_i e_i$, which is generally small, for discussion purposes. Consequently, the expected return to the U.S. dollar investor from investing in foreign security i can be approximated as,

$$\overline{R}_{i\$} \approx \overline{R}_i + \overline{e}_i \tag{15A.2}$$

Also, we can express the variance of dollar returns from the ith foreign security as follows:

$$\text{Var}(R_{i\$}) = \text{Var}(R_i) + \text{Var}(e_i) + 2\text{Cov}(R_i, e_i) \tag{15A.3}$$

Similarly, we can state the covariance between dollar returns from two different foreign securities as follows:

$$\text{Cov}(R_{i\$}, R_{j\$}) = \text{Cov}(R_i, R_j) + \text{Cov}(e_i, e_j) + \text{Cov}(R_i, e_j) + \text{Cov}(R_j, e_i) \tag{15A.4}$$

Now consider a simple exchange risk hedging strategy in which the U.S. dollar investor sells the expected foreign currency proceeds forward. In dollar terms, it amounts to exchanging the "uncertain" dollar return, $(1 + \overline{R}_i)(1 + e_i) - 1$, for the "certain" dollar return, $(1 + \overline{R}_i)(1 + f_i) - 1$, where $f_i = (F_i - S_i)/S_i$ is the forward exchange premium of the currency denominating security i. Although the expected foreign investment proceeds will be converted into U.S. dollars at the known forward exchange rate under this strategy, the unexpected foreign investment proceeds will have to be converted into U.S. dollars at the uncertain future spot exchange rate. The dollar rate of return under the hedging (H) strategy is thus given by

$$\overline{R}_{i\$H} = [1 + \overline{R}_i](1 + f_i) + [R_i - \overline{R}_i](1 + e_i) - 1 \tag{15A.5a}$$

$$= R_i + f_i + R_i e_i + \overline{R}_i(f_i - e_i) \tag{15A.5b}$$

Since the third and fourth terms of Equation 15A.5b are likely to be small in magnitude, the expected hedged return for the U.S. dollar investor can be approximated as follows:

$$\overline{R}_{i\$H} \approx \overline{R}_i + f_i \tag{15A.6}$$

Recall from the forward expectations parity discussion in Chapter 6 that f_i can be an unbiased estimate of $\overline{e}_i$, i.e., $f_i = \overline{e}_i$. Comparison of Equations 15A.1c and 15A.6 thus indicates that the expected return to the U.S. dollar investor is approximately the same whether the investor hedges the exchange rate risk in the investment, or remains unhedged.

To the extent that the investor establishes an effective hedge to eliminate exchange rate uncertainty, the $\text{Var}(e_i)$ and $\text{Cov}(R_i, e_i)$ terms in Equation 15A.3 will be close to zero. Similarly, the $\text{Cov}(e_i, e_j)$, $\text{Cov}(R_i, e_j)$, and $\text{Cov}(R_j, e_i)$ terms in Equation 15A.4 will be close to zero. Consequently, given that f_i is a constant, it follows that

$$\text{Var}(R_{i\$H}) < \text{Var}(R_{i\$}), \text{ and}$$

$$\text{Cov}(R_{i\$H}, R_{j\$H}) < \text{Cov}(R_{i\$}, R_{j\$}).$$

The empirical results presented in Exhibit 15.8 generally support these relationships. It thus follows that the risk-return efficiency is likely to be superior if the investor hedges the exchange rate risk when investing internationally.

15B Solving for the Optimal Portfolio

Here we explain how to solve for the optimal portfolio of risky securities when there exists a risk-free asset paying a certain risk-free interest rate, R_f. Once we assume that investors prefer more wealth to less and are averse to risk, we can solve for the "optimal" portfolio by maximizing the Sharpe ratio (SHPp) of the excess portfolio return to the standard deviation risk. In other words,

$$\text{Max SHPp} = [\overline{R}_p - R_f]/\sigma_p \tag{15B.1}$$

where $\overline{R}_p$ is the expected rate of return on the portfolio and σ_p is the standard deviation of the portfolio returns.

The expected portfolio return, $\overline{R}_p$, is just the weighted average of the expected returns to individual assets, $\overline{R}_i$, included in the portfolio, that is,

$$\overline{R}_p = \Sigma_i x_i \overline{R}_i \tag{15B.2}$$

where x_i denotes a fraction of wealth invested in the ith individual asset; the sum of fractions should add up to 1, that is, $\Sigma_i x_i = 1$. The portfolio risk, σ_p, on the other hand, is related to the variances and covariances of individual asset returns as follows:

$$\sigma_p = [\Sigma_i \Sigma_j x_i x_j \sigma_{ij}]^{1/2} \tag{15B.3}$$

where σ_{ij} denotes the covariance of returns to the ith and jth assets. What's inside the bracket is the variance of portfolio return.

Now let us consider a simple case where the portfolio includes only two risky assets, A and B. In this case, the risk and return of the portfolio will be determined as follows:

$$\overline{R}_p = x_A \overline{R}_A + x_B \overline{R}_B \tag{15B.4}$$

$$\sigma_p = [x_A^2 \sigma_A^2 + x_B^2 \sigma_B^2 + 2 x_A x_B \sigma_{AB}]^{1/2} \tag{15B.5}$$

Suppose we now want to solve for the optimal portfolio using the two assets. We then first substitute Equations 15B.4 and 15B.5 in Equation 15B.1 and maximize SHPp with respect to the portfolio weights x's to obtain the following solution:

$$x_A = \frac{[\overline{R}_A - R_f]\sigma_B^2 - [\overline{R}_B - R_f]\sigma_{AB}}{[\overline{R}_A - R_f]\sigma_B^2 + [\overline{R}_B - R_f]\sigma_A^2 - [\overline{R}_A - R_f + \overline{R}_B - R_f]\sigma_{AB}}$$

$$x_B = 1 - x_A \tag{15B.6}$$

EXAMPLE Suppose we are trying to construct the optimal international portfolio using the U.S. (US) and Netherlands (NL) stock market indexes. From the period 1980.1–2012.12, we obtain the following data (in percentage per month) for the two stock markets:

$$\overline{R}_{US} = 0.647; \qquad \sigma_{US}^2 = 21.07$$

$$\overline{R}_{NL} = 0.635; \qquad \sigma_{NL}^2 = 35.64$$

$$\sigma_{US,NL} = \sigma_{US}\sigma_{NL}\rho_{US,NL} = (4.59)(5.97)(0.73) = 20.00$$

Using the monthly risk-free rate of 0.023 percent, we can substitute the given data into Equation 15B.6 to obtain

$$x_{US} = \frac{(0.647 - 0.023)(35.64) - (0.635 - 0.023)(20.0)}{(0.647 - 0.023)(35.64) + (0.635 - 0.023)(21.07) - (0.647 - 0.023 + 0.635 - 0.023)(20.0)}$$

$$= 0.9606$$

$$x_{NL} = 1 - x_{US} = 1 - 0.9606 = 0.0394$$

The optimal international portfolio thus comprises 96.06 percent in the U.S. market and 3.96 percent in the Dutch market. The expected return and risk of the optimal portfolio can be computed as follows:

$$\bar{R}_{OP} = (0.9606)(0.647) + (0.0396)(0.635) = 0.647\%$$

$$\sigma_{OP} = [(0.9606)^2 (21.07) + (0.0394)^2 (35.64) + 2(0.9606)(0.0394)(20.0)]^{1/2}$$

$$= 4.58\%$$

PART FIVE

Financial Management of the Multinational Firm

PART FIVE covers topics on financial management practices for the MNC.

CHAPTER 16 discusses why MNCs make capital expenditures in productive capacity in foreign lands rather than just producing domestically and then exporting to overseas markets.

CHAPTER 17 deals with the international capital structure and the cost of capital of an MNC. An analytical argument is presented showing that the firm's cost of capital is lower when its shares trade internationally and if debt capital is sourced internationally.

CHAPTER 18 presents the adjusted present value (APV) framework of Donald Lessard that is useful for the parent firm in analyzing a capital expenditure in foreign operations.

CHAPTER 19 covers issues in cash management for the MNC. The chapter shows that if an MNC establishes a centralized cash depository and a multilateral system, the number of foreign cash flow transactions can be reduced, saving it money and giving it better control of its cash.

CHAPTER 20 provides a brief introduction to trade financing and countertrade. An example of a typical foreign trade transaction explains the three primary documents that are used in trade financing: letter of credit, time draft, and bill of lading.

CHAPTER 21 on the international tax environment opens with a discussion of the theory of taxation. Different methods of taxation are considered, and income tax rates in select countries are compared. The chapter concludes with a discussion of transfer pricing strategies, which might be a possible technique for an MNC to reduce its tax liabilities.

16

Foreign Direct Investment and Cross-Border Acquisitions

unctadstat.unctad.org

Provides FDI data in an interactive format.

IN THE EARLY 1980s, Honda, a Japanese automobile company, built an assembly plant in Marysville, Ohio, and began to produce cars for the North American market. These cars were substitutes for imports from Japan. As the production capacity at the Ohio plant expanded, Honda began to export its U.S.-manufactured cars to other markets, including its home market, Japan. A few key factors seem to have motivated Honda to make investments in America. First, Honda wanted to circumvent trade barriers imposed on Japanese automobile manufacturers; under the 1981 *Voluntary Restraint Agreement*, Japanese manufacturers were not allowed to increase their automobile exports to the U.S. market. Second, direct investments in America might have been an integral part of Honda's overall corporate strategy designed to bolster its competitive position vis-à-vis its domestic rivals, such as Toyota and Nissan. Following Honda's lead, Toyota and Nissan themselves subsequently made direct investments in America.

It is noteworthy that the Japanese government had been urging the automobile companies to begin production in the United States. In the early 1980s, Japan exported about two million cars a year to the United States, compared to about 20,000 cars imported from the United States. The Japanese government wished to forestall the kind of protectionist sentiment that led to U.S. import quotas on Japanese-made TVs. When TV import quotas were introduced in 1977, virtually all Japanese TV makers were forced to build plants in the United States.

Honda's decision to build a plant in Ohio was welcomed by the United Auto Workers (UAW), an American labor union, which regarded the plant as a major job opportunity for its members. Honda also received several forms of assistance from the state of Ohio, including improved infrastructure around the plant site, access to the Transportation Research Center operated by Ohio State University, abatement of property taxes, and setting up a special foreign trade zone that allowed Honda to import automobile parts from Japan at a reduced tariff rate.

Firms become *multinational* when they undertake **foreign direct investments (FDI)**. FDI often involves the establishment of new production facilities in foreign countries such as Honda's Ohio plant. FDI may also involve mergers with and acquisitions of existing foreign businesses. An example is provided by Ford, which acquired effective control of Mazda, a Japanese car manufacturer. Whether FDI involves a **greenfield investment** (that is, building brand-new production facilities) or **cross-border mergers and acquisitions**, it affords the multinational corporation (MNC) a measure of *control*. FDI thus represents an internal organizational expansion by MNCs.

According to a UN survey, the world FDI stock grew about twice as fast as worldwide exports of goods and services, which themselves grew faster than the world GDP by about 50 percent.[1] Indeed, FDI by MNCs now plays a vital role in linking national

---

[1]Source: *World Investment Report 2004*, UNCTAD, United Nations.

economies and defining the nature of the emerging global economy. By undertaking FDI on a global basis, such MNCs as General Electric, Toyota, British Petroleum, IBM, GM, Coca-Cola, McDonald's, Volkswagen, Siemens, and Nestlé have established their presence worldwide and become familiar household names. These MNCs deploy their formidable resources, tangible and intangible, irrespective of national boundaries, to pursue profits and bolster their competitive positions.

In this chapter, we discuss competing theories of FDI for the purpose of understanding the reasons firms undertake it. We also discuss in detail an increasingly popular mode of FDI, namely, cross-border mergers and acquisitions. In addition, we are going to discuss an extra dimension in FDI that would not particularly matter in domestic investments: how to measure and manage political risk associated with FDI. Our analysis of political risk is largely applicable to international portfolio investment as well. Once an MNC acquires a production facility in a foreign country, its operation will be subject to the "rules of the game" set by the host government. Political risk ranges from (unexpected) restrictions on the repatriation of foreign earnings to outright confiscation of foreign-owned assets. Needless to say, it is essential to the welfare of MNCs to effectively manage political risk. Before we discuss these issues, however, let us briefly review the global trends in FDI in recent years.

Global Trends in FDI

The recent trends in **FDI flows** are presented in Exhibit 16.1 and Exhibit 16.2. FDI flows represent new additions to the existing stock of FDI. As the exhibits show, during the six-year period 2010–2015, total annual worldwide FDI outflows amounted to about $1,394 billion on average. As can be expected, several developed countries are the dominant sources of FDI *outflows*. China is the only developing country with significant FDI outflows. During the six-year period 2010–2015, the United States, on average, invested about $320 billion per year overseas, followed by Japan, which invested about $111 billion per year. China is the third most important source of FDI outflows, investing about $98 billion per year on average during the six-year period. Germany ($84 billion) also invested heavily overseas. After these "big four" come the Netherlands ($58 billion), Canada ($53 billion), Switzerland ($47 billion), France ($39 billion), Italy ($29 billion), and Spain ($27 billion). The top 10 countries mentioned above account for about 62 percent of the total worldwide FDI outflows during this six-year period. This implies that MNCs domiciled in these countries should have certain comparative advantages in undertaking overseas investment projects. It is noted that China emerged as one of the top source countries for FDI. The U.K., which used to be a major source of FDI outflows, became an insignificant player due to divestment activities in recent years.

Exhibits 16.1 and 16.2 also show FDI *inflows* by country. During the six-year period 2010–2015, the United States received the largest amount of FDI inflows, $219 billion per year on average, among all countries. The next most popular destinations of FDI flows were China ($125 billion), the U.K. ($49 billion), Canada ($48 billion), Australia ($46 billion), the Netherlands ($36 billion), Germany ($34 billion), Mexico ($29 billion), France ($27 billion), and Spain ($26 billion). These 10 countries account for about 43 percent of the total worldwide FDI inflows, suggesting these countries must have locational advantages for FDI over other countries. In contrast to its substantial role as an originating country of FDI outflows, Japan plays a minor role as a host of FDI inflows; Japan received only about $0.1 billion worth of FDI, on average, per year during the period 2010–2015, reflecting a variety of legal, economic, and cultural barriers to foreign investment in Japan.

It is noteworthy that FDI flows into China have dramatically increased in recent years. The amount of inflow increased from $3.5 billion in 1990 to $136 billion in 2015. By 2015, China had emerged as the second most important host country for FDI,

EXHIBIT 16.1 — **Foreign Direct Investment—Outflows (Inflows) in Billions of Dollars**

Country	2010	2011	2012	2013	2014	2015	Annual Average
Australia	19.8	1.7	6.7	1.6	0.0	−16.7	2.2
	(36.4)	(58.9)	(59)	(57)	(39.6)	(22.3)	(45.5)
Canada	34.7	52.1	55.9	54.9	55.7	67.2	53.4
	(28.4)	(39.7)	(43.1)	(71.8)	(58.5)	(48.6)	(48.3)
China	68.8	74.7	87.8	107.8	123.1	127.6	98.3
	(114.7)	(124)	(121.1)	(123.9)	(128.5)	(135.6)	(124.6)
France	48.2	51.4	31.6	25.0	42.9	35.1	39.0
	(13.9)	(31.6)	(17)	(42.9)	(15.2)	(42.9)	(27.2)
Germany	125.5	77.9	62.2	40.4	106.2	94.3	84.4
	(65.6)	(67.5)	(28.2)	(11.7)	(0.9)	(31.7)	(34.3)
Italy	32.7	53.7	8.0	25.1	26.5	27.6	28.9
	(9.2)	(34.3)	(0.1)	(24.3)	(23.2)	(20.3)	(18.6)
Japan	56.3	107.6	122.5	135.7	113.6	128.7	110.7
	(−1.3)	(−1.8)	(1.7)	(2.3)	(2.1)	(−2.3)	(0.1)
Mexico	15.1	12.6	22.5	13.1	8.3	8.1	13.3
	(26.4)	(23.6)	(20.4)	(45.9)	(25.7)	(30.3)	(28.7)
Netherlands	68.4	34.8	6.2	70.0	56.0	113.4	58.1
	(−7.2)	(24.4)	(20.1)	(51.4)	(52.2)	(72.6)	(35.6)
Spain	37.8	41.2	−4.0	13.8	35.3	34.6	26.5
	(39.9)	(28.4)	(25.7)	(32.9)	(22.9)	(9.2)	(26.5)
Sweden	20.3	29.9	29.0	30.1	8.6	23.7	23.6
	(0.1)	(12.9)	(16.3)	(4.9)	(3.6)	(12.6)	(8.4)
Switzerland	85.7	48.1	43.3	38.6	−3.3	70.3	47.1
	(28.7)	(28.3)	(16)	(0.6)	(6.6)	(68.8)	(24.9)
United Kingdom	48.1	95.6	20.7	−18.8	−81.8	−61.4	0.4
	(58.2)	(42.2)	(55.4)	(47.6)	(52.4)	(39.5)	(49.2)
United States	277.8	396.6	318.2	307.9	316.5	300.0	319.5
	(198)	(229.9)	(188.4)	(211.5)	(106.6)	(379.9)	(219.1)
World	1,391.9	1,557.6	1,308.8	1,310.6	1,318.5	1,474.2	1,393.6
	(1,388.8)	(1,566.8)	(1,510.9)	(1,427.2)	(1,277.0)	(1,762.2)	(1488.8)

Note: FDI flows with a negative sign indicate that at least one of the three components of FDI (equity capital, reinvested earnings, or intra-company loans) is negative and is not offset by positive amounts of the other components. There are instances of reverse investment or disinvestment.

Source: *World Investment Report 2016*, UNCTAD.

EXHIBIT 16.2

Average Foreign Direct Investment per Year during 2010–2015 ($ billions)

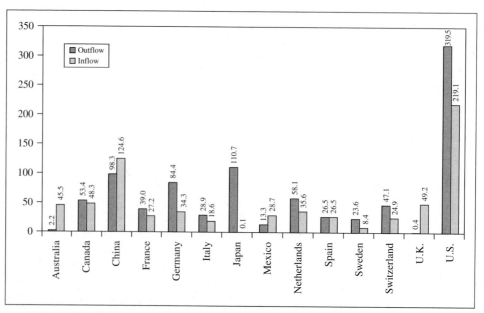

Source: Adapted from *World Investment Report 2016*, UNCTAD.

trailing only the United States. MNCs might have been lured to invest in China not only by lower labor and efficient manufacturing infrastructure but also by the desire to preempt the entry of rivals into China's potentially huge market.

Among developing countries, Mexico is another country that experienced substantial FDI inflows, $29 billion on average per year. It is well known that MNCs are investing in Mexico, a low-cost country, to serve the North American as well as Mexican markets. Considering that the wage rate in China has been rising fast in recent years, Mexico and other developing countries such as Indonesia and Vietnam may attract more FDI inflows in the future. It is also noteworthy that MNCs invested heavily, $26 billion per year, in Spain, where the costs of production are relatively low compared to other European countries such as France and Germany. Most likely, MNCs invested in Spain to gain a foothold in the huge single market created by the European Union, of which Spain is a member country.

It is noted that worldwide FDI, both inflows and outflows, declined significantly in 2008–2009 due to the global recession. However, it began to recover gradually since 2010.

Now, let us turn our attention to **FDI stocks**, which are the accumulation of previous FDI flows. The overall cross-border production activities of MNCs are best captured by FDI stocks. Exhibit 16.3 provides a summary of FDI stocks, both outward and inward, by country. The total worldwide FDI stock, which was about $514 billion in 1980, rose to about $7,400 billion in 2000 and $25,000 billion in 2015. In the case of the United States, FDI outward stock rose from $220 billion in 1980 to $5,983 billion in 2015. As of 2015, the United States, Germany, the U.K., France, Japan, Switzerland, Canada, the Netherlands, and China held the most outward FDI stocks. For FDI inward

EXHIBIT 16.3	Country	1990	1995	2000	2005	2010	2015
Foreign Direct Investment-Outward (Inward) Stocks in Billions of Dollars	Australia	30.1	41.3	92.5	159.2	449.7	396.4
		(75.8)	(104.2)	(121.7)	(210.9)	(527.1)	(537.4)
	Canada	78.9	110.4	442.6	399.4	998.5	1,078.3
		(113.1)	(116.8)	(325)	(356.9)	(983.9)	(756)
	China	2.5	17.3	27.8	46.3	317.2	1,010.2
		(14.1)	(129)	(193.3)	(317.9)	(587.8)	(1220.9)
	France	110.1	200.9	365.9	853.2	1,173.0	1,314.2
		(86.5)	(162.4)	(184.2)	(600.8)	(630.7)	(772)
	Germany	151.6	235.0	483.9	967.3	1,364.6	1,812.5
		(111.2)	(134)	(470.9)	(502.8)	(955.9)	(1121.3)
	Italy	56.1	86.7	170.0	293.5	491.2	466.6
		(58)	(64.7)	(122.5)	(219.9)	(328.1)	(335.3)
	Japan	201.4	305.5	278.4	386.6	831.1	1,226.5
		(9.9)	(17.8)	(50.3)	(100.9)	(214.9)	(170.7)
	Mexico	0.6	2.7	8.3	28.0	121.6	151.9
		(27.9)	(61.3)	(121.7)	(209.6)	(363.8)	(420)
	Netherlands	109.1	158.6	305.5	641.3	968.1	1,074.3
		(73.7)	(102.6)	(243.7)	(463.4)	(588.1)	(707)
	Spain	14.9	34.3	129.2	381.3	653.2	472.1
		(66.3)	(128.9)	(156.3)	(367.7)	(628.3)	(533.3)
	Sweden	49.5	61.6	123.6	202.8	374.4	345.9
		(12.5)	(32.8)	(93.8)	(171.5)	(347.2)	(281.9)
	Switzerland	65.7	108.3	232.2	394.8	1,041.3	1,138.2
		(33.7)	(43.1)	(86.8)	(172.5)	(610.9)	(833)
	United Kingdom	230.8	319.0	923.4	1,238.0	1,574.7	1,538.1
		(218)	(244.1)	(463.1)	(816.7)	(1057.2)	(1457.4)
	United States	435.2	705.6	1,316.2	2,051.3	4,809.6	5,982.8
		(394.9)	(564.6)	(1256.9)	(1625.7)	(3422.3)	(5588)
	World	1,758.2	2,897.6	7,436.8	10,671.9	20,803.7	25,044.9
		(1950.3)	(2992.1)	(7488.4)	(10129.7)	(20189.7)	(24983.2)

Source: Adapted from *World Investment Report 2009, 2012, 2016*, UNCTAD.

FDI Stocks among the Triad and Economies in Which FDI from the Triad Dominates, 2001 (billions of dollars)

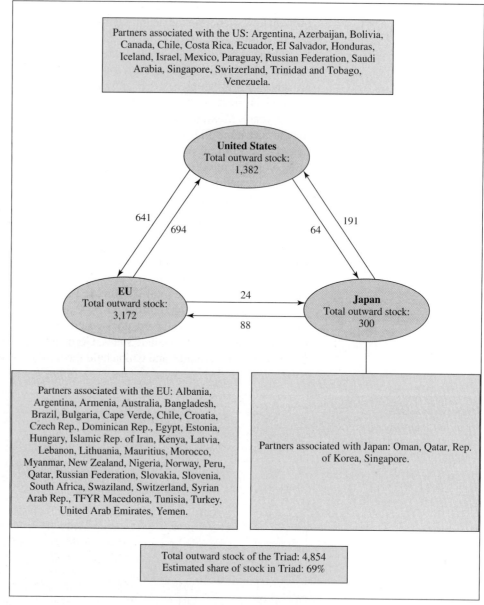

Partners associated with the US: Argentina, Azerbaijan, Bolivia, Canada, Chile, Costa Rica, Ecuador, El Salvador, Honduras, Iceland, Israel, Mexico, Paraguay, Russian Federation, Saudi Arabia, Singapore, Switzerland, Trinidad and Tobago, Venezuela.

United States
Total outward stock:
1,382

641

694

191

64

EU
Total outward stock:
3,172

24

88

Japan
Total outward stock:
300

Partners associated with the EU: Albania, Argentina, Armenia, Australia, Bangladesh, Brazil, Bulgaria, Cape Verde, Chile, Croatia, Czech Rep., Dominican Rep., Egypt, Estonia, Hungary, Islamic Rep. of Iran, Kenya, Latvia, Lebanon, Lithuania, Mauritius, Morocco, Myanmar, New Zealand, Nigeria, Norway, Peru, Qatar, Russian Federation, Slovakia, Slovenia, South Africa, Swaziland, Switzerland, Syrian Arab Rep., TFYR Macedonia, Tunisia, Turkey, United Arab Emirates, Yemen.

Partners associated with Japan: Oman, Qatar, Rep. of Korea, Singapore.

Total outward stock of the Triad: 4,854
Estimated share of stock in Triad: 69%

Note: Associate partners are the host economies in which the Triad member accounts for total FDI inward stocks or of total FDI inward flows within a 3-year average.

Source: UNCTAD *World Investment Report 2003:* www.unctad.org/wir.

stock, on the other hand, the United States, the U.K., China, Germany, France, Canada, and the Netherlands are the most important hosts. Exhibit 16.4 shows the direction of FDI stocks among the three major economic centers, that is, the United States, the European Union, and Japan. Clearly, much of the FDI stocks are concentrated in these three major economic centers.

Why Do Firms Invest Overseas?

Why do firms locate production overseas rather than exporting from the home country or licensing production to a local firm in the host country? In other words, why do firms seek to extend corporate *control* overseas by forming multinational corporations? Unlike the theory of international trade or the theory of international portfolio investment, we do not have a well-developed, comprehensive theory of FDI. But several theories can shed light on certain aspects of the FDI phenomenon. Many of the existing theories, such as Kindleberger (1969) and Hymer (1976), emphasize various *market imperfections*, that is, imperfections in product, factor, and capital markets, as the key motivating forces driving FDI.

In what follows, we are going to discuss some of the key factors that are important in firms' decisions to invest overseas:

- Trade barriers
- Imperfect labor market
- Intangible assets
- Vertical integration
- Product life cycle
- Shareholder diversification services

Trade Barriers

International markets for goods and services are often rendered imperfect by acts of governments. Governments may impose tariffs, quotas, and other restrictions on exports and imports of goods and services, hindering the free flow of these products across national boundaries. Sometimes, governments may even impose complete bans on the international trade of certain products. Governments regulate international trade to raise revenue, protect domestic industries, and pursue other economic policy objectives.

Facing barriers to exporting its products to foreign markets, a firm may decide to move production to foreign countries as a means of circumventing the trade barriers. A classic example for trade barrier-motivated FDI is Honda's investment in Ohio. Because the cars produced in Ohio would not be subject to U.S. tariffs and quotas, Honda could circumvent these barriers by establishing production facilities in the United States. The recent surge in FDI in countries like Mexico and Spain can be explained, at least in part, by the desire of MNCs to circumvent external trade barriers set up by NAFTA and the European Union.

Trade barriers can also arise *naturally* from transportation costs. Such products as mineral ore and cement that are bulky relative to their economic values may not be suitable for exporting because high transportation costs will substantially reduce profit margins. In these cases, FDI can be made in the foreign markets to reduce transportation costs.

Imperfect Labor Market

Suppose Samsung, a Korean conglomerate, would like to build production facilities for its consumer electronics products to serve the North American markets. Samsung could locate its production facilities anywhere in North America if the firm is concerned only with circumventing trade barriers imposed by NAFTA. Samsung initially chose to locate its production facilities in northern Mexico rather than in Canada or the United States, mainly because it wanted to take advantage of the lower costs of labor in Mexico.

Labor services in a country can be severely underpriced relative to their productivity because workers are not allowed to freely move across national boundaries to seek higher wages. Among all factor markets, the labor market is the most imperfect. Severe imperfections in the labor market lead to persistent wage differentials among countries. Exhibit 16.5 provides the hourly labor costs in the manufacturing sector for selected countries in 2012. Compared with Belgium, hourly compensation for factory workers is about $25 less in Spain. The hourly compensation is only $6.36 in Mexico, compared with $35.67 in the United States. The exhibit shows that the average hourly labor cost ranges from $57.79 in Switzerland to $0.37(!) in Bangladesh.

When workers are not mobile because of immigration barriers, firms themselves should move to the workers in order to benefit from the underpriced labor services. This is one of the main reasons MNCs are making FDIs in less-developed countries such as Mexico, China, India, and Southeast Asian countries like Thailand, Malaysia,

EXHIBIT 16.5 **Labor Costs around the Globe (2012)**	

Country	Average Hourly Cost ($)
Switzerland	57.79
Belgium	52.19
Sweden	49.80
Australia	47.68
Germany	45.79
France	39.81
Canada	36.59
United States	35.67
Japan	35.34
Italy	34.18
United Kingdom	31.23
Spain	26.83
Singapore	24.16
Korea, Republic	20.72
Israel	20.14
Brazil	11.20
Taiwan	9.46
Mexico	6.36
Philippines	2.10
China	1.64
India	1.45
Indonesia	1.15
Vietnam	0.73
Bangladesh	0.37

Source: U.S. Department of Labor, Bureau of Labor Statistics and Japan External Trade Organization.

and Indonesia, where labor services are underpriced relative to their productivity. The recent surge in investment in China by companies from Japan, South Korea, and Taiwan can be attributable, in part, to the highly productive, low-cost workforces in China. However, as labor costs in China began to rise, some of the manufacturing operations there have relocated to other Asian countries, where the wage rates are extremely low, such as Bangladesh, Cambodia, and Vietnam.

Intangible Assets

Coca-Cola has invested in bottling plants all over the world rather than, say, licensing local firms to produce Coke. Coca-Cola chose FDI as a mode of entry into foreign markets for an obvious reason—it wanted to protect the formula for its famed soft drink. If Coca-Cola licenses a local firm to produce Coke, it has no guarantee that the secrets of the formula will be maintained. Once the formula is leaked to other local firms, they may come up with similar products, which will hurt Coca-Cola's sales. This possibility is known as the *boomerang* effect. In the 1960s, Coca-Cola, which had bottling plants in India, faced strong pressure from the Indian government to reveal the Coke formula as a condition for continued operations in India. Instead of revealing the formula, Coca-Cola chose to withdraw from India.[2]

MNCs may undertake overseas investment projects in a foreign country, despite the fact that local firms may enjoy inherent advantages. This implies that MNCs should have significant advantages over local firms. Indeed, MNCs often enjoy comparative advantages due to special **intangible assets** they possess. Examples include technological, managerial, and marketing know-how, superior R&D capabilities, and brand power. These intangible assets are often hard to package and sell to foreigners. In

---

[2]Coca-Cola reentered the Indian market as India gradually liberalized its economy, improving the climate for foreign investments.

addition, the property rights in intangible assets are difficult to establish and protect, especially in foreign countries where legal recourse may not be readily available. As a result, firms may find it more profitable to establish foreign subsidiaries and capture returns directly by *internalizing* transactions in these assets. The internalization theory can help explain why MNCs, not local firms, undertake investment projects in foreign countries.

A strand of literature, including Caves (1982) and Magee (1977), places special emphasis on the role of market imperfections for intangible assets in motivating firms to undertake FDI. According to the **internalization theory** of FDI, firms that have intangible assets with a *public good* property tend to invest directly in foreign countries in order to use these assets on a larger scale and, at the same time, avoid the misappropriations of intangible assets that may occur while transacting in foreign markets through a market mechanism.[3]

Vertical Integration

Suppose Royal Dutch Shell purchases a significant portion of crude oil for its refinery facilities from a Saudi oil company that owns the oil fields. In this situation, Royal Dutch Shell can experience a number of problems. For example, Royal Dutch Shell, the downstream firm, would like to hold the crude oil price down, whereas the Saudi oil company, an upstream firm, would like to push the price up. If the Saudi company has stronger bargaining power, Royal Dutch Shell may be forced to pay a higher price than it would like to, adversely affecting the firm's profits. In addition, as the world's demand for refined oil fluctuates, one of the two firms may have to bear excessive risk. The conflicts between the upstream and downstream firms can be resolved, however, if the two firms form a vertically integrated firm. Obviously, if Royal Dutch Shell controls the oil fields, the problems will disappear. In recent years, Chinese firms actively pursued vertical integrations through overseas merger and acquisition (M&A) deals, especially in mining and resources sectors. For instance, Shandong Iron & Steel Group invested $1.5 billion to acquire a major stake in African Minerals of Sierra Leone in 2010. Also, Aluminum Corporation of China (Chinalco) bought 9 percent of Rio Tinto, a major Australian mining firm, for $14 billion, to ensure a reliable supply of minerals at reasonable prices. China's overseas M&A activities so far are heavily concentrated in resource-rich countries, such as Australia, Brazil, Canada, Mongolia, Sierra Leone, Guinea, and Indonesia.

Generally speaking, MNCs may undertake FDI in countries where inputs are available in order to secure the supply of inputs at a stable price. Furthermore, if MNCs have monopolistic/oligopolistic control over the input market, this can serve as a barrier to entry to the industry. Many MNCs involved in extractive/natural resources industries tend to directly own oil fields, mine deposits, and forests for these reasons. Also, MNCs often find it profitable to locate manufacturing/processing facilities near the natural resources in order to save transportation costs. It would be costly to bring bulky bauxite ore to the home country and then extract the aluminum.

Although the majority of vertical FDIs are *backward* in that FDI involves an industry abroad that produces inputs for MNCs, foreign investments can take the form of *forward* vertical FDI when they involve an industry abroad that sells an MNC's outputs. As is well known, U.S. car makers found it difficult to market their products in Japan. This is partly because most car dealers in Japan have a long and close business relationship with the Japanese car makers and are reluctant to carry foreign imports. To overcome this problem, U.S. car makers began to build their own network of dealerships in Japan to help sell their cars. This is an example of forward vertical FDI.

---

[3]Examples of public goods include public parks, lighthouses, and radio/TV broadcasting services. Once these goods are produced, it is difficult to preclude the public from using them, whether they are paying or not.

Linear Sequence in Manufacturing: Singer & Company

Singer was one of the first United States-based companies that internationalized its operations. In August 1850, I.M. Singer invented a sewing machine and established I.M. Singer & Company in New York in 1851 to manufacture and sell the machines in the United States. To protect this innovative product, Singer had applied for and obtained domestic and some foreign patents by 1851. Until 1855, the company concentrated on fine-tuning its operations in the domestic market.

The first step towards internationalizing took place in 1855, when Singer & Co. sold its French patent for the single thread machine to a French merchant for a combination of lump-sum payment and royalties. This proved to be a bad experience for Singer as the French merchant was reluctant to pay royalties and handled competitors' products, leading to disputes and discouraging Singer from selling foreign patents to independent businesspersons. By 1856, Singer stopped granting territorial rights to independents in the domestic market due to

bad experiences and began establishing its own sales outlets. Independent agents were not providing user instructions to buyers and failed to offer servicing. They were also reluctant to risk their capital by providing installment payments as well as carrying large inventories.

Learning from its domestic problems, Singer used franchised agents as a mode of entry abroad; they sold and advertised the company's product in a given region. By 1858, Singer had independent businesspersons as foreign agents in Rio de Janeiro and elsewhere. Between September 1860 and May 1861, the company exported 127 machines to agents in Canada, Cuba, Curacao, Germany, Mexico, Peru, Puerto Rico, Uruguay, and Venezuela. Due to its domestic experience, Singer sped up the linear sequence, sometimes simultaneously using both franchised agents and its own sales outlets.

Singer also started extending its policy of establishing sales outlets to foreign markets. By 1861, it had salaried

Product Life Cycle

According to Raymond Vernon (1966), firms undertake FDI at a particular stage in the life cycle of the products that they initially introduced. Vernon observed that throughout the 20th century, the majority of new products, such as computers, televisions, and mass-produced cars, were developed by U.S. firms and first marketed in the United States. According to Vernon's **product life-cycle theory**, when U.S. firms first introduce new products, they choose to keep production facilities at home, close to customers. In the early stage of the product life cycle, the demand for the new product is relatively insensitive to the price and thus the pioneering firm can charge a relatively high price. At the same time, the firm can continuously improve the product based on feedback from its customers at home.

As demand for the new product develops in foreign countries, the pioneering U.S. firm begins to export to those countries. As the foreign demand for the product continues to grow, U.S. firms, as well as foreign firms, may be induced to start production in foreign countries to serve local markets. As the product becomes standardized and mature, it becomes important to cut the cost of production to stay competitive. A foreign producer operating in a low-cost country may start to export the product to the United States. At the same time, cost considerations may induce the U.S. firms to set up production facilities in a low-cost foreign country and export the product back to the United States. In other words, FDI takes place when the product reaches maturity and cost becomes an important consideration. FDI can thus be interpreted as a *defensive* move to maintain the firm's competitive position against its domestic and foreign rivals. The International Finance in Practice box "Linear Sequence in Manufacturing: Singer & Company" provides an interesting historical example supporting the product life-cycle view of FDI.

The product life-cycle theory predicts that over time the United States switches from an exporting country of new products to an importing country. The dynamic changes in the international trade pattern are illustrated in Exhibit 16.6. The prediction of the product life-cycle theory is consistent with the pattern of dynamic changes observed for many products. For instance, personal computers (PCs) were first developed by U.S. firms (such as IBM and Apple Computer) and exported to overseas markets. As PCs became a standardized commodity, however, the United States became a

representatives in Glasgow and London. They established additional branches in England, to each of which the machines were sold on commission. By 1862, Singer was facing competition in England from imitators. Foreign sales of Singer machines increased steadily as the company was able to sell machines abroad at prices lower than in the United States because of the undervaluation of the dollar. In 1863, Singer opened a sales office in Hamburg, Germany, and later in Sweden. By 1866, the European demand for Singer machines surpassed supplies and competitors were taking advantage of Singer's inability to supply the machines. After the Civil War, the United States currency appreciated; at the same time, wages in the United States began to rise, increasing manufacturing costs and affecting firms' international competitiveness. As a result, some United States firms started establishing factories abroad.

In 1868, Singer established a small assembly factory in Glasgow, with parts imported from the United States. The venture proved to be successful and, by 1869, Singer decided to import tools from the United States to manufacture all parts in Glasgow. By 1874, partly due to the recession at home, Singer was selling more than half of its output abroad. Then, Singer started replacing locally financed independent agents

with salaried-plus-commission agents. By 1879, its London regional headquarters had 26 offices in the United Kingdom and one each in Paris, Madrid, Brussels, Milan, Basel, Capetown, Bombay, and Auckland.

By the 1880s, the company had a strong foreign sales organization, with the London regional headquarters taking the responsibility for sales in Australia, Asia, Africa, the southern part of South America, the United Kingdom, and a large part of the European continent. The Hamburg office was in charge of northern and middle Europe, while the New York office looked after sales in the Caribbean, Mexico, the northern part of South America and Canada. By 1881, the capacity in Singer's three factories in Glasgow was insufficient to meet demand. Therefore, in 1882, Singer established a modern plant in Kilbowie near Glasgow with the latest United States machine tools and with a capacity equivalent to that of its largest factory in the United States. In 1883, Singer set up manufacturing plants in Canada and Australia. Through experience, Singer learned that it could manufacture more cost effectively in Scotland than in the United States for sales in Europe and other markets.

Source: World Investment Report 1996, UNCTAD, p. 77.

net importer of PCs from foreign producers based in such countries as Japan, Korea, China, and Taiwan, as well as foreign subsidiaries of U.S. firms.

It should be pointed out that Vernon's theory was developed in the 1960s when the United States was the unquestioned leader in R&D capabilities and product innovations. Increasingly, product innovations are taking place outside the United States as well, and new products are introduced simultaneously in many advanced countries. Production facilities may be located in multiple countries from the inception of a new product. The international system of production is becoming too complicated to be explained by a simple version of the product life-cycle theory.

Shareholder Diversification Services

If investors cannot effectively diversify their portfolio holdings internationally because of barriers to cross-border capital flows, firms may be able to provide their shareholders with indirect diversification services by making direct investments in foreign countries. When a firm holds assets in many countries, the firm's cash flows are internationally diversified. Thus, shareholders of the firm can indirectly benefit from international diversification even if they are not directly holding foreign shares. Capital market imperfections thus may motivate firms to undertake FDI.

Although shareholders of MNCs may indirectly benefit from corporate international diversification, it is not clear that firms are motivated to undertake FDI for the purpose of providing shareholders with diversification services. Considering the fact that many barriers to international portfolio investments have been dismantled in recent years, enabling investors to diversify internationally by themselves, capital market imperfections as a motivating factor for FDI are likely to have become less relevant.

Cross-Border Mergers and Acquisitions

As previously mentioned, FDI can take place either through *greenfield investments*, which involve building new production facilities in a foreign country, or through *cross-border mergers and acquisitions*, which involve combining with or buying

EXHIBIT 16.6

The Product Life Cycle

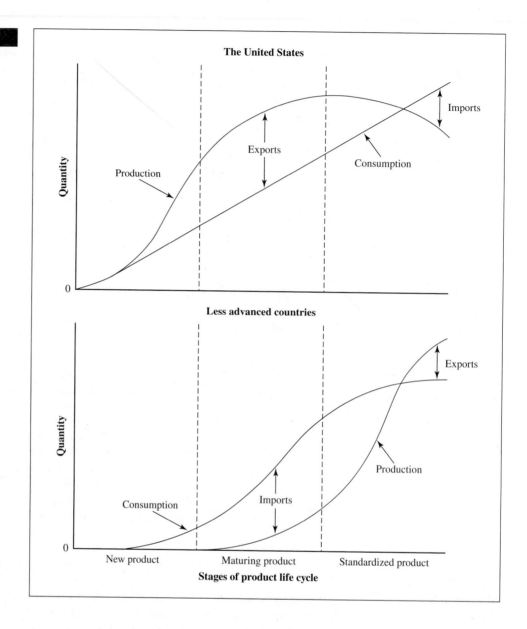

existing foreign businesses. In recent years, a growing portion of FDI has taken the form of cross-border mergers and acquisitions, accounting for more than 50 percent of FDI flows in terms of dollar amount. In 1998, for instance, British Petroleum purchased Amoco, a U.S. oil company, for $48 billion. In 2000, Vivendi, a French company, acquired Seagram, a major Canadian firm, for $40.4 billion. And Hoechst, a major German pharmaceutical company, was acquired by Rhone-Poulenc SA (Life Sciences), a French company, for $21.9 billion. In 2008, Thomson Corporation, a U.S. information services firm, acquired Reuters, a British news agency, for $17.6 billion. In 2009, Roche, a Swiss pharmaceutical giant, paid $46.7 billion to acquire Genentech, a highly successful U.S. biotech firm. In 2010, Kraft Foods, a U.S. firm, acquired Cadbury, a British confectionery producer, for $18.8 billion. To top it all, Vodafone, a British telecommunication company, paid $203 billion to acquire Mannesmann, a major German company, in 2000. Exhibit 16.7 lists major cross-border mergers and acquisition (M&A) deals that were consummated during 1998–2015. The rapid increase in cross-border M&A deals can be

EXHIBIT 16.7

Top 40 Cross-Border M&A Deals Completed during 1998–2015

No	Year	Deal Value ($ Billion)	Acquiring Company	Home Economy	Industry of the Acquiring Company	Acquired Company	Host Economy	Industry of the Acquired Company
1	2000	202.8	Vodafone Air Touch PLC	United Kingdom	Radiotelephone communications	Mannesmann AG	Germany	Radiotelephone communications
2	2014	130.3	Verizon Communications Inc	United States	Telephone communications, except radiotelephone	Verizon Wireless Inc	United States	Radiotelephone communications
3	2007	98.2	RFS Holdings BV	United Kingdom	Investors, nec	ABN-AMRO Holding NV	Netherlands	Investors, nec
4	1999	74.3	Royal Dutch Petroleum Co	Netherlands	Crude petroleum natural gas	Shell Transport & Trading Co	United Kingdom	Crude petroleum natural gas
5	2015	68.4	Actavis PLC	Ireland	Pharmaceutical preparations	Allergan Inc	United States	Pharmaceutical preparations
6	1998	60.3	Vodafone Group PLC	United Kingdom	Telecommunications	Air Touch Communications	United States	Telecommunications
7	2008	52.2	InBev NV	Belgium	Malt beverages	Anheuser-Busch Cos Inc	United States	Beverages and packaging
8	1998	48.2	British Petroleum Co PLC (BP)	United Kingdom	Oil and gas; petroleum refining	Amoco Corp	United States	Oil and gas; petroleum refining
9	2009	46.7	Roche Holding AG	Switzerland	Pharmaceutical preparations	Genentech Inc	United States	Biological products, except diagnostic substances
10	2000	46.0	France Telecom SA	France	Telephone communications, except radiotelephone	Orange PLC (Mannesmann AG)	United Kingdom	Telephone communications, except radiotelephone
11	2015	42.7	Medtronic Inc	United States	Electromedical and electrotherapeutic apparatus	Covidien PLC	Ireland	Surgical and medical instruments and apparatus
12	2014	42.2	CITIC Pacific Ltd	Hong Kong, China	Steel works, blast furnaces and rolling mills	CITIC Ltd	China	Investment advice
13	1999	40.5	Daimler-Benz AG	Germany	Transportation equipment	Chrysler Corp	United States	Transportation equipment
14	1999	40.4	Vivendi SA	France	Water supply	Seagram Co ltd	Canada	Motion picture and video tape production
15	2007	37.6	Rio Tinto PLC	United Kingdom	Gold ores	Alcan Inc	Canada	Aluminium, Alumina producer
16	1999	34.6	Zeneca Group PLC	United Kingdom	Drugs	Astra AB	Sweden	Drugs
17	1999	32.6	Mannesmann AG	Germany	Metal and metal products	Orange PLC	United Kingdom	Metal and metal products
18	2006	32.2	Mittal Steel Co NV	Netherlands	Steel works, blast furnaces and rolling mills	Arcelor SA	Luxembourg	Steel works, blast furnaces and rolling mills
19	2006	31.7	Telefonica SA	Spain	Telephone communications, except radiotelephone	O2 PLC	United Kingdom	Radiotelephone communications
20	2001	29.4	VoiceStream Wireless Corp	United States	Radiotelephone communications	Deutsche Telekom AG	Germany	Radiotelephone communications
21	2000	27.2	BP Amoco PLC	United Kingdom	Petroleum refining	ARCO	United States	Petroleum refining
22	2013	27.0	OAO Neftyanaya Kompaniya Rosneft	Russian Federation	Crude petroleum and natural gas	TNK-BP Ltd	British Virgin Islands	Crude petroleum and natural gas
23	2013	27.0	OAO Neftyanaya Kompaniya Rosneft	Russian Federation	Crude petroleum and natural gas	TNK-BP Ltd	British Virgin Islands	Crude petroleum and natural gas
24	2007	26.4	Investor Group	Italy	Investors, nec	Endesa SA	Spain	Public utility
25	2000	25.1	Unilever Group	United Kingdom	Creamery butter	Bestfoods	United States	Dried fruits, vegetables and soup mixes
26	2011	25.1	International Power PLC	United Kingdom	Electric services	GDF Suez Energy Europe & International	Belgium	Natural gas transmission
27	2008	23.1	Government of the Netherlands	Netherlands	National government	Fortis Bank Nederland(Holding) NV	Belgium/Netherlands	Banking
28	2014	23.1	Numericable Group SA	France	Cable and other pay television services	Societe Francaise du Radiotelephone SA	France	Telephone communications, except radiotelephone
29	2007	22.8	Shareholders	United States	Investors, nec	Tyco Healthcare Group Ltd	United States	Healthcare
30	2011	22.4	VimpelCom Ltd	Netherlands	Radiotelephone communications	Weather Investments Srl	Italy	Telephone communications, except radiotelephone
31	2007	22.2	Iberdrola SA	Spain	Electrical services	Scottish Power PLC	United Kingdom	Electrical services
32	1999	21.9	Rhone-Poulenc SA	France	Chemicals and allied products	Hoechst AG	Germany	Chemicals and allied products
33	2006	21.8	Airport Development	Spain	Special purpose finance company	BAA PLC	United Kingdom	Airports and airport terminal services
34	2013	21.6	SoftBank Corp	Japan	Radiotelephone communications	Sprint Nextel Corp	United States	Telephone communications, except radiotelephone
35	2011	21.2	Sanofi-Aventis SA	France	Pharmaceutical preparations	Genzyme Corp	United States	Biological products, except diagnostic substances
36	2007	21.0	Bank of America Corp	United States	National commercial banks	ABN AMRO North America Holding Co	United States	Banking
37	2015	20.6	Holcim Ltd	Switzerland	Cement, hydraulic	Lafarge SA	France	Cement, hydraulic
38	2015	20.4	Genesis International Holdings NV	Netherlands	Metal household furniture	Steinhoff International Holdings Ltd	South Africa	Metal household furniture
39	2007	19.6	AB Acquisitions Ltd	United States	Investors, nec	Alliance Boots PLC	United Kingdom	Pharmaceuticals, Healthcare, Beauty
40	2000	19.4	Zurich Allied AG	Switzerland	Life insurance	Allied Zurich PLC	United Kingdom	Life Insurance

Source: Adapted from *World Investment Report*, various issues (UNCTAD).

attributed to the ongoing liberalization of capital markets and the integration of the world economy.[4]

Firms may be motivated to engage in cross-border M&A deals to bolster their competitive positions in the world market by acquiring special assets from other firms or using their own assets on a larger scale. As a mode of FDI entry, cross-border M&As offer two key advantages over greenfield investments: speed and access to proprietary assets. A recent United Nations study aptly discusses why firms choose M&As as a mode of investment.[5]

Mergers and acquisitions are a popular mode of investment for firms wishing to protect, consolidate, and advance their global competitive positions, by selling off divisions that fall outside the scope of their core competence and acquiring strategic assets that enhance their competitiveness. For those firms, "ownership" assets acquired from another firm, such as technical competence, established brand names, and existing supplier networks and distribution systems, can be put to immediate use toward better serving global customers, enhancing profits, expanding market share, and increasing corporate competitiveness by employing international production networks more efficiently.

Recently, Chinese firms began to actively use cross-border M&As as a way of obtaining brand power and high technologies. For example, in 2010, the Chinese carmaker Zhejiang Geely Holding Group acquired Volvo, a Swedish carmaker famous for its safety technology, from Ford Motor Company for $1.3 billion. By doing so, Geely instantaneously obtained brand power, technology, and dealership networks of Volvo. In 2014, the Chinese insurance company Anbang acquired Waldorf Astoria, the famous hotel in New York City, for $1.95 billion. In 2015, China National Chemical, known as ChemChina, acquired Italian tire maker Pirelli for $7.9 billion and made a bid to acquire Swiss agrochemical company Syngenta AG for $48 billion. Clearly, open capital markets allow companies to strategically use cross-border M&A deals to gain access to brand power and technological and managerial know-how residing in target companies.

Cross-border M&A deals don't always work out as expected. The Daimler–Chrysler merger provides such an example. Intially, the combined company was expected to cut costs by as much as $3 billion annually and fill product and geographic gaps. In anticipation of the synergistic gains, stock prices of both companies rose upon the announcement of a $40.5 billion deal. However, the savings, technological synergies, and enhanced marketing power that both sides envisioned did not materialize. After continued profit decline, Chrysler was sold to private equity firm Cerberus for $7.4 billion in May 2007, ending a nine-year trans-Atlantic merger. This DaimlerChrysler saga clearly shows that cross-border business mergers do not always work as intended.

Cross-border acquisitions of businesses are a politically sensitive issue, as most countries prefer to retain local control of domestic firms. As a result, although countries may welcome greenfield investments, as they are viewed as representing new investment and employment opportunities, foreign firms' bids to acquire domestic firms are often resisted and sometimes even resented. Whether or not cross-border acquisitions produce **synergistic gains** and how such gains are divided between acquiring and target firms are thus important issues from the perspective of shareholder welfare and public policy. Synergistic gains are obtained when the value of the combined firm is greater than the stand-alone valuations of the individual (acquiring and target) firms.[6] If cross-border acquisitions generate synergistic gains and both the

---

[4]It is noted that UNCTAD lists some M&A deals within a country as cross-border deals arguing that "As long as the ultimate host economy is different from the ultimate home economy, M&A deals that were undertaken within the same economy are still considered cross-border M&As."

[5]Source: *World Investment Report 1996*, UNCTAD, p. 7.

[6]Synergistic gains may arise if the combined companies can save on the costs of production, marketing, distribution, and R&D and redeploy the combined assets to the highest-value projects.

acquiring and target shareholders gain wealth at the same time, one can argue that cross-border acquisitions are mutually beneficial and thus should not be thwarted both from a national and global perspective.

Synergistic gains may or may not arise from cross-border acquisitions, depending on the motive of acquiring firms. In general, gains will result when the acquirer is motivated to take advantage of the market imperfections mentioned earlier. In other words, firms may decide to acquire foreign firms to take advantage of mispriced factors of production and to cope with trade barriers.

As previously mentioned, imperfections in the market for *intangible assets* can also play a major role in motivating firms to undertake cross-border acquisitions. According to the internalization theory, a firm with intangible assets that have a public good property such as technical and managerial know-how may acquire foreign firms as a platform for using its special assets on a larger scale and, at the same time, avoid the misappropriation that may occur while transacting in foreign markets through a market mechanism. Cross-border acquisitions may also be motivated by the acquirer's desire to acquire and internalize the target firm's intangible assets. In this *backward-internalization* case, the acquirer seeks to create wealth by appropriating the rent generated from the economy of scale obtained from using the target's intangible assets on a global basis. The internalization thus may proceed *forward* to internalize the acquirer's assets, or *backward* to internalize the target's assets.

Reflecting the increased importance of cross-border acquisitions as a mode of FDI, several researchers investigated the effects of cross-border acquisitions. Doukas and Travlos (1988) investigated the impact of international acquisitions on the stock prices of U.S. bidding firms. The study shows that shareholders of U.S. bidders experience significant positive abnormal returns when firms expand into new industries and geographic markets. When firms already have operations in the target firm's country, U.S. shareholders experience no significant abnormal returns. Harris and Ravenscraft (1991), on the other hand, studied shareholder wealth gains for U.S. firms acquired by foreign firms. They concluded that U.S. targets experience higher wealth gains when they are acquired by foreign firms than when acquired by U.S. firms.

Morck and Yeung (1992) also investigated the effect of international acquisitions on the stock prices of U.S. firms. They show that U.S. acquiring firms with information-based intangible assets experienced a significantly positive stock price reaction upon foreign acquisition. This is consistent with the findings of their earlier work (1991) that the market value of the firm is positively related to its multinationality because of the firm's intangible assets, such as R&D capabilities, with public good nature. It is not the multinationality per se that contributes to the firm's value. Their empirical findings support the (forward-) internalization theory of FDI.

Eun, Kolodny, and Scheraga (1996), on the other hand, directly measured the magnitude of shareholders' gains from cross-border acquisitions, using a sample of major foreign acquisitions of U.S. firms that took place during the period 1979–90. Their findings are summarized in Exhibit 16.8. First, the exhibit shows that U.S. target shareholders realized significant wealth gains, $103 million on average, regardless of the nationality of acquirers. Second, the wealth gains to foreign acquiring shareholders varied greatly across acquiring countries. Shareholders of British acquirers experienced significant wealth reduction, −$123 million on average, whereas Japanese shareholders experienced major wealth increases, $228 million on average. Canadian acquisitions of U.S. firms produced modest wealth increases for their shareholders, $15 million on average.

Third, cross-border acquisitions are generally found to be synergy-generating corporate activities. Shareholders of the "paired" sample of U.S. targets and foreign acquirers experienced positive combined wealth gains, $68 million, on average. Synergistic gains, however, vary a great deal across acquiring countries. Japanese acquisitions generated large combined gains, $398 million, on average, which were shared by

EXHIBIT 16.8				Average Wealth Gains from Cross-Border Acquisitions: Foreign Acquisitions of U.S. Firms		
Country of Acquirer	Number of Cases	R&D/Sales (%)		Average Wealth Gains (in Million U.S.$)		
		Acquirer	Target	Acquirer	Target	Combined
Canada	10	0.21	0.65	14.93	85.59	100.53
Japan	15	5.08	4.81	227.83	170.66	398.49
U.K.	46	1.11	2.18	−122.91	94.55	−28.36
Other	32	1.63	2.80	−47.46	89.48	42.02
All	103	1.66	2.54	−35.01	103.19	68.18

Source: Reprinted from *Journal of Banking and Finance* 20, C. Eun, R. Kolodny, and C. Scheraga, "Cross-Border Acquisitions and Shareholder Wealth: Tests of the Synergy and Internalization Hypotheses," pp. 1559–82, © 1996 with kind permission from Elsevier Science-NL, Sara Burgerhartstreet 25, 1055 KV Amsterdam, The Netherlands.

target shareholders (43 percent) and acquiring shareholders (57 percent).[7] In contrast, British acquisitions produced a somewhat negative combined wealth gain, −$28 million on average, and caused a wealth transfer from acquiring to target shareholders.

Eun, Kolodny, and Scheraga argue that the significant gains for Japanese acquirers can be attributed to the successful internalization of the R&D capabilities of their targets, which have a much higher R&D intensity on average than the targets of acquirers from other countries. Thus, the desire to "backward" internalize the target's intangible assets appears to be an important driving force for Japanese acquisition programs in the United States. This supports the backward-internalization hypothesis.[8] In the case of British acquisitions, the average combined wealth gain was negative, and the acquiring shareholders lost substantial wealth. It thus appears that the managers of British firms often undertook negative NPV projects when they acquired U.S. firms. It is well known that corporate acquisitions can be driven by managers who pursue growth and diversification at the expense of shareholders' interests. As Jensen (1986) pointed out, managers may benefit by expanding the firm beyond the size that maximizes shareholder wealth for various reasons.[9]

Political Risk and FDI

In assessing investment opportunities in a foreign country, it is important for a parent firm to take into consideration the risk arising from the fact that investments are located in a foreign country. A sovereign country can take various actions that may adversely affect the interests of MNCs. In this section, we are going to discuss how to measure and manage **political risk**, which refers to the potential losses to the parent firm resulting from adverse political developments in the host country. Political risks range from the outright expropriation of foreign assets to unexpected changes in the tax laws that hurt the profitability of foreign projects.

Political risk that firms face can differ in terms of the incidence as well as the manner in which political events affect them. Depending on the incidence, political risk can be classified into two types:

1. *Macro risk*, where all foreign operations are affected by adverse political developments in the host country.

2. *Micro risk*, where only selected areas of foreign business operations or particular foreign firms are affected.

---

[7]This result is quite different from the findings of studies of domestic acquisitions, which show that target shareholders capture the lion's share of synergistic gains.

[8]Japanese acquirers themselves are highly R&D intensive. This suggests that Japanese acquisitions of U.S. firms may generate technological synergies, and that Japanese firms may be capable of using U.S. target firms' technical know-how.

[9]For example, managers' payments are often positively related to the size of the assets they control, not just profits.

The communist victory in China in 1949 is an example of macro risk, whereas the predicament of Enron in India, which we will discuss shortly, is an example of micro risk.

Depending on the manner in which firms are affected, political risk can be classified into three types:[10]

1. *Transfer risk*, which arises from uncertainty about cross-border flows of capital, payments, know-how, and the like.

2. *Operational risk*, which is associated with uncertainty about the host country's policies affecting the local operations of MNCs.

3. *Control risk*, which arises from uncertainty about the host country's policy regarding ownership and control of local operations.

Examples of transfer risk include the unexpected imposition of capital controls, inbound or outbound, and withholding taxes on dividend and interest payments. Examples for operational risk, on the other hand, include unexpected changes in environmental policies, sourcing/local content requirements, minimum wage law, and restriction on access to local credit facilities. Lastly, examples of control risk include restrictions imposed on the maximum ownership share by foreigners, mandatory transfer of ownership to local firms over a certain period of time (fade-out requirements), and the nationalization of local operations of MNCs.

Recent history is replete with examples of political risk. As Mao Ze-dong took power in China in 1949, his communist government nationalized foreign assets with little compensation. The same happened again when Castro took over Cuba in 1960. Even in a country controlled by a noncommunist government, strong nationalist sentiments can lead to the expropriation of foreign assets. For example, when Gamal Nasser seized power in Egypt in the early 1950s, he nationalized the Suez Canal, which was controlled by British and French interests. Politically, this move was immensely popular throughout the Arab world.

As Exhibit 16.9 shows, the frequency of expropriations of foreign-owned assets peaked in the 1970s, when as many as 30 countries were involved in expropriations each year. Since then, however, expropriations have dwindled to practically nothing. This change reflects the popularity of *privatization*, which, in turn, is attributable to widespread failures of state-run enterprises and mounting government debts around the world.

This, however, does not mean that political risk is a thing of the past. In 1992, the Enron Development Corporation, a subsidiary of the Houston-based energy company, signed a contract to build the largest-ever power plant in India, requiring a total investment of $2.8 billion. Severe power shortages have been one of the bottlenecks hindering India's economic growth. After Enron had spent nearly $300 million, the project was canceled by Hindu nationalist politicians in the Maharashtra state where the plant was to be built. Subsequently, Maharashtra invited Enron to renegotiate its contract. If Enron had agreed to renegotiate, it may have had to accept a lower profitability for the project. As can be seen from the Enron fiasco, the lack of an effective means of enforcing contracts in a foreign country is clearly a major source of political risk associated with FDI.

Political risk is not easy to measure. When Enron signed the contract to build a power plant in India, it perhaps could not have anticipated the victory of the Hindu nationalist party. Many businesses domiciled in Hong Kong were nervous about the intentions of Beijing in the post-1997 era. Difficult as it may be, MNCs still have to measure political risk for foreign projects under consideration. Experts of political risk analysis evaluate, often subjectively, a set of key factors such as:[11]

---

[10]Our discussion here draws on Kobrin (1979) and Root (1972).

[11]Our discussion here draws on Morgan Stanley's system of evaluating political risk.

Frequency of Expropriations of Foreign-Owned Assets

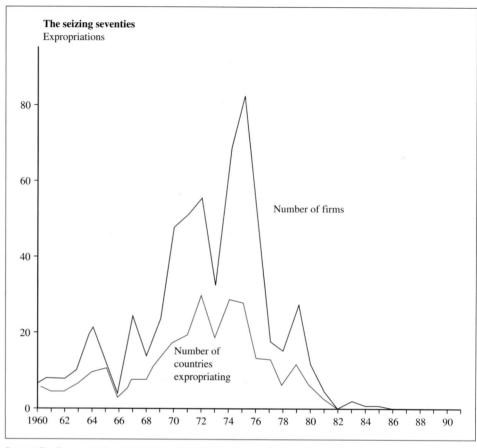

The seizing seventies
Expropriations

Source: *The Economist,* March 27, 1993, p. 19. © 1993 The Economist Newspaper Group, Inc. Reprinted with permission.

- *The host country's political and government system:* Whether the host country has a political and administrative infrastructure that allows for effective and streamlined policy decisions has important implications for political risk. If a country has too many political parties and frequent changes in government (like Italy, for example), government policies may become inconsistent and discontinuous, creating political risk.

- *Track records of political parties and their relative strength:* Examination of the ideological orientations and historical track records of political parties would reveal a great deal about how they would run the economy. If a party has a strong nationalistic ideology and/or socialist beliefs, it may implement policies that are detrimental to foreign interests. On the other hand, a party that subscribes to a liberal and market-oriented ideology is not very likely to take actions to damage the interests of foreign concerns. If the former party is more popular than the latter party and thus more likely to win the next general election, MNCs will bear more political risk.

- *Integration into the world system:* If a country is politically and economically isolated and segmented from the rest of the world, it would be less willing to observe the rules of the game. North Korea, Iraq, Libya, and Cuba are examples. If a country is a member of major international organizations, such as the EU, OECD, and WTO, it is more likely to abide by the rules of the game, reducing political risk. In the same vein, as China joins the World Trade Organization (WTO), MNCs operating in China may face less political risk.

- *The host country's ethnic and religious stability:* As can be seen from the civil war in Bosnia, domestic peace can be shattered by ethnic and religious conflicts, causing political risk for foreign business. Additional examples are provided by Nigeria, Rwanda, Northern Ireland, Turkey, Israel, Sri Lanka, and Quebec.

- *Regional security:* Real and potential aggression from a neighboring country is obviously a major source of political risk. Kuwait is an example. Countries like South Korea and Taiwan may potentially face the same risk depending on the future course of political developments in East Asia. Israel and its Arab neighbors still face this risk as well.

- *Key economic indicators:* Often political events are triggered by economic situations. Political risk thus is not entirely independent of economic risk. For example, persistent trade deficits may induce a host country's government to delay or stop interest payments to foreign lenders, erect trade barriers, or suspend the convertibility of the local currency, causing major difficulties for MNCs. Severe inequality in income distribution (for example, in many Latin American countries) and deteriorating living standards (as in Russia after the collapse of the Soviet Union) can cause major political disturbances. Argentina's protracted economic recession and the eventual collapse of the peso–dollar parity led to the freezing of bank deposits, street riots, and three changes of the country's presidency in as many months in 2002.

MNCs may use in-house experts to do the analysis. But often, MNCs use outside experts who provide professional assessments of political risks in different countries. For example, Morgan Stanley offers an in-depth analysis of country/political risks using a variety of data sources, including government and private sector publications, statistics provided by international organizations, newspaper articles, and on-site due diligence in countries with government officials and the private sector. Similarly, government agencies provide political risk analysis that can be useful to companies and investors. Exhibits 16.10 and 16.11 provide such analyses conducted by the Australian government for two countries: Vietnam and Turkey. The exhibits provide an example of how political risk analysis may be conducted.

transparency.org

Provides data about the Corruption Perceptions Index.

We next introduce the Corruption Perceptions Index (CPI) compiled annually by *Transparency International,* a global civil organization. The CPI provides a composite measure of perceived corruption in the public sector based on surveys and assessments from many institutions, such as the World Bank, Economist Intelligence Unit, and World Economic Forum. The level of perceived corruption in a particular country may serve as a useful gauge for the uncertainty about the rule of law and political risk, broadly defined, that MNCs and international investors may face in the country. Exhibit 16.12 presents the CPI for 2015. The index ranges from 0 (highly corrupt) to 100 (highly transparent). According to the CPI 2015, Denmark, Finland, and Sweden are the most transparent countries, followed by New Zealand, the Netherlands, Norway, Switzerland, Singapore, and Canada. Both Germany and the U.K. rank 10th, while the U.S. ranks 16th. Most developing countries rank lower—for example, Turkey 66th, both India and Brazil 76th, China 83rd, Indonesia 88th, Mexico 95th, Russia 119th, and Nigeria 136th. Afghanistan, Korea (North), and Somalia are the least transparent countries.

Let us now turn to the issue of how to manage political risk. First, MNCs can take a conservative approach to foreign investment projects when faced with political risk. When a foreign project is exposed to political risk, the MNC can explicitly incorporate political risk into the capital budgeting process and adjust the project's NPV accordingly. The firm may do so either by reducing expected cash flows or by increasing the cost of capital. The MNC may undertake the foreign project only when the adjusted NPV is positive. It is important here to recognize that political risk may be diversifiable to some extent. Suppose that an MNC has assets in, say, 30 different countries.

EXHIBIT 16.10   **Political Risk Analysis: Vietnam**

Sovereign Rating: Moody's: B1, Outlook: Stable; S&P: BB-, Outlook: Stable

Political Strengths
- Political stability with Communist Party in government since end of the country's civil war in 1975
- Widespread support for the CPV (Vietnam Communist Party) reflects its success in raising living standards and creating and maintaining security

Political Weaknesses
- Inconsistent and evolving regulations
- Unreliable legal system and corruption
- A lack of financial transparency, insufficient protection for minority owners, and poor corporate governance

Political & Governance Indicators

World Bank Ranking - Ease of doing business	90th/183
Freedom House - Political rights and civil liberties	Not Free
Transparency International Ranking—Corruption Perception Index	112th/180
OECD country risk rating (Scale: 0–7, 0 is least risk, 7 is highest risk)	5

Economic Strengths
- Transformation to market oriented economy since late 1980s
- High GDP growth facilitated by foreign investment
- Well educated and cheap labor force
- Sizable natural resources and advantageous location

Economic Weaknesses
- Large fiscal and trade deficits and weak banking system
- Plethora of state-owned enterprises and less diversification
- Industry and credit policies favor state-owned enterprises

Economic Indicators

GDP ($US bn)	199
GDP per capita ($US)	2,171
Real GDP growth (15-year average, %)	6.5
Fiscal balance (% of GDP)	−5.6
Public debt (% of GDP)	55.0
Foreign direct investment (% of GDP)	6.1
Current account (% of GDP)	0.7
External debt (% of GDP)	22.8
Foreign reserves (% of GDP)	16.8

Source: www.efic.gov.au, World Bank, and IMF, 2015 figures.

The collapse of the Soviet Union in the late 1980s forced Vietnam to transform from central planning and autarky to market orientation and international re-integration. Overall, this has been very successful. GDP growth has averaged nearly 8 percent a year, with foreign investment a key driver. Per capita income has risen from US$100 in 1990 to nearly US$2,200 in 2015. Vietnam has a number of attractions for investors and exporters: a large, young, and rapidly growing population; a labor force that is relatively well educated and cheap; sizable natural resources; an advantageous location; and a high level of political and social stability. Vigorous policy stimulus and spending helped Vietnam avoid the worst of the global financial crisis. But the authorities are now facing a fiscal deficit topping 6 percent of GDP, accelerating inflation, and a weakening banking system. In addition, a large trade deficit is putting strain upon the value of the dong—pegged to the US dollar—and has forced the central bank to run down reserves and devalue by 8 percent. Standard & Poor views the country's external foreign currency debt as speculative grade with a BB-rating and a stable outlook, and Moody's rating for the same is B1. Public debt is equivalent to 55 percent of GDP and contingent liabilities—in the banking sector and state-owned enterprises—are large.

The Vietnamese Communist Party (CPV) has been in government since the end of the country's civil war in 1975. The party has a firm grip on power, which ensures a high degree of political stability. Although the party's communist ideology has become less important over time, it led to a plethora of state-owned enterprises, which span most sectors and account for nearly 40 percent of GDP. Foreign investors face a number of challenges, including: inconsistent and evolving regulations, an unreliable legal system, a weak banking system, corruption, and industry and credit policies that favor state-owned enterprises.

Because the political risks in different countries may not be positively correlated, the political risk associated with a single country may be diversifiable to some extent. To the extent that political risk is diversifiable, a major adjustment to the NPV may not be necessary. This consideration also suggests that MNCs can use geographic diversification of foreign investments as a means of reducing political risk. Put simply, don't put all your eggs in one basket.

Second, once an MNC decides to undertake a foreign project, it can take various measures to minimize its exposure to political risk. For example, an MNC can form a joint venture with a local company. The idea is that if the project is partially owned

EXHIBIT 16.11	Political Risk Analysis: Turkey

Sovereign Rating: Moody's: Baa3, Outlook: Negative; S&P: BB+, Outlook: Negative

Political Strengths
- Transition to democracy at the end of 1970s
- Significant liberalization and stabilization by a drive to join European Union

Political Weaknesses
- Instability fuelled by conflict between the army and the civilian government
- Strained relations between religious conservatives and secular modernists

Political & Governance Indicators
- World Bank Ranking—Ease of doing business — 55th/183
- Freedom House—Political rights and civil liberties — Partly Free
- Transparency International Ranking—Corruption Perception Index — 66th/180
- OECD country risk rating — 4
  (Scale: 0–7, 0 is least risk, 7 is highest risk)

Economic Strengths
- Key dimensions of economic performance on par with central and eastern European countries
- Was able to weather the recent global economic crisis
- Debt is highly sought after by foreign investors
- Healthy growth forecast

Economic Weaknesses
- Mounting macroeconomic imbalances and major reliance on foreign financing
- Widening current account deficit, surging credit growth and building inflation pressures
- High business cycle and currency risk
- Lira is a volatile emerging market currency

Economic Indicators
GDP ($US bn)	722
GDP per capita ($US)	9,290
Real GDP growth (15 year average, %)	3.0
Fiscal balance (% of GDP)	−5.0
Public debt (% of GDP)	33.6
Foreign direct investment (% of GDP)	1.5
Current account (% of GDP)	−4.5
External debt (% of GDP)	55.3
Foreign reserves (% of GDP)	19.4

Source: www.efic.gov.au, World Bank, and IMF, 2015 figures.

At the end of the 1970s, Turkey was under martial law and handicapped by protectionism, triple-digit inflation, and financial crisis. It has since undertaken significant democratization, liberalization, and stabilization by a drive to join the European Union. Trade liberalization introduced by the late president Turgut Ozal in the 1980s helped to open the economy up. On key dimensions of economic performance such as per capita income, business climate, creditworthiness, and growth, Turkey is about on par with other Central and Eastern European countries. The Turkish economy really only began to demonstrate its full potential in the wake of a 2002 IMF-led stabilization program, which helped put in place policies that: sharply reduced inflation from 70 percent per annum to single digits, restored fiscal solvency, and unleashed GDP growth of almost 7 percent pa over 2002–2007. Turkey was able to weather the global financial and economic crises reasonably well. Its debt is highly sought after by foreign investors. And despite the lack of an investment-grade sovereign rating (S&P: BB+, Fitch: BB+, and Moody's: Baa3), the country's sovereign bond spreads are roughly in line with those of investment-grade emerging markets such as Russia and Brazil (BBB−).

But for all this progress, significant vulnerabilities remain. Mounting macroeconomic imbalances and a reliance on foreign financing are key economic challenges. The main near-term economic challenges are a widening current account deficit, surging credit growth, and building inflation pressures. Turkey also faces a sizable external financing requirement, which makes it vulnerable to domestic and international setbacks. In the political sphere, instability is fueled by conflict between the army and the civilian government and between religious conservatives and secular modernists. Exporters and investors in Turkey face high business cycle and currency risk; Turkish GDP growth has recently experienced a large bust and rebound, and the lira is a volatile emerging market currency.

by a local company, the foreign government may be less inclined to expropriate it since the action will hurt the local company as well as the MNC. The MNC may also consider forming a consortium of international companies to undertake the foreign project. In this case, the MNC can reduce its exposure to political risk and, at the same time, make expropriation more costly to the host government. Understandably, the host government may not wish to take actions that will antagonize many countries at the same time. Alternatively, MNCs can use local debt to finance the foreign project. In this case, the MNC has an option to repudiate its debt if the host government takes actions to hurt its interests.

EXHIBIT 16.12				Corruption Perceptions Index 2015—Transparency International				

Rank	Country/Territory	Score	Rank	Country/Territory	Score	Rank	Country/Territory	Score
1	Denmark	91	58	Romania	46	112	Honduras	31
2	Finland	90	60	Oman	45	112	Malawi	31
3	Sweden	89	61	Italy	44	112	Mauritania	31
4	New Zealand	88	61	Lesotho	44	112	Mozambique	31
5	Netherlands	87	61	Montenegro	44	112	Vietnam	31
5	Norway	87	61	Senegal	44	117	Pakistan	30
7	Switzerland	86	61	South Africa	44	117	Tanzania	30
8	Singapore	85	66	Sao Tome and	42	119	Azerbaijan	29
9	Canada	83		Principe		119	Guyana	29
10	Germany	81	66	The FYR of	42	119	Russia	29
10	Luxembourg	81		Macedonia		119	Sierra Leone	29
10	United Kingdom	81	66	Turkey	42	123	Gambia	28
13	Australia	79	69	Bulgaria	41	123	Guatemala	28
13	Iceland	79	69	Jamaica	41	123	Kazakhstan	28
15	Belgium	77	71	Serbia	40	123	Kyrgyzstan	28
16	Austria	76	72	El Salvador	39	123	Lebanon	28
16	United States	76	72	Mongolia	39	123	Madagascar	28
18	Hong Kong	75	72	Panama	39	123	Timor-Leste	28
18	Ireland	75	72	Trinidad and	39	130	Cameroon	27
18	Japan	75		Tobago		130	Iran	27
21	Uruguay	74	76	Bosnia and	38	130	Nepal	27
22	Qatar	71		Herzegovina		130	Nicaragua	27
23	Chile	70	76	Brazil	38	130	Paraguay	27
23	Estonia	70	76	Burkina Faso	38	130	Ukraine	27
23	France	70	76	India	38	136	Comoros	26
23	United Arab	70	76	Thailand	38	136	Nigeria	26
	Emirates		76	Tunisia	38	136	Tajikistan	26
27	Bhutan	65	76	Zambia	38	139	Bangladesh	25
28	Botswana	63	83	Benin	37	139	Guinea	25
28	Portugal	63	83	China	37	139	Kenya	25
30	Poland	62	83	Colombia	37	139	Laos	25
30	Taiwan	62	83	Liberia	37	139	Papua New	25
32	Cyprus	61	83	Sri Lanka	37		Guinea	
32	Israel	61	88	Albania	36	139	Uganda	25
32	Lithuania	61	88	Algeria	36	145	Central African	24
35	Slovenia	60	88	Egypt	36		Republic	
36	Spain	58	88	Indonesia	36	146	Congo Republic	23
37	Czech Republic	56	88	Morocco	36	147	Chad	22
37	Korea (South)	56	88	Peru	36	147	Congo, D.R.	22
37	Malta	56	88	Suriname	36	147	Myanmar	22
40	Cape Verde	55	95	Armenia	35	150	Burundi	21
40	Costa Rica	55	95	Mali	35	150	Cambodia	21
40	Latvia	55	95	Mexico	35	150	Zimbabwe	21
40	Seychelles	55	95	Philippines	35	153	Uzbekistan	19
44	Rwanda	54	99	Bolivia	34	154	Eritrea	18
45	Jordan	53	99	Djibouti	34	154	Syria	18
45	Mauritius	53	99	Gabon	34	154	Turkmenistan	18
45	Namibia	53	99	Niger	34	154	Yemen	18
48	Georgia	52	103	Dominican	33	158	Haiti	17
48	Saudi Arabia	52		Republic		158	Guinea-Bissau	17
50	Bahrain	51	103	Ethiopia	33	158	Venezuela	17
50	Croatia	51	103	Kosovo	33	161	Iraq	16
50	Hungary	51	103	Moldova	33	161	Libya	16
50	Slovakia	51	107	Argentina	32	163	Angola	15
54	Malaysia	50	107	Belarus	32	163	South Sudan	15
55	Kuwait	49	107	Côte d'Ivoire	32	165	Sudan	12
56	Cuba	47	107	Ecuador	32	166	Afghanistan	11
56	Ghana	47	107	Togo	32	167	Korea (North)	8
58	Greece	46				167	Somalia	8

Third, MNCs may purchase insurance against the hazard of political risk. Such insurance policies, which are available in many advanced countries, are especially useful for small firms that are less well equipped to deal with political risk on their own. In the United States, the **Overseas Private Investment Corporation (OPIC)**, a federally owned organization, offers insurance against (i) the inconvertibility of foreign currencies, (ii) expropriation of U.S.-owned assets overseas, (iii) destruction of U.S.-owned physical properties due to war, revolution, and other violent political events in foreign countries, and (iv) loss of business income due to political violence. OPIC's primary goal is to encourage U.S. private investments in the economies of developing countries. Alternatively, MNCs may also purchase tailor-made insurance policies from private insurers such as Lloyd's of London.

When the political risk faced by an MNC can be fully covered by an insurance contract, the MNC can subtract the insurance premium from the expected cash flows from the project in computing its NPV. The MNC then can use the usual cost of capital, which would be used to evaluate domestic investment projects, in discounting the expected cash flows from foreign projects. Lastly, it is pointed out that many countries have concluded bilateral or multilateral investment protection agreements, effectively eliminating most political risk. As a result, if an MNC invests in a country that signed the investment protection agreement with the MNC's home country, it need not be overly concerned with political risk.

One particular type of political risk that MNCs and investors may face is corruption associated with the abuse of public offices for private benefits. Investors may often encounter demands for bribes from politicians and government officials for contracts and smooth bureaucratic processes. If companies refuse to make *grease payments*, they may lose business opportunities or face difficult bureaucratic red tape. If companies pay, on the other hand, they may risk violating laws or being embarrassed when the payments are discovered and reported in the media. Corruption can be found anywhere in the world. But it is a much more serious problem in many developing and transition economies where the state sector is large, democratic institutions are weak, and the press is often muzzled. U.S. companies are legally prohibited from bribing foreign officials by the Foreign Corrupt Practices Act (FCPA). In 1997, the OECD also adopted a treaty to criminalize the bribery of foreign officials by companies. Bribery thus is both morally and legally wrong for companies from most developed countries. Another particular risk that companies may face is extortion demands from Mafia-style criminal organizations. For example, the majority of companies in Russia are known to have paid extortion demands. To deal with this kind of situation, it is important for companies to hire people who are familiar with local operating environments, to strengthen local support for the company, and to enhance physical security measures.

SUMMARY

This chapter discusses various issues associated with foreign direct investments (FDI) by MNCs, which play a key role in shaping the nature of the emerging global economy.

1. Firms become *multinational* when they undertake FDI. FDI may involve either the establishment of new production facilities in foreign countries or acquisitions of existing foreign businesses.

2. During the six-year period 2010–2015, total annual worldwide FDI outflows amounted to about $1,394 billion on average. The United States is the largest recipient, as well as initiator, of FDI. Besides the United States, Japan, China, and Germany are the leading sources of FDI outflows, whereas the United States, United Kingdom, China, Canada, and Australia are the major destinations for FDI in recent years.

3. Most existing theories of FDI emphasize various market imperfections, that is, imperfections in product, factor, and capital markets, as the key motivating forces driving FDI.

4. The *internalization* theory of FDI holds that firms that have intangible assets with a public good property tend to invest directly in foreign countries in order to use these assets on a larger scale and, at the same time, avoid the misappropriations that may occur while transacting in foreign markets through a market mechanism.

5. According to Raymond Vernon's product life-cycle theory, when firms first introduce new products, they choose to produce at home, close to their customers. Once the product becomes standardized and mature, it becomes important to cut production costs to stay competitive. At this stage, firms may set up production facilities in low-cost foreign countries.

6. In recent years, a growing portion of FDI has taken the form of cross-border acquisitions of existing businesses. *Synergistic* gains may arise if the acquirer is motivated to take advantage of various market imperfections.

7. Imperfections in the market for intangible assets, such as R&D capabilities, may play a key role in motivating cross-border acquisitions. The internalization may proceed *forward* to internalize the acquirer's intangible assets or *backward* to internalize the target's intangible assets.

8. In evaluating political risk, experts focus their attention on a set of key factors such as the host country's political/government system, historical records of political parties and their relative strengths, integration of the host country into the world political/economic system, the host country's ethnic and religious stability, regional security, and key economic indicators.

9. In evaluating a foreign investment project, it is important for the MNC to consider the effect of political risk, as a sovereign country can change the *rules of the game*. The MNC may adjust the cost of capital upward or lower the expected cash flows from the foreign project. Or, the MNC may purchase insurance policies against the hazard of political risks.

KEY WORDS

cross-border mergers and acquisitions, *404*
FDI flows, *405*
FDI stocks, *407*
foreign direct investments (FDI), *404*

greenfield investments, *404*
intangible assets, *410*
internalization theory, *411*
Overseas Private Investment

Corporation (OPIC), *425*
political risk, *418*
product life-cycle theory, *412*
synergistic gains, *416*

QUESTIONS

1. Recently, many foreign firms from both developed and developing countries acquired high-tech U.S. firms. What might have motivated these firms to acquire U.S. firms?

2. Japanese MNCs, such as Toyota, Toshiba, and Matsushita, made extensive investments in Southeast Asian countries like Thailand, Malaysia, and Indonesia. In your opinion, what forces are driving Japanese investments in this region?

3. Since NAFTA was established, many Asian firms, especially those from Japan and Korea, have made extensive investments in Mexico. Why do you think these Asian firms decided to build production facilities in Mexico?

4. How would you explain the fact that China emerged as one of the most important recipients of FDI in recent years?

5. Explain the internalization theory of FDI. What are the strengths and weaknesses of the theory?

6. Explain Vernon's product life-cycle theory of FDI. What are the strengths and weaknesses of the theory?

7. Why do you think the host country tends to resist cross-border acquisitions rather than greenfield investments?

8. How would you incorporate political risk into the capital budgeting process of foreign investment projects?

9. Explain and compare forward versus backward internalization.

10. What could be the reason for the negative synergistic gains for British acquisitions of U.S. firms?

11. Define *country risk*. How is it different from political risk?

12. What are the advantages and disadvantages of FDI as compared to a licensing agreement with a foreign partner?

13. What operational and financial measures can an MNC take to minimize the political risk associated with a foreign investment project?

14. Study the experience of Enron in India and discuss what we can learn from it for the management of political risk.

15. Discuss the different ways political events in a host country may affect local operations of an MNC.

16. What factors would you consider in evaluating the political risk associated with making FDI in a foreign country?

17. Daimler, a German carmaker, acquired Chrysler, the third largest U.S. automaker, for $40.5 billion in 1998. But after years of declining profit and labor problems, Daimler sold off Chrysler to the U.S. private equity firm Cerberus for $7.4 billion in 2007. Study the DaimlerChrysler saga and identify the main factors for the failure of this cross-border merger.

18. Lured by extremely low labor costs in Bangladesh, many MNCs in the so-called fast-fashion business, including H&M, Inditex (parent of the popular Zara brand), Marks&Spencer, and Gap, are heavily outsourcing to Bangladesh. As a result, the garment industry has become a major source of employment and income for Bangladesh. However, the industry has recently suffered a spate of disasters. In September 2012, about 110 workers died in a blaze at the Tazeen Fashions factory outside Dhaka, the capital city. What's worse, in April 2013, more than 1,100 workers perished in the collapse of the Rena Plaz building in Dhaka. In your opinion, (i) what are the root causes of the disasters? (ii) What should be done to prevent future disasters?

INTERNET EXERCISES

You are hired as a political consultant for General Motors Company, which is considering building automobile plants in three countries: Brazil, China, and Poland. Choose a country and analyze the political risk of investing in that country. In doing so, utilize websites such as www.cia.gov/library/publications/the-world-factbook or any other relevant Internet resources. You may prepare a final report to GM using a format similar to Exhibit 16.10.

MINI CASE **Enron versus Bombay Politicians**

On August 3, 1995, the Maharashtra state government of India, dominated by the nationalist, right-wing Bharatiya Janata Party (BJP), abruptly canceled Enron's $2.9 billion power project in Dabhol, located south of Bombay, the industrial heartland of India. This came as a huge blow to Rebecca P. Mark, the chairman and chief executive of Enron's international power unit, who spearheaded the Houston-based energy giant's international investment drive. Upon the news release, Enron's share price fell immediately by about 10 percent to

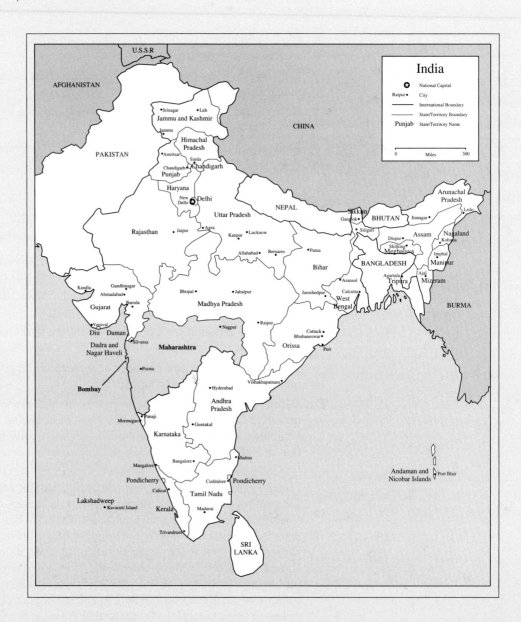

$33.50. Mark sprang to action to resuscitate the deal with the Maharashtra state, promising concessions. This effort, however, was met with scorn from BJP politicians. Enron's Dabhol debacle cast a serious doubt on the company's aggressive global expansion strategy, involving some $10 billion in projects in power plants and pipelines spanning across Asia, South America, and the Middle East.

Enron became involved in the project in 1992 when the new reformist government of the Congress Party (I), led by Prime Minister Narasimha Rao, was keen on attracting foreign investment in infrastructure. After meeting with the Indian government officials visiting Houston in May, Enron dispatched executives to India to hammer out a "memorandum of understanding" in just 10 days to build a massive 2,015-megawatt Dabhol power complex. New Delhi placed the project on a fast track and awarded it to Enron without competitive bidding. Subsequently, the Maharashtra State Electricity Board (MSEB) agreed to buy 90 percent of the power Dabhol produces. Two other U.S. companies, General Electric (GE) and Bechtel Group, agreed to join Enron as partners for the Dabhol project.

In the process of structuring the deal, Enron made a profound political miscalculation: It did not seriously take into consideration a rising backlash against foreign investments by an opposition coalition led by the BJP. During the state election campaign in early 1995, the BJP called for a reevaluation of the Enron project. Jay Dubashi, the BJP's economic advisor, said that the BJP would review all foreign investments already in India, and "If it turns out that we have to ask them to go, then we'll ask them to go." Instead of waiting for the election results, Enron rushed to close the deal and began construction, apparently believing that a new government would find it difficult to unwind the deal when construction was already under way. Enron was not very concerned with local political sentiments. Enron fought to keep the contract details confidential, but a successful lawsuit by a Bombay consumer group forced the company to reveal the details: Enron would receive 7.4 cents per kilowatt-hour from MSEB and Enron's rate of return would be 23 percent, far higher than 16 percent over the capital cost that the Indian government guaranteed to others. Critics cited the disclosure as proof that Enron had exaggerated project costs to begin with and that the deal might have involved corruption.

The BJP won the 1995 election in Maharashtra state and fulfilled its promise. Manohar Joshi, the newly elected chief minister of Maharashtra, who campaigned on a pledge to "drive Enron into the sea," promptly canceled the project, citing inflated project costs and too-high electricity rates. This pledge played well with Indian voters, many of whom had a visceral distrust of foreign companies since the British colonial era. (It helps to recall that India was first colonized by a foreign company, the British East India Company.) By the time the project was canceled, Enron already had invested some $300 million. Officials of the Congress Party who championed the Dabhol project in the first place did not come to the rescue of the project. The BJP criticized the Congress Party, rightly or wrongly, for being too corrupt to reform the economy and too cozy with business interests. In an effort to pressure Maharashtra to reverse its decision, Enron "pushed like hell" the U.S. Energy Department to make a statement in June 1995 to the effect that canceling the Enron deal could adversely affect other power projects. The statement only compounded the situation. The BJP politicians immediately criticized the statement as an attempt by Washington to bully India.

After months of nasty exchanges and lawsuits, Enron and Maharashtra negotiators agreed to revive the Dabhol project. The new deal required that Enron cut the project's cost from $2.9 billion to $2.5 billion, lower the proposed electricity rates, and make a state-owned utility a 30 percent partner in the project. A satisfied Joshi, the chief minister, stated: "Maharashtra has gained tremendously by this decision." Enron needed to make a major concession to demonstrate that its global power projects were still on track. The new deal led Enron to withdraw a lawsuit seeking $500 million in damages from Maharashtra for the cancellation of the Dabhol project.

Discussion Points

1. Discuss the chief mistakes that Enron made in India.

2. Discuss what Enron might have done differently to avoid its predicament in India.

REFERENCES & SUGGESTED READINGS

Aharoni, Yair. *The Foreign Investment Decision Process.* Cambridge, MA: Harvard Business School, 1966.

Caves, Richard. *Multinational Enterprise and Economic Analysis.* Cambridge, MA: Harvard University Press, 1982.

Doukas, John, and Nicholas Travlos. "The Effect of Corporate Multinationalism on Shareholders' Wealth: Evidence from International Acquisitions." *Journal of Finance* 43 (1988), pp. 1161–75.

Dunning, John. *Economic Analysis and the Multinational Enterprise.* New York: Praeger, 1975.

The Economist. "Multinationals, a Survey," March 27, 1993, pp. 4–20.

Eun, C., R. Kolody, and C. Scheraga. "Cross-Border Acquisitions and Shareholder Wealth: Tests of Synergy and Internalization Hypotheses." *Journal of Banking and Finance* 20 (1996), pp. 1559–82.

www.mhhe.com/er8e

Harris, Robert, and David Ravenscraft. "The Role of Acquisitions in Foreign Direct Investment: Evidence from the U.S. Stock Market." *Journal of Finance* 46 (1991), pp. 825–44.

Hymer, Stephen. *The International Operations of National Firms: A Study of Direct Foreign Investment.* Cambridge, MA: MIT Press, 1976.

Jensen, Michael. "The Takeover Controversy: Analysis and Evidence." *Midland Corporate Finance Journal* 5 (1986), pp. 1–27.

Kang, Jun-Koo. "The International Market for Corporate Control: Mergers and Acquisitions of U.S. Firms by Japanese Firms." *Journal of Financial Economics* 35 (1993), pp. 345–71.

Kindleberger, Charles. *American Business Abroad.* New Haven, CT: Yale University Press, 1969.

Kobrin, Stephen. "Political Risk: A Review and Reconsideration." *Journal of International Business Studies* 10 (1979), pp. 67–80.

Mandel, Robert. "The Overseas Private Investment Corporation and International Investment." *Columbia Journal of World Business* 19 (1984), pp. 89–95.

Magee, Stephen. "Information and the Multinational Corporation: An Appropriability Theory of Direct Foreign Investment." In Jagdish N. Bhagwati (ed.), *The New International Economic Order.* Cambridge, MA: MIT Press, 1977.

Morck, Randall, and Bernard Yeung. "Why Investors Value Multinationality." *Journal of Business* 64 (1991), pp. 165–87.

——. "Internalization: An Event Study Test." *Journal of International Economics* 33 (1992), pp. 41–56.

Ragazzione, Giorgio. "Theories of Determinants of Direct Foreign Investment." IMF Staff Papers 20 (1973), pp. 471–98.

Root, Franklin. "Analyzing Political Risks in International Business." In *The Multinational Enterprise in Transition*, ed. A. Kapoor and Philip Grub. Princeton: Darwin Press, 1972, pp. 354–65.

Rugman, Alan. "Internalization Is Still a General Theory of Foreign Direct Investment." Weltwirtschaftliche Archiv. 121 (1985), pp. 570–76.

Rummel, R. J., and David Heenan. "How Multinationals Analyze Political Risk." *Harvard Business Review* 56 (1978), pp. 67–76.

Vernon, Raymond. "International Investment and International Trade in the Product Cycle." *Quarterly Journal of Economics* 80 (1966), pp. 190–207.

——. "The Product Cycle Hypothesis in a New International Environment." *Oxford Bulletin of Economics and Statistics* 41 (1979), pp. 255–67.

17 International Capital Structure and the Cost of Capital

RECENTLY, MANY MAJOR firms throughout the world have begun to internationalize their capital structure by raising funds from foreign as well as domestic sources. As a result, these corporations are becoming *multinational* not only in the scope of their business activities but also in their **capital structure**. This trend reflects not only a conscious effort on the part of firms to lower the cost of capital by international sourcing of funds but also the ongoing liberalization and deregulation of international financial markets that make them accessible for many firms.

If international financial markets were completely integrated, it would not matter whether firms raised capital from domestic or foreign sources because the cost of capital would be similar across countries. If, on the other hand, these markets are less than fully integrated, firms may be able to create value for their shareholders by issuing securities in foreign as well as domestic markets.

As discussed in Chapter 13, cross-listing of a firm's shares on foreign stock exchanges is one way a firm operating in a segmented capital market can lessen the negative effects of segmentation and also internationalize the firm's capital structure.[1] For example, IBM, Honda Motor, and British Petroleum are simultaneously listed and traded on the New York, London, and Tokyo stock exchanges. By internationalizing its corporate ownership structure, a firm can generally increase its share price and lower its cost of capital.

In this chapter, we examine various implications of internationalizing the capital structure for the firm's cost of capital and market value. We also study various restrictions on foreign ownership of domestic firms and their effects on the firm's cost of capital. We are ultimately concerned with the MNC's ability to obtain capital at the lowest possible cost so that it can profitably take on the largest number of capital projects and maximize shareholders' wealth. We begin the chapter with a review of cost of capital concepts and basic asset pricing theory.

Cost of Capital

The **cost of capital** is the minimum rate of return an investment project must generate in order to pay its financing costs. If the return on an investment project is equal to the cost of capital, undertaking the project will leave the firm's value unaffected. When a firm identifies and undertakes an investment project that generates a return exceeding its cost of capital, the firm's value will increase. It is thus important for a value-maximizing firm to try to lower its cost of capital.

---

[1]Stapleton and Subrahmanyam (1977) pointed out that the firm may alternatively undertake foreign direct investment to mitigate the negative effects of segmented capital markets.

When a firm has both debt and equity in its capital structure, its financing cost can be represented by the **weighted average cost of capital**. It can be computed by weighting the after-tax borrowing cost of the firm and the cost of equity capital, using the capital structure ratio as the weight. Specifically,

$$K = (1 - \lambda) K_l + \lambda (1 - \tau)i \tag{17.1}$$

where

K = weighted average cost of capital,
K_l = cost of equity capital for a levered firm,
i = before-tax cost of debt capital (i.e., borrowing),
τ = marginal corporate income tax rate, and
λ = debt-to-total-market-value ratio.

In general, both K_l and i increase as the proportion of debt in the firm's capital structure increases.[2] At the optimal combination of debt and equity financing, however, the weighted average cost of capital (K) will be the lowest. Firms may have an incentive to use debt financing to take advantage of the tax deductibility of interest payments. In most countries, interest payments are tax deductible, unlike dividend payments. The debt financing, however, should be balanced against possible bankruptcy costs associated with higher debt. A trade-off between the tax advantage of debt and potential bankruptcy costs is thus a major factor in determining the optimal capital structure.

It is noted that the capital structure norm varies significantly across countries, largely reflecting differences in legal environments and institutional factors. As illustrated in Exhibit 17.1, a recent study by Fan, Titman, and Twite (2012) shows that the median debt ratio of firms varies from more than 0.50 for Korea to 0.099 for Australia. Developed countries like Germany, the United Kingdom, Sweden, the United States, and Canada have relatively low debt ratios, below 0.20. In contrast, many developing countries including Korea, Indonesia, Brazil, and India tend to have much higher debt ratios. The above study indicates that firms tend to use more debts in countries where tax benefits from debts are greater. In addition, firms tend to borrow more in countries with weaker laws and more government corruption. Firms can choose to use debts more in a country with a weaker legal system and more corruption as it is easier to expropriate outside equity holders than debt holders.

Choice of the optimal capital structure is important, since a firm that desires to maximize shareholder wealth will finance new capital expenditures up to the point where the marginal return on the last unit of new invested capital equals the weighted marginal cost of capital of the last unit of new financing to be raised. Consequently, for a firm confronted with a fixed schedule of possible new investments, any policy that lowers the firm's cost of capital will increase the profitable capital expenditures the firm takes on and increase the wealth of the firm's shareholders. Internationalizing the firm's cost of capital is one such policy.

Exhibit 17.2 illustrates this point. The value-maximizing firm would undertake an investment project as long as the internal rate of return (IRR) on the project exceeds the firm's cost of capital. It is noted that IRR is the discount rate that makes the net present value (NPV) of all expected future cash flows from a particular investment project equal to zero. When all the investment projects under consideration are ranked in descending order in terms of the IRR, the firm will face a negatively sloped IRR schedule, as depicted in the exhibit. The firm's optimal capital expenditure will then be determined at the point where the IRR schedule intersects the cost of capital.

Now, suppose that the firm's cost of capital can be reduced from K^l under the local capital structure to K^g under an internationalized capital structure. As the exhibit

---

[2]In Chapter 18, we distinguish between the cost of equity capital for a levered firm, K_l, and the cost of equity capital for an unlevered firm, K_u.

EXHIBIT 17.1   **Median Debt Ratios of Firms across Countries**

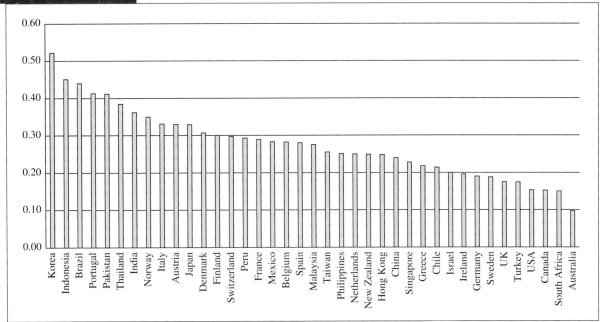

Note: The figure plots the median debt ratio across 39 countries over 1991–2006. The debt ratio is measured as total debt over the market value of the firm. Total debt is defined to be the book value of current and long-term interest-bearing debt. Market value of the firm is defined to be the market value of common equity plus book value of preferred stock plus total debt.

Source: The figure is constructed based on the data provided in Fan, Titman, and Twite (2012).

EXHIBIT 17.2

The Firm's Investment Decision and the Cost of Capital

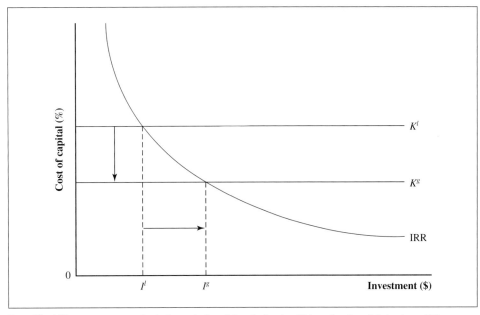

Note: K^l and K^g represent, respectively, the cost of capital under local and international capital structures; IRR represents the internal rate of return on investment projects; I^l and I^g represent the optimal investment outlays under the alternative capital structures.

illustrates, the firm can then increase its profitable investment outlay from I^l to I^g, contributing to the firm's value. It is important, however, to note that a reduced cost of capital increases the firm's value not only through increased investments in new projects but also through revaluation of the cash flows from existing projects.

Cost of Capital in Segmented versus Integrated Markets

The main difficulty in computing the financing cost (K) of a firm is related to the cost of equity capital (K_e). The cost of equity capital is the expected return on the firm's stock that investors require. This return is frequently estimated using the **Capital Asset Pricing Model (CAPM)**. The CAPM states that the equilibrium expected rate of return on a stock (or more generally any security) is a linear function of the systematic risk inherent in the security. Specifically, the CAPM-determined expected rate of return for the ith security is

$$\overline{R}_i = R_f + (\overline{R}_M - R_f)\,\beta_i \tag{17.2}$$

where R_f is the risk-free interest rate and $\overline{R}_M$ is the expected return on the **market portfolio**, the market-value-weighted portfolio of all assets. **Beta**, β_i, is a measure of systematic risk inherent in security i. **Systematic risk** is the nondiversifiable market risk of an asset. The CAPM equation shows that the expected return of security i, $\overline{R}_i$, increases in β_i, the greater the market risk, the greater the expected return. Beta is calculated as $Cov(R_i,R_M)/Var(R_M)$, where $Cov(R_i,R_M)$ is the covariance of future returns between security i and the market portfolio and $Var(R_M)$ is the variance of returns of the market portfolio.

Now, suppose that international financial markets are segmented and, as a result, investors can only diversify domestically. In this case, the market portfolio (M) in the CAPM formula would represent the domestic market portfolio, which is often proxied by the S&P 500 Index in the United States. The relevant risk measure in pricing assets will be the beta measured against the domestic market portfolio. In segmented capital markets, the same future cash flows are likely to be priced differently across countries, as they would be viewed as having different systematic risks by investors from different countries.

On the other hand, suppose that international financial markets are fully integrated and, consequently, investors can diversify internationally. In this case, the market portfolio in the CAPM formula will be the "world" market portfolio comprising all assets in the world. The relevant risk measure then should be the beta measured against the world market portfolio. In integrated international financial markets, the same future cash flows will be priced in the same way everywhere. Investors would require, on average, lower expected returns on securities under integration than under segmentation because they can diversify risk better under integration.[3]

EXAMPLE | 17.1: A Numerical Illustration

Suppose the domestic U.S. beta of IBM is 1.0, that is, $\beta_{IBM}^{U.S} = 1.0$, which is the average beta risk level. In addition, let us assume that the expected return on the U.S. market portfolio is 12 percent, that is, $\overline{R}_{U.S.} = 12\%$, and that the risk-free interest rate, which may be proxied by the U.S. Treasury bill rate, is 6 percent. If U.S. capital markets are segmented from the rest of the world, the expected return on IBM stock will be determined as follows:

$$\overline{R}_{IBM} = R_f + (\overline{R}_{U.S.} - R_f)\,\beta_{IBM}^{U.S}$$

$$= 6 + (12 - 6)(1.0) = 12\%.$$

Considering the domestic beta risk of IBM, investors would require 12 percent return on their investment in IBM stock.

Suppose now that U.S. capital markets are integrated with the rest of the world and that the world beta measure of IBM stock is 0.8, that is, $\beta_{IBM}^{W} = 0.8$. If we assume that the risk-free rate is 6 percent and the expected return on the world market

continued

---

[3]For a detailed discussion of the effect of integration/segmentation on the cost of capital, refer to Cohn and Pringle (1973) and Stulz (1995).

EXAMPLE 17.1: continued

portfolio is 12 percent, that is, $R_f = 6\%$ and $\bar{R}_w = 12\%$, we can compute the expected return on IBM stock as follows:

$$\bar{R}_{IBM} = R_f + (\bar{R}_w - R_f)\,\beta^W_{IBM}$$

$$= 6 + (12 - 6)\,(0.8) = 10.8\%.$$

In light of a relatively low world beta measure of 0.8, investors would require a lower return on IBM stock under integration than they would under segmentation.

Obviously, the integration or segmentation of international financial markets has major implications for determining the cost of capital. However, empirical evidence on the issue is less than clear-cut. Increasingly, researchers such as Harvey (1991) and Chan, Karolyi, and Stulz (1992) find it difficult to reject the international version of the CAPM, suggesting that international financial markets are integrated rather than segmented. Another group of researchers, including French and Poterba (1991), however, have documented that investors actually diversify internationally only to a limited extent, suggesting that international financial markets should be more segmented than integrated. In a study examining the integration of the Canadian and U.S. stock markets, on the other hand, Mittoo (1992) found that Canadian stocks cross-listed on U.S. exchanges are priced in an integrated market, and segmentation is predominant for those Canadian stocks that are not cross-listed.

These studies suggest that international financial markets are certainly not segmented anymore, but still are not fully integrated. If international financial markets are less than fully integrated, which may be the case, there can be systematic differences in the cost of capital among countries.

Does the Cost of Capital Differ among Countries?

The cost of capital is likely to vary across countries, due to international differences in the degree of financial integration, quality of corporate governance, macroeconomic conditions, and other factors. In a study, Lau, Ng, and Zhang (2010) document that the cost of equity capital indeed differs substantially across countries. For example, the estimated cost of capital is relatively low for many developed countries like Japan (7.4%), the United States (8.5%), and the U.K. (8.9%), but quite high for some of the developing countries like India (13.1%), South Africa (14.5%), and Brazil (16.8%). They report, among other things, that the cost of capital of a country is strongly related to the home bias in portfolio holdings, which reflects the country's degree of financial integration with the rest of the world.

Specifically, Lau et al. first compute the home bias of a country as the difference between the percentage of domestic mutual funds' holdings in domestic securities in a country and the country's weight in the world stock market capitalization. If a country's weight in the world market capitalization is 6 percent and domestic mutual funds collectively invest more than 6 percent of their investment funds in domestic securities, then the country is judged to exhibit a home bias. Lau et al. then compute the so-called "implicit cost of capital" (ICOC) as a proxy for the country's cost of capital. For each firm in a country, they estimate ICOC based on four different models, as implied by the current stock price and earning forecasts, and then take the average of the four estimates. For each country, the value-weighted ICOC estimate of all sample firms in the country is then used as the country's ICOC.[4]

---

[4]In computing ICOC, Lau et al. (2010) actually use the method that was previously employed by Hail and Leuz (2006). The basic premise of the ICOC method is that the ICOC is the internal rate of return (IRR) that equates current stock price to the present value of expected future steam of unexpected earnings. Refer to Hail and Leuz (2006) for details of the ICOC method.

Exhibit 17.3 provides both the degree of home bias and the ICOC for each of the 38 sample countries. Note that the degree of home bias reported in the exhibit is actually the percentage of domestic mutual funds' holdings in domestic securities in a country divided by the percentage weight of the country in the world market capitalization and is expressed in natural log. As can be seen from the exhibit, the degree of home bias ranges from 0.70 for the United States to 7.56 for Peru. The United States exhibits the lowest degree of home bias and, at the same time, has the lowest cost of capital (8.5%), whereas Peru exhibits the highest degree of home bias and has the second-highest cost of capital (16.5%), after Brazil (16.8%). Exhibit 17.4 plots the implicit cost of capital and the degree of home bias for different countries, showing that the two variables are positively related to each other. A higher home bias is associated with a higher cost of capital.

EXHIBIT 17.3

The Cost of Capital around the World

Country	World Market-Cap Weight (%)	Domestic Funds Local (%)	Home Bias	Implied Cost of Capital
Argentina	0.16	60.46	6.02	0.133
Australia	1.70	78.91	3.96	0.087
Austria	0.15	22.91	4.91	0.096
Belgium	0.63	17.71	3.31	0.088
Brazil	0.71	100.00	4.95	0.168
Canada	2.67	28.67	2.27	0.095
Chile	0.23	55.31	5.52	0.106
China	1.84	99.40	3.99	0.106
Czech Republic	0.06	58.59	7.08	0.110
Denmark	0.37	23.69	4.11	0.085
Finland	0.55	66.20	4.43	0.111
France	4.13	55.48	2.65	0.089
Germany	3.21	29.35	2.17	0.086
Greece	0.33	91.94	5.63	0.096
Hong Kong	2.08	22.51	2.34	0.101
India	0.71	99.51	4.98	0.131
Ireland	0.26	2.51	2.20	0.103
Italy	1.96	40.76	3.03	0.087
Japan	9.29	98.50	2.36	0.074
Luxembourg	0.12	12.21	4.54	0.077
Malaysia	0.43	99.90	5.44	0.100
Mexico	0.44	77.73	5.19	0.115
Netherlands	1.57	31.18	2.91	0.092
New Zealand	0.09	61.38	6.52	0.093
Norway	0.29	52.27	5.29	0.112
Peru	0.05	89.01	7.56	0.165
Philippines	0.12	99.52	6.71	0.098
Poland	0.12	82.46	6.69	0.119
Portugal	0.18	42.95	5.49	0.089
Singapore	0.51	20.00	3.52	0.100
South Africa	0.80	79.92	4.54	0.145
Spain	2.09	38.89	2.94	0.095
Sweden	1.00	48.36	3.93	0.090
Switzerland	2.24	21.08	2.17	0.084
Taiwan	1.10	100.00	4.51	0.113
Thailand	0.23	100.00	6.09	0.138
United Kingdom	7.64	42.95	1.71	0.089
United States	44.86	86.88	0.70	0.085

Note: The sample period of the study is 1998 to 2007.
Source: The world price of home bias, S.T. Lau et al., *Journal of Financial Economics* 97 (2010), pp. 191–217.

EXHIBIT 17.4

Implied Cost of Capital versus Home Bias

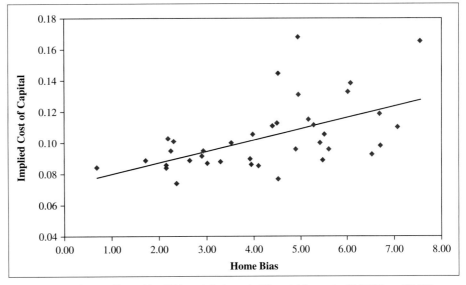

Source: The world price of home bias, S.T. Lau et al., *Journal of Financial Economics* 97 (2010), pp. 191–217.

When a country exhibits a high degree of home bias, as Peru does, the global risk sharing is hampered, thereby increasing the cost of capital for the country. Based on this finding, Lau et al. suggest that reduced home bias and greater global risk sharing would help reduce the cost of capital. In addition, they report that accounting transparency also helps reduce the cost of capital.

In perfect markets, firms would be indifferent between raising funds abroad or at home. When markets are imperfect, however, international financing can lower the firm's cost of capital. In Chapter 12, for example, we saw that Eurobond financing was typically a less expensive form of debt financing than domestic bond financing. We continue with this line of thinking in this chapter, where we explore ways of lowering the cost of equity capital through internationalizing the firm's ownership structure. Let us first examine the historical experiences of one firm, Novo Industri, that has successfully internationalized its cost of capital by cross-border listings. Our discussion here draws on Stonehill and Dullum (1982).[5]

CASE APPLICATION

www.novo.dk

The homepage of Novo provides basic information about the company.

Novo Industri

Novo Industri A/S is a Danish multinational corporation that controls about 50 percent of the world industrial enzyme market. The company also produces health care products, including insulin. On July 8, 1981, Novo listed its stock on the New York Stock Exchange, thereby becoming the first Scandinavian company to directly raise equity capital in the United States.

In the late 1970s, Novo management decided that in order to finance the planned future growth of the company, it had to tap into international capital markets. Novo could not expect to raise all the necessary funds exclusively from the Danish stock market, which is relatively small and illiquid. In addition, Novo management felt that the company faced a higher cost of capital than its main competitors, such as Eli Lilly and Miles Lab, because of the segmented nature of the Danish stock market.

Novo thus decided to internationalize its cost of capital in order to gain access to additional sources of capital and, at the same time, lower its cost of capital. Initially, Novo

---

[5]Stonehill and Dullum (1982) provide a detailed analysis of the Novo case.

EXHIBIT 17.5

Process of Internationalizing the Capital Structure: Novo

1977:	Novo increased the level of its financial and technical disclosure in both Danish and English versions. Grieveson, Grant and Co, a British stock brokerage firm, started to follow Novo's stock and issued the first professional security analyst report in English. Novo's stock price: DKr200–225.
1978:	Novo raised $20 million by offering convertible Eurobond, underwritten by Morgan Grenfell.
	Novo listed on the London Stock Exchange.
1980 April:	Novo organized a marketing seminar in New York City promoting its stock to U.S. investors.
1980 December:	Novo's stock price reached DKr600 level; P/E ratio rose to around 16.
1981 April:	Novo ADRs were listed on NASDAQ (5 ADRs = one share) Morgan Guaranty Trust Co. served as the depository bank.
1981 July:	Novo listed on NYSE.
	Novo stock price reached DKr1400. Foreign ownership increased to over 50 percent of the shares outstanding. U.S. institutional investors began to hold Novo shares.

Source: Arthur Stonehill and Kare Dullum, *Internationalizing the Cost of Capital* (New York: John Wiley & Sons, 1982).

increased the level of financial and technical disclosure, followed by Eurobond issue and the listing of its stock on the London Stock Exchange in 1978. In pursuing its goals further, Novo management decided to sponsor an American depository receipt (ADR) so that U.S. investors could invest in the company's stock using U.S. dollars rather than Danish kroners. Morgan Guarantee issued the ADR shares, which began trading in the over-the-counter (OTC) market in April 1981. On July 8, 1981, Novo sold 1.8 million ADR shares, raising Dkr. 450 million, and, at the same time, listed its ADR shares on the New York Stock Exchange. The chronology of these events is provided in Exhibit 17.5.

As can be seen from Exhibit 17.6, Novo's stock price reacted very positively to the U.S. listing.[6] Other Danish stocks, though, did not experience comparable price increases. The

EXHIBIT 17.6

Novo B's Share Prices Compared to Stock Market Indexes

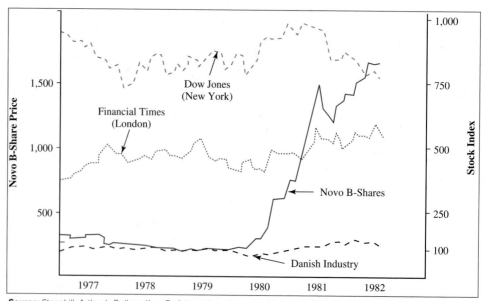

Source: Stonehill, Arthur I.; Dullum, Kare B., *Internationalizing the Cost of Capital: The Novo Experience and National Policy Implications.* John Wiley & Sons, 1982, p. 73. Note that Novo A shares are nontradable shares held by the Novo Foundation.

---

[6]It is noted that Novo has dual-class shares: A-shares that are held by the Novo Foundation and are nontradable and B-shares that are publicly tradable.

sharp increase in Novo's stock price indicates that the stock became fully priced internationally upon U.S. listing. This, in turn, implies that the Danish stock market was indeed segmented from the rest of the world. From the experiences of Novo, we can derive the following lesson: *Firms operating in a small, segmented domestic capital market can gain access to new capital and lower the cost of capital by listing their stocks on large, liquid capital markets like the New York and London Stock Exchanges.*

Cross-Border Listings of Stocks

www.adrbnymellon.com/
indices/composite-dr-index
/overview

Provides general information
about depositary receipts.

As we have seen from the case of Novo Industri, firms can potentially benefit from cross-border listings. As a result, cross-border listings of stocks have become quite popular among major corporations. Exhibit 17.7 presents the country-to-country frequency distribution of overseas listings that Sarkissian and Schill (2004) documented in their geographical analysis of cross-listings. As of 1998, their study period, there were 2,251 overseas listings. As can be seen from the bottom of Exhibit 17.7, U.S. and U.K. exchanges are, by far, the most popular hosts of overseas listings, probably reflecting the depth and credibility of these markets. Other important hosting markets include Belgium, France, Germany, Luxembourg, the Netherlands, and Switzerland, each hosting more than 100 foreign stocks. Examination of the exhibit suggests that to a certain extent, firms seem to prefer to list in neighboring markets. Out of the 266 Canadian overseas listings, 211 listings are on U.S. exchanges. New Zealand firms list heavily in Australia and vice versa. Similarly, Belgian firms list heavily in the Netherlands and vice versa. Sarkissian and Schill interpret this tendency as implying that the same proximity preference that is believed to be responsible for "home bias" in portfolio holdings may also influence firms' choice of overseas listing venues.

Exhibit 17.8 provides a partial list of overseas stocks that are cross-listed on the New York Stock Exchange (NYSE). Many well-known international companies such as BHP, Nokia, Deutsche Bank, Honda Motor, Infosys, ING, Unilever, BP, and China Mobile are all listed and traded on the NYSE. The London Stock Exchange (LSE) is another popular venue for cross-border listings. Exhibit 17.9 provides a list of foreign stocks listed on the LSE. It is noted that many companies from the British Commonwealth countries like Australia, Canada, and India are listed on the LSE. Reflecting London's traditional position as the center of European finance, many companies from the continental European countries, such as France, Germany, the Netherlands, Poland, and Russia, are also listed on the LSE. In addition, many high-profile U.S. companies, such as Bank of America, Boeing, General Motors, GE, IBM, and Pfizer, are also cross-listed on the LSE. Many exchanges of the world are now competing for cross-listings and trading volume of international stocks.

Generally speaking, a company can benefit from cross-border listings of its shares in the following ways:

1. The company can expand its potential investor base, which will lead to a higher stock price and a lower cost of capital.
2. Cross-listing creates a secondary market for the company's shares, which facilitates raising new capital in foreign markets.[7]
3. Cross-listing can enhance the liquidity of the company's stock.
4. Cross-listing enhances the visibility of the company's name and its products in foreign marketplaces.

---

[7]Chaplinsky and Ramchand (1995) report that, compared with exclusively domestic offerings, global equity offerings enable firms to raise capital at advantageous terms. In addition, they report that the negative stock price reaction that equity issue often elicits is reduced if firms have a foreign tranche in their offer.

EXHIBIT 17.7 **Country-to-Country Frequency Distribution of Foreign Listings**

Home Country	Australia	Austria	Belgium	Brazil	Canada	Denmark	France	Germany	H. Kong	Ireland	Italy	Japan	Luxem.	Malaysia	Nether.	N. Zealand	Norway	Peru	Singapore	S. Africa	Spain	Sweden	Switz.	UK	USA
Argentina				1									3										2	1	12
Australia					4			2				4	1			45			3				2	10	26
Austria			1				2	8							1										
Belgium							7	3					4		7		1						4		1
Brazil													5											1	21
Canada	4		8				6	2				1			4				1	1			8	20	211
Chile																									22
Colombia													3												1
Czech R.																								5	
Denmark																1						1	1	3	3
Finland							1	2														3		2	4
France			11		1			7			1	2	2		7				1		3		5	6	23
Germany		17	7				13				2	9	6		12				1		2	1	26	11	11
Greece													1		1									4	2
H. Kong	3											1					1		9					1	4
Hungary		1											5											4	1
India													48											17	
Indonesia													1											2	4
Ireland																								58	14
Israel			2																					4	59
Italy			2				4	5							1						1				14
Japan		1	5		1		30	52					21		19				6				14	29	28
Korea													12											14	3
Luxem.			5				3	1							2						1		1	6	3
Malaysia												1							1					5	
Mexico																									30
Nether.		4	11				9	20			1	1	6						1			1	12	13	26
N. Zealand	17																								5
Norway					1		1	2							1							2	1	5	6
Peru																									3
Philippines													5						1						1
Poland													1											7	
Portugal							1																	1	5
Singapore	2												2												1
S. Africa			9				15	5					4										4	40	11
Spain							4	4				4			1								2	4	5
Sweden		1	1		5		3	3				2					2		2				4	12	12
Switz.		1	1		1		5	10					4		1									1	5
Taiwan													14						1					10	2
Thailand													2						1						
Turkey													1											6	
UK	6		8		4	1	13	10	1	13		8	1	3	12		2		7	1			4		77
USA	8		31		27		32	42				23	1		71		3	2				5	67	104	
Venezuela													1												3
Total	40	25	106	1	37	8	148	179	1	13	4	60	150	3	140	45	10	2	34	2	4	17	157	406	659

Source: Sergei Sarkissian and Michael Schill. "The Overseas Listing Decision: New Evidence of Proximity Preference." *Review of Financial Studies* 17(2004).

EXHIBIT 17.8

Foreign Firms Listed on the New York Stock Exchange (selected)

Country	Firms
Australia	BHP Billiton, Samson Oil & Gas, Sims Group, Westpac Banking
Brazil	Banco Bradesco, Embraer, Petrobras, Telebras, VALE
Canada	Agrium, Barrick Gold, Canadian Pacific Railways, Domtar, RBC, Thomson Reuters, Toronto Dominion Bank
Chile	Banco de Chile, LAN Airlines, Vina Concha y Toro
China	China Eastern Airlines, China Life Insurance, Huaneng Power, PetroChina, China Mobile TAL Education
Finland	Nokia Corp.,
France	Constellium, Orange, Sanofi-Aventis, Sequans Communications, Total, Vivendi
Germany	Deutsche Bank, Orion Engineered Carbons, SAP, Voxeljet
India	ICICI Bank, Infosys, Tata Motors, Wipro
Israel	Blue Square, Cellcom Israel, Mobileye, Teva Pharmaceutical
Italy	ENI, Luxottica, Natuzzi, Telecom Italia
Japan	Canon, Honda Motor, Kyocera, Mizuho Financial, Nomura Holdings NTT Docomo, Sony, Toyota Motor
Korea	Korea Electric Power, Korea Telecom, Pohang Iron & Steel, SK Telecom
Mexico	Cemex, Empresas ICA, Grupo Simec Grupo Televisa
Netherlands	Aegon, AVG Technologies, Core Laboratories, Phillips Electronics, Unilever, ING
Norway	Marine Harvest, SeaDrill, Statoil
South Africa	Anglo Gold Ashanti, Gold Fields, Sasol
Spain	Banco Santander, Telefonica
Switzerland	ABB, Novartis, Tyco International, UBS
United Kingdom	Barclays, BP, BT Group, Diageo, GlaxoSmithKlein, HSBC, Lloyds, Prudential, Royal Bank of Scotland, Royal Dutch Shell

Source: *Datastream.*

EXHIBIT 17.9

Foreign Firms Listed on the London Stock Exchange (selected)

Country	Firms
Australia	Ironridge Resources, Prairie Mining, Range Resources, South32
Canada	Canadian Pacific Railways, Entertainment One, Falcon Oil & Gas, Republic Goldfields, Turbo Power Systems
China	Air China, China Petroleum & Chemical, Datang Intl Power Generation, Zhejiang Expressway
Egypt	Commercial Intl Bank, Suez Cement, Telecom Egypt
France	Compagnie de St-Gobain, Multi Units France, Total
Germany	BASF, Commerzbank, SQS Software Quality Systems
India	Lloyd Electric & Engineering, Reliance Industries, State Bank of India, Tata Power
Ireland	Abbey Plc, Bank of Ireland, Cairn Homes, Ryanair Hldgs
Israel	Bank Hapoalim, Dori Media Group, Metal-Tech
Japan	ANA, Mitsubishi Electric, Ricoh, Toyota Motor
Korea	Hyundai Motor, LG Electronics, Samsung Electronics, SK Telecom
Netherlands	European Assets Trust, Kimberly Enterprises, Nord Gold
Pakistan	Lucky Cement, MCB Bank, United Bank
Poland	Bank Pekao, Polski Koncern Naftowy Orlen, Telekomunikacja Polska
Russia	Gazprom, Lukoil, Sberbank, Severstal, Rosneft
Taiwan	Acer, Evergreen Marine, Hon Hai Precision Industry
Turkey	Finansbank, Turkiye Garanti Bankasi, Turkiye Petrol Rafinerileri
United States	Abbott Laboratories, Bank of America, Boeing, General Motors, General Electric, Honeywell, IBM, JPMorgan Chase, Pfizer

Source: London Stock Exchange.

5. Cross-listed shares may be used as the "acquisition currency" for taking over foreign companies.

6. Cross-listing may improve the company's corporate governance and transparency.

The last point deserves detailed discussion here. Consider a company domiciled in a country where shareholders' rights are not well protected, and controlling shareholders (e.g., founding families and large shareholders) derive substantial private benefits, such as perks, inflated salaries, bonuses, and even thefts, from controlling the company. Once the company cross-lists its shares on the New York Stock Exchange (NYSE), London Stock Exchange (LSE), or other foreign exchanges that impose stringent disclosure and listing requirements, controlling shareholders may not be able to continue to divert company resources to their private benefit. As argued by Doidge, Karolyi, and Stulz (2001), in spite of the "inconveniences" associated with a greater public scrutiny and enhanced transparency, controlling shareholders may choose to cross-list the company shares overseas, as it can be ultimately in their best interest to bond themselves to "good behavior" and to be able to raise funds to undertake profitable investment projects (thereby increasing share prices). This implies that if a foreign company does not need to raise capital, it may choose not to pursue U.S. listings, so that controlling shareholders can continue to extract private benefits from the company. The aforementioned study shows that other things being equal, those foreign companies that are listed on U.S. exchanges are valued nearly 17 percent higher, on average, than those that are not, reflecting investors' recognition of the enhanced corporate governance associated with U.S. listings. Since the London Stock Exchange also imposes stringent disclosure and listing requirements, foreign firms cross-listed on the exchange may also experience positive revaluation due to the effect of enhanced corporate governance.[8]

A study by Lang, Lins, and Miller (2003) shows that cross-listing can enhance firm value through improving the firm's overall information environments. Specifically, they show that foreign firms that cross-list in U.S. exchanges enjoy greater analyst coverage and increased forecast accuracy for firms' future earnings relative to those firms that are not cross-listed. They further show that firms that have greater analyst coverage and higher forecasting accuracy have a higher valuation, other things equal. These findings are consistent with the findings of other studies that cross-listed firms generally enjoy a lower cost of capital and better corporate governance.

Despite these potential benefits, not every company seeks overseas listings because of the costs.

1. It can be costly to meet the disclosure and listing requirements imposed by the foreign exchange and regulatory authorities.

2. Controlling insiders may find it difficult to continue to derive private benefits once the company is cross-listed on foreign exchanges.

3. Once a company's stock is traded in overseas markets, there can be volatility spillover from those markets.

4. Once a company's stock is made available to foreigners, they might acquire a controlling interest and challenge the domestic control of the company.

According to various surveys, disclosure requirements appear to be the most significant barrier to overseas listings. For example, adaptation to U.S. accounting rules, which is required by the U.S. Securities and Exchange Commission (SEC), is found

---

[8]As Dahya, McConnell, and Travlos (2002) point out, the standard of corporate governance has been raised significantly in the United Kingdom since the "Cadbury Committee" issued the *Code of Best Practice* in 1992, recommending that corporate boards include at least three outside directors and that the positions of chairman and CEO be held by different individuals.

EXHIBIT 17.10

Daimler's Net Profit/ Loss (DM bn): German vs. American Accounting Rules

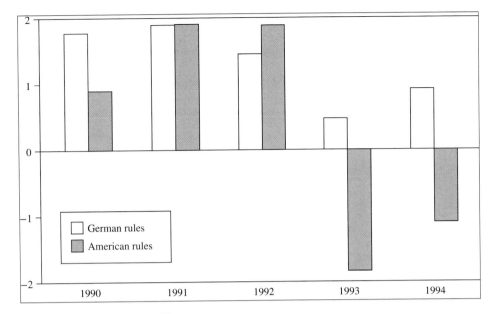

Source: *The Economist*, May 20, 1995.

to be the most onerous barrier facing foreign companies that consider NYSE listings. According to a German survey conducted by Glaum and Mandler (1996), one-third of the German sample firms are, in principle, interested in U.S. listings but view the required adaptation of financial statements to the U.S. Generally Accepted Accounting Rules (US-GAAP) as a major obstacle. Daimler, a German firm listed on the NYSE, employs US-GAAP as well as German accounting law and publishes two versions of consolidated financial statements with different reported earnings.[9] As can be seen from Exhibit 17.10, the company's net earnings were positive by German accounting rules but negative by American rules in 1993 and 1994. Also, as Gande and Miller (2012) documented, U.S. securities class-action lawsuits against foreign firms can be very costly in terms of the penalties and negative impact on the market values of foreign firms. In light of the costs and benefits of overseas listings, a foreign listing should be viewed as an investment project to be undertaken if it is judged to have a positive net present value (NPV) and thus adds to the firm's value.

In an extensive survey of the academic literature on the corporate decision to cross-list shares, Karolyi (1996) reports, among other things, that: (i) the share price reacts favorably to cross-border listings; (ii) the total postlisting trading volume increases on average, and, for many issues, home-market trading volume also increases; (iii) liquidity of trading in shares improves overall; (iv) the stock's exposure to domestic market risk is significantly reduced and is associated with only a small increase in global market risk; (v) cross-border listings resulted in a net reduction in the cost of equity capital of 114 basis points on average; and (vi) stringent disclosure requirements are the greatest impediment to cross-border listings. A detailed study by Miller (1999) also confirms that dual listing can mitigate barriers to international capital flows, resulting in a higher stock price and a lower cost of capital. Considering these findings, cross-border listings of stocks seem to have been, on average, positive NPV projects.

---

[9]Unlike U.S. accounting rules, German accounting rules are driven by tax considerations and creditor protection. For this reason, prudence, not a true and fair view, is the dominant accounting principle. German managers are granted broad discretion in accounting policy, and they try to achieve income smoothing.

In More Depth

Capital Asset Pricing under Cross-Listings[10]

To fully understand the effects of international cross-listings, it is necessary to understand how assets will be priced under the alternative capital market regimes. In this section, we discuss an **International Asset Pricing Model (IAPM)** in a world in which some assets are internationally tradable while others are not. For ease of discussion, we will assume that cross-listed assets are **internationally tradable assets** while all other assets are **internationally nontradable assets**.

It is useful for our purpose to recalibrate the CAPM formula. Noting the definition of beta, the CAPM Equation 17.2 can be restated as

$$\bar{R}_i = R_f + [(\bar{R}_M - R_f)/Var(R_M)]\, Cov(R_i, R_M) \tag{17.3}$$

For our purposes in this chapter, it is best to define $[(\bar{R}_M - R_f)/Var(\bar{R}_M)]$ as equal to $A^M M$, where A^M is a **measure of aggregate risk aversion** of all investors and M is the aggregate market value of the market portfolio.[11] With these definitions, Equation 17.3 can be restated as

$$\bar{R}_i = R_f + A^M M Cov(R_i, R_M) \tag{17.4}$$

Equation 17.4 indicates that, given investors' aggregate **risk-aversion measure**, the expected rate of return on an asset increases as the asset's covariance with the market portfolio increases.

Before we introduce the IAPM with cross-listing, however, let us first discuss the asset pricing mechanism under complete segmentation and integration as benchmark cases. Suppose that there are two countries in the world, the domestic country and the foreign country. In a **completely segmented capital market** where no assets are internationally tradable, they will be priced according to their respective **country systematic risk**. For domestic country assets, the expected asset return is calculated as

$$\bar{R}_i = R_f + A^D D Con(R_i, R_D) \tag{17.5}$$

and for foreign country assets, the expected asset return is calculated as

$$\bar{R}_g = R_f + A^F F Cov(R_g, R_F) \tag{17.6}$$

where $\bar{R}_i(\bar{R}_g)$ is the current equilibrium expected return on the ith (gth) domestic (foreign) asset, R_f is the risk-free rate of return that is assumed to be common to both domestic and foreign countries, $A^D(A^F)$ denotes the risk-aversion measure of domestic (foreign) investors, $D(F)$ denotes the aggregate market value of all domestic (foreign) securities, and $Cov(R_i, R_D)[Cov(R_g, R_F)]$ denotes the covariance between the future returns on the ith (gth) asset and returns on the **domestic (foreign) country market portfolio**.

By comparison, in **fully integrated world capital markets** where all assets are internationally tradable, each asset will be priced according to the **world systematic risk**. For both domestic and foreign country assets,

$$\bar{R}_i = R_f + A^W W Cov(R_i, R_W) \tag{17.7}$$

where A^W is the aggregate risk-aversion measure of world investors, W is the aggregate market value of the **world market portfolio** that comprises both the domestic and

---

[10]Readers may skip the theoretical discussion presented in this section and proceed to the numerical example without losing continuity.

[11]Here we assume, in fact, that investors' risk-aversion measure is constant.

foreign portfolios, and $Cov(R_i, R_w)$ denotes the covariance between the future returns of the ith security and the world market portfolio.

As we will see shortly, the asset pricing relationship becomes more complicated in **partially integrated world financial markets** where some assets are internationally tradable (that is, those that are cross-listed) while others are nontradable.

To tell the conclusion first, internationally tradable assets will be priced *as if* world financial markets were completely integrated. Regardless of the nationality, a tradable asset will be priced solely according to its world systematic risk as described in Equation 17.7. Nontradable assets, on the other hand, will be priced according to a world systematic risk, reflecting the spillover effect generated by the traded assets, as well as a country-specific systematic risk. Due to the **pricing spillover effect**, nontradable assets will *not* be priced as if world financial markets were completely segmented.

For nontradable assets of the domestic country, the pricing relationship is given by

$$\bar{R}_i = R_f + A^W W Cov^* (R_i, R_w) + A^D D [Cov (R_i, R_D) - Cov^*(R_i, R_D)] \tag{17.8}$$

where $Cov^*(R_i, R_D)$ is the *indirect* covariance between the future returns on the ith nontradable asset and the domestic country's market portfolio that is induced by tradable assets. Formally,

$$Cov^*(R_i, R_D) = \sigma_i \sigma_D \rho_{iT} \rho_{TD} \tag{17.9}$$

Where σ_i and σ_D are, respectively, the standard deviations of future returns of the ith asset and the domestic country's market portfolio; ρ_{iT} is the correlation coefficient between the ith nontradable asset and portfolio T of tradable assets, and ρ_{TD} is the correlation coefficient between the returns of portfolio T and the domestic country's market portfolio. Similarly, $Cov^*(R_i, R_w)$ is the *indirect* covariance between the ith nontradable asset and the world market portfolio. Nontradable assets of the foreign country will be priced in an analogous manner; thus, it is necessary to concentrate only on the pricing of nontradable assets in the domestic country.

Equation 17.8 indicates that nontradable assets are priced according to: (i) the **indirect world systematic risk**, $Cov^*(R_i, R_w)$, and, (ii) the *pure* domestic systematic risk, $Cov(R_i, R_D) - Cov^*(R_i, R_D)$, which is the domestic systematic risk, net of the part induced by tradable assets. Despite the fact that nontradable assets are traded only within the domestic country, they are priced according to an indirect world systematic risk as well as a country-specific systematic risk. This partial international pricing of nontradable assets is due to the pricing spillover effect generated by tradable assets. (The asset pricing spillover effect was first expounded in Alexander, Eun, and Janakiramanan, 1987.)

Although nontradable assets are exclusively held by domestic (local) investors, they are priced partially internationally, reflecting the spillover effect generated by tradable assets. As can be inferred from Equation 17.8, nontradable assets will not be subject to the spillover effect and will thus be priced purely domestically only if they are not correlated at all to tradable assets. This, of course, is not a very likely scenario. The pricing model also implies that if the domestic and foreign market portfolios can be exactly replicated using tradable assets, all nontradable, as well as tradable, assets will be priced fully internationally as if world financial markets were completely integrated.

The IAPM has a few interesting implications. First, international listing (trading) of assets in otherwise segmented markets directly integrates international capital markets by making these assets tradable. Second, firms with nontradable assets essentially get a **free ride** from firms with tradable assets in the sense that the former indirectly benefit from international integration in terms of a lower cost of capital and higher asset prices, without incurring any associated costs. Appendix 17A makes this point clear using numerical simulations.

The asset pricing model with nontraded assets demonstrates that the benefits from partial integration of capital markets can be transmitted to the entire economy through the pricing spillover effect. The pricing spillover effect has an important policy implication: *To maximize the benefits from partial integration of capital markets, a country should choose to internationally cross-list those assets that are most highly correlated with the domestic market portfolio.*

Consistent with the theoretical analyses presented above, many firms have indeed experienced a reduction in the cost of capital when their stocks were listed on foreign markets. In their study of foreign stocks listed on U.S. stock exchanges, Alexander, Eun, and Janakiramanan (1988) found that foreign firms from such countries as Australia and Japan experienced a substantial reduction in the cost of capital. Canadian firms, in contrast, experienced a rather modest reduction in the cost of capital upon U.S. listings, probably because Canadian markets were more integrated with U.S. markets than other markets when U.S. listings took place.

The Effect of Foreign Equity Ownership Restrictions

While companies have incentives to internationalize their ownership structure to lower the cost of capital and increase their market values, they may be concerned, at the same time, with possible loss of corporate control to foreigners. Consequently, governments in both developed and developing countries sometimes impose restrictions on the maximum percentage ownership of local firms by foreigners. In countries like India, Mexico, and Thailand, foreigners are allowed to purchase no more than 49 percent of the outstanding shares of local firms. These countries want to make sure that foreigners do not acquire majority stakes in local companies. France and Sweden once imposed an even tighter restriction of 20 percent. In Korea, foreigners were allowed to own only 20 percent of the shares of any local firm until recently.

In Switzerland, a local firm can issue two different classes of equity shares, bearer shares and registered shares. Foreigners are often allowed to purchase only bearer shares. In a similar vein, Chinese firms issue A shares and B shares, and foreigners are allowed to hold only B shares. Exhibit 17.11 lists examples of historical restrictions on foreign ownership of local firms for various countries. Obviously, these restrictions are imposed as a means of ensuring domestic control of local firms, especially those that are considered strategically important to national interests.[12]

Pricing-to-Market Phenomenon

Suppose that foreigners, if allowed, would like to buy 30 percent of a Korean firm, but they are constrained to purchase at most 20 percent due to ownership constraints imposed on foreigners. Because the constraint is effective in limiting desired foreign ownership, foreign and domestic investors may face different market share prices. In other words, shares can exhibit a dual pricing or **pricing-to-market (PTM) phenomenon** due to legal restrictions imposed on foreigners.

[12]Stulz and Wasserfallen (1995) suggest a theoretical possibility that firms may impose restrictions on foreigners' equity ownership to maximize their market values. They argue that when domestic and foreign investors have differential demand functions for a firm's stocks, the firm can maximize its market value by discriminating between domestic and foreign investors.

EXHIBIT 17.11	Restrictions on Equity Ownership by Foreigners: Historical Examples
Country	**Restrictions on Foreigners**
Australia	10% in banks, 20% in broadcasting, and 50% in new mining ventures.
Canada	20% in broadcasting, and 25% in bank/insurance companies.
China	Foreigners are restricted to B shares; locals are eligible for A shares.
France	Limited to 20%.
India	Limited to 49%.
Indonesia	Limited to 49%.
Mexico	Limited to 49%.
Japan	Maximum of 25–50% for several major firms; acquisition of over 10% of a single firm subject to approval of the Ministry of Finance.
Korea	Limited to 20%.
Malaysia	20% in banks and 30% in natural resources.
Norway	0% in pulp, paper, and mining, 10% in banks, 20% in industrial and oil shares, and 50% in shipping companies.
Spain	0% in defense industries and mass media. Limited to 50% for other firms.
Sweden	20% of voting shares and 40% of total equity capital.
Switzerland	Foreigners can be restricted to bearer shares.
U.K.	Government retains the veto power over any foreign takeover of British firms.

Source: Various publications of Price Waterhouse.

CASE APPLICATION

www.nestle.com

The homepage of Nestlé provides basic information about the company.

Nestlé[13]

The majority of publicly traded Swiss corporations have up to three classes of common stock: (i) registered stock, (ii) voting bearer stock, and (iii) nonvoting bearer stock. Until recently, foreigners were not allowed to buy registered stocks; they were only allowed to buy bearer stocks. Registered stocks were made available only to Swiss nationals.

In the case of Nestlé, a well-known Swiss multinational corporation that derives more than 95 percent of its revenue from overseas markets, registered shares accounted for about 68 percent of the votes outstanding. This implies that it was practically impossible for foreigners to gain control of the firm. On November 17, 1988, however, Nestlé announced that the firm would lift the ban on foreigners buying registered shares. The announcement was made after the Zurich Stock Exchange closed.

Nestlé's board of directors mentioned two reasons for lifting the ban on foreigners. First, despite the highly multinational nature of its business activities, Nestlé maintained a highly nationalistic ownership structure. At the same time, Nestlé made high-profile cross-border acquisitions, such as Rowntree (U.K.) and Carnation (U.S.). Nestlé's practices thus were criticized as unfair and incompatible with free-market principles. The firm needed to remedy this situation. Second, Nestlé realized that the ban against foreigners holding registered shares had the effect of increasing its cost of capital, negatively affecting its competitive position in the world market.

As Exhibit 17.12 illustrates, prior to the lifting of the ban on foreigners, (voting) bearer shares traded at about twice the price of registered shares. The higher price for bearer shares suggests that foreigners desired to hold more than they were allowed to in the absence of ownership restrictions imposed on them. When the ban was lifted, however, prices of the two types of shares immediately converged; the price of bearer shares declined by about 25 percent, whereas that of registered shares increased by about 35 percent. Because registered shares represented about two-thirds of the total number of voting shares, the total market value of Nestlé increased substantially when it fully internationalized its ownership structure. This, of course, means that Nestlé's cost of equity capital declined substantially.

Hietala (1989) documented the PTM phenomenon in the Finnish stock market. Finnish firms used to issue restricted and unrestricted shares, with foreigners allowed to purchase only

---

[13]The Nestlé case was briefly mentioned in Chapter 1. We offer an in-depth analysis of the case here.

EXHIBIT 17.12

Price Spread between Bearer and Registered Shares of Nestlé

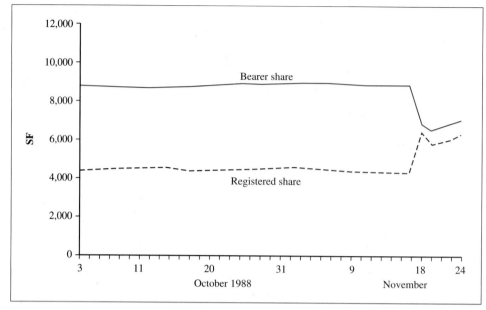

Source: *Financial Times,* November 26, 1988, p. 1.

unrestricted shares. Unrestricted shares accounted for at most 20 percent of the total number of shares of any Finnish firm. Because of this legal restriction, if foreigners desired to hold more than 20 percent of a Finnish firm, dual pricing could result. Indeed, Hietala found that most Finnish firms exhibited the PTM phenomenon, with unrestricted shares trading at roughly a 15 percent to 40 percent premium relative to restricted shares. Subsequently, Finland abolished restrictions imposed on foreigners altogether.

In More Depth

Asset Pricing under Foreign Ownership Restrictions[14]

In this section, we formally investigate how equilibrium asset prices are determined when foreigners are subject to ownership restrictions on the maximum proportionate ownership of domestic firms. As before, we assume that there are two countries in the world, the domestic country and the foreign country. For simplicity, we assume that the foreign country imposes an ownership constraint on investors from the domestic country, but that the domestic country does not impose any constraints on investors from the foreign country. Consequently, domestic country investors are restricted to holding at most a certain percentage of the shares of any foreign firms, whereas foreign country investors are not restricted in any way from investing in the domestic country.

Since we assume that there are no investment restrictions on domestic shares, both domestic and foreign country investors face the same price for the same domestic asset, which equals the perfect capital market price. As far as domestic assets are concerned, the law of one price prevails. For foreign shares, however, the PTM phenomenon applies.

Specifically, domestic country assets will be priced according to Equation 17.7, the fully integrated world capital market's IAPM. Foreign shares will be priced differently, depending upon whether the investor is from the foreign or domestic country. Investors

---

[14]Readers may proceed to the numerical example without losing continuity.

from the domestic country will pay a premium above and beyond the *perfect market price* that would prevail in the absence of restrictions, whereas investors from the foreign country will receive a discount from the perfect market price. This implies that the domestic country investors would require a lower return on foreign country shares than the foreign country investors.

Eun and Janakiramanan (1986) offer the following solutions for the equilibrium rates of return for foreign asset *i* from the domestic and the foreign country investors' perspectives, respectively:

$$\bar{R}_i^d = R_f + A^W W Cov\,(R_i, R_W) - (A^W W - \delta A^D D)[Cov\,(R_i, R_F) - Cov\,(R_i, R_S)] \qquad \textbf{(17.10)}$$

$$\bar{R}_i^f = R_f + A^W W Cov\,(R_i, R_W) + [(1 - \delta)A^D D - A^W W][Cov\,(R_i, R_F) - Cov\,(R_i, R_S)] \qquad \textbf{(17.11)}$$

where δ represents the fraction of the ith foreign firm that domestic country investors as a whole are allowed to own. In the above equations, portfolio *S* refers to the **substitution portfolio**, which is the portfolio of domestic country assets that is most highly correlated with the foreign market portfolio *F*. Portfolio *S* can thus be regarded as the domestic country investors' best *homemade* substitute for the foreign market portfolio *F*.

According to the above model, the equilibrium rates of return depend critically on (i) the severity of the ownership constraint (δ) and, (ii) the ability of domestic country investors to replicate the foreign market portfolio using their domestic assets, which is measured by the **pure foreign market risk**, $Cov(R_i, R_F) - Cov(R_i, R_S)$. In the special case where portfolio *S* is a perfect substitute for the foreign market portfolio *F*, we have $Cov(R_i, R_F) = Cov(R_i, R_S)$. In this event, the foreign asset will be priced as if world capital markets are fully integrated from both the domestic and foreign investors' perspectives, even though an ownership constraint is in force. In general, however, domestic country investors will pay premiums for foreign assets (that is, accept a lower rate of return than the perfect capital market rate) to the extent that they cannot precisely replicate the foreign market portfolio using domestic assets. Foreign country investors, on the other hand, will get a discount (that is, receive a higher rate than the perfect capital market rate).

EXAMPLE | 17.2: A Numerical Illustration

To illustrate the effect of foreign ownership restrictions on the firm's cost of equity capital, we conduct a numerical simulation using the model economy described in Exhibit 17.13.

Exhibit 17.13 provides the standard deviations and correlation matrix of our model economy. Firms D1 to D4 belong to the domestic country and firms F1 to F4 belong to the foreign country. For simplicity, the correlation matrix reflects the stylized fact that asset returns are typically less correlated between countries than within a country; the pairwise correlation is uniformly assumed to be 0.50 within a country and 0.15 between countries. Both domestic and foreign investors are assumed to have the same aggregate risk-aversion measure, and the risk-free rate is assumed to be 9 percent.

Exhibit 17.14 considers the case in which the foreign country imposes a 20 percent ownership constraint ($\delta_F = 20$ percent), whereas the domestic country does not impose any constraint on foreign investors. In this case, domestic country assets are priced as if the capital markets were completely integrated. Foreign country assets, however, are priced to market.

In general, the exhibit shows that the firm's cost of capital tends to be higher under the 20 percent ownership constraint than under complete integration. This

continued

EXAMPLE | 17.2: continued

implies that restricting foreign equity ownership in a firm will have a negative effect on the firm's cost of equity capital. For comparison purposes, we again provide the results obtained under complete segmentation and integration. Specifically, consider foreign firm F1. The exhibit shows that with the 20 percent ownership constraint, the firm's cost of capital is 22.40 percent, which is computed as a weighted average of the required returns by the domestic and foreign country investors in F1. Note that in the absence of the restriction, the firm's cost of capital would have been substantially lower, 19.03 percent. It is also noteworthy that when the PTM phenomenon prevails, the firm's cost of capital depends on which investors, domestic or foreign, supply capital. The exhibit also provides the case where both the domestic and foreign countries impose restrictions at the 20 percent level, that is, $\delta_D = 20\%$ and $\delta_F = 20\%$. Interpretation of this case is left to readers.

EXHIBIT 17.13   Description of the Model Economy

Firm	Expected Future Share Price ($)	Standard Deviation of Share Price ($)	Correlation Matrix						
			D2	D3	D4	F1	F2	F3	F4
D1	100	16	.50	.50	.50	.15	.15	.15	.15
D2	100	20		.50	.50	.15	.15	.15	.15
D3	100	24			.50	.15	.15	.15	.15
D4	100	28				.15	.15	.15	.15
F1	100	18					.50	.50	.50
F2	100	22						.50	.50
F3	100	26							.50
F4	100	30							

Note: Firms D1 to D4 are from the domestic country, whereas firms F1 to F4 are from the foreign country. The risk-free interest rate is assumed to be 9 percent. The domestic and foreign country investors are assumed to have the same aggregate (absolute) risk-aversion measure.

EXHIBIT 17.14

International Capital Market Equilibria: The Effect of Foreign Equity Ownership Restrictions

Asset	Complete Segmentation	σ-constraint $\delta_D = 20\%$ $\delta_F = 20\%$	σ-constraint $\delta_F = 20\%$	Complete Integration
A. Equilibrium Asset Prices ($)[a]				
D1	81.57	83.04/87.45	85.25	85.25
D2	78.53	80.45/86.22	83.34	83.34
D3	75.30	77.75/85.07	81.41	81.41
D4	71.88	74.86/83.82	79.34	79.34
F1	79.19	86.91/81.12	87.86/80.16	84.01
F2	75.87	85.66/78.31	86.87/77.11	81.99
F3	72.34	84.50/75.38	85.92/73.96	79.94
F4	68.62	83.24/72.28	84.90/70.62	77.76
B. Cost of Equity Capital (%)				
D1	22.59	19.15	17.30	17.30
D2	27.34	22.54	19.99	19.99
D3	32.80	26.24	22.84	22.84
D4	39.12	30.46	26.04	26.04
F1	26.28	21.54	22.40	19.03
F2	31.80	25.34	26.48	21.97
F3	38.24	39.96	32.82	25.09
F4	45.73	47.95	38.85	28.60

[a]The two figures indicate the asset prices for domestic/foreign country investors, respectively.

The Financial Structure of Subsidiaries

One of the problems faced by financial managers of multinational corporations is how to determine the financial structure of foreign subsidiaries. According to Lessard and Shapiro (1984), there are three different approaches to determining the subsidiary's financial structure:

1. Conform to the parent company's norm.
2. Conform to the local norm of the country where the subsidiary operates.
3. Vary judiciously to capitalize on opportunities to lower taxes, reduce financing costs and risks, and take advantage of various market imperfections.

Which approach to take depends largely on whether and to what extent the parent company is responsible for the subsidiary's financial obligations. When the parent is fully responsible for the subsidiary's obligations, the independent financial structure of the subsidiary is irrelevant; it is the parent's overall financial structure that becomes relevant. When the parent is legally and morally responsible for the subsidiary's debts, potential creditors will examine the parent's overall financial conditions, not the subsidiary's.

When, however, the parent company is willing to let its subsidiary default, or the parent's guarantee of its subsidiary's financial obligations becomes difficult to enforce across national borders, the subsidiary's financial structure becomes relevant. In this case, potential creditors will examine the subsidiary's financial conditions closely to assess default risk. As a result, the subsidiary should choose its own financial structure to reduce default risk and thus financing costs.

In reality, the parent company cannot let its subsidiary default on its debts without expecting its worldwide operations to be hampered in one way or another. Default by a subsidiary can deplete the parent's reputational capital, possibly increase its own cost of capital, and certainly make it difficult to undertake future projects in the country where default occurred. Various surveys, including one by Robert Stobaugh, strongly suggest that parent firms of MNCs indeed will not allow their subsidiaries to default, regardless of circumstances.

An immediate implication of the parent's legal and moral obligation to honor its subsidiary's debts is that the parent should monitor its subsidiary's financial conditions closely and make sure that the firm's overall financial conditions are not adversely affected by the subsidiary's financial structure. What really matters is the marginal impact that the subsidiary's financial structure may have on the parent's worldwide financial structure. The subsidiary's financial structure should be chosen so that the parent's overall cost of capital can be minimized.

In light of the above discussion, neither the first nor the second approach to determining the subsidiary's financial structure can be deemed appropriate. The first approach, which calls for replicating the parent's financial structure, is not necessarily consistent with minimizing the parent's overall cost of capital. Suppose the subsidiary can locally borrow at a subsidized interest rate because the host government is eager to attract foreign investments. In this situation, the subsidiary should borrow locally and exploit the lower interest rate, even if this means that the subsidiary's debt ratio will exceed the parent's norm. If deemed necessary, the parent can simply lower its own debt ratio. In other words, the distribution of debt between the parent and the subsidiary can be adjusted to take advantage of the subsidized loans. Also, in a special case where the subsidiary is operating in a country that regulates its financial structure, it would be difficult to replicate the parent's norm even if that were desirable.

The second approach, proposed by Stonehill and Stitzel (1969), calls for adopting the local financing norm. In essence, the approach is based on "When in Rome, do as the Romans do." By following the local norm, the firm can reduce the chance of being singled out for criticism. This approach makes sense only when the parent is not responsible for the subsidiary's obligations, and the subsidiary has to depend on local financing due to, say, segmentation of financial markets. Otherwise, it does not make much sense. Suppose each foreign subsidiary conforms to the local financing norm, which reflects the host country's cultural, economic, and institutional environments. Then, the parent firm's worldwide financial structure will be determined strictly in a "residual" manner. The overall financial structure so determined is not likely to be the optimal one that minimizes the parent's overall cost of capital. When the host country's norm reflects, for example, the immature nature of local financial markets, a subsidiary of the MNC with ready access to global financial markets should not slavishly follow the local norm. Doing so means that the MNC gives up its advantage in terms of a lower cost of capital.

This brings us to the third approach, which appears to be the most reasonable and consistent with the goal of minimizing the firm's overall cost of capital. The subsidiary should take advantage of subsidized loans as much as possible whenever available. It should also take advantage of tax deductions of interest payments by borrowing more heavily than is implied by the parent's norm when the corporate income tax rate is higher in the host country than in the home country, unless foreign tax credits are useful.

Apart from the tax factor, political risk is another factor that should be considered in choosing the method of financing the subsidiary. Political risk generally favors local financing over the parent's direct financing. The parent company can renounce the subsidiary's local debt in the event that the subsidiary's assets are expropriated. When the subsidiary is financed by local creditors and shareholders, the chance of expropriation itself can be lowered. When a subsidiary is operating in a developing country, financing from such international development agencies as the World Bank and International Finance Corporation will lower political risk. When the choice is between external debt and equity financing, political risk tends to favor the former. This is the case because the host government tolerates repatriation of funds in the form of interest much better than dividends.

To summarize, since the parent company is responsible, legally and/or morally, for its subsidiary's financial obligations, it has to decide the subsidiary's financial structure considering the latter's effect on the parent's overall financial structure. The subsidiary, however, should be allowed to take advantage of any favorable financing opportunities available in the host country, because that is consistent with the goal of minimizing the overall cost of capital of the parent. If necessary, the parent can adjust its own financial structure to bring about the optimal overall financial structure.

SUMMARY

In this chapter, we have discussed the cost of capital for a multinational firm. Reflecting the trend toward more liberalized and deregulated financial markets, major corporations of the world are internationalizing their capital structure by allowing foreigners to hold their shares and debts.

1. International comparison of the cost of funds indicates that while the costs of funds are converging among major countries in recent years, international financial markets are less than fully integrated. This suggests that firms can increase their market values by judiciously raising capital overseas.

2. When a firm is operating in a segmented capital market, it can reduce the negative effects by cross-listing its stock on foreign stock markets, thereby making the stock internationally tradable.

3. A firm can benefit from international cross-listings in terms of (a) a lower cost of capital and a higher stock price, and (b) access to new sources of capital.

4. When a firm's stock is cross-listed on foreign exchanges in an otherwise segmented capital market, the stock will be priced according to the world systematic risk as if international capital markets were fully integrated. Internationally non-tradable assets will be priced according to a country-specific systematic risk and an indirect world systematic risk, reflecting the pricing spillover effect generated by internationally tradable assets.

5. Although the trend is toward more liberal world financial markets, many countries still maintain restrictions on investment by foreigners, especially the maximum percentage ownership of a local firm by foreigners. Under an ownership constraint, foreign and domestic country investors may face different share prices, resulting in the pricing-to-market phenomenon (PTM). PTM generally raises the firm's overall cost of capital.

6. The parent company should decide the financing method for its own subsidiary with a view to minimizing the parent's overall cost of capital. To the extent that the parent is responsible for its subsidiary's financial obligations, the subsidiary's own financial structure is irrelevant.

KEY WORDS

beta, *434*
Capital Asset Pricing Model (CAPM), *434*
capital structure, *431*
completely segmented capital market, *444*
cost of capital, *431*
country systematic risk, *444*
domestic (foreign) country market portfolio, *444*
free ride, *445*
fully integrated world capital markets, *444*
indirect world systematic risk, *445*

International Asset Pricing Model (IAPM), *444*
internationally nontradable asset, *444*
internationally tradable asset, *444*
market portfolio, *444*
measure of aggregate risk aversion, *444*
partially integrated world financial markets, *445*
pricing spillover effect, *445*

pricing-to-market (PTM) phenomenon, *446*
pure foreign market risk, *449*
risk-aversion measure, *444*
substitution portfolio, *449*
systematic risk, *434*
weighted average cost of capital, *432*
world market portfolio, *444*
world systematic risk, *444*

QUESTIONS

1. Suppose that your firm is operating in a segmented capital market. What actions would you recommend to mitigate the negative effects?

2. Explain why and how a firm's cost of capital may decrease when the firm's stock is cross-listed on foreign stock exchanges.

3. Explain the pricing *spillover effect.*

4. In what sense do firms with nontradable assets get a *free ride* from firms whose securities are internationally tradable?

5. Define and discuss *indirect world systematic risk.*

6. Discuss how the cost of capital is determined in segmented versus integrated capital markets.

7. Suppose there exists a nontradable asset with a perfect positive correlation with a portfolio *T* of tradable assets. How will the nontradable asset be priced?

www.mhhe.com/er8e

8. Discuss what factors motivated Novo Industri to seek U.S. listing of its stock. What lessons can be derived from Novo's experiences?

9. Discuss foreign equity ownership restrictions. Why do you think countries impose these restrictions?

10. Explain the *pricing-to-market* phenomenon.

11. Explain how the premium and discount are determined when assets are priced to market. When will the law of one price prevail in international capital markets even if foreign equity ownership restrictions are imposed?

12. Under what conditions will the foreign subsidiary's financial structure become relevant?

13. Under what conditions would you recommend that the foreign subsidiary conform to the local norm of financial structure?

PROBLEMS

Answer problems 1, 2, and 3 based on the stock market data given by the following table.

	Correlation Coefficients				
	Telmex	Mexico	World	SD (%)	$\bar{R}$(%)
Telmex	1.00	.90	0.60	18	?
Mexico		1.00	0.75	15	14
World			1.00	10	12

The above table provides the correlations among Telmex, a telephone/communication company located in Mexico, the Mexico stock market index, and the world market index, together with the standard deviations (SD) of returns and the expected returns ($\bar{R}$). The risk-free rate is 5%.

1. Compute the domestic country beta of Telmex as well as its world beta. What do these betas measure?

2. Suppose the Mexican stock market is segmented from the rest of the world. Using the CAPM paradigm, estimate the equity cost of capital of Telmex.

3. Suppose now that Telmex has made its shares tradable internationally via cross-listing on the NYSE. Again using the CAPM paradigm, estimate Telmex's equity cost of capital. Discuss the possible effects of international pricing of Telmex shares on the share prices and the firm's investment decisions.

INTERNET EXERCISES

You are the controlling shareholder of Dragon Semicon based in Taiwan, a company with a strong growth potential. In order to fund future growth, you are considering listing the company stock either on the New York or the London stock exchange. Visit the websites of the two exchanges (www.nyse.com and www.londonstockexchange .com) and find out and compare their listing and disclosure requirements for foreign companies.

REFERENCES & SUGGESTED READINGS

Adler, Michael. "The Cost of Capital and Valuation of a Two-Country Firm." *Journal of Finance* 29 (1974), pp. 119–32.

Alexander, Gordon, Cheol Eun, and S. Janakiramanan. "Asset Pricing and Dual Listing on Foreign Capital Markets: A Note." *Journal of Finance* 42 (1987), pp. 151–58.

———. "International Listings and Stock Returns: Some Empirical Evidence." *Journal of Financial and Quantitative Analysis* 23 (1988), pp 135–51.

Bailey, Warren, and Julapa Jagtiani. "Foreign Ownership Restrictions and Stock Prices in the Thai Market." *Journal of Financial Economics* 36 (1994), pp. 57–87.

Black, Fisher. "International Capital Market Equilibrium with Investment Barriers." *Journal of Financial Economics* 1 (1974), pp. 337–52.

Bodie, Zvi, Alex Kane, and Alan J. Marcus. *Investments,* 2nd ed. Burr Ridge, Ill.: Irwin, 1993.

Chan, K. C., Andrew Karolyi, and Rene Stulz. "Global Financial Markets and the Risk Premium on U.S. Equity." *Journal of Financial Economics* 32 (1992), pp. 137−67.

Chaplinsky, Susan, and Latha Ramchand. "The Rationale for Global Equity Offerings." University of Virginia Working Paper, 1995.

Cohn, Richard, and John Pringle. "Imperfections in International Financial Markets: Implications for Risk Premia and the Cost of Capital to Firms." *Journal of Finance* 28 (1973), pp. 59−66.

Dahya, J., J. McConnell, and N. Travlos. "The Cadbury Committee, Corporate Performance, and Top Management Turnover." *Journal of Finance* 57 (2002), pp. 461−83.

Doidge, Craig, Andrew Karolyi, and Rene Stulz. "Why Are Foreign Firms Listed in the U.S. Worth More?" Ohio State University Working Paper (2001).

Errunza, Vihang, and Etienne Losq. "International Asset Pricing under Mild Segmentation: Theory and Test." *Journal of Finance* 40 (1985), pp. 105−24.

Eun, Cheol, and S. Janakiramanan. "A Model of International Asset Pricing with a Constraint on the Foreign Equity Ownership." *Journal of Finance* 41 (1986), pp. 897−914.

Fan, Joseph, Sheridan Titman, and Garry Twite. "An International Comparison of Capital Structure and Debt Maturity Choice." *Journal of Financial and Quantitative Analysis* 47 (2012), pp. 23−56.

French, K., and J. Poterba. "Investor Diversification and International Equity Markets." *American Economic Review* 81 (1991), pp. 222−26.

Gande, Amar, and Darius Miller. "Why Do U.S. Securities Laws Matter to Non-U.S. Firms? Evidence from Private Class-Action Lawsuits" (2012). Working Paper, Southern Methodist University.

Glaum, Martin, and Udo Mandler. "Global Accounting Harmonization from a German Perspective: Bridging the GAAP." Europa-Universitaet Viadrina Working Paper, 1996.

Hail, Luzi, and Christian Leuz. "International Differences in the Cost of Capital: Do Legal Institutions and Securities Regulation Matter?" *Journal of Accounting Research* 44 (2006), pp. 485−531.

Harvey, Campbell. "The World Price of Covariance Risk." *Journal of Finance* 46 (1991), pp. 111−57.

Hietala, Pekka. "Asset Pricing in Partially Segmented Markets: Evidence from the Finnish Markets." *Journal of Finance* 44 (1989), pp. 697−718.

Jayaraman, N., K. Shastri, and K. Tandon. "The Impact of International Cross Listings on Risk and Return: The Evidence from American Depository Receipts." *Journal of Banking and Finance* 17 (1993), pp. 91−103.

Karolyi, G. Andrew. "What Happens to Stocks That List Shares Abroad? A Survey of the Evidence and its Managerial Implications." University of Western Ontario Working Paper, 1996.

Lang, Mark, Karl Lins, and Darius Miller. "ADRs, Analysts, and Accuracy: Does Cross Listing in the United States Improve a Firm's Information Environment and Increase Market Value?" *Journal of Accounting Research* 41 (2003), pp. 317−45.

Lau, Sie T., Lilian Ng, and Bohui Zhang. "The World Price of Home Bias." *Journal of Financial Economics* 97 (2010), pp. 191–217.

Lee, Kwang Chul, and Chuck C. Y. Kwok. "Multinational Corporations vs. Domestic Corporations: International Environmental Factors and Determinants of Capital Structure." *Journal of International Business Studies* 19 (1988), pp. 195−217.

Lessard, D., and A. Shapiro. "Guidelines for Global Financing Choices." *Midland Corporate Finance Journal* 3 (1984), pp. 68−80.

Loderer, Claudio, and Andreas Jacobs. "The Nestlé Crash." *Journal of Financial Economics* 37 (1995), pp. 315−39.

McCauley, Robert, and Steven Zimmer. "Exchange Rates and International Differences in the Cost of Capital." In Y. Amihud and R. Levich (eds.), *Exchange Rates and Corporate Performance.* Burr Ridge, IL: Irwin, 1994, pp. 119−48.

Miller, Darius. "The Market Reaction to International Cross-listing: Evidence from Depository Receipts." *Journal of Financial Economics* 51 (1999), pp. 103−23.

Mittoo, Usha. "Additional Evidence on Integration in the Canadian Stock Market." *Journal of Finance* 47 (1992), pp. 2035−54.

Ross, Stephen A., Randolph W. Westerfield, and Jeffrey F. Jaffee. *Corporate Finance,* 3rd ed. Burr Ridge, Ill.: Irwin, 1987.

Sarkissian, Sergei, and Michael Schill. "The Overseas Listing Decision: New Evidence of Proximity Preference." *Review of Financial Studies* 17 (2004), pp. 769−809.

www.mhhe.com/er8e

Stapleton, Richard, and Marti Subrahmanyan. "Market Imperfections, Capital Market Equilibrium and Corporation Finance." *Journal of Finance* 32 (1977), pp. 307–21.

———. *Capital Market Equilibrium and Corporate Financial Decisions.* Greenwich, Conn.: JAI Press, 1980.

Stobaugh, Robert. "Financing Foreign Subsidiaries of U.S.-Controlled Multinational Enterprises." *Journal of International Business Studies* (1970), pp. 43–64.

Stonehill, Arthur, and Kare Dullum. *Internationalizing the Cost of Capital.* New York: John Wiley and Sons, 1982.

Stonehill, Arthur, and Thomas Stitzel. "Financial Structure and Multinational Corporations." *California Management Review* (1969), pp. 91–96.

Stulz, Rene. "On the Effect of Barriers to International Investment." *Journal of Finance* 36 (1981), pp. 923–34.

———. "Pricing Capital Assets in an International Setting: An Introduction." *Journal of Inter -national Business Studies* 16 (1985), pp. 55–74.

———. "The Cost of Capital in Internationally Integrated Markets: The Case of Nestlé." *European Financial Management* 1 (1995), pp. 11–22.

———. "Does the Cost of Capital Differ across Countries? An Agency Perspective." *European Financial Management* 2 (1996), pp. 11–22.

Stulz, Rene, and Walter Wasserfallen. "Foreign Equity Investment Restrictions, Capital Flight, and Shareholder Wealth Maximization: Theory and Evidence." *Review of Financial Studies* 8 (1995), pp. 1019–57.

Subrahmanyam, Marti. "On the Optimality of International Capital Market Integration." *Journal of Financial Economics* 2 (1975), pp. 3–28.

17A Pricing of Nontradable Assets: Numerical Simulations

To further explain the theoretical results presented in the preceding section, we provide a numerical illustration in which we assume a two-country and eight-firm world as described by Exhibit 17.13 to arrive at the equilibrium stock prices and expected rates of return, or costs of equity capital, under the alternative structures of international capital markets.

Exhibit 17A.1 presents the equilibrium asset prices and the costs of equity capital for each of the eight firms as computed according to the asset pricing models presented earlier. As the exhibit shows, cross-listing of domestic asset D1 on the foreign exchange in an otherwise segmented market decreases the equilibrium cost of equity capital from 22.59 percent (under segmentation) to 17.30 percent upon cross-listing. Clearly, international trading of the asset leads to a decrease in the cost of capital.

Once asset D1 is cross-listed, it will be priced (at $85.25) to yield the same expected rate of return that it would obtain under complete integration. Moreover, when the domestic asset is cross-listed, other domestic assets, which remain internationally nontradable, also experience a decrease in their costs of equity capital. Take asset D2 for example; the cost of capital falls from 27.34 percent under segmentation to 23.72 percent after cross-listing asset D1. This reflects the spillover effect generated by asset D1 when it becomes internationally tradable. Additionally, Exhibit 17A.1 shows that when foreign asset F1 is cross-listed in the domestic country, it will lower its own cost of equity capital as well as that of the other foreign firms. The exhibit shows that when F1 is cross-listed, its cost of equity capital falls from 26.28 percent to 19.03 percent, the same as if capital markets were completely integrated. Moreover, other foreign assets that remain internationally nontradable also experience a decrease in their costs of capital as a result of the spillover effect from the cross-listing of F1.

EXHIBIT 17A.1

International Capital Market Equilibria: The Effect of Cross-Listings

Asset	Complete Segmentation	Cross-Listings Asset D1	Cross-Listing Assets D1 and F1	Complete Integration
A. Equilibrium Asset Prices ($)				
D1	81.57	85.25	85.25	85.25
D2	78.53	80.83	80.37	83.34
D3	75.30	78.06	77.51	81.41
D4	71.88	75.10	74.45	79.34
F1	79.19	78.57	84.01	84.01
F2	75.87	75.11	78.36	81.99
F3	72.34	71.45	75.29	79.94
F4	68.62	67.59	72.02	77.76
B. Cost of Equity Capital (%)				
D1	22.59	17.30	17.30	17.30
D2	27.34	23.72	24.42	19.99
D3	32.80	28.11	29.02	22.84
D4	39.12	33.16	34.32	26.04
F1	26.28	27.28	19.03	19.03
F2	31.80	33.14	27.62	21.97
F3	38.24	39.96	30.97	25.09
F4	45.73	47.95	36.10	28.60

18 International Capital Budgeting

IN THIS BOOK, we have taken the view that the fundamental goal of the financial manager is shareholder wealth maximization. Shareholder wealth is created when the firm makes an investment that will return more in a present value sense than the investment costs. Perhaps the most important decisions that confront the financial manager are which capital projects to select. By their very nature, capital projects denote investment in capital assets that make up the productive capacity of the firm. These investments, which are typically expensive relative to the firm's overall value, will determine how efficiently the firm will produce the product it intends to sell, and thus will also determine how profitable the firm will be. In total, these decisions determine the competitive position of the firm in the product marketplace and the firm's long-run survival. Consequently, a valid framework for analysis is important. The generally accepted methodology in modern finance is to use the net present value (NPV) discounted cash flow model.

In Chapter 16, we explored why a MNC would make foreign direct investment in another country. In Chapter 17, we discussed the cost of capital for a multinational firm. We saw that a firm that could source funds internationally rather than just domestically could feasibly have a lower cost of capital than a domestic firm because of its greater opportunities to raise funds. A lower cost of capital means that more capital projects will have a positive net present value to the multinational firm. Our objective in this chapter is to detail a methodology for a multinational firm to analyze the investment in a capital project in a foreign land. The methodology we present is based on an analytical framework formalized by Donald Lessard (1985). The adjusted present value (APV) methodology is an extension of the NPV technique suggested for use in analyzing domestic capital expenditures. As will be seen, the APV methodology facilitates the analysis of special cash flows that are unique to international capital expenditures.

Most readers will already be familiar with NPV analysis and its superiority in comparison to other capital expenditure evaluation techniques as a tool for assisting the financial manager in maximizing shareholder wealth. Therefore, the chapter begins with only a brief review of the basic NPV capital budgeting framework. Next, the basic NPV framework is extended into an APV model by way of analogy to the Modigliani-Miller equation for the value of a levered firm. Following this, the APV model is extended to make it suitable for use by a MNC analyzing a foreign capital investment. The chapter includes a case application showing how to implement the APV decision framework.

Review of Domestic Capital Budgeting

The basic **net present value (NPV)** capital budgeting equation can be stated as:

$$NPV = \sum_{t=1}^{T} \frac{CF_t}{(1 + K)^t} + \frac{TV_T}{(1 + K)^T} - C_0 \tag{18.1}$$

where:

CF_t = expected after-tax cash flow for year t,
TV_T = expected after-tax terminal value, including recapture of working capital,
C_0 = initial investment at inception,
K = weighted-average cost of capital,
T = economic life of the capital project in years.

The NPV of a capital project is the present value of all cash inflows, including those at the end of the project's life, minus the present value of all cash outflows. The *NPV rule* is to accept a project if NPV ≥ 0 and to reject it if NPV < 0.

The internal rate of return (IRR), the payback method, and the profitability index are three additional methods for analyzing a capital expenditure. The IRR method solves for the discount rate, that is, the project's IRR, that causes the NPV to equal zero. In many situations a project will have only a single IRR, and the IRR decision rule is to select the project if the IRR $\geq K$. However, under certain circumstances a project will have multiple IRRs, thus causing difficulty in interpreting the simple decision rule if one or more IRRs are less than K. The payback method determines the period of time required for the cumulative cash inflows to "pay back" the initial cash outlay; the shorter the payback period the more acceptable is the project. However, the payback method ignores the time value of money and any cash flows after the payback period. The profitability index is computed by dividing the present value of cash inflows by the initial outlay; the larger the ratio, the more acceptable is the project. However, when dealing with mutually exclusive projects, a conflict may arise between the profitability index and the NPV criterion due to the scale of the investments. If the firm is not under a capital rationing constraint, it is generally agreed that conflicts should be settled in favor of the NPV criterion. Overall, the NPV decision rule is considered the superior framework for analyzing a capital budgeting expenditure.

For our purposes, it is necessary to expand the NPV equation. First, however, it is beneficial if we discuss annual cash flows. In capital budgeting, our concern is only with the change in the firm's total cash flows that are attributable to the capital expenditure. CF_t represents the *incremental* change in total firm cash flow for year t resulting from the capital project.[1] Algebraically CF_t can be defined as:

$$CF_t = (R_t - OC_t - D_t - I_t)(1 - \tau) + D_t + I_t(1 - \tau) \tag{18.2a}$$
$$= NI_t + D_t + I_t(1 - \tau) \tag{18.2b}$$

Equation 18.2a presents a very detailed expression for **incremental cash flow** that is worth learning so that we can easily apply the model. The equation shows that CF_t is the sum of three flows, or that the cash flow from a capital project goes to three different groups. The first term, as Equation 18.2b shows, is expected income, NI_t, which belongs to the equity holders of the firm. Incremental NI_t is calculated as the after-tax $(1 - \tau)$ value of the change in the firm's sales revenue, R_t, generated from the project, minus the corresponding operating costs, OC_t, minus project depreciation, D_t, minus interest expense, I_t. (As we discuss later in the chapter, we are only concerned with the interest expense that is consistent with the firm's optimal capital structure and the borrowing capacity created by the project.) The second term represents the fact that

---

[1]For simplicity, we assume that no additional capital expenditure or investment in working capital is required after inception.

depreciation is a *noncash* expense, that is, D_t is subtracted in the calculation of NI_t only for tax purposes. It is added back because this cash did not actually flow out of the firm in year t. D_t can be viewed as the recapture in year t of a portion of the original investment, C_0, in the project. The last term represents the firm's after-tax payment of interest to debtholders.

$$CF_t = (R_t - OC_t - D_t)(1 - \tau) + D_t \qquad\qquad (18.2\text{c})$$

$$= NOI_t(1 - \tau) + D_t \qquad\qquad (18.2\text{d})$$

Equation 18.2c provides a computationally simpler formula for calculating CF_t. Since $I_t(1 - \tau)$ is subtracted in determining NI_t in Equation 18.2a and then added back, the two cancel out. The first term in Equation 18.2c represents after-tax net operating income, $NOI_t(1 - \tau)$, as stated in Equation 18.2d.

$$CF_t = (R_t - OC_t)(1 - \tau) + \tau D_t \qquad\qquad (18.2\text{e})$$

$$= OCF_t(1 - \tau) + \tau D_t \qquad\qquad (18.2\text{f})$$

$$= \text{nominal after-tax incremental cash flow for year } t$$

Equation 18.2e provides yet an even simpler formula for calculating CF_t. It shows the result from Equation 18.2c of combining the after-tax value of the depreciation expense, $(1 - \tau)D_t$, with the before-tax value of D_t. The result of this combination is the amount τD_t in Equation 18.2e, which represents the tax saving due to D_t being a tax-deductible item. As summarized in Equation 18.2f, the first term in Equation 18.2e represents after-tax operating cash flow, $OCF_t(1 - \tau)$, and the second term denotes the tax savings from the depreciation expense.[2]

The Adjusted Present Value Model

To continue on with our discussion, we need to expand the NPV model. To do this, we substitute Equation 18.2f for CF_t in Equation 18.1, allowing us to restate the NPV formula as:

$$\text{NPV} = \sum_{t=1}^{T} \frac{OCF_t(1 - \tau)}{(1 + K)^t} + \sum_{t=1}^{T} \frac{\tau D_t}{(1 + K)^t} + \frac{TV_t}{(1 + K)^T} - C_0 \qquad\qquad (18.3)$$

In a famous article, Franco Modigliani and Merton Miller (1963) derived a theoretical statement for the market value of a levered firm (V_l) versus the market value of an equivalent unlevered firm (V_u). They showed that

$$V_l = V_u + \tau\text{Debt} \qquad\qquad (18.4\text{a})$$

Assuming the firms are ongoing concerns and the debt the levered firm issued to finance a portion of its productive capacity is perpetual, Equation 18.4a can be expanded as:

$$\frac{NOI(1 - \tau)}{K} = \frac{NOI(1 - \tau)}{K_u} + \frac{\tau I}{i} \qquad\qquad (18.4\text{b})$$

where i is the levered firm's borrowing rate, $I = i\text{Debt}$, and K_u is the **all-equity cost of equity** (i.e., the cost of equity for a firm financed only with equity).

Recall from Chapter 17 that the weighted average cost of capital can be stated as:

$$K = (1 - \lambda)K_l + \lambda i(1 - \tau) \qquad\qquad (18.5\text{a})$$

---

[2]Annual cash flows might also include incremental working capital funds. These are ignored here to simplify the presentation.

	Levered	Unlevered
Revenue	$100	$100
Operating costs	−50	−50
Net operating income	50	50
Interest expense	−10	−0
Earnings before taxes	40	50
Taxes @.40	−16	−20
Net income	24	30
Cash flow available to investors	$24 + 10 = $34	$ 30

where K_l is the cost of equity for a levered firm, and λ is the optimal debt ratio. In their article, Modigliani and Miller showed that K can be stated as:[3]

$$K = K_u(1 - \tau\lambda) \tag{18.5b}$$

Recall that Equation 18.2a can be simplified to Equation 18.2d. What this implies is that regardless of how the firm (or a capital expenditure) is financed, it will earn the same NOI. From Equation 18.5b, if $\lambda = 0$ (that is, an all-equity financed firm), then $K = K_u$ and $I = 0$; thus in Equation 18.4a $V_l = V_u$. However, if $\lambda > 0$ (that is, a levered firm), then $K_u > K$ and $I > 0$, thus $V_l > V_u$. For Equation 18.4b to hold as an equality, it is necessary to add the present value of the tax savings the levered firm receives. The main result of Modigliani and Miller's theory is that the value of a levered firm is greater than an equivalent unlevered firm earning the same NOI because the levered firm also has tax savings from the tax deductibility of interest payments to debtholders that do not go to the government. The following example clarifies the tax savings to the firm from making interest payments on debt.

EXAMPLE | 18.1: Tax Savings from Interest Payments
Exhibit 18.1 provides an example of the tax savings arising from the tax deductibility of interest payments. The exhibit shows a levered and an unlevered firm, each with sales revenue and operating expenses of $100 and $50, respectively. The levered firm has interest expense of $10 and earnings before taxes of $40, while the unlevered firm enjoys $50 of before-tax earnings since it does not have any interest expense. The levered firm pays only $16 in taxes as opposed to $20 for the unlevered firm. This leaves $24 for the levered firm's shareholders and $30 for the unlevered firm's shareholders. Nevertheless, the levered firm has a total of $34 (=$24 + $10) of funds available for investors, while the unlevered firm has only $30. The extra $4 comes from the tax savings on the $10 before-tax interest payment.

By direct analogy to the Modigliani-Miller equation for an unlevered firm, we can convert the NPV Equation 18.3 into the **adjusted present value (APV)** model:

$$APV = \sum_{\tau=1}^{T} \frac{OCF_t(1 - \tau)}{(1 + K_u)^t} + \sum_{t=1}^{T} \frac{\tau D_t}{(1 + i)^t}$$
$$+ \sum_{t=1}^{T} \frac{\tau I_t}{(1 + i)^t} + \frac{TV_T}{(1 + K_u)^T} - C_0 \tag{18.6}$$

---

[3]To derive Equation 18.5b from Equation 18.5a, it is necessary to know that $K_l = K_u + (1 - \tau)(K_u - i)$ (Debt/Equity).

The APV model is a **value-additivity** approach to capital budgeting. That is, each cash flow that is a source of value is considered individually. Note that in the APV model, each cash flow is discounted at a rate of discount consistent with the risk inherent in that cash flow. The OCF_t and TV_T are discounted at K_u. The firm would receive these cash flows from a capital project regardless of whether the firm was levered or unlevered. The tax savings due to interest, τI_t, are discounted at the before-tax borrowing rate, i, as in Equation 18.4b. It is suggested that the tax savings due to depreciation, τD_t, also be discounted at i because these cash flows are relatively less risky than operating cash flows if tax laws are not likely to change radically over the economic life of the project.[4]

The APV model is useful for a domestic firm analyzing a domestic capital expenditure. If APV $\geq$ 0, the project should be accepted. If APV < 0, the project should be rejected. Thus, the model is useful for a MNC for analyzing one of its domestic capital expenditures or for a foreign subsidiary of the MNC analyzing a proposed capital expenditure from the subsidiary's viewpoint.

Capital Budgeting from the Parent Firm's Perspective

The APV model as stated in Equation 18.6 is not useful for the MNC in analyzing a foreign capital expenditure of one of its subsidiaries from the MNC's, or parent's, perspective. In fact, it is possible that a project may have a positive APV from the subsidiary's perspective and a negative APV from the parent's perspective. This could happen, for example, if certain cash flows are blocked by the host country from being legally remitted to the parent or if extra taxes are imposed by the host country on foreign exchange remittances. A higher marginal tax rate in the home country may also cause a project to be unprofitable from the parent's perspective. If we assume the MNC owns the foreign subsidiary, but domestic shareholders own the MNC parent, it is the currency of the parent firm that is important because it is that currency into which the cash flows must be converted to benefit the shareholders whose wealth the MNC is attempting to maximize.[5]

Donald Lessard (1985) developed an APV model that is suitable for a MNC to use in analyzing a foreign capital expenditure. The model recognizes that the cash flows will be denominated in a foreign currency and will have to be converted into the currency of the parent. Additionally, Lessard's model incorporates special cash flows that are frequently encountered in foreign project analysis. Using the basic structure of the APV model developed in the previous section, Lessard's model can be stated as:

$$\text{APV} = \sum_{t=1}^{T} \frac{\bar{S}_t OCF_t(1 - \tau)}{(1 + K_{ud})^t} + \sum_{t=1}^{T} \frac{\bar{S}_t \tau D_t}{(1 + i_d)^t} + \sum_{t=1}^{T} \frac{\bar{S}_t \tau I_t}{(1 + i_d)^t} + \frac{\bar{S}_T TV_t}{(1 + K_{ud})^T}$$
$$- S_0 C_0 + S_0 RF_0 + S_0 CL_0 - \sum_{t=1}^{T} \frac{\bar{S}_t LP_t}{(1 + i_d)^t} \qquad (18.7)$$

Several points are noteworthy about Equation 18.7. First, the cash flows are assumed to be denominated in the foreign currency and converted to the currency of the parent at the expected spot exchange rates, $\bar{S}_t$, applicable for year t. The marginal

---

[4]Booth (1982) shows under what circumstances the NPV and APV methods will be precisely equivalent.

[5]When both $\text{NPV}_{parent} > 0$ and $\text{NPV}_{subsidiary} > 0$, the decision to make the capital expenditure is clear. Similarly, the decision to not invest is clear when $\text{NPV}_{parent} < 0$ and $\text{NPV}_{subsidiary} < 0$, as it is when $\text{NPV}_{parent} < 0$ and $\text{NPV}_{subsidiary} > 0$. However, when $\text{NPV}_{parent} > 0$ and $\text{NPV}_{subsidiary} < 0$, the firm should carefully review the assumptions used in calculating the two NPVs to be certain there is consistency between the analyses before making the investment.

corporate tax rate, τ, is the larger of the parent's or the foreign subsidiary's because the model assumes that the tax authority in the parent firm's home country will give a foreign tax credit for foreign taxes paid *up to* the amount of the tax liability in the home country. Thus, if the parent's tax rate is the larger of the two, additional taxes are due in the home country, which equals the difference between the domestic tax liability and the foreign tax credit. On the other hand, if the foreign tax rate is larger, the foreign tax credit more than offsets the domestic tax liability, so no additional taxes are due.[6] It is also noted that each of the discount rates has the subscript d, indicating that once the foreign cash flows are converted into the parent's home currency, the appropriate discount rates are those of the domestic country.

In Equation 18.7, the OCF_t represents only the portion of operating cash flows available for remittance that can be legally remitted to the parent firm. Cash flows earned in the foreign country that are blocked by the host government from being repatriated do not provide any benefit to the stockholders of the parent firm and are not relevant to the analysis. Additionally, cash flows that are repatriated through circumventing restrictions are not included here.

As with domestic project analysis, it is important to include only incremental revenues and operating costs in calculating the OCF_t. An example will help illustrate the concept. A MNC may currently have a sales affiliate in a foreign country who is supplied by merchandise produced by the parent or a manufacturing facility in a third country. If a manufacturing facility is put into operation in the foreign country to satisfy local demand, sales may be higher overall than with just a sales affiliate if the foreign subsidiary is better able to assess market demand with its local presence. However, the former manufacturing unit will experience **lost sales** as a result of the new foreign manufacturing facility; that is, the new project has *cannibalized* part of an existing project. Thus, incremental revenue is not the total sales revenue of the new manufacturing facility but rather that amount minus the lost sales revenue. However, if the sales would be lost regardless, say because a competitor who is better able to satisfy local demand is gearing up, then the entire sales revenue of the new foreign manufacturing facility is incremental sales revenue.

Equation 18.7 includes additional terms representing cash flows frequently encountered in foreign projects. The term S_0RF_0 represents the value of accumulated **restricted funds** (of amount RF_0) in the foreign land from existing operations that are freed up by the proposed project. These funds become available only *because* of the proposed project and are therefore available to offset a portion of the initial capital outlay. Examples are funds "whose use is restricted by exchange controls"[7] or funds on which additional taxes would be due in the parent country if they were remitted. RF_0 equals the difference between the face value of these funds and their present value used in the next best alternative. The extended illustration at the end of this chapter will help clarify the meaning of this term.

The term $S_0CL_0 - \sum_{t=1}^{T} \dfrac{\overline{S}_t LP_t}{(1 + i_d)^t}$ denotes the present value in the currency of

the parent firm of the benefit of below-market-rate borrowing in foreign currency. In certain cases, a **concessionary loan** (of amount CL_0) at a below-market rate of interest may be available to the parent firm if the proposed capital expenditure is made in the foreign land. The host country offers this financing in its foreign currency as a means of attracting economic development and investment that will create employment for

www.worldbank.org

This website of the World Bank provides information on doing business in the developing world, including information on financing instruments.

---

[6]This implicitly assumes that all net operating cash flows are remitted immediately to the parent firm and that the parent has no excess foreign tax credits. Chapter 21 covers the complicated topic of international taxation, withholding taxes, and foreign tax credits that may complicate Lessard's APV model and that can be incorporated in additional terms to the basic model. Additionally, Chapter 21 discusses transfer pricing strategies that may allow the firm to move taxable income from high to low tax regimes.

[7]Lessard (1985, p. 577).

its citizens. The benefit to the MNC is the difference between the face value of the concessionary loan converted into the home currency and the present value of the similarly converted concessionary loan payments (LP_t) discounted at the MNC's normal domestic borrowing rate (i_d). The loan payments will yield a present value less than the face amount of the concessionary loan when they are discounted at the higher normal rate. This difference represents a subsidy the host country is willing to extend to the MNC if the investment is made. It should be clear that the present value of the loan payments discounted at the normal borrowing rate represents the size of the loan available from borrowing at the normal borrowing rate with a debt service schedule equivalent to that of the concessionary loan.

Recall that to calculate the firm's weighted-average cost of capital, it is necessary to know the firm's optimal debt ratio. When considering a capital budgeting project, it is never appropriate to think of the project as being financed separately from the way the firm is financed, for the project represents a portion of the firm. When the asset base increases because a capital project is undertaken, the firm can handle more debt in its capital structure. That is, the borrowing capacity of the firm has increased because of the project. Nevertheless, the investment and financing decisions are separate. There is an optimal capital structure for the firm; once this is determined, the cost of financing is known and can be used to determine if a project is acceptable. We do not mean to imply that *each* and every capital project is financed with the optimal portions of debt and equity. Rather, some projects may be financed with all debt or all equity or a suboptimal combination. What is important is that in the long run the firm does not stray too far from its optimal capital structure so that overall the firm's assets are financed at the lowest cost. Thus, the interest tax shield term $S_t \tau I_t$ in the APV model recognizes the tax shields of the **borrowing capacity** created by the project *regardless* of how the project is financed. Handling the tax shields in any other way would bias the APV favorably or unfavorably, respectively, if the project was financed by a larger or smaller portion of debt. This is an especially important point in international capital budgeting analysis because of the frequency of large concessionary loans. The benefit of concessionary loans, which are dependent on the parent firm making the investment, is recognized in a separate term.[8]

Generality of the APV Model

Lessard's APV model includes many terms for cash flows frequently encountered in analyzing foreign capital expenditures. However, *all* possible terms are not included in the version presented as Equation 18.7. Nevertheless, the reader should now have the knowledge to incorporate into the basic APV model terms of a more unique nature for specific cash flows encountered in a particular analysis.

For example, there may be tax savings or deferrals that come about because of multinational operations. That is, the MNC may be able to shift revenues or expenses among its affiliates in a way that lowers taxes, or be able to combine profits or affiliates from both low- and high-tax environments in a manner that results in lower overall taxes. Tax deferrals are possible by reinvesting profits in new capital projects in low-tax countries.

Additionally, through interaffiliate transfer pricing strategies, licensing arrangements, royalty agreements, or other means, the parent firm might be able to repatriate some funds that are meant to be blocked, or restricted, by the host country.[9] These cash flows are the counterpart to the unrestricted funds available for remittance as part of operating cash flows. As with the cash flows arising from tax savings or deferrals, it may be difficult for the firm to accurately estimate the size of these cash flows or their duration. Since these cash flows will exist regardless of how the firm is financed, they should be discounted at the all-equity rate.

---

[8]Booth (1982) shows that tax shields calculated using the concessionary loan rates are also theoretically correct.
[9]Chapter 19 covers interaffiliate transfer pricing strategies, licensing arrangements, and royalty agreements as methods the parent firm might use to repatriate funds restricted by the host country.

One of the major benefits of the APV framework is the ease with which difficult cash flow terms, such as tax savings or deferrals and the repatriation of restricted funds, can be handled. The analyst can first analyze the capital expenditure as if these terms did not exist. Additional cash flow terms do not need to be explicitly considered unless the APV is negative. If the APV is negative, the analyst can calculate how large the cash flows from other sources need to be to make the APV positive, and then estimate whether these other cash inflows will likely be that large.

Estimating the Future Expected Exchange Rate

The financial manager must estimate the future expected exchange rates, $\bar{S}_t$, in order to implement the APV framework. Chapter 6 provided a wide variety of methods for estimating exchange rates. One quick and simple way to do this is to rely on PPP and estimate the future expected spot rate for year t as:

$$\bar{S}_t = S_0 (1 + \bar{\pi}_d)^t/(1 + \bar{\pi}_f)^t \tag{18.8}$$

where $\bar{\pi}_d$ is the expected long-run annual rate of inflation in the (home) domestic country of the MNC and $\bar{\pi}_f$ is the rate in the foreign land.

As noted in Chapter 6, PPP is not likely to hold precisely in reality. Nevertheless, unless the financial manager suspects that there is some systematic long-run bias in using PPP to estimate $\bar{S}_t$ that would result in a systematic over- or underestimate of the series of expected exchange rates, then PPP should prove to be an acceptable tool. Alternatively, the analyst may choose to use long-dated forward prices to estimate the future expected spot exchange rates, or use an IRP forecast.

CASE APPLICATION

The Centralia Corporation

The Centralia Corporation is a midwestern manufacturer of small kitchen electrical appliances. The market segment it caters to is the midprice range. It specializes in small and medium-size microwave ovens suitable for small homes, apartment dwellers, or office coffee lounges. In recent years it has been exporting microwave ovens to Spain, where they are sold through a sales affiliate in Madrid. Because of different electrical standards in various European countries, the ovens Centralia manufactured for the Spanish market could not be used everywhere in Europe without an electrical converter. Thus, the sales affiliate concentrated its marketing effort just in Spain. Sales are currently 9,600 units a year and have been increasing at a rate of 5 percent.

Centralia's marketing manager has been keeping abreast of integration activities in the European Union. All obstacles to the free movement of goods, services, people, and capital among the member states of the EU have been removed. Additionally, further integration promises a commonality among member states of rail track size, telephone and electrical equipment, and a host of other items. These developments have led the marketing manager to believe that a substantial number of microwave oven units could be sold throughout the EU and that the idea of a manufacturing facility should be explored.

The marketing and production managers have jointly drawn up plans for a wholly owned manufacturing facility in Zaragoza, which is located about 325 kilometers northeast of Madrid. Zaragoza is located just a couple hundred kilometers from the French border, thus facilitating shipment out of Spain into other EU countries. Additionally, Zaragoza is located close enough to the major population centers in Spain so that internal shipments should not pose a problem. A major attraction of locating the manufacturing facility in Zaragoza, however, is that the Spanish government has promised to arrange for a large portion of the construction cost of the production facility to be financed at a very attractive interest rate if the plant is built there. Any type of industry that will improve the employment situation would be a benefit, as the current unemployment rate in Spain exceeds 19 percent. Centralia's executive committee has instructed the financial manager to determine if the plan has financial merit. If the manufacturing facility is built, Centralia will no longer export units for sale in Europe. The necessary information follows.

On its current exports, Centralia receives $180 per unit, of which $35 represents contribution margin. The sales forecast predicts that 25,000 units will be sold within the EU during the first year of operation and that this volume will increase at the rate of 12 percent per year. All sales will be invoiced in euros. When the plant begins operation, units will be priced at €200 each. It is estimated that the current production cost will be €160 per unit. The sales price and production costs are expected to keep pace with inflation, which is forecast to be 2.1 percent per annum for the foreseeable future. By comparison, long-run U.S. inflation is forecast at 3 percent per annum. The current exchange rate is $1.32/€1.00.

The cost of constructing the manufacturing plant is estimated at €5,500,000. The borrowing capacity created by a capital expenditure of this amount is $2,904,000. The Madrid sales affiliate has accumulated a net amount of €750,000 from its operations, which can be used to partially finance the construction cost. The marginal corporate tax rate in Spain and the United States is 35 percent. The accumulated funds were earned under special tax concessions offered during the initial years of the sales operation, and taxed at a marginal rate of 20 percent. If they were repatriated, additional tax at the 35 percent marginal rate would be due, but with a foreign tax credit given for the Spanish taxes already paid.

The Spanish government will allow the plant to be depreciated over an eight-year period. Little, if any, additional investment will be required over that time. At the end of this period, the market value of the facility is difficult to estimate, but Centralia believes that the plant should still be in good condition for its age and that it should therefore have reasonable market value. All after-tax operating cash flows from the new facility will be immediately repatriated to the United States.

One of the most attractive features of the proposal is the special financing the Spanish government is willing to arrange. If the plant is built in Zaragoza, Centralia will be eligible to borrow €4,000,000 at a concessionary loan rate of 5 percent per annum. The normal borrowing rate for Centralia is 8 percent in dollars and 7 percent in euros. The loan schedule calls for the principal to be repaid in eight equal installments. In dollar terms, Centralia uses 12 percent as its **all-equity cost of capital**.

Here is a summary of the key points:

The current exchange rate in American terms is $S_0 = \$1.32/€1.00$.

$\overline{\pi}_f = 2.1\%$.

$\overline{\pi}_d = 3\%$.

The initial cost of the project in U.S. dollars is

$S_0 C_0 = \$1.32 \times €5,500,000 = \$7,260,000$.

For simplicity, we will assume that PPP holds and use it to estimate future expected spot exchange rates in American terms as:

$\overline{S}_t = 1.32(1.03)^t/(1.021)^t$.

The before-tax incremental operating cash flow per unit at $t = 1$ is €200 − 160 = €40. The nominal contribution margin in year t equals €40$(1.021)^{t-1}$.

Incremental lost sales in units for year t equals 9,600$(1.05)^t$.

Contribution margin per unit of lost sales in year t equals $35(1.03)^t$.

The marginal tax rate, τ equals the Spanish (or U.S.) rate of 35 percent.

Terminal value will initially be assumed to equal zero.

Straight-line depreciation is assumed; $D_t = €687,500 = €5,500,000/8$ years.

$K_{ud} = 12\%$.

$i_c = 5\%$.

$i_d = 8\%$.

In Exhibit 18.2 the present value of the expected after-tax operating cash flows from Centralia establishing the manufacturing facility in Spain is calculated. Column (a) presents the annual revenue in dollars from operating the new manufacturing facility. These are

EXHIBIT 18.2 — Calculation of the Present Value of the After-Tax Operating Cash Flows

Year (t)	$\bar{S}_t$	Quantity	$\bar{S}_t \times$ Quantity $\times €40 \times (1.021^{t-1})$ (a) $	Quantity Lost Sales	Quantity Lost Sales $\times \$35.00 \times (1.03)^t$ (b) $	$\bar{S}_t OCF_t$ (a + b) $	$\dfrac{\bar{S}_t OCF_t(1-\tau)}{(1+K_{ud})^t}$ $
1	1.3316	25,000	1,331,636	(10,080)	(363,384)	968,252	561,932
2	1.3434	28,000	1,536,175	(10,584)	(393,000)	1,143,175	592,366
3	1.3552	31,360	1,772,131	(11,113)	(425,029)	1,347,102	623,246
4	1.3672	35,123	2,044,331	(11,669)	(459,669)	1,584,662	654,603
5	1.3792	39,338	2,358,340	(12,252)	(497,132)	1,861,208	686,465
6	1.3914	44,059	2,720,581	(12,865)	(537,648)	2,182,932	718,862
7	1.4036	49,346	3,138,462	(13,508)	(581,467)	2,556,995	751,826
8	1.4160	55,267	3,620,530	(14,184)	(628,856)	2,991,674	785,386
							5,374,685

calculated each year by multiplying the expected quantity of microwave ovens to be sold times the year one incremental operating cash flow of €40 per unit. This product is in turn multiplied by the euro zone price inflation factor of 2.1 percent. For example, for year $t = 2$ the factor is $(1.021)^{t-1} = (1.021)$. The euro sales estimates are then converted to dollars at the expected spot exchange rates. Column (b) presents the annual lost sales revenues in dollars that are expected to result if the manufacturing facility is built and the parent firm no longer sells part of its production through the Spanish sales affiliate. These are calculated by multiplying the estimated quantity of lost sales in units by the current contribution margin of $35 per unit, which is in turn multiplied by a 3 percent U.S. price inflation factor. The incremental dollar operating cash flows are the sum of columns (a) and (b), which are converted to their after-tax value and discounted at K_{ud}. The sum of their present values is $5,374,685.

The present value of the depreciation tax shields τD_t is calculated in Exhibit 18.3. The tax savings on the annual straight-line depreciation of €687,500 is converted to dollars at the expected future spot exchange rates and discounted to the present at the domestic borrowing rate of 8 percent. The present value of these tax shields is $1,892,502.

The present value of the benefit of the concessionary loan is calculated in Exhibits 18.4 and 18.5. Exhibit 18.4 finds the present value of the concessionary loan payments in dollars. Since the annual principal payment on the €4,000,000 concessionary loan is the same each year, the interest payments decline as the loan balance declines. For example, during the first year, interest of €200,000 (= .05 × €4,000,000) is paid on the full amount

EXHIBIT 18.3
Calculation of the Present Value of the Depreciation Tax Shields

Year (t)	$\bar{S}_t$	D_t €	$\dfrac{\bar{S}_t \tau D_t}{(1+i_d)^t}$ $
1	1.3316	687,500	296,690
2	1.3434	687,500	277,134
3	1.3552	687,500	258,868
4	1.3672	687,500	241,805
5	1.3792	687,500	225,867
6	1.3914	687,500	210,980
7	1.4036	687,500	197,074
8	1.4160	687,500	184,084
			1,892,502

EXHIBIT 18.4

Calculation of the Present Value of the Concessionary Loan Payments

Year (t)	$\bar{S}_t$ (a)	Principal Payment (b) €	I_t (c) €	$\bar{S}_t LP_t$ (a) × (b + c) $	$\dfrac{\bar{S}_t LP_t}{(1 + i_d)^t}$ $
1	1.3316	500,000	200,000	932,145	863,097
2	1.3434	500,000	175,000	906,777	777,415
3	1.3552	500,000	150,000	880,890	699,279
4	1.3672	500,000	125,000	854,476	628,065
5	1.3792	500,000	100,000	827,528	563,202
6	1.3914	500,000	75,000	800,038	504,160
7	1.4036	500,000	50,000	771,999	450,454
8	1.4160	500,000	25,000	743,404	401,638
		4,000,000			4,887,311

EXHIBIT 18.5

Calculation of the Present Value of the Benefit from the Concessionary Loan

$$S_0 CL_0 - \sum_{t=1}^{T} \frac{\bar{S}_t LP_t}{(1 + i_d)^t} = \$1.32 \times €4,000,000 - \$4,887,311 = \$392,689$$

borrowed. During the second year interest of €175,000 (= .05 × (€4,000,000 − 500,000)) is paid on the outstanding balance over year two. The annual loan payment equals the sum of the annual principal payment and the annual interest charge. The sum of their present values in dollars, converted at the expected spot exchange rates, discounted at the domestic borrowing rate of 8 percent, is $4,887,311. This sum represents the size of the equivalent loan available (in dollars) from borrowing at the normal borrowing rate with a debt service schedule equivalent to that of the concessionary loan.

Exhibit 18.5 concludes the analysis of the concessionary loan. It shows the difference between the dollar value of the concessionary loan and the equivalent dollar loan value calculated in Exhibit 18.4. The difference of $392,689 represents the present value of the benefit of the below-market-rate financing of the concessionary loan.

The present value of the interest tax shields is calculated in Exhibit 18.6. The interest payments in column (b) of Exhibit 18.6 are drawn from column (c) of Exhibit 18.4. That is, we follow a conservative approach and base the interest tax shields on using the concessionary loan interest rate of 5 percent. The concessionary loan of €4,000,000 represents 72.73 percent of the project cost of €5,500,000. By comparison, the borrowing capacity created by the project is $2,904,000, which implies an optimal debt ratio λ for the parent firm of 40.0 percent = $2,904,000/$7,260,000 of the dollar cost of the project. Thus, only

EXHIBIT 18.6

Calculation of the Present Value of the Interest Tax Shields

Year (t)	$\bar{S}_t$ (a)	I_t (b) €	λ/Project Debt Ratio (c)	$\bar{S}_t \tau(.55) I_t$ (a × b × c × τ) $	$\dfrac{\bar{S}_t \tau(.55) I_t}{(1 + i_d)^t}$ $
1	1.3316	200,000	0.55	51,268	47,470
2	1.3434	175,000	0.55	45,255	38,799
3	1.3552	150,000	0.55	39,132	31,064
4	1.3672	125,000	0.55	32,897	24,181
5	1.3792	100,000	0.55	26,550	18,069
6	1.3914	75,000	0.55	20,088	12,659
7	1.4036	50,000	0.55	13,510	7,883
8	1.4160	25,000	0.55	6,815	3,682
					183,807

55.0 percent (= 40.0%/72.73%) of the interest payments on the concessionary loan should be used to calculate the interest tax shields. At the domestic borrowing rate of 8 percent, the present value of the interest tax shields is $183,807.

To calculate the amount of the freed-up restricted remittances it is first necessary to gross up the after-tax value of the net accumulation of €750,000, on which the Madrid sales affiliate has previously paid taxes at the rate of 20 percent. This amount is €937,500 = €750,000/(1 − .20). The dollar value of this sum at the current spot exchange rate S_0 is $1,237,500 = $1.32 (€937,500). If Centralia decided not to establish a manufacturing facility in Spain, the €750,000 should be repatriated to the parent firm. It would be required to pay additional taxes in the United States in the amount of $185,625 = (.35 − .20)$1,237,500. If the manufacturing facility is built, the €750,000 should not be remitted to the parent firm. Thus, freed-up funds of $185,625 result from the current tax savings, which can be applied to cover a portion of the equity investment in the capital expenditure.[10]

$$\begin{aligned} \text{The APV} &= \$5,374,685 + 1,892,502 + 392,689 + 183,807 + 185,625 \\ &\quad - 7,260,000 \\ &= \$769,308. \end{aligned}$$

There appears little doubt that the proposed manufacturing facility will be a profitable venture for Centralia. Had the APV been negative or closer to zero, we would want to consider the present value of the after-tax terminal cash flow. We are quite uncertain as to what this amount might be, and, fortunately, in this case we do not have to base a decision on this cash flow, which is difficult at best to forecast.

Risk Adjustment in the Capital Budgeting Analysis

The APV model we presented and demonstrated is suitable for use in analyzing a capital expenditure that is of average riskiness in comparison to the firm as a whole. Some projects may be more or less risky than average, however. The *risk-adjusted discount method* is the standard way to handle this situation. This approach requires adjusting the discount rate upward or downward for increases or decreases, respectively, in the systematic risk of the project relative to the firm as a whole. In the APV model presented in Equation 18.7, only the cash flows discounted at K_{ud} incorporate systematic risk; thus, only K_{ud} needs to be adjusted when project risk differs from that of the firm as a whole.[11]

A second way to adjust for risk in the APV framework is the *certainty equivalent method*. This approach extracts the risk premium from the expected cash flows to convert them into equivalent riskless cash flows, which are then discounted at the risk-free rate of interest. This is accomplished by multiplying the risky cash flows by a certainty-equivalent factor that is unity or less. The more risky the cash flow, the smaller is the certainty-equivalent factor. In general, cash flows tend to be more risky the further into the future they are expected to be received. We favor the risk-adjusted discount rate method over the certainty-equivalent approach because we find that it is easier to adjust the discount rate than it is to estimate the appropriate certainty-equivalent factors.[12]

---

[10]At the termination date, when all excess funds are repatriated to the parent firm, additional taxes will then be due on the accumulated funds. These are taken into consideration in the terminal value TV_T term.

[11]See Ross, Westerfield, and Jaffe (2008, Chapter 12) for a treatment of capital budgeting using discount rates adjusted for project systematic risk.

[12]See Brealey, Myers and Allen (2008, Chapter 10) for a more detailed discussion of the certainty equivalent method of risk adjustment.

Sensitivity Analysis

The way we have approached the analysis of Centralia's expansion into Spain is to obtain a point estimate of the APV through using expected values of the relevant cash flows. The expected values of these inputs are what the financial manager expects to obtain given the information he had at his disposal at the time the analysis was performed. However, each cash flow does have its own probability distribution. Hence, the realized value that may result for a particular cash flow may be different than expected. To examine these possibilities, the financial manager typically performs a sensitivity analysis. In a *sensitivity analysis,* different scenarios are examined by using different exchange rate estimates, inflation rate estimates, and cost and pricing estimates in the calculation of the APV. In essence, the sensitivity analysis allows the financial manager a means to analyze the business risk, economic exposure, exchange rate uncertainty, and political risk inherent in the investment. Sensitivity analysis puts financial managers in a position to more thoroughly understand the implications of planned capital expenditures. It also forces them to consider in advance actions that can be taken should an investment not develop as anticipated. Excel-based programs, such as Crystal Ball, can be easily used to conduct a Monte Carlo simulation of various probability assumptions.

Purchasing Power Parity Assumption

The APV methodology we developed assumes that PPP holds and that future expected exchange rates can be forecasted accordingly. As noted, relying on the PPP assumption is a common and conceptually satisfying way to forecast future exchange rates. Assuming no differential in marginal tax rates, when PPP holds and all foreign cash flows can be legally repatriated to the parent firm, it does not make any difference if the capital budgeting analysis is done from the perspective of the parent firm or from the perspective of the foreign subsidiary. To see this, consider the following simple example.

EXAMPLE | 18.2: The PPP Assumption in Foreign Capital Expenditure Analysis

A capital expenditure of FC30 by a foreign subsidiary of a U.S. MNC with a one-year economic life is expected to earn a cash flow in local currency terms of FC80. Assume inflation in the foreign host country is forecast at 4 percent per annum and at 2 percent in the United States. If the U.S. MNC's cost of capital is 7.88 percent, the Fisher equation determines that the appropriate cost of capital for the foreign subsidiary is 10 percent: $1.10 = (1.0788)(1.04)/(1.02)$. Consequently, the project NPV in foreign currency terms is $NPV_{FC} = FC80/(1.10) - FC30 = FC42.73$. If the current spot exchange rate is FC2.00/$1.00, $\bar{S}_1 (FC/\$) = 2.00\ (1.04)/(1.02) = 2.0392$ by PPP. In U.S. dollar terms, $NPV_\$ = (FC80/2.0392)/(1.0788) - FC30/2.00 = \$21.37$. Note that according to the *law of one price,* $NPV_{FC}/S_0 (FC/\$) = NPV_\$ = FC42.73/2.00 = \$21.37$. This is the expected result because both the exchange rate forecast and the discount rate conversion incorporate the same differential in expected inflation rates. Suppose, however, that $\bar{S}_1(FC/\$)$ actually turns out to be FC5.00/$1.00, that is, the foreign currency depreciates in real terms versus the dollar, then $NPV_\$ = -\$0.17$ and the project is unprofitable from the parent's perspective.

Real Options

Throughout this chapter, we have recommended the APV framework for evaluating capital expenditures in real assets. The APV was determined by making certain assumptions about revenues, operating costs, exchange rates, and the like. This approach treats risk through the discount rate. When evaluated at the appropriate discount rate, a positive APV implies that a project should be accepted and a negative APV implies that it should be rejected. A project is accepted under the assumption that all future operating decisions will be optimal. Unfortunately, the firm's management does not know at the inception date of a project what future decisions it will be confronted with because complete information concerning the project has not yet been learned. Consequently, the firm's management has alternative paths, or options, that it can take as new information is discovered. Options pricing theory is useful for evaluating investment opportunities in real assets as well as financial assets, such as foreign exchange that we considered in Chapter 7. The application of options pricing theory to the evaluation of investment options in real projects is known as **real options**.

The firm is confronted with many possible real options over the life of a capital asset. For example, the firm may have a *timing option* about when to make the investment; it may have a *growth option* to increase the scale of the investment; it may have a *suspension option* to temporarily cease production; and, it may have an *abandonment option* to quit the investment early. All of these situations can be evaluated as real options.

In international capital expenditures, the MNC is faced with the political uncertainties of doing business in a foreign host country.[13] For example, a stable political environment for foreign investment may turn unfavorable if a different political party wins power by election—or worse, by political coup. Moreover, an unexpected change in a host country's monetary policy may cause a depreciation in its exchange rate versus the parent firm's home currency, thus adversely affecting the return to the shareholders of the parent firm. These and other political uncertainties make real options analysis ideal for use in evaluating international capital expenditures. Real options analysis, however, should be thought of as an extension of discounted cash flow analysis, not as a replacement of it, as the following example makes clear.

EXAMPLE | 18.3: Centralia's Timing Option

Suppose that the sales forecast for the first year for Centralia in the case application had been for only 22,000 units instead of 25,000. At the lower figure, the APV would have been −$55,358. It is doubtful that Centralia would have entered into the construction of a manufacturing facility in Spain in this event. Suppose further that it is well known that the European Central Bank has been contemplating either tightening or loosening the economy of the European Union through a change in monetary policy that would cause the euro to either appreciate to $1.45/€1.00 or depreciate to $1.20/€1.00 from its current level of $1.32/€1.00. Under a restrictive monetary policy, the APV would be $86,674, and Centralia would begin operations. On the other hand, an expansionary policy would cause the APV to become an even more negative −$186,464.

Centralia believes that the effect from any change in monetary policy will be known in a year's time. Thus it decides to put its plans on hold until it learns what the ECB decides to do. In the meantime, Centralia can obtain a purchase option for a year on the parcel of land in Zaragoza on which it would build the manufacturing facility by paying the current landowner a fee of €5,000, or $6,600.

---

[13]It may be helpful to review the discussion on political risk in Chapter 16.

The situation described is a classic example in which real options analysis is useful in evaluating a capital expenditure. In this situation, the purchase option of €5,000 represents the option premium of the real option and the initial investment of €5,500,000 represents the exercise price of the option. Centralia will only exercise its real option if the ECB decides to follow a restrictive policy that would cause the APV to be a positive $86,674. The €5,000 seems like a small amount to allow Centralia the flexibility to postpone making a costly capital expenditure until more information is learned. The following example explicitly values the timing option using the binomial options pricing model.

EXAMPLE | 18.4: Valuing Centralia's Timing Option

In this example, we value the timing option described in the preceding example using the binomial options pricing model developed in Chapter 7. We use Centralia's 8 percent borrowing cost in dollars and 7 percent borrowing cost in euros as our estimates of the domestic and foreign risk-free rates of interest. Depending upon the action of the ECB, the euro will either appreciate 10 percent to $1.45/€1.00 or depreciate 9 percent to $1.20/€1.00 from its current level of $1.32/$1.00. Thus, $u = 1.10$ and $d = 1/1.10. = .91$. This implies that the risk-neutral probability of an appreciation is $q = [(1 + i_d)/(1 + i_f) - d]/(u - d) = [(1.08)/(1.07) - .91]/(1.10 - .91) = .52$ and the probability of a depreciation is $1 - q = .48$. Since the timing option will only be exercised if the APV is positive, the value of the timing option is $C = .52($86,674)/(1.08) = $41,732$. Since this amount is in excess of the $6,600 cost of the purchase option on the land, Centralia should definitely take advantage of the timing option it is confronted with to wait and see what monetary policy the ECB decides to pursue.

SUMMARY

This chapter presents a review of the NPV capital budgeting framework and expands the methodology into the APV model that is suitable for analyzing capital expenditures of a MNC in a foreign land.

1. The NPV capital budgeting framework in a domestic context is reviewed. The NPV is the difference between the present value of the cash inflows and outflows. If NPV $\geq$ 0 for a capital project, it should be accepted.

2. The annual after-tax cash flow formula was thoroughly defined and presented in a number of variations. This was necessary to expand the NPV model into the APV model.

3. The APV model of capital budgeting was developed by analogy to the Modigliani-Miller formula for the value of a levered firm. The APV model separates the operating cash flows from the cash flows due to financing. Additionally, each cash flow is discounted at a rate of discount commensurate with the inherent risk of the individual cash flow.

4. The APV model was further expanded to make it amenable for use by a MNC parent analyzing a capital project of a foreign subsidiary. The cash flows were converted into the parent firm's home currency, and additional terms were added to the model to handle cash flows that are frequently encountered in international capital projects.

5. A case application showing how to apply the APV model was presented and solved.

KEY WORDS

adjusted present value
(APV), *461*
all-equity cost
of capital, *466*
all-equity cost
of equity, *460*

borrowing capacity, *464*
concessionary
loan, *463*
incremental cash
flow, *459*
lost sales, *463*

net present
value (NPV), *459*
real option, *471*
restricted
funds, *463*
value-additivity, *462*

QUESTIONS

1. Why is capital budgeting analysis so important to the firm?
2. What is the intuition behind the NPV capital budgeting framework?
3. Discuss what is meant by the *incremental* cash flows of a capital project.
4. Discuss the nature of the equation sequence, Equations 18.2a to 18.2f.
5. What makes the APV capital budgeting framework useful for analyzing foreign capital expenditures?
6. Relate the concept of *lost sales* to the definition of incremental cash flows.
7. What problems can enter into the capital budgeting analysis if project debt is evaluated instead of the *borrowing capacity* created by the project?
8. What is the nature of a *concessionary* loan and how is it handled in the APV model?
9. What is the intuition of discounting the various cash flows in the APV model at specific discount rates?
10. In the Modigliani-Miller equation, why is the market value of the levered firm greater than the market value of an equivalent unlevered firm?
11. Discuss the difference between performing the capital budgeting analysis from the parent firm's perspective as opposed to the subsidiary's perspective.
12. Define the concept of a real option. Discuss some of the various real options a firm can be confronted with when investing in real projects.
13. Discuss the conditions under which the capital expenditure of a foreign subsidiary might have a positive NPV in local currency terms but be unprofitable from the parent firm's perspective.

PROBLEMS

1. The Alpha Company plans to establish a subsidiary in Hungary to manufacture and sell fashion wristwatches. Alpha has total assets of $70 million, of which $45 million is equity financed. The remainder is financed with debt. Alpha considered its current capital structure optimal. The construction cost of the Hungarian facility in forints is estimated at HUF2,400,000,000, of which HUF1,800,000,000 is to be financed at a below-market borrowing rate arranged by the Hungarian government. Alpha wonders what amount of debt it should use in calculating the tax shields on interest payments in its capital budgeting analysis. Can you offer assistance?
2. The current spot exchange rate is HUF250/$1.00. Long-run inflation in Hungary is estimated at 10 percent annually and 3 percent in the United States. If PPP is expected to hold between the two countries, what spot exchange rate should one forecast five years into the future?
3. The Beta Corporation has an optimal debt ratio of 40 percent. Its cost of equity capital is 12 percent and its before-tax borrowing rate is 8 percent. Given a marginal tax rate of 35 percent, calculate (a) the weighted-average cost of capital, and (b) the cost of equity for an equivalent all-equity financed firm.

4. Zeda, Inc., a U.S. MNC, is considering making a fixed direct investment in Denmark. The Danish government has offered Zeda a concessionary loan of DKK 15,000,000 at a rate of 4 percent per annum. The normal borrowing rate for Zeda is 6 percent in dollars and 5.5 percent in Danish krone. The load schedule calls for the principal to be repaid in three equal annual installments. What is the present value of the benefit of the concessionary loan? The current spot rate is DKK5.60/$1.00 and the expected inflation rate is 3 percent in the United States and 2.5 percent in Denmark.

5. Delta Company, a U.S. MNC, is contemplating making a foreign capital expenditure in South Africa. The initial cost of the project is ZAR10,000. The annual cash flows over the five-year economic life of the project in ZAR are estimated to be 3,000, 4,000, 5,000, 6,000, and 7,000. The parent firm's cost of capital in dollars is 9.5 percent. Long-run inflation is forecasted to be 3 percent per annum in the United States and 7 percent in South Africa. The current spot foreign exchange rate is ZAR/USD = 3.75. Determine the NPV for the project in USD by:

   a. Calculating the NPV in ZAR using the ZAR equivalent cost of capital according to the Fisher effect and then converting to USD at the current spot rate.

   b. Converting all cash flows from ZAR to USD at purchasing power parity forecasted exchange rates and then calculating the NPV at the dollar cost of capital.

   c. Are the two dollar NPVs different or the same? Explain.

   d. What is the NPV in dollars if the actual pattern of ZAR/USD exchange rates is: $S(0) = 3.75$, $S(1) = 5.7$, $S(2) = 6.7$, $S(3) = 7.2$, $S(4) = 7.7$, and $S(5) = 8.2$?

6. Suppose that in the case application in the chapter the APV for Centralia had been −$60,000. How large would the after-tax terminal value of the project need to be before the APV would be positive and Centralia would accept the project?

7. With regard to the Centralia case application in the chapter, how would the APV change if:

   a. The forecast of $\bar{\pi}_d$ and/or $\bar{\pi}_f$ is incorrect?

   b. Depreciation cash flows are discounted at K_{ud} instead of i_d?

   c. The host country did not provide the concessionary loan?

INTERNET EXERCISES

Many articles on the importance of concessionary financing can be found on the Internet by searching under the keywords *concessionary financing*.

MINI CASE 1

Dorchester, Ltd.

Dorchester, Ltd. is an old-line confectioner specializing in high-quality chocolates. Through its facilities in the United Kingdom, Dorchester manufactures candies that it sells throughout Western Europe and North America (United States and Canada). With its current manufacturing facilities, Dorchester has been unable to supply the U.S. market with more than 225,000 pounds of candy per year. This supply has allowed its sales affiliate, located in Boston, to be able to penetrate the U.S. market no farther west than St. Louis and only as far south as Atlanta. Dorchester believes that a separate manufacturing facility located in the United States would allow it to supply the entire U.S. market and Canada (which presently accounts for 65,000 pounds per year). Dorchester currently estimates initial demand in the North American market at 390,000 pounds, with growth at a 5 percent annual rate. A separate manufacturing facility would, obviously, free up the amount currently shipped to the United States and Canada. But Dorchester believes that this is only a short-run problem. They believe the economic development taking place in Eastern Europe will allow it to sell there the full amount presently shipped to North America within a period of five years.

Dorchester presently realizes £3.00 per pound on its North American exports. Once the U.S. manufacturing facility is operating, Dorchester expects that it will be able to initially price its product at $7.70 per pound. This price would represent an operating profit of $4.40 per pound. Both sales price and operating costs are expected to keep track with the U.S. price level; U.S. inflation is forecast at a rate of 3 percent for the next several years. In the U.K., long-run inflation is expected to be in the 4 to 5 percent range, depending on which economic service one follows. The current spot exchange rate is $1.50/£1.00. Dorchester explicitly believes in PPP as the best means to forecast future exchange rates.

The manufacturing facility is expected to cost $7,000,000. Dorchester plans to finance this amount by a combination of equity capital and debt. The plant will increase Dorchester's borrowing capacity by £2,000,000, and it plans to borrow only that amount. The local community in which Dorchester has decided to build will provide $1,500,000 of debt financing for a period of seven years at 7.75 percent. The principal is to be repaid in equal installments over the life of the loan. At this point, Dorchester is uncertain whether to raise the remaining debt it desires through a domestic bond issue or a Eurodollar bond issue. It believes it can borrow pounds sterling at 10.75 percent per annum and dollars at 9.5 percent. Dorchester estimates its all-equity cost of capital to be 15 percent.

The U.S. Internal Revenue Service will allow Dorchester to depreciate the new facility over a seven-year period. After that time the confectionery equipment, which accounts for the bulk of the investment, is expected to have substantial market value.

Dorchester does not expect to receive any special tax concessions. Further, because the corporate tax rates in the two countries are the same—35 percent in the U.K. and in the United States—transfer pricing strategies are ruled out.

Should Dorchester build the new manufacturing plant in the United States?

MINI CASE 2

Strik-it-Rich Gold Mining Company

The Strik-it-Rich Gold Mining Company is contemplating expanding its operations. To do so it will need to purchase land that its geologists believe is rich in gold. Strik-it-Rich's management believes that the expansion will allow it to mine and sell an additional 2,000 troy ounces of gold per year. The expansion, including the cost of the land, will cost $2,500,000. The current price of gold bullion is $1,400 per ounce and one-year gold futures are trading at $1,484 = $1,400(1.06). Extraction costs are $1,050 per ounce. The firm's cost of capital is 10 percent. At the current price of gold, the expansion appears profitable: NPV = ($1,400 − 1,050) × 2,000/.10 − $2,500,000 = $4,500,000. Strik-it-Rich's management is, however, concerned with the possibility that large sales of gold reserves by Russia and the United Kingdom will drive the price of gold down to $1,100 for the foreseeable future. On the other hand, management believes there is some possibility that the world will soon return to a gold reserve international monetary system. In the latter event, the price of gold would increase to at least $1,600 per ounce. The course of the future price of gold bullion should become clear within a year. Strik-it-Rich can postpone the expansion for a year by buying a purchase option on the land for $250,000. What should Strik-it-Rich's management do?

**REFERENCES
& SUGGESTED
READINGS**

Ang, James S., and Tsong-Yue Lai. "A Simple Rule for Multinational Capital Budgeting." *The Global Finance Journal* 1 (1989), pp. 71–75.

Booth, Lawrence D. "Capital Budgeting Frameworks for the Multinational Corporation." *Journal of International Business Studies* (Fall 1982), pp. 113–23.

Brealey, Richard A., Stewart C. Myers, and Franklin Allen. *Principles of Corporate Finance,* 9th ed. New York: McGraw-Hill/Irwin, 2008.

Endleson, Michael E. "Real Options: Valuing Managerial Flexibility (A)." *Harvard Business School Note* (March 31, 1994).

Holland, John. "Capital Budgeting for International Business: A Framework for Analysis." *Managerial Finance* 16 (1990), pp. 1–6.

Lessard, Donald R. "Evaluating International Projects: An Adjusted Present Value Approach." In Donald R. Lessard (ed.), *International Financial Management: Theory and Application,* 2nd ed. New York: Wiley, 1985, pp. 570–84.

Luehrman, Timothy A. "Capital Projects as Real Options: An Introduction." *Harvard Business School Note* (March 22, 1995).

Luehrman, Timothy A. "Investment Opportunities as Real Options: Getting Started on the Numbers." *Harvard Business Review* (July–August 1998), pp. 51–67.

Luenberger, David G. "Evaluating Real Investment Opportunities." In Chapter 12, "Basic Options Theory," in *Investment Science.* New York: Oxford University Press, 1998, pp. 337–43.

Modigliani, Franco, and Merton H. Miller. "Corporate Income Taxes and the Cost of Capital: A Correction." *American Economic Review* 53 (1963), pp. 433–43.

Ross, Stephen A., Randolph W. Westerfield, and Jeffrey F. Jaffe. *Corporate Finance,* 8th ed. New York: McGraw-Hill/Irwin, 2008.

Shapiro, Alan C. "Capital Budgeting for the Multinational Corporation." *Financial Management* (Spring 1978), pp. 7–16.

Multinational Cash Management

OUR PRIMARY CONCERN in this chapter is with the efficient management of cash within a MNC. We are concerned with the size of cash balances, their currency denominations, and where these cash balances are located among the MNC's affiliates. Efficient cash management techniques can reduce the investment in cash balances and foreign exchange transaction expenses, and it can provide for maximum return from the investment of excess cash. Additionally, efficient cash management techniques result in borrowing at the lowest rate when a temporary cash shortage exists. The chapter begins with a case application that develops a centralized cash management system for a MNC. The system we develop includes interaffiliate netting and a centralized cash depository. The benefits of a centralized system are clearly detailed.

The Management of International Cash Balances

Cash management refers to the investment the firm has in **transaction balances** to cover scheduled outflows of funds during a cash budgeting period and the funds the firm has tied up in precautionary cash balances. **Precautionary cash balances** are necessary in case the firm has underestimated the amount needed to cover transactions. Good cash management also encompasses investing excess funds at the most favorable rate and borrowing at the lowest rate when there is a temporary cash shortage.

Many of the skills necessary for effective cash management are the same regardless of whether the firm has only domestic operations or if it operates internationally. For example, the cash manager of a domestic firm should source funds internationally to obtain the lowest borrowing cost and to place excess funds wherever the greatest return can be earned. Firms with multinational operations, however, regularly deal in more than one currency, and hence the cost of foreign exchange transactions is an important factor in efficient cash management. Moreover, multinational operations require the firm to decide on whether the cash management function should be centralized at corporate headquarters (or elsewhere) or decentralized and handled locally by each affiliate. In this chapter, we make a strong case for centralized cash management.

CASE APPLICATION

Teltrex's Cash Management System

We use a case problem for a company named Teltrex International to illustrate how a centralized cash management system works. Teltrex is a U.S. multinational firm with headquarters in California's Silicon Valley. It manufactures low-priced quartz watches which it markets throughout North America and Europe. In addition to its manufacturing facilities in California, Teltrex has three sales affiliates in Canada, Germany, and the United Kingdom.

EXHIBIT 19.1		Cash Receipts and Disbursements Matrix for Teltrex ($000)					
		Disbursements					
Receipts	U.S.	Canada	Germany	U.K.	External	Total Internal	Total Receipts
U.S.	—	30	35	60	140	125	265
Canada	20	—	10	40	135	70	205
Germany	10	25	—	30	125	65	190
U.K.	40	30	20	—	130	90	220
External	120	165	50	155	—	—	490[a]
Total Internal	70	85	65	130	—	350	—
Total Disbursements	190	250	115	285	530[b]	—	1,370[c]

[a]Total cash disbursed by the U.S. parent firm and its affiliates to external parties.

[b]Total cash received by the U.S. parent firm and its affiliates from external parties.

[c]Balancing check figure.

Note: $350,000 is shifted among the various affiliates; $530,000 − $490,000 = $40,000 = increase in cash balances for Teltrex during the week.

The foundation of any cash management system is its cash budget. The **cash budget** is a plan detailing the time and the size of expected cash receipts and disbursements. Teltrex prepares a cash budget in advance for the fiscal year (updating it periodically as the year progresses), using a weekly time interval as the planning frequency. Exhibit 19.1 presents a payments matrix for one week during the cash budget planning horizon; it summarizes all interaffiliate cash receipts and disbursements of Teltrex *and* the receipts from and disbursements to external parties with which Teltrex does business. Exhibit 19.1 is denominated in U.S. dollars, the reporting currency of the parent firm. However, the functional currency of each foreign affiliate is the local currency.

Exhibit 19.1 shows, for example, that the U.S. parent expects to receive the equivalent of $30,000 in Canadian dollars from its Canadian affiliate, the equivalent of $35,000 in euros from its German affiliate, and the equivalent of $60,000 in British pounds sterling from its affiliate in the United Kingdom. In total, it expects to receive $125,000 from interaffiliate transactions. Additionally, the U.S. parent expects to receive $140,000 from external parties, say, from sales in the United States. In total, the parent expects to receive $265,000 in cash during the week. On the disbursements side, the U.S. parent expects to make payments in dollars in the amounts of $20,000 to its Canadian affiliate, $10,000 to its German affiliate, and $40,000 to its British affiliate. It also expects to make external disbursements of $120,000 to, say, suppliers for component parts and to cover other operating costs. Analogous cash flows exist for the three affiliates.

Exhibit 19.1 shows that the equivalent of $350,000 in interaffiliate cash flows are expected to flow among the parent and its three affiliates. Note that no increase in cash in the MNC occurs as a result of interaffiliate transactions. Interaffiliate transactions effectively represent taking money out of one pocket of the MNC and putting it into another. However, Teltrex expects to receive the equivalent of $530,000 from external parties and to make payments of $490,000 to other external parties. From these external transactions, a net increase of $40,000 in cash among the affiliates is expected during the week.

Netting Systems

Let's first consider the interaffiliate transactions that make up part of Exhibit 19.1. Later we will examine the transactions Teltrex expects to have with external parties. Exhibit 19.2 presents only the portion of Teltrex's receipts and disbursements matrix from Exhibit 19.1 that concerns interaffiliate cash flows.

Exhibit 19.2 shows the amount that each affiliate is to pay and receive from the other. Without a netting policy, 12 foreign exchange transactions will take place among the four affiliates. In general, if there are N affiliates, there will be a maximum of $N(N − 1)$ transactions; in our case $4(4 − 1) = 12$. Exhibit 19.3 diagrams these 12 transactions.

EXHIBIT 19.2	Teltrex's Interaffiliate Cash Receipts and Disbursements Matrix ($000)					
	Disbursements					
Receipts	U.S.	Canada	Germany	U.K.	Total Receipts	Net[a]
U.S.	—	30	35	60	125	55
Canada	20	—	10	40	70	(15)
Germany	10	25	—	30	65	0
U.K.	40	30	20	—	90	(40)
Total Disbursements	70	85	65	130	350	0

[a]Net denotes the difference between total receipts and total disbursements for each affiliate.

EXHIBIT 19.3

Teltrex's Interaffiliate
Foreign Exchange
Transactions Without
Netting ($000)

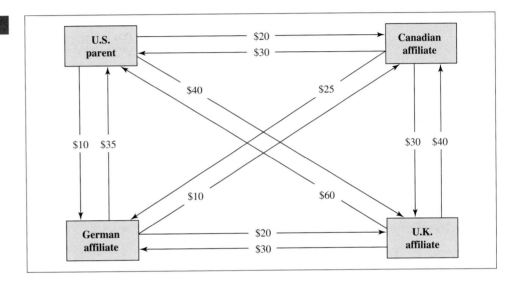

Exhibit 19.3 indicates that the equivalent of $350,000 in funds flows among the four affiliates in 12 foreign exchange transactions. This represents a needless use of administrative time in arranging the transactions and a waste of corporate funds in making the transactions. The cost of transferring funds is in the range of .25 percent to 1.5 percent of the transaction; this includes transaction expenses and the opportunity cost of funds tied up in interaffiliate float. If we assume a cost of .5 percent, the cost for transferring $350,000 is $1,750 for the week.

The 12 transactions can be reduced at least by half through bilateral netting. Under a **bilateral netting** system, each pair of affiliates determines the net amount due between them, and only the net amount is transferred. For example, the U.S. parent and the Canadian affiliate would net the $30,000 and the $20,000 to be received from one another. The result is that only one payment is made; the Canadian affiliate pays the U.S. parent an amount equivalent to $10,000. Exhibit 19.4 shows the results of bilateral netting among Teltrex's four affiliates.

From Exhibit 19.4, it can be seen that a total of $90,000 flows among the four affiliates of Teltrex in six transactions. Bilateral netting can reduce the number of foreign exchange transactions among the affiliates to $N(N-1)/2$, or less. The equivalent of $260,000 in foreign exchange transactions is eliminated through bilateral netting. At .5 percent, the cost of netting interaffiliate foreign exchange transactions is $450, a savings of $1,300 (= $1,750 − 450) over a non-netting system.

Exhibit 19.2 implies a way to limit interaffiliate transfers to no more than $(N-1)$ separate foreign exchange transactions. Rather than stop at bilateral netting, the MNC can establish a multilateral netting system. Under a **multilateral netting** system, each affiliate nets all its interaffiliate receipts against all its disbursements. It then transfers or receives the balance,

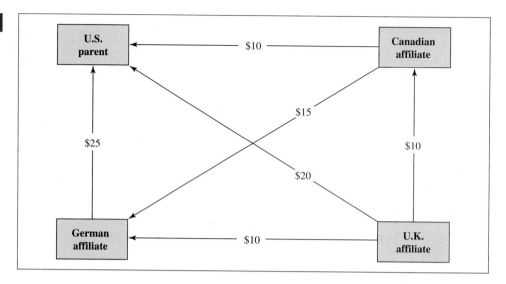

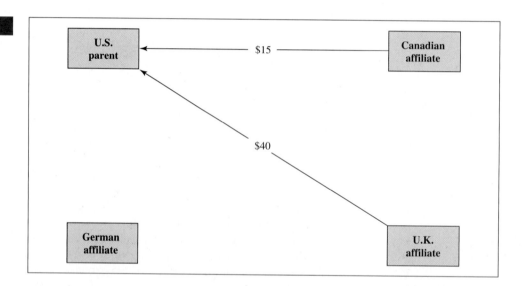

respectively, if it is a net payer or receiver. Recall from Exhibit 19.1 that total interaffiliate receipts will always equal total interaffiliate disbursements. Thus, under a multilateral netting system, the net funds to be received by the affiliates will equal the net disbursements to be made by the affiliates.

Exhibit 19.5 illustrates a multilateral netting system for Teltrex. Because the German affiliate's net receipts equal zero, only two foreign exchange transactions are necessary. The Canadian and U.K. affiliates, respectively, pay the equivalent of $15,000 and $40,000 to the U.S. parent firm. At .5 percent, the cost of transferring $55,000 is only $275 for the week, a savings of $1,475 (= $1,750 − 275) with a multilateral netting system. Moreover, multilateral netting reduces foreign exchange risk because currency flows are reduced. In a typical multilateral netting operation, it is common to cut FX volume and expense by up to 70 percent.

Centralized Cash Depository

A multilateral netting system requires a certain degree of administrative structure. At the minimum, there must be a netting center manager who has an overview of the interaffiliate cash flows from the cash budget. The **netting center** manager determines the amount of

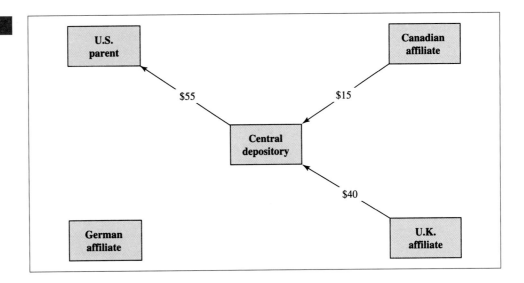

the net payments and which affiliates are to make or receive them. A netting center does not imply that the MNC has a central cash manager, however. Indeed, the multilateral netting system presented in Exhibit 19.5 suggests that each affiliate has a local cash manager who is responsible for investing excess cash and borrowing when there is a temporary cash shortage. Probably 50 percent of all netting operations worldwide do not go beyond this level of sophistication of international cash management.

Exhibit 19.6 presents a modified diagram of multilateral netting for Teltrex with the addition of a centralized depository. Under a centralized cash management system, unless otherwise instructed, all interaffiliate payments will flow through the *central cash depository*.

As Exhibit 19.6 shows, the Canadian affiliate remits the equivalent of $15,000 to the central depository and the U.K. affiliate remits the equivalent of $40,000. In turn, the central depository remits $55,000 to the U.S. parent. One might question the wisdom of this system. It appears as if the foreign exchange transactions have doubled from $55,000 in Exhibit 19.5 to $110,000 in Exhibit 19.6. But that is not the case. The Canadian and U.K. affiliates might be instructed to remit to the central depository in U.S. dollars. Alternatively, the central depository could receive the remittances in Canadian dollars and British pounds sterling and exchange them for dollars before transferring the funds to the U.S. parent. (There is the expense of an additional wire transfer, however.)

The benefits of a central cash depository derive mainly from the business transactions the affiliates have with external parties. Exhibit 19.7 presents a table showing the net amount of external receipts and disbursements each affiliate of Teltrex is expected to have during the week, as originally presented in Exhibit 19.1.

As Exhibit 19.7 shows, the U.S. parent expects to have net receipts of $20,000 by the end of the week. Analogously, in dollars, the German affiliate expects net receipts of $75,000. The Canadian affiliate expects a cash shortage of $30,000, and the U.K. affiliate expects a cash shortage of $25,000. In total, $40,000 of net receipts are expected for the MNC as a whole.

Affiliate	Receipts	Disbursements	Net
United States	$140,000	$120,000	$20,000
Canada	135,000	165,000	(30,000)
Germany	125,000	50,000	75,000
United Kingdom	130,000	155,000	(25,000)
			$40,000

EXHIBIT 19.8

Flow of Teltrex's Net Cash Receipts from Transactions with External Parties with a Centralized Depository ($000)

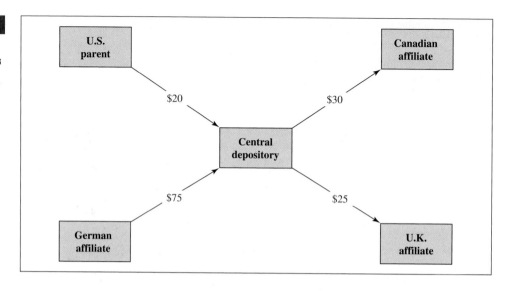

www.treasury
-management.com

This is the website of the online magazine *Treasury Management International. TMI* articles are written by corporate treasurers. Many articles on international cash management can be found at this site.

With a **centralized cash depository**, excess cash is remitted to the central cash pool. Analogously, the central cash manager arranges to cover shortages of cash. The central cash manager has a global view of the MNC's overall cash position and needs. Consequently, there is less of a chance for *mislocated funds;* that is, there is less chance for funds to be denominated in the wrong currency. Moreover, because of his global perspective, the central cash manager will know the best borrowing and investing rates. A centralized system facilitates *funds mobilization,* where systemwide cash excesses are invested at the most advantageous rates and cash shortages are covered by borrowing at the most favorable rates. Without a centralized cash depository, one affiliate might end up borrowing locally at an unfavorable rate, while another is investing temporary surplus funds locally at a disadvantageous rate. Exhibit 19.8 diagrams the cash payments for Teltrex depicted in Exhibit 19.7, showing the flows to and from the central cash pool.

Exhibit 19.8 shows that the U.S. parent will remit $20,000 of excess cash from transactions with external parties to the central cash pool, and similarly, the German affiliate will remit the $75,000 it has obtained. Both the Canadian and U.K. affiliates will have their cash shortages of $30,000 and $25,000, respectively, covered by the central pool. In total, a net increase of $40,000 is expected at the central cash depository at the end of the week. The diagram shows that a total of $150,000 of cash is expected to flow to ($95,000) and from ($55,000) the cash depository.

In More Depth

Bilateral Netting of Internal and External Net Cash Flows

Up to this point, we have handled the multilateral netting of interaffiliate cash flows (Exhibit 19.6) *and* the net receipts of the affiliates from the transactions with external parties (Exhibit 19.8) as two separate sets of cash flows through the central cash depository. While it was easier to develop the concepts in that manner, it is not necessary, practical, or efficient to do it that way in practice. Instead, the two sets of net cash flows can be bilaterally netted, with the resulting net sums going through the central depository. This will further reduce the number, size, and expense of foreign exchange

EXHIBIT 19.9

Net Cash Flows of Teltrex
Affiliates through the
Central Cash Depository

Affiliate	Net Receipts from Multilateral Netting[a] (a)	Net Excess Cash from Transactions with External Parties[b] (b)	Net Flow[c] (a − b)
United States	$55,000	$20,000	$35,000
Canada	($15,000)	($30,000)	$15,000
Germany	0	$75,000	($75,000)
United Kingdom	($40,000)	($25,000)	($15,000)
			($40,000)

[a]Net receipt from (payment to) the central depository resulting from multilateral netting, as shown in Exhibit 19.6.

[b]Net excess (shortage) of cash to be remitted to (covered by) the central depository, as shown in Exhibit 19.7.

[c]A positive amount in this column denotes a payment to an affiliate from the central cash depository; a negative amount denotes a payment from the affiliate.

EXHIBIT 19.10

Net Cash Flows of Teltrex
Affiliates through the
Central Cash Depository
after Netting Multilateral
Netting Payments and Net
Payments from External
Transactions ($000)

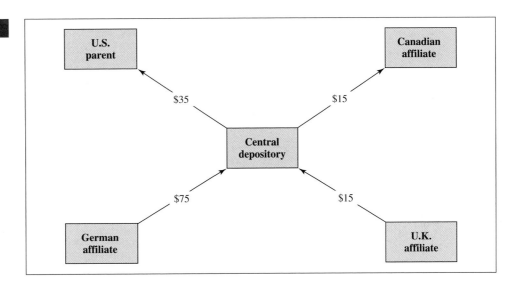

transactions for the MNC. Exhibit 19.9 calculates the net amount of funds from Teltrex affiliates to flow through the central depository.

Exhibit 19.9 shows the result of netting the cash receipts that would flow through the central cash depository via multilateral netting with the net cash flows that would flow through the central depository as a result of external transactions. As the exhibit shows, the U.S. parent will receive a single payment from the cash pool of $35,000 and the Canadian affiliate will receive $15,000. The German affiliate will remit to the central depository $75,000 and the U.K. affiliate will remit $15,000. In total, the central depository receives $90,000 and disburses $50,000, for an expected net increase in cash of $40,000 for the week. Instead of two separate sets of cash flows totaling $55,000 from the multilateral netting and $150,000 from transactions with external parties, there is only one set of cash flows after the netting totaling $140,000. Thus, there is a savings on foreign exchange transactions of $65,000 for the week. Exhibit 19.10 diagrams the resulting $140,000 of cash flows for Teltrex that are calculated in Exhibit 19.9.

Reduction in Precautionary Cash Balances

An additional benefit of a centralized cash depository is that the MNC's investment in precautionary cash balances can be substantially reduced without a reduction in its ability to cover unforeseen expenses. To see how this is accomplished, consider the

EXHIBIT 19.11

Transaction and
Precautionary Cash
Balances Held by Each
Teltrex Affiliate under
a Decentralized Cash
Management System

Affiliate	Expected Transactions (a)	Standard Deviation (b)	Expected Needs plus Precautionary (a + 3b)
United States	$120,000	$50,000	$ 270,000
Canada	165,000	70,000	375,000
Germany	50,000	20,000	110,000
United Kingdom	155,000	65,000	350,000
Total	$490,000		$1,105,000

receipts and disbursements each affiliate of Teltrex expected to make with external parties during the week. Assume, for simplicity, that each affiliate will have to make *all* its planned payments to external parties before it receives any cash from other external sources. For example, from Exhibit 19.7, the Canadian affiliate expects to have to pay to external parties the equivalent of $165,000 before it receives any of the expected $135,000 in receipts. Thus, the Canadian affiliate will need a transactions balance of $165,000 to cover expected transactions.

As previously mentioned, a firm keeps a precautionary cash balance to cover unexpected transactions during the budget period. The size of this balance depends on how safe the firm desires to be in its ability to meet unexpected transactions. The larger the precautionary cash balance, the greater is the firm's ability to meet unexpected expenses, and the less is the risk of financial embarrassment and loss of credit standing. Assume that cash needs are normally distributed and that the cash needs of one affiliate are independent from the others. If Teltrex follows a conservative policy, it might keep three standard deviations of cash for precautionary purposes, in addition to the cash needed to cover expected transactions for the planning period. Thus, the probability that Teltrex would experience a cash shortage is only .13 of 1 percent; it will have sufficient cash to cover transactions 99.87 percent of the time.

Under a decentralized cash management system, each affiliate would hold its own transaction balance and precautionary cash. Exhibit 19.11 shows the total cash held for transactions and precautionary purposes by each affiliate and by Teltrex as a whole.

As can be seen from Exhibit 19.11, Teltrex needs the equivalent of $490,000 in cash to cover expected transactions and an additional $615,000 in precautionary balances to cover unexpected expenses, for a total of $1,105,000. A centralized cash management system will greatly reduce the investment in precautionary cash balances. Under a centralized system, the amount of cash held by the MNC is viewed as a portfolio. Each affiliate will continue to hold cash sufficient to cover its expected cash transactions, but the precautionary cash balances are held by the central cash manager at the central cash depository. In the event one of the affiliates experiences a cash shortage, funds are wired from precautionary cash held in the central cash pool.

From portfolio theory, the standard deviation of the portfolio of cash held by the centralized depository for N affiliates is calculated as:[1]

$$\text{Portfolio Std. Dev.} = \sqrt{(\text{Std. Dev. Affiliate 1})^2 + \cdots + (\text{Std. Dev. Affiliate } N)^2}$$

For our example,

$$\text{Portfolio Std. Dev.} = \sqrt{(\$50,000)^2 + (\$70,000)^2 + (\$20,000)^2 + (\$65,000)^2}$$
$$= \$109,659.$$

---

[1]The standard deviation formula assumes that interaffiliate cash flows are uncorrelated with one another.

Thus under a centralized system, only $328,977 (= 3 \times \$109,659$) needs to be held for precautionary purposes by Teltrex's central cash manager. A total of $818,977 (= \$490,000 + \$328,977$) is held by Teltrex. The reduction in precautionary cash balances under the centralized system is $286,023 (= \$1,105,000 - \$818,977$), a sum that most likely can be used more profitably elsewhere, rather than standing by as a potential safety net.

Cash Management Systems in Practice

Multilateral netting is an efficient and cost-effective mechanism for handling interaffiliate foreign exchange transactions. Not all countries allow MNCs the freedom to net payments, however. Some countries allow interaffiliate transactions to be settled only on a gross basis. That is, all receipts for a settlement period must be grouped into a single large receipt and all disbursements must be grouped into a single large payment. The reason for requiring gross settlement is precisely the opposite of the reason that MNCs desire to net. By limiting netting, more needless foreign exchange transactions flow through the local banking system, thus generating income for the local banks that handle them.

A study by Collins and Frankle (1985) surveyed the cash management practices of the *Fortune* 1000 firms. The researchers received a 22 percent response rate from their questionnaire. Of the responding firms, 163 were involved in international operations. Thirty-five percent of the international respondents reported using some type of intracorporate netting and 23 percent had centralized funds concentration.

In another study, Bokos and Clinkard (1983) found that the most frequently cited benefits of a multilateral netting system were:

1. The decrease in the expense associated with funds transfer, which in some cases can be over $1,000 for a large international transfer of foreign exchange.

2. The reduction in the number of foreign exchange transactions and the associated cost of making fewer but larger transactions.

3. The reduction in intracompany float, which is frequently as high as five days even for wire transfers.

4. The savings in administrative time.

5. The benefits that accrue from the establishment of a formal information system, which serves as the foundation for centrally managing transaction exposure and the investment of excess funds.

www.euronetting.com

This is the website of EuroNetting, an online netting company that enables companies worldwide to manage their intercompany netting activities.

There are several commercial multilateral netting packages available that offer full international cash management services. For example, EuroNetting is a 100 percent web browser-based system for both the netting center and the participants. It is used by approximately 50 companies with about 8,000 associated users worldwide to manage their interaffiliate reconcilement and netting activities. The EuroNetting system facilitates both balance and invoice-level netting with participant settlement in any currency. The system incorporates a comprehensive set of hedging capabilities and interfaces with most popular bank settlement systems and treasury workstations. Wall Street Systems' Wallstreet Treasura is another international cash management system that allows the corporation to achieve global cash visibility by connecting to all the firm's banks to position cash and reconcile daily cash and liquidity. It allows the firm to make daily, weekly, and monthly cash forecasts, facilitates interaffiliate loans, and can accommodate foreign exchange transactions. Bank of America Merril Lynch's CashPro Accelerate is a similar cash management system that integrates with the firm's general ledger. It provides for streamline cash position reporting in multiple bank accounts around the globe. Daily currency exchange rates are built into the system to allow viewing cash balances in different currencies. It is capable of providing updated cash balances every five minutes.

SUMMARY

This chapter discussed cash management in the multinational firm. Special attention was given to the topic of multilateral netting. A case application was used to show the benefits of centralized cash management.

1. A multilateral netting system is beneficial in reducing the number of and the expense associated with interaffiliate foreign exchange transactions.

2. A centralized cash pool assists in reducing the problem of mislocated funds and in funds mobilization. A central cash manager has a global view of the most favorable borrowing rates and most advantageous investment rates.

3. A centralized cash management system with a cash pool can reduce the investment the MNC has in precautionary cash balances, saving the firm money.

KEY WORDS

bilateral netting, *479*
cash budget, *478*
cash
   management, *477*

centralized cash
   depository, *482*
multilateral
   netting, *479*

netting center, *480*
precautionary cash
   balances, *477*
transaction balances, *477*

QUESTIONS

1. Describe the key factors contributing to effective cash management within a firm. Why is the cash management process more difficult in a MNC?

2. Discuss the pros and cons of a MNC having a centralized cash manager handle all investment and borrowing for all affiliates of the MNC versus each affiliate having a local manager who performs the cash management activities of the affiliate.

PROBLEMS

1. Assume that interaffiliate cash flows are uncorrelated with one another. Calculate the standard deviation of the portfolio of cash held by the centralized depository for the following affiliate members:

Affiliate	Expected Transactions	Standard Deviation
U.S.	$100,000	$40,000
Canada	$150,000	$60,000
Mexico	$175,000	$30,000
Chile	$200,000	$70,000

INTERNET EXERCISES

1. EuroNetting, an online netting company, offers a multilateral service that enables companies to run their netting efficiently over the Internet. See their website at www.euronetting.com to view their product offerings. EuroNetting is used by approximately 50 companies with about 10,000 associated users worldwide to manage their intercompany reconcilement and netting activities.

2. Students interested in a professional designation in international cash management should explore the online program leading to a Certificate in International Cash Management (CertICM) at the Association of Corporate Treasurers website, www.treasurers.org. The six-month program requires 200 hours of self-study, after which there is a three-hour written exam.

MINI CASE 1

Efficient Funds Flow at Eastern Trading Company

The Eastern Trading Company of Singapore purchases spices in bulk from around the world, packages them into consumer-size quantities, and sells them through sales affiliates in Hong Kong, the United Kingdom, and the United States. For a recent month, the following payments matrix of interaffiliate cash flows, stated in Singapore dollars, was forecast. Show how Eastern Trading can use multilateral netting to minimize the foreign exchange transactions necessary to settle interaffiliate payments. If foreign exchange transactions cost the company .5 percent, what savings result from netting?

Eastern Trading Company Payments Matrix (S$000)

	Disbursements				
Receipts	Singapore	Hong Kong	U.K.	U.S.	Total Receipts
Singapore	—	40	75	55	170
Hong Kong	8	—	—	22	30
U.K.	15	—	—	17	32
U.S.	11	25	9	—	45
Total disbursements	34	65	84	94	277

MINI CASE 2

Eastern Trading Company's New MBA

The Eastern Trading Company of Singapore presently follows a decentralized system of cash management where it and its affiliates each maintain their own transaction and precautionary cash balances. Eastern Trading believes that it and its affiliates' cash needs are normally distributed and independent from one another. It is corporate policy to maintain two and one-half standard deviations of cash as precautionary holdings. At this level of safety there is a 99.37 percent chance that each affiliate will have enough cash holdings to cover transactions.

A new MBA hired by the company claims that the investment in precautionary cash balances is needlessly large and can be reduced substantially if the firm converts to a centralized cash management system. Use the projected information for the current month, which is presented below, to determine the amount of cash Eastern Trading needs to hold in precautionary balances under its current decentralized system and the level of precautionary cash it would need to hold under a centralized system. Was the new MBA a good hire?

Affiliate	Expected Transactions	One Standard Deviation
Singapore	S$125,000	S$40,000
Hong Kong	60,000	25,000
United Kingdom	95,000	40,000
United States	70,000	35,000

REFERENCES & SUGGESTED READINGS

Bokos, W. J., and Anne P. Clinkard. "Multilateral Netting." *Journal of Cash Management* 3 (1983), pp. 24–34.
Collins, J. Markham, and Alan W. Frankle. "International Cash Management Practices of Large U.S. Firms." *Journal of Cash Management* 5 (1985), pp. 42–48.

20 International Trade Finance

IN MODERN TIMES, it is virtually impossible for a country to produce domestically everything its citizens need or demand. Even if it could, it is unlikely that it could produce all items more efficiently than producers in other countries. Without international trade, scarce resources are not put to their best uses.

International trade is more difficult and risky, however, than domestic trade. In foreign trade, the exporter may not be familiar with the buyer, and thus may not know if the importer is a good credit risk. If merchandise is exported abroad and the buyer does not pay, it may prove difficult, if not impossible, for the exporter to have any legal recourse. Additionally, political instability makes it risky to ship merchandise abroad to certain parts of the world. From the importer's perspective, it is risky to make advance payment for goods that may never be shipped by the exporter.

The present chapter deals with these issues and others. The chapter begins with an example of a simple yet typical foreign trade transaction. The mechanics of the trade are discussed, delineating the institutional arrangements that have been developed over time to facilitate international trade in light of the risks we have identified. The three basic documents needed in a foreign trade transaction—a letter of credit, a time draft, and a bill of lading—are discussed in detail. It is shown how a time draft becomes a banker's acceptance, a negotiable money market instrument.

The second part of the chapter discusses the role of the Export-Import Bank, an independent government agency founded to offer competitive assistance to U.S. exporters through loans, financial guarantees, and credit insurance. The chapter concludes with a discussion of various types of countertrade transactions. Countertrade transactions can collectively be defined as foreign trade transactions in which the seller provides the buyer with goods or services in return for a reciprocal promise from the seller to purchase goods or services from the buyer.

A Typical Foreign Trade Transaction

To understand the mechanics of a typical foreign trade transaction, it is best to use an illustration. Consider a U.S. importer, who is an automobile dealer, and who desires to purchase automobiles from a Japanese exporter, the manufacturer. The two do not know one another and are obviously separated by a great distance. If the Japanese manufacturer could have his way, he would have the U.S. importer pay *cash in advance* for the shipment, since he is unfamiliar with the creditworthiness of the auto dealer.

If the auto dealer could have his way, he ideally would prefer to receive the cars on consignment from the auto manufacturer. In a *consignment* sale, the exporter retains title to the merchandise that is shipped. The importer only pays the exporter once he sells the merchandise. If the importer cannot sell the merchandise, he returns it to the exporter. Obviously, the exporter bears all the risk in a consignment sale. Second best for the auto dealer would be to receive the car shipment on credit and then to make payment, thus not paying in advance for an order that might not ever be received.

How can the situation be reconciled so that the foreign trade transaction is satisfactory for both the exporter and the importer? Fortunately for the auto dealer and the auto manufacturer, they are not the first two parties who have faced such a dilemma. Over the years, an elaborate process has evolved for handling just this type of foreign commerce transaction. Exhibit 20.1 presents a schematic of the process that is typically followed in foreign trade. Working our way through Exhibit 20.1 in a narrative fashion will allow us to understand the mechanics of a trade and also the three major documents involved.

EXHIBIT 20.1   **Process of a Typical Foreign Trade Transaction**

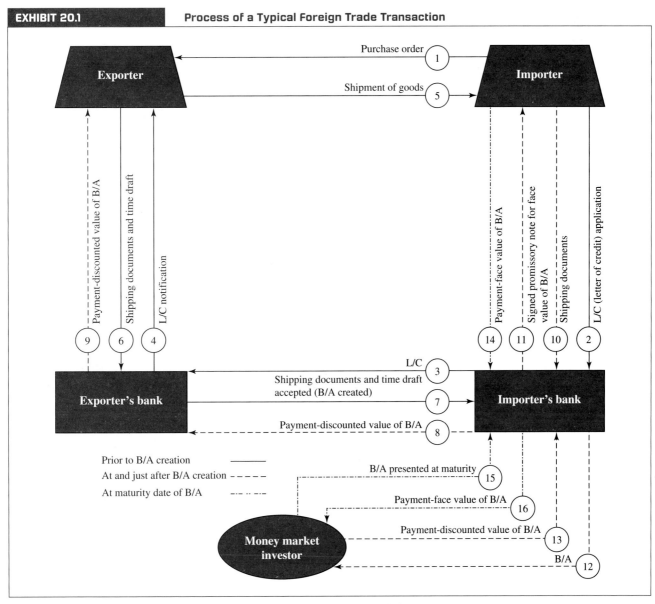

Source: Adapted from *Instruments of the Money Market*, Federal Reserve Bank of Richmond, 1986.

Exhibit 20.1 begins with (i) the U.S. importer placing an order with the Japanese exporter, asking if he will ship automobiles under a letter of credit. If the auto manufacturer agrees to this, he will inform the U.S. importer of the price and the other terms of sale, including the credit terms. For discussion purposes, we will assume the length of the credit period is 60 days. The U.S. importer will (ii) apply to his bank for a letter of credit for the merchandise he desires to purchase, providing his bank with the terms of the sale.

A **letter of credit (L/C)** is a guarantee from the importer's bank that it will act on behalf of the importer and pay the exporter for the merchandise if all relevant documents specified in the L/C are presented according to the terms of the L/C. In essence, the importer's bank is substituting its creditworthiness for that of the unknown U.S. importer.

The L/C is (iii) sent via the importer's bank to the exporter's bank. Once the L/C is received, the exporter's bank will (iv) notify the exporter. The Japanese exporter will (v) then ship the cars.

After shipping the automobiles, the Japanese exporter will (vi) present to his bank a (60-day) time draft, drawn according to the instructions in the L/C, the bill of lading, and any other shipping documents that are required, such as the invoice and a packing list. A **time draft** is a written order instructing the importer or his agent, the importer's bank, to pay the amount specified on its face on a certain date (that is, the end of the credit period in a foreign trade transaction). A **bill of lading (B/L)** is a document issued by the common carrier specifying that it has received the goods for shipment; it can serve as title to the goods. The exporter's bank (vii) presents the shipping documents and the time draft to the importer's bank. After taking title to the goods via the bill of lading, the importer's bank accepts the time draft, creating at this point a **banker's acceptance (B/A)**, a negotiable money market instrument for which a secondary market exists. The importer's bank charges an acceptance commission, which is deducted at the time of final settlement. The acceptance commission is based on the term-to-maturity of the time draft and the creditworthiness of the importer.

One of several things can happen with the B/A. It can be returned to the Japanese exporter, who will hold it for 60 days and then present it for payment to the importer's bank at maturity. Should the exporter suddenly find he needs funds prior to the maturity date, the B/A can be sold at a discount in the money market. Since their risks are similar, banker's acceptances trade at rates similar to rates for negotiable bank certificates of deposit. Alternatively, as in Exhibit 20.1, the Japanese exporter could instruct its bank to have the B/A (viii) discounted by the importer's bank and (ix) pay that amount to it. Analogously, the exporter's bank may decide to hold the B/A to maturity as an investment, and pay the Japanese exporter the discounted equivalent.

The U.S. importer (x) signs a (60-day) promissory note with his bank for the face value of the banker's acceptance, due on the maturity date of the B/A. In return, the exporter's bank (xi) provides the auto dealer with the shipping documents needed to take possession of the automobiles from the common carrier.

If the B/A is not held by the Japanese exporter or the exporter's bank, the importer's bank may hold it for 60 days until maturity when it will collect the face value from the U.S. importer via the promissory note. Alternatively, as in Exhibit 20.1, the importer's bank may (xii) sell the B/A in the money market to an investor at a (xiii) discount from face value. At maturity, the importer's bank will (xiv) collect the face value of the B/A via the promissory note from the U.S. importer, the money market investor will (xv) present the B/A for payment to the importer's bank, and the importer's bank will (xvi) pay the face value of the B/A to the investor. In the event of default by the U.S. importer, the importer's bank will seek recourse against the importer. B/As usually have maturities ranging from 30 days to 180 days; as such they are only short-term sources of trade financing.

EXAMPLE | 20.1: Cost Analysis of a Banker's Acceptance

As mentioned in the previous discussion of the schematic describing a typical foreign trade transaction, the exporter may hold the B/A to maturity and collect payment at that time. Alternatively, the exporter may discount the B/A with the importer's bank or sell it at a discount in the money market.

Suppose the face amount of the promissory note is $1,000,000 and the importer's bank charges an acceptance commission of 1.5 percent. Since the note is for 60 days, the exporter will receive $997,500 = $1,000,000 × [1 − (.015 × 60/360)] if he decides to hold the B/A until maturity. Thus, the acceptance commission is $2,500.

If 60-day B/A rates are 5.25 percent and the exporter discounts the B/A with the importer's bank, he will receive $988,750 = $1,000,000 × [1 − ([.0525 + .0150] × 60/360)]. Thus, the importer's bank receives a discount rate of interest of 6.75 percent = 5.25 + 1.50 percent on its investment. At maturity the importer's bank will receive $1,000,000 from the importer. The bond equivalent yield it receives on its investment (which is figured on the actual number of days in a year instead of a 360-day banker's year) is 6.92 percent, or .0692 = ($1,000,000/$988,750 − 1) × 365/60.

The exporter pays the acceptance commission regardless of whether he discounts the B/A or holds it to maturity, hence it is not marginal to a decision to discount the B/A. The bond equivalent rate the exporter receives from discounting the B/A is 5.38 percent, or .0538 = ($997,500/$988,750 − 1) × 365/60. If the exporter's opportunity cost of capital is greater than 5.38 percent compounded bi-monthly (an effective annual rate of 5.5 percent), discounting makes sense; if not, the exporter should hold the B/A to maturity.

Forfaiting

www.tradeandforfaiting.com

The website of the Association of Trade and Forfaiting in the Americas, Inc. It provides information on forfaiting for exporters, importers, and financial institutions.

Forfaiting is a type of medium-term trade financing used to finance the sale of capital goods. Forfaiting involves the sale of promissory notes signed by the importer in favor of the exporter. The *forfait,* usually a bank, buys the notes at a discount from face value from the exporter. In this way, the exporter receives payment for the export and does not have to carry the financing. The forfait does not have recourse against the exporter in the event of default by the importer. The promissory notes are typically structured to extend out in a series over a period of from three to seven years, with a note in the series maturing every six months. Since forfaiting transactions are typically used to finance capital goods, they usually are for amounts of $500,000 or more. Forfaiting began in Switzerland and Germany, but it has now spread throughout most of Western Europe and into the United States. Forfait transactions are typically denominated in Swiss francs, euros, and U.S. dollars.

The International Finance in Practice box "First Islamic Forfaiting Fund Set Up" discusses how forfaiting meets Islamic finance practices.

Government Assistance in Exporting

www.export.gov

A U.S. government website with information on export counseling, programs and services, and financing and insurance.

Success in international trade is fundamentally important for a country. Success in exporting implies that there is demand for a country's products, that its labor force is benefiting from employment, and that some resources are used for technological advancement. To be successful in international trade requires a country's export-oriented firms to be good marketers, that is, to be competitive in terms of product offerings, promotion, price, delivery capability, and service provided to importers. Equally important, however, is for firms to be competitive in terms of extending credit to importers.

Because of the benefits that accrue from exporting, the governments of most developed countries offer competitive assistance to domestic exporters in the form of

First Islamic Forfaiting Fund Set Up

While selling debt at a reduced value, strictly forbidden under the terms of Islamic finance, is inherent in forfaiting as this involves the sale of a discounted letter of credit (LC), Norton Rose and WestLB have recently managed to structure a forfaiting fund aimed at institutional investors requiring Islamically compliant investment opportunities.

The WestLB-Tricon Forfaiting Fund is a Bermuda-registered entity allowing investors to participate in a Shari'ah compliant investment strategy involving commodity and trade finance, including forfaiting asset receivables. Islamic finance is a relatively new field that has only existed for around two decades, and financing solutions to accommodate it continue to be rolled out.

Mohammed Paracha, an associate and London-based member of Norton Rose's Islamic finance group, tells *Trade Finance*: "Financial institutions have for some time recognized that the requirements of Middle Eastern investors are not being met. With so much wealth in the region, people are looking at innovative ways to tap into Islamic money, and it was decided that there was a need to get Islamic money into a product that

could be combined with forfaiting assets, and we have been able to develop an investment fund which has been structured to adhere to Shari'ah principles whilst at the same time making use of forfaiting assets."

It is understood that the fund is now up and running, and that its investment strategy includes investing in LCs (or similar trade paper) across all sectors, though screening is required to ensure that the products underlying the LCs do not run counter to Shari'ah principles. According to Paracha, the structure is a complex one. He says: "It was quite a difficult exercise, and there had to be a sign-off by Islamic scholars to verify that Shari'ah strictures had been met with. There was also the issue of working across UK and Bermudan jurisdictions."

Paracha continues: "We also had to be careful in ensuring that the pool of non-Islamic forfaiting assets was not used to directly satisfy the Islamically compliant obligations under the commodity and trade financing arrangements."

---

subsidized credit that can be extended to importers. Also, credit insurance programs that guarantee financing extended by private financial institutions are common. In this section, we discuss the main features of programs available to U.S. exporters.

The Export-Import Bank and Affiliated Organizations

In 1934, the **Export-Import Bank (Ex-Im Bank) of the United States** was founded, and subsequently chartered in 1945, as an independent government agency to facilitate and finance U.S. export trade. Ex-Im Bank's purpose is to provide financing in situations where private financial institutions are unable or unwilling to because: (i) the loan maturity is too long; (ii) the amount of the loan is too large; (iii) the loan risk is too great; or (iv) the importing firm has difficulty obtaining hard currency for payment.

To meet its objectives, Ex-Im Bank provides service through several types of programs. Some of the most important of these are working capital guarantees, direct loans to foreign borrowers, loan guarantees, and credit insurance.[1]

Through its *Working Capital Guarantee Program,* Ex-Im Bank facilitates the expansion of U.S. exports by encouraging commercial lenders to make working capital loans to U.S. exporters. The Ex-Im Bank loan guarantee covers 90 percent of the loan principal and accrued interest, and it is backed by the full faith and credit of the U.S. government.

Through its *Medium and Long-Term Loan Program,* Ex-Im Bank will facilitate direct credit to foreign buyers of U.S. exports. Disbursements go to the U.S. exporter, and the export products go to the foreign importer. The *Long-Term Program* covers repayment terms in excess of seven years and a loan amount greater than $10 million. The *Medium-Term Program* covers repayment terms of seven years or less and loan

---

[1]Much of the discussion in this section is drawn from the Export-Import Bank website, www.exim.gov.

amounts of $10 million or less. Both programs cover financing up to 85 percent of the export contract value. The *Private Export Funding Corporation (PEFCO),* established in 1970 by a group of commercial banks and industrial corporations, frequently cooperates in loans with the Ex-Im Bank under these programs by providing liquidity via the purchase of notes issued by Ex-Im Bank to finance the loans.

Through its *Medium and Long-Term Guarantee Program,* Ex-Im Bank guarantees the loans made by private financial institutions to foreign importers. Interest charged on these loans is usually at a floating rate. The guarantees, which commit the full faith and credit of the U.S. government, cover financing up to 85 percent of the export contract value. The guarantees cover 100 percent of the loan principal and accrued interest against loss due to commercial and political risks. Guarantees covering only political risks are available.

Through its *Export Credit Insurance Program,* Ex-Im Bank helps U.S. exporters develop and expand their overseas sales by protecting them against loss should a foreign buyer or other foreign debtor default for political or commercial reasons. Insurance policies may cover both comprehensive commercial and political credit risks, or only specific political risks.

In the United Kingdom, the *Exports Credits Guarantee Department (ECGD)* performs functions similar to those of the Ex-Im Bank. Formed in 1919, the ECGD provides assistance to exporters through direct insurance coverage against nonpayment by the importer due to commercial and political risks and by guaranteeing bank loans to foreign borrowers. The exporter, who is considered to be the true beneficiary, pays to ECGD the guaranteed bank loan insurance premium.

www.eximbankindia.com

Website of the Export-Import Bank of India. The EXIM India was set up in 1981 to finance, facilitate, and promote India's international trade. It is the counterpart of the Ex-Im Bank of the United States. There are several websites providing information about various countries' export-import banks.

www.ecgd.gov.uk

The official website of the Export Credits Guarantee Department (ECGD).

Countertrade

www.globaloffset.org

Official site of the Global Offset and Countertrade Association (GOCA). The GOCA provides a forum for companies involved in countertrade and a resource for companies exploring the possibilities held by countertrade and offset.

Countertrade is an umbrella term used to describe many different types of transactions, each "in which the seller provides a buyer with goods or services and promises in return to purchase goods or services from the buyer."[2] Countertrades may or may not involve the use of money. If money is not exchanged, the trade is a type of barter. Regardless, countertrade usually results in a two-way flow of commodities.

Countertrade arrangements can be traced back to prehistoric times and they have been used throughout history whenever money was scarce. While it is difficult to determine the exact volume of countertrade, the practice is nevertheless widespread. According to Hammond (1990), some estimates put countertrade at only 5 percent of total world trade, whereas other estimates are as high as 40 percent. Moreover, countertrade transactions are not accounted for in official trade statistics. In the new millennium, the IMF, the World Bank, and the U.S. Department of Commerce estimate that as much as half of all international trade transactions will be conducted as countertrade.[3] Most recently, a surge of countertrade activity occurred in the 1980s, when the Third World debt crisis left the debtor countries without sufficient foreign exchange reserves or bank lines of credit to carry on normal commerce.[4]

Forms of Countertrade

Hennart (1989) identifies six forms of countertrade: barter, clearing arrangement, switch trading, buy-back, counterpurchase, and offset. The first three do not involve the use of money, whereas the latter three do.

Barter is the direct exchange of goods between two parties. While money does not exchange hands in a barter transaction, it is common to value the goods each party exchanges in an agreed-upon currency. It is often necessary to place a monetary value on the goods for accounting, taxation, and insurance purposes.

---

[2]Definition from Hennart (1989).

[3]See Anyane-Ntow and Harvey (1995, p. 47) for this estimate.

[4]See Chapter 11 for a discussion of the extent and severity of the Third World debt crisis.

Hammond (1990) describes barter as "a rather primitive way to do business. It fosters bilateral trade which, in turn, under mercantilist economies and imperialistic policies, fostered a tight system of colonial dependency with protected markets and captive sources of raw materials." He notes that barter flourished until after World War II when the Bretton Woods fixed exchange rate system was established that provided for currency convertibility and fostered free trade.

Today, barter transactions are typically one-time exchanges of merchandise that take place when circumstances warrant. Schaffer (1989) describes a modern example of barter that took place between General Electric (GE) and Romania. GE had agreed to sell Romania a turbine generator for cash. The Romanian loan financing subsequently fell through, and in order to complete the deal, GE agreed to accept Romanian products, which it in turn sold for cash through its trading company.

A *clearing arrangement* (also called a bilateral clearing agreement) is a form of barter in which the counterparties (governments) contract to purchase a certain amount of goods and services from one another. Both parties set up accounts with each other that are debited whenever one country imports from the other. At the end of an agreed-upon period of time, any account imbalances are settled for hard currency, or by the transfer of goods. The clearing arrangement introduces the concept of credit to barter transactions, and means bilateral trade can take place and does not have to be immediately settled. Account balances are periodically determined and any trade imbalances are settled in an agreed-upon currency. Anyane-Ntow and Harvey (1995) note that bilateral clearing agreements have usually taken place between Third World and Eastern European countries. They cite the 1994 agreement between China and Saudi Arabia with a $1 billion target as an example.

A *switch trade* is the purchase by a third party of one country's clearing agreement imbalance for hard currency, which is in turn resold. The second buyer uses the account balance to purchase goods and services from the original clearing agreement counterparty who had the account imbalance. Anyane-Ntow and Harvey (1995) give the example of a switch trade when the United States exported fertilizers to Pakistan through a Romanian-Pakistani clearing agreement.

A *buy-back transaction* involves a technology transfer via the sale of a manufacturing plant. As part of the transaction, the seller agrees to purchase a certain portion of the plant output once it is constructed. As Hennart (1989) notes, money enters into the agreement in two ways. First, the plant buyer borrows hard currency in the capital market to pay the seller for the plant. Second, the plant seller agrees to purchase enough of the plant output over a period of time to enable the buyer to pay back the borrowed funds. A buy-back transaction can be viewed as a form of direct investment in the purchasing country. Examples of buy-back transactions include Japan's agreements with Taiwan, Singapore, and Korea to exchange computer chip production equipment for a certain percentage of the output.[5]

A *counterpurchase* is similar to a buy-back transaction, but with some notable differences. The two counterparties are usually an Eastern importer and a Western exporter of technology. The major difference between a buy-back and a counter-purchase transaction is that in the latter, the merchandise the Western seller agrees to purchase is unrelated and has not been produced on the exported equipment. The seller agrees to purchase goods from a list drawn up by the importer at prices set by the importer. Goods on the list are frequently items for which the buyer does not have a ready market. As an example of a counterpurchase, Anyane-Ntow and Harvey (1995) cite the agreement to exchange Italian industrial equipment for Indonesian rubber.

An *offset transaction* can be viewed as a counterpurchase trade agreement involving the aerospace/defense industry. Offset transactions are reciprocal trade

---

[5]See Anyane-Ntow and Harvey (1995, p. 48).

Armed Forces Tops in Countertrade List

The Armed Forces of the Philippines (AFP) leads all government agencies in countertrade transactions, accounting for a total of $143.4 million worth from 1989 to August 2004 based on figures provided by the Philippine International Trading Corporation (PITC). Countertrade refers to reciprocal and compensatory agreements involving the purchase of goods or services by the seller from the buyer of this product or arrangements where the seller assists the buyer in reducing the net cost of the purchase through some form of compensatory financing.

The AFP yesterday announced that the Philippines recently benefited from two countertrade transactions by the military. In February last year, the Philippine Army procured $2.1 million worth of Squad Automatic Weapons from FN Herstal of Belgium, with a countertrade commitment of $1.8 million or 85 percent of the contract price.

The program has paved the way for the development of Philippine semi-processed rubber exports worldwide through a financing scheme packaged by Raifeissen Centrobank of Austria, the designated trading partner of FN Herstal under the Countertrade Program of the Philippines.

The assistance has opened doors to new exports markets including the Czech Republic, Australia, Italy, Germany, and New Zealand, officials added. The AFP also purchased $7.6 million worth of HF/SSB Transceivers and Manpack Communications equipment from Harris Corp. in December 2003 and February 2004. As a direct beneficiary of the countertrade program, the military received some $6.1 million worth of offset activities.

Under the arrangement Harris Corporation is obligated to an 80 percent offset of some $6.2 million and a 20 percent counterpurchase or $1.5 million. Some of the offset benefits included software upgrades for 324 Manpack Communication units, donation of additional Manpack batteries, donation of one automated test set and spare modules, officials said.

The government countertrade program was established under Executive Order 120, which provides that all government procurements equivalent of $1 million and above have to have a countertrade component of at least 50 percent of the value of the supply contract. In response, the Department of National Defense issued Dept. Circular 4 dated July 20, 2001, requiring countertrade to be part of the AFP's acquisition program for all projects costing more than $1 million.

The AFP is closely followed by the National Food Authority with a total of $136.6 million worth of countertrade transactions. More than $300 million worth of Philippine products have been exported under the Countertrade Program of the Government through its foreign procurement.

agreements between an industrialized country and a country that has defense and /or aerospace industries. Hammond (1990) cites the example of the sale of F-16 jet fighters manufactured by General Dynamics to Turkey and Greece in exchange for olives, hydroelectric power projects, the promotion of tourism, and aircraft coproduction.

The International Finance in Practice box "Armed Forces Tops in Countertrade List" discusses how the Armed Forces of the Philippines uses offset transactions and counterpurchases to obtain military equipment.

Some Generalizations about Countertrade

Countertrade transactions became very prominent in international trade in the 1980s and 1990s. Arguments both for and against countertrade transactions can be made. Hammond (1990) notes that there are both negative and positive incentives for a country to be in favor of countertrade. Negative incentives are those that are forced upon a country or corporation whether or not it desires to engage in countertrade. They include the conservation of cash and hard currency, the improvement of trade imbalances, and the maintenance of export prices. Positive reasons from both the country and corporate perspectives include enhanced economic development, increased employment, technology transfer, market expansion, increased profitability, less costly sourcing of supply, reduction of surplus goods from inventory, and the development of marketing expertise.

Those against countertrade transactions claim that such transactions tamper with the fundamental operation of free markets, and, therefore, resources are used inefficiently. Opponents claim that transaction costs are increased, that multilateral trade is restricted by fostering bilateral trade agreements, and that, in general, transactions that do not make use of money represent a step backward in economic development.

Hennart (1989) empirically studied 1,277 countertrade transactions. Of these transactions, 694 were clearing arrangements, 171 were classified as barters, 298 as counterpurchases, 71 as buy-backs, and 43 as offsets. The countries involved were classified into the World Bank categories of: Developed, Organization of Petroleum Exporting Countries (OPEC) Members, Centrally Planned Economies (CPE), Middle-Income, and Low-Income.

Hennart found that each country grouping had a propensity to engage in certain types of countertrade transactions. OPEC and middle-income countries used more counterpurchases; CPEs more buy-backs; and developed and middle-income countries engaged in more offsets. Barter was most common between two middle-income countries and between developed and middle-income countries.

Hennart claims the high frequency of buy-backs among CPEs is consistent with their use as a substitute for foreign direct investment. The reasons that CPEs and low-income countries do not actively engage in offset transactions are twofold: historically, CPEs have not been allowed to purchase Western weapons, and low-income developing countries cannot afford sophisticated weapons systems typically sold via offset transactions. Barter between two middle-income countries (the most frequent) is consistent with the two countries desiring to avoid the repayment of external debt. The absence of barter between two OPEC countries and between two developed countries is consistent with the use of barter to bypass cartels and commodity arrangements. The analysis of Marin and Schnitzer (1995) is consistent with Hennart's conclusions.

Whether countertrade transactions are good or bad for the global economy, it appears certain that they will increase in the near future as world trade increases.

SUMMARY

Export and import transactions and trade financing are the main topics discussed in this chapter.

1. Conducting international trade transactions is difficult in comparison to domestic trades. Commercial and political risks enter into the equation, which are not factors in domestic trade. Yet it is important for a country to be competitively strong in international trade in order for its citizens to have the goods and services they need and demand.

2. A typical foreign trade transaction requires three basic documents: letter of credit, time draft, and bill of lading. A time draft can become a negotiable money market instrument called a banker's acceptance.

3. Forfaiting, in which a bank purchases at a discount from an importer a series of promissory notes in favor of an exporter, is a medium-term form of trade financing.

4. The Export-Import Bank provides competitive assistance to U.S. exporters through direct loans to foreign importers, loan guarantees, and credit insurance to U.S. exporters.

5. Countertrade transactions are gaining renewed prominence as a means of conducting international trade transactions. There are several types of countertrade transactions, only some of which involve the use of money. In each type, the seller provides the buyer with goods or services in return for a reciprocal promise from the seller to purchase goods or services from the buyer.

KEY WORDS

banker's acceptance
 (B/A), *490*
bill of lading (B/L), *490*
countertrade, *493*

Export-Import Bank
 (Ex-Im Bank) of the
 United States, *492*
forfaiting, *491*

letter of credit
 (L/C), *490*
time draft, *490*

QUESTIONS

1. Discuss some of the reasons why international trade is more difficult and risky from the exporter's perspective than is domestic trade.

2. What three basic documents are necessary to conduct a typical foreign commerce trade? Briefly discuss the purpose of each.

3. How does a time draft become a banker's acceptance?

4. Discuss the various ways the exporter can receive payment in a foreign trade transaction after the importer's bank accepts the exporter's time draft and it becomes a banker's acceptance.

5. What is a forfaiting transaction?

6. What is the purpose of the Export-Import Bank?

7. Do you think that a country's government should assist private business in the conduct of international trade through direct loans, loan guarantees, and/or credit insurance?

8. Briefly discuss the various types of countertrade.

9. Discuss some of the pros and cons of countertrade from the country's perspective and the firm's perspective.

10. What is the difference between a buy-back transaction and a counterpurchase?

PROBLEMS

1. Assume the time from acceptance to maturity on a $2,000,000 banker's acceptance is 90 days. Further assume that the importing bank's acceptance commission is 1.25 percent and that the market rate for 90-day B/As is 7 percent. Determine the amount the exporter will receive if he holds the B/A until maturity and also the amount the exporter will receive if he discounts the B/A with the importer's bank.

2. The time from acceptance to maturity on a $1,000,000 banker's acceptance is 120 days. The importer's bank's acceptance commission is 1.75 percent and the market rate for 120-day B/As is 5.75 percent. What amount will the exporter receive if he holds the B/A until maturity? If he discounts the B/A with the importer's bank? Also determine the bond equivalent yield the importer's bank will earn from discounting the B/A with the exporter. If the exporter's opportunity cost of capital is 11 percent, should he discount the B/A or hold it to maturity?

INTERNET EXERCISES

The chapter indicated that banker's acceptances were negotiable money market instruments. You might be interested in including B/As in your portfolio. Fiscal Agents Savings and Investment Centre is an investment advisory service dedicated to finding financial solutions that suit the needs and goals of its clients. Search www.fiscalagents .com to learn what Fiscal Agents has to say about B/As as an investment.

www.mhhe.com/er8e

www.mhhe.com/er8e

MINI CASE

American Machine Tools, Inc.

American Machine Tools is a midwestern manufacturer of tool-and-die-making equipment. The company has had an inquiry from a representative of the Moldovan government about the terms of sale for a $5,000,000 order of machinery. The sales manager spoke with the Moldovan representative, but he is doubtful that the Moldovan government will be able to obtain enough hard currency to make the purchase. While the U.S. economy has been growing, American Machine Tools has not had a very good year. An additional $5,000,000 in sales would definitely help. If something cannot be arranged, the firm will likely be forced to lay off some of its skilled workforce.

Is there a way that you can think of that American Machine Tools might be able to make the machinery sale to Moldova?

REFERENCES & SUGGESTED READINGS

Anyane-Ntow, Kwabena, and Santhi C. Harvey. "A Countertrade Primer." *Management Accounting* (April 1995), pp. 47–50.

Hammond, Grant T. *Countertrade, Offsets and Barter in International Political Economy.* New York: St. Martin's Press, 1990.

Hennart, Jean-Francois. "Some Empirical Dimensions of Countertrade." *Journal of International Business Studies* (Second Quarter, 1989), pp. 243–70.

Marin, Dalia, and Monika Schnitzer. "Tying Trade Flows: A Theory of Countertrade with Evidence." *The American Economic Review* 85 (1995), pp. 1047–64.

Neumeir, Shelley. "Why Countertrade Is Getting Hot." *Fortune,* June 29, 1992, p. 25.

Schaffer, Matt. *Winning the Countertrade War.* New York: John Wiley and Sons, 1989.

21 International Tax Environment and Transfer Pricing

ONE PURPOSE OF this chapter is to provide a brief introduction to the international tax environment that will be useful to multinational firms in their tax planning and also informative to investors in international financial assets. Tax regulation is a complex topic at the domestic level. It is obviously a much more complex topic at the international level. Hence, this chapter is designed to serve only as an introduction.

The chapter begins with a discussion of the two main objectives of taxation: tax neutrality and tax equity. After this theoretical foundation has been established, the main types of taxation are discussed. Next follows discussions of how taxes are typically levied throughout the world, the purpose of foreign tax credits, and tax treaties between nations. Since it is not possible to thoroughly address taxation from the viewpoint of all national taxpayers, by necessity the perspective is from the U.S. taxpayer's viewpoint when the discussion needs to be country specific.

Some taxation issues have been introduced earlier in other chapters because a thorough presentation of the topic under discussion required it. For example, Chapter 18 on international capital budgeting required some elementary knowledge of the concepts of worldwide taxation of active foreign-source income and foreign tax credits applied against a MNC's domestic tax liability. This topic will be revisited in this chapter to provide a more detailed and structured understanding of these issues.

The second purpose of this chapter is to explore transfer pricing issues. This is accomplished through a case application that is used to illustrate transfer pricing strategies and the unbundling of services as two means for a MNC to reposition cash between affiliates and, under certain circumstances, reduce its overall income tax liability. The chapter concludes with a discussion on moving blocked funds from a host country that has imposed foreign exchange restrictions.

The Objectives of Taxation

Two basic objectives of taxation have to be discussed to help frame our thinking about the international tax environment: tax neutrality and tax equity.

Tax Neutrality

Tax neutrality has its foundations in the principles of economic efficiency and equity. Tax neutrality is determined by three criteria. **Capital-export neutrality** is the criterion that an ideal tax should be effective in raising revenue for the government and not have any negative effects on the economic decision-making process of the taxpayer. That is, a good tax is one that is efficient in raising tax revenue for the government and does not prevent economic resources from being allocated to their most appropriate use no matter where in the world the highest rate of return can be earned. Obviously, capital-export neutrality is based on worldwide economic efficiency.

A second neutrality criterion is **national neutrality**. That is, taxable income is taxed in the same manner by the taxpayer's national tax authority regardless of where in the world it is earned. In theory, national tax neutrality is a commendable objective, as it is based on the principle of equality. In practice, it is a difficult concept to apply. In the United States, for example, foreign-source income is taxed at the same rate as U.S.-earned income and a foreign tax credit is given against taxes paid to a foreign government. However, the foreign tax credit is limited to the amount of tax that would be due on that income if it were earned in the United States. Thus, if the tax rate paid on foreign-source income is greater than the U.S. tax rate, part of the credit may go unused. Obviously, if the U.S. tax authority did not limit the foreign tax credit to the equivalent amount of U.S. tax, U.S. taxpayers would end up subsidizing part of the tax liabilities of U.S. MNCs' foreign earned income.

The third neutrality criterion is **capital-import neutrality**. To illustrate, this criterion implies that the tax burden a host country imposes on the foreign subsidiary of a MNC should be the same regardless of the country in which the MNC is incorporated and the same as that placed on domestic firms. Implementing capital-import neutrality means that if the U.S. tax rate were greater than the tax rate of a foreign country in which a U.S. MNC earned foreign income, additional tax on that income above the amount paid to the foreign tax authority would *not* be due in the United States. The concept of capital-import neutrality, like national neutrality, is based on the principle of equality, and its implementation provides a level competitive playing field for all participants in a single marketplace, at least with respect to taxation. Nevertheless, implementing capital-import neutrality means that a sovereign government follows the taxation policies of foreign tax authorities on the foreign-source income of its resident MNCs and that domestic taxpayers end up paying a larger portion of the total tax burden. Obviously, the three criteria of tax neutrality are not always consistent with one another.

Tax Equity

The underlying principle of **tax equity** is that all similarly situated taxpayers should participate in the cost of operating the government according to the same rules. Operationally, this means that regardless of the country in which an affiliate of a MNC earns taxable income, the same tax rate and tax due date apply. A dollar earned by a foreign affiliate is taxed under the same rules as a dollar earned by a domestic affiliate of the MNC. The principle of tax equity is difficult to apply; as we will see in a later section, the organizational form of a MNC can affect the timing of a tax liability.

Types of Taxation

This section discusses the three basic types of taxation that national governments throughout the world use in generating revenue: income tax, withholding tax, and value-added tax.

Income Tax

Many countries in the world obtain a significant portion of their tax revenue from imposing an **income tax** on personal and corporate income. An income tax is a **direct tax**, that is, one that is paid directly by the taxpayer on whom it is levied. The tax is levied on **active income**, that is, income that results from production by the firm or individual or from services that have been provided.

One of the best guides detailing corporate income tax regulations in most countries is PriceWaterhouseCoopers' *Corporate Taxes: Worldwide Summaries*. Exhibit 21.1 is

EXHIBIT 21.1

Corporate Percentage Income Tax Rates from Certain Countries[a]

Country	Tax Rate	Country	Tax Rate	Country	Tax Rate	Country	Tax Rate
Albania	15	Czech Republic	19	Kuwait	0	Qatar	10
Algeria	26	Denmark	22	Kyrgyzstan	10	Romania	16
Angola	30	Dominica, Commonwealth of	28	Lao, People's Democratic Republic	24	Russian Federation	20
Antigua & Barbuda	25	Dominican Republic	27	Latvia	15	Rwanda	30
Argentina	35	Ecuador	22	Lebanon	15	St. Kitts and Nevis	33
Armenia	20	Egypt	22.5	Libya	20	St. Lucia	30
Aruba	25	El Salvador	30	Liechtenstein	12.5	Saudi Arabia	20
Australia	30	Equatorial Guinea	35	Lithuania	15	Senegal	30
Austria	25	Estonia	20	Luxembourg	21	Serbia	15
Azerbaijan	20	Fiji	20	Macau	12	Singapore	17
Bahrain	0	Finland	20	Macedonia	10	Sint Maarten	34.5
Barbados	25	France	33.33	Madagascar	21	Slovak Republic	22
Belarus	18	Gabon	30	Malawi	30	Slovenia	17
Belgium	39.99	Georgia	15	Malaysia	24	South Africa	28
Bermuda	0	Germany	≤ 33	Malta	35	Spain	25
Bolivia	25	Ghana	25	Mauritius	15	Sri Lanka	12
Bosnia Herzegovina	10	Gibraltar	10	Mexico	30	Swaziland	27.5
Botswana	22	Greece	29	Moldova	12	Sweden	22
Brazil	25.5	Greenland	25	Mongolia	25	Switzerland	11.5–24.2
Bulgaria	10	Guatemala	31.8	Montenegro	9	Taiwan	17
Cabo Verde	25	Guyana	40	Morocco	31	Tajikistan	15
Cambodia	20	Honduras	25	Mozambique	32	Tanzania	30
Cameroon	33	Hong Kong	16.5	Myanmar	25	Thailand	20
Canada	15	Hungary	19	Namibia	32	Timor-Leste	10
Caribbean Netherlands	0	Iceland	20	Netherlands	25	Trinidad & Tobago	25
Cayman Islands	0	India	33.6	New Zealand	28	Tunisia	25
Chad	35	Indonesia	25	Nicaragua	30	Turkey	20
Channel Islands, Guernsey	0	Iraq	15	Nigeria	30	Turkmenistan	8
Channel Islands, Jersey	0	Ireland	12.5	Norway	25	Uganda	30
Chile	24	Isle of Man	0	Oman	12	Ukraine	18
China	25	Israel	25	Pakistan	32	United Arabs Emirates	≤ 55
Colombia	25	Italy	27.5	Panama	25	United Kingdom	20
Congo, Democratic Republic of	35	Ivory Coast	25	Papua New Guinea	30	United States	35
Congo, Republic of	30	Jamaica	33.33	Paraguay	10	Uruguay	25
Costa Rica	30	Japan	23.9	Peru	28	Uzbekistan	7.5
Croatia	20	Jordan	14	Philippines	30	Venezuela	34
Curacao	22	Kazakhstan	20	Poland	19	Vietnam	20
Cyprus	12.5	Kenya	30	Portugal	21	Zambia	35
		Korea	22	Puerto Rico	39	Zimbabwe	25.75

[a]The table lists normal, standard, or representative upper-end marginal tax rates for nonfinancial corporations or corporations without an industry-specific tax rate.

Source: Derived from PriceWaterhouseCoopers. *Corporate Taxes: Worldwide Summaries*, www.pwc.com, 2015/16.

derived from the PriceWaterhouseCoopers summaries. It lists the normal, standard, or representative upper-end marginal income tax rates for domestic nonfinancial corporations for 155 countries for tax year 2016. As the exhibit shows, national tax rates vary from a low of zero percent in such tax haven countries as Bahrain, and the Cayman Islands, to 40 percent or more in some countries. The current U.S. marginal tax rate of 35 percent is positioned toward the upper end of the rates assessed by the majority of countries.

Withholding Tax

www.taxsites.com/international
.html

www.worldwide-tax.com

These websites provide tax and accounting information by country.

A **withholding tax** is a tax generally levied on passive income earned by an individual or corporation of one country within the tax jurisdiction of another country. **Passive income** includes dividends and interest income, and income from royalties, patents, or copyrights paid to the taxpayer by a corporation. A withholding tax is an **indirect tax** that is borne by a taxpayer who did not directly generate the income. The tax is withheld from payments the corporation makes to the taxpayer and turned over to the local tax authority. The withholding tax assures the local tax authority that it will receive the tax due on the passive income earned within its tax jurisdiction.

Many countries have **tax treaties** with one another specifying the withholding tax rate applied to various types of passive income. Exhibit 21.2 lists the *basic* withholding tax rates the U.S. imposes on other countries through its tax treaties with them for 2013. For specific types of passive income, the tax rates may be different from those presented in the exhibit.[1] Withholding tax rates imposed through tax treaties are bilateral; that is, through negotiation two countries agree as to what tax rates apply to various categories of passive income.

Note from Exhibit 21.2 that withholding tax rates vary by category of passive income from zero to 30 percent. It is also noteworthy that withholding tax rates vary significantly among countries within an income category. For example, the United States withholds 0 percent on interest income from taxpayers residing in most Western European countries, but 30 percent from taxpayers residing in Pakistan. The exhibit also shows that the United States withholds 30 percent of passive income from taxpayers that reside in countries with which it does not have withholding tax treaties. Exhibit 21.2 also indicates that according to the withholding tax treaty with a country, the *general* tax rate on dividends paid to foreign payees from portfolio investment in a U.S. firm is frequently higher than the *direct* dividend rate applied to investors with a substantial ownership share.

Value-Added Tax

ec.europa.eu/taxation_customs
/taxation/vat

Use the site map at this website to find a discussion of the practical aspects of value-added taxation in the European Union.

A **value-added tax (VAT)** is an indirect national tax levied on the value added in the production of a good (or service) as it moves through the various stages of production. There are several ways to implement a VAT. The "subtraction method" is frequently followed in practice.

EXAMPLE | 21.1: Value-Added Tax Calculation

As an example of the subtraction method of calculating VAT, consider a VAT of 15 percent charged on a consumption good that goes through three stages of production. Suppose that Stage 1 is the sale of raw materials to the manufacturer at a cost of €100 per unit of production. Stage 2 results in a finished good shipped to retailers at a price of €300. Stage 3 is the retail sale to the final consumer at a price of €380. €100 of value has been added in Stage 1, resulting in a VAT of €15. In Stage 2 the VAT is 15 percent of €300, or €45, with a credit of €15 given against the value added in Stage 1. In Stage 3, an additional VAT of €12 is due on the €80 of value added by the retailer. Since the final consumer pays a price of €380, he effectively pays the total VAT of €57 (= €15 + €30 + €12), which is 15 percent of €380. Obviously, a VAT is the equivalent of imposing a national sales tax. Exhibit 21.3 summarizes the VAT calculation.

---

[1]See the United States Internal Revenue Service website at www.irs.gov for exceptions to the basic withholding tax rates.

| Country | Interest Paid by U.S. Obligors— General | Dividends[b] | | Royalties-Industrial Know-How/ Patents[c] |
		Paid by U.S. Corporations— General	Qualifying for Direct Dividend Rate	
Nontreaty countries	30	30	30	30
Australia	10	15	5	5
Austria	0	15	5	0
Bangladesh	10	15	10	10
Barbados	5	15	5	5
Belgium	0	15	5	0
Bulgaria	5	10	5	5
Canada	0	15	5	0
China, People's Republic of	10	10	10	10
Commonwealth of Independent States	0	30	30	0
Cyprus	10	15	5	0
Czech Republic	0	15	5	10
Denmark	0	15	5	0
Egypt	15	15	5	30/15
Estonia	10	15	5	10
Finland	0	15	5	0
France	0	15	5	0
Germany	0	15	5	0
Greece	0	30	30	0
Hungary	0	15	5	0
Iceland	0	15	5	5/0
India	15	25	15	15
Indonesia	10	15	10	10
Ireland	0	15	5	0
Israel	17.5	25	12.5	15
Italy	10	15	5	8
Jamaica	12.5	15	10	10
Japan	10	10	5	0
Kazakhstan	10	15	5	10
Korea, South	12	15	10	15
Latvia	10	15	5	10
Lithuania	10	15	5	10
Luxembourg	0	15	5	0
Malta	10	15	5	10
Mexico	15	10	5	10
Morocco	15	15	10	10
Netherlands	0	15	5	0
New Zealand	10	15	5	5
Norway	0	15	15	0
Pakistan	30	30	15	0
Philippines	15	25	20	15
Poland	0	15	5	10
Portugal	10	15	5	10
Romania	10	10	10	15
Russia	0	10	5	0
Slovak Republic	0	15	5	10
Slovenia	5	15	5	5
South Africa	0	15	5	0
Spain	10	15	10	10
Sri Lanka	10	15	15	10
Sweden	0	15	5	0
Switzerland	0	15	5	0
Thailand	15	15	10	15
Trinidad and Tobago	30	30	30	15
Tunisia	15	20	14	15
Turkey	15	20	15	10
Ukraine	0	15	5	10
United Kingdom	0	15	5	0
Venezuela	10	15	5	10

[a]The exhibit shows the basic treaty withholding tax rates; see the original source for exceptions and rates that apply to special situations.

[b]No U.S. tax is imposed on a dividend paid by a U.S. corporation that received at least 80 percent of its gross income from an active foreign business for the three-year period before the dividend is declared.

[c]Royalties on industrial equipment, film and television, and copyrights are different. For Egypt and Iceland, the know-how/patents royalties are different from one another.

Source: Derived from United States Internal Revenue website, www.irs.gov, April 2013.

EXHIBIT 21.3

Value-Added Tax Calculation

Production Stage	Selling Price	Value Added	Incremental VAT
1	€100	€100	€15
2	€300	€200	€30
3	€380	€80	€12
			Total VAT €57

In many European countries (especially the EU) and also Latin American countries, VAT has become a major source of taxation on private citizens. Many economists prefer a VAT in place of a personal income tax because the latter is a disincentive to work, whereas a VAT discourages unnecessary consumption. A VAT fosters national saving, whereas an income tax is a disincentive to save because the returns from savings are taxed. Moreover, national tax authorities find that a VAT is easier to collect than an income tax because tax evasion is more difficult. Under a VAT, each stage in the production process has an incentive to obtain documentation from the previous stage that the VAT was paid in order to get the greatest tax credit possible. Of course, some argue that the cost of record keeping under a VAT system imposes an economic hardship on small businesses.

A problem with a VAT, is that not all countries impose the same VAT tax rate. For example, in Denmark the VAT rate is 25 percent, but in Germany it is only 19 percent. Consequently, consumers who reside in a high-VAT country can purchase goods less expensively by simply shopping across the border in a lower-VAT country. Indeed, *The Wall Street Journal* reports that Danish customers frequently *demand* the lower German VAT rate on their purchases in Denmark![2] This problem should eventually be resolved among the EU countries where VAT is expected to be harmonized at the standard rate of 19 percent.

National Tax Environments

The international tax environment confronting a MNC or an international investor is a function of the tax jurisdictions established by the individual countries in which the MNC does business or in which the investor owns financial assets. There are two fundamental types of tax jurisdiction: the *worldwide* and the *territorial*. Unless some mechanism were established to prevent it, double taxation would result if all nations were to follow both methods simultaneously.

Worldwide Taxation

The **worldwide** or **residential** method of declaring a national tax jurisdiction is to tax national residents of the country on their worldwide income no matter in which country it is earned. The national tax authority, according to this method, is declaring its tax jurisdiction over people and businesses. A MNC firm with many foreign affiliates would be taxed in its home country on its income earned at home and abroad. Obviously, if the host countries of the foreign affiliates of a MNC also tax the income earned within their territorial borders, the possibility of double taxation exists, unless a mechanism is established to prevent it.

Territorial Taxation

The **territorial** or **source** method of declaring a tax jurisdiction is to tax all income earned within the country by any taxpayer, domestic or foreign. Hence, regardless of the nationality of a taxpayer, if the income is earned within the territorial boundary of a country, it is taxed by that country. The national tax authority, according to this method, is declaring its tax jurisdiction over transactions conducted within its borders. Consequently, local firms and affiliates of foreign MNCs are taxed on the income earned in the *source* country. Obviously, if the parent country of the foreign affiliate

---

[2]See Horwitz (1993).

also levies a tax on worldwide income, the possibility of double taxation exists, unless a mechanism is established to prevent it.

Foreign Tax Credits

The typical approach to avoiding double taxation is for a nation not to tax foreign-source income of its national residents. An alternative method, and the one the United States follows, is to grant to the parent firm **foreign tax credits** against U.S. taxes for taxes paid to foreign tax authorities on foreign-source income. In general, foreign tax credits are categorized as direct or indirect. A *direct* foreign tax credit is computed for taxes paid on active foreign-source income of a foreign branch of a U.S. MNC or on the withholding taxes withheld from passive income distributed by the foreign subsidiary to the U.S. parent. For foreign subsidiaries of U.S. MNCs, an *indirect* foreign tax credit is computed for income taxes *deemed paid* by the subsidiary. The deemed-paid tax credit equals the pro rata portion of the earnings that were actually distributed. For example, if a wholly owned foreign subsidiary pays out dividends equal to 50 percent of its earnings, the deemed-paid tax credit is 50 percent of the foreign income taxes paid by the foreign subsidiary.

In a given tax year, an *overall limitation* applies to foreign tax credits; that is, the maximum total tax credit is limited to the amount of tax that would be due on the foreign-source income if it had been earned in the United States. The maximum tax credit is figured on worldwide foreign-source income; losses in one country can be used to offset profits in another. Excess tax credits for a tax year can be carried back one year and forward ten years. Examples of calculating foreign tax credits for U.S. foreign branch and subsidiary operations are provided in the next section. Value-added taxes paid may not be included in determining the amount of the foreign tax credit, but they are nevertheless indirectly expensed as part of the cost of a good or service.

Individual U.S. investors may take a tax credit for the withholding taxes deducted from the dividend and interest income they received from the foreign financial assets in their portfolios.

Organizational Structures

Branch and Subsidiary Income

An overseas affiliate of a U.S. MNC can be organized as a branch or a subsidiary. A **foreign branch** is not an independently incorporated firm separate from the parent; it is an extension of the parent. Consequently, active or passive foreign-source income earned by the branch is consolidated with the domestic-source income of the parent for determining the U.S. tax liability, regardless of whether or not the foreign-source income has been repatriated to the parent. A **foreign subsidiary** is an affiliate organization of the MNC that is independently incorporated in the foreign country, and one in which the U.S. MNC owns at least 10 percent of the voting equity stock. A foreign subsidiary in which the U.S. MNC owns more than 10 percent but less than 50 percent of the voting equity is a *minority foreign subsidiary* or an *uncontrolled foreign corporation*. Foreign-source income derived from a minority foreign subsidiary is taxed in the United States only when remitted to the U.S. parent firm via a dividend. A foreign subsidiary in which the U.S. MNC owns more than 50 percent of the voting equity is a *controlled foreign corporation*. In general, foreign-source income from a controlled foreign corporation will be passive, in the form of a dividend paid to the U.S. parent, and not taxable in the United States until remitted. However, certain types of undistributed income from a controlled foreign corporation is taxed by the United States as earned, even if it has not been repatriated to the parent. A more detailed explanation is reserved for later in this section.

> **EXAMPLE | 21.2:** Foreign Tax Credit Calculations
>
> Exhibit 21.4 presents examples of calculating the foreign tax credits for a wholly owned foreign subsidiary of a U.S. MNC in the host countries of Finland and Pakistan. The examples use the actual domestic marginal income tax rates presented in Exhibit 21.1 and the withholding tax treaty rates with respect to the United States. The

continued

EXAMPLE | 21.2: continued

examples show the total tax liability for $100 of foreign taxable income when any excess foreign tax credits can be used and when they cannot. As a rule, excess tax credits can be carried back one year and forward ten years. The examples assume that *all* after-tax foreign-source income available for remittance is immediately remitted to the U.S. parent.

Exhibit 21.4 indicates that when the U.S. MNC can use the full excess tax credits, the total tax liability is $35 per $100 of foreign taxable income, or 35 percent, the same amount due on $100 of taxable income earned in the United States. This is true regardless of the foreign affiliate's location and regardless of the size of the income tax and withholding tax rates. A MNC that consistently generates excess foreign tax credits will never be able to use them in the allowable time. Thus, the more typical situation is that excess foreign tax credits go unused.

When excess tax credits go unused, the foreign tax liability for a foreign subsidiary is greater than the corresponding U.S. tax liability when: [foreign income tax rate + withholding tax rate − (foreign income tax rate × withholding tax rate)] is greater than the U.S. income tax rate of 35 percent. To illustrate, a foreign subsidiary in Pakistan for which excess foreign tax credits cannot be used has a total tax liability of: 32 + .0875 − (.32 × .0875) = .3795, or 37.95 percent versus 35 percent in the United States.

These days, many countries impose a branch profits withholding tax in addition to an income tax on taxable income earned by a branch operation of a MNC. Thus, in these countries it matters little whether the MNC establishes its foreign affiliate as a branch operation or a wholly owned subsidiary.

Tax Havens

A **tax haven** country is one that has a low corporate income tax rate and low withholding tax rates on passive income. Some major tax haven countries, which are suggested by the income tax rates presented in Exhibit 21.1, are Bahrain, Bermuda, Cayman Islands, Channel Islands (Guernsey and Jersey), Hong Kong, and the Isle of Man. Additionally, in Hong Kong foreign-source income is exempt from taxation, whereas in Panama, dividends paid from foreign source income are taxed at the low rate of 5 percent.

Tax havens were once useful as locations for a MNC to establish a wholly owned "paper" foreign subsidiary that in turn would own the operating foreign subsidiaries of the MNC. Hence, when the tax rates in the host countries of the operating affiliates were lower than the tax rate in the parent country, dividends could be routed through

---

EXHIBIT 21.4

Examples of Calculating U.S. Foreign Tax Credits for Subsidiary Operations

	Finland	Pakistan
Foreign income tax rate	20%	32%
Withholding tax rate	0%	8.75%
Taxable income	100	100
Foreign income tax	−20	−32
Net available for remittance	80	68
Withholding tax[a]	−0	−6
Net cash to U.S. parent	80	62
Gross-up: Income tax	20	32
Gross-up: Withholding tax	0	6
U.S. taxable income	100	100
U.S. income tax at 35%	35	35
Less foreign tax credit:		
Income tax	−20	−32
Withholding tax	0	−6
Net U.S. tax (excess credit)	15	(3)
Total tax: Excess credit used	35	35
Total tax: Excess credit not used	35	38

[a]100 percent of the funds available for remittance are assumed to be declared as dividends.

the tax haven affiliate for use by the MNC, but the taxes due on them in the parent country could continue to be deferred until a dividend was declared by the tax haven subsidiary. These days the benefit of a tax haven subsidiary for U.S. MNCs has been greatly reduced by two factors: One is that the present corporate income tax rate in the United States is not especially high in comparison to most non-tax haven countries, thus eliminating the need for deferral; the second factor is that the rules governing controlled foreign corporations (the topic to be discussed next) have effectively eliminated the ability to defer passive income in a tax haven foreign subsidiary. As the International Finance in Practice box "On or Off? It's a Matter of Degree" indicates, the definitions of an offshore financial center and a tax haven can be confusing.

Controlled Foreign Corporation

The Tax Reform Act of 1986 created a new type of foreign subsidiary called a controlled foreign corporation. The purpose of the reform was to prevent the tax deferral of certain income in tax haven countries. A **controlled foreign corporation (CFC)** is a foreign subsidiary that has more than 50 percent of its voting equity owned by U.S. shareholders. A U.S. shareholder is any U.S. citizen, resident, partnership, corporation, trust, or estate that owns (or indirectly controls) 10 percent or more of the voting equity of the CFC. Thus, six nonaffiliated U.S. shareholders each owning exactly 10 percent of the voting equity would be required for a foreign corporation to be designated a CFC. Alternatively, a wholly owned subsidiary of a U.S. MNC would be a CFC.

In the case of a CFC, certain types of undistributed income, known as Subpart F income, are subject to immediate taxation. In 2006, Congress passed the Tax Increase Prevention and Reconciliation Act (TIPRA) of 2005 that redefined Subpart F income. Under TIPRA, **Subpart F income** includes: insurance income; foreign base company income (i.e., passive, sales, shipping, and oil-related income); income from countries subject to international boycotts; illegal bribes, kickbacks, or similar payments; and income from countries where the United States has severed diplomatic relations.

Tax Inversion

As noted in Exhibit 21.1, the upper-end marginal corporate federal income tax rate on taxable income for the United States is 35 percent, which taxes on worldwide income no matter where it is earned. A perusal of Exhibit 21.1 indicates that this is high in comparison to most countries. To put matters in perspective, the combined federal- and state-average income rate in the U.S. is 39 percent versus 25 percent among the 34 mostly-rich OECD member countries. Also, as previously noted, undistributed after-tax income of a foreign subsidiary of a U.S. MNC (other than Subpart F income of a CFC) is not taxed until it is remitted to the parent. When remitted, the U.S. parent will receive a tax credit for taxes paid to a foreign host-country on income earned by the foreign subsidiary in that country. However, several U.S. MNCs (e.g., Dell Computer, General Electric, Hewlett-Packard, and Sonoco Products) have been reluctant to repatriate foreign-source income if it has been earned in low-tax host-countries and the repatriation will result in large additional taxation in the U.S., even given the foreign tax credit offset. Collectively, it has been estimated that U.S. MNCs have $2.1 trillion in cash residing offshore with the hope that the U.S. will reduce the corporate income tax rate or declare a tax holiday temporarily lowering the tax rate on foreign source income. Obviously, the tax revenue generated from the repatriation of these funds would assist the U.S. Treasury with federal budget deficits and the after-tax amount would become available as dividends available to corporate shareholders.

Nevertheless, none of this is likely to come about anytime soon. In fact, beginning in 2014, several large U.S. firms have sought to engage in a tax inversion. A **tax inversion** is a maneuver in which a firm (usually U.S.) acquires or merges with a foreign rival incorporated in a low-tax country, then shifts its domicile abroad to reap tax benefits. The new firm will be able to access its non-U.S. profits at a much lower rate than if the

On or Off? It's a Matter of Degree

What exactly is an offshore financial centre? At its broadest, it is any financial centre that takes in a large chunk of foreign funds—in other words, almost every financial capital in the world. Much of the business conducted in places such as New York, London or Hong Kong is from outside America, Britain or China.

Britain is arguably one of the biggest personal-tax havens in the world. So-called "resident non-domiciles"—people who live in Britain but claim domicile abroad—do not have to pay tax on offshore income. America, for its part, soaks up huge amounts of offshore cash because it takes little of the money held in its banks by non-resident foreigners. Foreigners' bank deposits in America add up to $2.5 trillion, well over twice as much as those in Switzerland.

But as most people understand the term, "OFC" means a smaller jurisdiction where the lion's share of the institutions are controlled by non-residents and many of them are in the financial sector or set up for financial reasons. The volume of business conducted by these financial institutions often far outstrips the needs of the local economy.

When OFCs combine all these attributes with a low- or no-tax regime they are tagged as "tax havens," especially if they also have strict banking-secrecy rules, light supervision and a slack grip on business within their borders. Panama, for instance, still allows bearer shares that can be anonymously owned and traded.

The Financial Stability Forum (FSF), a group that monitors threats to the global financial system, has put together a list of 42 jurisdictions that it defines as OFCs. The OECD in 2000 compiled a narrower list of 35 tax havens. There is a great deal of overlap between the two.

Dividing the world into onshore and offshore financial centres is difficult because "It is a matter of degree, not substance," says one European bank regulator. For example, many people consider Bermuda an OFC, but it is packed with actuaries pricing reinsurance risks. Jersey, where the financial sector accounts for over half of all tax revenues, is home to a sophisticated banking industry, cooperates with other governments on

tax matters and requires banks and other licensed institutions to have a "real presence" on the island.

More confusingly, some jurisdictions straddle both categories. One example is Luxembourg, a tiny country sandwiched between Belgium, France and Germany and one of Europe's most important financial centres. A founder-member of the EU, Luxembourg is considered a well-managed, soundly regulated financial centre with real expertise. It is home to more than 2,200 investment funds with almost €1.8 trillion under management. It is also the euro zone's biggest private-banking centre. The financial-services industry contributes a third of Luxembourg's output and, including its indirect contribution (accountants, lawyers and the like), supplies around 40 percent of Luxembourg's tax take.

Luxembourg is sometimes lumped with tax havens because of various scandals involving companies based there, including the notorious BCCI and, more recently, Clearstream. But although Luxembourg got most of the bad press, BCCI was operated out of London and Clearstream is mainly a French affair.

Ireland and Singapore are big in manufacturing but also have thriving financial centres that cater to offshore business. Singapore has strict rules on banking secrecy and does not consider foreign tax evasion a crime. Some people consider Switzerland as a tax haven because of its low tax rates and its fabled banking secrecy.

But onshore economies can be opaque too. A report issued by a government agency in America last April found that few states collect information on the true owners of companies set up within their borders. Delaware and Nevada are particularly lax.

Mr. Owens at the OECD prefers to differentiate between well and poorly regulated financial centres rather than onshore or offshore ones. Well-regulated centres cooperate with foreign tax and other authorities and have sound supervision; poorly regulated ones hide behind secrecy. Low or no taxes on their own, says Mr. Owens, do not constitute a harmful tax practice.

Source: © The Economist Newspaper Limited, London, February 24, 2007.

old firm had repatriated the income. Moreover, U.S. employment is potentially adversely affected. After the inversion, it is likely that job growth in the new company will largely be overseas and some U.S. jobs will likely move offshore. Consequently, the U.S. is likely to lose out on future tax revenue from lower U.S. earned income by the newly created foreign firm. To stem the tide of these inversions, the Obama administration has attempted to brand these tax maneuvers as unpatriotic. And the Treasury has attempted to stymie tax inversions with new restrictions that make inversions more difficult to structure. The real problem of course is the high U.S. corporate income tax rate. It is understandable that U.S. companies object to paying such high taxes. An overhaul of the U.S. tax system is needed to get U.S. tax rates in line with other developed countries.[3]

---

[3]This section is loosely based on the articles "How to Stop the Inversion Perversion," *The Economist,* July 26, 2014, p. 12; and "Inverted Logic," *The Economist,* August 15, 2015, p. 12.

Transfer Pricing and Related Issues

Within a large business firm with multiple divisions, goods and services are frequently transferred from one division to another. The process brings into question the **transfer price** that should be assigned, for bookkeeping purposes, to the goods or services as they are transferred between divisions. Obviously, the higher the transfer price, the larger will be the gross profits of the transferring division relative to the receiving division. Even within a domestic firm, it is difficult to decide on the transfer price. Within a MNC, the decision is further compounded by exchange restrictions on the part of the host country where the receiving affiliate is located, a difference in income tax rates between the two countries, and import duties and quotas imposed by the host country. The following case application illustrates the important transfer pricing issues.

CASE APPLICATION

Mintel Products Transfer Pricing Strategy

Low versus High Markup Policy

Mintel Products, Inc., manufactures goods for sale in the United States and overseas. Finished goods are transferred from the parent firm to its wholly owned sales affiliate for overseas retail sale. Mintel's financial manager, Hilary Van Kirk, has decided that the firm's transfer pricing strategy should be reevaluated as part of a routine review of the operations of the sales affiliate. Van Kirk has decided to explore both a low and a high markup policy. The analysis is to be done in U.S. dollars. She notes that both the parent firm and the sales affiliate have a 40 percent income tax rate, that the variable production cost of one unit is $1,500, and that the unit retail sales price charged by the sales affiliate to the final customer is $3,000. As a first step in her analysis, Van Kirk prepares Exhibit 21.5. The upper portion of the exhibit presents the analysis of a low markup policy, where the transfer price is set at $2,000. The lower portion of the exhibit analyzes the effect of a high markup policy, where the transfer price is $2,400 per unit.

Van Kirk notices from Exhibit 21.5 that the low markup policy results in larger pretax income, income taxes, and net income per unit in the selling country. On the other hand, the high markup policy has the opposite effect, that is, higher taxable income, income taxes, and net profit per unit in the manufacturing country. She also notes that because the income tax rates are the same in both countries, the consolidated results are identical regardless of whether the MNC follows a low or high transfer pricing scheme.

Exchange Restrictions

Van Kirk wonders if Mintel should be indifferent between the low and high markup policies, since the consolidated results are the same. She reasons, however, that if the distribution country imposes exchange restrictions limiting or blocking the amount of profits that can be repatriated to the manufacturing parent, Mintel would no longer be indifferent between the two markup policies. It obviously would prefer the high markup policy. According to Exhibit 21.5, the higher markup allows $240 per unit to be repatriated to the parent that otherwise may have been blocked. This amount represents the $400 higher markup minus the $160 additional taxes paid in the parent country.

Van Kirk notes that the high markup policy is disadvantageous from the host country's perspective. If the transferring affiliate attempts to reposition funds by changing from the low to the high markup policy, the exchange controls have been partially bypassed and there is a loss of tax revenue in the host country. Thus, the host country may take measures to enforce a certain transfer price. She decides she needs to brush up on how this might be accomplished and also to consider the effect of a difference in income tax rates between the two affiliates.

EXHIBIT 21.5

Low versus High Transfer Pricing Strategy between Mintel Affiliates with the Same Income Tax Rate

	Manufacturing Affiliate	Sales Affiliate	Consolidated Company
Low Markup Policy			
Sales revenue	$2,000	$3,000	$3,000
Cost of goods sold	1,500	2,000	1,500
Gross profit	500	1,000	1,500
Operating expenses	200	200	400
Taxable income	300	800	1,100
Income taxes (40%)	120	320	440
Net income	180	480	660
High Markup Policy			
Sales revenue	$2,400	$3,000	$3,000
Cost of goods sold	1,500	2,400	1,500
Gross profit	900	600	1,500
Operating expenses	200	200	400
Taxable income	700	400	1,100
Income taxes (40%)	280	160	440
Net income	420	240	660

Differential Income Tax Rates

As a second step, Van Kirk prepares Exhibit 21.6, which examines the low versus high markup policies when the tax rate in the transferring country is assumed to be 25 percent, or 15 percent less than the marginal tax rate of 40 percent in the receiving country.

Van Kirk notes from Exhibit 21.6 that the consolidated taxable income is $1,100 under both markup policies. However, Mintel would no longer be indifferent when there is a differential in the income tax rates. In the absence of governmental restrictions on the transfer price, the MNC would prefer a high markup policy when the tax rate in the parent country is lower than the tax rate in the receiving country. Consolidated net income for Mintel would be $60 [= ($2,000 − 2,400) 3 (.25 − .40)] per unit greater under the high versus the low markup

EXHIBIT 21.6

Low versus High Transfer Pricing Strategy between Mintel Affiliates with Differential Income Tax Rates

	Manufacturing Affiliate	Sales Affiliate	Consolidated Company
Low Markup Policy			
Sales revenue	$2,000	$3,000	$3,000
Cost of goods sold	1,500	2,000	1,500
Gross profit	500	1,000	1,500
Operating expenses	200	200	400
Taxable income	300	800	1,100
Income taxes (25%/40%)	75	320	395
Net income	225	480	705
High Markup Policy			
Sales revenue	$2,400	$3,000	$3,000
Cost of goods sold	1,500	2,400	1,500
Gross profit	900	600	1,500
Operating expenses	200	200	400
Taxable income	700	400	1,100
Income taxes (25%/40%)	175	160	335
Net income	525	240	765

policy. The high markup policy results in $400 per unit of taxable income being shifted from the receiving country to the transferring country, where it is taxed at a 15 percent lower rate. Consequently, the consolidated income taxes paid by Mintel drop from $395 to $335 per unit.

If the tax rate in the receiving country is lower than in the parent country, it is not clear that a low markup policy should be pursued. Van Kirk recalls that U.S. MNCs are taxed on their worldwide income. Hence, income repatriated to the U.S. parent from a receiving country with a low tax rate would be "grossed up" to its pretax amount so that U.S. taxes could be figured. A credit for the taxes paid in the receiving country would be given against taxes owed in the United States. Thus, pursuing a low markup policy would not result in a dollar tax savings if net income was to be repatriated. However, if the net income of the foreign subsidiary was to be reinvested in the host country, the low markup policy would result in a tax savings and allow more funds for reinvestment. Nevertheless, this would only be temporary, Van Kirk reasons. At some point, profitable investment opportunities would be exhausted, and the parent firm and its stockholders would desire some return on the investment made—and this means repatriation.

Regulations Affecting Transfer Prices

www.ustransferpricing.com

This website provides news and resources relating to transfer pricing in the United States for international tax professionals.

Van Kirk believes that governmental authorities within a host country would be quite aware of the motives of MNCs to use transfer pricing schemes to move blocked funds or evade tax liabilities. After doing some research, she learns that most countries have regulations controlling transfer prices. In the United States, Section 482: Allocation of Income and Deductions Among Taxpayers of the U.S. Internal Revenue Code stipulates that the transfer price must reflect an *arm's-length price*, that is, a price the selling affiliate would charge an unrelated customer for the good or service. The Internal Revenue Service (IRS)..."may distribute, apportion, or allocate gross income, deductions, credits, or allowances between or among such organizations...[if it is] necessary in order to prevent evasion of taxes or clearly to reflect the income of any such organizations..." Moreover, in the event of conflict, the burden of proof lies with the taxpayer to show that the IRS has unreasonably established the transfer price and determined taxable income.

She learns that there are three basic methods prescribed by the IRS, and recognized internationally, for establishing arm's-length prices of tangible goods. The method considered the best is to use a *comparable uncontrolled price* between unrelated firms. While this method seems reasonable and theoretically sound, it is difficult to use in practice because many factors enter into the pricing of goods and services between two business enterprises. The Code allows for some adjustments because differences in the terms of sale, the quantity sold, quality differences, and the date of sale are all factors that can realistically affect the sale price among various customers. Thus, what is a reasonable price for one customer may not be reasonable for another. The next best method is the *resale price* approach, which can be used if, among other things, there is no comparable uncontrolled sales price. Under this method, the price at which the good is resold by the distribution affiliate is reduced by an amount sufficient to cover overhead costs and a reasonable profit. However, it may be difficult to determine the value added by the distribution affiliate. The third method is the *cost-plus* approach, where an appropriate profit is added to the cost of the manufacturing affiliate. This method assumes that the manufacturing cost is readily accountable. Additionally, a group of methods collectively referred to as *fourth methods* can be applied to approximate arm's-length prices when the three basic methods are not applicable. The fourth methods include those based on financial and economic models and econometric techniques. The comparable uncontrolled price method and fourth methods are used for determining an arm's-length transfer price for intangible goods, whereas cost methods are used for pricing services.

The Organization for Economic Cooperation and Development Model Tax Convention sets out the same methods as the IRS Code for use by member countries. Van Kirk concludes that all methods present operational difficulties of some type and are also difficult for the taxing authority to evaluate. Thus, transfer pricing manipulation cannot be completely

Transfer Pricing: An Important International Tax Issue

A recent article in *Business Wire* cites a new survey by Ernst & Young that transfer pricing is the most important international tax issue that multinational corporations (MNCs) currently face.

According to the survey, 86 percent of MNC parent company respondents and 93 percent of subsidiary identified transfer pricing as the most important international tax matter they are currently dealing with. The respondents indicated that audits by tax authorities are becoming standard practice.

A transfer price is the price at which a transaction between units of a multinational corporation takes place, including the intercompany transfer of goods, property, services, loans and leases.

The E&Y survey indicated that 59 percent of all MNCs with revenues of US$5 billion or more, and 71 percent of all U.S.-based MNCs regardless of revenues, had been subject to a transfer pricing audit within the past four years. MNCs believe that an audit is more likely because more countries are adopting transfer pricing legislation, and those countries that already have legislation are stepping up their enforcement efforts. The survey respondents also believe that audits will become more challenging because revenue authorities are more sophisticated.

According to *Business Wire*, the survey indicated that if an MNC is subject to an adjustment as the result of a transfer pricing audit, there is almost a one-in-three chance that it will be threatened with a penalty, and a one-in-seven chance that one will actually be imposed. In addition, E&Y's survey revealed that 40 percent of the reported transfer pricing adjustments resulted in double taxation.

The Ernst & Young survey found that MNC experiences with the competent authority process, which is a tax treaty process under which two governments agree to resolve the issue, vary. In many cases, although the competent authority process may take a year or two to reach resolution, the authorities eliminate or reduce the double taxation. Those MNCs who have used the competent authority process generally appear to have had a favorable experience. Most would go to competent authority again or even consider an Advance Pricing Agreement.

The survey found that many multinationals fail to reexamine their transfer pricing policies in the wake of mergers or acquisitions. "Because of the increasing scrutiny of transfer pricing policies, it is essential for a MNC to review the impact of any business change on its risk profile. In many cases, this will highlight the multinational's need to re-design core elements of its transfer pricing policies," according to Robert D. M. Turner, Ernst & Young's Global CEO of Transfer Pricing Services.

Mr. Turner pointed out that while 46 percent of the survey's parent company respondents had been through a merger or acquisition in the last two years, only 18 percent of these MNCs either recognized the need or used the opportunity to reexamine their overall transfer pricing policies.

The E&Y survey revealed that while the sale of tangible goods remains the most commonly audited transaction among MNCs, the percentage of audits of tangible goods transactions is decreasing, however, while the percentage of audits relating to service and intangible property transactions is increasing. Mr. Turner also noted that "intercompany services are becoming a much larger part of the 'services economy' and we are seeing services transactions with larger monetary value."

Business Wire, "Transfer Pricing is the Most Important International Tax Issue," November 5, 2003.

---

controlled and the potential exists for maneuverability by the MNC to reposition funds or reduce its tax liability.

The International Finance in Practice box "Transfer Pricing: An Important International Tax Issue" discusses a recent survey by the international accounting firm Ernst & Young.

Import Duties

After some reflection, Van Kirk concludes that import duties must also be considered. When a host country imposes an *ad valorem* import duty on goods shipped across its borders from another country, the import tax raises the cost of doing business within the country. An ad valorem duty is a percentage tax levied at customs on the assessed value of the imported goods. She reasons that an import tax will affect the transfer pricing strategy a MNC uses, but that, in general, the income tax will have the greatest after-tax effect on consolidated net income. To analyze the effect of an import duty on Mintel, she prepares Exhibit 21.7, which shows the low versus high transfer price alternatives presented in Exhibit 21.6 with the imposition of a 5 percent import duty by the receiving country.

Comparison of Exhibits 21.6 and 21.7 shows Van Kirk that under the low markup policy, Mintel would receive $60 less (= $645 − 705) per unit if a 5 percent import duty was

EXHIBIT 21.7

Low versus High Transfer Pricing Strategy between Mintel Affiliates with Differential Income Tax Rates and a 5 Percent Import Duty

	Manufacturing Affiliate	Sales Affiliate	Consolidated Company
Low Markup Policy			
Sales revenue	$2,000	$3,000	$3,000
Cost of goods sold	1,500	2,000	1,500
Import duty (5%)	—	100	100
Gross profit	500	900	1,400
Operating expenses	200	200	400
Taxable income	300	700	1,000
Income taxes (25%/40%)	75	280	355
Net income	225	420	645
High Markup Policy			
Sales revenue	$2,400	$3,000	$3,000
Cost of goods sold	1,500	2,400	1,500
Import duty (5%)	—	120	120
Gross profit	900	480	1,380
Operating expenses	200	200	400
Taxable income	700	280	980
Income taxes (25%/40%)	175	112	287
Net income	525	168	693

imposed by the host country. The $60 represents the after-tax cost of the $100 import duty on the $2,000 per unit transfer price cost of the good. Mintel would still prefer the high markup policy as before, however, as it results in an increase in net income from $645 to $693 per unit. The difference in the net incomes between the two markup policies is only $48, in comparison to $60 without the 5 percent import tax. The loss of $12 represents the after-tax cost of an additional $20 of import duty per unit when the transfer price is $2,400 instead of $2,000 per unit.

Unbundling Fund Transfers

As Van Kirk knows, host countries are well aware of transfer pricing schemes used by MNCs to evade taxes within its borders or to avoid exchange restrictions. She wonders if there are ways to avoid suspicion from host country governmental authorities, and the administrative hassle likely to arise from such an inquiry, when the firm is merely trying to repatriate a sufficient amount of funds from a foreign affiliate to make the investment worthwhile. To learn more about transfer pricing strategies and related issues, she decides to attend a one-day seminar on the topic she saw advertised by a professional organization to which she belongs. She hopes it is beneficial, as the registration fee is $1,500 for the day!

As it turns out, the money was well spent. In addition to making the acquaintance of financial managers from other companies, one thing Van Kirk learned at the conference was that a MNC is likely to fare better if, instead of lumping all costs into a single transfer price, the parent firm unbundled the package to recognize the cost of the physical good and each service separately that it provides the affiliate. A detailing of the charges makes it easier, if ever necessary, to present and support to the taxing authority of a host country that each charge is legitimate and can be well substantiated. For instance, in addition to charging for the cost of the physical good, the parent firm could charge a fee for technical training of the affiliate's staff, a share of the cost of worldwide advertising or other corporate overhead, or a royalty or licensing fee as payment for use of well-recognized brand names, technology, or patents. The royalty or licensing fee represents remuneration for expense previously incurred by the parent for development or having made the product one that is desirable to own.

EXHIBIT 21.8

Low versus High Transfer Pricing Strategy for Mintel with Low Transfer Price and Additional Royalty Charge with Differential Income Tax Rates

	Manufacturing Affiliate	Sales Affiliate	Consolidated Company
Low Markup Policy			
Sales revenue	$2,000	$3,000	$3,000
Cost of goods sold	1,500	2,000	1,500
Gross profit	500	1,000	1,500
Operating expenses	200	200	400
Taxable income	300	800	1,100
Income taxes (25%/40%)	75	320	395
Net income	225	480	705
High Markup Policy			
Sales revenue	$2,400	$3,000	$3,000
Cost of goods sold	1,500	2,400	1,500
Gross profit	900	600	1,500
Operating expenses	200	200	400
Taxable income	700	400	1,100
Income taxes (25%/40%)	175	160	335
Net income	525	240	765
Low Markup Policy and Royalty			
Sales revenue	$2,000	$3,000	$3,000
Royalty and fee income	400	—	—
Cost of goods sold	1,500	2,400	1,500
Gross profit	900	600	1,500
Operating expenses	200	200	400
Taxable income	700	400	1,100
Income taxes (25%/40%)	175	160	335
Net income	525	240	765

As a final step in her analysis, Van Kirk prepares Exhibit 21.8, which reproduces the low versus high markup policy analysis for Mintel with differential income tax rates presented in Exhibit 21.6. In addition, Exhibit 21.8 shows that a $2,000 transfer price and $400 per unit charge for royalties and fees results in the same consolidated net income of $765 as does the high markup policy with a $2,400 transfer price. By comparison, the low markup policy only provides $705 per unit consolidated net income. This is the case, regardless of whether a portion of the $480 net income of the sales affiliate is repatriated to the manufacturing affiliate as a dividend, because the tax rate in the distribution country is higher. As Van Kirk learned at the conference, the strategy of recognizing specific services may be acceptable to the host government, whereas the high markup policy may not, if $2,400 appears to be more than an arm's-length price for the transferred good.

The International Finance in Practice box "Wake Up and Smell the Coffee" describes a transfer pricing and royalty payment arrangement used by Starbucks in Great Britain to keep taxes low. This arrangement is similar to the "low markup policy and royalty" arrangement described in Exhibit 21.8.

Miscellaneous Factors

Transfer pricing strategies may be beneficial when the host country restricts the amount of foreign exchange that can be used for importing specific goods. In this event, a lower transfer price allows a greater quantity of the good to be imported under

Wake Up and Smell the Coffee

"THIS is an unprecedented commitment," said Kris Engskov, the boss of Starbucks in Britain and Ireland, on December 6th, announcing that the coffee retailer will volunteer to the British taxman around £10m ($16m) a year more in 2013–14 than it is required to pay by law. It is doing so not under any pressure from the authorities, which had not been party to the firm's decision to donate an extra shot of cash to the exchequer, but to please British consumers furious not, as you might expect, at the high price of a latte, but at how little tax the firm pays in their country. "We've heard that loud and clear from our customers," said Mr Engskov.

Alas, this pioneering effort to transform tax into a marketing expense did not elicit the hoped-for gratitude. On December 8th, UK Uncut, a group which campaigns against government austerity and corporate tax avoidance, staged protests at dozens of British Starbucks stores. Campaigners point out that since first opening its doors in Britain in 1998, Starbucks has paid only £8.6m in corporate income taxes there. In testimony last month before a parliamentary committee, Starbucks had said this was because it had made a profit in only one year in Britain, although it also admitted that its British business had made large payments for coffee to a profitable Starbucks subsidiary in Switzerland and large royalty payments to another profitable subsidiary in the Netherlands for use of the brand and intellectual property.

Starbucks is not thought to be using the "Dutch Sandwich" and "Double Irish," even if these sound like items on its menu. They are legal tax-avoidance techniques believed to have been used by, among others, Google, which was also called to testify before Parliament. Most of Google's revenues in Europe are booked in Dublin, then shifted via royalty payments to a Dutch subsidiary, before whatever is left is recognized as profits by a subsidiary in Bermuda, which levies no income tax. Another online giant, Amazon, told parliamentarians that its low British corporate-tax bill—£1.8m in 2011—was due to its British operations merely providing back-office services to its main Europe-wide business, which is based in low-tax Luxembourg.

Although Starbucks denies using tax havens, it admits to having negotiated a secret low rate of tax with the Dutch taxman for its subsidiary in Amsterdam. Worldwide, it says it pays out over 30 percent of its profits in tax. Many other firms are making extensive use of havens. A study published last year by ActionAid, an activist charity, said 98 of the firms in the FTSE 100 index have at least one subsidiary in a haven. An increasingly popular strategy is to transfer ownership of the multinational's main intellectual property to a subsidiary in a tax haven, then charge other subsidiaries in higher-tax countries for use of it. Data compiled by the OECD, a rich-country think-tank, highlight how many patents are owned by outfits in such unlikely innovation hubs as Barbados, the Cayman Islands and Bermuda.

In both Britain and America, businesses have been lobbying for cuts in marginal corporate-tax rates, even if this meant losing a few small loopholes, and had started to get somewhere. Their arguments were bolstered by a study in June from the Centre for Business Taxation at Oxford University, which found that the two countries had among the world's highest effective tax rates (ie, after allowances). Barack Obama, having failed in 2011 with an attempt to cut America's headline tax rates while eliminating some exemptions, has made a similar proposal as a carrot to the Republicans in the "fiscal cliff" talks.

Now, though, the public outrage being whipped up over the most lucrative avoidance strategies may cause politicians to shift their focus from making taxes more business-friendly to shoring up the tax base. George Osborne, Britain's chancellor of the exchequer, has responded to the furor over Starbucks, Google, and Amazon by promising to use the country's imminent chairmanship of the G8 club of rich countries to wage war on tax havens. Politicians elsewhere, also facing swelling deficits, may join him in that.

Source: © The Economist Newspaper Limited, London, December 15, 2012.

a quota restriction. This may be a more important consideration than income tax savings, if the imported item is a necessary component needed by an assembly or manufacturing affiliate to continue or expand production.

Transfer prices also have an effect on how divisions of a MNC are perceived locally. A high markup policy leaves little net income to show on the affiliate's books. If the parent firm expects the affiliate to be able to borrow short-term funds locally in the event of a cash shortage, the affiliate may have difficulty doing so with unimpressive financial statements. On the other hand, a low markup policy makes it appear, at least superficially, as if affiliates, rather than the parent firm, are contributing a larger portion to consolidated earnings. To the extent that financial markets are inefficient, or securities analysts do not understand the transfer pricing strategy being used, the market value of the MNC may be lower than is justified.

Obviously, transfer pricing strategies have an effect on international capital expenditure analysis. A very low (high) markup policy makes the adjusted present value (APV) of a subsidiary's capital expenditure appear more (less) attractive. Consequently, in order to obtain a meaningful analysis, arm's-length pricing should be used in the APV analysis to determine after-tax operating income, regardless of the actual transfer price employed. A separate term in the APV analysis can be used to recognize tax-savings from transfer pricing strategies. This was the recommended approach detailed in Chapter 18.

Advance Pricing
Agreement

An **advance pricing agreement (APA)** is a binding contract between the IRS and a multinational firm by which the IRS agrees to not seek a transfer pricing adjustment under Section 482 of the Internal Revenue Code for some set of transactions called *covered transactions*. The APA program provides a means to resolve transfer pricing issues before they arise in an audit. The APA process increases the efficiency of tax administration by encouraging taxpayers to present to the IRS all relevant information for it to properly conduct a transfer pricing analysis. For the taxpayer, the program creates greater certainty regarding the transfer pricing method (TPM). An APA covering a specific TPM can be negotiated up to five years in advance.

APAs can be unilateral, bilateral, or multilateral. A unilateral APA involves a negotiated TPM between the taxpayer and the IRS for U.S. tax purposes. In the event of a tax dispute with a foreign tax administration, the taxpayer may request that the U.S. Competent Authority (IRS representative) initiate a mutual agreement proceeding with the foreign tax administration, assuming an applicable tax treaty exists between the two countries. However, if the Competent Authorities for the two countries are unable to resolve the issue, it is the taxpayer who suffers. A bilateral or multilateral APA is an agreement between the taxpayer and one or more foreign tax administrations under the mutual agreement procedure specified in tax treaties. The taxpayer is assured that the income associated with covered transaction will not be subject to double taxation by any taxing authority. Consequently, they are of benefit to the taxpayer. In January 2007, a bilateral APA involving Wal-Mart Stores, Inc., was concluded between the United States and China. It is expected to serve as a model for future APAs between the two countries.

Blocked Funds

For a variety of reasons, a country may find itself short of foreign currency reserves, and thus impose exchange restrictions on its own currency, limiting its conversion into other currencies so as not to further reduce scarce foreign currency reserves. When a country enforces exchange controls, the remittance of profits from a subsidiary firm to its foreign parent is blocked. The blockage may be only temporary, or it may be for a considerable period of time. A lengthy blockage is detrimental to a MNC. Without the ability to repatriate profits from a foreign subsidiary, the MNC might as well not even have the investment as returns are not being paid to the stockholders of the MNC.

Prior to making a capital investment in a foreign subsidiary, the parent firm should investigate the potential of future funds blockage. This is part of the capital expenditure analysis outlined in Chapter 18. The APV framework developed in that chapter only considers the expected operating cash flows that are available for repatriation.

Unexpected funds blockage after an investment has been made, however, is a political risk with which the MNC must contend. Thus, the MNC should be familiar with methods for moving blocked funds so as to benefit its stockholders. Several methods for moving blocked funds have already been discussed in this chapter and others. For example, transfer pricing strategies and unbundling services are methods the MNC might be able to use to move otherwise blocked funds. These methods were covered earlier in this chapter. Moreover, in Chapter 8, leading and lagging of payments were discussed primarily as a means of controlling transaction exposure. However, leading and lagging payments may be used as a strategy for repositioning funds within a MNC. Additional strategies that may be useful for moving blocked funds are *export creation* and *direct negotiation*.

Export creation involves using the blocked funds of a subsidiary in the country in which they are blocked to pay for exports that can be used to benefit the parent firm or other affiliates. Thus, instead of using repatriated funds to pay for goods or services that will benefit the MNC, blocked funds are used. Examples include: using consulting firms located in the host country where funds are blocked, instead of a firm in the parent country, to provide necessary consulting work that benefits the MNC; transferring personnel from corporate headquarters to the subsidiary offices where they will be paid in the blocked local currency; using the national airlines of the host country when possible for the international travel of all MNC executives, where the reservations and fare payments are made by the subsidiary; and holding business conferences in the host country, instead of elsewhere, where the expenses are paid by the local subsidiary. All of these possibilities not only benefit the MNC, since these goods and services are needed, but they also benefit various industries within the host country.

Host countries desire to attract foreign industries that will most benefit their economic development and the technical skills of their citizens. Thus, foreign investment in the host country in industries that produce export goods, such as automobiles or electronic equipment, or in industries that will attract tourists, such as resort hotels, is desirable. This type of investment provides good employment and training for the country's citizens and is also a source, rather than a use, of foreign exchange. The host country should not expect a MNC to make beneficial investment within its borders if it is not likely to receive an appropriate return. Consequently, MNCs in desirable industries may be able to convince the host country government through direct negotiation that funds blockage is detrimental to all.

SUMMARY

This chapter provided a brief introduction to the international tax environment that confronts MNCs and investors in international financial assets. Additionally, attention was given to the topic of transfer pricing. A case application was used to examine transfer pricing strategies.

1. The twin objectives of taxation are tax neutrality and tax equity. Tax neutrality has its foundations in the principles of economic efficiency and equity. Tax equity is the principle that all similarly situated taxpayers should participate in the cost of operating the government according to the same rules.

2. The three basic types of taxation are income tax, withholding tax, and value-added tax. Corporate income tax rates from many countries were listed and compared. Similarly, the withholding tax rates for certain countries for various types of foreign-source income for which the United States has bilateral tax treaties were listed and compared.

3. Nations often tax the worldwide income of resident taxpayers and also the income of foreign taxpayers doing business within their territorial boundaries. If countries simultaneously apply both methods, double taxation will result unless a mechanism is established to prevent it. The concept of the foreign tax credit as a means to eliminate double taxation was developed. Examples were presented from the perspective of a U.S. MNC showing the calculation of the foreign tax credits for branch and subsidiary operations in three countries with different corporate income tax rates.

www.mhhe.com/er8e

4. Different forms of organizational structure were explained. Transfer pricing strategies, subsidiary operations in tax haven countries, foreign-controlled corporations, and foreign sales corporations were also defined and discussed.

5. Transfer pricing strategies are a means to reposition funds within a MNC and a possible technique for reducing tax liabilities and removing blocked funds from a host country that has imposed foreign exchange restrictions.

6. Unbundling fund transfers, export creation, and direct negotiation are other means for removing blocked funds from a host country that is enforcing foreign exchange restrictions.

KEY WORDS

active income, *500*
advance pricing
   agreement (APA), *516*
capital-export
   neutrality, *499*
capital-import
   neutrality, *500*
controlled foreign
   corporation (CFC), *507*
direct tax, *500*
foreign branch, *505*
foreign subsidiary, *505*

foreign tax credits, *505*
income tax, *500*
indirect tax, *502*
national
   neutrality, *500*
passive income, *502*
residential
   taxation, *504*
source taxation, *504*
Subpart F income, *507*
tax equity, *500*
tax inversion, *507*

tax haven, *506*
tax neutrality, *499*
tax treaties, *502*
territorial
   taxation, *504*
transfer price, *509*
value-added tax
   (VAT), *502*
withholding tax, *502*
worldwide
   taxation, *504*

QUESTIONS

1. Discuss the twin objectives of taxation. Be sure to define the key words.

2. Compare and contrast the three basic types of taxation that governments levy within their tax jurisdiction.

3. Show how double taxation on a taxpayer may result if all countries were to tax the worldwide income of their residents and the income earned within their territorial boundaries.

4. What methods do taxing authorities use to eliminate or mitigate the evil of double taxation?

5. How might a MNC use transfer pricing strategies? How do import duties affect transfer pricing policies?

6. What are the various means the taxing authority of a country might use to determine if a transfer price is *reasonable?*

7. Discuss how a MNC might attempt to repatriate blocked funds from a host country.

PROBLEMS

1. There are three production stages required before a pair of skis produced by Fjord Fabrication can be sold at retail for NOK2,300. Fill in the following table to show the value added at each stage in the production process and the incremental and total VAT. The Norwegian VAT rate is 25 percent.

Production Stage	Selling Price	Value Added	Incremental VAT
1	NOK 450		
2	NOK1,900		
3	NOK2,300		
			Total VAT

2. The Docket Company of Asheville, NC, USA, is considering establishing an affiliate operation in the city of Wellington, on the south island of New Zealand. It is undecided whether to establish the affiliate as a branch operation or a wholly owned subsidiary. New Zealand taxes the income of both resident corporations and branch operations at a flat rate of 28 percent. New Zealand withholds taxes at 5 percent on dividends for an investor who holds at least 10 percent of the shares in the subsidiary company that pays the dividend; 0 percent if the investor holds 80 percent or more of the shares in the subsidiary company and meets other criteria; 15 percent in all other cases. New Zealand does not withhold taxes on branch income. The United States has an income tax rate of 35 percent on income earned worldwide, but gives a tax credit for taxes paid to another country. Based on this information, is a branch or subsidiary the recommended form for the affiliate?

3. Affiliate X sells 10,000 units to Affiliate Y per year. The marginal tax rates for X and Y are 20 percent and 30 percent, respectively. The transfer price per unit is currently set at $1,000, but it can be set as high as $1,250. Calculate the increase in annual after-tax profits if the higher transfer price of $1,250 per unit is used.

4. Affiliate A sells 5,000 units to Affiliate B per year. The marginal income tax rate for Affiliate A is 25 percent and the marginal income tax rate for Affiliate B is 40 percent. The transfer price per unit is currently $2,000, but it can be set at any level between $2,000 and $2,400. Derive a formula to determine how much annual after-tax profits can be increased by selecting the optimal transfer price.

5. Affiliate A sells 5,000 units to Affiliate B per year. The marginal income tax rate for Affiliate A is 25 percent and the marginal income tax rate for Affiliate B is 40 percent. Additionally, Affiliate B pays a tax-deductible tariff of 5 percent on imported merchandise. The transfer price per unit is currently $2,000, but it can be set at any level between $2,000 and $2,400. Derive (a) a formula to determine the effective marginal tax rate for Affiliate B, and (b) a formula to determine how much annual after-tax profits can be increased by selecting the optimal transfer price.

INTERNET EXERCISES

WWW

1. The website www.taxsites.com/international.html is a comprehensive site that provides links to many other websites. For example, go to the Worldwide-Tax link and learn about the history of taxation.

2. The Transfer Pricing Management Benchmarking Association conducts benchmarking studies to identify the best transfer pricing processes that will improve the overall operations of its members. Its website is tpmba.com. Go to this website to learn about the objectives of the association and the events it sponsors. You may be interested in receiving its free newsletter.

MINI CASE 1

Sigma Corp.'s Location Decision

Sigma Corporation of Boston is contemplating establishing a wholly owned subsidiary operation in the Mediterranean. Two countries under consideration are Spain and Cyprus. Sigma intends to repatriate all after-tax foreign-source income to the United States. In the United States, corporate income is taxed at 35 percent. In Cyprus, the marginal corporate tax rate is 10 percent. In Spain, corporate income is taxed at 30 percent. The withholding tax treaty rates with the United States on dividend income paid is 5 percent from Cyprus and 10 percent from Spain.

The financial manager of Sigma has asked you to help him determine where to locate the new subsidiary. The location decision of Cyprus or Spain will be based on which country has the smaller total tax liability.

MINI CASE 2

Eastern Trading Company's Optimal Transfer Pricing Strategy

The Eastern Trading Company of Singapore ships prepackaged spices to Hong Kong, the United Kingdom, and the United States, where they are resold by sales affiliates. Eastern Trading is concerned with what might happen in Hong Kong now that control has been turned over to China. Eastern Trading has decided that it should reexamine its transfer pricing policy with its Hong Kong affiliate as a means of repositioning funds from Hong Kong to Singapore. The following table shows the present transfer pricing scheme, based on a carton of assorted, prepackaged spices, which is the typical shipment to the Hong Kong sales affiliate. What do you recommend that Eastern Trading should do?

Eastern Trading Company Current Transfer Pricing Policy with Hong Kong Sales Affiliate

	Singapore Parent	Hong Kong Affiliate	Consolidated Company
Sales revenue	S$300	S$500	S$500
Cost of goods sold	200	300	200
Gross profit	100	200	300
Operating expenses	50	50	100
Taxable income	50	150	200
Income taxes (20%/17.5%)	10	26	36
Net income	40	124	164

REFERENCES & SUGGESTED READINGS

Bischel, Jon E., and Robert Feinscheiber. *Fundamentals of International Taxation,* 2nd ed. New York: Practicing Law Institute, 1985.

Horwitz, Tony. "Continental Shift: Europe's Borders Fade and People and Goods Can Move Freely." *The Wall Street Journal,* May 18, 1993.

"How to Stop the Inversion Perversion," *The Economist,* July 26, 2014.

"Inverted Logic." *The Economist,* August 15, 2015.

Isenberg, Joseph. *International Taxation: U.S. Taxation of Foreign Taxpayers and Foreign Income,* Vols. I and II. Boston: Little, Brown, 1990.

Kaplan, Richard L. *Federal Taxation of International Transactions: Principles, Planning and Policy.* St. Paul, Minn.: West, 1988.

Kuntz, Joel D., and Robert J. Peroni. *U.S. International Taxation,* Vols. I and II. Boston: Warren, Gorham and Lamont, 1994.

Metcalf, Gilbert E. "Value-Added Taxation: A Tax Whose Time Has Come?" *Journal of Economic Perspectives* 9 (1995), pp. 121–40.

Glossary

A

Active Income Income that results from production or services provided by an individual or corporation.

Adjusted Present Value (APV) A present value technique that discounts a firm's cash flows at different rates depending on the risk of the cash flows.

Agency Market A market in which the broker takes the client's order through the agent, who matches it with another public order.

Agency Problem Managers who are hired as the agents working for shareholders may actually pursue their own interests at the expense of shareholders, causing conflicts of interest. Agency problems are especially acute for firms with diffused share ownership.

All-Equity Cost of Capital The required return on a company's stock in the absence of debts.

All-in-Cost All costs of a swap, which are interest expense, transaction cost, and service charges.

American Depository Receipt (ADR) A certificate of ownership issued by a U.S. bank representing a multiple of foreign shares that are deposited in a U.S. bank. ADRs can be traded on the organized exchanges in the United States or in the OTC market.

American Option An option that can be exercised at any time during the option contract.

Appreciate In the context of a domestic currency, a decrease (an increase) in a foreign exchange rate relative to another currency when stated in terms of the domestic (foreign) currency.

Arbitrage The act of simultaneously buying and selling the same or equivalent assets or commodities for the purpose of making certain, guaranteed profits.

Ask Price *See* Offer Price.

B

Balance of Payments A country's record of international transactions presented in a double-entry bookkeeping form.

Balance Sheet Hedge Intended to reduce translation exposure of an MNC by eliminating the mismatch of exposed net assets and exposed net liabilities denominated in the same currency.

Bank Capital Adequacy The amount of equity capital and other securities a bank holds as reserves against risky assets to reduce the probability of a bank failure.

Banker's Acceptance (B/A) A negotiable money market instrument for which a secondary market exists and is issued by the Importer's Bank once the bill of lading and time draft are accepted. It is essentially a promise that the bank will pay the draft when it matures.

Basel Accord Established in 1988 by the Bank for International Settlements, this act established a framework to measure bank capital adequacy for banks in the Group of Ten and Luxembourg.

Bearer Bond A bond in which ownership is demonstrated through possession of the bond.

Bid Price The price at which dealers will buy a financial asset.

Bilateral Netting A system in which a pair of affiliates determines the net amount due between them and only this amount is transferred.

Bill of Lading (B/L) In exporting, a document issued by a common carrier specifying that it has received goods for shipment and that can also serve as title to the goods.

Bimetallism A double standard maintaining free coinage for both gold and silver.

Brady Bonds Loans converted into collateralized bonds with a reduced interest rate devised to resolve the international debt crisis in the late 1980s. Named after the U.S. Treasury Secretary Nicholas Brady.

Bretton Woods System An international monetary system created in 1944 to promote postwar exchange rate stability and coordinate international monetary policies. Otherwise known as the gold-exchange system.

Brexit British decision to leave the European Union based on the outcome of the referendum held in June 2016.

C

Cadbury Code The Cadbury Committee appointed by the British government issued the *Code of Best Practice* in corporate governance for British companies, recommending, among other things, appointing at least three outside board directors and having the positions of CEO and board chairman held by two different individuals.

Call Market A market in which market and limit orders are accumulated and executed at specific intervals during the day.

Call Option An option to "buy" an underlying asset at a specified price.

Capital Account Balance-of-payment entry capturing all sales and purchases of financial assets, real estate, and businesses.

Capital-Export Neutrality The idea that an ideal tax is one which is effective in raising revenue for the government and, at the same time, does not prevent economic resources from being deployed most efficiently no matter where in the world the highest return can be earned.

Capital-Import Neutrality The idea that an ideal tax burden imposed by a host country on a foreign subsidiary of an MNC should be the same regardless of which country the MNC is incorporated in and should be the same burden as placed on domestic firms.

Cash Budget In cash management, a plan that details the time and size of expected receipts and disbursements.

Cash Management The handling of cash within a firm such as the investment a firm has in transaction balances, funds tied up in precautionary cash balances, investment of excess funds at the most favorable rate, and borrowing at the lowest rate when there is a temporary cash shortage.

Centralized Cash Depository In an MNC, it is a central cash pool in which excess cash from affiliates is collected and invested or used to cover system-wide shortages of cash.

Closed-End Country Fund (CECF) A country fund (fund invested exclusively in the securities of one country) that issues a given number of shares that are traded on the host country exchange as if it were an individual stock. These shares are not redeemable at the underlying net asset value set in the home market.

Comparative Advantage David Ricardo used the notion of comparative advantage to justify international trade. Specifically, if countries specialize production in those industries where they can produce goods and services more efficiently (in relative terms) than other countries, and engage in trade, all countries will be better off.

Competitive Effect Refers to the effect of exchange rate changes on the firm's competitive position, which, in turn, affects the firm's operating cash flows.

Complete Contract Refers to the contract that specifies exactly what each party will do under all possible future contingencies.

Concessionary Loan A loan below the market interest rate offered by the host country to a parent MNC to encourage capital expenditures in the host country.

Contingent Claim Security *See* Derivative Security.

Contingent Exposure The risk due to uncertain situations in which a firm does not know if it will face exchange risk exposure in the future.

Continuous Market A market in which market and limit orders can be executed any time during business hours.

Controlled Foreign Corporation (CFC) A foreign subsidiary in which U.S. shareholders own more than 50 percent of the voting equity stock.

Conversion Effect Refers to the fact that the dollar amount converted from a given cash flow from foreign operation will be affected by exchange rate changes.

Convertible Bond A bond that can be exchanged for a predetermined number of equity shares of the issuer.

Corporate Governance The economic, legal, and institutional framework in which corporate control and cash flow rights are distributed among shareholders, managers, and other stakeholders of the company.

Counterparty One of the two parties involved in financial contracts who agrees to exchange cash flows on particular terms.

Countertrade Transactions in which parties exchange goods or services. If these transactions do not involve an exchange of money, they are a type of barter.

Country Risk In banking and investment, it is the probability that unexpected events in a country will influence its ability to repay loans and repatriate dividends. It includes political and credit risks.

Covered Interest Arbitrage A situation that occurs when IRP does not hold, thereby allowing certain arbitrage profits to be made without the arbitrageur investing any money out of pocket or bearing any risk.

Cross-Currency Interest Rate Swap Typically called a "currency swap." One counterparty exchanges the debt service obligations of a bond denominated in one currency for the debt service obligations of the other counterparty that are denominated in another currency.

Cross-Exchange Rate An exchange rate between a currency pair where neither currency is the U.S. dollar.

Cross-Hedging Involves hedging a position in one asset by taking a position in another asset.

Cross-Listing The act of directly listing securities on foreign financial exchanges. Cross-listing will require meeting the listing and disclosure standards of foreign exchanges.

Cumulative Translation Adjustment (CTA) Used in the current rate method of translating foreign currency financial statements, this equity account allows balancing of the balance sheet by accounting for translation gains and losses.

Currency Board An extreme form of the fixed exchange rate regime under which local currency is fully backed by the U.S. dollar or another chosen standard currency.

Currency Swap One counterparty exchanges the debt service obligations of a bond denominated in one currency for the debt service obligations of the other counterparty denominated in another currency.

Current Account Balance-of-payment entry representing the exports and imports of goods and services, and unilateral transfer.

Current/Noncurrent Method In dealing with foreign currency translation, the idea that current assets and liabilities are converted at the current exchange rate while noncurrent assets and liabilities are translated at the historical exchange rates.

Current Rate Method In dealing with foreign currency translation, the idea that all balance sheet accounts are translated at the current exchange rate except stockholder's equity, which is translated at the exchange rate on the date of issuance.

D

Dealer Market A market in which the broker takes the trade through the dealer, who participates in trades as a principal.

Debt-for-Equity Swap The sale of sovereign debt for U.S. dollars to investors desiring to make equity investment in the indebted nation.

Depreciate In the context of a domestic currency, an increase (a decrease) in a foreign exchange rate relative to another currency when stated in terms of the domestic (foreign) currency.

Derivative Security A security whose value is contingent upon the value of the underlying security. Examples are futures, forward, and options contracts.

Direct Tax A tax paid directly by the taxpayer on whom the tax is levied.

Diversification of the Market A strategy for managing operating exposure in which a firm diversifies the market for its product. Thus, exchange rate changes in one country may be offset by opposite exchange rate changes in another.

Dodd-Frank Act The Dodd-Frank Wall Street Reform and Consumer Protection Act of 2010 aims to identify and reduce the systemic risk of the entire financial system by regulating Wall Street and big banks.

Draft A written order instructing the importer or his agent to pay the amount specified on its face at a certain date.

Dual-Currency Bond A straight fixed-rate bond that pays coupon interest in the issue currency, but at maturity pays the principal in a currency other than the issue currency.

E

Economic Exposure The possibility that cash flows and the value of the firm may be affected by unanticipated changes in the exchange rates.

Edge Act Bank Federally chartered subsidiaries of U.S. banks that may engage in the full range of international banking operations. These banks are located in the United States.

Efficient Market Hypothesis Hypothesis stating that financial markets are informationally efficient in that the current asset prices reflect all the relevant and available information.

Elasticity of Demand A measure of the sensitivity of demand for a product with respect to its price.

EURIBOR The rate at which interbank deposits of the euro are offered by one prime bank to another in countries that make up the EMU as well as prime banks in non-EMU EU countries and major prime banks in non-EU countries.

Euro The common European currency introduced in 1999 of the 11 countries of the EU that make up the EMU.

Eurobond A bond issue denominated in a particular currency but sold to investors in national capital markets other than the issuing country.

Eurocurrency A time deposit of money in an international bank located in a country other than the country that issues the currency.

European Central Bank (ECB) The central bank of the 11 countries that make up the EMU, responsible for maintaining price stability via monetary policy.

European Currency Unit (ECU) A basket currency made up of a weighted average of the currencies of the 12 members of the European Union. The precursor of the euro.

European Monetary System (EMS) Replaced the snake in 1979. A system to establish monetary stability in Europe and promote European economic and political unification.

European Monetary Union (EMU) The monetary union of 11 countries of the EU that irrevocably fixed their exchange rates and use the common euro currency.

European Option An option that can be exercised only at the maturity date of the contract.

European Union (EU) A regional economic integration in Western Europe, currently with 15 member states, in which all barriers to the free flow of goods, capital, and people have been removed. EU plans to complete economic unification including a single currency.

Eurosystem The monetary authority composed of the European Central Bank (ECB) and the central banks of euro-zone countries responsible for implementing the common monetary policy.

Exchange Rate Mechanism (ERM) The procedure, prior to the introduction of the euro, by which EMS member countries collectively manage their exchange rates based on a parity grid system, a system of par values between ERM countries.

Exchange Rate Pass-Through The relationship between exchange rate changes and the price adjustments of internationally traded goods.

Exchange-Traded Funds (ETF) The portfolios of securities that are traded on the stock exchanges like individual securities.

Exercise Price The prespecified price paid or received when an option is exercised.

Export-Import Bank (Ex-Im Bank) of the United States Chartered in 1945, it is an independent government agency that facilitates and finances U.S. export trade by financing exports in situations where private financial institutions are unable or unwilling to provide financing.

Exposure Coefficient The coefficient obtained from regressing the home currency value of assets on the foreign exchange rate under consideration. This provides a measure of the firm's economic exposure to currency risk.

Exposure Netting Hedging only the net exposure by firms that have both payables and receivables in foreign currencies.

F

Financial Hedging Refers to hedging exchange risk exposure using financial contracts such as currency forward and options contracts.

Fisher Effect Theory stating that the nominal interest rate is the sum of the real interest rate and the expected inflation rate.

Flexible Sourcing Policy A strategy for managing operating exposure that involves sourcing from areas where input costs are low.

Floating-Rate Note (FRN) Medium-term bonds that have their coupon payments indexed to a reference rate such as the three-month U.S. dollar LIBOR.

Foreign Bond Refers to a bond offered by a foreign borrower to the investors in a national capital market and denominated in that nation's currency. Example: An American company selling yen-denominated bonds in Japan to local investors.

Foreign Branch An overseas affiliate of an MNC that is not an independently incorporated firm but is rather an extension of the parent.

Foreign Direct Investment (FDI) Investment in a foreign country that gives the MNC a measure of control.

Foreign Exchange (FX) Markets Encompass the conversion of purchasing power from one currency into another, bank deposits of foreign currencies, and trading in foreign currency spot, forward, futures, swap, and options contracts.

Foreign Exchange Risk The risk of facing uncertain future exchange rates.

Foreign Subsidiary An affiliate organization of an MNC that is independently incorporated in a foreign country.

Foreign Tax Credit Used to avoid double taxation on a parent firm with foreign subsidiaries. It is the credit given to the parent firm against taxes due in the host country based on the taxes paid to foreign tax authorities on foreign-source income.

Forfaiting A form of medium-term trade financing used to finance exports in which the exporter sells promissory notes to a bank at a discount, thereby freeing the exporter from carrying the financing.

Forward Expectations Parity Theory stating that the forward premium or discount is equal to the expected change in the exchange rate between two currencies.

Forward Market A market for trading foreign exchange contracts initiated today but to be settled at a future date.

Forward Market Hedge A method of hedging exchange risk exposure in which a foreign currency contract is sold or bought forward.

Forward Premium/Discount The amount over (under) the spot exchange rate for a forward rate that is often expressed as an annualized percent deviation from the spot rate.

Forward Rate Agreement An interbank contract that is used to hedge the interest rate risk in mismatched deposits and credits.

Free Cash Flow It represents a firm's internally generated fund in excess of the amount needed to finance all investment projects with positive net present values.

Functional Currency For a foreign subsidiary of an MNC, it is the currency of the primary economic environment in which the entity operates. This is typically the local currency of the country in which the entity conducts most of its business.

Futures A standardized foreign exchange contract with a future delivery date that is traded on organized exchanges.

G

General Agreement on Tariffs and Trade (GATT) A multilateral agreement between member countries to promote international trade. The GATT played a key role in reducing international trade barriers.

Gold-Exchange Standard A monetary system in which countries hold most of their reserves in the form of a currency of a particular country. That country is on the gold standard.

Gold Standard A monetary system in which currencies are defined in terms of their gold content. The exchange rate between a pair of currencies is determined by their relative gold contents.

Gresham's Law Under the bimetallic standard, the abundant metal was used as money while the scarce metal was driven out of circulation, based on the fact that the ratio of the two metals was officially fixed.

H

Hedger One who attempts to eliminate the risk of an unfavorable price change in an asset by taking an offsetting position in another asset, usually a derivatives contract.

Hedging through Invoice Currency A method of hedging exchange risk exposure by invoicing in terms of the home currency of the firm.

Home Bias In portfolio holdings, the tendency of an investor to hold a larger portion of the home country securities than is optimum for diversification of risk.

I

Income Tax A direct tax levied on the active income of an individual or corporation.

Indirect Tax A tax levied on a taxpayer's income that was not directly generated by the taxpayer and serves as passive income for the taxpayer.

Initial Performance Bond An initial collateral deposit needed to establish an asset position.

Interest Rate Parity (IRP) An arbitrage equilibrium condition holding that the interest rate differential between two countries should be equal to the forward exchange premium or discount. Violation of IRP gives rise to profitable arbitrage opportunities.

International Banking Facility (IBF) Banking operation within domestic U.S. banks that act as foreign banks in the U.S. and, as such, are not bound by domestic reserve requirements or FDIC insurance requirements. They seek deposits from non-U.S. citizens and can make loans only to foreigners.

International Fisher Effect A theory stating that the expected change in the spot exchange rate between two countries is the difference in the interest rates between the two countries.

International Monetary System The institutional framework within which international payments are made, movements of capital are accommodated, and exchange rates among currencies are determined.

Intrinsic Value The immediate exercise value of an American option.

J

Jamaica Agreement International monetary agreement in January 1976 by which flexible exchange rates were accepted and gold was abandoned as an international reserve asset.

J-curve Effect Refers to the initial deterioration and eventual improvement of the trade balance following the depreciation of a country's currency.

L

Law of One Price The requirement that similar commodities or securities should be trading at the same or similar prices.

Lead/Lag Strategy Reducing transaction exposure by paying or collecting foreign financial obligations early (lead) or late (lag) depending on whether the currency is hard or soft.

Letter of Credit (L/C) A guarantee from the Importer's Bank that it will act on behalf of the importer and pay the exporter for merchandise if all documentation is in order.

Limit Order An order away from the market price that is held until it can be executed at the desired price.

Liquidity The ability of securities to be bought and sold quickly at close to the current quoted price.

London Interbank Offered Rate (LIBOR) The interbank interest rate at which a bank will offer Eurocurrency deposits to another bank in London. LIBOR is often used as the basis for setting Eurocurrency loan rates. The loan rate is determined by adding a risk premium to LIBOR.

Louvre Accord An agreement in 1987, prompted by the dollar's decline, in which the G-7 countries (i) cooperate to achieve greater exchange rate stability and (ii) consult and coordinate their macroeconomic policies.

M

Maastricht Treaty Treaty signed in December 1991 states that the European Union will irrevocably fix exchange rates among member countries by January 1999 and introduce a common European currency that will replace individual national currencies.

Maintenance Performance Bond Collateral needed to maintain an asset position.

Managed-Float System Established by the Louvre Accord in 1987, it allows the G-7 countries to jointly intervene in the exchange market to correct over- or undervaluation of currencies.

Market Completeness A market is complete if each state of the economy is matched by security payoff.

Market Imperfections Various frictions, such as transaction costs and legal restrictions, that prevent the markets from functioning perfectly.

Market Order An order executed at the best price available (market price) when the order is received in the market.

Marked-to-Market The process of establishing daily price gains and losses in the futures market by the change in the settlement price of the futures contract.

Merchant Bank A bank that performs traditional commercial banking as well as investment banking activities.

Monetary/Nonmonetary Method In dealing with foreign currency translation, the idea that monetary balance sheet accounts such as accounts receivable are translated at the current exchange rate while nonmonetary balance sheet accounts such as stockholder's equity are converted at the historical exchange rate.

Money Market Hedge A method of hedging transaction exposure by borrowing and lending in the domestic and foreign money markets.

Multilateral Netting A system in which all affiliates each net their individual interaffiliate receipts against all their disbursements and transfer or receive the balance, respectively, if they are net payers or net receivers.

Multinational Corporation (MNC) Refers to a firm that has business activities and interests in multiple countries.

N

National Neutrality The idea that an ideal tax on taxable income would tax all income in the same manner by the taxpayer's national tax authority regardless of where in the world it is earned.

Negotiable Certificate of Deposit (NCD) A negotiable bank time deposit.

Net Present Value (NPV) A capital budgeting method in which the present value of cash outflows is subtracted from the present value of expected future cash inflows to determine the net present value of an investment project.

Netting Center In multilateral netting, it determines the amount of net payments and which affiliates are to make or pay them.

North American Free Trade Agreement (NAFTA) Created in 1994, it includes the United States, Canada, and Mexico as members in a free trade area. NAFTA aimed to eliminate tariffs and import quotas over a 15-year period.

Notional Principal A reference amount of principal used for determining payments under various derivative contracts.

O

Offer Price The price at which a dealer will sell a financial asset.

Offshore Banking Center A country in which the banking system is organized to allow external accounts beyond the normal economic activity of the country. Their primary function is to seek deposits and grant loans in currencies other than the host country currency.

Open Interest The total number of short or long contracts outstanding for a particular delivery month in the derivative markets.

Operating Exposure The extent to which the firm's operating cash flows will be affected by random changes in the exchange rates.

Operational Hedging Long-term, operational approaches to hedging exchange exposure that include diversification of the market and flexible sourcing.

Optimum Currency Area A geographical area that is suitable for sharing a common currency by virtue of a high degree of factor mobility within the area.

Option A contract giving the owner the right, but not the obligation, to buy or sell a given quantity of an asset at a specified price at some date in the future.

Options Market Hedge Use of put and call options to limit the downside risk of transaction exposure while preserving the upside potential. The price of such flexibility is the option premium.

Over-the-Counter (OTC) Market Trading market in which there is no central marketplace; instead, buyers and sellers are linked via a network of telephones, telex machines, computers, and automated dealing systems.

P

Par Value The nominal or face value of stocks or bonds.

Passive Income Income not directly generated by an individual or corporation, such as interest income, royalty income, and copyright income.

Plaza Accord G-5 agreement in 1985 that depreciation of the dollar is desirable to correct the U.S. trade deficits.

Political Risk Potential losses to the parent firm resulting from adverse political developments in the host country.

Portfolio Risk Diversification Portfolio risk is minimized by investing in multiple securities that do not have strong correlations between one another.

Precautionary Cash Balance Emergency funds a firm maintains in case it has underestimated its transaction cash balance.

Price-Specie-Flow Mechanism Under the gold standard, it is the automatic correction of payment imbalances between countries. This is based on the fact that, under the gold standard, the domestic money stock rises or falls as the country experiences inflows or outflows of gold.

Primary Market The market in which new security issues are sold to investors. In selling the new securities, investment bankers can play the role of either broker or dealer.

Privatization Act of a country divesting itself of ownership and operation of business ventures by turning them over to the free market system.

Product Differentiation Creating a perception among consumers that a firm's product(s) are different from those offered by competitors, thereby reducing price sensitivity of demand.

Purchasing Power Parity (PPP) A theory stating that the exchange rate between currencies of two countries should be equal to the ratio of the countries' price levels of a commodity basket.

Put An option to sell an underlying asset at a prespecified price.

Q

Quality Spread Differential (QSD) The difference between the fixed interest rate spread differential and the floating interest rate spread differential of the debt of two counterparties of different creditworthiness. A positive QSD is a necessary condition for an interest swap to occur that ensures that the swap will be beneficial to both parties.

Quantity Theory of Money An identity stating that for each country, the general price level times the aggregate output should be equal to the money supply times the velocity of money.

R

Random Walk Hypothesis A hypothesis stating that in an efficient market, asset prices change randomly (i.e., independently of historical trends), or follow a "random walk." Thus, the expected future exchange rate is equivalent to the current exchange rate.

Real Exchange Rate Measures the degree of deviation from PPP over a period of time, assuming PPP held at the beginning of the period.

Real Option The application of options pricing theory to the evaluation of investment options in real projects.

Registered Bond A bond whose ownership is demonstrated by associating the buyer's name with the bond in the issuer's records.

Reinvoice Center A central financial subsidiary of a multinational corporation where intrafirm transaction exposure is netted, and the residual exposure is managed.

Reporting Currency The currency in which an MNC prepares its consolidated financial statements. Typically this is the currency in which the parent firm keeps its books.

Residential Taxation *See* Worldwide Taxation.

Residual Control Rights Refers to the right to make discretionary decisions under those contingencies that are not specifically covered by the contract.

Reversing Trade A trade in either the futures or forward market that will neutralize a position.

S

Sarbanes-Oxley Act The U.S. Congress passed this law in 2002 to strengthen corporate governance. The act requires the creation of a public accounting oversight board. It also requires that the CEO and the CFO sign off on the company's financial statements.

Secondary Market A market in which investors buy and sell securities to other investors; the original issuer is not involved in these trades. This market provides marketability and valuation of the securities.

Shareholder Wealth Maximization This represents the most important objective of corporate management that managers of companies should keep in mind when they make important corporate decisions. Managers can maximize shareholder wealth by maximizing the market value of the firm.

Sharpe Performance Measure (SHP) A risk-adjusted performance measure for a portfolio that gives the excess return (above the risk-free interest rate) per standard deviation risk.

Shelf Registration Allows a bond issuer to pre-register a securities issue that will occur at a later date.

Single-Currency Interest Rate Swap Typically called an "interest rate swap." There are many variants; however, all involve swapping interest payments on debt obligations that are denominated in the same currency.

Smithsonian Agreement In December 1971, the G-10 countries agreed to devalue the U.S. dollar against gold and most major currencies in an attempt to save the Bretton Woods system.

Snake European version of fixed exchange rate system that appeared as the Bretton Woods system declined.

Source Taxation *See* Territorial Taxation.

Special Drawing Rights (SDRs) An artificial international reserve created by the International Monetary Fund (IMF) that is a currency basket currently composed of four major currencies.

Specialist On exchange markets in the United States, each stock is represented by a specialist who makes a market by holding an inventory of the security.

Speculator One who attempts to profit from a favorable, but uncertain, price change in an asset by acquiring a position in it.

Spot (Exchange) Rate Price at which foreign exchange can be sold or purchased for immediate (within two business days) delivery.

Straight Fixed-Rate Bond Bonds with a specified maturity date that have fixed coupon payments.

Striking Price *See* Exercise Price.

Stripped Bond A synthetic zero coupon bond created by an investment bank by selling the rights to a specific coupon payment or the bond principal of a coupon bond, typically a U.S. Treasury bond.

Subpart F Income Income of controlled foreign corporations that is subject to immediate U.S. taxation; includes income that is relatively easy to transfer between countries and is subject to a low foreign tax levy.

Swap Bank A generic term to describe a financial institution that facilitates currency and interest rate swaps between counterparties.

Swap Broker Function of a swap bank in which it matches counterparties but does not assume any risk of the swap; however, it does receive a commission for this service.

Swap Dealer Function of a swap bank in which it makes a market in one or the other side of a currency or interest rate swap.

Swap Transaction The simultaneous spot sale (purchase) of an asset against a forward purchase (sale) of an approximately equal amount of the asset.

Syndicate A group of Eurobanks banding together to share the risk of lending Eurocredits.

Systemic Risk The risk of collapse of the entire financial system, as opposed to the risk associated with any one individual component, market, or sector.

T

Tax Equity The idea that all similarly situated taxpayers should participate in the cost of operating the government according to the same rules.

Tax Haven A country that has a low corporate income tax rate and low withholding tax rates on passive income.

Tax Inversion A maneuver in which a firm (usually U.S.) acquires or merges with a foreign rival incorporated in a low-tax country, then shifts its domicile abroad to reap tax benefits.

Tax Neutrality A principle in taxation, holding that taxation should not have a negative effect on the decision-making process of taxpayers.

Technical Analysis A method of predicting the future behavior of asset prices based on their historical patterns.

Temporal Method In dealing with foreign currency translation, the idea that current and noncurrent monetary accounts as well as accounts that are carried on the books at current value are converted at the current exchange rate. Accounts carried on the books at historical cost are translated at the historical exchange rate.

Territorial Taxation A method of declaring tax jurisdiction in which all income earned within a country by any taxpayer, domestic or foreign, is taxed.

Theory of Comparative Advantage An argument that supports the existence of international trade. This theory states that it is mutually beneficial for countries to specialize in the production of goods that they can produce most efficiently and then engage in trade.

Time Draft A written order instructing the importer or the importer's bank to pay a specific sum of money on a certain date. Used in import-export trade financing.

Tobin Tax A tax on the international flow of hot money proposed by Professor Tobin for the purpose of discouraging cross-border financial speculation.

Transaction Balance Funds a firm has marked to cover scheduled outflows during a cash budgeting period.

Transaction Exposure The potential change in the value of financial positions due to changes in the exchange rate between the inception of a contract and the settlement of the contract.

Transfer Price The price assigned, for bookkeeping purposes, to the receiving division within a business for the cost of transferring goods and services from another division.

Translation Exposure The effect of an unanticipated change in the exchange rates on the consolidated financial reports of an MNC.

Triangular Arbitrage The process of trading U.S. dollars for a second currency and subsequently trading this for a third currency. This third currency is then traded for U.S. dollars. The purpose of such trading is to earn arbitrage profit via trading from the second currency to the third.

Triffin Paradox Under the gold exchange standard, the reserve-currency country should run a balance of payments deficit, but this can decrease confidence in the reserve currency and lead to the downfall of the system.

U

Uncovered Interest Rate Parity This parity condition holds that the difference in interest rates between two countries is equal to the expected change in exchange rate between the countries' currencies.

Universal Bank International banks that provide such services as consulting in foreign exchange hedging strategies, interest rate and currency swap financing, and international cash management.

V

Value-Added Tax (VAT) An indirect national tax that is levied on the value added in the production of a good or service as it moves through the various stages of production.

W

Withholding Tax An indirect tax levied on passive income earned by an individual or corporation of one country within the tax jurisdiction of another country.

World Beta A measure of the sensitivity of an asset or portfolio to the world market movements. This is a measure of the world systematic risk.

World Equity Benchmark Shares (WEBS) WEBS are exchange-traded, open-end country funds designed to closely track national stock market indexes. WEBS are traded on the American Stock Exchange (AMEX).

World Trade Organization (WTO) Permanent international organization created by the Uruguay Round to replace GATT. The WTO has the power to enforce international trade rules.

Worldwide Taxation A method of declaring national tax jurisdiction in which national residents of the country are taxed on their worldwide income regardless of which country it is earned in.

Y

Yankee Bond (Stock) Bond (stock) directly sold to U.S. investors by foreign companies.

Z

Zero-Coupon Bond A bond that pays no coupon interest and simply returns the face value at maturity.

Index